A DEMOCRACY
AT WAR

A DEMOCRACY AT WAR

*America's Fight at Home and Abroad
in World War II*

William L. O'Neill

HARVARD UNIVERSITY PRESS
Cambridge, Massachusetts
London, England

Third printing, 1999

This Harvard University Press paperback edition published by
arrangement with The Free Press, a Division of Macmillan, Inc.

First Harvard University Press paperback edition, 1995

Library of Congress Cataloging-in-Publication Data

O'Neill, William L.
  A democracy at war: America's fight at home and abroad in World War II / William L. O'Neill.
    p. cm.
  Includes bibliographical references (p.) and index.
  ISBN 0–674–19737–2 (pbk.)
  1. World War, 1939–1945—United States. 2. United States—History—1933–1945. I. Title.
D769.064   1993   93–15677
940.54'0973—dc20   CIP

Map by George Ward from *Tennozan* by George Feifer. Copyright © 1992 by George Feifer.
Reprinted by permission of Ticknor & Fields/Houghton Mifflin Co. All rights reserved.

From *There's a War to Be Won* by Geoffrey Perret. Map copyright © 1991 by Anita Karl and
Jim Kemp. Reprinted by permission of Random House, Inc.

Maps from *The Great Crusade: A New Complete History of the Second World War* by
H.P. Willmott (The Free Press, 1990).

*To my parents, Helen E. and John P. O'Neill,
who held our share of the home front; to the
war generation as a whole; and especially to the
gallant fighting men to whom so much is owed.*

Contents

Introduction

This is a history of the people's war, not as the phrase was used then to describe a liberal-left agenda, but the actual war that Americans fought to preserve their way of life. Leaders are important to this story, because decisions made at all levels of command caused the deaths of many servicemen and determined conditions on the home front. I am particularly concerned with the war generation itself, the men and women, mostly in their teens and twenties, who carried the heaviest load. Everyone contributed to the war effort in some way, if only by paying taxes. Some 80 percent of civilians bought war bonds as well. Children collected scrap. Millions of adults, and many teens, worked in defense plants. The greatest sacrifices were made by the men in the armed forces, and especially those who risked, and often gave, their lives in the struggle. The women who loved and supported them suffered too, living through the years of separation and dread even if their men came back.

Because in a democracy tough decisions require popular support, this is also a book about politics, not partisan politics so much as the struggles between the Administration and Congress, among the various armed services, between Britain and the United States, and between both of the two great Western Allies and the Soviet Union. The resulting compromises determined the course of the war and its aftermath, often in ways that are not well understood today. Many members of the war generation are still alive, and know the war as they experienced it better than does any historian. But, with hindsight, and the revelation of things once secret, and thanks to many fine works of scholarship, one can now outline the American war in ways not possible earlier.

It will be argued here that the United States fought under major handicaps. One was a failure to understand the facts of international life, and therefore both to prepare for war and to intervene soon enough. Another was the politicians' fear that if they asked for too many sacrifices they would make the war unpopular and be swept from office. Thus, the military draft was never broad enough, and there was no labor draft at all, despite public-opinion polls that supported a greater effort. A third weakness was prejudice—against refugees, Jews in particular, Negroes, Japanese–Americans, and to a degree women, which deprived the nation of skills and willing hands to such an extent that the Army succeeded only by asking the impossible of many fighting men. These were the liabilities of American democracy, bad habits as well as bad morals, that made victory more difficult to achieve than it needed to have been.

And yet, America had great vitality, too, which helped right the balance. Materially the United States was far and away the world's leading industrial nation. There were social and moral strengths as well, without which physical assets alone would have been inadequate. Family life was solid and the basis of national might. The average years of schooling had been greatly extended, and literacy was widespread. To what now seems an amazing degree, Americans of many different ethnic backgrounds lived and worked together. People of all races and religions shared a common faith in hard work, individual obligation, and a respected legitimate authority. The young Americans who were called upon to fight and die for their country, had been raised to believe in it, to prize loyalty to neighborhood and nation, and to do what was asked of them. Consequently, the United States met the world crisis with a relatively homogenous, well-disciplined, and well-educated work force, a huge industrial capacity, and a generation of young men who would prove to be excellent warriors.

The subject of this book, then, is how and why America won the war despite its late start, cumbersome political system, and debilitating prejudices. Productive of many lessons, awe inspiring in part, it is a story that cannot be told too frequently or reexamined often enough.

William L. O'Neill

Highland Park, New Jersey

Wellfleet, Massachusetts

Acknowledgments

As always I am grateful to Rutgers University for its support of scholarship, and to Georges Borchardt for the best possible representation. Joyce Seltzer edited the manuscript with a loving attention to detail and a ruthless drive for clarity, both of which I appreciate. My colleagues Warren F. Kimball and David M. Oshinsky read an earlier version of this work and provided much helpful criticism. I am indebted also to Warren for his publications on Roosevelt, and to David for his friendship. Stephen E. Ambrose, whose writings on Eisenhower and the campaigns in Europe have been a major source of information and inspiration, gave the final version a very close reading, saving me from error and offering valuable suggestions and encouragement. My daughter Kate O'Neill has been a bright light for me in a dark time. My deepest thanks to everyone.

1
Day of Infamy

They came in low over the water, 40 torpedo bombers streaking for Battleship Row. Above and beyond them were 140 fighters, dive bombers, horizontal bombers, and, an hour behind them, a second and equally powerful group.[1] A Japanese force of six carriers had launched the first wave in a quarter of an hour. All its planes were in the air within 90 minutes, an impressive display of strength and expertise which no other navy could match. At 7:55 A.M. on December 7, 1941, loudspeakers aboard warships in Pearl Harbor crackled to life with warnings—"Air Raid. This is no shit" carrying the most conviction.

Moments later, two torpedoes slammed into the battleship *Oklahoma*, followed by three others. She soon capsized, many survivors walking up the sides as she rolled over into the mud. *Maryland*, tied up alongside her, sustained only a handful of casualties and no serious harm. *Pennsylvania* was in dry dock and so escaped with little damage. *California* took two torpedoes but settled upright, her guns firing throughout the attack. *West Virginia*, counterflooded by her crew, also sank in place. Many of her guns continued to fire, despite sheets of flames washing across her decks, until she had to be abandoned. *Tennessee*, wedged inboard of *West Virginia* and unable to move, took two bomb hits but did not sink, and sustained few

1

casualties. *Arizona* exploded after a bomb hit its forward magazine. A thousand sailors went down with her, four-fifths of the entire crew. They are entombed in her still.

Many were trapped when *Oklahoma* capsized, some rescued by sailors who worked day and night, others perishing in spite of heroic efforts. The first two men found were suffocated by their rescuers' acetylene torch, which used up all the air. Switching to pneumatic drills and air hammers was slower and not necessarily safer, for the escaping air permitted water levels to rise, drowning individuals who were on the brink of salvation. In 36 hours, 32 men were pulled out alive, more than from some other ships, especially those with men who were trapped below decks when their vessels settled on the bottom.

Of the 94 ships in Pearl Harbor, most had only one boiler lit and so could not get underway. The destroyers needed an hour to make steam, the larger ships at least two. Destroyer *Helm*, one of a handful with steam up, moved out smartly, Quartermaster Frank Handler at the wheel. Though he had never steered the ship through Pearl's difficult channel, and lacked a working compass, when the skipper said "Go" he stormed out to sea, ignoring the 14-knot speed limit. To the captain of supply ship *Antares*, hovering anxiously at the channel mouth, "one of the most beautiful sights I ever saw" was *Helm* bursting out of the pall of smoke at 30 knots.[2] As fast as they could others followed. Destroyer *Blue* commanded by Ensign Nathan Asher, the senior of four officers aboard, came out early. Behind her was *Aylwin*, conned by Ensign Stanley Caplan, USNR, a 26 year-old chemistry graduate.[3]

The battlewagons were easy prey, moored together two by two, the insiders unable to move, the outsiders exposed to torpedoes. Apart from *California*, only *Nevada* was anchored alone, and only she had steam up when the attack began and was able to sortie. She was commanded by a middle aged reservist who happened to be the senior officer on board. When he took her out jaws dropped, as everyone knew it required four tugs to get a capital ship out of harbor. Despite being holed in the bow *Nevada* made for deep water, her guns firing so rapidly that at times awed watchers in the hills could not see the ship for her smoke. She was on fire as well, flames sweeping her decks and raging up from below as Japanese planes swarmed around her. Down by the bow, oil streaming from her ruptured bunkers and smoke from her guns and fires, *Nevada* drove on, until ordered to beach by the harbor commander, who feared she would sink in Pearl's twisting channel and lock out the carrier force. Once aground, and despite additional bomb hits, her crew put out the fires and saved their ship, which had given the Navy cause for pride at a time when there was little of it. Despite taking a torpedo in the bow and at least 10 bomb hits, *Nevada* had only 29 men killed, one difference between being a fighting ship and riding helpless at anchor.

The only big ship to make it out under fire was the light cruiser *St. Louis*, which sortied at 9:31 a.m. Later, a flag officer who saw her charge remembered excitedly that she "was moving beyond all knots I had ever seen in the channel . . . Everyone at the ship seemed at their battle stations and no one seemed to give a damn as that cruiser dashed out to sea . . . That skipper was really moving and it looked as though no one but God himself was going to stop him."[4] No one did, *St. Louis* crashing through obstacles at "Emergency Full," and narrowly escaping two torpedoes fired by a Japanese midget sub. Five of these minisubs, having piggybacked in on fleet submarines, participated in the attack. But the tiny submersibles did no harm, unlike the lethal torpedo bombers. As a senior American air officer later remarked of those planes "Their accuracy was uncanny . . . Evidently they were further advanced than the U.S. in torpedoes and torpedo planes."[5] It was the beginning of wisdom for the US Navy.

The first wave of carrier-based attackers encountered little opposition, but the second, arriving at 8:40 a.m., did not find things so easy, for now the guns were being manned—catch-as-catch-can in most cases. At one of *Pennsylvania's* 5-inch guns, three men did the work of 15. *Tennessee's* 5-inchers were firing so fast that their paint peeled off in long strips. Smaller AA guns were firing, too, and their gunners were beginning to score. Still, the Japanese hit virtually all their intended targets.

The Army's Schofield Barracks was bombed and strafed. Soldiers returned fire with machine guns mounted on railings, benches, even a field altar, with a chaplain assisting (this giving rise to a popular song, "Praise the Lord and Pass the Ammunition"). Hickam and Wheeler Fields, the main Army Air Force bases, lost nearly all their aircraft, which were neatly grouped together for protection against sabotage, making them easy targets. Few planes escaped damage at naval air stations, either. Army fighter pilots were on four-hour alert against an attack that took only two hours to complete. A mere handful of brave pilots got their planes into the air, but then they were as likely to be hit by friendly fire as by the enemy's. When aircraft from *Enterprise*, which was 200 miles offshore, tried to land that night, four were shot down by jumpy gunners.

Fires broke out in Honolulu, some as a result of enemy action, most from unfused American antiaircraft shells that rained down on the city. Apart from civil defense vehicles, traffic consisted largely of servicemen trying desperately to reach their duty stations—in private cars, taxi cabs, and anything else that moved. One officer was pursued across half the city by a Japanese pilot who fired many bursts without ever hitting his target. Others were not so lucky. As vehicles converged on the waterfront, so did enemy strafers.

For the Japanese, December 7 brought some surprises. It puzzled them that the U.S. Pacific Fleet could be so completely undefended. That no search planes provided advance warning. That there was no combat air patrol over Oahu. That American warships were in peacetime "Condition 3" of readiness, which meant that no heavy guns were manned, and neither were the plotting rooms and ammunition magazines. Some machine guns were attended, but the ready ammunition boxes were locked. Only officers of the deck had keys!

Despite the shock of the attack, there was little panic. Enlisted men and junior officers alike broke open ammunition magazines and jumped to their guns. Small boats returned officers and men to their ships despite repeated attacks from the air. Junior officers, like Lieutenant Commander Francis J. Thomas of *Nevada*, assumed temporary commands above their rank and handled their ships superbly. Ensign W. H. Sears, USNR, of *West Virginia* embodied their fighting spirit. Boarding the first small craft at hand, he wound up on the cruiser *Phoenix*. Finding that it had no need of a turret officer, he dove into the oil covered waters as it steamed by *West Virginia*, and swam to his burning ship.

Civil Defense forces were splendid, too. A Major Disaster Council had planned for such an event, and its efforts now bore fruit. Civilian volunteers manned their posts at once, provisional police directed traffic, and medical teams reported for duty, often with no more prompting than a radio announcer's startling exclamation "This is the real McCoy." Local merchants donated trucks which served as emergency ambulances. This exigency had been planned for as well, medical personnel gutting the trucks and fitting them with prepared frames holding four litters apiece. So many donors responded to appeals for blood that the containers ran out. A visiting VIP from New York, Dr. John J. Moorhead, who had been an Army surgeon in World War I, ended up heading a scratch team that operated for 11 hours straight. In the course of this marathon he was commissioned again, ending the day as a "bird" (full) colonel. Fidelity and initiative proved routine on December 7. And, though they made the defeat only a little less great, they were omens of things to come.

Because of time differences it was afternoon in Washington when Secretary of the Navy Frank Knox received the first message from Hawaii. "AIR RAID PEARL HARBOR—THIS IS NO DRILL." At 1:40 p.m. Knox called President Franklin D. Roosevelt, who was in the Oval Office chatting with Harry Hopkins. At first Roosevelt seemed relieved to have the suspense ended at last, but as the day wore on and the damage reports kept coming, in his mood changed to anger.

Prime Minister Winston Spencer Churchill was at Chequers, the PM's official country house, on December 7. By chance he was alone, except for US Ambassador John G. Winant and Averell Harriman, the director of Lend-Lease aid to Britain, when he turned on a small American radio given him by Hopkins. On the BBC's regular newscast he heard a brief announcement that the Japanese had attacked Hawaii. He immediately telephoned Roosevelt, who told him the news was true, adding "We are all in the same boat now."

Churchill, in his grand but for the most part discreet memoirs, made no secret of his own feelings. For the leader of an embattled empire, "to have the United States at our side was to me the greatest joy. I could not foretell the course of events. I do not pretend to have measured accurately the martial might of Japan, but now at this very moment I knew the United States was in the war, up to the neck and in to the death. So we had won after all!"[6] He also learned that the Germans had failed to take Moscow and were now being pushed back. When he turned in that night, it was to enjoy "the sleep of the saved and the thankful."

Most Americans got the news in bits and pieces over the radio, and were anything but thankful. Some found out when athletic and cultural events were interrupted by announcements. For example, at Griffith Stadium in Washington, D.C., a crowd of 27,000 remained in the dark even though the PA system began calling upon notables to report to their offices. Yet spectators were distracted less than might be supposed, since the game between the Redskins and the Philadelphia Eagles was exceptionally exciting. Pat O'Brian, a wire service reporter, found out only after being instructed to limit his coverage because it was unimportant. When he indignantly wired back that it was a "damn important game," someone at Associated Press replied "Japs just kicked off. War now."[7]

Though the full story was slow to come out, the Navy could not deny that this was its worst day ever, and a debacle for the Army, too. America lost 188 planes, and 159 others were damaged, 18 warships were sunk or disabled, including seven battleships; and 2,403 Americans, including civilians, were killed and 1,178 wounded. Japan lost 29 planes and pilots, five midget submarines and one fleet sub, plus their crews. The Navy alone lost more men than it had in the Spanish–American and First World Wars combined.

In two hours the Imperial Japanese Navy had turned America's Pacific fortress into a shambles. Flames swept over once powerful warships, columns of smoke darkened the skies, and oil covered the waters of Pearl Harbor, its debris, and the bodies of men washing up on shore: ghastly evidence of the nation's failure. The military had blundered, to be sure, but not the armed forces alone. American democracy as well was responsible for the tragic events of December 7, and for the melancholy days that followed, when gallant men made desperate stands on island after island.

2

America in 1941

More than 60 years have passed since the Second World War was set in motion by Japan's seizure of Manchuria in 1931. Nearly half a century separates us from its conclusion in Tokyo Bay, almost equaling the span of time between the finale of the Civil War at Appomattox and that of World War I at Versailles. Before long World War II will be as remote to us as the Civil War was to those who fought the Axis powers. America has changed so much that those who grew up in the interwar years remember a nation that, to a significant degree, no longer exists. Understanding how war came to America requires a look at that lost democracy.

To modern eyes the most striking feature of American cities in 1941 was the absence of people of color. Strict laws denied admission to non-whites. The entire continent of Asia had an immigration quota of exactly zero, one of many points of contention between the United States and Japan. African–Americans, then called Negroes, were 10 percent of the population. The great majority, 10 million out of 13 million, were concentrated in the Southern and border states, mostly in rural areas. Outside the South, what most impressed foreign visitors was the remarkably varied ethnic backgrounds of white Americans.

Many Americans of North European descent had been greatly alarmed by the flood of immigrants from Southern and Eastern Europe who began pouring into Atlantic ports after the Civil War. Some charged that Americans were committing "race suicide" by allowing the dregs of Europe to settle here and outbreed the native born. Yet, by 1941 the great problem of how to "Americanize" these new immigrants had been solved without anyone seeming to notice. Partly this was a function of schools that determinedly taught the children of Poles, Greeks, Slavs, and dozens of other nationalities, that George Washington was their founding father and Longfellow their greatest poet. Although this approach may have been hard on ethnic pride, its extentions helped to make from many peoples one nation.

Ironically, it was the virtual closing of America's gates, first by World War I and then by strict nationality quotas, that provided the time needed to absorb the earlier waves of newcomers and educate their children.[1] As a result, though white Americans were ethnically very diverse (a "mongrel people," Hitler called them) recent immigrants were better assimilated than at any time in memory. While Americans were profoundly divided during the Roosevelt era, first over the New Deal, then over whether or not to join other liberal democracies in the struggle to deter war, and finally over whether to join Britain in the battle against fascism, they enjoyed a degree of cultural unity that was high by any standard.

The integration of so many new ethnic groups into the mainstream of national life was the greatest American accomplishment of this era. The greatest national failure was the continued oppression and segregation of blacks, especially in the South. There were 133.4 million Americans in 1941, of whom 13.7 million were classified by the Census Bureau as "Negro and other." Except as providers of entertainment and manual labor, minorities had little influence on American life. Racial segregation was universal, mandated by law in the Southern states and everywhere else by custom.

White women were almost invariably better off than blacks of both sexes, but unlike today their choices were limited, and most, whether they liked it or not, and a great many did—served as full-time housewives. In 1940, of 65.6 million women, 13.8 million were employed, of whom all but 4.2 million were single. Most working women were young, and expected to leave the work force after marriage. The majority of employed women either were unskilled factory operatives, servants, menials, shop clerks, secretaries and clerical workers, or else served in "helping professions" like teaching and nursing that were poorly paid and lacked opportunities for advancement.

Women of this era voted and served on juries. A few held public office. Otherwise, the first feminist movement had come and gone without leaving many traces.[2] Like the discrimination that kept blacks out of many fields, that against women also made America less ready for war than it otherwise would have been. The relatively small number of working women, and the attitudes that made them scarce, would hurt later on when more hands were desperately needed.

Because the divorce rate was much lower then than it is today, and illegitimate births were infrequent, most children, regardless of race or background, were raised by both their parents. Crime rates were low, few were addicted to narcotics, the streets were safe and clean, and the urban environment was generally wholesome. Even in the Great Depression Americans continued to respect governmental authority, an attitude reinforced by the New Deal, which had restored confidence to America even if not full employment. A law-abiding and moderate people, Americans were not drawn to the radical ideologies of fascism or Communism that attracted many followers abroad. Organized crime and some labor conflicts excepted, there was little violence in the 1930s although political dissatisfaction ran high.

While the United States had few military personnel, only 458,000 servicemen in 1939, America was better prepared to make war than it looked on paper. Despite hard times it was the world's foremost industrial nation, having produced in the previous year 28.7 percent of world's manufacturing output, compared to Germany's 13.2 percent and Japan's 3.8 percent. Beyond that, Americans were a proud people who subscribed to a common culture based on work, family, respect for institutions, and faith in self and nation. It was these intangibles that the Axis powers neglected to take into account when declaring war on the United States. Aware of the nation's industrial strength, they discounted it, regarding Americans as soft, enfeebled by ethnic and racial divisions, an excessive love of material goods, and a contempt for martial values. Rarely has prejudice had a more fateful outcome.

While Americans had a common culture, they were politically divided. At home Franklin D. Roosevelt's New Deal was still the central issue. Democrats, white ethnics and blacks, especially, swore by Roosevelt and credited the New Deal with having put the country back on its feet. Republicans, the more affluent in particular, hated Roosevelt and the New Deal, which they confounded with socialism. In foreign affairs the line was drawn between internationalists (called "interventionists" after the war in Europe broke out), who believed that the United States should support European democracy, and isolationists, who were against becoming involved in Europe regardless of circumstances. The predominance of the latter had limited the President's options for years. By 1941, however, there was a large middle group with tendencies in both directions.

Beginning in 1935, while Roosevelt was introducing the sweeping measures known collectively as his Second New Deal, and was trying to decide what to do about Supreme Court attacks on his First, the Old World claimed more and more of his attention. In February Benito Mussolini, the Fascist dictator of Italy, sent additional forces to East Africa in support of his demands upon Ethiopia. In March Germany revealed that it was defying the Versailles peace treaty by building an air force and creating a 550,000-man army. Roosevelt then asked Congress for a $1.1 billion defense budget, which, though puny in relation to future needs, would be the largest peacetime military appropriation in American history.

An avalanche of isolationist sentiment resulted. On April 6, 1935, the eighteenth anniversary of American entry into the First World War, 50,000 veterans held a peace march in Washington. On April 12 some 175,000 college students staged a one hour antiwar strike. Walter Millis published his best selling *Road to War: America, 1914–1917*, which blamed American entry on the nation's failure to remain genuinely neutral. The public demanded legislation to prevent history from repeating itself. Isolationists wanted a bill that would oblige the government to embargo arms, ban loans to belligerents, and limit trade with them, if and when a war broke out. Roosevelt tried to stop the bill, and then, when passage became inevitable, lobbied for changes that would enable him to discriminate between victim and aggressor nations. But, as passed by the Senate on August 20, 1935, the Neutrality Act required Roosevelt to embargo the sale of arms and munitions to all combatants.

German and Japanese aggression might have inspired Americans to clamor for rearmament and collective security agreements with their past and future allies. But national sentiment after World War I took an opposite course. A Gallup poll taken in 1935 found that fully 70 percent of respondents agreed that intervention in the Great War had been a mistake.[3] In part this conviction arose from ethnic resentment, for many German–Americans, Irish–Americans, and other groups who had opposed American entry in the first place never became reconciled to it.

Moreover, President Woodrow Wilson, in seeking to build support for intervention, had made promises he could not keep—that an Allied victory would end all wars and make the world safe for democracy. Inevitably the defeat of Germany had no such results. And, just as inevitably, failure led to bitterness. The Allies, glorified during the war beyond their merits, suffered an excessive loss of reputation afterward for failing to behave like angels. Germany, reviled while the fighting lasted, came to be seen as a scapegoat when the Allies insisted on making it assume all responsibility for the war and pay what were regarded as exorbitant reparations.

A demonology arose in consequence that blamed American entry on false Allied propaganda and greedy businessmen, the so-called "merchants of death," who had allegedly sacrificed American boys for the sake of filthy lucre. These half-truths enabled Americans to forget how war fever had raged in 1917, and to nurture feelings of betrayed innocence. Never again, the majority swore, would they become victims of deceit and their overgenerous natures. Isolationists could draw not only upon recent experience but also from a heritage of self-imposed unilateral and hemispheric restrictions.[4] For most of its history the United States had gotten along very well without allies. As a rule it had intervened only in North America and the Caribbean. Since 1814 there had never been a time when national survival was at risk. The oceans were all but uncrossable moats, requiring only a modest fleet to secure American beaches. Absolute security created a mood resembling absolute indifference to what happened in the rest of the world. Occasionally an exciting crisis, like the War with Spain or World War I, briefly captured public attention. But both of these had unpleasant results, which only served to underscore the desirability of noninvolvement.[5]

The failure to understand that technology was rendering these assumptions obsolete extended very broadly. Even most military leaders did not think much beyond their responsibility for continental defense. This was less true of the Navy, which would be the first to fight in case of an invasion. It was also charged with protecting the Philippines, and therefore could not avoid thinking about how it would respond if the archipelago were threatened. Despite the legacy of Admiral Alfred Mahan, its greatest theorist, who had argued that control of the seas was the key to America's future, even the Navy failed to anticipate what would result if the balance of power in Europe and Asia was destroyed.

Military leaders, being American, could not avoid sharing their countrymen's impatience with traditional ideas about world politics and the principles of statecraft. This can be seen in the hostility that met the work of Nicholas John Spykman, Sterling Professor of International Relations at Yale University from 1934 until his death at the age of 50 in 1943. Born in the Netherlands, Spykman had attended Delft University and the University of Cairo before earning his graduate degrees at Yale. He had also been a journalist in the Near, Middle, and Far East, bringing to the study of foreign relations an unusually broad background. Spykman was an authority on geopolitics, a European discipline that attached great weight to geography and national resources. His most important work, *America's Strategy in World Politics: The United States and the Balance of Power*, published soon after Pearl Harbor, argued that America could no longer afford to see itself as entirely self-sufficient.[6]

A citizen since 1928, Spykman wanted his fellow Americans to realize that an aggressive nation was always a danger to others, at least hypothetically, and that the solution was to neutralize it by allying with another state, or combination of states, powerful enough to offset its strength and reestablish equilibrium. This had always been true of close neighbors, but as modern technology made even distant states potential enemies, it was now true of them as well. Furthermore, the best time to restore the balance of power was before an aggressive state became a neighbor.

Spykman understood that this was extremely hard for a democracy to do, since maintaining the balance of power required, when all else failed, the employment of force in ways repugnant to most Americans. As he observed, "This preference of the good man for dying on his own soil instead of abroad is a serious handicap to the democratic state. Most of the successful wars of history have been carried out on other people's territory."[7] There can be no victory without offensive action, he continued, and there are great advantages if this takes place as far from home as possible. Spykman directly challenged the prevailing belief that America should never go to war unless the Western Hemisphere was invaded.

Spykman argued that maintaining the balance of power in Europe had been critical to Britain's security. He pointed out that as its potential enemies became capable of striking over greater distances, the United States was finding itself in somewhat the same geographical position. To Europe, England was an offshore island. America was becoming an offshore continent to Europe and Asia both; it could not afford to have either dominated by a hostile nation. If such a danger threatened, America had to take steps to restore the balance of power, through diplomacy or, as a last resort, military action. By failing to do so, the United States had allowed Germany and Japan to threaten the entire Eurasian land mass. By 1941 only Russia and China barred the way. If they collapsed the New World would be encircled. In that event the United States would ultimately fall as well, since "allies across the ocean are as indispensable to us as allies across the Channel have been to Great Britain."[8]

Spykman dismissed a postwar world federation as unworkable. So also was the notion of an Anglo–American hegemony, because sea powers cannot dominate the world, and attempting to do so would only unite the land powers against them. In any case, Britain would probably not want Germany reduced to nothing, as that would destroy the balance of power in Europe. "A Russian state from the Urals to the North Sea can be no great improvement over a German state from the North Sea to the Urals. Russian air fields on the Channel are as dangerous as German air fields to British territorial security."[9] This was to anticipate both the debate with Britain over grand strategy during the war, and the difficulties with Russia later.

Spykman's book appeared only a few months after Pearl Harbor had silenced the isolationists who were his principal target. Yet, the fact that Americans were now at war did not mean that they were any more comfortable with power politics. It was immediately recognized that his analysis, if correct, not only was a critique of past policy, but also had grave implications for the future. All reviewers acknowledged the force of his argument, which was variously described as "hard-boiled," "pragmatic," "realistic," "coldly reasoned, icily detached," and "callous," though usually "brilliant" also. Nearly everyone complained of his lack of "idealism," as if by talking about the world in a more high-minded way one could somehow change it.[10]

Spykman was doomed to fail in the short run because Americans had no tolerance for arguments based on geopolitical realities. Only two kinds of discourse were permissible when it came to foreign relations. One was the rhetoric of isolationists, the other of Woodrow Wilson. The first was dominant through the 1930s, the second coming into play after war broke out. Neither served the country well, and both made it extremely hard to think about national security in terms of American interests. The simple truth was, as Spykman argued, that the United States could not afford to remain aloof if either Europe or Asia fell under the domination of a hostile power. The prudent course for America in the 1930s would have been to throw its weight as early as possible on the side of states whose interests were closest to its own.

To prepare only to resist invasion raised the prospect of having to fight an overwhelmingly powerful enemy after all potential allies had been defeated, the very situation that traditional statecraft existed to prevent.

America's distance from Europe, an asset for as long as the United States could afford to ignore the Continent, had enabled Americans to get along without a significant military establishment, without allies, and without thinking seriously about world politics. This gave rise to the habit of turning one's back on distasteful foreign quarrels, or, as during World War I, of accepting the bizarre idea that America had both the duty and the means to create a democratic planet. Traditional isolation prevented Americans from realizing why other democratic states sought allies, spheres of influence and to maintain the balance of power. Such pursuits were regarded not as the means by which nations tried to remain secure in a dangerous world, the same world in which Americans lived, too, much as they denied it, but as the causes of Europe's problems.

A further obstacle to the exercise of an enlightened self-interest was the American political system itself, which had been designed to prevent sudden policy changes no matter how urgently needed. The separation of powers, revered by generations of Americans, was the principal reason. A president might well decide that an aggressor should be stopped preemptively, but if Congress did not agree there was little he could do about it. In the 1930s Congress never agreed. Isolationism was strongest in the Midwest, which, as "one man, one vote" had not yet been mandated by the Supreme Court, was overrepresented, not just in the Senate but in the House of Representatives, too. Localism was also strengthened by the old American principle that he governs best who governs least, particularly in Washington. This adage had been eroded to some extent by Roosevelt's New Deal, which, faced with a national economic disaster, was forced to seek national remedies. But the New Deal was widely seen as an exception to the rule that grass roots decisions were best.

Compounding the problem of how to devise a rational foreign policy was the public-opinion poll. In 1935 when Dr. Gallup started conducting his surveys, the public was able to express itself between elections as well as by means of them. In addition to appearing frequently, opinion polls were highly accurate. In 1940, the last preelection Gallup poll found that 52 percent of Americans planned to vote for Roosevelt, and as 54.5 percent actually did, the margin of error was only 2.5 percent—a small discrepancy even by present standards. A boon to historians, polls were then, as they still are, the curse of representative government, because they hold congressmen hostage to shallowly rooted opinions.

These obstacles to effective leadership blocked FDR. Whereas today Congress gives the President broad latitude in both foreign and military affairs, in the thirties it did not. Roosevelt's foreign policy was often frustrated or undermined by a Congress that was most sensitive to local concerns and pressure groups. The force of isolationism, the belief that the world balance of power had nothing to do with America, the short-term orientation of Congress, joined to make forming a wise national security policy all but impossible.

The four Neutrality Acts passed between 1935 and 1939 embodied the prevailing climate of opinion. Based on the theory that all wars were bad, and making no distinction between aggressors and victims, the acts prohibited everything Congress believed had led America into the First World War. Among the activities banned were giving loans and credits to belligerents, the shipment of arms or munitions to them, travel by American citizens on belligerent vessels, and the arming of American merchant ships. Roosevelt exploited the limited room for maneuver the Acts left him as best he could. When Italy invaded Ethiopia in October 1935 he embargoed both sides as provided for under the Neutrality Act, but only because Italy alone would feel the effects since Ethiopia had no money with which to purchase arms. Roosevelt had some discretion in that he could refuse to identify a conflict as a war and thus avoid having to embargo any nation. That is what he did when Japan invaded China, because, since Japan produced its own arms, an embargo would have benefited it.

In 1938, when Czechoslovakia's fate hung in the balance, Roosevelt did little to prevent the young democracy from being betrayed. He was, however, free with advice, counseling London to resist Hitler, and assuring a French visitor "You may count on us for everything except troops and loans," a promise he knew to be empty.[11] On September 21, when Czechoslovakia gave way to Allied pressure and agreed to hand over its frontier to Germany, and with it the ability to resist Nazi aggression, Roosevelt shared the general relief. He urged all the principals to keep negotiating, appealing personally to Mussolini and Hitler in the name of peace. After Prime Minister Neville Chamberlain accepted Hitler's invitation to visit Munich, where the details of

Czechoslovakia's ruin would be ironed out, Roosevelt immediately wired Chamberlain "Good man."

Munich did not buy peace but only fed the dictator's appetite, as Winston Churchill, then a mere backbencher, had said it would. On October 9, 1938, Hitler announced that he would further strengthen his western defenses. Two days later, Roosevelt said that he would spend another $300 million on armaments, and told reporters that he would probably ask Congress for an additional half a billion. Sharing the general view that Germany's air force was unbeatable, a fiction that Colonel Charles A. Lindbergh had unwittingly done so much to promote, Roosevelt toyed with various schemes to enhance Western air power. At a White House conference on November 14 he told the military that he wanted an Army Air Corps of 10,000 planes and the capacity to produce 20,000 aircraft a year. This was a popular course.[12] The polls had consistently showed support for a larger military, and for more aircraft most of all. Owing to its superior publicity machine, the Army Air Corps—which civilians called the "Air Force," as if it were already independent—always received higher ratings than the Army ground forces and the Navy.[13]

The War Department threw cold water on Roosevelt's proposal; claiming it would result in planes without pilots, airfields, or support facilities, and so most of the new aircraft would be grounded. Roosevelt had to settle for 6,000 planes, aircraft procurement being tied to the acquisition of air bases and flight personnel. The chiefs were right that the armed services could not as yet absorb large numbers of aircraft, but had Roosevelt insisted on a crash program, there would have been aircraft to spare for the Allies in 1940, the year when their need would prove greatest. The upshot must have inclined FDR to trust his own judgment more, for he would frequently overrule the service chiefs thereafter, usually with good results.[14]

On August 22, 1939 Stalin agreed to a Nazi–Soviet nonaggression pact that saved Hitler from having to fight a war on two fronts and ensured the defeat of France. Eighteen days earlier Roosevelt had sent a prophetic telegram to Moscow urging Stalin not to deal with Berlin, and warning against just such an outcome. He also predicted that if France fell, Russia's turn would come next. Stalin paid the message no mind, though perhaps he remembered it two years later when the Panzers were at his gates. Not anticipating that turn of events, Communists everywhere were soon hailing the Pact as a masterstroke that had saved Russia from immediate attack. In later years they would say that it earned Russia time to become better prepared. Further, it was rationalized, Stalin had no choice but to accept the deal once the Munich Conference had shown that the Allies would continue to appease Hitler.

In actual fact Stalin betrayed the anti-Fascist cause not after Munich, when the Allies surrendered to German demands, but after they had guaranteed the territorial integrity of Poland and shown a willingness to fight. Stalin seems to have assumed that if fighting broke out the result would be another stalemate, as in World War I. This led him to conclude that, with Germany and the Allies bogged down on a new Western Front, he would be free to swallow fresh territories and digest them at leisure. Thus, the Pact contained secret provisions allowing Russia, under conditions soon realized, to take a part of Finland, which Stalin attacked that winter, Estonia, Latvia, eastern Poland, and the Rumanian province of Bessarabia, while western Poland and Lithuania were reserved for the Germans. An historic act of villainy, the Pact was an historic error, too, which nearly destroyed the Soviet Union. As Churchill put it, the subsequent invasion of Russia would show Stalin and his underlings to be "the most completely outwitted bunglers of the Second World War."[15] Although there were other contenders for this title, the Soviet claim was a strong one.

As a result of the Pact, on September 1, 1939 Germany invaded Poland with 1.5 million men and six Panzer (armored) divisions. The Poles, outnumbered, outgunned, and only half-mobilized, never had a chance, becoming the first victims of Hitler's blitzkrieg, the "lightning war" that no one had anticipated. Only a French attack on Germany's lightly defended Western frontier might have saved Poland, but the French were unready and unwilling to stir from their famous Maginot Line. Panzer attacks quickly broke the Poles, and soon their armies were either surrounded or in flight. Poland's doom was sealed on the seventeenth, when Russia began occupying eastern Poland and, with Hitler's reluctant consent, Lithuania and the other Baltic states. On the twenty-eighth, Warsaw was taken after a two week siege, and Poland ceased to exist.

Although Poland's prewar government had been far from ideal, having seized its share of Czechoslovakia after Munich; Poles were "the bravest of the brave, too often led by the vilest of the vile," Churchill later wrote.[16] Yet, they fought gallantly, and did not deserve what befell them. Poland's agony would be the longest and among the most terrible of any country in Europe.

The United States, to no one's surprise, was impotent during the crisis. Roosevelt sent off the usual notes with the usual lack of success. Two days after war broke out he gave a "Fireside Chat" assuring Americans that the United States would remain neutral. But, public opinion, though solidly opposed to entering the war, was not exactly neutral. Polls showed that 80 percent wanted the Allies to win, and more than half favored giving aid to France and Britain so long as doing so presented little risk. Thus encouraged, Congress finally revised the Neutrality Act, permitting the sale of weaponry to Allied nations on a cash-and-carry basis, which, as the United States had few munitions to sell, was next to meaningless in practice.

When Hitler launched his blitzkrieg in the West on May 10, 1940, America had done nothing either to deter his attack or enable the Allies to withstand it. On May 28, 1940, Belgium surrendered to Germany, moving the United States up to eighteenth place in Army size, just ahead of Bulgaria. Chief of Staff George C. Marshall testified before Congress that in a pinch he might be able to field 80,000 troops, a great exaggeration, while the Army Air Corps could send 160 pursuit ships aloft—some of them recent models. When war broke out Roosevelt had feared to offend isolationists by pointing out the need for a real defense program. But, in May he asked Congress for $1.8 billion in additional military spending, over half of it for the Army. And he proposed that the nation commit itself to a 50,000 plane air force and additionally acquire the capability to manufacture 50,000 aircraft a year—arousing considerable disbelief, since industry was then producing at the rate of 2,000 such machines annually. In 1941 the industry would produce almost 20,000 planes, and ultimately 300,000. These were popular steps, as the Gallup organization had revealed that only a small minority of Americans believed the armed forces to be strong enough to guard the United States against attack.

To arm the nation required time, so Roosevelt took his first gamble. Britain had saved its soldiers at Dunkirk in June 1940, but they had left their weapons ashore. Disregarding his military advisors, who correctly pointed out that America had nothing to spare, FDR ordered General Marshall to strip the armories and arsenals and send everything possible to Britain, which now, in its darkest hour, was finally being given resolute leadership by its new PM, Winston Churchill. By October 1940 the United States had delivered to the British 970,000 rifles, 87,500 machine guns, 895 French "75s" and great quantities of ammunition. Though mostly of World War I vintage, these munitions were useful for training troops and equipping Britain's last line of defense, the overage Home Guard. Old weapons were better than none, and providing them was to offer real support. Also encouraging was Roosevelt's promise to supply Britain with 14,000 aircraft by April 1942. This was Roosevelt at his best, cool, intrepid, decisive, the qualities that in the end would always redeem his failings. He also made Henry Stimson, who had been Taft's Secretary of War and Hoover's Secretary of State, Secretary of War again, while Frank Knox, a newspaper publisher, became Secretary of the Navy. These Republicans succeeded the two most isolationist members of FDR's Cabinet, and gave his defense policy a bipartisan flavor in time for the upcoming election. Though FDR preferred to work directly with the service chiefs, Knox and Stimson would become influential figures in the war effort, and major political assets.[17]

Roosevelt already had the best Army chief a president could want in George Cattlett Marshall, Jr. A 1901 graduate of Virginia Military Institute, he had served in the Philippines and elsewhere, attended and taught at many service schools, and, during the Great War, as Chief of Operations of First Army helped plan its offensives. Marshall influenced many junior officers during his later tour as Assistant Commandant of the Infantry Training School at Fort Benning, Georgia. In his training program Marshall reduced all tactics to one—the holding attack. As Geoffrey Perret says:

> It could be taught in less than five minutes. It didn't matter what the terrain was like, what the weather was like, or what size force was involved—it was always the same. You used some of your troops to advance and pin down the enemy with fire, while other troops under your command tried to find a way to strike the enemy in the flank or rear. If you could spare them you held some troops in reserve so you could exploit success or, if things went wrong, shore up your position."[18]

Benning was the test site for the new Army that Marshall would build to implement this idea.

He experimented with infantry battalions in order to discover the optimum size, which proved to be about 850 men, still the standard in most armies. Disliking the Army's World War I "square" infantry division of four regiments, he established that a triangular division of three regiments was more mobile and efficient. To make up for its smaller size he added firepower: a field artillery battalion to each regiment, a heavy weapons company (mortars and machine guns) to each battalion, and a weapons platoon to each company. Later a tank battalion would be attached to most infantry divisions. This gave the triangular division several times the firepower of its predecessor. It also met the needs of a holding attack, providing one unit for maneuver and one for fire support while keeping one in reserve. The result of Marshall's labors was *Infantry in Battle* (1934), a text produced by the Infantry School that communicated his ideas and methods throughout the Army, laying the groundwork for his transformation of it when he became Chief of Staff in 1939.

As its chief, Marshall built the Army from scratch. Working with the small cadre of professional officers, and with ideas tested in the excellent Army schools, he forged a mighty weapon. Its basis was the 12 million citizen–soldiers who would serve under him during the war, the best educated men of any army. Between 1900 and 1920 there had been a revolution in American education, free public high schools becoming open to nearly everyone. Marshall had seen the results at first hand when he was assigned to Roosevelt's Civilian Conservation Corps, which put unemployed young men to work on outdoor projects. He was impressed by these youngsters, and as chief of staff based the Army's training camps and schools on the well-founded assumption that they would make fine troops.

Churchill called Marshall "the architect of victory," which was generous considering how often they were at odds over military planning. Marshall was distinguished by his intelligence, fairness, strength of character, and integrity. Most who worked for or with him held Marshall in awe, and were at least slightly afraid of him, not because he was a bully like Admiral King—though he did have a temper—but because to fail Marshall was unthinkable. Austere, aloof, coldly formal, almost the only man Roosevelt did not call by his first name, trying that only once, Marshall brought out the best in his senior officers. Most owed their appointments and promotions to having impressed him previously. Two hundred men he met at Benning alone became Generals, their names taken from a little black book in which he recorded his impressions. Despite his lack of the common touch, Marshall was respected by Congress for his knowledge, authority, and forthrightness. This combination of powerful support and unbeatable qualities was of immense value to the President and the country alike.

Roosevelt would sorely try the patience of Marshall and his new service secretaries by refusing to get very far ahead of public opinion, regardless of the military risks. As he had to win reelection before all else, and knowing how much opposition there would be to his seeking an unprecedented third term, Roosevelt moved slowly on preparedness—wasting 1940. This frustrated Marshall although he later conceded that Roosevelt had done about as much as the political situation allowed. If he erred on the side of caution, in doing so Roosevelt stored up political capital for the times when he had to be daring.

While America failed until the election was over to mobilize for war, events waited for no man or nation. Having conquered France and driven Britain from Europe, Hitler assumed that Churchill would strike a bargain with him, giving Germany a free hand on the Continent in return for the secure possession of its Empire. The advantage to Britain being so obvious, Hitler was infuriated by its refusal to negotiate. He therefore unleashed his U-boats on British shipping. As Britain braced itself for the onslaught, Churchill asked Roosevelt for 50 or 60 old destroyers, mothballed veterans of World War I, to help keep her sea lanes open. "Mr. President, with great respect I must tell you that in the long history of the world, this is a thing to do now."[19] The Prime Minister knew that the next few months would decide Britain's fate, and that of the Free World also.

Roosevelt wished to oblige Churchill, but the law seemed to forbid that. A group of private citizens suggested getting around the law by exchanging destroyers for military bases on British territory in the Americas. The destroyer deal could be put forward as strengthening national defense, which indeed it would. The Cabinet liked this proposal, especially such hawks as Knox, Stimson, and Ickes, and so did the Republican Presidential candidate, Wendell Willkie, whose support was considered crucial. Unfortunately, for political reasons he could not reveal his position. To make matters worse, the Selective Service bill, the first step toward building an army, was stalled in Congress, and might go down to defeat if the destroyer deal proved unpopular.

Yet, Britain was fighting for its life. Because the job would hardly be worth having if he gained reelection by letting Britain go under, Roosevelt took another chance. On September 3, 1940 the destroyer deal was announced to widespread recriminations, both for its own sake and because the President had bypassed Congress. Some argued that it was a bad idea, not only because it violated neutrality but also because if Britain were defeated, the destroyers being traded to the Royal Navy could be turned against the United States. To FDR and his supporters, however, that made it all the more vital that Britain not lose the war.[20]

Willkie finally endorsed FDR's decision but condemned his

methods, calling his failure to involve Congress "the most dictatorial and arbitrary act of any President of the United States."[21] It was high-handed, no doubt, but Roosevelt had taken a courageous position for this exchange amounted to much more than simply turning over a handful of obsolete ships. In fact, materially the deal was not to Britain's advantage, since the bases were worth far more than the old "four-stackers" that Britain gained in return. The swap's true importance was that it brought America closer to entering the war, if not as an active participant, at least as an arms supplier. This was a bold step considering that Roosevelt had not yet been reelected.

Willkie, a dark horse who had gained the GOP Presidential nomination by appealing to the rank and file over the heads of party bosses, was in deep trouble as election day drew near. He was a moderate who believed in both preparedness and aid to Britain, and thus failed to present himself as much of an alternative to the President. He campaigned vigorously, Roosevelt hardly at all, yet in October the President was comfortably ahead in the polls and Willkie beside himself. Desperate for office, Willkie abandoned not only his own principles, but also the liberal, internationalist advisors who shared them. Instead, he harkened to the Republican Old Guard, which believed that fear mongering was in order. Claiming that Roosevelt was bent on war and that American boys were already in troopships bound for Europe, Willkie began pandering to isolationism. As Robert Sherwood later observed: "The campaign really descended to the lower depths and became, for two impassioned weeks, pretty much of a national disgrace."[22] Despite the danger to America, Willkie's recklessness paid off.

Because all indicators suggested that Willkie was gaining ground, Democratic leaders panicked, begging Roosevelt to go the limit for his and the party's sake. Reluctantly he obliged, saying in Boston on October 30 that the American people need have no fear. "Your boys are not going to be sent into any foreign wars."[23] This was a low point, indeed, for both candidates knew that the chances of avoiding war were between slim and nonexistent. Democracy survived this charade somehow, though it must be said in defense of Roosevelt that he had little choice once Willkie's campaign caught fire. For this lie, plus his own brilliant campaign, Roosevelt was rewarded on election day with a majority of 5 million popular and 367 electoral votes.

After the 1940 elections were safely past, Roosevelt came to grips with Britain's most pressing need, which was credit to sustain its American purchases. When Great Britain declared war its liquid reserves were sufficient to cover only a few months of fighting. Somehow the British muddled through, but by the fall of 1940 they were out of cash. Roosevelt had pledged that in 1941 they could buy enough equipment for 10 divisions and 12,000 more aircraft in addition to the 14,000 already committed. However, he did not wish to confront the issue of payment while still running for reelection. London held its peace until November 23, when the British Ambassador, Lord Lothian, cheerfully told reporters "Well, boys, Britain's broke; it's your money we want."[24] At last people knew the truth, it remained to be seen if they would accept the consequences. These amounted in the short run to repealing or amending the Neutrality laws forbidding loans to belligerents, requiring them to purchase arms on a cash-and-carry basis. It also meant making huge loans to Britain, a crucial step, as everyone knew, down the road to war under Wilson.

Polls showed that most Americans still hoped to remain neutral. They favored aid to Britain, but to what extent and at what risk was uncertain. Gallup indicated that 90 percent of the people surveyed favored more aid to Britain, and 60 percent believed that it was more important to aid Britain than to stay out of the conflict, but only 12 percent would vote for a declaration of war on Germany. Roosevelt lacked a clear mandate, and he could not bypass Congress because he needed it to legislate the mobilization of men and material. Everything hung in the balance. Britain could not carry the burden alone any more, and if it fell there would be no security for America. People sensed this, but could not bring themselves to accept the obvious conclusion. The times called for inspired leadership and Roosevelt would provide it.

At first Roosevelt stalled and went on vacation, letting the pressure of events build up. Upon his return to Washington he met with the press and announced his answer to Britain's need, the program that became known as Lend-Lease. This was simply a method to supply Britain on credit, precisely what the isolationists feared. But Roosevelt had packaged it cleverly. The United States was not going to loan the British money, never fear; still less would it give away munitions. It was simply going to remove the "silly, foolish old dollar sign" by lending armaments to the British, which they would later pay for in kind or return.

Roosevelt compared Lend-Lease to a garden hose which one unhesitatingly lends to a neighbor if his house is on fire—receiving it or a replacement back when the fire is out. Reporters asked whether doing so would involve convoying goods to Britain. Roosevelt denied this, possibly even to himself. He acknowledged that it would require congressional approval, but refused to admit that it increased the risk of war. No one asked what repayment "in kind" meant, although that was the key question. If it referred to surplus weaponry after the war, then Lend-Lease would actually be a gift.[25] No doubt reporters failed to ask the question because they did not wish to hear the answer.

Thanks to their support the press conference was a triumph. Introducing Lend-Lease in this casual way made it seem less significant than it was. That the garden hose metaphor worked despite being a fiction might be interpreted to mean the public was exceedingly gullible. A better explanation is that Americans wanted to do the right thing, and would act responsibly if offered a face saving way to get around the prevailing dogmas. Years of antiwar propaganda had made it hard to look squarely at the truth—that Britain's fight was America's as well—yet people were waking up.

Roosevelt capped his performance with a Fireside Chat on December 29, assuring his radio audience that he was not speaking of war but rather about national security. The issue was how to keep the nation "out of a last-ditch war for the preservation of American independence and all the things that American independence means to you and to me and to ours."[26] Never in American history had the danger been so great, for, as the Tripartite Pact showed, the Axis powers were seeking world domination. If Britain fell all Americans would live at the point of a gun, and to survive "We would have to convert ourselves permanently into a militaristic power on the basis of a war economy." There was no hiding out in our hemisphere, because airplanes had reduced the travel time between for example Africa and Brazil to five hours. There was only one hope: to keep Britain and its allies fighting by making ourselves "the great arsenal of democracy."

It was a magnificent speech in support of a grand decision. The timing was right also, witness a Gallup poll released the same day, showing that 60 percent of the American people favored aid to Britain, even at the risk of war. Yet, when asked if they favored the President's bill, the public's response was hardly overwhelming. A poll released on February 10 found that 54 percent favored it and 22 percent were opposed, while 15 percent offered only qualified support.

Despite the isolationists' opposition, the Lend-Lease bill, HR-1776, passed with resounding majorities in the Senate on March 8, 1941, and in the House three days later, aided by polls showing that, thanks to aggressive promotion, the public now supported it by margins of two to one. Though it lifted British morale, and Churchill called it a "new Magna Carta," Lend-Lease initially had little effect, as the weapons Britain could buy with its new charge account existed only on paper. Though $14 billion was appropriated under Lend-Lease, in 1941 Britain would receive only $1 billion worth of munitions, all that could be spared, given American unreadiness.

Lend-Lease was enacted only after Britain had been compelled to prove that the cupboard really was bare by opening its books. In December 1940, and again in the following March, U.S. warships went to South Africa to take delivery of all the gold that the British Empire then possessed. Besides taking British assets, drastic restrictions were written into the Act to prevent Britain from reexporting Lend-Lease goods. London thought these measures were actually designed to give American businessmen easier admission to imperial markets.

This set the pattern for many later negotiations in which Americans would obtain commercial advantage from British weaknesses. Throughout the war American suspicion of British designs became the justification for sharp business practices. This behavior, although not very friendly, was impossible to prevent. American political leaders feared exposing themselves to charges of having been hoodwinked yet again by clever British diplomats, as their predecessors supposedly had been during World War I. By seeming to drive a hard bargain, politicians tried to insure themselves against any such backlash. No matter: Yet, whatever the cost to His Majesty's Government, Britain received in Lend-Lease and other aid much more than it lost as a result of these actions.

Though often represented as foreign aid, Lend-Lease was really in America's interest. Its formal title, "An Act to Promote the Defense of the United States," was the literal truth. Isolationists echoed Senator Burton K. Wheeler, who claimed that Lend-Lease resembled the New Deal's farm program in that it "will plow under every fourth American boy," a phrase that Communist folk-singers set to music.[27] Overseas there was grumbling that, through Lend-Lease, America was prepared to fight to the last Briton. Still, as a promise of things to come, Lend-Lease was vitally important and did much to cement Anglo–American relations. The appointments of Harry Hopkins as head of Lend-Lease, and Averell Harriman as overseer of its distribution in the United Kingdom, both good friends of Britain, helped take some of the sting out of its growing dependency.

While Congress discussed the pros and cons of Lend-Lease, German preparations for Operation Barbarossa, the Nazi invasion of

Russia, were going ahead. Germany would soon have 3.3 million men in 142 divisions deployed on its Eastern Front. Peculiarly, although so great a force could not be concealed, its purpose remained unclear: Hitler might be bluffing, or he might be planning to take the Suez Canal. A campaign in Russia would delay the invasion of Britain, and, for many analysts, that was almost too good to be true.

A further worry was the rising threat of German submarines, which were growing in number and ranging farther afield. They had sunk 41 Allied vessels in March 1941 alone. Together with those sunk by aircraft and surface raiders, British ship losses amounted to 500,000 tons a month. Annualized this would result in the destruction of one-quarter of Britain's merchant marine, more than three times the tonnage it could replace. In response, on March 15, Roosevelt mobilized the Atlantic Fleet, beginning a series of steps that would result in America's joining the Battle of the Atlantic without a declaration of war.

Churchill wanted America to start fighting Germany in the Atlantic at once, or at least provide the Royal Navy with more destroyers. Roosevelt remained hesitant. In March a Gallup poll showed that 83 percent of the public would vote to remain neutral, although 67 percent now favored more aid to Britain even at the risk of war. Another Gallup poll, released on April 23, showed that only 41 percent of respondents wished to see the U.S. Navy escort convoys, though 71 percent said they would support the move if it appeared that Britain would collapse otherwise. No one could say how the public would react if convoying led the Navy to fire upon U-boats. To compound Roosevelt's problems, the weak Atlantic Fleet would not be fit for action until mid-May at the earliest. If in the interim more destroyers were given to Britain, the Fleet would be weaker still, and slower to put to sea.

Though public-opinion polling had only just begun, the drawbacks were already evident. Government by poll meant trying to square a circle, because the public's position all too often owed nothing to logic. If Britain's survival was important to the United States, then it could not wait to see whether Britain was going to fall. If, on the other hand, British survival did not matter, then the United States ought to have stayed at peace, regardless of events. Instead, a series of polls released in April showed that 68 percent of respondents believed that the United States should declare war if there was no other way to defeat Germany and Italy, and 82 percent believed that the United States was going to enter the war anyway, but only 19 percent favored declaring war now. If any sense could be made of these results, the public seemed to feel that the United States must and would enter the war, but should wait until the very last minute—when, obviously, the likelihood of defeat would be greatest.

During March the first German offensive in Libya, where Hitler had intervened to save Italy from disaster, threw the British into retreat. On April 6 Germany invaded Yugoslavia, which had a new government that refused to cast its lot with Hitler, and also Greece, where hapless Italian invaders had been bogged down since October. Since delay appeared ever more risky, FDR authorized the transfer of a handful of ships from Pearl Harbor to the Atlantic. On April 10, with the Danish government-in-exile concurring, he took over Greenland's defense, thus entering the North Atlantic combat zone that Hitler had proclaimed in March. By this time Roosevelt had already provided Britain with 10 Coast Guard cutters and 60 patrol planes, authorized American yards to repair British vessels, turned over 1 million tons of confiscated Axis shipping, and approved construction of 200 additional vessels for the British Merchant Marine.

In late April the U.S. Atlantic Fleet extended its patrols, but denied Churchill's request to put the Azores and Cape Verde Islands under surveillance, because an American carrier force could visit the area for only one or two days out of every ten. Stretched thin as it was, the Navy was still better off than the Army and its Air Corps. Not wanting to alarm the public, General Marshall told a Senate committee that in terms of readiness the Army was "over the hump," while the aptly named Brigadier General Larry L. Twaddle, head of the Operations and Training Division of the General Staff, went so far as to say "We have created a fighting army in less than a year."[28]

Actually, the 1st Infantry Division was almost ready, and to it might be added the understrength 1st Marines, a combined force of 25,000 men. In all its commands, the Air Corps had a total of 53 heavy bombers, 91 medium bombers, 92 light bombers, and 327 fighters, compared to the 2,700 aircraft and hundreds of divisions, including those of its allies, that Germany was about to launch against Russia.[29] To be sure, there was the Pacific Fleet, with its 12 battleships, three carriers, two dozen cruisers, and 50 destroyers, but while FDR worried about how to use them, Greece fell, the British forces who had come to its aid falling back on Crete.

According to plans worked out with the British ahead of time, when America entered the war it would turn its strength against Germany, remaining at peace with Japan. By this reasoning the Pacific Fleet, or a good part of it, should be sent to the North Atlantic, leaving the Air Corps to defend Hawaii, as General Marshall suggested. Hull balked at the idea. Weakening the Pacific Fleet would encourage Japanese militarists and undermine his talks with Tokyo's ambassador. Roosevelt compromised by ordering the transfer of three battleships, four cruisers, and 13 more destroyers to the Atlantic, too few vessels to satisfy Stimson and those eager to assist Britain, too many if Hull was right. Thus, the United States drifted toward war in the midst of a strategic vacuum.

To interventionists these steps were excessively gradual. Stimson, who had an uncomplicated view of foreign relations, was especially eager for action. In his memoirs Stimson wrote: "The final issue of policy was always one of right and wrong, not peace and war."[30] In this spirit he urged Roosevelt to drive forward, start naval convoying at once, and quickly get into the fight. Britain had lost 1.5 million tons of shipping in the first four months of 1941. As it produced only 2.1 million tons a year, Britain was running out of freighters. Stimson had considerable respect for FDR, but could not help wishing that at this critical moment Theodore Roosevelt were President. TR would have brushed the "contemptible" isolationists aside and braced the nation to its duty.

Events forced Roosevelt's hand just the same, even if all too slowly. On May 20 the British were driven from Crete. Polls taken afterward showed that a majority of Americans were now in favor of convoying, and Roosevelt decided to occupy Iceland, which was not the same thing but would give America a base in the mid-Atlantic that could support convoy operations. On May 27 Roosevelt issued a declaration of unlimited national emergency, and then—to the despair of many— undercut its effectiveness in a press conference on the following day. Caught between Hitler and isolationism, Roosevelt was still taking a step backward for every step or two ahead.

A columnist in the *London Daily Mirror* could be forgiven for saying of the Americans "They seem to have taken up permanent residence on the brink. The runners are on their marks! The starter pulls the trigger! There is an explosion like a feather falling on velvet . . . Don't miss the next tense installment of this gripping drama next week . . . next month . . . sometime . . . never."[31]

On June 22 Germany invaded Russia, transforming the war. It was Hitler's biggest blunder to date, and Roosevelt knew it. Russia might hold out. If it didn't, at least more time would be gained to pursue victory in the Atlantic. This was so obvious that even such an isolationist publication as *The Saturday Evening Post* got the point, observing that all Hitler could get by invading Russia was a long war, the last thing he needed. "None of this quite makes sense," it remarked, expressing the general confusion.[32] Germany's invasion of Russia did ensure its defeat. The war would cost Germany 13.6 million casualties, the total of dead, wounded, and taken prisoner. Of these 10 million would be incurred on the Eastern Front. Without the Soviets no Allied coalition could hope to retake Europe, but, thanks to Hitler, when the time came, Russia would be in the fight.

Churchill at once gave a broadcast offering aid to Moscow, though he had nothing much to spare. On July 7 an American occupation force landed in Iceland, giving the United States a forward base commanding the sea lanes upon which Britain's survival depended. On July 10 Roosevelt met with Soviet Ambassador Constantine Oumansky, and, supported by a Gallup poll showing that 72 percent of respondents wanted Russia to defeat Hitler, offered limited help. About this time he also ordered the Navy to prepare for escort duty. The Atlantic Fleet was still not up to the mark, but for various reasons U-boat activities fell off and from late June until early September no convoyed ships were lost. This pause gave the Navy much needed time to prepare for its daunting task. Yet, as little use was made of the time gained thereby, interventionists became increasingly anxious.

To *Life* magazine it seemed as if the American defense effort was all talk. Roosevelt had spoken of the need for total defense. "But the fact is that this spring, after one year of total verbal defense, we are producing mechanical luxuries that compete with defense not merely in normal but in boom quantities. He has encouraged this country to remain asleep and to dream that it could defeat Hitler without sacrifice, or even without inconvenience."[33] Though unjust to FDR, who was doing his best, this was not far off the mark.

On August 4 Roosevelt slipped quietly out of New London, transferring at sea to the cruiser *Augusta* for a rendezvous with Churchill. They met in a bay off Argentia, Newfoundland to pursue what turned out to be somewhat different agendas. Churchill hoped for American promises of additional support, especially against Japan which both knew was gearing up for offensive action, possibly in Southeast Asia. Roosevelt wanted a joint statement of principles that would establish the basis for a democratic war effort. With Woodrow Wilson's errors in mind, Roosevelt would see to it that the United States did not announce its war aims unilaterally as before. Wilson had proclaimed his Fourteen Points without gaining pledges of support for them from the Allies, which weakened him at Versailles. Roosevelt intended that this time the Allies would commit to America's goals before it entered the war.[34]

Roosevelt must have had additional things in mind, since agreement on generalities did not really require a summit. Probably he meant to encourage Churchill, and to placate interventionists, who were dismayed by the slow progress toward war. Whatever the case, since Roosevelt attached great importance to personal contacts, he was eager to take Churchill's measure. They had met only once, and then cursorily during the previous war. Further, he loved the romance of it, the secret arrangements, code names, cover stories, which satisfied his appetite for theater and surprises.

The document that resulted from this meeting, what became known as the Atlantic Charter, was not very important. It included the usual Wilsonian principles: self-determination of peoples (Churchill, who still hoped to save the British Empire, crossing his fingers); freedom of trade; freedom of the seas (more crossed fingers); disarmament; and eventually some kind of collective security system. Roosevelt was vague about Japan, but he could promise the PM an American convoy system, having already decided upon it. Then too, at Argentia his tentative interest in supporting Russia received much encouragement, from Churchill and from the Eastern Front itself, where Russia seemed to be holding.

As the conference was largely symbolic, its value depended upon the weight given to symbols. To Roosevelt and his supporters Argentia was a great success, which may have been true so far as publicity went. Robert Sherwood, whose biography of Hopkins is lucid and essential, but also one-sided, maintained that the Atlantic Charter was the "cornerstone" of the United Nations. To the British, who had hoped for more definite commitments, the conference was disappointing, though, as usual, Churchill put the best possible face on things. To isolationists the Charter was a mask behind which Roosevelt had secretly agreed to invade Europe. This, unfortunately, was one claim that had no basis at all in fact. At the very least Argentia did no harm, which is more than can be said of later conferences.

The distance still to be traveled was underlined on August 12, Argentia's last day, when the House extended the term of enlistment for draftees from one year to two and a half by the margin of a single vote, following the polls, it seems, as Gallup had recently disclosed that public opinion was evenly split. Had this vote gone the other way the first draft of conscripts would have gone home in October, leaving the Army in a shambles.[35] Though disaster was averted, as a measure of American nonchalance, the close vote and divided public opinion spoke volumes, and did little for British spirits, which declined further when Roosevelt, on his return to Washington, kept insisting that America was no closer to war than when he left. This was a necessary feature of the odd dialectic between President and people, in which FDR gave assurances he did not mean, and they pretended to believe him. Gradually, Americans were becoming aware that the war could not be fought only by surrogates. But the old clichés died hard, and Roosevelt still felt obliged to pay them lip service.

Thus, while the machinery of intervention was cranking up, nothing forced a decision, not even an initial skirmish on September 4 when the U.S. destroyer *Greer* tracked a U-boat in the American defense zone. Though under strict orders not to attack American warships, the German commander could not be certain who was stalking him, and when a British aircraft bombed it, U-652 retaliated by firing off two torpedoes. The Greer then made depth charge attacks upon it until twilight ended hostilities. Roosevelt used this incident to authorize convoying on a larger scale than had been planned, and over the radio told Americans that, in defense of the freedom of the seas, he was instructing naval vessels to shoot Axis warships on sight. It was an order approved by 62 percent of those Gallup polled.

In October and November Roosevelt accelerated and greatly broadened Lend-Lease to Russia, at the expense of both British and American needs. In this he was again supported by the polls, though there was substantial opposition within the Administration, and around the country, to aiding the Soviets. The Stalin–Hitler Pact had not been forgotten, nor Russia's annexation of the Baltic States, nor its Winter War against Finland in 1939–40. Some agreed with Senator Harry Truman that the two despots should be left alone to wipe each other out. The military believed that because America's defenses were so weak, nothing could be spared for Russia. Roosevelt understood that aid was essential, not only to keep Russia alive, but even more to get what would certainly be a closer association with the Soviets off to a good start. Thus he took another step toward war.

In October Roosevelt asked Congress to further revise the Neutrality Act so that American merchantmen could be armed, 72 percent of the public approving, and indicated that he favored allowing U.S. ships to operate in war zones and enter belligerent ports. While Congress was reflecting on these proposals, the destroyer *Kearny* was torpedoed, at a cost of 11 lives. On October 31, a U-boat sank the *Reuben James*, with the loss of 115 sailors. The public remained apathetic, only 26 percent wanting to get into the war, making no such demands as had followed submarine attacks a quarter of a century earlier. Its passivity dashed Roosevelt's hope that an incident at sea would inspire Congress to declare war, and Hitler stubbornly refused to solve FDR's problem by declaring war on the United States. By following the rules of American politics Roosevelt had achieved only failure. Never was it more important to fight Germany than after Russia came into the picture. Yet the United States seemed about as far away from intervening as ever. It remained for Japan, though at a fearful price, to save the Allied cause.

Historians have been critical of Roosevelt for not taking the lead more aggressively during this time of crisis. The truth is that great leadership only goes so far. In difficult times great followership is required as well. Americans would rise to the challenge eventually, but not of their own free will. One may criticize Roosevelt over small things—the timing of individual moves, the slowness of his naval escalation. But, even when the Atlantic Fleet was actually at war, people remained listless. It was American democracy that failed the test, not just, or even particularly, the American President.

3

The Lion and the Albatross

FDR and Lindy

Franklin Delano Roosevelt was the greatest American political hero of his time, and Charles A. Lindbergh the greatest popular hero. Each embodied a different side of the great debate over American foreign policy. Lindbergh was the foremost isolationist in the land and became the principal spokesman of the anti-interventionist movement. Roosevelt was always the leading advocate of aid to the Allies. That the unequal struggle between them lasted so long and was so bitterly fought testified not just to the renown of Lindbergh, but to the public division that crippled preparedness. Though they were as unlike each other as two Americans could be, together they represented the views of most citizens on the issue of intervention. Beyond FDR was the minority of committed interventionists. Beyond Lindbergh lay the demented right wing of anti-Semites and xenophobes. Between them stretched the moderate middle that each hoped to win over. Behind them were long, twisting roads that made each the enemy of the other. That such dissimilar men could frame the debate says much about the nature of American democracy, but, as events were to show, only one was a real democrat.

We see Roosevelt in documentary films today as the newsreels recorded him, the great head frequently tossed, the big frame, the flashing smile, the sweeping gestures, the rich voice with its peculiar diction. He was the most controversial president of this century, despised by conservatives and yet admired, even adored, by millions upon millions of people. Electorally he owned the cities of the North, and anyplace else that happened to have a working class majority. He was, it seems fair to say, the all time master of the electoral process. Accusations that he was a revolutionary socialist and a demagogue have faded. More durable is the memory of him as the paragon of statesmen, so much so that even Republican presidents like to be compared with him. Roosevelt now seems to have been the father of modern America, and its greatest leader, a view which, although not exactly wrong, leaves out the complexities that baffled those who knew him best.

As a youth Franklin Delano Roosevelt showed little interest in war and statecraft. He loved the Navy, to be sure, but more because he adored ships and the sea than out of lust for martial glory. In this, as in so many other ways, he differed from his famous cousin Theodore—a boxer, wrestler, and big-game hunter who relished blood and battle. Before he had fired a shot in anger, TR told officers at the Naval War College "No triumph of peace is quite so great as the supreme triumphs of war." After he led his Rough Riders to victory in Cuba, TR bragged to his friend Cabot Lodge that he had shot a Spaniard to death, doubling him over as "neatly as a jackrabbit."[1]

Like TR Franklin was athletic, but he disdained contact and blood sports in favor of swimming, sailing, and tennis. During World War I, while Theodore was moving heaven and earth to get command of a division, Franklin retained his post as Assistant Secretary of the Navy. FDR was not a pacifist and attempted to get into action as an officer commanding naval guns on the Western Front, an effort which, had Theodore been in Franklin's shoes, certainly would have succeeded. The crucial distinction was that while both were ardent interventionists, Theodore loved war and Franklin didn't. What he did enjoy was supreme command; and, when he finally achieved it, FDR would make many decisions himself of a kind that presidents before him had left to the military.

The effort to understand him has defeated many biographers, for Roosevelt was an enigmatic man whose inner life remains mysterious. He did not keep a diary or write revealing letters, and if he confided his secrets to intimate friends none ever revealed them. In the absence of confessional literature, historians have tended to take Roosevelt at face value. Here the problem has been to determine which of his faces to take. Many biographers have seen him as an heroic leader, intrepid, farsighted, and resourceful. There is much in the record to support this view, but at the same time, and some have refused to acknowledge this, FDR was devious and secretive as a matter of course—which makes him difficult to understand, even when one respects what seem to have been his motives. He was at once a lion and a fox, and the challenge facing his biographers has always been to reconcile the two.[2]

Roosevelt was born with a silver spoon in his mouth as the son of James Roosevelt, a wealthy gentleman farmer, and Sara Delano, whose family was even richer. Though the child of doting parents, Roosevelt was severely tested in boyhood. James was much older than Sara, his second wife, and began suffering from heart trouble when Franklin was nine. James would spend the last decade of his life as a semi-invalid. To protect him from worry, Sara and Franklin sometimes went to extreme lengths. Soon after James became ill, Franklin's head was badly cut in their private railroad car. To keep his father from learning of this, Franklin had Sara clean him up, then donned a hat to conceal the wound, and remained on the observation platform for hours until the gash was solidly crusted over. In addition to finding out about deceiving others for their own good, he thus learned, as Geoffrey Ward puts it, that "Unpleasant facts about which little could be done were best simply ignored."[3] The result was fortitude overlaid with a bright line of patter.

The greatest challenge that young Franklin had to meet was his mother's possessiveness. She did not want to share him with anyone except his father, and she wanted Franklin to do nothing inconsistent with his social position, that is to say, very little. She did not even want him to go to boarding school, though for future gentlemen that was now a must. Franklin loved his mother, but he seems to have understood early on that he would never amount to anything unless he escaped her loving grasp. In order to enter Groton, he was obliged to confront her directly. But as a rule he got his way through manipulation rather than defiance, exercising his charm to the fullest and avoiding disagreeable truths. This would always be Roosevelt's way of dealing with both social and political relationships.

Franklin also acquired—though not from Sara, who had high behavioral standards but was not ambitious for him—a powerful drive to succeed. Like most upper-class boys of his time, Roosevelt had little interest in academic honors. He was hungry for distinction and approval, and did not get enough of either at Groton. At Harvard

College he was also disappointed, failing of election to Porcellian (the most elite fraternity) a snub which rankled for decades. However, Roosevelt was voted editor in chief of the college newspaper in January, 1903, an honor that led him to remain at Harvard for another year, nominally as a graduate student.

On March 17, 1905 Franklin married his fifth cousin, Eleanor, President Theodore Roosevelt's niece, a misalliance that would be hard on both of them, especially Eleanor. Young Franklin was vain, pleasure-loving, ambitious, superficial, and self-possessed, while Eleanor was his opposite, her childhood having been blighted by loss. Her mother, Anna Hall Roosevelt, died of diphtheria in 1892 when Eleanor was not quite eight; her brother Elliott died from the same disease in 1893; and her father, TR's brother, of alcoholism in 1894. All three were carried off within a period of 21 months. Besides Eleanor, only her brother Hall survived, to become an alcoholic like his father. Until she was 15, Eleanor was raised by her Grandmother Hall, whose stern regime deprived her of much-needed affection.

In 1899 Eleanor had been sent to an English boarding school, where she spent the happiest part of her youth. In New York society, Eleanor felt inadequate, "But at Allenswood where friendship, loyalty, and intellect took precedence, she shone."[4] Her first experience with success, it planted seeds that would one day flower beyond anyone's expectations. Yet she remained sensitive and needy in ways Franklin could not meet. It was to prove a mixed blessing for both of them that they fell in love and were married.

In short order, Eleanor had five children. Franklin meanwhile studied law at Columbia. Admitted to the bar in 1907, he was elected to the New York State Senate in 1910, and appointed Assistant Secretary of the Navy by Woodrow Wilson in 1913, a post he held until nominated for Vice President by the Democrats in 1920. His relationship with Eleanor failed to follow this same upward course. Too many babies, too much interference by Sara, and too frequent absences by Franklin, made marriage something less than the blissful state Eleanor had pictured. In 1918 she learned that Franklin was having an affair with her own secretary and confidante. The marriage survived because divorce would have ruined Franklin's political career. Eleanor never forgave the betrayal, even though she herself was unable to provide Franklin with the same uncritical devotion as did Lucy Mercer.[5]

If no longer a love match, the Roosevelts' marriage went beyond mere convenience, this becoming evident when Franklin was struck down by poliomyelitis in 1921. Almost dying at first, he suffered great pain for a long time, and was crippled by the disease. The supreme crisis of his life, it was also the making of him as a leader. Perhaps he might have gotten through the ordeal on his own. He showed immense courage from the start, exhibiting not simply the graceful doggedness of his childhood but an attitude so positive as to seem barely credible. Far from merely brushing off sympathy or sorrow, he made his bedside a place of good cheer and high spirits. Nothing in his life better became him than the manner in which he almost left it, and he would be brave and gallant about his disability ever after.

As a cripple Roosevelt developed qualities he had never displayed in a life marked until then by privilege and good fortune: patience, dedication, acceptance of limitations, and the courage not to give up after failing in the presence of others. The methods he had used earlier were of little help; polio could not be charmed or deceived or manipulated. He had to fight it head-on, not to beat the disease, which was impossible, but to keep it from ruining his life. That he did so was his greatest victory, and the foundation of all that followed. The old faults remained, to plague those who would have to work for and with him, yet beneath them ran a vein of iron that otherwise might never have been uncovered.

Eleanor was his salvation during the worst years of FDR's illness. She was as determined as Franklin that he not retreat to the life of a country squire, as Sara Roosevelt expected. Eleanor formed an alliance with Louis Howe, Franklin's chief political aide, an untidy Irish–American commoner whose intimacy with Franklin she had previously resented. Howe moved into their house, and together he and Eleanor kept Franklin's career going while FDR struggled to get back on his feet. Because the nerves in his legs had been destroyed he never did, despite the efforts of many doctors and his purchase of a spa in Warm Springs, Georgia, which he believed had restorative powers.

Franklin learned to move horizontally for short distances, using crutches or canes or companions—this involving throwing his hips forward, one at a time, his braced legs following—and, by developing his upper body, managed to give the impression of radiant health. His skill at deception, and his talent for presenting himself in the best possible light, now combined to create an aura of strength and vigor that would enable him to win and hold the confidence of most Americans. He was a cripple all the same, and, however much he disguised it, Franklin remained, as a patient at Warm Springs wrote, "like ourselves, a polio first, and man and President after that. Only we could sense the endless tedium of his days, the being lifted in and out of chairs, of bed, bathtub, pool. And know that war and politics and the glory of his fame were outside of all this, strung like beads on the thread of the waiting days. . . ."[6]

With Howe's assistance, and with Eleanor serving as his eyes and ears in the places his legs could not take him, and as his conscience also, which was not exactly what he wanted in a wife but benefited from just the same, Roosevelt was elected Governor of New York in 1928. He had expected to run four years later, agreeing with Howe and Eleanor that Herbert Hoover would serve two terms in the White House, making 1932 the year for Albany and 1936, when the incumbent would have to step down, the year to run for President. But Al Smith needed someone to carry New York in his uphill fight against Hoover, and Roosevelt understood the first law of political life, which decreed that if he now failed to help Smith, New York's most important Democrat, Smith would not help him later. Fate, as if to make up for Roosevelt's legs, had dealt him the winning hand. He would be Governor of what was then America's most populous state when the Depression came, and thus in the best possible place for gaining the Democratic Presidential nomination in 1932, just when Hoover's political collapse would make the office available to a Democrat.

Roosevelt's luck was the nation's, too. Had he not been a governor in 1932, someone else would have been nominated by the Democrats, and Roosevelt would probably not have gotten the nod until 1940, and perhaps never. Even if he had gained the presidency at last, Roosevelt would have been learning his job at a moment in history when the nation required an experienced leader. Roosevelt's effectiveness during the war owed much to his previous two terms, including his early foreign policy ventures, which met with indifferent success.[7]

By 1940 Roosevelt was an accomplished policymaker. He enjoyed the trust of most Americans, and so had greater room for maneuver than if he had just stepped into office. He was a world-famous leader, which helped him deal with Churchill and Stalin. And he had the self-assurance that comes from having run a great country for years. He would require all these advantages to meet the demands of war, but, and here the timing was everything, they would be available when needed.

The man who guided America through depression and war was a study in contradictions. On one level he reminded people of his cousin Theodore, having a ready laugh, exuberant charm, and the ability to give off, even from his wheel chair, a sense of vibrant energy. On another level, the deepest and most authentic, some believed, Roosevelt was a closed book. It was this inner core, this private self, that led one of his long-time secretaries to insist that no one really knew him, and President Truman to say that Roosevelt didn't give a damn for anyone else in the world, an impression that was shared by a surprisingly large number of people who knew him better than Truman did. Dean Acheson, who worked for them both, greatly preferred Truman, resenting Roosevelt's familiarity with subordinates, which Acheson considered patronizing. Still, he admitted, this was a small thing compared to the primary impression Roosevelt made, the "essence" of which was "force."[8]

James MacGregor Burns writes of FDR's "bewildering complexity," since Roosevelt could be "bold or cautious, informal or dignified, cruel or kind, intolerant or long-suffering, urbane or almost rustic, impetuous or temporizing, Machiavellian or moralistic," all compounded by his "mercurial capacity to move from one mood to another, to deal with portentous public events with little private evasions, to lose himself" in bits of foolishness and seemingly aimless flights of fancy.[9] He was also a chronic dissembler, not averse to the outright lie, and short on loyalty.

To Joseph Alsop, a relative as well as a journalist who covered him, Roosevelt was, at bottom, "a truly good man." That is to say, he was against the bad men and bad things of this world, and a "stout friend" to all who struggled for fairness and decency. "In truth, he loved the light and loathed the darkness, and in hard and testing times he was also inspired and sustained—a point no longer fashionable to make but a true point none the less—by a simple, rather old-fashioned, but deep and unshakable Christian faith."[10]

Roosevelt's Christianity did not keep him from being a great user of people, including his nearest and dearest. Eleanor could attest to that, as also Marguerite Le Hand, known to intimates as "Missy," who worked at his campaign headquarters in 1920, and soon thereafter, at the age of 23, became his personal secretary, possibly his mistress, and certainly his "office wife"—with him much more than his real one. For the better part of two decades she was the person closest to Roosevelt. Yet, after she was felled by a stroke in 1941, FDR dropped her. Thereafter, Eleanor and members of his official family continued to remember Missy with gifts and letters, but Roosevelt seems not to have had any contact with her after November, 1941, although she lived for another 32 months. Following her death, and just before his own, FDR named a cargo ship in her honor, wiring the yard his hope "that a craft which bears so honored a name will make a safe journey and always find a peaceful harbor," a case, surely, of late being as bad as never.[11]

If there is no agreement on Roosevelt's character and leadership, few question his skills as politician and orator whose popularity was closely tied to his mastery of rhetoric. Equally fluent on the stump or on air, he was the most eloquent President since Lincoln, and the most versatile communicator. Roosevelt was the first President to hold regular press conferences, and the first to exploit the mass media, as with his famous "Fireside Chats," seemingly casual radio talks in which he spoke as if a guest of each listening family. These were highly successful, in part because he used them sparingly, giving only 16 during his first two terms in office.

Whatever the form he employed, Roosevelt knew exactly what he needed, and, though he could not write well himself, he was a skillful editor.[12] He would explain at length to Harry Hopkins, Robert Sherwood, a successful playwright, and Judge Samuel I. Rosenman— the last two doing most of the actual writing—whatever points he wished to make. The writers would then go off with their notes, his dictation, and various research materials, until they had produced an enormous rough draft for FDR's inspection.

Roosevelt would as a rule say it was too long, then make further additions. The writers would cut and rewrite, FDR would add more material, and the process would go on until as many as a dozen drafts (by some accounts 21) had been sacrificed to produce a final version.

The result seldom bore any sign of the labor that went into composing it. As a rule, FDR's speeches sounded fresh, were invariably simple, and at their best contained memorable phrases— "the only thing we have to fear is fear itself"—which became part of the language. Nor did Roosevelt ignore delivery. He made a point of employing frequently used words and phrases, talking more slowly than most politicians, his rate being 100 words a minute when 105 to 110 was usual. FDR always knew the exact number of words he could speak in a half hour, this figure varying from speech to speech, depending on how difficult the contents were and what he was trying to put over. In addition, his timing was perfect.

Roosevelt was not only the first President to hold regular press conferences, but remains the all-time champion. He held his initial meeting with reporters just four days after being inaugurated. The newsmen were so impressed with the differences between him and

Hoover that they broke into applause when he finished. Roosevelt played the press deftly, and by meeting with reporters two or three times a week provided them with reams of copy. As early as 1934 the United Press alone was distributing three times as much information from Washington as it had during Hoover's presidency. This increase in traffic made Washington press bureaus much more important than before, giving journalists every incentive to not bite the hand that fed them.

Roosevelt socialized with the press, invited it to previously closed functions, and raised the standing of reporters in general. A favored few were given "exclusives", though not so frequently as to antagonize the others. Newspapers were his most frequent medium of communication, and FDR manipulated them skillfully in order to both enhance his image and build support for his programs (despite the owners, 90 percent of whom opposed him). In all these ways Roosevelt added a new dimension to democratic leadership and set a standard never since equaled.

Still, rhetoric had its limits, as was demonstrated by the President's Navy Day speech on October 27, 1941. This was the strongest anti-German speech Roosevelt would give before Pearl Harbor. He declared that in firing upon American warships the Germans had attacked America itself. He said that he possessed a Nazi map of South and Central America realigning it into five vassal states; also a Nazi plan to "abolish all existing religions." Roosevelt therefore called upon Congress in the most urgent terms to arm American merchant ships. FDR was rebuked for this speech, not only by isolationists but by moderates, their charge being that the plan and map he had cited were not official German documents but the ravings of Nazi fanatics. In this view the President should be more straightforward, and discuss the national interest rather than the evils of Nazism, on which there already was widespread agreement. Supporters of the President maintained that the moderates' outlook was unrealistic: People respond to emotions, not to reasoned expositions, was their view.[13] The fact was, however, that FDR had been more temperate in the past without achieving striking results.

This, one of Roosevelt's most belligerent speeches, had remarkably little effect on Congress, which slowly and grudgingly did amend the Neutrality Act so that cargo ships could be armed, but gave FDR less support than it , and especially the Democrats, had on Lend-Lease. Nor did the public respond well, support for armed merchant ships actually declining after the President's speech. Roosevelt had done all that rhetoric could, exhausting the means available to a democratic leader. It remained for America's prospective enemies to determine when—or even if—it would go to war.

Of the opponents who prevented Roosevelt from taking a more aggressive stand, none was more formidable than Charles A. Lindbergh, "Lucky Lindy" to millions of fans, "the Lone Eagle" to newsmen. Though he never held office, or even ran for one, Lindbergh was more dangerous than any politician. Unlike Wendell Willkie, who might have turned Roosevelt out of office but would not have abandoned Britain, Lindbergh was a threat to democracy's survival.

With the passage of time, Lindbergh's original fame as the first to fly solo to Europe, and the notoriety following the murder of his infant son, have eclipsed his career in politics. He is the Lone Eagle in memory still. Lindbergh's fame derived only partially from his flight across the Atlantic in 1927. Extravagantly admired for this feat, he was honored even more for his deportment and what was taken to be his character. Americans saw him as fearless, modest, boyish, and unspoiled by his incomparable fame and the wealth it generated, some earned and some acquired by his marriage to Anne Morrow—the daughter of Dwight Morrow, America's Ambassador to Mexico and a former Morgan partner.

But people were mistaken. Distant and reserved, Lindbergh was also arrogant, overconfident, rigid, intolerant, and self-righteous. His reserve, mistaken for shyness, was the outward expression of his inner disdain for the mobs that trailed him everywhere. His aloofness ripened into contempt after the kidnaping and murder of his first child in 1932, or rather following the media circus that attended both it and the subsequent trial and execution of Bruno Hauptmann.

To escape the storm of publicity the Lindberghs fled to Great Britain in 1935. Lindbergh was as popular there as in America, but, thanks to British respect for privacy, he felt more at ease. This did not prevent him from giving aid and comfort to Nazi Germany, soon to be at war with his British hosts. Despite his origins as the son of a populist congressman from Minnesota, which ought to have made him at least as great a democrat as the patrician Roosevelt, Lindbergh was deeply conservative. A self-made engineer (he was a student at the University of Wisconsin for only three semesters), Lindbergh admired the German people for their efficiency and technological prowess, and the Nazis for having successfully exploited these national traits.

Lindbergh had supported the crusade of his father, Congressman C.

A. Lindbergh, against American participation in World War I, a stand which destroyed the elder Lindbergh's political career. This experience was much on Lindbergh's mind during his own similar campaign a generation later. So too was the idea that another Great War, no matter who won it, would destroy Western civilization and leave Soviet Communism as the only real victor, a common view among conservative isolationists.

Through the efforts of an American military attaché in Berlin, who hoped he would learn something useful, Lindbergh made several visits to Germany at the invitation of the Nazis. The first was for 11 days in July and August 1936, followed by two others, one of several weeks in 1937 and a final one from October 11 to 29, 1938. The visits were much alike. Lindbergh would meet a large number of leading figures in German aviation, tour airfields and factories, and be flattered by officials. On his third visit he was awarded a Nazi decoration by Hermann Goering himself, arousing, for the first time, press criticism in America. Lindbergh was genuinely impressed by the technical advances and extensiveness of German military aviation. In this he was only half right. Germany did have advanced military airplanes, but the gigantic aircraft industry that Lindbergh surveyed was an illusion. By duping him into believing they were much more productive than was actually the case, the Nazis persuaded Lindbergh that German air power was invincible.

While exaggerating their strength in aircraft, the Germans were also concealing from Lindbergh advances in rocketry, which would soon lead to production of the world's first ballistic missile. Years afterward, Lindbergh confronted one of those who had misled him, Adolf Baumker, formerly chief of research and development for the Luftwaffe, and latterly an American rocket scientist. Lindbergh reminded Baumker that when he visited Germany he was told that he would see everything, but hadn't. Baumker replied "Did you really expect to get the truth out of us?" To which Lindbergh replied simply "Yes, I did."[14] Ignorant of history and politics and already disposed in their favor, Lindbergh was an easy mark.

A poor intelligence agent, Lindbergh became an effective sapper of Allied morale. On September 21, 1938 America's Ambassador to Great Britain, the isolationist Joseph Kennedy, asked Lindbergh to give an estimate of German air strength. Lindbergh wrote a report unwittingly overstating both the number of German war planes and the productive capacity behind them. Prime Minister Neville Chamberlain possessed this document when he left for his meeting with Hitler at Bad

Godesberg on the twenty-second, a precursor to the infamous Munich agreement.[15] Britain and France would have betrayed Czechoslovakia in any case, but the Munich agreement was something Lindbergh had worked hard for, and with which he was delighted. For the remainder of his time in Europe he continued to promote appeasement, even as Britain and France mobilized for war.[16]

When at last war did break out Lindbergh severed his informal connection with the Army Air Corps, freeing himself to fight against American intervention. An arch-conservative commentator named Fulton Lewis, Jr. arranged for Lindbergh to air his opinions over the Mutual radio network. His talk, carried by three networks, proved to be the first of five nationally broadcast radio addresses he would give in the first 15 months of the war. He would also speak at two public meetings, testify before two committees of Congress, write three articles for national magazines, and advise many leaders, all before he joined America First.

Throughout Lindbergh maintained that the United States had nothing at stake in Europe, the war being a family affair within Western civilization. It was not a struggle for freedom and democracy, as Roosevelt insisted, but only a dispute among neighbors. Lindbergh found it tragic that Europeans were killing each other when the real enemy lay to the east, from which might come "either a Genghis Khan or the infiltration of inferior blood." Germany was essential to the salvation of the white race, threatened as it was by a "pressing sea of Yellow, Black and Brown."[17] Lindbergh said repeatedly that he did not favor a German victory, nor did he wish to see the British Empire collapse. What he hoped for was a negotiated peace that would leave the West strong enough to withstand both Russia and Japan.

Lindbergh would never admit that democratic Britain and France were morally superior to Hitler's Germany. He was always raking up Allied shortcomings and failures in order to offset his grudging admissions of Nazi brutality. Lindbergh would not concede that there was any difference between selfish foreign policies, which he attributed to the Allies, and enslaving one's neighbors. Lindbergh's perversity hurt his case, and ultimately his good name.

A compassionate, deeply sensitive person, Anne Morrow Lindbergh supported her husband throughout the ordeal and after, at great cost to her own reputation. Before the war she probably agreed with his politics. After hostilities commenced only loyalty to him explains her isolationism. Her diary entries show her to be instinctively pro-Ally, sickened by Nazi cruelty, and put off by the narrow nationalism of

America First. In her diary she wrote that the interventionists possessed the "fundamental truth" of our times, that "one must lose one's life to save it," meaning that to intervene on Britain's side was to risk one's life for another, thereby rising above the coarse values of "a materialistic age." The greatest leaders, to her, were those like Churchill, and possibly even Roosevelt, who grasped this higher truth.[18]

Perhaps Lindbergh had some excuse for his position during the first nine or ten months of war. After Polish resistance was extinguished on October 6, 1939, German expansion came to a halt. It looked like the First World War all over again, another stalemate giving Americans time to leisurely consider their future. After Dunkirk and the fall of France that was no longer true. News of these catastrophes—which plunged many Americans into gloom and led some to rethink the wisdom of having failed to support the Allies when doing so could have made the difference—did not disturb Lindbergh's adamantine complacency.

At first Lindbergh acted by himself, but soon he was drawn to the America First Committee. The AFC grew out of a Yale student group organized by Kingman Brewster, a future president of Yale, and R. Douglas Stuart, a law student. They quickly won support from prominent business and political leaders, and on September 4, 1940, America First was born in Chicago. Stuart was the national director and Robert Wood, a retired general and board chairman of Sears, Roebuck and Company, became the AFC's national chairman. Some 50 individuals served on the board of America First at one time or another, including journalist John T. Flynn; Chester Bowles, an advertising man and subsequently governor of Connecticut; Mrs. Bennett Champ Clark, the wife of a prominent isolationist senator from Missouri; Alice Roosevelt Longworth, TR's daughter; Eddie Rickenbacker of Eastern Airlines and a former war hero; Kathleen Norris, a popular novelist; and actress Lillian Gish.

Well-financed and reasonably independent, America First at its peak would have 850,000 members. While a majority were Republicans, it appealed to liberal and left-wing isolationists as well, including the socialist leader Norman Thomas. Many on the liberal-left who did not share Lindbergh's political views agreed with America First that the United States should remain neutral. They judged European democracies to be unworthy of American support owing to various flaws—such as the harsh terms the Allies had imposed upon Germany after World War I, or because they were colonial powers. Many believed that American purity might be soiled by alliances with decadent European nations. *The New Republic* spoke for this school of thought, asserting that it "is not a mark of barren isolationism to believe with all one's heart and soul that the best contribution Americans can make to the future of humanity is to fulfill democracy in the United States."[19]

Perhaps even before, but certainly after, Lindbergh gave his maiden speech for America First on April 17, 1941, it was far and away the most important isolationist organization, and one of the largest nonpartisan political movements in American history. Lindbergh would speak to 13 AFC rallies, usually to overflow crowds. No other "America Firster" had anything like his appeal. However, Lindbergh's ability to command public attention was not infinite. Despite his unrivaled access to the mass media, a Gallup poll released on May 9, 1941 revealed that 42 percent of the public had no idea of his position on foreign policy.

As events stiffened the national backbone, Roosevelt went after Lindbergh. With FDR's encouragement William Allen White, an influential political journalist even though his home base was a tiny newspaper in Emporia, Kansas, formed the Committee to Defend America by Aiding the Allies. It became a major counterweight to America First without White, who soon became alarmed by the drift toward intervention and resigned as chairman on January 2, 1941, the Committee to Defend continuing as before. A smaller, more militant group, Fight for Freedom, regarded the policy of all aid short of war as pusillanimous and worked doggedly to secure American intervention. When it attacked America First no holds were barred, including charges that Lindbergh and other prominent Committee members were fascists.

Roosevelt was not above joining the fight himself. In a press conference on April 25, 1941, he compared Lindbergh to Clement L. Vallandigham. Diligent research by newsmen established that Vallandigham had been a leading Copperhead, that is, a Northerner who sympathized with the South during the Civil War. This implied that Lindbergh was a traitor, and he therefore resigned his Army Air Corps commission, charging Roosevelt with having questioned his loyalty, character, and motives. That was true, yet it only touched the surface of Roosevelt's feeling, for he too believed that Lindbergh was a Nazi. Secretary of the Interior Harold Ickes regarded Lindbergh as, if not a Party member, at least the foremost Nazi sympathizer in America.

Justly famed for his acid wit, Ickes once remarked that the AFC ought to be called the "America Next Committee."[20]

On Bastille day, 1941, after repeated efforts, Ickes finally got under Lindbergh's skin by calling him a "Knight of the German Eagle"—a reference to Lindbergh's Nazi decoration (the Service Cross of the Order of the German Eagle with the Star). Lindbergh responded with an angry letter of protest to FDR that delighted Ickes. In his journal Ickes, who relished his reputation as "the old curmudgeon," gloated that Lindbergh's whimpers showed him to be slipping. Ickes rubbed salt into the wound at his next press conference, saying that Lindbergh, by preaching defeatism and promoting disunity, was doing Hitler's dirty work.

Earlier, Lindbergh's wife had written in her diary that "he cares as little for blame as he once did for praise."[21] Perhaps that had been true once, but by 1941 Lindbergh was feeling the heat. He had been unprepared for the ferocious assaults on him by Administration spokesmen like Ickes and Robert Sherwood, who accused Lindbergh of having a "poisoned mind." He was even less ready to find himself deserted by many old friends. Some of the French were understanding, but all, some hotly, regretted his efforts to deny France essential aid. Both the Lindberghs suffered in consequence. Anne wrote that Charles keenly missed their good will, since the French reception of him in 1927 had been so pure and spontaneous. She particularly minded their estrangement from Antoine de Saint-Exupéry, a noted author and pilot who had written a preface to the French edition of one of Anne's books and whose friendship she cherished.

British critics hit Lindbergh hard, especially Harold Nicolson. A writer and Member of Parliament, Nicolson had rented his country home to the Lindberghs, and knew them fairly well. In an article republished by *The New York Times*, Nicolson speculated that Lindbergh's treatment at the hands of the press after his son's murder had unhinged him, leading him to despise the press, and then the freedom of the press, and in the end freedom itself. Nicolson cut Lindbergh to the quick when he wrote "Let us not allow this incident to blind us to the great qualities of Charles Lindbergh. He is and always will be not merely a schoolboy hero, but a schoolboy."[22] American friends deserted Lindbergh as well, including Henry Breckenridge, his attorney for many years, and Harry Guggenheim, who had sponsored Lindbergh's flight around the world in 1927. Even family did not agree with him, Anne's mother and sister, who had married a Welshman, becoming active members of Fight for Freedom. Lindbergh's own mother disapproved, too, despite his father's legacy.

Their new isolationist friends did not make up for those they had lost, at least to Anne. While she admired some of them—Phil La Follette, former Governor of Wisconsin; General Wood; Senator Burton K. Wheeler; and a few others—and even though the young isolationists were fine, "The older generation are pretty seedy and washed out. All the good ones are on the other side."[23] She did not blame Charles for this, except indirectly, as when she told him that they were now exiles. "There is no place for us today, and no people."[24]

Lindbergh did not give an inch in the face of overwhelming political, social, and kin pressure, but counterattacked instead, ruining America First. For some time isolationists had been warning Lindbergh that his hard line gave needless offense. He was always being asked to condemn fascism and express greater sympathy for the Allied cause. This only made him more defiant. By September 1941 Lindbergh had taken all the criticism he could stand and decided to reply in kind, rationalizing that as intervention could not be stopped it was time to name those responsible while he still could. Anne persuaded him to modify his remarks a little. What remained was bad enough.

On September 11, 1941, in Des Moines, Iowa, Lindbergh gave a speech entitled "Who Are the War Agitators?" As he saw it the small minority of Americans who were dragging this nation into war consisted of three groups: "the British, the Jewish, and the Roosevelt Administration." They planned "first, to prepare the United States for foreign war under the guise of American defense; second, to involve us in the war step by step, without our realization; third, to create a series of incidents which would force us into the actual conflict."[25]

Lindbergh knew who his enemies were, but was wrong to suggest that interventionists had anything more in common than unity of purpose. There was no Anglo–Jewish–White House conspiracy at work. Each group had different goals, and different methods as well. Few interventionists worked in secret, the whole point being to win over Americans to their side. Although by the time of Lindbergh's Des Moines speech Roosevelt was attempting to manufacture an incident that would provoke Germany to a declaration of war, or else allow him to ask Congress for one, there is no evidence that FDR plotted with anyone to that end. The interventionist conspiracy was dreamed up by Lindbergh out of sheer frustration.

Lindbergh had been warned by his wife not to criticize the Jews.

She hated the speech as soon as she read it in draft. It would make people think he was anti-Semitic. Worse still, Anne believed, it would incite hatred of the Jews, even if inadvertently. According to her diary, she told him "I would prefer to see this country at war than shaken by violent anti-Semitism."[26] Anne pled with him in vain. Charles had persuaded himself that being right was everything. As it turned out, whatever truth there was in his talk, and it was slight, mattered less than his having tried to make American Jews collectively responsible for intervention. Fight for Freedom laid into him, but so did nearly everyone else.

Roosevelt prudently kept still, leaving his press secretary, Stephen T. Early, to observe that there was a "striking similarity" between Lindbergh's charges and "the outpourings of Berlin in the last few days." Wendell Willkie called Lindbergh's speech "the most un-American talk made in my time by any person of national reputation." Governor Thomas E. Dewey of New York, the next Republican presidential nominee, said it was "an inexcusable abuse of the right of freedom of speech."[27] The Hearst newspapers, which were isolationist, also criticized Lindbergh's statement. Even the *Chicago Tribune*, rabidly anti-Roosevelt and Anglophobic, assured readers that it did not endorse Lindbergh's remarks.

America First lost more than prestige in consequence. Frank E. Gannett told General Wood that his newspaper chain would have to retreat because, after Lindbergh's statement, he could not afford being identified with the Committee. Norman Thomas, a staunch ally until then, declined to speak at any more AFC rallies. Oswald Garrison Villard, an old Progressive who was fighting intervention for a second time, resigned from the AFC's council. The uproar led America First to cancel a major rally it had planned to hold in Washington later that month. By making the Committee appear to be anti-Semitic Lindbergh had thrown America Firsters on the defensive, where they remained until Pearl Harbor finished them off.

In promoting appeasement and military unpreparedness Lindbergh damaged his country to a greater degree than any other private citizen in modern times. That he meant well makes no difference, nor does the fact that numerous Americans agreed with him. Many young isolationists would serve in the military and atone with their lives for previous error. Lindbergh, who had learned nothing from this experience, would suffer only loss of popularity and temporary difficulties in finding suitable employment.[28]

The question of American intervention in the European War, which pitted Roosevelt and Lindbergh against each other, was the greatest challenge American democracy had faced thus far in the twentieth century. Lindbergh advocated a passive role for fear that a total war effort would destroy American freedoms, whatever the fighting's outcome. To Roosevelt inaction meant running the greater risk that America would find itself alone in the world, and lose its democratic character in the resulting struggle.

History's verdict is clear. It proved possible to fight a global war without suspending the Constitution. Though we cannot know exactly what would have happened if the isolationists had won, it is obvious that the passive course they urged endangered American democracy far more than they realized. While they failed in the end, they delayed American mobilization for war to a perilous degree, endangering liberty at home as well as everywhere else. The most precious freedom a democrat has is the right to propagate error, but to be wrong on so fundamental a point endangers democracy itself. The glory of our system of government is, therefore, also its greatest weakness. This was never more alarmingly demonstrated than in 1941.

4

The Force of Events

The struggle over whether America should go to war was centered on Germany. In one of the war's many ironies, the United States would engage Japan first, even though it did not threaten American security, as Germany did, and could have been ignored. That instead Japan became a national obsession resulted less from a sober examination of the issues than from American democracy's habit of taking sides in foreign quarrels on the basis of emotion. Its fear that a war with Germany would result in heavy casualties greatly influenced America's reluctance to confront the Nazi threat. With Japan, however, which did not inspire the same respect, Americans were chiefly propelled by a maudlin attachment to China. Sentimentality, not statecraft, would be the engine that drove America to war.

Though Japan, for centuries a hermit kingdom, was not forced to treat with other states until 1853, it lost no time becoming a regional power. Successful wars with China and Russia gained it Formosa, Korea, and a sphere of influence in South Manchuria. After siding with the Allies in World War I, it took over Germany's Pacific islands—notably the Marshalls, Marianas, and Carolines, names that meant nothing to Americans then, but which one day would be household words. Japan was far from satisfied with its achievements, remarkable though they were, and as it became more powerful the West sought to contain it. In 1915 Japan took advantage of the Great War to present China with a set of demands that would have made North China a Japanese protectorate. After the war President Woodrow Wilson stepped in, saving China from dismemberment.

The years from 1922 to 1936 were notable for arms-control agreements that limited naval weapons and allowed Japan three capital ships for every five separately possessed by Britain and the United States. To the West this formula seemed to guarantee peace and usher Japan into the ranks of great powers. Many in Japan, especially the Navy, regarded these agreements as stains on the national honor. Militarists exploited this feeling and "5-5-3" became an ultranationalist slogan.[1] Worse still, from the Japanese point of view, was the Nine Power Treaty of 1922 that guaranteed the independence and territorial integrity of China, obliging Japan once again to relinquish part of its Great War spoils—namely, China's Shantung Province, formerly a German concession.

In 1921 Britain took a fateful step by ending its almost 20-year-old alliance with Japan. London did so because Washington pressed it to choose between Japan and the United States. Cutting this tie heightened Japan's insecurity while removing a check on its appetite. Japan was further insulted by the US Immigration Act of 1924, which prohibited the Japanese, along with all other Asians, from becoming residents. The ban was total, ruling out even token admissions that might have saved Japanese face. These events strengthened Japanese chauvinism, militarism, and adventurism, while further weakening the parties arguing for restraint.

In September 1931 Japan's Kwantung Army occupied all of Manchuria, which was nominally Chinese, provoking a worldwide outpouring of censure. This resolution of a territorial dispute by force violated the Covenant of the League of Nations, which Japan had signed, and it appeared to violate also the Nine Power Treaty, whose signatories were bound to respect the Open Door Policy—an American belief that all great powers should have equality of access to, and treatment by, China—as well as China's sovereignty, integrity, and independence. Manchuria accelerated the militarization of Japan and set it upon a collision course with America. Except for Nazi Germany, whose rise and fall the military government of Japan paralleled, no regime in modern history was as self-destructive, nor, save for Germany and Russia, as devastating to others.

Though the Kwantung Army seems to have acted on its own, there were compelling reasons behind Japan's seizure of Manchuria that received little attention in the West. By 1931 Manchuria had become central to Japanese development. It was the only haven for Japanese emigrants at a time of rapid population growth on their home islands, and Manchuria provided Japan with half its food and pig iron, and a third of its coal. Then too, Manchuria was Japan's first line of defense against the Soviet Union, which was reinforcing its military presence in sensitive border areas. While technically a part of China, it had been many years since a Chinese government actually ruled Manchuria. The Japanese-owned South Manchurian Railway Company controlled the local economy. Japanese troops based in the railway zone were the strongest regional force. The local warlord, a former Manchurian bandit named Chang Tso-lin, though nominally subject to China, was a Japanese pawn.

In the late 1920s China under Chiang Kai-shek began to assert its rights in Manchuria, following the migration to it of millions of Chinese citizens. By 1928, when Chang Tso-lin was assassinated, he had already begun succumbing to Chinese pressure. His son and heir, Chang Hsueh-liang, proved even more responsive to Chinese nationalism and formally accepted the sovereignty of the Kuomintang, or National People's Party (KMT), Chiang Kai-shek's political vehicle, over the whole of Manchuria. At the same time China, which though weak was also belligerent, moved against Japanese interests, notably by building parallel lines to those of the South Manchurian Railway, which threatened Japan's position. These developments were especially alarming to Japan because since 1929, when the American stock market crashed, its foreign trade had been cut in half, and its exports to America reduced by even more than that. Any hope of regaining its lost American business was ruled out in 1930 by the prohibitive Smoot–Hawley Tariff. Economic hardship made Manchuria even more important to Japan, and its seizure was a direct response to the growing Chinese threat.

Japan defended its actions by invoking the Monroe Doctrine, arguing that continental East Asia was as important to it as Latin America was to the United States. Trade with China and Manchuria, where it had invested 82 percent of its overseas capital, was essential to Japan's economy. Manchuria, its buffer against Russia, was strategically far more important to Japan than the Caribbean was to America. In recognition of this, Theodore Roosevelt had spoken approvingly of a Japanese Monroe Doctrine, a phrase which later administrations tried to forget. Japan felt justified in ignoring the Nine Power Treaty since, at the time of signing, Japan had specified that it did not regard the treaty as applying to Manchuria or Inner Mongolia.

Morally, too, Japan felt that it had a strong case, since there was support for its rule among the inhabitants of Manchuria. Though ethnically Chinese, given a choice between being ruled by Stalin's Russia, the chaotic and corrupt Kuomintang, and Japan, which were their only alternatives, some Manchurians seemed to prefer the latter—especially after the Japanese consolidated their rule, suppressing banditry and building roads and other public works. That, at least, was the opinion of America's Ambassador to Japan, Joseph C. Grew, who in 1934 reported that the Manchukuans were living "with a considerable degree of contentment," so much so that if things got worse, North China might wish to join them voluntarily.[2]

Though aware of some of these mitigating circumstances, Secretary of State Henry L. Stimson denounced Japanese operations in Manchuria as a clear case of aggression that violated the Nine Power Treaty, the Covenant of the League, and the Kellogg–Briand Pact of 1928, a pledge that all the great nations had virtuously signed outlawing war. Beyond safeguarding the peace, Stimson wished to maintain the Open Door and defend China, to which many Americans were sentimentally attached as a result of generations of missionary work. During the 1930s there were three times as many American missionaries in China as in Japan, important members of what later came to be known as the China Lobby. It included not only missionaries but their relatives, members of the supporting churches back home, educators who had taught in China at one time or another, and interested businessmen. Collectively they had a strong influence on public opinion, more than offsetting America's economic ties with Japan.

Henry Louis Stimson was already a distinguished public servant when he entered Hoover's Cabinet. He would become one of the very few Americans of his generation to play a major role in the Second World War, a nineteenth-century man in the middle of the twentieth century's greatest and most terrible events. A graduate of Andover, Yale, and Harvard Law, Stimson joined the Wall Street firm of Root and Clarke in 1893. Elihu Root, an extremely successful corporation lawyer, was then on the verge of a new career that would take him to the top of the national security establishment (which he served both as Secretary of War and as Secretary of State) and Stimson along with him. Through Root's influence, Stimson became a US attorney in New York, and the Republican candidate for governor of New York in 1910.

He took his mentor's old job as secretary of war under Taft for two years, and when America entered the Great War commanded a field artillery battalion in France (preferring ever after to be addressed as colonel). Later, he served briefly as governor general of the Philippines, and in 1929 was made secretary of state by President Herbert Hoover.[3]

Stimson vainly hoped to isolate Japan by persuading other powers to emulate his policy of refusing to extend diplomatic recognition to Manchukuo. He regarded the League of Nations as the proper instrument for restraining Japan, but as a nonmember the United States was unable to utilize it. Great Britain, the most important Western power in the Far East, refused to go along with nonrecognition, the others following suit. Stimson had managed to offend Japan without accomplishing anything, which typified relations between it and the United States.[4] With all respect to Stimson, a decent man and a patriot, his instinctive response to Japanese aggression made for good morals but bad politics. It was a mistake to offend Japan, far and away Asia's most important state and a key element in the local balance of power, except for a compelling reason, which China's claim to Manchuria was not.

Since the incident was closed when Franklin Roosevelt entered the White House, relations with Japan were unimportant to him and so required little care. While he dwelt on problems at home, Japan's Army was growing stronger and increasing its pressure on China. This came to a head on July 7, 1937, when Japanese troops held a shootout with Chinese soldiers at the Marco Polo Bridge outside of Peking, that developed into a full-scale invasion of China. As in 1931, where the Army led, Tokyo followed. Unlike Manchuria, however, which Japan had seized out of necessity, the attempted conquest of China was lawless and unconscionable. Though Japan had substantial investments in China, unlike Manchuria it was not critical to the Empire. Japan invaded China opportunistically because the national government was insecure and faced a growing challenge from the Communist movement led by Mao Tse-tung, and because the European powers were preoccupied with Hitler.

War in China presented Roosevelt's Administration with a dilemma. Viewed strictly in terms of national self-interest, there was much to be said for appeasing Japan in the short run. Americans had a large stake in good relations with Japan, where their investments totaled $466 million, twice as much as in China. Forty-eight percent of American exports to the Far East went to Japan, and 21 percent of America's Far Eastern imports came from it, in dollar terms much less than before the crash, but still a substantial figure. American commerce with Japan was three times that with China, and produced a favorable balance of trade. If forced to choose between the two countries, economics dictated that the United States side with Japan.

Further, by resisting Soviet pressure, Japan strengthened the balance of power in East Asia. As there was no chance of China playing such a role in the foreseeable future, security requirements also might have inclined this country to favor Japan. The alternative, challenging Japanese imperialism, meant risking a war that would damage trade, endanger the Philippines, America's Far Eastern commonwealth, which it could not protect and yet had to defend, cost much in lives and money, and, if won, still leave East Asia vulnerable to the Soviets. If Japan refused ever to leave China, the United States would someday be forced to act, but to do so later instead of sooner was clearly the wisest path.

Domestic American politics, not grand strategy, ruled out conciliation. Roosevelt was among those holding a sentimental regard for China, where at various times his mother and many of his Delano relatives had lived and traded. Most Americans shared his prejudice against Japan, and like him wished to save China, preferably on the cheap. Japan antagonized everyone, not only by wantonly invading China but by committing horrendous atrocities there. During the Rape of Nanking in 1937, a six-week orgy of violence perpetrated against the inhabitants of what had been China's capital, several hundred thousand Chinese were slaughtered. This was fully reported in the West by journalists and by the foreign embassies in Nanking, as were other cases of Japanese barbarism. Before they were finished with China, "the forgotten holocaust," Japan's military would kill some 6 million civilians.[5]

Japan's drive into China inflamed public opinion, thereby making it difficult to compromise with the Island Empire, even had that been possible. As Japan became more predatory, it became harder and harder for Washington to exercise restraint. In time it ceased to matter that America's investment in Japan was so large, that Japan helped contain the Soviet Union, that Japan had legitimate grievances against the United States, or that, as war with Germany became more likely, it made no sense to fight Japan as well. None of these considerations made Japanese aggression less odious, and Japan was chiefly to blame for the worsening state of its diplomatic relations. The United States had hoped that a friendly East Asian power would arise capable of enforcing regional stability, and for some time the choice was open. There were many advantages to having Japan play the part, beginning with the fact that no other nation could. Japan's own acts forced the United States to support China, which was unable to police East Asia but seemed the only alternative.

If China had not captured the American imagination it might just have been possible to work out a more satisfactory Far Eastern policy. However, the American public was flooded with books and articles glorifying the Chinese people. These included the novels of Pearl Buck, notably *The Good Earth* (1931), and many nonfiction works, such as Freda Utley's *China at War* (1939). Infused with an understandable compassion for the suffering Chinese, such writings did little to inform Americans about their limited options in Asia. After Pearl Harbor China became America's favorite ally, further muddying the political waters.

As more drivel appeared in the press concerning China than any other ally, few Americans understood its real situation. During peacetime the central government under Generalissimo Chiang Kai-shek controlled at best only 10 provinces, while at least 18 were governed by local elites and warlords. The ruling Kuomintang Party (KMT) was backed by landowners and had neither the will nor the way to keep them from exploiting their peasants, the vast majority of China's 400 million people. The KMT itself was a collection of rival factions that Chiang played off against each other in order to keep himself in power.

During the decade preceding Japan's attack Chiang had accomplished little or nothing for China, to a large extent because of his preoccupation with the threat posed to him by the indigenous Communist movement. In 1927 he almost wiped out the Communist Party (CCP), but the survivors retreated to Kiangsi Province—and then in 1934, under pressure from Chiang's forces, made their famous Long March, a 6,000-mile trek to Yenan in North China, where they were putting down roots under Mao Tse-tung when the Japanese invaded.

Reporters in China seldom told the truth about Chiang's appallingly corrupt and brutal government for a variety of reasons. Doing so meant being denied permission to cover it in future. More than that, most reporters were anti-Japanese even before Pearl Harbor and did not want to write anything that would benefit the Empire. Thus, as one journalist put it, no one could visit the KMT's wartime capital,

Chungking, "without going into ecstasies over the beauty of [Chiang's wife], the heroic determination of the G-mo [Chiang], the prowess of the Chinese armies and the general nobility of all hands."[6] This remained standard practice until late in the war, too late to put American relations with China on a realistic footing. Seldom did the democratic influence on American foreign policy have such negative consequences.

The men responsible for America's Far Eastern policy were sharply divided over how to deal with Japan. Of those who took a hard line on the Axis, often called at the time "all-outers," the most important was Secretary of the Treasury Henry Morgenthau, Jr., a key member of Roosevelt's official family. Morgenthau was a Hudson Valley neighbor of FDR and had been his friend and political associate since 1915, despite being morose and thin-skinned, qualities that normally did not appeal to the gregarious Roosevelt. A gentleman farmer, Morgenthau rose from chairman of the New York Agricultural Advisory Commission to his secretaryship in 1934. He displayed marked executive skills, but, more importantly, he lacked personal ambition and was devoted to the President.

Being honest and loyal qualified Morgenthau for the many important tasks he was assigned, and his disinterested recommendations carried greater weight than most other advice received by Roosevelt. Because economic weapons were the main ones available for use against Japan, Treasury had to participate in the making of Far Eastern policy. Though Morgenthau would accomplish great things in other areas, notably as the father of Lend-Lease, he was excessively harsh toward Japan because of his mistaken belief that economic reprisals against it would be safe and effective.

The men who favored a conciliatory policy toward Japan, such as Ambassador Grew and William Bullitt, regarded themselves as "realists." Their opponents scorned them as "idealists," weak-minded believers in Wilsonian slogans. In fact, the differences between the two factions concerned priorities and timing more than substance. All agreed that Japan could not be allowed to rampage indefinitely. Realists wished to delay confrontation, hoping that Japan might change. If it did not, the Japanese should be placated until the European crisis was over. The hawks did not want war either, but mistakenly believed that strong sanctions would prevent it.

Secretary of State Cordell Hull, a veteran of 23 years in the Congress, knew little about foreign affairs. He was, however, a leading opponent of tariffs and believed evangelically in free trade, his preferred method of reform being the reciprocal trade agreement. All this commended him to Roosevelt, who did not wish to appoint an experienced statesman since he meant to be his own secretary of state. At the same time, it was useful to have a secretary who was popular on the Hill, and with the public, and with whose economic beliefs the President largely agreed. To look after things for him, in 1937 Roosevelt installed an old friend, Sumner Welles, as Under Secretary.

Although he was conservative on domestic issues, Hull's Wilsonian view of foreign affairs pleased many liberals. He believed that world peace depended upon all nations respecting the rule of law. From 1937 on he felt that Japan threatened both the peace, and the free exchange of goods and services, upon which international order and American prosperity depended. This was a typical American view that did not take account of the need to actively maintain the balance of power in Asia if good will proved inadequate. Hull remained in office for 12 years, longer than any other Secretary of State. Roosevelt, however, mistrusted Hull's department, preferring to rely on personal emissaries and on old friends like Welles.

Roosevelt's quandary remained that in opposing Japan he had little to offer save bluff. Despite the recommendations of virtually all his advisors, he refused for years to build the fleet up to London Naval Treaty limits. When he finally began a naval construction program in 1936, it was too late for purposes of deterrence. Further, while the public increasingly demanded that Japan be stopped, it ruled out the threat of force. Two Gallup polls released in September 1937 summed up FDR's dilemma. When asked on which side of the China War their sympathies lay, 43 percent named China, and only 2 percent Japan. But when the question was whether the United States should remove its (very small) forces from China, 54 percent answered yes. In February 1938, though 59 percent of respondents now sympathized with China, only 36 percent were willing to allow the shipment of arms and ammunition from this country to it. Public opinion tied Roosevelt's hands, which was a good thing, and would have been better still had the public not later changed its mind.

This left economic sanctions as the sole means of threatening Japan; yet here, too, little had changed since 1931. Businessmen did not want to see trade with Japan limited—and sanctions, if applied, might backfire: The United States could find itself warring against Japan. Or perhaps Japan might invade Southeast Asia to find reliable supplies of the oil that, together with scrap metal, was its principal import from America. Neither prospect pleased anyone, so the United

States continued to sell Japan the very materials it was using against China.

These constraints kept American relations with Japan in an unsettled state, to everyone's annoyance. Japan resented American criticism. The American public was dissatisfied with a policy that failed to protect China. The British deplored Washington's lack of consistency. In 1937 Sir Ronald Lindsay, London's Ambassador to Washington, expressed a common British view when he informed his superiors that "America is the despair of the diplomat."[7] The British understood why. They knew that the decentralized American system of government prevented any administration from pursuing unpopular policies, since it could not rely on the support of Congress,unlike His Majesty's Government, which could count on having a majority in Parliament, and up to six years between elections, even longer in a crisis. While the electorate passed judgment on HMG in the end, it was not forced to bend with every political breeze, as so often happened in Washington. Britain's problem was that its ends, protection of the Empire, outran its means in the Orient. The nature of American politics was thus much more than an academic issue to Britain.

In September 1937 Britain suggested that the United States join in trying to mediate the Sino–Japanese War. Roosevelt and Hull declined, citing their preference for "cooperation on parallel but independent lines."[8] Obviously something had to be done, yet isolationism ruled out decisive measures. The result was Roosevelt's famous "Quarantine the Aggressors" speech given in Chicago on October 5, 1937. Avoiding specifics, he declared that the rise of international lawlessness obliged peace-loving states to consider imposing a quarantine, just as when "an epidemic of physical disease starts to spread, the community approves and joins in a quarantine of the patients in order to protect the health of the community against the spread of the disease."[9]

Did this mean imposing sanctions, reporters wanted to know. Not at all, Roosevelt answered, characteristically taking back what he had just seemed to offer. His speech only expressed an attitude not a program, Roosevelt explained, though he was earnestly looking for one, and would rejoice when he found it. The public shared his unwillingness to back up morality with muscle. Far from embracing collective security, people now favored withdrawing America's troops from China.[10] The United States wanted influence without responsibility, which was embarrassing in the short term and ultimately futile.

Over the next few years conditions grew worse. China, contrary to

Japanese expectations, refused to surrender. While Japan won all the battles and occupied much of its coast, Chiang's government kept the war alive by retreating into China's interior. Like some huge primitive organism, China could not fight and yet would not die, presenting Japanese militarists with a quandary they had failed to foresee. Disengaging from China was unthinkable, because they would lose face, but, as the war was unwinnable, Japan's prestige declined anyway. Meanwhile, its economy strained to support the high cost of aggression.

Japan's treatment of this self-inflicted wound evolved in fits and starts, though certain broad outlines can be detected. One was the search for allies that finally brought Japan into alignment with Hitler and Mussolini. Another was the impulse to win the war by broadening it, outflanking and isolating China, while also gaining additional wealth and resources. This would take Westerners by surprise, since they believed that Japan's involvement in China reduced its ability to provoke trouble elsewhere. However, the Japanese never forgot that the longer they were bogged down in China, the better for Soviet Russia—which gained potentially at least, from whatever weakened Japan.

In November 1938 Japan brazenly announced that it was creating a "new order" in East Asia, closing the Open Door over American protests. In December Roosevelt authorized a loan of $25 million to China. This was the first direct assistance to China in four years, if large American silver purchases are not counted. A small step in its own right, the loan was part of a growing determination in Washington to fight fire with economics. The popular misconception that sanctions would not incite hostilities encouraged Roosevelt in the summer of 1938 to ask for a "moral embargo" of aircraft sales, and the denial of credits to Japan. He persisted despite the efforts of Ambassador Grew, who twice visited him in Washington during the summer of 1939, arguing that sanctions had to fail and might provoke war.

On July 26, 1939, following a British retreat before Japanese pressure in China, Roosevelt decided to give the six-months' notice required to abrogate a commercial treaty with Japan that dated from 1911, a step meeting with the approval of 81 percent of those Americans polled by Gallup. Though encouraging to London, his action still did not involve the coordinated military policy and economic sanctions that Britain hoped for. It also fell short of what the public wanted, which were an arms embargo against Japan and a boycott of Japanese products.

The outbreak of war in Europe further weakened Britain's position in Asia. Avoiding a Japanese conflict was more important than ever, yet the preoccupation of the European imperial powers with Germany created fresh opportunities for Japanese expansion. It was essential to Britain that China continue fighting so as to tie down the Japanese Army. But being stuck in China would lead Japan to seek a way out of the quagmire by widening the war. That was foreshadowed on September 15, 1939, when Japan signed an armistice with the Soviet Union.

An undeclared war had been going on between the two nations since the Japanese occupied Manchuria, which bordered on the Soviet Union and its client state Outer Mongolia. Between 1932 and 1938 there were at least 500 border incidents, many on the Mongolian frontier, leading in 1936 to a mutual assistance pact between Mongolia and the Soviet Union. Incidents developed into pitched battles, followed by a ceasefire in 1938. During the next year Japanese forces crossed the Mongolian border again, and in August were soundly beaten. Led by General Georgi Zhukov, a future Field Marshal, the Soviets counterattacked, and with their superior armor and air power overwhelmed the aggressor. This rout forced Japan to reconsider its position. The resulting armistice helped turn Japan's attention southward—and finally to Pearl Harbor.

The outbreak of war in Europe created a temptation for Japan's military leaders that they could not resist. Having failed to crush China, they saw in the weakening of the colonial powers an opportunity to cut China's links to the outside world. Tokyo demanded that the Allies withdraw their support of China, ordered France to close the Indochinese border, insisted that Britain shut down China's supply lines through Hong Kong and Burma, and declared the "regions of the South Seas" to be part of its Greater East Asia Co-Prosperity Sphere. This was a device by which Japan hoped to rally the oppressed peoples of Asia to its side. Represented as a policy of "Asia for the Asians," at a time when much of the continent was still ruled by Europe, the slogan had considerable appeal. Asians knew a great deal about mistreatment by Europeans. Of Japan's far more lethal aims they as yet had little knowledge.

Britain, France, and China called vainly upon Washington to assist them against Japan. Roosevelt and Hull believed that strong action, such as economic reprisals against Japan, might trigger a war that America was unprepared to fight. Some felt that sanctions would be effective, because Japan was so dependent upon the United States—

which provided it with 80 percent of its oil, 90 percent of its gasoline, 74 percent of its scrap metal, and 60 percent of its machine tools. Roosevelt was unwilling at first to gamble on that assumption. Protests were in order, but not sanctions. On the other hand, America would not retreat in the face of aggression.[11]

To maintain this delicate balance Roosevelt kept the Pacific Fleet in Hawaii after summer maneuvers, instead of allowing it to return as usual to bases on the West Coast. Later, at Stimson's request, he agreed to provide a supply train that would enable it to operate in the Western Pacific. Meanwhile, the lack of such a train made basing the Fleet in Hawaii an empty gesture, while also putting it at risk, as the Japanese did not fail to notice. Finally, after much bureaucratic jockeying, on July 25, 1940 Roosevelt signed an order embargoing aviation fuel and lubricants, and the type of scrap metal used in making steel.

An effort at deterrence, this order almost slid over into brinkmanship. Without telling the President, Morgenthau had it expanded to cover all petroleum and petroleum products. Roosevelt actually signed the document, which would have gone into effect had not Under Secretary of State Welles, whose signature was also required, noticed the change and gotten the original language restored. As this incident suggests, not only were Roosevelt and Hull having trouble developing a workable policy toward Japan, they were also finding it increasingly difficult to restrain their hawks.

Japan was not deterred by the limited embargo. In August and September Tokyo forced Britain to withdraw its troops from Shanghai, the Dutch to consider making economic concessions in the East Indies, and the French to recognize Japanese claims in Indochina. On September 26, when it appeared that the Battle of Britain was won, and after Japanese troops had entered Indochina, Roosevelt embargoed all iron and steel scrap. The next day Tokyo signed a Tripartite Pact with Rome and Berlin which specified that they would help each other if any of them were attacked by a nation at present neutral. Undaunted, Stimson, Morgenthau, and Ickes called again for a total oil embargo. Additionally, Stimson wanted Roosevelt to send a naval force to Singapore, as Churchill had requested, and another to the Netherlands East Indies—even though the Navy was too small to meet its existing commitments.

The Chiefs of Staff were against tangling with Japan. Although like most Westerners they underrated the Japanese, the service heads knew how unready America was for war. Instead of sending ships in harm's way, the Navy asked permission to withdraw the Pacific Fleet from Hawaii. FDR turned the Navy down, but he discouraged the hawks also, telling Morgenthau to mind his own business.[12] There would be no additional sanctions until the following summer.

This lull did not mean that Roosevelt had rallied the foreign-policy establishment behind him. Not counting those wishing to placate Japan, who had already lost, there were three important schools of thought battling for supremacy by the latter half of 1940. Roosevelt would, at various times, appear to endorse all of them. The growing defense bureaucracy was bringing into government service more and more hawks. The middle course championed by Hull, which called for taking a firm line against Japan that stopped short of making dangerous threats, continued to enjoy FDR's favor.

The military took a third position based on a hardheaded assessment of America's limited resources. Despite Stimson's eagerness to stop Japan, the Army knew that it could not undertake operations in both Europe and the Pacific. The Army General Staff wanted to pull out of the Western Pacific altogether. Admiral Harold R. Stark, chief of naval operations, was leaning in that direction, too. On November 4, 1940 he and his staff released Plan Dog, which called, in the case of a two-ocean war, for a holding action against Japan while offensive operations were confined largely to the Atlantic. This approach ran counter to that of Stimson and Knox, who, with many hawks, wanted a stronger military presence in the Pacific, and a commitment to defend Singapore and the rest of Southeast Asia. On January 16, 1941, FDR endorsed Plan Dog, seeming to fall in with the Navy. Yet he also authorized the Asiatic Fleet's commander to withdraw from the Philippines at his own discretion, and further authorized him to either fall back on Hawaii or advance to Singapore, as circumstances dictated. Five days later he sent Grew a letter emphasizing Singapore's importance. More waffling was to come.

In 1941 as the United States began contemplating a naval war with Germany, it made good sense to improve Japanese–American relations and, if possible, drive a wedge between the principal Axis powers. Washington began trying to do so in April, encouraged by the appointment of Admiral Kichisaburo Nomura, a known anti-Fascist, as Japan's Ambassador. Nomura would meet with Secretary Hull 45 times, Under Secretary Welles six times, and Roosevelt on eight occasions, none of which stopped the two countries from continuing to misunderstand each other. Just as this series of talks began, news reached Washington on April 13 that Japan and Soviet Russia had signed a nonaggression pact, specifying that if one went to war with a third power, the other would remain neutral. The implications, which Welles called "very sinister," were grasped at once. If the pact held, Japan would gain freedom of action in Southeast Asia. Talks between Hull and Nomura now acquired a greater urgency, especially after June 22, when Germany invaded Russia.

To Washington Germany's attack meant that Japan's rear was safe, as the Soviets would not want to fight in both Asia and Europe. To Tokyo, however, it raised the possibility of an Anglo–British–Soviet alliance that would isolate the Empire. Japanese leaders thought about taking advantage of Russia's European war by attacking Siberia. But the Kwantung Army was still heavily outnumbered by Soviet border forces, whose recent shattering defeat at their hands had been an unforgettable lesson. Further, as the Imperial Navy pointed out, while an attack on the Soviet Union would probably lead to war with Britain and America as well, if Japan advanced to the south, Russia, having its hands full, would probably remain neutral.

This was correct so far as it went, though it omitted larger considerations, the main one being that Japan was embarking upon a course that would bring it into conflict with the United States, and therefore certain ruin. Cooler heads realized this. In August 1941, as an instance, Colonel Hideo Iwakuro had explained at an Army–Navy conference that America outproduced Japan in steel 20 to 1, and that its other superiorities were more or less as great. Therefore, all things taken into account, America's war potential was 10 times that of Japan.[13] A lesser but still vital point was that Britain, and the United States even more, while obstacles to Japanese expansion, did not threaten the nation's survival. Soviet Russia, unlike the others, was a contender with Japan for supremacy in East Asia and, ideologically at least, committed to the Empire's destruction. Ambition pointed Japan one way, security another. That ambition would prevail was a foregone conclusion. Even as the Japanese debated each other, preparations for taking southern Indochina went forward.

Japanese planners had been working on the conquest of Southeast Asia as early as July 1940, though no target date had been set. The campaign might lead to war with the United States, but Japan hoped that, being weak militarily, and with its eyes turned toward Europe, America would not fight. These were, in fact, compelling motives for an American policy of restraint. The United States was unready for war with Germany, Roosevelt's efforts to provoke one notwithstanding, still less for a second conflict across the broad Pacific. London and

Washington agreed that Germany, as the greater menace, must be disposed of first. But by the summer of 1941 an Anglo–American war with Japan was looming, despite numerous diplomatic contacts and discussions. They were all getting nowhere because of the deadlock over China. Japan insisted on a free hand, while the United States demanded that it withdraw altogether.

This stalemate doomed hopes for fruitful negotiation because China was the baseline from which Japan's military leaders would not retreat; London and Washington alike were putting excessive faith in the threat of sanctions. Even if sanctions failed, Churchill believed, Japan would never dare take on the U.S. Pacific Fleet—and that, in any event, Britain's mighty fortress of Singapore, the key to Southeast Asia, was known by the Japanese to be impregnable. For this reason the Japanese would not attack it, and if they did, it could be defended until America came to the rescue. The British desire to avoid war with Japan was greater even than Roosevelt's. But Britain's position was so complicated that London could not always determine precisely what was in its own best interest.

Although it had already begun preparing for such an event, not until the summer of 1941 did Japan come to regard war with the United States as unavoidable. This determination resulted from America's response to Japan's occupation of southern Indochina, which began on July 24. The United States knew something was up thanks to Operation Magic, a triumph of the codebreaker's art, which enabled American intelligence to read Japanese radio traffic. Because of decryptions and other forms of intelligence Washington was aware of Japanese ship movements, though not their destinations. Wherever the Japanese were going, it did not appear that they could be stopped.

American, British, and Dutch planners had worked out a tentative defense plan in April, ABD-1. Even assuming American cooperation, it suffered from a fatal defect. Few British or American capital ships could be spared, so if the three nations chose to fight in Southeast Asia, most likely at the so-called Malay Barrier, where Malaya overlapped Sumatra, they could muster just one small British carrier, eight cruisers (plus another six in Australia and New Zealand), and 24 destroyers, the American force consisting of a pair of old cruisers and 13 World War I four-stackers. Japan could brush this little fleet aside. If the Japanese went on to Malaya, they would encounter a British defense consisting of 180 aircraft, mostly obsolete, plus an infantry corps that relied heavily on new Indian recruits and possessed few heavy guns and no armor.

In the Philippines there was even less. It had long been correctly regarded as indefensible because its garrison consisted of fewer than 11,000 American troops, 165 obsolete aircraft, and 6,500 Philippine Scouts, the native light infantry. In case of war with Japan the Philippines would have to be abandoned. Yet, as actual war impended, common sense disappeared. In January 1941 the General Staff rejected the advice of its War Plans Division to evacuate the islands. Instead, it chose to add some 2,000 troops and double the number of Scouts. Month by month the trickle of reinforcements increased, until by July it included scarce front-line fighter planes. On July 26, after the first Japanese landings in southern Indochina, President Roosevelt called the Philippine Army into service and restored General Douglas MacArthur to active duty as commander of American forces in the Far East.

These steps did not frighten Japan, although the threat of an oil embargo did. In the 10 months following the ban on aviation fuel Japan had purchased almost four times as much regular gasoline, whose octane level was easy to raise, and nearly three times as much lubricating oil as in all of 1939. American Cabinet hawks demanded an end to this flow, and the public seemed to back them. Not so the Navy, which argued that an oil embargo was certain to force a Japanese attack upon British and Dutch possessions, resulting in a Pacific war that would be contrary to American interests. As Japan closed in on Indochina Roosevelt weighed the pros and cons, read the Magic intercepts, and decided to freeze Japanese assets in the United States and establish a complex system of licensing that would inhibit the oil trade without closing it off. The order was issued on July 26, 1941, putting an end to a long period of Presidential inaction.

In May Secretary of the Interior Harold Ickes and his colleagues had despaired over Roosevelt's failure to provide clear direction. Mobilization was limping along without a central leader. The dead hand of the State Department, which everyone in Washington blamed for the foreign policies they disagreed with, was held to be keeping Roosevelt from taking stronger measures against the Axis. Ickes was so worked up that in his role as petroleum coordinator he personally halted a shipment of oil bound for Japan, an order Roosevelt angrily reversed. Ickes felt vindicated by the embargo order, and was certain that, with the British and Dutch following suit, it would discourage Japanese adventurism.

Unlike those expecting Japan not to fight, Ickes, who lacked any expert knowledge but was extremely self-confident, hoped that Japan would, because, in combination with the Allies, "We could probably crush her within a few months," thereby releasing warships for duty in the Atlantic.[14] Ickes had nothing but scorn for the State Department "appeasers" who, he wrongly believed, wished to reopen trade with Japan. In that event, Ickes wrote in his diary, he would have resigned from the Cabinet. "I believe that the President would have lost the country on this issue and that hell would have been to pay generally."[15]

As Latin America followed Washington's lead, all possible sources of supply could be closed on a moment's notice. The theory was that a partial and ambiguous embargo would restrain Japan without provoking it to attack Southeast Asia. In fact, a choice was required between militancy and appeasement. Unknown to Hull and Roosevelt, on a lower level the logic had been grasped. Led by Assistant Secretary of State Dean Acheson, government officials applied the embargo in such a way as to make it virtually complete. The countdown to war had begun.

America's military leaders now committed themselves to holding the Philippines. As it would take a miracle to save the islands, the chiefs convinced themselves that deliverance was at hand in the form of the B-17 bomber. The Boeing Flying Fortress, the world's first operational four-engine bomber, could deliver a payload of 4,000 pounds from an altitude of 25,000 feet. Financial constraints and teething troubles had kept the B-17 from going into mass production, but 25 were manufactured in June, and Roosevelt had just placed an order for 500 heavy bombers a month. Even higher hopes were vested in the new B-24 Liberator, which had a somewhat greater range and bombload but was not yet operational.

A strong force of heavy bombers based on Luzon, the military reasoned, could not only defend the Philippines but, with auxiliary fields in Singapore, the Netherlands East Indies, Australia, and New Guinea, draw a curtain of air power across Southeast Asia. Further, being able to strike Formosa, South China, and—if given the use of Soviet bases—even Japan itself, B-17s might constitute a deterrent to Japanese expansion. To air officers the Philippines offered a chance to show off their principal weapon and advance their effort to become the war-winning service.[16] Little wonder that to civilian and military leaders alike the prospects seemed irresistible.

Apart from the shortage of bombers, there was only one flaw in this exciting concept. Neither the B-24 nor the B-17 had ever been tested against naval objectives. When war came, it would soon become clear that from the high altitudes where they were supposed to fight they could not hit a moving target, or even a ship at anchor. But, for now, no one bothered to ask what the planes weren't capable of.

By summer's end America's Japanese policy was moving in opposite directions. With one hand the Administration continued to reinforce the Philippines. On September 12, 1941 nine Flying Fortresses arrived in Manila, having taken only a week to get there from Hawaii, proving that rapid reinforcement was feasible. General Marshall ordered a second group of 35 sent in December. They would double the Philippine striking force and move the Army toward the total of 165 Flying Fortresses it was hoping to achieve by spring.

The War Department overflowed with enthusiasm, Stimson telling Roosevelt and the Cabinet that heavy bombers had transformed world strategy. The Flying Fortress might prevent Japanese aggression or, if war came, nullify it. Fantasies proliferated, the Flying Fortress, in imagination, sinking fleets, smashing Japanese cities, and decimating the population. These visions were unconstrained by the limited number of B-17s, or by the fact that Russia had not agreed to allow shuttle bombing from its territory, or that the heavy bomber was an untested weapon.

Meanwhile, the Administration, learning that its nominally partial embargo had actually become a complete one, decided that seeming to back down would be more harmful than continuing the boycott. On September 5 Secretary Hull authorized State to manipulate the licensing system in such a way as to cut off the flow of oil, thus sanctioning the policy already in force. Though no public announcement was made, the British and Dutch were notified on the thirteenth. On the twenty-sixth, the intricacies of the undeclared embargo were explained to them, so that all might act in concert. This was done in haste because, as the Germans were advancing in Russia again, and since Magic indicated that Japanese military preparations were accelerating, Roosevelt wished to forestall a Japanese attack on Soviet Asia.

He was succeeding better than he knew, for the embargo had already convinced Japanese generals that they must obtain reliable supplies of oil before attempting anything else. For the same reason the Imperial Japanese Navy was also convinced that an attack must be made to the south—and soon. Japan's Combined Fleet outnumbered the ABD forces by 11 battleships to 9, and 10 carriers to 3, but the Imperial Navy was a diminishing asset. When the American shipbuilding program matured the IJN would be hopelessly outclassed. The Japanese estimated that whereas they now had 70 percent as many warships as America, giving them local superiority in the Pacific, their relative strength would decline to 50 percent in 1943, and in 1944 to 30 percent. If Japan was to strike America at all, there was no time like the present.

At an Imperial Conference on September 6 the Japanese agreed to go with their plan of attack. Hirohito attempted to slow the rush toward war by reciting a poem of his grandfather, the Emperor Meiji:

> *All the seas, everywhere,*
> *are brothers one to another*
> *Why then do the winds and waves of strife*
> *rage so violently through the world?*[17]

The Emperor's poetry recitation, though it startled the military, did not stop them. Their only concession was that negotiations with the United States might go on, in the remote chance of a breakthrough. Otherwise, the decision to attack would be made in October. The odds against peace were worse than they suspected. Roosevelt had no intention of backing down and was only playing for time.

Why the President did not stall more fruitfully remains an open question. Stimson, his normally good judgment warped by dreams of aerial glory, was assuring the President that "From being impotent to influence events in that area we suddenly find ourselves vested with the possibility of great effective power."[18] Marshall too was swept along by the tide of excitement, telling Admiral Stark that heavy bombers would certainly stop the "Malaysian thing," probably cancel the "Siberian thing," and might even force Japan out of the Axis. Further, as Britain was sending naval reinforcements to Singapore, the doomed *Repulse* and *Prince of Wales*, the whole balance of military power appeared to be tilting in ABD's favor. Even if accurate, which they weren't, these calculations were based on military units in transit. Time was needed for them to arrive, as Stimson and Knox kept saying.

Probably the overestimation of Western military strength by American leaders at this time arose out of a desperate need to save Russia from a Japanese attack, which could only be done by inciting a strike to the south that was sure to be overpowering. No one wanted to admit this, hence the delusion that a handful of bombers and capital ships would make all the difference. Real faith in heavy bombers would have led Washington to buy more time until they were ready for use. Yet, the Administration made no concessions to Japanese negotiators, even though it knew from Magic intercepts that Japan was preparing to attack.

Disgusted by Hull's "pathetic" diplomacy, Under Secretary of the Treasury Harry Dexter White put forward a daring last minute proposal. It entailed moving the Pacific Fleet to the Atlantic, where it was desperately needed, resuming normal trade with Japan, and allowing at least a token number of Japanese citizens to qualify as immigrants. In return Japan was to withdraw from China, but not Manchuria, give China a reconstruction loan with funds loaned to it by the United States, sell up to 50 percent of its merchant marine to the United States, and sign a nonaggression pact with the leading Asian powers. This remarkable plan addressed Japan's legitimate needs, and would have strengthened the United States enormously in its struggle with Hitler. There is no way of determining whether it had any chance of success because Hull, over the objections of his Far Eastern section, quashed it. So perished the last slim chance of avoiding, or even delaying, war in the Pacific.

In November, to be sure, last-ditch efforts were made to work out a *modus vivendi*, or interim agreement, the military advising Roosevelt and Hull that time was still needed for the Philippine reinforcement. Forty-eight heavy bombers were scheduled to leave for the islands between December 3 and 10. Another 82 would fly out during the next 10 weeks. Half of a pursuit group of 105 Curtiss P-40s was at sea, and the other half would sail in December. Fifty-two dive bombers were scheduled to arrive by Christmas. The largest contingent of troops ever, some 21,000 men, was to embark in early December. Without this reinforcement there was little chance of holding the Philippines. Indeed, the danger was becoming so great that Admiral Hart, who commanded the Navy's Asiatic Fleet, received orders to move his ships south from Manila Bay, putting them beyond the reach of Japanese aircraft based on Formosa.

Magic revealed that the Japanese government had established a November 25 deadline for making diplomatic progress, in the absence of which military operations were to follow. Yet when they assembled on the twenty-fifth Roosevelt, Stimson, Knox, Stark, and Hull confined themselves to discussing how Japan could be manipulated into firing first. On November 26, with full awareness that the deadline had passed and that Japanese troop convoys were in the South China Sea, the Administration confronted Japan with 10 proposals, one of which called for the Japanese to withdraw from China. Diplomacy had come to an end. On November 27 the Army and Navy sent war warnings to their Pacific commanders, the Navy cautioning that it anticipated a Japanese attack against the Philippines, or Thailand, the Kra Isthmus, where Thailand and Malaya met, or Borneo. In the event of an attack upon Thailand alone, the United States would not intervene—otherwise it would.

At the top, however, there was still uncertainty as to where the line would actually be drawn. On December 1 Roosevelt told the British Ambassador that if Japan attacked Thailand he would support British action. As to what that support would consist of, he could not say. In case of a Japanese assault on British or Dutch territory, "We should obviously all be in the same boat together"—whatever that meant. On December 3, for the first time, he gave a firm guarantee, telling Halifax that if Japan struck he would authorize military action.[19] Admiral Phillips of the Royal Navy flew from Singapore to Manila for talks on how to coordinate naval operations. Admiral Hart ordered Destroyer Division 47 in Borneo to sail for Singapore.

On December 6 (Washington time), Roosevelt learned that Japanese convoys were entering the Gulf of Siam. He immediately sent a peace message to Emperor Hirohito. The next morning Japanese aircraft destroyed most of the American fighter force in Hawaii on the ground, and wrecked the battleship fleet. Some hours later Japan struck again, crippling the Philippine defenses. On December 8, the United States declared war on Japan, and on the eleventh, Hitler issued a declaration of war against the United States. At last the long wait was over.

The most telling charge against Roosevelt's Administration is not that it deliberately allowed Pearl Harbor to be attacked so as to get into the war, as was, and has continued to be, often said, but that its Far Eastern policy was shamefully bad. After deciding that Germany was the greater threat to vital American interests, the Administration should have bent over backward to reach agreement with Japan. That failing, a *modus vivendi* to buy time was absolutely essential. But Washington did nothing, allowing a Japanese deadline that it knew meant war to pass without making any effort to avoid or postpone the conflict. There was no excuse for the peculiar mixture of fear, fatalism, and belligerence that overcame government leaders. Nor was there any excuse for Roosevelt's allowing middle-level managers to, in effect, make crucial decisions, nor for the strategic vacuum in which all of this occurred.[20] That it was the popular course and supported by opinion surveys did not make it good policy. Events dictated the government's actions, which were too little and too late if boldness was needed, and too belligerent if it was not.

The American people were at fault as well. In contrast to their earlier reluctance, and despite their continuing fear of a war with Germany, they were now demanding that Japanese aggression be stopped at all costs. In February 1941 polls showed that 39 percent of the people were willing to risk war to keep Japan from seizing Singapore and the NEI. By September 70 percent were in favor of risking war to keep Japan from becoming more powerful. In the week preceding Pearl Harbor, with Japanese–American relations at their lowest ebb, 64 percent of respondents indicated that they were ready for a fight in the Pacific. "U.S Cheerfully faces war with Japan" was the title of *Life*'s last prewar comment on the state of American morale, which, even to that interventionist magazine, seemed strange under the circumstances. For "a nation poised on the precipice of two-ocean war," it wrote, "the U.S. was extraordinarily complacent last week. No one seemed afraid of war. Congressional leaders reported that a declaration of war against Japan would slide through both houses easily." "Americans felt confident," *Life* noted with less assurance than usual, "rightly or wrongly, that the Japs were pushovers."[21]

That particular misjudgment would soon be corrected. What would remain a problem for American democracy was the attitude that, even on a subject about which it knew almost nothing, the public's will should prevail. Without these polls, and its other methods of determining opinion, the Administration would not have dared to drift into a war with the wrong enemy in the wrong place at the wrong time—a war, further, which it lacked the means to fight. The military may have been intoxicated by the B-17, but only weeks before Pearl Harbor *Life* had thrown cold water on these illusions, pointing out to its millions of readers that the nation still lacked "an adequate two-ocean Navy and a properly trained Army."[22]

Public opinion had blocked the war with Hitler that it was critically important to win. Now it sanctioned a war that the country could not afford against a great power that it had no immediate need to fight. Responsibility for the calamities that followed was, therefore, widely shared. That may be the reason why, after Pearl Harbor, public outrage was directed mainly against Japan's alleged duplicity, rather than at an Administration whose miscalculations invited the surprise attack. Almost everyone had much to answer for, and on some level seemed to know it.

5

The Government
Cannot Mobilize

B ad as America's diplomacy was, its defenses were even worse. Had it been strongly armed Germany and Japan would not have declared war. Or, if they had done so despite the odds, retribution would have been swift and lethal. Instead, peacetime mobilization lagged, ensuring that when war came disaster would follow disaster. Yet, for years before Pearl Harbor polls had shown that a majority of Americans favored rearmament—on its merits to be sure, but also because defense orders would create more jobs at a time of high unemployment: 15 percent of the work force remaining idle as late as 1940.

Why necessity and a popular mandate did not inspire vigorous preparations goes back to the democratic process. For one, it seems to have been a fixed rule that politicians did not believe that people were willing to sacrifice, no matter what the polls said. A strong defense effort would have created many jobs, but also higher taxes and fewer consumer goods. Congress and the President alike shrank from testing voter resolution on these sensitive topics.

Moreover, a strong defense meant strengthening the executive branch, which alone could oversee it. Congress had reservations about this, and so did the President, because expansion raised knotty questions about delegating power, recruiting personnel, and managing the aims of contending interest groups. In retrospect it all seems perfectly obvious. A collapsing world order made military strength the number one national priority. America had the means to build a great armed force and should have done so at once. However, to contemporaries balancing long term need against short-term pain, it was not that easy.

At first few voices were raised on behalf of preparedness. Chief among them was Bernard M. Baruch, who, as chairman of the War Industries Board in 1918, had directed American mobilization.[1] The son of an immigrant Jewish physician, Baruch was born in South Carolina on August 19, 1870. Although he moved 10 years later with his family to New York, he would always claim to be a Southerner. Baruch quickly made his fortune. After graduating from City College he entered the securities business, buying his own seat on the stock exchange at the tender age of 27. He opened his own firm in 1903, by which time he was already rich. Baruch was a bear on Wall Street, one who gambled that stock values would drop. That shaped his career in government, where few would match his zeal as an inflation fighter.

Woodrow Wilson appointed Baruch to his "War Cabinet," an informal body of agency heads that met with the President weekly. As chairman of the War Industries Board Baruch succeeded even though the WIB never had enough clout. Most of the time it had to depend on voluntary compliance because Baruch lacked the power to draw up a master plan and compel obedience to it, which allowed war agencies to work at cross-purposes. That the United States had little at stake in the Great War made this system tolerable, but a poor model for any real crisis.

Throughout the interwar years Baruch repeatedly stressed how important it was to build upon America's World War I experience. No one put the case as strongly as he, or was so explicit about what should be done. He wanted the WIB revived as an advisory commission that would, in an emergency, be given complete control of mobilization. In addition, price control was essential to maintain a stable economy. Remembering his mistaken belief in 1918 that demobilization would take care of itself, he insisted that planning for reconversion should take place before the first shots were fired.

Baruch's failure as an advocate was very nearly total. Isolationists were quick to reject his stand. Roosevelt was not impressed by it either because the WIB approach meant filling Washington with temporary "dollar-a-year men," executives on loan from business who still drew their company pay—taking only a token sum from the government.

Such men were usually Republicans. Further, since they had corporate jobs to fall back upon, they were too independent. Thus, when Assistant Secretary of the Army Louis A. Johnson approached FDR in 1937 with the idea of creating an advisory board on industrial mobilization to be headed by Baruch, the President turned him down. When Baruch asked Roosevelt directly for such a board, the President rebuffed him also. FDR was supported by Secretary of War Henry H. Woodring, an isolationist who believed that national defense should be rooted in the theory that America was never going to fight. This put him in conflict with Johnson, his right-hand man, which was typical of Roosevelt.

By 1939, however, FDR seemed more receptive to Baruch's ideas. In May the War Department developed a new industrial mobilization plan that differed from earlier ones in conferring upon a war resources administrator centralized control of the economy, precisely what Baruch had asked for. On August 8 when he was once more approached by Johnson, now acting secretary since Woodring was on vacation, Roosevelt authorized the formation of a civilian review board to study the new plan and suggest improvements. In doing so Roosevelt made it plain that he did not want Baruch to serve on the panel, recommending Edward R. Stettinius, Jr. instead. Stettinius, a Roosevelt supporter, had risen to become chairman of U.S. Steel, and so was acceptable to business. He was famous for his good looks and impeccable grooming, and to many epitomized the back-slapping, glad-handing executive. His ready smile prompted Latin Americans to name him "the teeth" (los dientes).[2] As always with Roosevelt, family connections helped. When FDR was assistant secretary of the Navy, Stettinius's father, a Morgan partner, had been his opposite number in the War Department. Roosevelt would come to value Stettinius as an administrator who did not make waves. His pliancy—spinelessness some called it—would carry him far. Besides Chairman Stettinius, most other members of the new War Resources Board were businessmen as well.

Leading New Dealers, including Secretary of Labor Frances Perkins, Secretary of Agriculture Henry Wallace, and Lauchlin Currie, FDR's principal economic advisor, were dismayed at the Board's conservative makeup. In addition, many New Dealers were opposed to rearmament on principle. They worried that preparedness would undermine reform, as in Wilson's day. That the WRB was made up chiefly of businessmen only confirmed their suspicions, which would have been even more intense had Baruch served on the Board—one reason why Roosevelt kept him off it. Another may have been that, with Baruch as chairman, the hopes of those favoring a strong defense would be raised excessively, leading to bitterness later.

Despite Baruch's absence, the WRB arrived at conclusions similar to his and endorsed, with some changes, the new plan for mobilization. FDR forthwith dismissed the Board and suppressed its report. The explanation for FDR's apparent reversal begins with his approach, not just to mobilization but also to leadership. Many noticed at the time that Roosevelt habitually set his appointees upon collision courses with one another. It was no accident that Woodring the isolationist had a hawk as assistant secretary. It had not been by chance earlier that Roosevelt divided responsibility for relief projects between dynamic Harry Hopkins and cautious Harold Ickes. It was no coincidence later on when Roosevelt inserted himself between Churchill and Stalin. Divide and conquer was his rule, broken only when there seemed no alternative.

According to Eliot Janeway, what the President intended was:

> to claim credit for the successes of the mobilization effort and to blame the leaders he appointed for its failures. From the White House, the problem of mobilization could never seem as simple as Roosevelt's appointees invariably regarded it, and it could never be solved by the simple expedient of his delegating his powers to them. What Roosevelt delegated, accordingly, was always responsibility and never authority.[3]

Defense advocates wanted a single agency with a single head to direct the sprawling mobilization process, which Roosevelt was determined to avoid. His method, obscure at first, became clearer with his abolition of the War Resources Board in November 1939, after Poland had fallen, a time when it should have been self-evident that America ought to prepare for the worst.

New Dealers rejoiced at the WRB's demise, mistakenly seeing it as a blow against privilege and a boost to reform, issues of much greater concern to them than overseas aggression. It might be supposed that as anti-Fascists New Dealers would have gotten behind strong military and foreign policies. Such was not the case. Though some, like Ickes, were, or soon would become, hawks, most New Dealers were isolationists. Even after Pearl Harbor they wanted a politically correct war effort more than an efficient one.

For this reason New Dealers never supported full mobilization if that required, as it did, putting all power over it in the hands of a businessman—or someone acceptable to business. Whenever the need for a mobilization "czar" was addressed, New Dealers balked, certain that Baruch, or a man like him, would be appointed. Accordingly, for Roosevelt a weak mobilization in the prewar era was politically expedient, appealing as it did to both liberal and conservative isolationists. On July 1, 1939, the day he received his first preparedness budget, Roosevelt ordered the Chiefs of Staff and the Army–Navy Munitions Board, plus a handful of planning and management agencies, directly into the Executive Office of the President. In war, as in peace, all roads would lead to the White House. This centralization was portrayed as an aid to efficiency. In fact it would set civilians against the military, cut the service secretaries out of the power loop, and leave Roosevelt as the only one fully informed.

On May 25, 1940, while France was falling, Roosevelt took additional steps. By executive order he formed an Office of Emergency Management in the White House, through which he proposed to direct mobilization. He invoked the Defense Act of 1916 to create a new Advisory Commission to the moribund Council of National Defense that would report directly to him. Its members included William S. Knudsen of General Motors, a famous production man, Stettinius again, Sidney Hillman, FDR's link to the trade unions, and Leon Henderson, a dedicated and versatile New Deal economist. There was no head, each man being expected to render only his professional advice. The word commonly used to describe this powerless commission was "monstrosity." It seemed as if FDR wanted to give a sop to hawks, yet one so obviously hopeless that isolationists would not mind it.

The President's reorganization ensured once again that there would be no super agency to bleed away his power. Thus, the time gained by staying out of the war would continue to be wasted. He would not form a War Cabinet on the British model, or even on that of Wilson. Roosevelt also ignored the WRB's other recommendations, the most important of which was that large additions be made to the stockpile of strategic raw materials, for which money had already been appropriated. Instead, Secretary of Commerce and Chairman of the Reconstruction Finance Corporation Jesse H. Jones, formerly a small time banker, hoarded the Rubber Reserve Corporation's purchasing fund, searching for bargains that did not exist because war was inflating commodity prices. In consequence, at the time of Pearl

Harbor America would have only enough natural rubber for a year of peacetime production, about 600,000 tons, whereas it was estimated that in war the country would need 700,000 annually.

The WRB had recommended that a foreign trade policy, coordinated by the State and War Departments, be implemented to support rearmament. That was not done either. The Board drew up an emergency labor plan involving a War Labor Administration, which was also disregarded. There remained no way of adapting the manpower supply to defense requirements, and no way to mediate labor disputes. When strikes broke out in defense plants they would be at the expense of production. A full year was lost as a direct consequence of Roosevelt's approach to mobilization. This was deliberate. The President genuinely wanted a stronger national defense, but first he wanted to be reelected in 1940. If this necessitated appointing the wrong men to key mobilization jobs, setting them at cross purposes, and creating a maze of overlapping and poorly defined authorities to give the impression of doing much while actually doing little, so be it.

Roosevelt's Advisory Council, known as the NDAC, though weak was not idle. The usual bureaucratic expansion took place, and as part of it unlucky Donald M. Nelson entered American history. This came about because one of the numerous anomalies faced by mobilizers was that government agencies were competing with one another for the same or similar materials, and for products manufactured by the same plants. To remedy this it was decided on June 28, 1940 to appoint a coordinator of national defense purchases. At that time Nelson was director of purchasing for the Treasury Department, a position that had been created in May because Great Britain and France were frantically buying aircraft in the United States, bidding against each other as well as the US Army and Navy.

Roosevelt assigned Secretary Morgenthau to solve this problem, and Morgenthau asked General Robert E. Wood of Sears, Roebuck and Company to lend one of his vice presidents, a production man named E. Penn Brooks, to the Treasury. Brooks could not be spared, so Wood volunteered Nelson instead. Nelson was a chemical engineer who had been with Sears since 1912, most recently as chairman of the firm's Executive Committee. A merchandiser, and a large jovial man who looked the part, Nelson knew something about production as well, so even if he wasn't Morgenthau's first choice, and despite the implication that Sears could manage without him, Nelson got the job. He did well enough at it so that when NDAC needed a purchasing agent he was the obvious choice.

Nelson tried to escape his fate, reminding everyone that he was only on loan for two months. But he was summoned to Roosevelt's office, and, once buttered up by the master's hand, Nelson could deny him nothing. After agreeing to serve, Nelson discovered that the NDAC was not much better than no agency at all. It "operated in a climate of uncertainty; its powers were blurred around the edges; its job was ill defined or not defined at all," he would later write.[4]

Knudsen's task on the NDAC was supposedly to tool industry up for war production, "one of the biggest jobs ever done in this world," Nelson would call it. However, Knudsen was expected to accomplish his historic task without affecting the civilian economy. Since any meaningful defense program must inevitably reduce the supply of consumer goods, Knudsen's task was manifestly impossible. If Roosevelt had wanted him to succeed, Knudsen would not have been named head of a subcommittee of an advisory committee modeled on a creation of Wilson's that had failed dismally in 1917—as Roosevelt, who helped supplant it at the time, knew perfectly well.

Roosevelt's guile did not end there. Since even the very limited mobilization he allowed was likely to raise prices, some mechanism was needed to offset the law of supply and demand. Baruch wanted the government to control everything. As organized labor was crucial to his reelection, Roosevelt could not freeze wages. Accordingly, he could not freeze profits or prices, either. He found the answer in antitrust action, or rather the threat of it. Thurman Arnold, his assistant attorney general in charge of the Antitrust Division, was put to work inspecting defense contracts. This alarmed big businessmen who wanted competition suspended for the duration, though it pleased small manufacturers who resented the practice of giving defense contracts mostly to large corporations.

Though Roosevelt knew that antitrust suits would not increase production, he did not say so, thus retaining his freedom of action. The threat that he might unleash Arnold on them helped him deal with big business, while the hope that he would move against errant corporations kept liberals from jumping ship. None of this did mobilization any good, but then, it was not supposed to.

Donald Nelson resigned his post as coordinator of defense purchases as soon as the votes were counted in November. The result was another summons to the White House and more soft soap. Roosevelt talked about a great many subjects not including Nelson's resignation, a standard Presidential tactic. When he left the Oval Office after an hour spent listening to FDR's views on everything under the sun, Nelson was charmed, baffled, and still coordinator of purchasing. No wonder, he reflected later, that people all over the world trusted and believed in Roosevelt as if he were almost a god.

Divine attributes notwithstanding, Roosevelt still had no intention of giving mobilizers the authority they needed. After Pearl Harbor he would delegate of necessity, but until then he continued to guard his power. Sitting in the middle of his spider's web, Roosevelt knew all, controlled all, and gave away nothing. However, with the election past, calls for a more serious mobilization could no longer be resisted.

In response to popular demand NDAC was swept away. On January 7, 1941 FDR unveiled a new monstrosity called the Office of Production Management. It consisted of Knudsen, Hillman, Stimson, and Knox, who would make policies, which Hillman and Knudsen, as co-directors, would then carry out. As Janeway put it, Roosevelt had "substituted two centers of power for seven circuits of conversation." When he announced it, the press could not understand how the thing was supposed to work. Roosevelt compared OPM's dual leadership to a law firm, which it in no way resembled. One exchange with a reporter went as follows:

"Why is it you don't want a single responsible head?"

"I have a single responsible head; his name is Knudsen & Hillman."

"Two heads."

"No, that's one head. In other words, aren't you looking for trouble? Would you rather come to one law firm or two?"[5]

And so on, into the darkening gloom.

On March 11, 1941 Roosevelt signed the Lend-Lease Act, which would in time greatly expand the shipment of munitions to Great Britain. As the threat of inflation could no longer be ignored Roosevelt, instead of giving control of prices to OPM, created the Office of Price Administration and Civilian Supply, under his budget chief Leon Henderson. This further complicated an already bewildering power structure.

Meanwhile, contracts were being let, production was rising, and shortages were becoming acute. Though the utilities denied it, electric power was one of them. Fuel shortfalls led Roosevelt to appoint Ickes as Petroleum Coordinator of National Defense on May 28, 1941. This tied the transportation and power crises together, since a shortage of tanker trucks and railroad tank cars was developing. There were so many shortages that it is difficult to say, even now, which was the most crippling. The rubber shortage would soon begin to hurt. On May 16, 1940, when Roosevelt had issued his call for the production of 50,000 military aircraft, industry was capable of producing only half the needed aluminum. Alcoa, the aluminum trust, offered to double its production capacity, that being the only way to expand output quickly. Precious months slipped by without action while policymakers debated whether they ought to condone monopoly—even though Stimson would rather have had some sinful aluminum right away instead of waiting a year for the virtuous stuff.

At a guess, the shortage of steel hurt most because it was used in practically everything. Cargo ships were a case in point. In order to transport Lend-Lease supplies abroad it was necessary to expand the merchant fleet. By early 1941 contracts had been let to build 1,200 cargo vessels, the famous Liberty Ships, even though steel was already scarce. OPM did not prevent the military and the Maritime Commission from competing for steel, nor did it raise production to the point where all needs could be met. Thus even the modest production goal of 1941 was not reached, still less that of 1942, which called for eight times as many Liberty Ships as had been built in the previous year. Not until September 1941 was it decided to expand the steel industry, and as late as July OPM was assigning priorities to users without having any statistical data on either steel production or inventories. As a result, it issued more priority orders for steel than the industry could meet, so, everyone ignored them.

Shortages, and the government's failure to provide leadership, forced manufacturers to bend the rules. Henry J. Kaiser could not have become the most famous industrialist of the war had he lacked that ability. A heavy-construction man who had built many roads and dams, he found his true calling in the war as an industrialist. Though in peacetime he had never laid a keel, he became the world's biggest shipbuilder. In time he would build war planes as well, and employ 250,000 workers, for whom he provided housing, recreational facilities, and medical care, a rarity among big businesses. His contempt for established procedures sometimes got him into trouble, but more often enabled Kaiser to accomplish what others refused to attempt. This made him a favorite of the press, for in an age of "can-do" manufacturers, few did more than he.[6]

Shipbuilding was a case in point. In 1941 it took a year to build a Liberty Ship. Kaiser's dozen yards, which ultimately built a third of the 2,708 Liberty Ships made during the war, would cut that to a matter of days, assembling the *Robert E. Peary* in fewer than five.[7] These production feats consumed vast quantities of steel. When steel companies refused to provide the volume he needed, Kaiser convinced government to put him in the business. This led other suppliers to meet his needs until his own furnaces were running. The users who would otherwise have gotten the steel that Kaiser received had to do without. Coups such as his made a mockery of planning, as also of OPM, but—given Washington's maze of red tape—men like Kaiser had no choice but to slash their way through it.

For auto makers, on the other hand, it remained business as usual. In 1941, as in 1917, they went on producing civilian vehicles while attempting to gear up for war. The companies hoarded materials, and enlarged passenger-car inventories, at the expense of their own defense contracts. At the same time, they were laying men off by closing down assembly lines so as to install the new equipment required for war production. As late as the summer of 1941 the all-important machine-tools industry was still working only one shift a day. With Japanese–American relations worsening fast, it was time to end the anarchy that characterized what passed for mobilization.

Roosevelt's answer to bureaucratic confusion and production delays was yet another monstrosity, the Supplies Priorities and Allocations Board. He created it on August 28, 1941, when Russia's survival, and therefore the only real hope of defeating Germany, hung in the balance. Even so, SPAB was no super agency empowered to make things work. Instead, it further complicated the bureaucratic structure. SPAB was supposed to lay down general policies for OPM to administer. It would have made more sense to vest OPM with authority to create its own directives, but that would have gone a long way toward giving OPM actual control of production, which would never do, and it wouldn't do either to have SPAB acquire such power.

To guard against this the President made cross-appointments bewildering even to those who held them. The new Board consisted of Hillman, Knox, Knudsen, and Stimson, who were also in OPM, plus Vice President Henry A. Wallace, who was, in addition, Chairman of the recently established Economic Defense Board, and Harry Hopkins, who took charge of whatever Roosevelt was most interested in at the moment. As if these overlapping directorates were not enough, FDR also chose Nelson to be the Executive Director of SPAB without relieving him of his post with OPM. Thus, Nelson remained Knudsen's subordinate as chief of purchasing for OPM, while becoming his superior as head of SPAB. Roosevelt also appointed Henderson to SPAB, while at the same time he split Henderson's agency into two parts, an Office of Price Administration and a Division of Civilian Supply. OPA remained independent while DCS became a unit of the Office of Production Management, and therefore subject to the policies laid down by SPAB.

This meant that Henderson was subordinate to Knudsen in his capacity as a division head in OPM, but his equal as a member of SPAB. It also made Henderson his own superior, for on SPAB he was one of those issuing directives which as a division chief of the OPM he had to implement. Moreover, by dividing OPACS, Roosevelt had separated price control from production control, thus complicating— and possibly even jeopardizing—both activities.

Bernard Baruch was so alarmed by this chaos that he came out of his closet briefly, telling reporters that SPAB was only a "faltering step forward." Admonished by Roosevelt, he then backed down in public, while continuing privately to warn everyone that SPAB could not work. Apart from its bizarre structure, SPAB would fail because the wrong man was in charge. While Baruch no longer considered himself eligible to become head of mobilization, others hoped it was not too late for him to serve in that capacity. Nelson and Knudsen were good operationally, but not as policymakers. Baruch had the right policies and the management skills to go with them. Politically his appointment would be popular and yet no threat, since Baruch, though influential, had no broad political base and, in any case, at 71 was too old to use high office as a springboard to the White House, if that was what worried Roosevelt. But Nelson seemed the safer choice, so he got the job, a place of sorts in history, and incredible aggravation.

Though Roosevelt would not mobilize, he did accept that the nation needed an Army. To create one there had to be a draft, which was sure to arouse fierce opposition. So, once again citizens would have to take charge. A unique feature of American democracy was the extent to which, given the suspicion of government, controversial initiatives had to be undertaken by private parties. So it was with Selective Service. On June 11, with France on the brink of surrender, public opinion favored a one-year draft. This was Grenville Clark's opportunity, and he was prepared to seize it. Clark, then 57, stood at the highest level of the social and professional hierarchy. The product of an affluent old family, he was a graduate of Harvard College (Class of 1903), and of Harvard Law. In 1909 he and Elihu Root formed what would become the famous law firm of Root, Clark, Buckner and Ballantine. During the First World War he was a leader of the Plattsburg camp movement, which trained civilians to become future officers and promoted American intervention.

Despite his wealth, distinction, interest in public affairs, and rugged good looks, Clark preferred to operate behind the scenes rather than hold office. Thus, his first important move in 1940 was to convene, on May 22 in the Harvard Club of New York, a meeting of 100 leading members of the Military Training Camps Association. These men were Plattsburg alumnae, and graduates of Ivy League colleges, conservatives, Anglophiles, successful businessmen, and professionals. Most were veterans of the Great War, which was consistent with all of the above. They included Colonel William J. Donovan, who would head the legendary Office of Strategic Services, forerunner of the CIA in World War II, Judge Robert P. Patterson, soon to become Henry Stimson's right hand man in the War Department, TR's son Archibald B. Roosevelt, Elihu Root, Jr., and, most importantly, Julius Ochs Adler, Vice President and General Manager of *The New York Times*, who put his great paper behind the conscription movement.

The Plattsburgers quickly endorsed compulsory military training and all aid to the Allies short of war. They began lobbying for a draft at once, working on General Marshall and, through Justice Felix Frankfurter, a law school classmate of Clark's, Roosevelt himself. But, in this election year, Roosevelt was reluctant to ask for conscription.

On June 3 another meeting was held in Adler's office to form the National Emergency Committee of the MTCA. Within four days it had a thousand members, and in three weeks raised $39,000, more than they would actually need to finance the lobbying effort. On June 20 their conscription bill was introduced in Congress. They had wanted the Administration to adopt it, that failing, the bill to be a bipartisan measure. The Democrats would not back it without White House approval, so in the end both sponsors were Republicans: Representative James W. Wadsworth of New York, and Senator Edward R. Burke of Nebraska.

Secretary Stimson favored the bill. General Marshall hesitated at first, as he wanted it to be the result of civilian pressure. Stimson worked on the Army and FDR alike. Clark and his friends tirelessly lobbied Congress, and appealed for public support, which they received in generous measure. Shortly before the passage of Burke–Wadsworth polls showed that 71 percent of all respondents favored it, as also a remarkable 65 percent of males aged 16 to 24, the men who were to be conscripted. On July 12, General Marshall testified before Congress, lending strong support to the draft. Finally, on August 2, the President stuck his neck out and endorsed Selective Service in plain language. From the standpoint of national security this was long overdue. But if it took a little courage on Roosevelt's part, it required much more from Wendell Willkie.

Willkie was under immense pressure to oppose the draft, since his campaign had little chance if the antiwar movement abandoned it. All the same, on August 17 in a campaign speech, Willkie said "I cannot ask the American people to put their faith in me without recording my conviction that some form of selective service is the only democratic way to secure the trained and competent manpower we need for national defense."[8] Willkie did not endorse Burke–Wadsworth, or even the principle of peacetime conscription, but what he said was enough. To all intents and purposes the draft bill was now bipartisan. Nine days later Willkie finished the job by endorsing Burke–Wadsworth. In taking this chance Willkie won an honored place for himself in posterity's eyes, despite his subsequent demagoguery.

Over frantic efforts by isolationists to block, cripple, or at least delay Burke–Wadsworth, it passed by comfortable margins. When Roosevelt signed it on September 16 General Marshall was present at the ceremony. He later remarked that "Grenville Clark should have been here instead of me."[9] Stimson and Wadsworth expressed similar feelings, as well they might, since without him and the Plattsburgers there would have been no draft in 1940, and perhaps the National Guard and Organized Reserves would not have been called to active duty, either—a step authorized by Congress on August 27. Eventually these things would have been done, but when and at what cost no one can say. After Pearl Harbor Clark launched a similar campaign for national service that failed. In the postwar he devoted himself to world federalism, which failed also. No matter, what he accomplished in 1940 was more than enough for one lifetime.

To the surprise of many, Selective Service worked well, and enjoyed a fair degree of public approval. There was no wholesale refusal to register, as in 1917, even though some men endeavored to persuade draft boards that they were physically or emotionally unfit. Because it soon became clear that local boards preferred to draft singles, there were about half a million more marriages than expected in late 1940 and 1941. To be on the safe side, many civilians became fathers as well, judging by the upsurge of births in 1941 and 1942. Boards could afford to be tolerant, since they had to produce fewer than a million men during the first 13 months of conscription. The main obstacle was simply that an Army numbering only 270,000 officers and men in 1940 could not grow by more than 500 percent in the course of one year without having serious problems.

A great network of training facilities had to be built almost from scratch. Most of these would be in the South and West, usually in rural areas with few or no amenities. So also the camps themselves, in which barracks had to go up first, and canteens and Post Exchanges (PXs), where the men shopped for personal items, later. Often the soldier's first home in the Army was a tent, even in the frigid northern states. Uniforms too were in short supply, and many a GI began his career outfitted like a doughboy from World War I, down to the hated leg wrappings that the Army called "puttees." A favorite word was "simulate," the soldier being called upon to drill with a simulated rifle that was actually a broom handle, and fire a simulated gun, really a wooden pole. In maneuvers trucks with signs reading "tank" became simulated armor.

Ill-clad and ill-housed, though amply fed, the recruit found himself in an alien world where everyone who wore even one stripe on his sleeve was entitled to scream at him, and where endless hours were spent at what the Army in its jocular way referred to as "policing": picking up from all kinds of surfaces, or pretending to, everything classified as litter—even if it was underwater. Kitchen police, the wretched KPs that few escaped becoming, toiled away in coal-fired kitchens for up to 16 hours at a stretch when it was their regular turn—which came with horrifying regularity, and also was used as "company punishment". When all else failed, idleness was averted by sudden assignments to clean up either someone else's mess somewhere, or the home barracks, again. The training itself was endlessly repetitious. Camp life, never much fun, was singularly unpleasant under these conditions, and also appeared, to the GIs being told what to do, at least, lacking in meaningful purpose.

In the summer of 1941, when a bill extending their term of enlistment was introduced, many conscripts wrote to their Congressmen in protest. The acronym OHIO, meaning "Over the Hill in October," appeared on walls, the implication being that mass desertions would take place if tours of duty were lengthened. Reporters seeking to explain the Army's low morale did not have to dig very deep. As Edgar Snow, a journalist who had made his reputation with a book on Asian Communism—*Red Star Over China* (1938)—put it "They were ready to die for their country, but they didn't want to be bored to death; and they were tired of playing soldier."[10] By the fall there were over 1.5 million men in the Army. Of these half a million were regulars who had enlisted for three years, 280,000 were National Guardsmen and the rest "selectees," as conscripts were called. Boredom was especially concentrated among the guardsmen and selectees who were assigned to infantry divisions. Men in elite units, like the new armored divisions, had more interesting work and were less likely to complain.

There was plenty to complain about, even in the best-motivated outfits. For example, training with simulated weapons could never be very realistic. At one camp Snow discovered that there were only four rifles for a unit of 55 men! As Brigadier General Omar Bradley, Commandant of the Infantry School, pointed out, it took about 13 weeks to train a qualified rifleman. After that he was supposed to have advanced training as part of a combat team. Without weapons this training could not take place, so the soldier was obliged to repeat what he had already learned, a disheartening experience.

On top of all this, the camps themselves were still poorly supplied with amenities, or even basics. In the South and Southwest, where most camps were located, there were only 21 recreational facilities for men with overnight or weekend passes. On average, the camps had one service club for every 20,000 men, and a total of just 97 guest houses with 5,000 beds, allowing only one out of every 300 men to have an overnight visitor. Worst of all, the country was at peace, which made the men intolerant of their facilities. When the shooting began there would be much less talk about the defects of Army bases.

In the absence of a real war, the Army made do with war games, which proved much better than nothing. Half a million men were brought together for maneuvers in Louisiana and South Carolina. The first took place in September 1941, and featured a tremendous flanking attack by Major General George S. Patton's 2nd Armored Division, which covered 400 miles on back roads to surprise the defenders of Shreveport. An investigation disclosed that this unauthorized movement had been funded by Patton himself, who purchased out of his own deep pockets the gasoline his tankers needed. Unorthodox by peacetime standards, it was a precursor of the more drastic methods he would employ in Europe.

Though the rules governing these training efforts were highly unrealistic, with umpires being allowed to declare tanks destroyed by simulated hand grenades and machine guns, as would never happen in combat, the games served a useful purpose. Lessons were learned, unfit commanders were weeded out, and the troops had been given something to do besides drill or "police." A few were so carried away by the spirit of things that they cursed umpires over disputed calls. At least one man burst into tears of frustration. Eric Sevareid, a young reporter at the time, drew the obvious conclusion. "What the new soldier lacks is not morale but incentive. . . . "[11] On December 7, 1941, this would be provided.

After Pearl Harbor it was obvious that SPAB and OPM must go: There had to be a wholehearted mobilization directed by someone with authority. Roosevelt could no longer avoid having a powerful assistant to coordinate production. What he could avoid was a "ministry of supply" comparable to Britain's. On January 15, 1942, Roosevelt told Henry Wallace and Donald Nelson that a new instrument, the War Production Board, would take charge of mobilization, with Nelson as Chairman, whose decisions, the President announced, "will be final." On paper WPB looked like the answer to Baruch's prayers. The powers given it were those outlined in the suppressed report submitted by the War Resources Board in 1939, so WPB bore at least some resemblance to the super agency that Baruch had been asking for all along. But its authority was not complete, and even if it had been, WPB required aggressive leadership, which Nelson could not provide. Hopkins would have been a good choice, but, considering his frail health, he was already overextended.

To those like Baruch who favored complete centralization, Nelson was bound to be a disappointment, and not just because of his failings as an administrator. WPB was a big improvement over its predecessors, but it had not been given control over the entire war procurement and production effort. Nelson was obliged to compete with the military services, which retained their authority to place orders, thus undermining WPB in ways that Nelson should not have permitted. He had to contend with international raw materials and allocations boards, and with various little czars who had considerable autonomy. A more forceful individual might have created order out of this madness, but most likely not even Baruch could have done the job without broader powers. As it was, everyone raided, or tried to raid, each other's programs in order to obtain the crucial materials they needed to meet inflated production quotas.

In the first six months of 1942 $100 billion worth of war contracts were placed, requiring levels of output that could not be achieved in one year, or possibly even two. Meanwhile, competition for scarce materials led to crippling shortages. To ease these, Nelson put forward a Production Requirements Plan, which, by allowing any manufacturer with a contract to set his own priorities, made everything worse.

To control prices an Office of Economic Stabilization was created, and on October 3 Roosevelt named Supreme Court Justice James Byrnes to direct it. Byrnes, a former Senator and future Secretary of State, was a conservative Democrat from South Carolina. Although no friend of the New Deal, he was a skillful negotiator, popular with Congress, and, above all, loyal to Roosevelt. Byrnes's job was to halt inflation and he soon learned that controlling the flow of scarce resources was essential to his task. In less than a month Byrnes acquired a way to do so called the Controlled Materials Plan, which went into effect on November 2.

The CMP established a strict priorities system for three vital materials—steel, copper, and aluminum—which were doled out in relation to the user's order of importance. This gave Byrnes control over production. The post–Pearl Harbor target figures of $60 billion worth of military output in 1942, and $110 billion in 1943, had to be abandoned. Even so, thanks to the CMP, munitions production reached a level of $60 billion in 1943, and rather more than that in 1944. Little known at the time and quickly forgotten, CMP was critical to the entire war effort.

Byrnes did not have to worry about rubber shortages because that problem was already on the way to being solved when he took charge of stabilization. This was not because the rubber crisis was easy to meet. On the contrary, since the rubber shortage mandated rationing, it was one of the hardest decisions facing Roosevelt. People hated rationing, and the thought of having to conserve rubber was especially distasteful. Rubber rationing would pinch consumers severely, because Americans depended to a large extent on rubber-eating automobiles for transportation. Limiting rubber supplies meant limiting the motorist's freedom to travel, regarded by Americans as an essential human right. Yet, of all raw materials, rubber was in shortest supply.

Roosevelt knew that conservation was essential, but hesitated to impose rationing in the face of public disapproval. He was supported by Harold Ickes, who stubbornly insisted that there was no shortage, even though a synthetic-rubber industry barely existed and natural-rubber imports would be limited to about 175,000 tons in 1942, Japan having seized most of the world's rubber trees. By summer rubber stockpiles were shrinking so fast that in June, Nelson and Leon

Henderson told FDR that action had to be taken. Roosevelt's response was not to impose gasoline rationing, the logical way to conserve rubber, and necessary in the Northeast, where gasoline was running short, but to go on the air and ask citizens to turn in their rubber goods for recycling. This produced 450,000 tons of rubber in the form of old tires, overcoats, shoes, gloves, bathing caps, and the like, a temporary expedient that failed to solve the problem.

Congress, abandoning its usual obstructionism, forced Roosevelt to act by passing a bill that established a Rubber Supply Agency with the usual czar as its head. His assignment would be to create a great industry that would make rubber out of alcohol, the raw material Congress preferred because it would generate windfall profits for agriculture. Oil was the alternative, but its use would do nothing to win votes in the politically powerful farm belt. To keep the WPB from being further undermined, Roosevelt vetoed this bill, but he also announced that a committee had been formed to deal with the rubber crisis. It would be headed by Bernard Baruch. Since gasoline rationing was inevitable, Roosevelt needed the support of the one mobilizer above all others who inspired public confidence.

Baruch was appointed in August and within a month he and his colleagues, Presidents James B. Conant of Harvard and Karl T. Compton of MIT, issued their Rubber Survey Report. It disposed of the alcohol question by recommending that synthetic rubber be made of petroleum. It called for a rubber administrator to be named by WPB. The committee wanted a national speed limit of 35 miles per hour, and a gasoline-rationing program sufficient to bring down the average distance traveled by automobiles from 6,700 to 5,000 miles a year. Baruch's committee succeeded in turning public opinion around, showing that people would do what was asked of them as long as they understood the reasons.

Given a green light Nelson moved quickly for once, and though only 234,000 tons of synthetic rubber would be manufactured in 1943, annual production ultimately rose to 800,000 tons. Meanwhile, gasoline rationing stretched natural rubber supplies enough to cover the gap. Whether Nelson, as he suggests, or Baruch deserves the most credit for this is unimportant. Nelson's WPB did most of the work and Baruch and his colleagues made that possible. Together with unsung bureaucrats, they enabled the nation to roll to victory on synthetic rubber tires.

Baruch was right in believing that taxes were the most effective way to limit inflation, for price controls would never be comprehensive. At the same time, without price controls taxation alone would not work because corporations could meet the added cost by raising prices. However, Roosevelt was against large tax increases because nobody liked them. Morgenthau opposed broadly based taxes, such as a national sales tax, because they were unfair to poorly paid workers. He opposed compulsory savings programs, another way to do the job, for similar reasons. The Victory Tax of 1942 did embody compulsory savings, but it was unpopular and Morgenthau led a successful fight to repeal it in 1943.

Much more effective was the Revenue Act of 1942, which transformed the government's approach to taxation. It was the brainchild of yet another private citizen—Beardsley Ruml, the treasurer of Macy's, who bore the same relation to taxes as Grenville Clark to the draft. The son of a physician in Cedar Rapids, Iowa, Ruml distinguished himself as a lad by his close attention to the penny. Once his father was having a garage built, and offered his children a cent a nail to retrieve the ones that workmen dropped. Rather than picking them up by hand young Beardsley obtained a magnet, which he dragged up and down the property until, tiring of the sport, he rented it out to his younger brother.

After graduating from Dartmouth Ruml went to the University of Chicago, then having a golden age under its wunderkind President, Robert Maynard Hutchins, who made Ruml dean of social sciences in 1932, at the age of 37. Somewhat eccentric, Ruml was a real life version of the fictional "Man Who Came to Dinner." At a party hosted by a University of Chicago trustee he asked to lie down, as he was feeling unwell. He remained in the bed for weeks—until finally he took a train to New York and had a mastoid operation to correct what proved to be the source of his problem.

Two years later Ruml left Chicago to become treasurer of R. H. Macy and Company, a misleading title in that he did not preside over company finances so much as generate ideas. This was to Macy's advantage, because Ruml developed an inexpensive form of installment buying, geared to the needs of war workers, that was highly profitable for the firm and also planted the seed of his "pay-as-you-go" tax proposal. In addition to his job at R. H. Macy, he served as chairman of the Board of the Federal Reserve Bank of New York, which ensured him of an audience.

Ruml was given to colorful leisure costumes, such as peasant blouses, pastel corduroy pants, and Hawaiian shirts, which, had he been less well-connected, would have led to his expulsion from polite society in that age of rigid dress codes. Ruml hated exercise even more than most men of his generation, declaring proudly "I spent many years getting into condition for a sedentary life, and having gotten into condition, I never broke training."[12] Ruml stayed in private life for the money, no doubt, but also because he liked working through others rather than trying to implement his own ideas, which were sometimes controversial as he drew on the new and still hotly debated Keynesian economics. One friend called him a cuckoo because he went about laying eggs in other people's nests. All the same, Ruml was a shrewd judge of what would work, and also of what would sell, hence the passage of the Current Tax Payment Act of 1943, despite Secretary Morgenthau's opposition.

Ruml led a body of businessmen, called the Committee for Economic Development, who were dedicated to remodeling the federal tax structure. Ruml's group favored lowering the amount of money exempt from income taxes, so as to include the nonpaying majority of Americans. The Revenue Act of 1942 made this change, and in the next year Congress adopted another idea of Ruml's, the "collection-at-the-source," or "pay-as-you-go," income tax plan, whereby payments were deducted from employee paychecks. Thus, whereas only 7 million Americans filed income tax returns in 1941, in 1944 some 42 million would do so. The income tax was an effective inflation fighter. It was also a reasonably fair tax, compared with most others.

The new tax formula aroused little opposition outside of government—patriotism being one reason, the psychology of it another. The IRS discovered, as merchants had earlier, that individuals found small installment payments relatively painless compared to forking over a lump sum. Government made it easier still by its payroll withholding plan. Even people who had never heard of pay-as-you-earn liked the idea at once. Gallup pollers found that as late as December 1942 only 44 percent of respondents knew what the Ruml plan was. However, when pay-as-you-earn was explained to them, 71 percent endorsed it. By January 1943 when the publicity mills had done their work, 81 percent of Americans knew of the Ruml plan, and 90 percent of the informed majority favored it.

The system as a whole remained inequitable because the excess profits of business were never fully taxed. Further, a key feature of Ruml's plan, forgiveness of 1942 taxes, was anathema to Morgenthau, who called it "rather disgusting" because it would allow the rich to escape paying taxes on 1942 incomes swollen by war profits.[13] However, for the majority of workers pay-as-you-go would have been a burden, forcing them to pay taxes on current income at the same time as they were making payments on money earned in the previous year. Led by Morgenthau the Administration waged a tremendous fight against tax forgiveness. It lost, beaten not only by Republican legislators happy to benefit the rich again, but also by popular enthusiasm for forgiveness—the average American, as usual, failing to display class resentment.

The final bill, entitled the Current Tax Payment Act of 1943, made 70 percent of taxpayers current, while the rest were forgiven 75 percent of their taxes for either 1942 or 1943, whichever figure was lowest.[14] Partly as a result of the wartime tax structure, the distance between high and middle income earners narrowed for the only time in modern history. By comparison with recent years, when the income of the top 1 percent of earners has risen greatly in relation to everyone else's, the wartime tax compromises approached perfection.

This was so despite the failure of Roosevelt's most celebrated tax initiative, the "super-tax" he proposed in 1942. His idea was to confiscate all income above $25,000 a year ($50,000 for families) after the federal income tax had been paid. When Congress dismissed the proposal, Roosevelt imposed it on salaries by executive order in October 1942. It was so widely attacked as socialistic or worse that Congress had no trouble repealing it in the following March, most Democrats joining in. Roosevelt did not issue his order chiefly as a revenue measure, since the cap itself was extremely high. Because it applied only to after-tax salaries, an individual would have had to earn $67,200 before it took effect, a figure so large that it was estimated only between 2,000 and 3,000 Americans would pay any super tax at all. People supported the super tax by margins of 2 to 1, apparently because it affected not the upper class as a whole but only the obscenely rich. Its defeat shows again FDR's limited influence on Capitol Hill.

All the same, inflation was brought under control, unlike during World War I, and, it was done in such a way as to move excess cash into savings, so there would be ample funds after the war to support high levels of investment and consumption. Holding the line was not easy: Special interest groups were always lobbying Congress to exempt them from price or wage controls—the farm lobby in particular. Roosevelt acted to protect stabilization, playing the lion's part again by vetoing an inflationary farm bill, issuing a Hold-the-Line wage order, and taking other steps offensive to special interests. In consequence, after May 1943, the cost of living rose by only 1 percent. As so often before, after maddening delays Roosevelt provided decisive leadership.

Baruch exercised his greatest influence upon mobilization in 1942, the most dangerous year of the war. He was particularly good at resolving deadlocks. These were frequent, for while Roosevelt insisted on making all important decisions himself, he was a procrastinator, abhorred conflict, and discouraged aides from bringing feuds to his attention. Since Roosevelt would not settle disputes, log jams resulted which Baruch sometimes cleared. With his great reputation, diplomatic gifts, boardroom skills, deal-making instincts, and numerous personal allies, Baruch flourished in the Byzantine maze of power that Roosevelt had built around himself. As he held no office and sought none, Baruch had—or gave the appearance of having—nothing at all to lose. This inspired a confidence in him that he traded upon shrewdly.

Baruch was manipulative, opinionated, egotistical, and obsessed with appearances. His vanity was awe inspiring, even by Washington standards. He cultivated the press diligently, using it to build up his image as the nation's elder statesman. Besides nourishing his self-conceit, Baruch's access to reporters, especially Arthur Krock of *The New York Times*, who idolized him, constituted a source of power equally as useful to him as his access to the White House. Like a versatile running back, he could go inside or outside as needed.

When fighting inflation, Baruch showed his hand by speaking openly to the press. When it came to war production he was the consummate insider. Though he supported Nelson up to a point, Baruch's favorite administrator was Ferdinand Eberstadt, an aristocratic member of the governing elite. Formerly a Wall Street lawyer and broker, Eberstadt worked closely with Under Secretary of the Navy James Forrestal.[15] As the first civilian head of the Army–Navy Munitions Board Eberstadt performed outstandingly. It was he, more than anyone else, who invented the Controlled Materials Plan, leading Nelson to make him its administrator. But as Nelson's second in command Eberstadt occupied an altogether too important post so far as New Dealers were concerned.

New Dealers mistrusted Eberstadt, whom they regarded as a Prussian and a stalking-horse for Lieutenant General Brehon Somervell, the much feared chief of the Army Service Forces. This was probably untrue, for Eberstadt believed in civilian control, and, by tactfully curbing its appetite for materials, kept the Army in check.[16]

What most alienated New Dealers was not Eberstadt's political philosophy, but a dispute that went to the very heart of mobilization.

New Dealers wanted to maintain, if not actually expand, the output of consumer goods. As they saw it, munitions ought to be turned out in addition to, rather than instead of, civilian products. They favored butter over guns, not so much from lack of patriotism as because they failed to appreciate either the demands of war or the limitations of industry. Eberstadt took the opposite view, as did Baruch, holding that civilian production should be stabilized, and all excess capacity devoted to making munitions. This struggle would last until V-J Day, but, since New Dealers failed to gain the upper hand, it did not seriously endanger war production, as otherwise might have happened.

New Dealers backed Nelson because the alternatives to him, mainly Baruch, seemed worse, rather than out of any pronounced enthusiasm. In late 1942, the low point of mobilization, when it became clear that the optimistic goals set earlier could not be met, they favored bringing Charles Wilson of General Electric into the WPB. With advocates of a total war effort demanding his head Nelson's position was shaky. Assigning a production man to assist him would help, and Wilson, though not a liberal, would want the power that Eberstadt had, thus killing two birds with one stone. Roosevelt obliged, since doing so created his favorite managerial relationship. As he once told Frances Perkins, "A little rivalry is stimulating, you know. It keeps everybody going to prove he is a better fellow than the next man. It keeps them honest, too."[17]

Wilson did indeed crowd Eberstadt out, but in doing so antagonized the War and Navy Departments, who had nothing against Wilson but regarded Eberstadt more highly. Nor did adding Wilson to Nelson's team improve the latter's standing. By early 1943 it was obvious that Nelson had to go. On February 5 Byrnes wrote the President that the time had come to put Baruch in charge of WPB. The War Department supported him, as did Congress, Wilson, Eberstadt, and Hopkins. Appointing Baruch would silence press and business critics of the WPB, thus providing Roosevelt with a public relations bonanza. These were compelling reasons, and for a short time Roosevelt bought them, offering Baruch the job he had held with such distinction a quarter of a century earlier.

Baruch hesitated, which gave Nelson time to fire Eberstadt and make it impossible for Roosevelt to replace him. Nelson wanted to get rid of Eberstadt anyway, but now if Nelson were fired it would seem to be as a result of having discharged Eberstadt. Liberals were certain to complain bitterly if Nelson were let go in any case, but they would be especially outraged if it appeared that their man had been dismissed for removing the hated Eberstadt. It was no time to keep Nelson in office for petty political reasons, nor to lose the gifted Eberstadt, but that is precisely what happened. In the event, Nelson's days were numbered. Through a clever trick he had saved himself without answering his critics. They, and his own weak leadership, would finish him off in the end.

Typically, Roosevelt decided to solve his mobilization problems by creating a brand-new agency. The WPB lived on, but under the shadow of the new Office of War Mobilization created by FDR in May 1943. To general amazement, OWM was not a monstrosity. Byrnes gave up his job as economic stabilizer to head it, continuing to operate with a small staff led by the faithful, to Roosevelt, Benjamin Cohen. In this way the nation came as close as it ever would to having a mobilization director. Creating OWM was an extreme act on Roosevelt's part, since sharing power went so strongly against his grain. He hated it when the press called Byrnes "Assistant President" and "Chief of Staff," titles awarded Byrnes even before his promotion. Yet Byrnes could be relied on. He was cautious and diplomatic. His office would be in the White House, under Roosevelt's supervision. Things could be worse, would have been worse, from FDR's point of view, had he stuck with Baruch.

Such decisive action contrasted sharply with the general muddle. Everywhere in Washington there existed duplication and confusion, overlapping grants of authority, and divided tasks. A host of agencies fought each other to gain power, funds, and breathing space. Decisions were made on the basis of immediate or local needs, rather than according to an overall design, or anything resembling one. What planning did take place was short-term and specific.

Roosevelt's working habits contributed to this disorder. Access to him was limited and capricious. Important men cooled their heels outside his office while nobodies who had caught his eye engaged the President's attention. Letters were answered or not as fancy dictated. Often the President made conflicting pronouncements on the same subject, leaving frustrated officials to find out for themselves what his intentions were. He ignored all complaints, and they were incessant, or else airily dismissed them. Not even discovering that enemy news agencies were using the "mess in Washington" to support Japanese morale made any difference to the man who was apparently responsible for it.

In some respects the American war effort resembled that of Nazi Germany. This would have come as a surprise to Americans at the time, who believed that Germany was a model of Teutonic precision and police-state efficiency. In fact, the Nazi state was remarkable for its overlapping authorities and plagued by bureaucratic chaos. As in America, personalities were vitally important, favored administrators expanding their reach at the expense of those outside the magic circle of power. As also in America the supreme leader, for political reasons, did not wish mobilization to inconvenience civilians. Though Hitler increased armament production before the war, he resisted stockpiling essential materials and cutting back on inessentials. As in America again, German munitions were produced over and above consumer goods more than might be expected. America got away with doing so because of its immense industrial base and because it still produced most of its raw materials.[18] Germany made up for domestic shortages by plundering captive nations. Even so, theft had its limits. In 1942 Hitler was obliged to put the economy on a war footing at last.

After the death of Minister of Armaments and War Production Fritz Todt, Hitler installed Albert Speer, his favorite architect, as head of mobilization. Perhaps coincidentally, this appointment took place two and a half years after Germany went to war, almost the same length of time that passed between Pearl Harbor and Roosevelt's assignment of Byrnes to OWM. Speer tripled war production in 1942 and 1943, and in some areas more than that, as by increasing tank production sixfold in two years. Still more could have been done, for, like Donald Nelson and even James Byrnes, Speer never had full control of the domestic war effort. Manpower was directed by another Minister, who seldom took account of Speer's requirements. And, again as in America, powerful leaders, such as Nazi Party chief Martin Bormann and his gauleiters, opposed total mobilization as harmful to civilian morale.

There were other reasons why Speer was unable to make the best use of Germany's human and material resources. Like Roosevelt, Hitler made a practice of assigning one or more agencies or individuals to perform the same task. "That way," he used to tell Speer, eerily echoing Roosevelt, "the stronger one does the job."[19] Another handicap was that Nazi dogma, and their reluctance to work in industry, prevented Speer from mobilizing German women.

Businessmen showed Speer photographs of workers changing shifts in the same ammunition factory 24 years apart. Yet, while in 1918 the employees had been predominantly women, in 1942 most were men. To Speer's disgust they remained so, Nazi leaders refusing to compromise their ideology despite the labor shortage. Further, even more than Americans, they insisted on maintaining peacetime standards of comfort and luxury. As late as 1944 factories manufacturing such items as rugs and picture frames were exempted from the war effort. For these and other reasons, ammunition production never reached World War I levels, even though bureaucratization was far greater, the Ordnance Office alone having a staff 10 times as big as in the previous war.

By this standard the American war effort looks more impressive than when studied by itself. On the other hand, if compared with Great Britain's, the shortcomings become apparent. Churchill, who was both Prime Minister and Minister of Defence, conducted national affairs with the aid of a five-man War Cabinet—a highly efficient mechanism that had no counterpart in America. There was no mobilization czar in Britain either, for, like Roosevelt, Churchill did not wish to share power. To a large extent the War Cabinet made one unnecessary. While he created some new ministries, notably the Ministry of Production in 1942, much of the war effort was administered through existing agencies by professional civil servants. Though some business executives were brought into government, Britain got along without the horde of dollar-a-year men (the WPB alone had 800) who in America did, along with much good, much to promote big business.[20]

Once Byrnes became Director of War Mobilization, the war effort was at least adequately managed, yet American mobilization never was what it could have been. Paul Koistinen, the leading authority on this subject, estimates that the United States could easily have increased its supply of munitions by 10 to 20 percent.[21] Production during the war was only about what could have been achieved in peacetime, given full employment. The results were striking just the same.

Much criticism of Roosevelt's wartime leadership missed the point, which was that even if Roosevelt had made efficiency his god, the American system of government would still have obstructed him. Here again the comparison with Great Britain is useful. In America individualism, pluralism, and mistrust of government made extemporizing not just desirable but absolutely necessary. Americans put a premium on leadership as well, the success or failure of any war agency depending to a large extent on whoever happened to run it. As the existing bureaucracy was relatively small and inelastic, it seemed easier, and was culturally more acceptable, to solve each new problem by creating a new organization and inviting businessmen to staff it. The tradition of public service being weak, and civil service a synonym for time wasting incompetence, business was the primary source of executive talent.

Business was also the interest group that worried Roosevelt most. A *Fortune* magazine survey published in November 1941 revealed that three-quarters of all businessmen feared that Roosevelt would use the war crisis to promote what they saw as undesirable reforms. Because some businessmen were still resisting mobilization, it was all the more important for Roosevelt to appease corporate America. Since expanding the federal service would only have further upset it, Roosevelt followed the easier course of creating temporary new bodies for business leaders to run. Despite his mistrust of dollar-a-year men, expediency won out.

The best commentator on America in wartime was not a journalist, or even an American. Isaiah Berlin, later a renowned philosopher but then an obscure Oxford don, spent most of the war in Washington providing the British government with weekly reports that were notable for their dry wit and shrewd judgments. He was startled to find that power in Washington resided more in the man than in the agency. Except for the State Department:

> The relationships between the powerful satraps who governed provinces of the Administration, and between the groups of officials who "worked for" them (and their relationships to individual journalists) seemed to me to be far more important than relations between established institutions, knowledge of which was indispensable to the understanding of the ways in which the British Civil Service, and to some degree, British Ministers too, thought and functioned.[22]

Contrary to American practice, British leadership was collegial rather than individualistic. Churchill was as domineering as Roosevelt, but all did not hinge on him personally, as with the President.

Unlike Churchill, who led a true coalition government and was sheltered to some extent from political pressure, Roosevelt was nagged unceasingly by independent legislators. This was true even before November 1942, when conservatives won so many seats that during the next two years it was, in all but name, a Republican Congress. Because of a light Democratic turnout, the GOP was only 13 seats short of a majority in the House, and missed controlling the Senate by just nine. If North Africa had been invaded a week earlier, instead of on November 8, the results might well have been different, for Operation Torch was popular at home and would have benefited the Democrats. Instead, their margin was so thin that in 1944, just before the general election, the Democrats lost their majority altogether as a result of by-elections. The 1942 results strengthened the conservative wing of each party, and, as Southern Democrats frequently voted with Republicans, the Seventy-eighth Congress ended many worthwhile New Deal programs.

Any review of the difficulties he faced must inevitably cast Roosevelt's apparently negative methods in a different light. Critics deplored, and rightly so, the costs of America's way of making war. His defenders observed that things worked out all right despite the terrible muddle. This is to miss the point again. Given the American system of government and the intensity of partisan politics, Roosevelt's style of leadership was not simply the result of personality quirks, but essential to his success.

Because American government is organized to prevent decisions from being made, and elected officials have little protection against interest groups, nothing important can be done until the need is overwhelmingly obvious. Thus, Roosevelt would delay making hard decisions as long as he could, put as many stalking-horses and sacrificial victims in place as needed, and only when the outcry was at its height install the appropriate man or measure. Roosevelt was a great user of men, sometimes using them up it is true, but more often skillfully manipulating them, as in his complex relations with Baruch.

Roosevelt's understanding of the political system, and his appetite for intrigue, even if sometimes overdone, were crucial aspects of his leadership. They go a long way toward explaining why American planning and management during the Second World War was so much better than in the First. Despite all that went wrong, a great armed force was trained and equipped, inflation curbed, taxes raised, profits and wages kept under control, and essential requirements met. Advocates of a total effort were bound to be disappointed by the necessary compromises and delays—which even Baruch, despite all his experience, seems never to have understood. But domestic liberals would be disappointed too, often out of necessity given their bias in favor of consumption.

There is no need to praise every step Roosevelt took, for many were indefensible. On the whole, however, given the environment in which he had to work, Roosevelt solved the great problems about as quickly as he could. It is not on FDR's shoulders that blame should be placed for the holdups and confusion, but rather on American democracy, which he managed so skillfully that it avoided defeating itself.

6

Rout and Recovery

Japan's attack on Hawaii exposed the shortcomings of American national security policy as nothing else could have done. The nation had failed to ready itself for a war everyone knew was coming. Political games were played as usual while the sands of time ran out. Mobilization limped along, the constant reshuffling of personnel only making things worse. The military had based its plans upon what now stood exposed as illusions. Diplomacy was bankrupt. Yet, beyond the chaos in Washington were enormous strengths, a people whose resolution would not fail, a productive system that would stun the world, a generation of young men bred to peace who would prove to be awesome in battle. Unwittingly, the Japanese had lit a fire that would consume them.

Even the Imperial Navy's victory at Pearl Harbor was less than it seemed to be, for closer analysis showed that only tactical gains had been won, rather than a strategic advantage. The United States lost many aircraft, ships, and men; the Japanese very few. But because its aircraft carriers were at sea, the Pacific Fleet retained its offensive punch and was far from beaten. This doomed Japan's hope for a quick end to the war, and, hard as it was to see at the time, made the attack on Hawaii a colossal blunder.

To make matters worse for the enemy, Vice Admiral Chuichi

Nagumo had denied his air commander permission to launch a second strike, thus sparing the shipyards, dry docks, machine shops, and especially tank farms, upon which everything depended. Had these been wiped out, the Fleet would have withdrawn to its mainland bases, and there would have been no triumph at Midway to redeem Pearl Harbor. Even the battle damage at Pearl was less serious than it looked. Except for *Arizona* and *Oklahoma*, the battleships would be repaired, modernized, and put to useful service.

The political benefits resulting from Japan's attack were great, for it silenced isolationists and united Americans. Polls showed that a large majority supported the fullest possible effort, including a national service plan similar to that of Great Britain—a level of mobilization beyond what even the government wanted. Opposition to the draft collapsed. Despite complaints about rationing and shortages on the home front, civilians were prepared to assume heavy burdens. Yet, because Pearl Harbor had accomplished what FDR could not, it aroused the suspicion of many.

The debate over whether Roosevelt knew of Pearl Harbor in advance has diverted attention from the larger failings of American policymakers. Despite two congressional investigations and a stream of books to the contrary, there has never been the slightest evidence to show that the attack on Hawaii was anything less than a complete surprise to American leaders.[1] All arguments that Roosevelt knew of it in advance turn on the fact that Pearl Harbor solved Roosevelt's most pressing problem, which was how to get into the fight against Hitler. Though the road to war with Germany finally led through Japan, there was no guarantee that it would. Indeed, the odds were high that, with the United States bogged down in the Pacific, Germany would continue its policy of refusing the bait since American neutrality was so advantageous to it. Roosevelt would then have been trapped in the wrong war, and, with public indignation at fever pitch, it would have been difficult to continue aiding Britain and Russia.

Hitler declared war on the United States for several reasons. He did not want Japan to be overwhelmed by the American response. His patience in the face of America's undeclared war on German U-boats, and its aid to Britain and Russia, was running out. He seems also to have been strongly influenced by Rainbow Five, the secret plan for a two-ocean war, which had been leaked to the *Chicago Tribune*. It revealed that the United States did not expect to be able to fight in Europe until 18 months after war broke out, a time by which Hitler expected the war to be over.[2] That Hitler would react as FDR needed him to was not something the President could count on, and to deliberately take so great a risk was inconsistent with Roosevelt's nature.

Washington knew weeks in advance that Japan was on the move, and sent war warnings out on November 27 precisely for that reason. It was probable that Japan would avoid U.S. territories altogether in hopes that America would stay neutral. If Japan did attack, the most logical targets were American air and naval bases in the Philippines, which potentially threatened a Japanese invasion effort anywhere in Southeast Asia. No responsible person believed that Hawaii was at risk. Roosevelt appears to have counted upon Japan's behaving as Germany did in the thirties, gobbling up small states first before taking on the great powers. Odd as it seems in retrospect, the high command believed that Hawaiian defenses were adequate to meet any challenge. Assuming those defenses had been vigilantly manned, they might even have been correct.

Apart from complacency, the military high command was to blame for failing to make the war warnings more specific, to list the precautions it wanted, and to establish close communications between the Army and Navy. All the same, Washington had a right to expect that senior commanders would know their duties without having to be reminded. Hawaii should have been on full alert, and the Philippines, which were on the invasion route, if anything even more so. That the defenders were caught completely by surprise was the fault of local headquarters. Thus, the Hawaiian Army and Navy commanders were promptly sacked, as MacArthur should have been.

Though their defenders made much of Washington's failure to provide timely and specific instructions, ordinary common sense should have been enough, the press alone providing ample notice. In May the journalist Edgar Snow had told *Saturday Evening Post* readers exactly what to expect. Like Snow, *Life* magazine feared a Pacific blitzkrieg, pointing out that an American economic embargo would provoke a swift response. "For Japan, the immediate future was death or glory," it accurately predicted.[3]

Earlier in the year *Life* had put its finger on what was undoubtedly a major reason for the composure with which people viewed a possible war with Japan. In March Gallup had found that 39 percent of respondents thought the United States should intervene to keep Japan from seizing Singapore and the Netherlands East Indies. Why were so many Americans willing to fight for the distant colonies of nations with which they were not allied? The reason, *Life* thought, was that "There seemed to be no fierce emotional resistance to war in the Pacific, as there is among many people to war in Europe. The strong American hatred of war has really been hatred of the bloody slaughter which Americans associate with the last war. For most Americans a naval war at arm's length, such as a war with Japan would be, holds no terror."[4]

If *Life* correctly gauged the degree of American smugness at the time, and the polls supported its assessment, two things become more clear. At the highest level, official drift must have been encouraged by the knowledge that a war with Japan would enjoy popular support. This would help explain why there were no frantic last minute political efforts to discourage a Japanese attack. On the operational level, since the Pacific commanders, like the American people as a whole, underrated the Japanese, they failed to take obvious defensive steps, ignoring the war warnings from Washington and also the many clues that afterward leaped out at critics.

It is true that the signals of an impending attack were part of a broad stream of intelligence reports that pointed in many directions, and also that much vital intelligence was narrowly held, and failed to reach Pacific commanders. But they knew that the Imperial Japanese Navy had changed its call signals twice in one month, twice a year being usual. Naval intelligence had lost track of the Japanese carriers, which were observing radio silence. An illegal FBI phone tap revealed shortly before December 7 that the Japanese consulate in Honolulu was burning its documents. Just before enemy aircraft arrived, the destroyer *Ward* sank an unidentified submarine right outside Pearl Harbor—an event that ought to have set off alarms, but didn't. Neither did the sighting, at 7:02 A.M. local time, by an experimental radar station, of a large number of incoming aircraft—which proved to be the attacking force.

When the Japanese air fleet arrived it found a military establishment that was still observing peacetime conventions. Though it trained hard on weekdays, the Fleet still took weekends off. Numerous sailors were ashore. Most of the ships had cold boilers and so could not take evasive action. The battleships were not protected by antitorpedo nets. Antiaircraft guns were largely unmanned and without ammunition. At Hickam and Wheeler Fields, the main air bases, conditions were even worse. To protect against sabotage aircraft were grouped together for easy guarding—which made them easy targets. The fighter planes were on four-hour alert, apparently in expectation that Japan would give advance notice—despite its history of surprise attacks. No reconnaissance flights were being made. The Army was responsible for defending Pearl Harbor, but the only long-distance patrol planes were Navy PBYs and their commander had five different superiors, none of them an Army officer. The two services went their separate ways, Japanese aircraft flying between them.

In the Philippines as well peacetime habits were to blame for America's losses. General MacArthur learned of the Pearl Harbor attack at 3:30 A.M. local time, and had received official confirmation by 5:00. However, when at noon the Japanese attacked Clark Field, 50 miles northwest of Manila, they found its bombers parked neatly along the runways and no American fighters in sight. MacArthur lost half his aircraft on that first day, and with them the Philippines—yet no one accused him of conspiring to bring on war. It was military bungling that brought disaster to the archipelago, as earlier to Hawaii.

Incompetence was not the only cause, for as would be true throughout the war, military planning was closely tied to politics, to deeply rooted national beliefs, to the ebb and flow of public opinion— in short, to all that made American democracy what it was. A less insular people would have insisted upon having a military establishment second to none. A less confident people would have taken the Japanese threat seriously rather than trusting in racist stereotypes. Americans believed that, being slight of stature, the Japanese were also weak, that they had inner-ear defects and myopic eyes which prevented them from being good pilots, that they lacked mechanical skills and were otherwise handicapped.[5] These attitudes contributed both to the drift toward war and the failure to prepare for it. These same reasons explain why Japan's audacity came as a much greater shock than if it had been displayed by Europeans.

Yet, such are the fortunes of war that, had the Japanese plan been less brilliant, Japan would have been better off. This was because the Pacific commander, Admiral Husband E. Kimmel, had devised a strategy, codenamed Plan 0-1, that called for the Fleet to sortie at once when war broke out and raid Japanese bases in the Marshall Islands. His idea was to draw out the Imperial Japanese Navy, which would be defeated by his battle line because of its 3 to 2 advantage in 16-inch guns. Among the many difficulties Kimmel did not take into account was that Japan's carriers outnumbered his, 10 to 3. Kimmel was a battleship Admiral and didn't understand that the carrier was no longer an auxiliary vessel but rather the primary weapon of naval war. If Plan O-1 had brought the two sides together it would have given the Japanese an opportunity to destroy America's carriers as well as the battle line. Fate was on America's side again, though no one knew this yet.[6]

Admiral Morison was more right than he knew when he observed that:

> The surprise attack on Pearl Harbor, far from being a "strategic necessity" as the Japanese claimed even after the war, was a strategic imbecility. One can search military history in vain for an operation more fatal to the aggressor. On the tactical level, the Pearl Harbor attack was wrongly concentrated on ships rather than permanent installations and oil tanks. On the strategic level it was idiotic. On the high political level it was disastrous.[7]

Despite these silver linings, the clouds of war hung heavily over America in the aftermath of Pearl Harbor. While its enemies were fully armed, the United States was practically naked. The Army still did not have a single combat-ready division. The Air Force had lost most of its front-line planes. The Pacific Fleet was heavily outnumbered in every type of ship. To avoid antagonizing Japan, America had failed to develop an advanced anchorage on Guam, which meant, for want of a supply train, that the Fleet was tied to Hawaii. The Imperial Japanese Navy, in contrast, had built a string of island bases and could go wherever it pleased.

Japanese planners had devised a complex and far-reaching network of operations designed to win the Pacific War in short order. The raid on Hawaii coincided with landings in southern Siam and northern Malaya. They were followed by other attacks that quickly reduced most of Southeast Asia. Air strikes against the Philippines were supposed to coincide with those against Pearl Harbor, but in fact they did not, because pilots of Japan's Eleventh Imperial Air Fleet based on Formosa were grounded by a heavy fog. Having lost the element of surprise, Japanese airmen were prepared for heavy casualties. Yet, when they belatedly arrived over Clark Field, the main American bomber base, they encountered little resistance. A hundred aircraft were destroyed at Clark and its neighboring fighter base—including 18 Flying Fortresses, half the strategic bomber force that was supposed to make the Philippines defensible.

Final responsibility for this debacle belonged to General Douglas MacArthur, head of both the American and Philippine Commonwealth forces. Soldiering was in MacArthur's blood. His father, Lieutenant General Arthur MacArthur, had commanded troops during the Philippine Insurrection at the turn of the century, and young Douglas followed his lead, graduating first in his class from West Point in 1903. During World War I MacArthur was the youngest brigadier in the

Army, enabling him to become the only American commander to serve as a general officer in both world wars. He was appointed Army chief of staff in 1930. In that capacity MacArthur is best remembered for ordering an attack upon unarmed veterans who were camped in Washington while lobbying for early payment of their World War I bonuses. In 1935 he was named military advisor to the Philippine Commonwealth, and in 1936 promoted to field marshal in command of the Philippine Army. Retired from the U.S. Army in 1937, he returned to active duty in 1941.

The Army had sent most of its available Flying Fortresses to the Philippines without adequate radar equipment, antiaircraft units, or fighter protection. Knowing this, MacArthur had ordered all his B-17s sent to Mindanao where they would be relatively safe. Yet when Japan struck only half the Fortresses had been moved. The Air Force did not reconnoiter Formosa, from which any Japanese air attack would come, and failed even to provide adequate cover for its own bases. MacArthur and his senior officers had different versions as to who was at fault, but all shared the blame in varying degrees—and, under different circumstances, would have had to answer for it.

MacArthur was never accused of treason for his complete lack of readiness, or even of incompetence, because his troops fought magnificently after the Japanese landed and wiped out recollections of the initial errors—plus those he perpetrated later. Moreover, in the early months America badly needed a hero, and MacArthur, for lack of an alternative, had to fill the bill. *Newsweek* ran his picture on its cover of March 9, 1942, calling MacArthur "The War's No. 1 Hero." Streets were named after him, and even a beauty contest was held to select the "MacArthur Girl." Party politics contributed to the adulation. Those who accused Roosevelt of conspiring in the attack on Pearl Harbor were mostly Republicans eager to glorify MacArthur and run him for President in 1944. Thus, MacArthur never had to account for his Philippine mistakes, flagrant though they were.

In the weeks that followed, Japan attacked other American possessions in the Pacific. Guam in the Marianas, a refueling stop for Pan American Clippers, was the first to fall. Its tiny garrison of 427 Marines and sailors, plus a few hundred native troops, had only 170 rifles among them and few automatic weapons. On December 10 they were overrun by 5,400 Japanese soldiers. At Wake Island, 2,300 miles west of Hawaii, there were fewer than 600 Americans, 12 obsolescent Marine fighter planes, two 5-inch naval guns, and a dozen antiaircraft weapons. On December 7 a Japanese air raid destroyed eight of the fighters. Wake was then attacked by a Japanese force comprised of three light cruisers, six destroyers, two patrol boats, and two transports. Marine gunners promptly sank one destroyer, and a Marine pilot another, driving the task force off. The Japanese returned in greater strength on December 23 (December 22, Hawaiian time) and inundated the garrison—which fought valiantly all the same, 122 men being killed before Major James P. Devereux surrendered Wake in order to keep a thousand civilians alive. For their valor the Marines were brutally mistreated in prison camps, Japan having ceased to observe the conventions governing treatment of POWs.

Making December 22 an even darker day, at dawn (local time) 43,000 Japanese troops came ashore on Lingayen Gulf with orders to take Luzon, and then the other Philippine Islands. To defend these territories General MacArthur commanded a force three times as large on paper, but his army consisted largely of some 100,000 Philippine reservists, who were ill-trained, poorly armed, and usually broke under fire. One American general described them simply as a "mob." They should never have been called up, nor, after the fighting began, kept in service. MacArthur's effectives consisted of miscellaneous Army units, the 4th Marine Regiment, and 12,000 Philippine Scouts—about 30,000 regulars in all. The Japanese not only outnumbered MacArthur's combat-ready force, but had total air and naval mastery. On that basis, their plan realistically allowed 50 days for seizing the islands.

MacArthur waited too long before deciding to concentrate his troops on Bataan, a 30-mile-long peninsula that, together with the island of Corregidor, controlled Manila Bay. Bataan was covered with mountains and jungles, making it highly suitable for a stand. But it had not been fortified or provisioned beforehand, or during the several weeks that elapsed between the first air strikes and Japan's invasion. This was because MacArthur planned to attack the Japanese at their landing points, and in his arrogance regarded preparations to hold Bataan as defeatist. When he did give the order to retreat on December 23, it was too late to stock Bataan with even the bare essentials.

MacArthur, acceding to the request of President Manuel Quezon, left a huge store of rice behind for civilian use. A fifth of this stockpile, some 10 million bushels, would have fed the men on Bataan for a year. The rice remained behind, only to be destroyed by Japanese bombers. Years later it was revealed that the Philippine Commonwealth had presented MacArthur with half a million dollars, the equivalent of perhaps $5 million today, and that, though contrary to Army regulations, MacArthur had been allowed to keep it by Roosevelt and

Marshall.[8] The gift was improper all the same, and suggests that MacArthur's objectivity—never his strong point—had been further compromised by Quezon.

Japanese forces occupied Manila on January 2, 1942, and the evacuation to Bataan, superbly directed by Major General Jonathan Wainwright, was largely complete by the sixth. The garrison on Bataan consisted of about 15,000 American and 65,000 Filipino troops, who were short of ammunition, medical supplies, and food. Bataan, with its swamps and jungles, was a malarial nightmare whereon, for lack of quinine, thousands of soldiers were soon racked by chills and fevers. Against all odds, the garrison fought a tremendous delaying battle. When its first line of defense was outflanked, it fell back upon a second line halfway down the peninsula, stopping Lieutenant General Masaharu Homma's 14th Army in its tracks. By the time his 50 days were up, Homma had taken 7,000 casualties, lost an additional 10,000 to 12,000 men to malaria and other diseases, and could not launch another assault. He was obliged to pull back and seek reinforcements.

Not counting the minor action at Wake, this was the first setback Japan experienced in its spectacular round of conquests, giving the Americans and Filipinos on Bataan almost two more months of freedom. But, since Japan controlled the Western Pacific, Bataan could not be reinforced or resupplied, and so its defenders were steadily worn down by starvation, disease, air attacks, and Japanese raiding parties. On February 23 President Roosevelt sought to lift their morale with a radio broadcast. Unhappily, in doing so he disclosed that no help was coming. Little wonder the doomed men circulated verses such as this:

We're the battling bastards of Bataan:
No mama, no poppa, no Uncle Sam,
No aunts, no uncles, no nephews, no nieces,
No rifles, no planes, or artillery pieces,
And nobody gives a damn.[9]

The soldiers also made reference to "Dugout Doug," which was unfair since MacArthur habitually walked around in the open during air raids on Corregidor to inspire his troops—on the theory, it appears, that fighting men would be encouraged by the sight of their commander taking pointless risks.

Their desperate situation was concealed by the media. A photo essay on Bataan by *Life* said: "In their first impact with the enemy, as seen in these pictures, Americans showed themselves to be fighters—cleverer, tougher and more resolute than their enemies. Above all, their faces and bearing show here that they were enjoying the war, that the co-operative job of war was simply more fun than any singlehanded job of peace they had ever known."[10] This was a reversion to the fraudulent cheerleading of the last war, and would have inspired much profane humor on Bataan if the troops had seen it.

MacArthur earned the contempt of his men by setting foot on Bataan exactly once—in keeping with his regal view of command—by having the food reserves of starving infantrymen removed to Corregidor, where the daily ration was three or four times what those on Bataan were getting, and by excluding the 4th Marines from a list of proposed Presidential unit citations, observing that the Marine Corps had gotten enough glory in World War I. Of 142 communiques issued by MacArthur's command during the first three months of the war, 109 mentioned only one soldier—himself.[11] He also made it a habit of assuring his men, sincerely at first, that help was coming. Thus, when the troops learned they were on their own, morale declined even further.

MacArthur was the most pompous, grandiose, and mendacious American commander in World War II, and the most relentless publicity-seeker. He mistrusted almost everyone outside his inner circle of sycophants, which General Marshall once told him was not a staff but a court, finding sinister motives in the most ordinary behavior. Yet, Roosevelt chose to give MacArthur a major command, an appointment which was to shape in large measure the entire Pacific War.

Undoubtedly FDR made MacArthur an official hero so as to placate the former isolationists in Congress. It was politically useful to have a leader whom conservatives were obliged to support, and yet who was far away from Washington and so could not figure in the next election.[12] A strong point of the American system during World War II was that party politics ordinarily had little effect upon the selection of major commanders. MacArthur was the chief exception to this rule, and, events would prove, a wholly justified one. Roosevelt, and the nation too, would ultimately profit from this decision, whatever the reasons behind it.

On March 11, 1942 MacArthur, his wife, his son Arthur, and Arthur's Chinese nurse, boarded PT-41 for a rough and dangerous 500-mile passage to Mindanao, followed by a long flight to Australia. Upon arrival he gave a press conference and a promise, saying "I came through, and I shall return." Meanwhile, the Bataan front crumbled under renewed Japanese attacks. On April 9 some 76,000 men, most too weak to fight, laid down their arms. The great fortress of Corregidor, just off Bataan and the key to Manila Bay, held out under continuous bombardment until May 6, when Japanese landings forced Wainwright, now a lieutenant general, to surrender all Philippine and American forces—not just on Luzon but throughout the islands.

Several thousand American and Filipino troops on various islands did go underground, but most obeyed Wainwright's order to surrender. That was unfortunate for them, because Japanese captivity proved to be worse than anything faced by guerrillas. During the Bataan Death March, as the forced trek to their stockades would later be called, some 7,000 American and Filipino POWs perished, most of them brutally murdered after collapsing during the 65 mile journey to Camp O'Donnell—where thousands more expired of wounds, disease, and malnutrition. Almost half of the Americans taken in the Philippines would not survive their imprisonment.

These horrors resulted from America's being unprepared for war and resolving to defend the Philippines without the means to do so. They were compounded by MacArthur's refusal to accept reality before, and even during, the final stand on Bataan. For MacArthur's mistakes he alone was at fault. All else must be blamed on the military and the Administration, and beyond them the public at large, which tolerated a mobilization effort that doomed the men in the Philippines to death or agonizing captivity. Thanks to the garrison's valiant stand, everyone forgave themselves, or were forgiven. Democracy's failure remained inexcusable.

MacArthur's arrival in Australia forced the services to outline a Pacific strategy. Japan's success had invalidated the prewar plans, yet the speed of events had left little time for reflection. As MacArthur demanded men and munitions, and with the nation expecting action in the Pacific, the service chiefs could no longer avoid laying plans for the middle distance. They had assumed that a Pacific War would be fought by the Navy. However, Japan's vast territorial conquests meant that the Army would be involved as well. A new strategy was required, but intimately linked to it was the question of supreme command. This complicated everything, for the Navy would not allow the Pacific Fleet to be commanded by a general, while it was equally inconceivable that MacArthur take orders from an admiral.

Service pride and rivalry dictated the outcome, which was to reshape strategy in such a way as to avoid having a Supreme Commander. Admiral Ernest J. King, Marshall's opposite number, was slow to see the danger to his service. At a meeting of the American Joint Chiefs of Staff on March 2, 1942, he proposed setting up strong points in preparation for an advance through the New Hebrides Islands, the Solomons, and the Bismarck Archipelago. Such a movement would secure Australia and pave the way for a return to the Philippines. The land forces required for this offensive would be directed by Admiral Chester W. Nimitz, King's newly appointed Pacific Fleet commander.

However, Australia and New Zealand had recently proposed forming an "ANZAC Council," which would be superior in the Pacific to the Allied Combined Chiefs of Staff (CCS), a body formed after Pearl Harbor to oversee all British and American operations. This suggestion opened the door to an Army power play. On March 7, through the CCS, Marshall and his planners supported the ANZAC proposal and, in connection with it, asked for the creation of a Southwest Pacific Area, to be commanded by MacArthur, that would include such naval and Marine forces as were required to further its mission. In one stroke the Army had taken over King's strategy, while also reaching for the means to implement it.

When the Joint Chiefs met on March 9 King attacked the ANZAC plan and the Army's proposed new theater, which threatened the Navy's independence and control of its aircraft carriers. After heavy negotiations a deal was struck on March 30. Marshall dropped the ANZAC proposal, and King agreed that MacArthur should have his theater, to consist initially of Australia, the Netherlands East Indies, and New Guinea. The Navy got everything else—a vast region designated as the Pacific Ocean Areas, which it subdivided into the South, Central, and North Pacific Areas. By forcing the issue, Marshall had gained the Army a theater of its own while also usurping King's strategy, for Australia was the key to any advance up the South Sea island chains that led to mainland Asia. King's response would be to devise a new strategy utilizing the Central Pacific that would compete with his original scheme as executed by MacArthur.

The Army had gained more than it realized, for no one anticipated the tremendous effort Australia would put forth—not only militarily but as a source of supply. Thanks to Aussie dedication, as well as that of his own men, MacArthur would work wonders in the Southwest Pacific. Even so, installing two separate commands in one region was among the worst American decisions of the war. Because of it MacArthur never had enough men and ships, while the Navy embarked on a wasteful drive that tied up immense resources to little purpose. There was nothing peculiar to the United States about this. Germany's command structure was terrible. Japanese interservice feuds were far worse than those of America. Just the same, Army–Navy turf battles made the Pacific War costlier than it needed to have been, and led to major strategic errors.

The valiant American defense of Bataan held up Japan for several months. This delay proved critically important to Australia, which may well have been saved by it, because the time gained was just enough to organize a successful defense. Otherwise, the Japanese swept all before them—seizing Burma, Malaya, the NEI, the Philippines, and islands without number. In the six months following Pearl Harbor, Japan made itself master of Southeast Asia, an area comprising 1 million square miles and 150 million people.

As Japan swept the Allies before it Washington could do little, since America's strategy, such as it was, of defending the Philippines with heavy bombers had been ruined on December 8. A week after Pearl Harbor Brigadier General Dwight D. Eisenhower joined the Army's War Plans Division. Marshall put him in charge of the Philippines, telling Eisenhower to do his best to save them. That was plainly impossible. Reinforcements did not exist, and, even if they had, the Pacific Fleet, still reeling from the blows sustained on December 7, could not be sent across 5,000 miles of enemy-infested ocean—and lacked the supply train that would enable it to fight even if it got there. Prewar planning had assumed that, if necessary, the Fleet could operate out of Manila Bay. That most of Luzon was now in enemy hands ruled out any chance of relief.

Yet, overwhelming as the rout was, and weak though the USN remained for many months afterward, at the very apex of Japan's success the tide would turn because of just two battles. The first of these, the Battle of the Coral Sea, put an end to Japanese expansion. At Midway its main attack force would be shattered. These defeats came about partly because in the late spring of 1942 many Japanese officers were suffering from what they came to call "Victory Disease," the symptoms being euphoria and carelessness. Intoxicated by success, rather than consolidating their gains they proceeded at once with further offensive actions.

Their first effort was to occupy Tulagi in the Solomon Islands, and other points in the region—notably Port Moresby, New Guinea, so as to gain control of the Coral Sea and neutralize Australia. As usual the enemy plan was exceedingly complex, requiring not only great skill on the Imperial Japanese Navy's part, but American conformity to its expectations.[13] Moreover, the Japanese paid little attention to security. That lapse was more dangerous than they knew, for, although outnumbered and outgunned, the USN had an overwhelming intelligence edge.

Naval Intelligence was monitoring 60 percent of Japanese radio transmissions over its Mid-Pacific Direction-Finding Net. This chain of stations tracked individual ships over thousands of miles of ocean by a process known as radio traffic analysis. It had missed the Japanese fleet that maintained radio silence before it attacked Pearl Harbor, but radio silence was not characteristic of the Imperial Japanese Navy, whose ships otherwise were always chattering away, to America's great benefit. Further, Navy codebreakers were able to decrypt a significant amount of the IJN's operational code, which yielded priceless data.

By April 20 Admiral Nimitz knew that in two weeks' time a Japanese carrier task force would enter the Coral Sea bound for Port Moresby. Though it was in MacArthur's theater, the divided command arrangement stipulated that fast carrier operations would remain under Navy control wherever they took place. Accordingly, Nimitz sent Frank Jack Fletcher to defend the Coral Sea with *Lexington* and *Yorktown*. Nimitz had no replacement carriers, but the Allies could not afford to lose Australia, and so the risk had to be taken.

On May 1 both U.S. carrier groups were in place. They and the Japanese strike force, which included two big carriers and one light, blundered back and forth for days, always missing each other. The battle was finally joined on May 7. When it was over Japanese planes had sunk an American destroyer and an oil tanker, and scored numerous hits on *Lexington* and *Yorktown*, "Lady Lex" suffering most because she had been built on a battle cruiser hull and was less maneuverable than *Yorktown*, a carrier from keel up. At this point America was far ahead, the Japanese having lost a light carrier and the use temporarily of its big carriers—the badly damaged *Shokaku* for two crucial months, and *Zuikaku* until June 12 because of heavy losses by its air group. The tally changed at 12:47 P.M., when *Lexington* started erupting. She had taken two torpedoes and three bomb hits during the battle, but her crew had gained control of the fires and relit her boilers. She was steaming home at 25 knots when gasoline fumes from her ruptured tanks exploded.

Remarkably, though 36 planes went down with her, only some 200 lives were lost out of a complement of nearly 3,000. *Lexington*, with *Saratoga*, the biggest combat vessel in the Navy, was famous as a happy ship, and greatly missed by her crewmen. She was missed by Admiral Nimitz, too, especially since he was now left with only three carriers to face the Japanese onslaught. Though the loss of *Lexington* made the Coral Sea a tactical win for the Japanese, it remained a strategic victory for the United States, because after the battle Japan was obliged to call off its invasion of Port Moresby for lack of air support. The Battle of the Coral Sea had saved Australia from either invasion or blockade.

This was the high-water mark of Japan's advance in the Pacific and a crucial setback, for the two Japanese fleet carriers would not return to service in time for Midway—much reducing the tactical odds in that all-important engagement. Because Coral Sea was the first naval battle fought entirely by aircraft, both sides made many mistakes. But the enemy committed more of them, and the USN was learning fast. One thing it had failed to learn was not to gild the lily. It reported two Japanese carriers sunk, inspiring speculation at home that the war would be won that year.

Midway did not have to be embroidered. It was the first great American victory of the war and prevented Japan from renewing its march across the Pacific. Midway resulted from the Imperial Japanese Navy's decision to draw out the American carriers. Attacking Midway, the westernmost of the inhabited Hawaiian islands, would lure the Pacific Fleet to its doom. Taking Midway would also close a gap in Japan's defensive screen, through which an American task force had slipped to launch 16 Army medium bombers against Tokyo. This famous raid, led by Lieutenant Colonel James H. Doolittle on April 18, 1942, did little material damage—but had, in principle, endangered Emperor Hirohito's life, and humiliated the military. Overnight Midway, which some Japanese planners had considered marginal, became an essential target.

On paper the IJN at this stage of the war was impossible to beat. For the attack on Midway, Admiral Isoroku Yamamoto would have at his disposal 11 battleships, 5 fleet and 3 light carriers, 12 cruisers, 43 destroyers, and some 700 aircraft. The United States would deploy only 3 fleet carriers with 233 combat aircraft, 8 cruisers, 15 destroyers, and a further 121 planes based on Midway. To make matters worse, the Japanese carriers were in prime condition and manned by seasoned crews and aviators. On the other hand, while *Enterprise* was in good shape, *Yorktown* had been damaged at the Coral Sea, and *Hornet* was newly commissioned and its air group lacked experience. Worse still, by this time the Navy knew that its aircraft were seriously deficient. The Grumman Wildcat fighter was no match for Japan's Zero, a splendid fighter plane which came as a nasty surprise to American military leaders even though it had been used in China for years. To protect against it, Wildcat pilots adopted an intricate defensive maneuver, the "Thach weave"—named after its inventor, Lieutenant Commander James Thach. This was a handy survival tool, but no substitute for better aircraft.

More inferior still was the obsolete Douglas Devastator, a torpedo plane that lacked self-sealing fuel tanks and was so slow that if unescorted it became a flying coffin. The ill-named Devastator featured a top speed (loaded) of 115 MPH, a range of 455 miles, and was armed with 2 machine guns, and a 1,300-pound torpedo. Its opposite number, the Japanese Kate, had a speed of 220 MPH, a range of 1,220 miles, 4 machine guns, and a 1,764-pound torpedo. In addition, the superb Japanese Long Lance torpedo was 10 times as effective as its American counterpart. The USN's Mark XIV submarine torpedo had a small warhead, a tendency to broach in the water, or, alternatively, to run too deep, unreliable firing mechanisms, and so little speed that at long range a Japanese ship could outrun it. Its aerial version, the Mark XIII, had all these defects plus others. A much better torpedo bomber, the Grumman Avenger, would soon join the fleet—but too late to save the Devastator crews at Midway. There were no improved torpedoes in sight, one of the Navy's major failings in World War II.

Midway, as the IJN's General Staff had pointed out, was not the best place for a decisive engagement, being too far from Japan and too close to Hawaii for comfort. Even so, the disparity in strength, both in numbers and quality, was so overwhelming that Japan would have won at Midway had Yamamoto done the obvious thing. That would have been to concentrate his forces, threaten Midway, and, when the American carriers arrived to defend it, crush them with his overwhelming firepower. Instead, he decided to attack Midway first, locking his fleets in place instead of going after the much more important carriers. He then drew up a complicated plan which entailed a broad dispersal of force. So ill-conceived a plan was unworthy of the officer who had designed the attack on Pearl Harbor.

Some of his vessels, including two light carriers, were to support an invasion of the Aleutian Islands as a feint; the four big carriers of his

First Mobile Force were to bomb Midway, and a Midway Occupation Force was to take it; while far behind these would be his Main Body with a light carrier and the rest of the surface fleet. Even by Japanese standards—which overvalued surprise and diversionary tactics, while failing to allow for the unexpected—this was a remarkably intricate plan of attack involving too many separate units. Thus, in the decisive carrier duel the odds would be about even, rather than, as easily could have been arranged, hugely in Japan's favor.

In addition to Japanese mistakes, the USN would benefit from its mastery of cryptoanalysis. By April the codebreakers at Station Hypo in Pearl, plus those in Washington and Australia, were reading much of the enemy's traffic. Thanks to codebreakers, Nimitz had been able to deploy his carriers to their best advantage in the Coral Sea. Now Naval Intelligence scored its greatest coup of the war by decrypting Yamamoto's plan for Midway. Luckily, for the USN, it had been sent over the air in full, and the crack cryptoanalysts of Fleet Radio Unit, Pacific, directed by Commander Joseph J. Rochefort, read it chapter and verse.[14] When the American carriers sortied, they knew exactly where to go. This time they—not Vice Admiral Chuichi Nagumo, who had commanded at Pearl and now at Midway—would do the unforeseen.

On May 27 *Yorktown* arrived at Pearl Harbor from the Coral Sea with internal damage and serious leaks caused by bomb explosions. The first estimate for repairs was 90 days. Nimitz gave the yard 72 hours. Had the Japanese addressed their own damaged carriers similarly, all might have been different. Fourteen hundred skilled workers immediately swarmed over the ship. On the twenty-ninth, *Yorktown* was out of dry dock and loading fuel and replacement planes, acquiring an air group composed of elements from three different carriers. The next day at 9:00 A.M., with hundreds of workmen still aboard, they would be taken off before the battle, it sailed for Midway and glory.

Enterprise and *Hornet* were already at sea, under the command of Rear Admiral Raymond A. Spruance, who had never before been responsible for even a single carrier. Admiral William F. Halsey, the most experienced and belligerent air admiral, a favorite back home and with his men, too, should have led at Midway, but had come down with a skin disease. On Halsey's advice, Nimitz replaced him with Spruance, the leader of Halsey's cruiser division. Poised, remote, intellectual, the opposite of colorful "Bull" Halsey, Spruance would prove himself to be a master of carrier warfare. Command of the battle was vested in Admiral Fletcher on *Yorktown*, who made several important decisions—one of them being to have the two task forces operate separately and at a distance from each other. As a result, when *Yorktown* came under attack the other two carriers would be out of danger. The most important tactical decisions were made by Spruance, who, if he had done nothing more in his career, would still rank with the greatest American admirals.[15]

The strategic planning for Midway must be credited to Nimitz. He took the risk of placing full trust in his codebreakers. He elected not to play it safe, despite the odds, but to defend Midway at all costs. In choosing Spruance to replace Halsey he found exactly the right commander. He ordered his task forces to take station northeast of Midway, out of range of enemy scouts, while aircraft from the island would do their searching for them. As he had hoped, the American carriers retained the element of surprise and were placed to strike the enemy as soon as he was discovered.

On June 3 a long-range PBY Catalina Flying Boat spotted the Midway Occupation Force, which subsequently was attacked all day by planes from the island—one of which managed to slightly damage a tanker. On June 4 Nagumo launched a strike against Midway, and soon after his carriers were spotted by another PBY. Midway then launched its own strikes, while the American carriers, still undetected, turned southwest to close with the enemy. Nagumo's aircraft easily wiped out the obsolete Marine fighters based on Midway, but heavy anti-aircraft fire destroyed 38 of his own planes, and put 30 more out of action. Nagumo thus was deprived of a third of his combat aircraft, and now had fewer war planes than the advancing American carriers. In addition, he had to attack Midway again, as it had not been disabled. This meant rearming his torpedo planes with bombs and changing the ordnance of his dive bombers from armor-piercing to high-explosive.

While the dangerous procedure took place, Nagumo was repeatedly attacked by planes from Midway. Six Navy torpedo bombers and four Army B-26 bombers armed with torpedoes bored in, scoring no hits and losing all but three aircraft. At this point a Japanese search plane made the first sighting of American warships. Then 16 Marine dive bombers attacked his fleet, doing no damage because of intense Japanese fire while losing half their number. Fifteen B-17s passed overhead, their bombs falling harmlessly into the water. Another Marine dive bomber formation attacked, making no hits but sustaining only one loss.

Nagumo was then advised of the presence of at least one American carrier. Though he had 36 dive bombers ready to go, Nagumo, cautious as ever, chose a textbook response. He would wait until all planes had been fueled and rearmed once again with antiship ordnance, and then send out a balanced attack force—mindful that the American planes attacking from Midway without fighter protection were being slaughtered. Thus passed Nagumo's last chance to win.

Fletcher gave Spruance, whose task force was closer to the enemy, orders to attack it on sight. Spruance decided to hit the Japanese early and hard, in hopes of catching them with their decks full of planes being serviced after bombing Midway. At maximum range he launched everything he had, 68 dive bombers, 30 torpedo planes, and 20 fighters, retaining only the Wildcats of his combat air patrol. This bold decision was a difficult one, since it meant that the torpedo planes, with their limited range, might not make it back. The fighters too were jeopardized—and, as it happened, all of *Hornet's* would be forced to ditch. After a slow and ragged start, which obliged Spruance to order his squadrons to attack singly instead of in air groups, his planes were off by 8:00 A.M. Fletcher began launching a much smaller force at 8:30.

The American squadrons were supposed to time their flights so that dive bombers went in ahead of the vulnerable torpedo planes—which would attack under fighter protection. Many pilots lacked the experience needed to bring three different types of aircraft with different flying speeds and launching times to the target in formation, and some squadrons lost sight of each other. Because Nagumo had changed course and Midway neglected to report this to Spruance, *Hornet's* fighters and dive bombers never found their targets. This left Lieutenant Commander J. C. Waldron's Torpedo 8 on its own. It was a green squadron, most of its pilots having never taken off with a torpedo aboard, let alone fired one in combat. Though they knew they were flying to almost certain death, not one held back when Waldron led them into battle. All 15 American planes were destroyed, few if any even releasing their torpedoes. Only one man from Torpedo 8 lived to tell the story.

Torpedo 6 from *Enterprise* made the next run. Unlike Waldron's men, these were experienced flyers; but, without fighter support, all that deft piloting could do was save four of the 14 planes that attacked—none scoring a hit. *Yorktown's* Torpedo 3 arrived last, escorted by six ships of Fighting 3 led by Commander Thach, whose obsolete Wildcats were overwhelmed by Zeros. Torpedo 3 lost 10 of 12 Devastators, again without hitting a target. At that moment, 10:22 A.M. local time, Thach recalled, he saw a glint in the sun and then a "beautiful silver waterfall." It was the Dauntless dive bombers of *Enterprise* and *Yorktown* screaming down through the empty sky.

By accident *Yorktown*'s air group had arrived at the same time as Lieutenant Commander Clarence McClusky of *Enterprise* and his 32 dive bombers, who had finally found the Mobile Force after a desperate search in which they used up most of their fuel. Since the Japanese combat air patrol had been drawn down to sea level by the torpedo plane attacks, all four enemy carriers were now unprotected. *Enterprise* pilots delivered lethal blows to *Akagi* and *Kaga*, while planes from *Yorktown* left *Soryu* a flaming hulk. In a mere three minutes the Pacific War had turned against Japan.

Only *Hiryu* survived to launch two waves against *Yorktown*, her veteran pilots breaking through the American CAP to put three bombs and two torpedoes into the great carrier. *Hiryu*'s dispensation was brief. In the evening, 24 dive bombers from *Enterprise*, 10 of them *Yorktown*'s, found that last Japanese carrier and sent her to the bottom.

Spruance retired to the east that night, preventing the Japanese battleships from engaging him under cover of darkness. Next day, planes from *Enterprise* found two damaged Japanese cruisers, sinking one and putting the other out of action for a year. With his bunkers emptying fast, his air groups reduced to a handful of planes, at risk of running into the enemy's battle line, or Japanese aircraft based on Wake, Spruance turned back on June 6 and made for Pearl Harbor.

Yorktown failed to return. She had survived the first wave of attackers despite serious damage, thanks to heroic efforts by her engineers and boiler-room men. "One hour and ten minutes after the bomb exploded in the stack, *Yorktown* lowered the breakdown flag and hoisted the signal: 'My speed five.' A spontaneous cheer rang out from every ship in the carrier's screen, encircling her in a golden ring of joy and affection." [16] She was making 20 knots when the second Japanese wave broke through, leaving her in flames. Even though soon abandoned, *Yorktown* would not sink and was brought under tow by a minesweeper while damage parties reboarded her. Had there been a fleet tug at hand, or even a cruiser, *Yorktown* might have been saved, but little *Viero* could barely move her. When an enemy submarine fired its fatal torpedoes, *Yorktown* was almost dead in the water.

Midway gave the IJN a blow from which it would never recover. Despite the heavy odds against them, the Americans inflicted much more harm than they suffered, losing one carrier to the enemy's four, less than a thousand men to the enemy's 3,000, and 150 aircraft, including those based on Midway, to Japan's 322. Japan would miss most the over 100 veteran pilots who were killed at a time when it had only 1,000 carrier pilots and was producing perhaps only 100 a year. The loss was greatly aggravated by the IJN's self-defeating habit of keeping its veteran flyers in action until they were used up. Its naval aviators became fewer and greener, while those of the USN—whose veterans were rotated home to train new pilots—became more numerous and proficient. Though Japan built new carriers, its naval air arm would never again be as good as it had been at Pearl Harbor. Midway was America's revenge for Pearl, and the assurance of final victory.

For once, *Life* magazine understated the case. Having been misled by Navy bulletins on the Battle of the Coral Sea, it regarded Midway with caution. *Life* acknowledged that a major victory had been won, reporting that five enemy carriers had gone down and 10,000 Japanese killed (the Navy once again gilding its lily). It warned that people who said Japan's offensive power had been crippled might be wrong. "Others more conservative and probably more correct cautiously warn that Japan can better afford carrier losses than the U.S., that Japan was still on the offensive, that the Aleutian Islands were in danger. A blow had been struck for our side but there were many rounds still to be fought."[17] This was about half right. There were many more rounds to go, but Midway had forced Japan to give up the strategic initiative.

During the Battle of Midway the Americans committed serious mistakes traceable to inexperience. The veteran Japanese made graver errors for which they had no excuse. True, the Americans enjoyed some luck, but, what they didn't make themselves, they took full advantage of. It was lucky, for example, that Nagumo issued faulty orders, but part of the reason he did was that his carriers were under incessant attack, first from Midway and then by carrier-based torpedo bombers, attacks that were pressed home with magnificent courage. These kept the Japanese too busy to think, forcing some of their errors. In the end, the seemingly fruitless sorties by Army, Marine, and Navy pilots made a difference that proved crucial.

The self-sacrifice of American flyers exposed a cherished Japanese delusion. Many Japanese believed that, though weaker industrially, they would win because Americans were soft, they themselves being battle-hardened samurai eager to die for Hirohito. Midway gave the lie to this prejudice. The United States did lack a warrior heritage. Military service, except by citizen–soldiers during wartime, was not highly valued. No American was ready to die for Franklin Roosevelt. Few if any regarded a glorious death in battle as the highest human achievement. Though brought up by peace-loving parents, young Americans proved at Midway, as they would throughout the war, that one need not be raised as a warrior to display martial virtues.

This point was critically important, for Americans were being asked to fight with inferior weaponry, a skillful, experienced, and well-armed foe. Understandably, Washington was reluctant to admit how poorly it had armed America's fighting men—who, in addition to being outnumbered, were effectively outgunned as well. Before the war high officials had repeatedly boasted that America's planes were the best in the world, while Japan supposedly had only copies of outdated Western models. When Japan's Zero burst upon the scene, military commentators scoffed at its lack of armor and its small-caliber guns. After Midway the Navy still claimed that its Wildcat could outfight the Zero, a claim which all pilots, and even some reporters, knew to be false, and had the nerve to praise the Devastator, a proven death trap.[18]

The Army too could not admit its failure to give fighter pilots an adequate weapon. Lacking a good interceptor, it celebrated the one it had. In January, after Senator Harry S Truman's investigating committee charged that most of the Army's fighter planes were no good, General Arnold went so far as to say that the P-40 was superior to Britain's Hurricane—which, even if true, was irrelevant, since Japan was using the Zero. Most reporters repeated these claims, though *Newsweek* printed a column by John Lardner that refuted them in the very same issue as another story full of Pentagon falsehoods. From Australia he reported that pilots were telling him that Zeros could fly rings around their P-40s. A "good and brave" pilot had said "When you fly a P-40 against a Zero, you can make one pass at him. Then, if you miss, you better get the hell out of there."[19]

Though the people at home did not know it, their outnumbered fighting men were being asked to compensate for inadequate arms with raw courage, and to a remarkable degree they were doing so. The armed forces in the Pacific at this stage of the war included several broad categories. Many enlisted men, and virtually all the noncoms, were regulars who had signed on before the draft. Less well-educated than draftees, but carefully chosen from among a large pool of applicants created by the Great Depression, they fought bravely under the worst conditions. The officers were a mixture of professionals and reservists, the latter especially being typical middle class young Americans from all walks of life. Torpedo 8 included a former college track star, an ex-insurance man, a Kansas City meat packer, a Harvard law student, and a Navy enlisted man who had been appointed to

Annapolis and was one of the few USNA graduates in the squadron. Even before Midway, but especially there, men from widely diverse backgrounds were showing that, given good leadership and half a chance, Americans would not be beaten.

In his history/memoir *Goodbye Darkness*, William Manchester recalls what a "tightly disciplined society" America had in those days, how rigid the standards were, how strong the pressures to conform. Respect for authority was general and began with the family unit. This had much to do with the success of young Americans in battle. "Sheathed in obedience, reinforced by Marine Corps pride and the conviction that the war was just, the men wearing green camouflaged helmets could outfight the Japanese, and they did it again and again."[20] Not just Marines, but also the brave airmen who gave their lives in doomed attacks at Midway, and the gallant soldiers at Bataan who fought on after hope was lost, were prototypes of an enemy unlike any Japan had faced. Resolute in the face of giant odds, certain of final victory, Americans would wage an implacable war such as Japan had never imagined.

The combination of courage and quality displayed by its young fighters was America's secret weapon. Ironically, the very same democratic forces that kept the country from preparing for this war had shaped its youth in such a way as to enable them to win it. The contribution of public schools cannot be overestimated, not only educationally but in other ways that Americans considered equally important. Despite the Duke of Wellington's belief that Waterloo had been won on the playing fields of Eton, no country, not even Great Britain, emphasized as America did team sports and athletic competition. At much expense, and as a rite not only of passage but almost of citizenship, few school districts failed to ensure that every able-bodied young male had the chance to play football and basketball—and usually other sports also. As a result, the young Americans of that era were team players and fierce competitors, their discipline and will to win having deep community roots. Localism, the curse of effective national government, was at the same time not only intrinsic to American democracy, but a superb maker of men.

7

The People Are Willing

After Pearl Harbor a flood of volunteers overwhelmed recruiting offices, especially in the South. When the entire Lepanto, Arkansas football team joined the Navy, one member attempted suicide after failing to pass his physical. "I was afraid folks would think I was yellow because I didn't get into the service," he explained.[1] Millions who were ineligible to serve wished to know what civilians could do to further the war effort. Washington went into overtime, and the armed forces were committed to battle, but there did not seem much for ordinary people to do, however motivated.

The "mess in Washington," as everyone called it, aroused much popular wrath. Though they had accepted the leisurely pace of rearmament, people now expected everything to be done at once, and were angry over practices they had tolerated until December 7. But years of neglect precluded speed, especially by a system of government not geared for swift decisions. *Life* magazine, long a critic of American unreadiness, was surprisingly forbearing at first. Soon after America entered the war, it printed a long article by Milton Mayer that praised Washington for doing a good job under the circumstances:

> To carp at the waste, the stupidity, the disorganization and the red tape—and there is plenty to carp at—is to forget that we Americans

have always insisted that the government is best which governs least. To carp is to forget that the traditional American attitude has exalted efficiency in business and inefficiency in government. To carp is to forget that government men who have never thought of producing and production men who have never thought of governing have been thrown together to do a government–production job in a hurry.[2]

This was wisdom from a most unlikely source.

Most Americans believed that government did not need to be overly effective because the people themselves could manage. While they overstated its benefits, voluntarism was a fact of life, and Americans were capable—within limits—of doing what elsewhere were functions of government. This attribute manifested itself immediately after Pearl Harbor. Agencies like the Red Cross and local civilian defense offices were overwhelmed with offers to help. Because many commodities would soon be scarce, scrap drives were organized that collected not only rubber items but paper, fats, bones, a wide variety of metal goods, and other essential materials.

Towns convened meetings to discuss ways of aiding the war effort. Citizens' committees sprang up. Neighborhoods organized. When a Milwaukee air-raid warden could not afford a telephone, the other families on his block agreed to donate 10 cents a month apiece so he could subscribe to the service. In Chicago 23,000 block captains were sworn in at a mass ceremony by the head of the Office of Civilian Defense. West Coast hospitals reeled before waves of enthusiastic blood donors. The hottest literary property of 1942 was the Red Cross first aid manual, which, though not considered a book and therefore omitted from best seller lists, sold 8 million copies. Farmers began plowing at night in order to put their spring crops in early. Shipyard employees in San Francisco offered to work Sundays for free. That summer an event called The National Salvage Fair was held in New York as part of a campaign to establish Salvage Sewing Workrooms in which volunteers could use mill ends and scraps of cloth to make garments for the needy and establish a clothing reserve.

Though very much in the American grain, efforts such as these suffered from the limitations intrinsic to thousands of uncoordinated local schemes, often inspired by an excess of willing hands rather than any clear sense of purpose. By summer *Life* was overflowing with complaints. Congress was not doing a good job. Neither were the people. All the powerful interest groups continued to pursue their own agendas. Every scrap campaign had failed, the rubber drive most of all.

People were still motoring frivolously. Washington was asking too little, and getting what it asked for. Everyone was living their dream of a "Hollywood war," instead of facing up to the real one in which sacrifices would have to be made.[3]

These complaints were well founded. In 1941 when aluminum was in short supply, the call went out for housewives to turn in their pots and pans. Ten thousand tons of aluminum would build 4,000 fighter planes was what they were told. Obedient to duty's call, women stripped their kitchens and donated 70,000 tons of aluminum, apparently solving the problem. It transpired that only virgin aluminum was suitable for aircraft, so the donated cookware gathered dust until it was finally sold to scrap dealers. Then the stuff was turned into new pots and pans, women buying back what they had previously given.

More serious than bungling was government's reluctance to take full advantage of civilian support for the war effort, especially that of women. The public was encouraged to buy war bonds and practice conservation. Otherwise, it often seemed as if Washington did not want public participation in national defense, which had been the case before Pearl Harbor. In January 1941 one of Dr. Gallup's polls had revealed that 67 percent of those questioned were willing "to spend one hour each day training for home guard, nursing, first aid work, ambulance driving," and similar activities.

Though officials frequently remarked on the gravity of the world situation and the need to prepare for hardships, they seldom took their own advice. When asked what people could do, Frank Bane, Chief of the National Defense Advisory Commission's Division on State and Local Cooperation, suggested that it might be nice if women living near Army posts would help entertain the troops. They could also work as volunteers in the overburdened health and welfare programs of "war boom" towns, laudable suggestions, to be sure, but hardly a call to action.[4]

In August the president of the General Federation of Women's Clubs—an old, large, and conservative body—complained that women were being discriminated against "intolerably" in the civil-defense program.[5] The Office of Civilian Defense did not even have a women's division. There were only seven women in the entire federal government at the policymaking level. Women were excluded from serving in Civil Aeronautics Authority programs for training student pilots. The female Assistant National Civilian Defense Director had just resigned because Director Fiorello La Guardia disapproved of her efforts to have the WPA survey and catalogue volunteer associations around the country, many of them women's groups, as possible contributors to civil defense.

Women were joining the Red Cross and other emergency related bodies in large numbers, but not because government was encouraging them to, or promising that if war came it would utilize their services. This lack of interest would not change very much after Pearl Harbor. In the age of total war the United States would make a semitotal effort, a limitation that was prefigured by government's earlier policy on civilian defense. This prejudice against women would seriously weaken the war effort.

It was obvious that vast numbers of men in uniform would be performing clerical tasks and other duties that were not gender-specific. Yet military leaders were slow to admit that women could do these jobs as well as, if not better than, men, thereby freeing able-bodied males for combat. Early in 1942 the Army agreed to accept 10,000 volunteers for a Women's Army Auxiliary Corps only because a bill introduced in Congress by Representative Edith Nourse Rogers (R, MA) forced its hand. The Navy went on refusing to accept women in any capacity. There were plenty of men as yet undrafted, the military's reasoning went—which was true at the time, but this surplus did not last, forcing a change of heart.

Washington's attitude was particularly galling in light of the popular support for a more serious war effort. In January 1942 Gallup reported that 68 percent of the public favored a labor draft for women aged 21 to 35; among women, the majority in favor rose to 73 percent. Women in the suggested age group were most enthusiastic of all, fully three-quarters of respondents asking for such a draft. In March another poll disclosed that support for registering all adults, and assigning as many as needed to war work—what later would be called national service—was supported by a ratio of almost two to one. It seems clear that a selective labor draft, focusing upon young women but selectively including other women and men, too, had all the support it needed. Magazines regularly predicted the enactment of legislation to that effect. But Congress refused to pass such a bill, even in 1944 when Roosevelt finally got around to asking for it.

Despite popular acceptance of the idea national service aroused the opposition of labor and business leaders alike, who wanted the assignment of civilians to remain voluntary. Secretary Stimson argued that it was not only necessary, but desirable as well, telling Congressmen that such a bill would "extend the principles of democracy and justice more evenly throughout our population."[6] Roosevelt thought so, too, but the force of selfishness was irresistible and Congress, eager to avoid antagonizing important interest groups, let the bill die in committee.

Lacking official outlets, women formed numerous paramilitary groups of their own, including the Powder Puff Platoon of Joplin, Missouri, the Green Guards of Washington, and the Women's Defense School of Boston, which taught a course in field cooking modeled on that of the Army. Some 25,000 women volunteered for the Women's Ambulance and Defense Corps of America, whose slogan was "The Hell We Can't." Its more than 50 chapters trained women to serve as air-raid wardens, security guards, and couriers for the armed forces. However, most who wished to contribute joined the Red Cross, which, with 3.5 million female volunteers, was by far the most important outlet for patriotic womanhood.

Some government agencies actually recognized opportunity when they saw it. The Office of Civilian Defense employed a number of female volunteers. The Office of Price Administration used 50,000 women in five states to conduct a three-day canvas in July 1942, during which they briefed 450,000 retailers on the new price regulations. For the most part, though, except for defense contractors who gradually warmed to the idea of hiring women workers, volunteer organizations remained the main outlets.

Of these latter groups, the most controversial was the American Women's Voluntary Services, founded by a group of Anglophile socialites in 1940 to prepare women for emergency work in a London-style blitz. It soon enrolled 350,000 members in almost every state. To refute mockers who accused them of being social butterflies out on a lark, AWVS cast a remarkably broad net for the times, organizing several units in Harlem, at least one Chinese chapter, a number of Hispanic units, and one affiliate consisting entirely of Taos tribeswomen. Defying local taboos, the New Orleans chapter bravely included Negro women. When it became evident that America was not going to be attacked by German bombers, the AWVS took on new assignments. In New York members sold $5 million worth of war bonds. In California there were AWVS "chuckwagons" that delivered food, including late-night snacks, to Coast Guard stations and remote military sites. In San Francisco AWVS women taught Braille to blinded veterans. Others organized agricultural work camps in California and Colorado. Some New York suburbs had ambulances staffed entirely by AWVS members.

Though it was the biggest, AWVS was by no means the only volunteer women's organization that made a place for itself in the war effort. At least three other women's groups provided land and air ambulance services. There were also volunteer groups of working women, such as WIRES (Women in Radio and Electric Service), WAMS (Women Aircraft Mechanics), and WOWS (Women Ordnance Workers)—the latter of whom by 1943 had a membership of 33,000 in dozens of munitions plants. As part of an elaborate recruiting campaign, Oldsmobile created WINGS (also known as the "Keep 'Em Winning Girls"), workers who were given uniforms with a torch-and-wing insignia on the front pocket. So that housewives should not feel excluded, the *Ladies Home Journal* organized WINS (Women in National Service), saying that housewives were "the largest army in the nation fighting on the home front."[7] The outpouring of female volunteers in a host of organizations enabled women to accomplish much, and suggested how much more they might have done had there been a system in place to take full advantage of their enthusiasm. Even as it was, when in April 1942 ten thousand women volunteers marched down Fifth Avenue in New York there were so many different uniforms that no one could identify them all.

Ernest K. Lindley whose *Newsweek* column was refreshingly candid on many subjects, did not mince words about the failure of government to mobilize its people. The executive branch consistently underestimated the intelligence and patriotism of American citizens, in his opinion, but Congress was even worse, its members seeming to assume "that their constituents put personal convenience above winning the war and preserving the American economic system." He was certain that the "American people, as their sons, brothers, and fathers in the armed services prove, have more courage and determination than these office seekers credit them with having."[8]

While the numerous complaints about government's incompetence and neglect were fully justified, it was important to keep in mind that the mills of American democracy were supposed to grind slowly. Though this was not apparent at first, the mess in Washington would improve. Private initiatives too would become more fruitful. Scrap drives got better, the rule seeming to be that behind every successful local drive there was one especially determined person. In Seattle, which had a very big one, that man was a local jeweler by the name of Leo Weisfield.

A landmark effort was the great Nebraska scrap drive of 1942, inspired by Henry Doorly, publisher of the state's biggest newspaper, the Omaha *World–Herald*. A unique feature of his plan was that prizes worth up to $2,000 in war bonds would be given to individuals and organizations who collected the most scrap, regardless of whether it was sold to dealers or donated gratis. This was a significant feature, not just because it meant that donors could mingle patriotism with profit, but because scrap dealers had the heavy equipment required to salvage large metal structures.

The drive collected 135 million tons of scrap, the equivalent of 103 pounds for every person in Nebraska. By comparison, the previous national scrap campaign collected only 213 million tons in its first two weeks, an average of barely more than a pound and a half for each American. Many Nebraska companies donated trucks, 40 a day on average, which were employed to transport scrap. The *World–Herald* itself contributed nine tons of old press parts which a frugal foreman had been stockpiling for 30 years. In the town of Oldrege a local department-store owner and a farm-implement dealer set up a nonprofit corporation that paid $10 a ton for salvage, a dollar and a half above the going rate. To finance it they borrowed money from the local bank, and with the aid of hundreds of volunteers ended up breaking even—a feat they accomplished by sorting the scrap, which enabled them to resell it to dealers for a premium that covered their overpayments.

Rural salvage was the most rewarding because of its scale. While townspeople were turning in old appliances, the countryside yielded up treasures in the form of disused iron bridges, farm machinery, and 537 tons of abandoned track donated by the Burlington Railroad. When the prizes were given out, the individual winner was a section hand for the Burlington who brought in 97,000 pounds of scrap. The winning business was a dinette in Norfolk whose owner hired two women to run the place while he collected 81,000 pounds of salvage. The junior prize went to the Omaha Future Farmers of America, who took time out from agricultural pursuits to amass a staggering 445,000 pounds.

The most successful state drive yet, the Nebraska model was widely copied, demonstrating that the will was there and could be mobilized with inventive planning. If the weakness of democracy was inefficient government, the strength was volunteerism, especially when it exploited the national love of competition.

An example of what could be done with official support was gasoline rationing, which went into effect on December 1, 1942—tardily, of course, but as so often happened, delay was needed to convince people that the rubber crisis really existed. Americans who hated rationing, complied with the rules as a whole, despite the inevitable chiseling and the rise of black marketeers and forgers of gas-ration permits. It helped that most people walked to work (40 percent) or took public transportation (23 percent).[9] Even the 36 percent who commuted by car accepted gasoline rationing after the Baruch Report came out. Though only 49 percent of all Americans saw a need for it when first proposed, by the end of 1942 the great majority of motorists (73 percent) supported gasoline rationing. The 35 MPH speed limit won almost universal approval, 89 percent of car owners backing it. Fortunately, though the black market in gasoline eventually became a big business, it never grew so large as to jeopardize the war effort.

Rationing, an inconvenience to some, meant real sacrifice for others—such as small businesses that depended on the drive-in trade. Nine hundred restaurants in Los Angeles alone closed within the first two weeks after rationing took effect. Labor and other kinds of shortages would also devastate small businessmen and farmers. In Arkansas, 6,000 small businesses would fail by 1943 for lack of workers, while the state's farm population declined from 667,000 in 1940 to 292,000 by the spring of 1944.

In January 1943 pleasure driving was banned completely on the East Coast, where a genuine gasoline shortage existed, virtually emptying the streets of major cities. Compliance was encouraged by police officers, who confiscated the gas-ration books of offending drivers. If after a court hearing the accused were found guilty of frivolous motoring, the fine was in gasoline coupons rather than cash— a powerful and effective deterrent. More important than stiff fines was patriotism, since experience would demonstrate that programs with which most Americans did not agree were ultimately unenforceable.

Conversely, programs that Americans believed in could not be stopped. Victory gardens were a case in point. Food production and conservation had been strongly encouraged in the First World War, and many families that did not ordinarily grow their own produce established kitchen gardens in response. People took it for granted that food would be short this time as well. They began planting vegetables in the spring, despite the Department of Agriculture, which initially dragged its feet. By April 1942, at least 6 million gardens were being cultivated, inspiring Secretary of Agriculture Claude Wickard to call for 18 million victory gardens—a goal that was easily reached. In 1943, more than 8 million tons of produce was grown on 20 million individual plots many of them very small. In cities with populations above 100,000, victory gardens averaged only 500 square feet in size— that is, about 20 by 25 feet—but nevertheless amounted collectively to 7 million acres, an area the size of Rhode Island.

Victory gardens appeared everywhere, not only on private lots but in parks, before the San Francisco City Hall, in the yards of schools and prisons, wherever there was arable soil, and hands to do the tilling. The Agriculture Department reported that the amount of vegetables grown in victory gardens exceeded "the total commercial production for fresh sale for civilian and non-civilian use."[10] This was all the more impressive because, after being grown, much of this produce had to be canned—hence the slogan, "Eat what you can and can what you can't," no small thing, as a mistake could result in glass canisters exploding, or even bacterial growths that were potentially lethal.

Most of the conservation burden fell on women—and children, too, who were good collectors of scrap. In the fully mobilized household there were separate holders for tins, rags, bottles, paper, and bones. Tin cans were washed and flattened. Tinfoil and rubber bands were collected in balls. Bottle caps, chewing gum wrappers, and flashlight batteries were saved for later recycling. Because it was used to make munitions, schools had "Fat Parades," enabling children to make ceremonial deposits of accumulated kitchen grease. In rural areas they collected milkweeds, whose silken fibers would be stuffed into life jackets.[11]

The Office of Civilian Defense gave a "V–Home Award," inspired by the Army–Navy E for excellence in production, as "'a badge of honor for those families which have made themselves into a fighting unit on the home front,' by conserving food, salvaging vital materials, buying war bonds, and refusing to spread rumors.'"[12] It never caught on, however. Few families wanted credit for supporting the war effort at home in whatever small ways they could. What did spread were the stars people spontaneously hung in their windows to indicate that a family member was in uniform—or, if a gold star was displayed, that one had sacrificed his life for his country. These were the true badges of honor, recognized as such by everyone.

Efforts to employ the war effort for political ends, or to artificially implant political ideas, almost always failed. This was especially trying for progressives, as they often called themselves, those left-liberals who looked to Vice President Henry Wallace for guidance domestically and sympathized with Russia.[13] Progressives differed from most Americans in having highly doctrinaire war aims, which were articulated by the liberal weeklies *The Nation* and *The New Republic*, by the New York daily newspaper *PM*, and by such left-wing journalists as I. F. Stone and Max Lerner. In addition to Allied victory, they wanted social reforms in the United States and social revolutions elsewhere. If conducted along these lines, World War II supposedly would become a people's war—an altogether finer thing than a war fought merely in self-defense.

Lerner explained that in Russia "The thoroughgoing organization of the war economy, the civilian resistance, the guerilla warfare could only be achieved in a war that had become democratic in its inner nature."[14] Except to progressives, the reason why America shunned this global crusade was clear. There was no base of support for a people's war, as most voters failed to see any need for radical changes, either at home or abroad—except the obvious one of destroying militant fascism. Americans were fighting because they had been attacked. Their war aims did not extend beyond defeating the enemy and ensuring peace. This led progressives to conclude that somehow government must convince Americans to demand what they so obviously did not want.

Secretary of the Treasury Morgenthau agreed with progressives on this, up to a point. He wanted bonds sold widely and in such a way as to make Americans "war-minded." He believed this was even more important than helping finance defense purchases. To sell bonds was to sell the war, so bond drives were aimed at the average American rather than at wealthy investors—which meant, in turn, drawing heavily on the popular culture. Movie stars played important parts, with Hollywood organizing seven tours that played in 300 communities. Dorothy Lamour alone, the star of a series of "Road" pictures with Bob Hope and Bing Crosby, was credited with selling $350 million worth of bonds. Carole Lombard, a popular movie actress, gave her life to the cause, dying in a plane crash on her way home from a bond tour. In addition to bonds, "war stamps" costing only pennies were sold— mainly to children, though sometimes to adults, as when scantily-clad showgirls covered their flesh with 10¢ savings stamps for happy businessmen to peel off and purchase. Every form of hucksterism was employed in this cause, few managing to escape it.

In practice, however, bond drives did not educate Americans or raise their political consciousness, but instead, like commercial advertising, reinforced existing values. Progressives believed that Americans would have gotten excited about the people's war if only President Roosevelt had talked it up. This ignored the fact that no one had ever been able to talk Americans into accepting any major policy shifts with which they disagreed, and it was the people who lacked interest in a social revolution.

Despite occasional lapses, Roosevelt did not truly believe in propaganda. In 1917, precisely because opinion was divided on the merits of intervention, Washington had cranked up a vast publicity machine to bolster the war effort. A Committee on Public Information was created to that end, which distributed 75 million pamphlets, issued 6,000 press releases, placed ads in leading magazines, enlisted a corps of "Four-Minute Men" who gave short, canned talks emphasizing German atrocities, and in other ways sought to promote war fever. The intellectual content of most of this is suggested by some of the war films endorsed by CPI, such as "The Prussian Cur" and "The Kaiser, the Beast of Berlin."

The ads too spoke for themselves. One, headed "Spies and Lies," urged people to inform on anyone who belittled the war effort, cried for peace or spread pessimistic stories. Another, headlined "Bachelor of Atrocities," called upon college students to resist the "Prussian Python," and warned that the "Hohenzollern fang strikes at every element of decency and culture and taste that your colleges stand for."[15] The popular *Literary Digest* asked readers to send it editorials that might be seditious or treasonable. The Pittsburgh Press Club boasted that it had developed an intelligence program that kept 27 Pennsylvania counties under surveillance for the Justice Department. These instances were but small parts of a gigantic national campaign to silence dissent and encourage patriotism.

After World War I many felt that this mixture of propaganda and intimidation had encouraged the violation of basic American rights, inflamed passions, contributed to vigilante action, stimulated xenophobia, oversimplified the issues, and aroused unrealistic expectations. FDR was not going to repeat the mistake. Public relations was one thing, a ministry of domestic propaganda another. Congress seconded his motion, conservatives fearing that government propaganda campaigns would glorify Roosevelt, the New Deal, and liberal internationalism—what Congresswoman Clare Boothe Luce referred to as "globaloney."

Roosevelt wished to communicate with the public, and understood that there were limits to what could be accomplished by means of Fireside Chats and official press releases. Characteristically, he set out to meet this need by creating a "thicket of competing, overlapping agencies, none of them with a clear mandate."[16] First came the Office of Government Reports, a bureau that was supposed to clarify the general confusion surrounding national defense, and still remain innocuous enough to survive congressional scrutiny. In August 1940 Roosevelt invented an Office of the Coordinator of Inter-American Affairs, headed by Nelson D. Rockefeller. Next the President established a Division of Information within the Office of Emergency Management. On May 20, 1941 he created the Office of Civilian Defense, under Fiorello La Guardia, the irrepressible mayor of New York. OCD was supposed to protect civilians, but also build their morale—the latter an assignment La Guardia ignored. In July 1941 Roosevelt formed the Office of the Coordinator of Information to wage psychological warfare overseas. Later it was assigned a Foreign Information Service, headed by Robert Sherwood, which subsequently became the Voice of America.

In the fall, responding to criticism of these half-measures, Roosevelt authorized an Office of Facts and Figures, transferring to it the function of building morale. The title was meant to suggest that OFF would have somewhat the same relation to propaganda as did the Census Bureau. Roosevelt named Archibald MacLeish, the Librarian of Congress and an ardent interventionist, to be its chief, confusing the issue as usual. OFF never could decide what it was supposed to be doing, its scattered efforts pleasing few. Especially resented was a series of radio programs, which began airing in February 1942 on all the networks, called "This Is War." Of the first broadcast, which employed the standard pop-culture mix of show business and Madison Avenue, Raymond Moley, a disgruntled former New Dealer, had this to say: "It was as if Mr. MacLeish had handed a man who wanted 'accurate' information about Denmark a copy of *Hamlet*."[17]

In June 1942 OFF was replaced by the Office of War Information, headed by veteran newsman Elmer Davis. He was responsible for both foreign and domestic programs, but his greatest difficulties were at home, since he had to deal with such basic questions as how much truth it was safe to tell, and (more important still) what kind of war the nation was supposed to be having. All-outers favored a maximum publicity barrage in the interests of maximum effort. Progressives wanted the people's war enshrined in every heart. As Roosevelt failed to provide guidance, and Congress was actively hostile, both strategies languished. In 1943 the freshly elected conservative Congress, which was busily destroying New Deal programs, reduced OWI's budget for domestic programs to under $3 million. Davis was forced to close 12 regional branches and suspend his publications. Congress left overseas operations alone, but thereafter domestic war information was supplied through commercial news channels.

Given Washington's lack of interest in propaganda, writers eager to aid the war effort were inspired to create their own. West Coast patriots formed the Hollywood Writer's Mobilization. Its counterpart on the East Coast was organized by Rex Stout, author of the popular Nero Wolfe detective novels, who launched the Writer's War Board two days after Pearl Harbor. Initially it helped sell war bonds, but soon grew "into a liaison office between writers and government departments, a kind of unpaid extension of the Office of War Information."[18] Looking back, a former member described its purpose thusly. "The government was slow; we were fast. They were timid; we were bold. They used official gobbledygook; we had some wit. World War II was strangely unemotional and needed a WWB to stir things up."[19] As this suggests, the mobilized wordsmiths put a high premium on ardor.

Members not only wrote advertising copy for war bonds, but used every known outlet to reach the public. The WWB itself might instigate a campaign; other times it responded to official requests. An example of the latter case occured when the Air Force wanted to promote the enlistment of flight crew other than pilots. WWB's contribution included 12 short stories, 24 syndicated columns, three radio broadcasts, one novel, one handbook, and two popular songs— one of them entitled "I Wanna Marry a Bombardier." The campaign had to be terminated after it produced a surplus of volunteers. Because WWB and the Hollywood Writer's Mobilization were private organizations, they carried on without a break when OWI's funding was slashed in 1943. Thus, government failure to recruit writers was, from the propaganda standpoint, a blessing in disguise. Writers, without being either censored or coerced, helped the military to solve many problems.

These were America's strengths, a lack of regimentation, the refusal to indoctrinate; and most of all the initiative of ordinary people organizing, conserving, collecting, recycling, buying war bonds—or if, like writers and entertainers, they had special skills, devoting them to public service. That government never found a way of fully exploiting their eagerness to help was its biggest wartime failure, and a curious one in light of the opinion polls showing a willingness to give beyond what was ever asked of civilians.

The degree of American mobilization fell short not because men and women were unwilling to sacrifice more, but because leaders shrank from the prospect. The "mess in Washington" was not to blame, because, what with so many people being faced with a need to do everything at once, confusion and inefficiency could hardly be avoided. More serious was the refusal of Congress to take more than minimal chances. Understandably, this was less clear early on than later. At first it was easy to man both the factories and the armed forces, because unemployment was still high and the military's ability to process recruits as yet limited. In time there would be a labor shortage, and then there would still be no national service bill—and too few men would be drafted. No doubt congressmen were patriotic, but it was "politics as usual" during the war, involving frequent elections and all that went with them, including fears that voters would retaliate if there was a labor draft, regardless of what the polls seemed to say.

This was not a case of too much democracy, but in a real sense of too little; a matter of putting personal and partisan advantage ahead of what voters made clear they wanted. It might have helped if general elections had been suspended, as in Great Britain. That failing, the country would depend on what the people themselves could do. As it turned out, that was a great deal. Yet voluntarism could never completely replace sensible national policies that made the best use of all Americans. The will was there at the grass roots. It just never quite reached the top.

All these things and others notwithstanding, civilians contributed more to the winning of World War II than to any previous American conflict—on the homefront, but directly too in the battle against the U-boats. In this campaign the front lines were manned not just by sailors and fliers, but by civilian seamen of the U.S. merchant fleet, thousands of whom lost their lives to keep Britain and Russia going. Many more would have died had it not been for a handful of men in government and business who played key roles at critical points that were to make a tremendous difference.

Among the many shocks Americans had to absorb after Pearl Harbor was the discovery of how vast the Earth remained. Before the war, much publicity had been given to the lightning speed of global communications, and how aircraft had shrunk the planet. After all, clipper ships could fly from San Francisco to Manila in less than a week. A military mission could leave London for Cairo and arrive there the same day. The telephone and telegraph provided virtually instant contact. But, as *Life* pointed out:

> It was all an illusion. Fighter planes cannot fly from San Francisco to Manila. Nor can armies be ferried from London to Egypt by plane. An order for steel is only a piece of yellow radiogram paper until a trudging nine-knot freighter has spent 50 days plowing the Pacific to dump its cargo in Calcutta. The globe cannot be measured by the speed of planes or of streamlined ships or of radio messages. The yardstick is the freighter making 250 miles a day. With war, the world has grown vast and confusing again."[20]

Vast and confusing to be sure for the Allies who were entirely dependent on those trudging freighters. Nowhere was their passage more crucial than in the storm-tossed North Atlantic, the lifeline between the American arsenal, Great Britain, Russia, and the fighting fronts. To lose the Battle of the Atlantic was to lose the war. Yet few realized what a near thing it was, and how much the outcome depended on Roosevelt personally.

FDR had not appointed Ernest J. King to be Commander in Chief, U.S. Fleet (Cominch) because he liked the man.[21] Almost no one liked King, who was rude, overbearing, and quick-tempered. King was an outstanding sea officer, and had been effective as commander of the Atlantic Fleet during the exacting undeclared naval war with Hitler in 1941. After Pearl Harbor, Roosevelt wanted a tough man to whip the Navy into shape, and there was no doubt about King's abilities— harshly though he employed them.

King had graduated from Annapolis in 1901 and reached the rank of Captain when he was 40, a rapid rise he owed in part to opportunities for advancement provided by World War I. In 1923 he was given command of the submarine base at New London, and two years later brought up the sunken S-51, an object of great public interest. Raising this boat made King famous, putting him ahead of all other Navy captains. In 1927 he entered aviation school and soloed, though he never flew alone again. Still, he now had his pilot's wings and was qualified to command an aircraft carrier. In 1930 King was given

Lexington, which he turned into a tight ship, earning promotion to Rear Admiral at the age of 54 in 1932.

Other promotions followed, surprising some as Roosevelt did not know King personally—a grave handicap to the career of any flag officer. In 1938 during a Fleet exercise, King successfully attacked Pearl Harbor by taking advantage of a weather front and detaching his fast carriers from the slow battleships. This was contrary to Navy doctrine, but foreshadowed the tactics Japan would use in 1941. In the following year he was not selected for higher command, being named instead to the General Board, an advisory panel that was ordinarily the last stop before being put out to pasture. He was saved from retirement and oblivion because he impressed Secretary of the Navy Charles Edison who recommended to Roosevelt that he put King in charge of the fleet. That did not happen right away, but, following a series of lesser assignments, King became C in C, U.S. Fleet—that is, operational head of the Navy—soon after Pearl Harbor. As Cominch, his lightning bolts would be feared throughout the service.

King drove the Navy relentlessly toward his idea of perfection, subject only to Roosevelt's interference. Historians have pointed out that FDR stuck his nose into Navy business so often because he loved the service and could not resist treating it as a hobby, which was undoubtedly true. His actions also suggest that Roosevelt understood that King was inflexible and unlikely to admit a mistake. General Marshall claimed that as many as six weeks might go by without his seeing Roosevelt. Roosevelt had great confidence in Marshall, and so could afford to leave him alone. King, on the other hand, was called to the White House almost weekly at first, Presidential dabbling probably accounting for some of these visits, uncertainty about King others. Whatever their rationale, these meetings were to prove of cardinal importance.

The Battle of the Atlantic was the most important of all. Had it been lost there would have been no Allied invasion of France, no Lend-Lease convoys to Russia, and therefore no victory. Shipping was critical to every Allied operation, and the greatest number of ships lost went down in the North Atlantic. The U-boat threat, Churchill would admit later, was the only one "that really frightened me during the war." Even though German U-boats were capable of operating in American waters, the military had given little thought to antisubmarine warfare (ASW) before Pearl Harbor. The Navy sought to justify this nearly fatal lapse by saying that subchasers, being small, could be quickly built, and so it made more sense in prewar days to use scarce funds for capital ships. That had also been the Royal Navy's defense when it was caught off guard in 1939. But while British admirals could not know for certain what the war at sea would be like until it broke out, there was no such excuse for the Americans, who ought to have learned from Britain's experience. Since they did not, the Western Hemisphere became a happy hunting ground for U-boat captains, beginning on December 31, 1941, when they first arrived off shore.

During the next several months, 61 ships were sunk off the East Coast. In February and March, 42 ships went down in the Caribbean and eight in the Gulf of Mexico. U-boats struck at will, attacking on the surface even in broad daylight. For ASW operations throughout the length and breadth of what it called the Eastern Sea Frontier, the Navy had available perhaps 20 vessels, not one of which was fast enough to catch a U-boat running on the surface, and about 100 aircraft, none suited to antisubmarine warfare or capable of long patrols. The Army was asked to help out, contributing 100 two-engine aircraft, nine B-17s, and a handful of other planes. They were not equipped to track, still less destroy, U-boats, and the crews had no ASW training. The only bright spot in this picture was that Hitler had neglected U-boats before the war, and Germany was still building relatively few of them. Even so, the handful deployed were tremendously effective. Indeed, if Hitler had seen their value in time, the war might have developed quite differently.

The first American improvements began on March 4, 1942, when a group of oil industry executives worried by tanker losses met with representatives of the War and Navy Departments. Why couldn't coastal cities be blacked out, they wanted to know, since many losses came at night when merchant ships were silhouetted against the bright lights of the mainland? Why couldn't the Navy route merchantmen closer to shore, and allow them to enter protected waters at night? The executives had other ideas as well, some of which King accepted—a measure of how bad things were, as he usually ignored outsiders. By early April the Navy had established a limited convoy system. By the middle of May a coastal blackout was in force, despite numerous complaints that it would damage the tourist season. In March, the Civil Air Patrol began making offshore flights, and gradually the AAF's I Bomber Command developed an ASW capability. The oilmen had made their mark.

Still, after six and a half months, the United States had sunk only eight U-boats while losing over 360 merchant ships. As late as June 15 two American merchantmen were torpedoed off Virginia Beach in full view of bathers. Some insiders regarded its complete unreadiness as entirely the Navy's fault, a consequence of an obsession with size which led it to neglect submarine and antisubmarine warfare alike. President Roosevelt had urged the Bureau of Ships and the General Board of the Navy to build a small-craft fleet, but, as he once remarked, "The Navy couldn't see any vessel under a thousand tons."[22] Perhaps owing to this experience, Roosevelt would issue direct orders, rather than mere suggestions, when the Battle of the Atlantic worsened.

Over time enough subchasers and ASW aircraft were scraped together to make the East Coast unhealthy for U-boats. By late summer most German subs were redeployed to the western Caribbean—where, by the end of September, 173 merchantmen had gone down. On October 15, 1942, I Bomber Command became the Army Air Forces Antisubmarine Command (AAFAC). The Air Force had discovered that the Very Long Range Liberator was its best weapon against the U-boat, and also that searching out U-boats was more effective than simply escorting convoys—though that had to be done as well. Its views were opposed by the Navy, which wanted the VLR Liberators itself and viewed escorting convoys as the ASW tactic of choice.

This interservice bickering and competition took place against a background of steadily mounting ship losses. Though hemispheric waters grew safer, the mid-Atlantic became increasingly dangerous. After January 1943 no merchantman was destroyed within a 600-mile radius of any Allied air base, yet the loss rate soared. This was the work of Admiral Karl Doenitz, head of the U-boat force, and, since January 30, Commander in Chief, Navy. His promotion was a result of Hitler's decision to forget the surface fleet and concentrate on submarines. Fortunately for the Allies, he did so too late—yet Doenitz still managed to wreak havoc by concentrating his vessels in a patch of the North Atlantic that was beyond the reach of land based aircraft. Up to 80 boats at a time worked the area with devastating results. In the first three weeks of March 1943 alone, the Allies lost 750,000 tons of shipping, a rate that, if continued for long, would have destroyed their merchant fleets—or at least that of Great Britain. Roosevelt now came to the rescue.

The Anglo–American alliance worked best at sea, and nowhere else did the two nations cooperate more closely than in their joint use of merchant shipping. In 1942 the amount of American shipping in British service doubled, while Britain transported many American troops and significantly increased the number of warships that protected Atlantic convoys. Nonetheless, in 1942 Britain lost almost 6 million tons of shipping, a third more than in 1941, while American losses came to fewer than 2.5 million tons. In the same year American yards turned out almost 4 million tons of shipping, giving the United States a net gain of 1.5 million tons, while Britain suffered a net loss in excess of 2 million.

The combination of shipping losses and a great increase in military cargo, a result chiefly of the American overseas buildup, was overwhelming Britain's merchant marine. Before the war British imports had amounted to 50 million tons a year. In 1942 this figure fell to 23 million, forcing Britain to draw down its reserves. Worse yet, imports during the fourth quarter were coming in at an annual rate of only 20 million tons, at least 6 million tons below actual consumption. In January 1943 imports fell to the lowest level of the war, leaving Britain with no more than a few months' supply of foodstuffs.

Roosevelt had already agreed on November 30, 1942 to assign Britain 2.5 million tons of shipping. But much of it was yet to be built. In the meantime, sinkings continued to rise while the needs of the Mediterranean were proving to be greater than expected. While North Africa was supposed to require only 66 ships a month, over a four-month period it actually used more than 400, much of the overage being provided by Britain. In January Churchill took the extreme step of switching to Atlantic routes 52 of 92 monthly sailings scheduled for India. Despite such drastic measures, Britain remained short of merchant vessels at a time when Americans were making ever greater demands on them. Britain was counting on enough U.S. shipping to transport 7 million tons of domestic cargo in 1943, but American planners were assuming that Britain would require less than a third of that, and also expecting that Britain would turn back a good part of this tonnage to carry supplies to American troops in the UK. The gap between the two sets of plans amounted to about 6 million tons, more than a quarter of the entire volume of cargo destined for American forces overseas that year.

What actually happened was that troop and cargo movements from the United States to Britain almost ceased, thanks to the invasion of Africa and the great upsurge in U-boat activity. On March 12 Britain revealed its shipping requirements to the American service heads. The figures seemed to indicate that if 27 million tons of goods were shipped to Britain, the least it could get by with, there would be almost no merchant vessels left to support American forces. The Joint Chiefs were furious, demanding that Britain reduce imports to whatever level was required for American troop movements to continue on schedule. Britain could not back down because, while America's overseas activities were in a sense elective, if Britain's basic needs were not met the national—and therefore the Allied—war effort would collapse. The Joint Chiefs refused to admit this, insisting that shipping agreements made at the Casablanca Conference in January 1943, which did not conform to current realities, be carried out regardless.

Only Roosevelt could break the deadlock. He was given the means to do so by Lewis Douglas, deputy administrator of the War Shipping Administration. During the last week of March Douglas convinced Harry Hopkins that FDR's commitment of November 30 had to be honored. Since the Joint Chiefs would not budge, they should be ignored. On March 29 Hopkins, Douglas, and Foreign Minister Anthony Eden met with Roosevelt, no military being present. Crunching the numbers, Douglas showed that the chiefs were, as usual, exaggerating their requirements. Further, because of increasing production, an adequate number of merchant ships should be available by mid–year. Accordingly, if military shipping demands for the third quarter of 1943 were cut back, it would be possible to meet the essential needs of Great Britain at little expense to America's war effort. FDR accepted this analysis and took one of his bigger gambles.

Overruling the Joint Chiefs, Roosevelt stood by his promise. In May he directed the WSA to provide Britain with 150 to 200 merchant ships over a 10-month period. From a low point of 4.5 million tons in the first quarter, British imports rose to 7.5 million in the second, exceeding requirements. Douglas had been right about the military's inflated projections. It turned out that the Army could not fully use even the reduced tonnage made available to it.

Roosevelt won his gamble not only because more shipping was built, because ASW weapons became better and more numerous, and because the Navy became more cooperative, but also thanks to force deployments for which he was personally responsible. One reason for Germany's success was that the U-boats were directed by a single commander, whereas the various Allied services often worked at cross purposes. As the official Air Force history puts it, the antisubmarine war "suffered from complicated and divided command and from a wasteful duplication of effort. Little attempt had been made to standardize communications, intelligence reporting, training, or tactical doctrine, either among the nations concerned or between the U.S. Army and the U.S. Navy."[23]

The intelligence failure may have been most serious, for by 1943

(ABOVE) The USS *Arizona* explodes at her mooring in Pearl Harbor on December 7, 1941. The Japanese surprise attack stunned an America unready for war. *(Navy)*

(LEFT) President Franklin D. Roosevelt signs the declaration of war against Japan, after Pearl Harbor silenced the isolationists and united the country behind him. *(National Park Service)*

(OPPOSITE, TOP) American prisoners on the Bataan Death March, April 1942. Overwhelmed by superior Japanese firepower, they paid the price for democracy's unpreparedness. *(Marine Corps)*

(OPPOSITE, BOTTOM) Dust storm at a relocation camp in Manzanar, CA. Here, innocent Japanese-Americans were imprisoned by a nation in search of scapegoats. Although America remained democratic throughout the war in that majority rule was preserved, the Bill of Rights was all but suspended for the duration. *(Lange—WRA)*

(LEFT, TOP) After Pearl Harbor, virtually every American contributed in some way to the war effort. Movie star Rita Hayworth does her bit by donating her car bumpers to a scrap drive. Film stars also sold war bonds and entertained the troops at home and abroad. *(OWI)*

(LEFT, BOTTOM) Between shortages and government-imposed rationing, American people grew accustomed to queuing up for scarce items. In cities, lines might extend for blocks. *(OWI)*

(ABOVE) Despite its late start, industry was soon producing weapons in massive numbers, with the help of women workers like these building a Flying Fortress bomber at the Douglas Aircraft Company plant in Long Beach, CA. (*Palmer, OWI*)

(RIGHT) Contrary to prevailing stereotypes, few jobs were so hard, dirty, or dangerous that women could not fill them. Working on the B & O Railroad. (*Women's Bureau*)

(TOP) Women clean blast furnaces at U.S. Steel's plant in Gary, Indiana. They wear oxygen masks because toxic gas emissions could kill. *(Women's Bureau)*

(BOTTOM) Racial prejudices were set aside as well. An integrated team of riveters worked at the Lockheed Aircraft Corporation, Burbank, CA. *(Women's Bureau)*

(TOP) Generalissimo and Madame Chiang Kai-shek with Lieutenant General Joseph W. Stilwell, Burma, April 1942, before the Allies were driven out of Burma by Japanese forces. China was victimized not only by the Japanese, but also by the hapless and corrupt regime of Chiang Kai-Shek. *(Eldridge—Army)*

(BOTTOM) An Army medium bomber rises from the USS *Hornet* on April 15, 1942, bound for Tokyo. Seemingly a futile gesture, the "Doolittle Raid" would prompt the Japanese to attack Midway Island, giving the United States its first great victory in World War II. *(Navy)*

(TOP) Lieutenant General George S. Patton confers with Lieutenant Colonel Lyle Bernard, commander of the 30th Infantry Regiment, which had gone ashore behind enemy lines in Sicily, August 1943. Their achievement was a bright moment in an otherwise badly managed Allied campaign. Patton was among the few commanders to enhance his reputation in North Africa and Sicily, and was the only one in the Mediterranean to take advantage of Allied sea power. *(Army)*

(BOTTOM) B-17s destroying a Focke Wulf plant in Marienburg, Germany, October 1943. The Eighth Air Force's commander, Major General Ira C. Baker, would call it "the classic example of precision bombing," although most other strategic bombing attacks against Germany and Japan contributed little to victory. *(Army Air Forces—OWI)*

(ABOVE) On the eve of victory, D-Day minus 1. General Dwight D. Eisenhower, the Supreme Commander, talks with troopers of the 101st Airborne Division. Operation Overlord, the biggest and most important amphibious assault of the war, owed much of its success to Eisenhower's decision that day not to wait for better weather. *(Moore—Army)*

(BELOW) Brigadier General Anthony C. McAuliffe, artillery commander of the 101st Airborne, addresses his glider pilots before the division's jump in support of the unsuccessful Operation Market Garden, September 18, 1944. This costly failure ended any hope of defeating Germany that year. *(Klosterman—Army)*

Ultra, Britain's codebreaking operation, was turning out a steady flow of decrypted enemy radio messages. Ultra was a great help in locating U-boats, not only so that they could be attacked but also because convoys could be rerouted away from wolf packs—easily the most effective way of defending them. However, for lack of coordination, this priceless data did not always reach those who needed it. Further, the US Navy retained operational control over AAFAC units and exercised it constantly, rather than laying down policy and allowing air officers to carry it out—the procedure followed with much success by the Royal Navy and RAF Coastal Command.

Yet, the tide of battle would soon turn. On March 1, 1943, at King's invitation, a secret Washington Convoy Conference opened with 100 participants representing the armies and navies of the United States, Britain, and Canada. At the end of 12 days they agreed to divide the oceans into zones of responsibility for ASW purposes. King then formed what was called the Tenth Fleet, an advisory group within his own headquarters which became the nerve center of America's ASW campaign. Improved coordination and communication were accompanied, among other measures, by more sophisticated detection devices, better use of Ultra decrypts, and an increase in land-based aircraft, and also in escort vessels, including small carriers. Many officers had tended to think of the U-boat war as something to be won by a single new weapon or strategy: more and faster escorts, more and faster merchantmen, better radar, bombing the U-boat pens in France—whatever. The frustrating thing about the ASW question was that it did not have a single answer.

Admiral Morison later summed up the problem by writing:

> [It] was like lifting an immense jellyfish. Grasping it with two hands accomplished nothing, but with hands-all-around and heaving together, one could really do something to the so-and-so. Progress was made against the submarine only by seven-rayed cooperation: between the United States, British, Canadian and Brazilian Navies, among different branches of the American armed forces and merchant marine, between all bureaus of the Navy Department, between naval officers specially detailed for anti-submarine work and the Operations Research Group of civilian scientists, between foreign policy and military operations, and between the armed forces and the public."[24]

To combat what was never more than a few hundred U-boats at any given time required huge numbers of men and munitions and cost many billions of dollars.

While ASW was a collective effort, some tactics and weapons were superior to others. Here Roosevelt made another big difference. In 1943 the most desperately needed ASW aircraft was the Very Long Range Liberator. The Navy had 112 of these, most of which King was hoarding in the Pacific. The AAFAC had two squadrons, but they were operating in North Africa. This left only 18 VLRs in RAF Coastal Command to cover the entire Atlantic. Somehow Roosevelt, who almost never concerned himself with tactics, learned of this. On March 18, 1943, during the worst month of the U-boat war, he asked for the exact locations of every VLR Liberator. Upon being informed that they were mostly in the wrong places he ordered what proved to be a momentous redeployment. Roosevelt's lifelong interest in naval matters was now to greatly benefit the Allied cause.[25]

By mid-April 41 VLRs were flying above the North Atlantic, and U-boats could no longer surface without risk anywhere in its broad reaches. More B-24s would be built than any other type of heavy bomber. Although Liberators went on many important missions, these precious 41 may have contributed as much to victory as all the rest put together. In addition, by mid-May, escort carriers could give air protection to convoys everywhere in the Atlantic. During April and May Doenitz lost 56 boats, a casualty rate so high that he was forced temporarily to abandon the North Atlantic. The British, whose experience fighting U-boats much exceeded that of Americans, contributed greatly to this outcome, yet Roosevelt's interventions may have been what provided the margin of victory.

It had taken only five weeks to eliminate the U-boat menace! Two starkly contrasting figures sum things up. In April, Allied shipping losses amounted to 245,000 tons; in June, 18,000. It was the most important defeat for German arms since World War I.[26] Soon, American shipyards were producing in volume, and by October 1943 all the shipping lost since 1939 had been replaced. Doenitz roared back later with more and better U-boats, but the Allies kept ahead of him. By 1944, despite a great increase in Allied traffic, the tonnage— not the number of vessels, but their combined weight—of U-boats lost exceeded that of Allied merchant ships. All told, of 1,162 U-boats commissioned during the war, 941 were sunk or captured. Seventy-five percent of those who fought the undersea war for Hitler became casualties, a rate unmatched by any other fighting service of any belligerent nation.

Planes operating off the escort or "jeep" carrier, designated CVE, the fleet carrier being CV, became the most effective antisubmarine weapons, though land-based aircraft and surface warships remained important. This too was Roosevelt's doing, for if Admiral King had gotten his way there would not have been enough escort carriers to go around. King favored CVs, and in June 1942, when the famous industrialist Henry J. Kaiser proposed building 30 escort carriers, the Navy rejected his offer. But Kaiser was big enough so that he didn't have to take no for an answer, going directly to Roosevelt—who reversed the decision. In time Kaiser's yards would be launching a CVE every week. Escort carriers, which held up to 30 aircraft, were immensely valuable to the Allies and, thanks to Roosevelt, joined the fleet when most needed.

Deadly hunter–killer groups were built around these vessels that played havoc with Doenitz's U-boats. In the Pacific they were useful, too, providing close support to amphibious troops from inshore waters where the fast carriers dared not go. Ultimately, even King recognized their value, and they were built in large numbers—especially the *Casablanca* class, of which 49 were launched. In the Battle of Leyte Gulf, escort carriers would actually engage a Japanese battleship force and save the invasion fleet.

In the lesser war between the services over control of ASW, a compromise was reached after long feuding. In the summer of 1943 air and naval officers agreed that the Army would withdraw from the antisubmarine war entirely, while the Navy would in exchange forgo strategic bombing. Admiral King vetoed the deal at first, wanting to keep his heavy bomber force, but unbent in the end and a trade was effected. The AAFAC gave its VLR Liberators to the Navy, in return for conventional B-24s. The Navy finally admitted that the AAFAC doctrine of search and destroy was more effective than simply escorting convoys.

It says much for Admiral King's value to Roosevelt that the President kept him on as Cominch despite his mishandling of the U-boat war. Britain received its vital supplies in the critical spring and summer of 1943 only because Roosevelt overruled King and the other chiefs on the issue of shipping. The Battle of the Atlantic was won with escort carriers which FDR had compelled the Navy to purchase, and with VLR aircraft which he personally ordered sent where they were most needed.[27] No wonder FDR kept a close eye on King, and a good thing for the Allies that he did.

The Battle of the Atlantic took the lives of many brave sailors, most of them technically noncombatant merchant seamen. Britain, which had the world's largest merchant navy before the war, correspondingly suffered most. All told, 30,000 British mariners died, a fifth of the prewar service. John Keegan rightly says that they "were quite as certainly front-line warriors as the guardsmen and fighter pilots to whom they ferried the necessities of combat. Neither they nor their American, Dutch, Norwegian fellow mariners wore uniform and few have any memorial. They stood nevertheless between the Wehrmacht and the domination of the world."[28]

That they did so with such effectiveness owed a great deal to Roosevelt, who made many of the key decisions himself and forced the services to cooperate with each other. It owed a great deal as well to the civilians who intervened in such critical ways—to Hopkins and Douglas and Henry Kaiser and the unsung oil executives. The country was lucky to have such men, and to have a President who often enough was willing to listen. Those invaluable few went a long way to make up for the shortcomings of the American system.

Staving off defeat at sea was an absolutely vital step, but to achieve victory more was needed. Hitler would not be beaten by defensive measures, vital though they were. To win the war, the Allies would require an offensive strategy. This would prove hard to get.

8

Operation Torch and the Great Debate over Strategy

After mobilizing the home front and defeating its enemies, America's next greatest challenge in the war was dealing with its allies. In time Russia would present the greatest problems, but, since the Soviets and Americans agreed on strategy, for most of the war the hardest bargaining was with Great Britain, and, to a much lesser degree, Fighting France. United as the British and Americans were by their democratic values, they were separated by distinctive histories, and by radically different geopolitical interests that gave them separate answers to the question of how to defeat Hitler. Until Overlord, America's fight with Britain would be over grand strategy, the total conduct of the war—in Asia as well as Europe. After France was invaded the focus would be on battlefield issues. What united both levels of negotiation was that for several years Britain successfully advanced military policies that effectively prolonged the war. These debates were, therefore, much more significant than was realized at the time, or than many historians have been willing to admit.

The issue was joined immediately after Pearl Harbor when Churchill hurried to Washington for what was codenamed the Arcadia Conference (December 22, 1941 to January 3, 1942). He wanted reassurance, which he promptly received, that America's fury over the Japanese attack would not lead it to forget that Germany was the

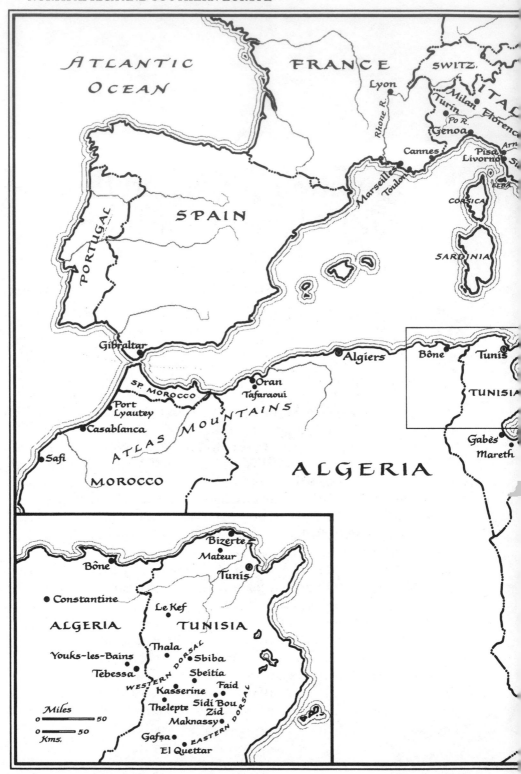

AUSTRIA
HUNGARY
ROMANIA
Venice
Trieste
YUGOSLAVIA
BULGARIA
Bologna
Viterbo
Civitavecchia
Tiber-R.
Rome
Pescara
Foggia
ALBANIA
TURKEY
Anzio
Bari
Garigliano-R.
Naples
Taranto
Brindisi
Volturno-R.
Salerno
GREECE
CAPRI
Gulf of Salerno
Marsala
Palermo
Messina
Reggio Calabria
SICILY
Mt. ETNA
Agrigento
Syracuse
Licata
Gela
CRETE
PANTELLERIA
MALTA

MEDITERRANEAN SEA

Tripoli
Benghazi
Tobruk
Alexandria
El Alamein
Cairo

LIBYA
EGYPT

Miles
0   300
                     300
Kms.

©A·Karl/J·Kemp, 1991

greater menace. Agreement was also soon reached on the immediate problems in Asia, the Allies establishing a unified command, ABDA (American, British, Dutch, Australian), to direct the Pacific War.

A declaration of what President Roosevelt at the last moment thought to call the "United Nations," a brief statement of support for the Atlantic Charter, was written and ultimately agreed to by every Allied state. As signed by Churchill and Roosevelt on August 11, the Charter laid down eight principles that were to guide the Allied war effort. The most important asserted the right of peoples to choose their own government, endorsed free trade, economic cooperation, freedom of the seas, and reduction of armaments. It appeared to say that a Wilsonian peace was what Roosevelt meant to establish.

Collaboration was troubled at first by the absence of liaison arrangements. The British had a command structure refined by years of experience. Their Chiefs of Staff (COS), consisting of the Chief of the Imperial General Staff, the first sea lord, and the chief of air staff, served under the War Cabinet and the Defence Committee and met with Churchill, who was both Prime Minister and minister of defence, on a daily basis. Decisions once made were transmitted to those with a need to know by a highly efficient secretariat. The three service heads were in direct and constant touch with each other, as well as with their civilian masters. All issues were thoroughly discussed, usually with the aid of well-drawn position papers. Service rivalries were minimized. Communication among the services, and between them and civilian agencies, was as full and fast as necessary. No other great power had anything resembling this tightly knit yet highly flexible system.

British efficiency and close communication were less evident when it came to operations. Britain had its share of military fiascos, for example the Dieppe raid of August 1942, when everything that could go wrong did. But in their relations with American commanders the British presented a united front—which contrasted sharply with the lack of interservice cooperation among their opposite numbers in Washington—and were far ahead of their allies when it came to staff work.

When Britain's military representatives arrived for the Arcadia Conference they were shocked by America's command-and-control procedures, which barely seemed to exist. President Roosevelt was remote, by tradition and habit alike, from his military chiefs, who often were represented in the White House by a single naval ensign. As Churchill met every day both with Roosevelt and with his own chiefs, British officers often knew more about Roosevelt's intentions than did the American brass. In the absence of structural links between the President and his armed services, Roosevelt could freely indulge his taste for secretiveness and informality.

Field Marshal Sir John Dill, the ranking British officer at Arcadia, informed General Sir Alan Brooke, Chief of the Imperial General Staff and Chairman of the COS, that there was no American equivalent to the COS, the Army and Navy going in separate and sometimes opposite directions. In order to get the planning sessions started, FDR created on the spot an entity named the Joint Chiefs of Staff (JCS), which in its final form would consist of General Marshall, General Henry H. Arnold of the Army Air Force, which Marshall treated like a separate service, and Admiral King, with Admiral William D. Leahy, FDR's friend and personal Chief of Staff, serving as de facto Chairman. At its first meeting with the British the embryonic JCS had no staff, no agenda, and no one assigned to take minutes.

Dill told Brooke "There are no regular meetings of their Chiefs of Staff, and if they do meet there is no secretariat to record their proceedings. They have no joint planners and executive planning staff. Then there is the great difficulty of getting the stuff over to the President. He just sees the Chiefs of Staff at odd times, and again no record. There is no such thing as a Cabinet meeting." Dill concluded "[This] whole organization belongs to the days of George Washington."[1] There would be few improvements. Meetings of the JCS regularized but did not eliminate interservice competition. FDR went on bypassing the military departments. Communication among the services, and between them and civilian agencies, remained haphazard.

Despite these difficulties, an adequate mechanism for directing the Allied war effort was speedily put together. A Combined Chiefs of Staff (CCS), consisting of the COS and JCS, was formed with headquarters in Washington. As the British chiefs would be absent most of the time, a British Joint Staff Mission was formed under Dill to work with the JCS on a daily basis. After considerable argument, a Combined Munitions Assignment Board was also established under the CCS, to allocate supplies and weaponry.

The success of these arrangements owed much to Marshal Dill. A strong spokesman for British interests, Dill nonetheless came to be esteemed by the American military above any other Briton. This was especially true of Marshall, who liked Dill so much that, after Dill's death of natural causes in 1944, Marshall managed to have his friend's remains laid to rest in Arlington National Cemetery, despite its rule prohibiting the burial of foreigners, and persuaded Congress to pass a resolution of gratitude for Dill's services. No doubt this only confirmed Churchill's view that Dill had gone native, which was unfair since Dill served as a genuinely honest broker between Washington and London.

On the American side Harry Hopkins played something like Dill's part. Hopkins was the most unpopular and misunderstood of the President's close advisors because he symbolized the alleged wastefulness of New Deal spending on welfare and unemployment. After graduating from Grinnell College in 1912, he became a social-work executive, serving from 1923 to 1933 as director of the New York Tuberculosis and Health Association. Careless with his personal funds and something of a playboy, he was also a passionate reformer, a workaholic, an excellent administrator, and an inspiring leader. In 1931 Governor Franklin Roosevelt made him executive director of New York's Temporary Emergency Relief Administration. After being elected President, FDR put the dynamic Hopkins in charge of emergency relief nationwide. Hopkins would go on to become FDR's most reliable troubleshooter. He had a kind of genius for insider politics that became especially important in wartime when Roosevelt's preference for backstairs negotiations, his immobility, and the lack of institutional arrangements, made Hopkins invaluable. Churchill called him "Lord Root of the Matter" for his skill at focusing debate.[2]

Hopkins's importance was related not to his various jobs, as head of Lend-Lease, for example, but from his closeness to Roosevelt. Hopkins and his daughter actually lived in the White House during the early war years, and it was as FDR's most trusted advisor that he was everywhere welcomed. Only in America was so much power vested in someone without portfolio, or even a staff, a peculiarity that says as much about the ad hoc quality of American democracy as it does about Roosevelt.

Hopkins lobbied hard for the people he believed in, such as Marshall, who needed the President's ear but sometimes had difficulty getting it. Trusted by the British, and by the Russians to the degree to which they were capable of trusting anyone, he was at times Roosevelt's alter ego in diplomacy, and practically a member of the Joint Chiefs of Staff and the CCS. A key, if also sometimes a rather shadowy figure, Hopkins was one of the most important men in the war effort. Except for the two heads of state, and at times Stimson, Hopkins was the only civilian involved at the highest level in the great strategic debate that began at Arcadia.

Although the British disagreed among themselves over priorities, and Churchill changed his mind frequently, what they kept coming back to was a Mediterranean, or "peripheral," strategy. After France collapsed in 1940 Britain used its naval superiority to blockade the European coast, while also attempting to weaken the Third Reich through aerial bombardment. In time, it hoped, uprisings would break out on the Continent, which Britain could assist with commando raids and landing parties. To that end Britain needed to gain control of the areas surrounding Europe—notably the Middle East, North Africa, and the Mediterranean. This was an appropriate strategy for a seafaring nation and had been Britain's traditional formula for maintaining the balance of power in Europe until the First World War, in which it fielded great armies as if it were a Continental state.

Germany's invasion of Russia in June 1941 supplied the missing link, as Britain's foreign policy had always hinged on being allied with European states possessing the armies needed to complement British sea power. American entry into the war meant that the vast resources of the world's greatest industrial nation would be at the service of the Allies, transforming the nature of their struggle. That was fine with Churchill, but Britain's basic aims—to minimize losses and avoid risk—would not change, despite the fact that more could now be accomplished. Moreover, the better the Soviets defended themselves, the less reason there would be for Britain to engage in large-scale ground combat. This put the British squarely at odds with America, for the U.S. Army's heritage was one of directly engaging the enemy with maximum force and battering it into submission. It had done this in the Civil and First World Wars and planned to do so again.

In addition to its long-range strategic interests, Britain had pressing current needs that Churchill was eager to see met. For one, Britain's only important land campaign was taking place in North Africa, where its Eighth Army was fighting General Erwin Rommel's formidable desert warriors. Even as Churchill and Roosevelt met in Washington, Rommel's Panzer Army Africa was giving the British yet another beating.

Churchill and his chiefs of staff were eager to avenge their numerous defeats at the hands of the German Army. They also desperately needed to relieve the strain on their shipping caused by Axis control of the western Mediterranean. Britain's convoys were prevented from using the Suez Canal to reach the Far East and had to sail around South Africa. Doing so doubled the transit time, the trip to

India and back lasting up to half a year. This meant that there were only enough ships to transport 40,000 to 50,000 thousand troops out of Britain each month, barely enough to replace the men lost to battle and sickness overseas. Britain wanted American support for a campaign to seize French North Africa, defeat Rommel, and, by means of new naval and air bases, regain control of the Mediterranean.

Although Roosevelt would make the final decisions, Britain's chief antagonist in the long struggle that led up to the invasion of Normandy in 1944 was George Catlett Marshall. Like Secretary of War Stimson, always his staunchest ally, he had little enthusiasm for Operation Gymnast, a proposal for invading North Africa in 1942 that Churchill favored. Conversely, the War Department had set its mind on going to France at the earliest opportunity and did not wish to get involved in secondary theaters.

Nothing was settled at Arcadia because of the Pacific crisis, but the debate was resumed again in April 1942 when Marshall and Hopkins arrived in London to sell to the British the U.S. Army's plan for an invasion of France. Americans regarded this as making far greater sense than an invasion of North Africa. They viewed England as the most convenient staging area for an attack on Germany: the North Atlantic route to it was comparatively short and well-protected, and had to be kept open in any event; no dispersion of effort would be required to mount assaults from Britain; and bases there would enable the Allies to go forward under stronger air cover than could be provided anywhere else. France's Channel coast was also the invasion site closest to the Ruhr, Germany's industrial heart, without which the Wehrmacht must speedily collapse. The Ruhr/Rhine industries were the great strategic prize of the war, and therefore, to Americans, the obvious Allied target.

Building up forces in Great Britain would also be an implicit threat to Nazi-occupied Europe, forcing Germany to beef up its garrison in France, and thus draining troops from the Eastern Front.[3] Above all else, attacking in Europe would bring American strength to grips with major enemy forces, preventing it from being dribbled away in lesser operations that would neither save the Red Army from defeat nor quickly end the war. The Army's greatest fear at this time was that Soviet Russia would cave in under German pressure, hence the need for action.

Powerful as this argument seemed to Americans, it made little impression on British leaders, especially General Sir Alan Brooke. A fine soldier, Brooke was also an amateur naturalist, a gardener, and an admirer of fine horses. All this commended him to Marshall, who loved the outdoors and was an ardent rider. Marshall was grateful that Brooke exercised some restraint over Churchill's impulsive imagination, which was forever throwing out bizarre military schemes. But Brooke was hard to get along with, icy and patronizing, quick to anger, and short on tact. He looked down on the American officers, who had so much less experience of war than their British counterparts.

Marshall acknowledged America's greenness, but remained convinced that his was the better strategy. It consisted of three parts. Bolero was the codename for assembling men and supplies in Great Britain during 1942 for a 1943 invasion of France. The attack itself, codenamed Roundup, would consist of 5,800 combat planes, of which 3,250 would be American, and 48 divisions, 30 of them US. There could also be a small-scale landing in France, codenamed Sledge-hammer, in the fall of 1942, if the Eastern Front appeared likely to collapse. That would be a hazardous—perhaps suicidal—effort justified only by an extreme emergency.

On April 12, 1942 Churchill wired Roosevelt that he and the COS were "in entire agreement in principle with all you propose." This was an outright lie.[4] The British disliked Sledgehammer intensely, and, whereas Marshall saw it as a gamble worth taking if Russia appeared to be near defeat, Churchill would never consent to it. Since Britain would have to supply virtually all the troops for a 1942 operation, there would never be one. Not wishing to antagonize their new ally, the British dissembled. On April 14 Churchill told Hopkins and Marshall that Great Britain accepted the American proposal, so long as it did not jeopardize India or the Middle East. The Americans returned home believing that Britain was committed to Sledgehammer if need be, and Roundup for certain, whereas in reality the one was doomed and the other doubtful.

Marshall worked hard to keep Roosevelt from diverting elsewhere men and materials intended for Britain, reminding the President that Britain was preparing to take great risks in support of Sledgehammer. It was Sledgehammer that Roosevelt had in mind on May 29 when he instructed Foreign Commissar V. M. Molotov to notify Marshal Stalin that the Second Front in Western Europe, for which Moscow was clamoring, would be opened "this year"—a promise that Marshall, aware of Sledgehammer's provisional status, tried to keep him from making. FDR stuck his neck out anyway because he had to tell Molotov that he could not make good on his earlier promise of more Lend-Lease aid, and in fact was going to have to reduce shipments to Russia by almost 40 percent. It was easier for FDR to present this bad news when he could claim that the demands of Sledgehammer were responsible, even though they weren't—shipping losses and production failures being to blame.

Though Marshall and the Army were thinking of Sledgehammer in military terms, to Roosevelt its main virtues were political. While the debate over how to defeat Hitler went on, there was another discussion taking place on how to deal with Russia. Here too, Britain and the United States had different points of view. Stalin was pressing for a postwar settlement even before it was clear that Russia would survive another German offensive. He was particularly eager to have Soviet Russia's absorption of the Baltic States, gained as a result of the Stalin–Hitler Pact, confirmed by his Western Allies.

Britain was inclined to go along with Stalin for reasons of expediency. Foreign Minister Anthony Eden believed that Russia might defeat Germany before the Allies invaded Europe. It would then establish Communist governments everywhere and free itself from dependence on the Allies. As early as February 18, 1942, the Foreign Office had sent a strong message to Washington, arguing that the danger of such an outcome was

> in itself a powerful reason for establishing close relations with Russia while her policy is still in a fluid state in order to exercise as much influence as possible on her future course of action. It would be unsafe to gamble on Russia emerging so exhausted from the war that she will be forced to collaborate with us without our having to make any concessions to her. On the contrary common prudence requires us to lay our plans on the assumption that, if we want Russia's collaboration with us after the war, we shall have to be prepared to make such a policy advantageous to her. The application of this policy will be [a] laborious and lengthy process. If we are to adopt it we must start now and not wait until the war is over.[5]

That summed up the problem neatly. The chances of avoiding trouble with Russia after Germany's defeat were slight, but to the degree any existed they depended upon pursuing just such a course. Unless Soviet territorial demands were granted, agreement on anything else would be unlikely.

The State Department was torn between moral scruples on the one hand, and fear of seeming to acquiesce in Soviet expansion on the other. It objected that to make territorial agreements at that time would (1) violate the Atlantic Charter, (2) endanger the peace negotiations—just as the secret treaties of World War I had compromised the Versailles Conference, (3) encourage the Soviets to make greater demands, (4) damage America's reputation, and (5) make Russia the dominant power in Eastern Europe. In contrast to the British position, the American seemed irrelevant. Points 1 and 4 were true but trivial; point 3 was false, since Stalin would always make greater demands and never needed encouragement to do so; and point 5 denied the central fact. If the Grand Alliance prevailed, Russia was going to control much of Europe. Saving the rest would depend both on how much territory the Allies liberated and what kind of bargain was made with Russia in advance.

Roosevelt agreed with State. A deal with Russia conceding territory could only hurt him politically. He would wait and see how the war developed before talking about postwar boundaries. Roosevelt saw delay as a means of keeping his hands free, while to Eden it ran the risk of eliminating options. The British wished to confirm Stalin's frontiers as a political substitute for the military assistance the Allies could not provide. Roosevelt preferred military assistance to political commitments and did not want to be limited by Allied unreadiness, hence his support for a cross-Channel attack in 1942 despite the obvious hazards. There was the additional benefit that if Sledge-hammer succeeded, Germany might be beaten before Russia overran Eastern Europe. On the other hand, Roosevelt was a realist. If the British declined to go ahead in 1942, he would not try to force them.

This exchange over boundaries demonstrated the limits that American democracy imposed on Roosevelt, who could not afford to take an expedient view of the postwar settlement, as Churchill did. The public accepted that war was cruel. It refused to admit that cruel choices must be made about the postwar world, as well—apparently believing that a proper peace would redeem the harsh acts of wartime. George F. Kennan, the great theorist and historian of American diplomacy, wrote not long after the war that:

> The real source of the emotional fervor which we Americans are able to put into a war lies less in any objective understanding of the wider issues involved than in a profound irritation over the fact that other people have finally provoked us to the point where we had no alternative but to take up arms. This lends to the democratic war effort a basically punitive note, rather than one of expediency."[6]

If this meant that Americans supported bombing enemy civilians, it also meant that they would demand a peace settlement based on Wilsonian principles. Churchill could afford to seem cynical, Roosevelt dared not.

The bad news was brought to Washington in early June by Britain's chief of combined operations, Admiral Lord Louis Mountbatten—a relative of the royal family and a dashing young officer of infinite charm. Supposedly he was there to check out the landing craft situation. Actually it was to argue against Sledgehammer, giving for the first time Britain's real position in this backstairs way. Impressed by his case, and no doubt recognizing a lost cause when he saw one, Roosevelt suggested that American troops might go instead to Libya or Morocco. Marshall and Stimson were shocked upon being informed of FDR's change of heart—which they learned about not from the President, but from British members of the CCS who showed them Mountbatten's summary of his conversation with Roosevelt. Churchill had already warned Molotov that Britain could not promise to launch a cross-Channel attack in 1942, but would do so if it could, which was still disingenuous as the conditions Britain had established for Sledgehammer could not be realized except through divine intervention.

On June 11 the three powers issued a communique promising, among other things, an invasion of France in August or September, even though each knew that such an event was unlikely. Indeed, Churchill had just told Molotov "that a landing on the Continent this year which was doomed to failure, and resulted in another Dunkirk with considerable slaughter, would do nothing to help the Russians and would, moreover, prejudice the larger scale operations planned for 1943."[7] Britain publicly embraced what it privately scorned because on May 25 the Soviets had signed a treaty of alliance with London that failed to provide for territorial concessions. They did so having learned from Ambassador Winant the previous day that Roosevelt would not commit himself to postwar boundaries, but was interested in a Second Front in 1942, a new Lend-Lease agreement, and a postwar Soviet relief program.

Russia still preferred the Second Front, but, given British opposition to it, Roosevelt's tentative package was the best it could get. Britain, though opposed to the Second Front now, wanted a nonterritorial treaty, and thus paid lip service to the one so as to secure the other. In addition, the British did not wish to contradict FDR. They feared also that a public statement which misled the Allied peoples might benefit Germany. Russia knew Britain's real position, but settled for lip service because even that would help morale in the Soviet Union, and because after the pledge was broken it would be a useful card to play in future hands of diplomatic poker.

Roosevelt committed prematurely to a Second Front because of Soviet pressure, and also to mollify public opinion at home, forestall the "Pacific Firsters," and block the Anglo–Soviet frontiers treaty. He then used Sledgehammer to justify cuts in Lend-Lease to Russia, even though he knew Britain was against the proposed operation and that it would be too small to meet Russia's needs.

From the very start, then, the Grand Alliance entailed more intricate bargaining and games of feigned, and sometimes real, deception than the public realized—or could be allowed to know, in light of what that would have done to morale and the entire war effort. To save democracy it was sometimes necessary to misinform the people, a practice that itself threatened the democratic state, and yet, in this case anyway, a risk that had to be taken.

Since the U.S. Army was still preparing to invade France, a showdown between the Allies could no longer be avoided. On June 17–18, 1942, Churchill and Brooke flew to Washington by Pan American Clipper. Ordinarily the British presented a common front in negotiations, but at this time, while Churchill and Brooke both opposed Sledgehammer, they differed as to whether Gymnast should be put in its place—Brooke having strong reservations about going into French North Africa. Though Roosevelt was coming around to Churchill's view, Marshall and Stimson held their ground. When Churchill returned to England the issue was still undecided.

In an effort to block Gymnast, Marshall and King sent Roosevelt a memorandum proposing that if Bolero, the buildup for the cross-Channel attack, did not continue as scheduled, the United States ought to forget about sending troops to Europe and concentrate on Japan. The Navy had always wanted this, King going along with the Europe First strategy only because he had to, but Marshall was bluffing. Worse still, FDR knew it and called him. Upon receipt of the memo, Roosevelt demanded that the chiefs immediately produce detailed plans and specifications for their new Pacific strategy, along with estimates of its probable effect upon the Soviets and the Middle East. No such documents existed, so King had a proposal thrown together which FDR scathingly rejected on July 14:

I have carefully read your estimate of Sunday. My first impression is that it is exactly what Germany hoped the United States would do following Pearl Harbor. Secondly it does not in fact provide use of American troops in fighting except in a lot of islands whose occupation will not affect the world situation this year or next. Third: it does not help Russia or the Near East. Therefore it is disapproved as of the present."[8]

Roosevelt was willing to use the Pacific War as an excuse for delaying aid to Britain and Russia. He would not allow it to be used against himself.

When Marshall, Hopkins, and King left for Britain on July 16 the Army's chief was not optimistic. Roosevelt insisted that American troops go into action against Germany in 1942. If Sledgehammer were scuttled, Gymnast would remain the only alternative. Marshall came to understand that Roosevelt could not afford to wait another year before attacking German forces, however much doing so made military sense, since during that time pressure at home to upgrade the Pacific War might well become impossible to resist. As he dryly remarked "We failed to see that the leader in a democracy has to keep the people entertained."[9]

The polls would bear Roosevelt out. Americans cared more about the Pacific War than they did the fight against Germany. In February 1943, as an instance, after American troops had been mauled in Tunisia, and with the Allies facing some quarter of a million Axis troops there, 53 percent of Americans still thought Japan was America's "chief enemy," only 34 percent nominating the Germans. If the North African operations were designed mainly to build political support for the war against Hitler, they remained compelling for that reason.

Marshall still felt that Roosevelt had made a mistake, but—right or wrong—in the end it was Roosevelt who determined American strategy, unlike Churchill, who, while he argued with and even stormed at his chiefs, did not overrule them. Thus, when the British officially rejected Sledgehammer on July 22, Marshall had to accept North Africa as an invasion site, in obedience to Roosevelt's demand for action against Germany that year, even though he agreed with the bitterly disappointed Eisenhower that the twenty-second might go down as "the blackest day in history."[10]

American leaders feared that Gymnast would expand, jeopardizing the main cross-Channel invasion scheduled for 1943. This was indeed likely, and all the more so as the War Department had wasted so much time arguing for Sledgehammer, which never had a chance. The six to eight available divisions, most if not all British, would not have enough landing craft, would be operating at the extreme limit of Allied fighter range, would divert relatively few Germans from the Eastern Front, and would not be strong enough to withstand German counterattacks.

Against this formidable array of objections Marshall could only claim that the Soviets would appreciate the effort. Important as it was to hearten the Russians, however, the sacrifice of scarce divisions in aid of a futile gesture made no sense to the British then, or to most historians later. If the question of how to defeat Germany had not gotten entangled with the issue of how to aid Russia, things might have been different, since, on its merits, there was little to recommend Sledgehammer. But with Stalin demanding a Second Front, and given the fear that Russia might collapse or make a deal with Germany, which Stalin did consider, it was hard for Americans to think clearly about the proposed operation.

On the larger issue Marshall cannot be faulted. Victories in North Africa and the Mediterranean added the equivalent of 2 million tons of shipping when the Suez Canal became accessible, and provided the Allies with valuable experience, but otherwise did little to defeat Hitler. Germany had to be beaten in Europe. The more time that was spent on peripheral campaigns the longer the war would last. Hence the importance of Roundup and the danger posed by Torch.

The invasion of North Africa was popular at home because it came at a time when America's forces on Guadalcanal and New Guinea were getting nowhere. As the Pacific War lagged, it was good news to have the United States closing in at last on the Nazi monster. Yet the decision to invade, and the outcome as well, were poorly understood at the time. The Mediterranean campaigns, portrayed then as logical steps, are among the most dubious of the war.

On August 25, 1942, President Roosevelt, having lost patience with the slowness of military planners, ordered that the North African campaign be launched on or before October 30. Five days later he told Admiral Leahy and General Arnold that the invasion, now known as Operation Torch, had first claim on available resources. With time running out the Allies now had to determine the size and purpose of Torch.

Party politics governed this schedule. With Sledgehammer dead Roosevelt needed a substitute for it, as the public was demanding results. There would be congressional elections on the third of November, and, with mobilization still limping along and the Pacific

War dragging, the Democrats needed a feat of arms to retain their position. To his everlasting credit, Roosevelt did not flinch when notified just before election day that Torch would have to come after it. This postponement, aggravated by a low voter turnout, cost Roosevelt the Congress. Though he could be petty about small things and was not entirely free of malice, on the big ones FDR showed character. He understood the rules of the democratic game and did not seek to change them, nor would he prejudice military operations for the sake of partisan advantage. That was part of the American way of war as practiced by Roosevelt.

Churchill wanted Torch mounted on the largest possible scale. A small operation would not draw many German troops out of Russia and thus could not be represented to Stalin, who was getting the news about Allied intentions piecemeal, as a Second Front. In addition, Churchill hoped to seize all of North Africa and beyond, making Torch, in his words, "a springboard, not a sofa." However, Marshall wanted a limited operation that would not compromise Roundup, whereas the British wished to land as far east as possible, so as to seize Tunisia before the Axis did.

In its final form Torch, under the command of Marshall protégé Lieutenant General Dwight D. Eisenhower, was larger than Marshall desired, but more cautious than if Britain had gotten its way. Even so, it represented a significant win for Churchill, who not only got an operation on the scale that he wanted, but persuaded Stalin to accept it in lieu of a Second Front. The plan was for three task forces of 35,000 to 40,000 men each to land at widely separated points. A Western Task Force would sail directly from the United States to land near Casablanca on the Atlantic coast of Morocco. A Center Task Force, also consisting entirely of American troops, would sail from Britain to Oran on the Mediterranean coast. A joint Anglo–American Eastern Task Force would seize Algiers.

The great flaw in this plan, as the British had maintained from the start, and which Eisenhower saw also as soon he became responsible for it, was that taking Casablanca offered no important benefits. Tunisia, only 100 miles from Sicily and the best place for a German buildup, was the strategic prize. If the Allies could get there first, Hitler would lose Rommel's army, and with it North Africa. Eisenhower tactfully pointed out the irrelevance of Casablanca in a message to the War Department by quoting a British General who allegedly said "It doesn't accomplish anything. What is the reason for going at all if we don't gain Tunisia? We cannot get Tunisia unless we do it quickly and attack as far east as Bone"—which was close to the Tunisian border.[11] Marshall was adamant, thinking Bone too much of a risk, so the best chance of making Torch pay off was lost before it started.

Britain's contribution—40 percent of the troops and nearly all Allied naval strength in the Mediterranean—was played down as much as possible. Partly this may have been, as critics have charged, because Roosevelt wanted it to seem an American effort so as to impress the voters. But many planners held that French colonial forces would look benevolently upon a purely American invasion. The Vichy government under Marshal Henri Pétain had been allowed by Hitler to retain control of France's colonial empire, on the condition that it be defended. Thus, French garrisons had fought against both the British and the Free French when they took Syria in 1941 and Madagascar in 1942. While the French were furious with Britain for sinking their warships after France surrendered to Germany, it was believed they bore no grudges against the United States and would not fire on Americans.

That was a forlorn hope. Even though Vichy was a tool of the Germans, most French officers went along with it for a host of reasons: because they were used to obeying orders and believed in the chain of command; because they saw Vichy as the legitimate government and the Free French, led by Charles de Gaulle, as rebels against it; because they feared that the collapse of existing authority would mean increased rebelliousness throughout the French empire, and a stronger Communist movement at home; because their pensions were at stake; and because of what might happen to relatives in France if they defected. The Allies knew this, and complex negotiations designed to win over the Vichyites in North Africa preceded Torch. But the Allies, justifiably afraid of leaks, did not entrust their French contacts with the date Torch was to begin. On November 8, when the landings commenced, what the French would do was unclear.

This made Eisenhower anxious, for he had understood from the start that the success of Torch depended "more upon political attitudes and reactions in Northern Africa than upon strictly military factors." Nor did it relieve him to know that all of Churchill's assumptions had to be correct, that "Spain will do nothing, France['s] resistance will be negligible, and Germany's reaction will be encountered only through Tunis."[12] Little wonder that it seemed to him the Allies had embarked on a "desperate" enterprise.

Admiral Jean Darlan, commander of Vichy's military, who by

accident was in Algiers on November 8, initially ordered his forces to resist, then that evening announced a ceasefire in Algiers, and two days later extended it throughout North Africa. Marshal Petain in Vichy promptly countermanded these instructions. Amid the resulting confusion in Oran and Morocco fighting, some of it heavy, continued for days. The Moroccan operation was a shambles, thanks to bad intelligence and inexperience, although its commander, Major General George S. Patton, Jr., would soon prove himself to be one of the war's outstanding combat leaders. Yet, luck was with the Americans. Along the treacherous Moroccan coast wave action was exceptionally low; the Vichy French could not bring their superiority in manpower to bear; Spain, which had 100,000 troops in its part of Morocco, did not enter the war; divisional commanders displayed initiative after failing to make contact with Patton; and American forces quickly gained control of the sea and air. French resistance collapsed after three days.

Probably things worked out better than they should have, given the planning errors. There was no need to take Morocco, which could have been bypassed, as the British recommended. If landings had been made farther east in the Mediterranean, as Britain wanted, the Allies would have seized Tunisia before Germany had a chance to secure it. The Moroccan fiasco was both unnecessary and only the beginning of America's troubles in the Mediterranean. It was a measure of Eisenhower's stature that he did not pretend that Torch had begun any way but badly. To the man who had succeeded him as head of the Operations Division he summed it up as follows. "I think the best way to describe our operations to date is that they have violated every recognized principle of war, are in conflict with all operational and logistic methods laid down in text-books, and will be condemned, in their entirety, by all Leavenworth and War College classes for the next twenty-five years."[13]

After Torch Germany occupied the rest of France, ending the pretense that Vichy was independent. It did not get the French fleet, which was scuttled in Toulon, as promised. Although the Allies had hoped it would sail to join them, destruction was the next best thing, and the Allies could live with it. Far more troublesome were such questions as how to deal with the Vichy forces in North Africa, and who was to govern it after the Allies landed. Charles de Gaulle, a true patriot who had risked everything for the sake of France, was a possible choice. But the Vichyites, still the administrators of French North Africa, hated de Gaulle, since if he was a patriot they were traitors. They would obey Darlan to support the fiction that they had been right all along.

The question of North Africa's government, on one level a matter of tactics, tested in a deeper way the Allied commitment to democratic values. Putting Darlan in charge might make North Africa easier to take, but he was a Nazi collaborator and the author of Vichy's anti-Semitic decrees. De Gaulle was the clear choice morally. He had defied the Nazis in their hour of triumph and raised a standard to which Frenchmen could repair throughout France's still far-flung empire.

In preinvasion days America's favorite was General Henri Giraud, who had escaped from prison to join the Allies and possessed the great merit of not being de Gaulle, whom American leaders disliked for his arrogance. Giraud was the candidate of Robert Murphy, FDR's personal emissary in North Africa and a foreign service officer with considerable Vichy experience but little knowledge of the region. Speaking from ignorance, Murphy assured Eisenhower that French colonial troops would rally round Giraud as soon as they heard his name. Admiral Darlan had feelers out and might also be won over. Eisenhower was getting nothing from Washington on this, and a meeting with Churchill produced no guidance either.

On his own authority, Eisenhower offered to make Giraud commander in chief of French forces in North Africa and governor general of the region. But Giraud insisted that, as ranking officer, he should be the supreme commander of Torch as well—a manifestly absurd idea. After the landings began he changed his mind, accepted the offer, and in a radio broadcast instructed France's colonial forces to cooperate with the Allies. Everyone ignored Giraud, Murphy's assurances to the contrary, for, unlike de Gaulle, he had no personal following.

Facing up to Giraud's uselessness, General Eisenhower put Darlan in charge of French North Africa. He alone, the theory went, could guarantee an orderly transfer of authority and, most important of all, induce the Vichy troops in Tunisia, where there had been no landings, to cooperate. The chances of this were fading fast on November 11 when Eisenhower made the appointment, but a slim chance seemed better than none, considering the stakes. As fate would have it, the stupefyingly contrary French in Tunisia allowed German forces to land unopposed, dooming the Allies to a long and bitter campaign instead of the walkover they hoped for and needed. Had the French in Tunisia responded to Darlan's call, enabling the Allies to get there first, the infamous agreement would have gone down easier. Bad as it was in other ways, the worst thing about the "Darlan Deal" was that it yielded few benefits. Democratic principles had been sacrificed in vain.

Churchill and Roosevelt backed Eisenhower's decisions (as time would make clear, FDR invariably allowed his commanders to make their own local arrangements), even though this prompted cries of outrage from the liberal-left in America and Great Britain, who viewed it as a betrayal of the cause. In Vichy itself the moral dimension appeared somewhat more complex, one of Marshal Pétain's staff observing "We live in a sad time when we cannot trust our own traitors any more."[14] The bargain made Darlan high commissioner in North Africa, with Giraud under him as commander in chief of French forces.

The only thing to be said for the deal is that Darlan was expendable. And Darlan knew this, complaining that his friends were saying that the Allies would squeeze him dry and cast him aside like a lemon. He was right. In an unsent cable to Eisenhower FDR had said of Darlan: "It is impossible to keep a collaborator of Hitler and one whom we believe to be a Fascist in civil power any longer than is absolutely necessary."[15] Churchill took the same view, describing the bargain in a wire to Roosevelt as "a temporary expedient."

Luckily, on December 24 a young French monarchist assassinated Darlan. This relieved the Allies, as Churchill wrote, "of their embarrassment at working with him, and at the same time left them with all the advantages he had been able to bestow during the vital hours of the Allied landings."[16] If those advantages were slighter than Churchill wished to admit, the embarrassment had been real enough. In any case, Giraud was at hand and Eisenhower immediately put him in Darlan's place. The way was now clear to unite the French military units in Africa with de Gaulle's Free French movement. However, Giraud, a three-star general, would not serve under de Gaulle, a mere brigadier, while to Gaullists Giraud was not much of an improvement over Darlan. Despite the American preference for Giraud, de Gaulle would win out in the end.

In retrospect it seems clear that de Gaulle should have been recognized at once as the embodiment of Free France—yet this was not so obvious at the time. He had not been elected to anything, and Roosevelt believed that the French themselves should determine who would lead them. De Gaulle's haughtiness did not endear him to the Allies, whose hand he was always biting. Yet, de Gaulle was a true republican, for all his regal bearing, and, beyond that, there was no good alternative to him, which is why he would prevail.

With Roosevelt it was always difficult to tell where principle ended and opportunism began, but de Gaulle had no doubt as to what he had in mind.

> President Roosevelt, under cover of proclamations to the contrary, intended that French affairs should fall within his own sphere of influence, that the leading strings of our divisions should end up in his hand, and that the public powers eventually emerging from this disorder should derive from his arbitration.[17]

Perhaps there was something to this. On the other hand, FDR was always looking ahead, and, anticipating deep divisions in postwar France, did not want the United States to be tied to a man like de Gaulle, who might well be repudiated by the French. Neither Roosevelt nor any other Allied leader realized that de Gaulle would make good on his claim to represent—indeed, to personify—France. In this critical time, de Gaulle played his cards with great finesse. He did not reproach the Allies for failing to include Fighting France in their invasion of French territory, or even for not informing him of Torch, but instead called upon Frenchmen to rise in support of the landings. From that moment, all things worked to his advantage.

In time it became evident that the French in North Africa would not accept Giraud and his Vichyites as legitimate rulers. A clumsy power-sharing arrangement fared no better. Finally, Giraud resigned as co-president of the French Committee for National Liberation (CFLN)—the umbrella group for all anti-Vichy Frenchmen—and closed his separate recruiting offices. In 10 months de Gaulle had swallowed him up. On November 9, 1943, a government in exile was created, and from that day on there was but one Army, one Navy, and one leader of all the Fighting French, for the first time since 1940.

If de Gaulle, with his hostility toward them, was very difficult for a Briton or a Yank to admire, it was hard not to respect him. Churchill did, despite himself, saying to his translator once, after a stormy meeting with de Gaulle: "There is no doubt about it! C'est un grand animal!"[18] In his memoirs, de Gaulle is straight-faced about how he had forced himself upon the Anglo–Americans, saying only "Their policy came to terms with what it could not prevent. The common effort was to gain much thereby."[19]

If little in this story reflects great credit on American political skill or moral vision, it illustrates certain pitfalls that a democracy at war risked. Roosevelt was forced to weigh, against the uncertain political needs of the future, the often conflicting requirements of military expediency and the promotion of democratic values. To choose Darlan was to cast one's lot for immediate military advantage, or so it seemed. To choose de Gaulle was the morally superior choice, yet one that might well compromise relations with liberated France were de Gaulle not received by it as the national savior. As always, personalities complicated matters. Ultimately, striking the right balance was so difficult that errors could hardly be avoided.

While the intrigue progressed, the war did also. Only a few days before Torch began, Lieutenant General Bernard Law Montgomery's Eighth Army administered a severe defeat to Rommel at El Alamein in the Western Desert. El Alamein was the farthest point of Germany's advance in North Africa, and Britain's victory there ensured both the safety of Egypt and the vital Suez lifeline. Though slow off the mark, Eighth Army eventually began pursuing Rommel while, from the opposite direction, Allied units advanced to within 12 miles of Tunis. Then the rainy season and thickening German defenses put the offensive on hold and gave Hitler time to send in more reinforcements.

This was either an inspired move or yet another example of Hitler's lack of military judgment. The obvious response was for Germany to have pulled Rommel's army out after El Alamein, because that defeat and Torch combined had made North Africa untenable for the Axis— which was precisely what Rommel advised. Instead, Hitler poured men and supplies into Tunisia, delaying defeat until the following May but losing at the surrender a quarter of a million Axis troops, half of them German. If Hitler had sent a force this size to Rommel earlier, the Desert Fox could have taken Egypt and secured the entire Mediterranean. Hitler had failed to act when a German victory was possible, and now he was sending men on a doomed mission when they were desperately needed in Russia—where the Soviets were destroying an entire German army at Stalingrad. Also needed were the many aircraft that had to be transferred to Africa because Allied naval and intelligence superiority made movement by sea extremely dangerous. Their hopeless last stand would, in terms of men and munitions, cost the Germans dearly.

On the other hand, while Hitler seems to have reinforced Tunisia for his usual poor reasons (he could not bear to admit defeat, or tolerate losses of territory), doing so prolonged the fighting there for up to five additional months. During that time, and partly because of the

Tunisian campaign, the Allies abandoned their plan to invade France in 1943, enabling the Nazi regime to survive for an additional year. From this standpoint, Hitler's refusal to leave Africa was a tactical mistake which, in one of the war's cruelest ironies, brought him strategic benefits.

Given the need to "entertain" American voters, Torch did little harm to the common war effort. Not so the chain of decisions that began at Casablanca in January. By then the political and military advantages of Torch had been largely realized. American voters had accepted the decision to defeat Hitler first. Allied control of the Mediterranean was close to being won. Further adventures along its shores could only be undertaken if the Allies forgot about invading France in 1943, the worst possible outcome in terms of shortening the war—yet, owing to British persistence, exactly what would happen.

9

The Sea of Dreams

B ritain's continuing effort to scuttle Roundup did not surprise the
War Department. Though often misrepresented as political rubes,
Army planners were always on guard against what they thought of as
British imperialism. Just before the Casablanca Conference, the Army
and Army Air Forces Joint Strategic Survey Committee gave General
Marshall a paper arguing that the British were pursuing a hidden
agenda contrary to American interests. While paying lip service to
Roundup, their real intent was to prevent an early cross-Channel
attack, despite its military advantages. What Britain secretly wanted,
the Joint Committee believed, was to pursue its traditional policy of
holding the balance of power in Europe. The British could not do so if
an overwhelmingly strong Germany was replaced by an equally potent
Russia. "It would be in strict accord with that policy, however," his
planners told Marshall, "to delay Germany's defeat until military
attrition and civilian famine had materially reduced Russia's potential
toward domination in Europe."[1]

Brigadier General Albert C. Wedemeyer, chief of the Army's
Strategy and Policy Group, shared this view, warning Marshall that
American military operations would suffer if Britain were allowed to
pursue its politically motivated agenda. Years later, in his memoirs,
Wedemeyer conveniently forgot his advice to Marshall in 1942 and

1943, instead censuring Churchill and Roosevelt for having failed to maintain the balance of power in Europe. This was because he had learned from Alan Brook's published diaries that Churchill had no geopolitical masterplan but rather was chiefly interested in winning the war. Thus, in 1958, Wedemeyer condemned Churchill for not pursuing the course that in 1943 he had urged Marshall to keep Britain from following. In the postwar era many conservative critics of Roosevelt would argue that FDR should have been thinking up ways to keep Russia out of Europe. Wedemeyer was in the unique position of having helped formulate the strategy that he later denounced Roosevelt for following.

Except for his lapse of memory, Wedemeyer would have been able to explain why Allied leaders and planners, himself included, had paid little attention to the postwar menace he was later to chastise everyone else for ignoring. In 1943 few realized how quickly Russia would recover from the losses of the previous two years. Further, the Army assumed that if Stalin did seek to expand, he would be most interested in Turkey and the Balkans, Russia's traditional interests. In the unlikely event that Russia did threaten Western Europe, it would be up to Britain and other endangered nations to contain the Soviets. No one, and certainly not Wedemeyer, anticipated the collapse of British power that would do so much to invalidate these assumptions. Everyone, including Wedemeyer, was mainly concerned that Russia stay in the war and continue pinning down the bulk of the German Army. It made a difference as well that Russia and the United States agreed on how to defeat Hitler, only the British lagging. There was no shame in having held these opinions, which made perfect sense at the time.[2]

After Torch the Allies had to determine their strategy for 1943, which would inevitably govern the war's subsequent course and bring the Allies to grips with Russia. The most radical proposal still was America's plan for a cross-Channel attack. The most cautious was offered by the British chiefs, who advised Churchill in early November 1942 that, after North Africa was secure, the Allies should occupy Sardinia and Sicily. Churchill was outraged to be given such a timid proposal, and argued instead for an invasion of Italy or Southern France. If North Africa was secured by the end of January, it might even be possible to launch Roundup in August or September, the PM remarked—though how seriously is difficult to say as his opinions tended to be unstable. The debate among British leaders was resolved before they left for the fateful summit in Casablanca that began on

January 13, 1943. There they would propose following up North Africa with an invasion of Sicily.

Unlike the British commanders, who met frequently and worked out their plans in detail, the Americans convened only once, on January 7, without reaching agreement. At this time American officers lacked experience at joint and combined planning. Army and Navy planners did not work closely with the British, or even with each other. Roosevelt seldom offered foreign policy guidelines, and the State Department was never consulted. In the resulting policy vacuum each service went its own way. On January 7, Marshall informed Roosevelt that his planners were divided over what to do next. He personally still wanted Roundup to follow directly upon the conquest of North Africa. Roosevelt pointed out that after Tunisia fell, half a million Allied troops would become available. He wanted to know how they would be used, indicating by his questions that he had in mind a Mediterranean target. As so often, the meeting ended with nothing having been resolved, the drift, however, being in Sicily's direction.

When they left for Africa the American chiefs not only lacked a program but were accompanied, at Roosevelt's insistence, by only a handful of aides. The British had a clear agenda, a large and excellent staff, and a communications ship that kept them in continuous touch with London. A greater edge was that during the immediate future any major Allied operation would depend upon Britain's contributing the lion's share. Britain had the advantage at Casablanca and would make the most of it.

The conference lasted for two weeks and was marked by heated debates between the American and British chiefs. The American chiefs gave in finally and accepted operation Husky, the projected invasion of Sicily. At the same time, the Combined Chiefs established August 1, 1943, as D-Day for the cross-Channel attack, which they knew Husky might well prevent. It was agreed that first priority must be given to the Battle of the Atlantic, since Allied shipping losses were becoming so heavy as to jeopardize the entire war effort. Husky came next, and their third objective would be to bring Turkey into the war on the Allied side—a favorite pipe dream of Churchill's that would never materialize.

At Casablanca the British chiefs wore down even Marshall with their doggedness. Perhaps the British genuinely believed that the Mediterranean was awash with opportunity. One thing everyone understood was that campaigning there would never take place on a large enough scale to incur extremely high casualties or jeopardize the war effort, while Roundup meant taking just such a chance. On the other hand, Roundup also promised to pay rich dividends which, Britain to the contrary, the Mediterranean never would.³ Whatever their motives, the British favored a low risk strategy—and at Casablanca would get it.

Among other decisions made at Casablanca was to go ahead with Operation Pointblank, the Combined Bomber Offensive against Germany. Churchill wanted the U.S. Army Air Force to join the RAF in its nighttime raids on Germany. But the Air Force's bombers, at that time few in number, had been designed for daylight precision bombing and would be relatively ineffective at night. Major General Ira Eaker, who commanded America's heavy bombers in England, explained this to Churchill, as also the demoralizing effect upon Germany if it were to be bombed both night and day. Eaker's phrase, "round the clock bombing," appealed to Churchill, and, since the Air Force was adamant, he graciously accepted defeat. Thus, the green light was given at Casablanca for the Combined Bomber Offensive that would end in defeat 10 months later.

The doctrine of unconditional surrender, which Roosevelt announced on January 24, 1943, although the only feasible course, should not have been publicly asserted. At their most extreme, critics would later say that it undermined the anti-Nazi resistance in Germany, and may have caused the coup attempt of July 20, 1944 to fail, thus creating a political vacuum in Eastern Europe to Russia's great advantage. As European wars had usually been ended by negotiations, unconditional surrender was a radical change that received much criticism.

Unconditional surrender had been recommended by Roosevelt's advisors as a sign to Stalin of Western resolve. It would also prevent Germany from claiming afterward that it had not been defeated in battle, but only at the peace conference—reviving the "stab in the back" myth that flourished after the previous war. Churchill, though surprised by the timing, did not object to Roosevelt's statement, because unconditional surrender was one of the few items that the Big Three seemed to agree on, though Stalin less so than the others.

Where Germany was concerned it made little difference. Even if the plot by German generals against Hitler had succeeded, in 1944 they hoped for surrender terms that the Allies would never have given them. At Teheran Stalin said that rather than calling for unconditional surrender, which would unify the Germans, it would have been better simply to send them a stern ultimatum. Actually, given Hitler's absolute control over Germany almost to the day of his death, the outcome would have been the same whatever route was taken.

Unconditionality complicated negotiations, and may have delayed Italy's surrender, thus making it easier for Germany to occupy the peninsula after Mussolini's overthrow. It certainly delayed the surrender of Japan. As the Emperor's safety was a prerequisite to any capitulation, there would have to be—and in the end there was—a compromise on this point. Otherwise, the "unconditional surrender" doctrine had little effect.

Though Roosevelt was delighted to have agreement, and the British were pleased about getting their way, the military decisions made at Casablanca were ill-advised. Husky would lead to the cancellation of Roundup, delaying victory by at least a year. Operation Pointblank was a sentence of death for many American air crews that served no valid military purpose. The hope that Turkey could be drawn into the war was a delusion. Operation Anakim, a proposed effort to retake Burma which the Americans argued for strenuously, would have little effect on the war. Only the decision to give first priority to the North Atlantic made sense, yet the Allies would have been very dim indeed not to realize that, if this particular battle was lost, they would soon be out of business.

Finally, despite the agreement to invade Sicily next, the grand strategy for defeating Hitler had not yet been completed. On Marshall's side a faint hope still flickered that Husky had not doomed Roundup. Churchill was determined that it would, however, and meant to go the extra mile to prevent not only an invasion of France in 1943 but in 1944 as well. Hard though the bargaining had been at Casablanca, it would get rougher still.

Casablanca justifiably increased the fear of Army planners that Britain would continue proposing Mediterranean ventures until Russia had broken Hitler. But Roosevelt was less worried about Britain's aims than by short tempers in Moscow. Stalin was not going to accept the Combined Bomber Offensive as a substitute for the Second Front. He was livid over the Allies' repeated failures to make good on their promise to invade France. He would be angrier still if Allied troops were unemployed after Sicily fell.

Roosevelt did not have to be sold on the merits of invading France, but he needed to offer Stalin an interim operation if Roundup was put off—and this need became especially acute after the Allies suspended their convoys to Russia in March 1943, after suffering heavy ship losses. As theater commander, Eisenhower also wished to see the mighty forces he led put to further use, pointing out that after Sicily it would not take much more effort to land on the Italian coast. To Marshall's planners this was action for the sake of doing something rather than as part of a larger design. Knocking Italy out of the war made no strategic sense. It would tie up huge amounts of Allied shipping to support the civilian population, in return for very small military assets—chiefly air bases in the south. Eisenhower himself had pointed this out to Marshall in April.

On May 11 the last Axis army in Tunisia surrendered, bringing the total of captured enemies to a quarter million, in addition to many more who had been killed or evacuated because of wounds. The North Africa campaign had been messy and long. During it, the United States Army experienced what would turn out to be its only defeat by the German Army—at Sidi-bou Zid in February. Yet, Torch had paid for itself in many ways. By committing so many resources to it Hitler made it a worthwhile front that eased the pressure on Russia. In addition to ending in victory for the Allies, it was a valuable learning experience for American commanders. Politically essential in any case, it might have been strategically important as well had it not led to Sicily, and on to the Italian mainland.

As Tunisia fell, another Allied conference was convening in Washington. Known as Trident, its discussions were often stormy because Marshall had begun putting his foot down. Brooke noted in his diary on May 17, 1943:

> The Americans are taking up the attitude that we led them down the garden path by taking them to North Africa. That at Casablanca we again misled them by inducing them to attack Sicily. And now they do not intend to be led astray again. Added to that the swing towards the Pacific is stronger than ever, and before long they will be urging that we should defeat Japan first![4]

The British were starting to pay for their earlier successes. They had been able to force Marshall to accept Torch, but they could not make him like it. Now that more time was being lost while the British continued to come up with proposals for landing in various places on the margin of Europe, the Americans were becoming peevish. Brooke would not admit that America would never share Britain's view of the Mediterranean, and he always seemed taken aback when putting off the cross-Channel attack led America to divert resources to the Pacific.

Trident began with Churchill arguing for an Italian campaign to follow the conquest of Sicily, while Roosevelt worried that it might compromise next year's cross-Channel attack. After days of tough bargaining, during which each side promoted its sideshows in the Mediterranean and the Pacific respectively, a compromise was hammered out. Upon taking Sicily the Allies would eliminate Italy from the war by means of unspecified actions. These would come to an end on November 1, after which troops would be concentrated in England for a cross-Channel assault on May 1, 1944.

Stalin responded angrily to the cancellation of Roundup, since the Germans were gearing up for their great offensive at Kursk and needed to be diverted. In a blunt exchange with Churchill, he pointed out that a cross-Channel attack in 1943 would "save millions of lives in the occupied regions of Western Europe and Russia," and would reduce the "colossal sacrifices of the Soviet armies," with which, by comparison, "the losses of the Anglo–American troops could be considered as modest."[5]

This cable was hotly resented by all who saw it as being rude, tactless, and, though the British conceded nothing, all too accurate. While Stalin was unable to change Allied policy, he could send out alarming signals—and proceeded to do so. He recalled his Ambassadors from London and Washington, the Communist press renewed its demands for a Second Front in Europe, Stalin omitted the usual congratulatory message after the Allied invasion of Sicily, and, most ominously of all, once Hitler's summer offensive was broken, he formed a "Free Germany" committee which suggested that a Soviet puppet state might be created to succeed the Third Reich. Stalin aroused, as he meant to, fears that the Soviets might go their own way or even sign a separate peace. Nothing could be done about this at the time for Husky was too far advanced.

On July 10, 1943 the greatest fleet ever assembled to that date, an armada of 3,200 ships, arrived off the coast of Sicily. In three days, 150,000 troops hit the beaches, followed soon by 300,000 more. Although Sicily was defended on paper by 350,000 Axis troops, most were Italians who wished only to surrender. The real opposition was provided by a German army corps that never exceeded 60,000 men. The Allies ought to have brushed it aside. Instead, the campaign lasted for 38 days and ended with the entire German force escaping to Italy after suffering fewer battle deaths than the Allies. The Sicilian campaign, given the lack of enemy strength, was more of a mess than Torch, even the British War Office calling it "a strategic and tactical failure." It took too long to execute, and gained only air bases that could have been obtained more easily by taking Corsica and Sardinia. Italy could then have been neutralized by air, thus avoiding the need to invade it.

In addition to being misconceived, Husky was poorly designed. Eisenhower unwisely left the Sicilian campaign in the hands of General Sir Harold Alexander—who, though well-liked by Americans, had been promoted above his merits. The planning for Husky was sloppy and late, little effort being made to exploit the Allied superiority in air and naval power. There was no planning beyond the beachheads, so the Allies followed up their landings with too many unimaginative frontal attacks and a campaign of attrition. Air commanders went their own way, failing to provide adequate ground support or anticipate that the Germans would withdraw across the Strait of Messina—though it was the only escape route. As Husky was a combined operation, both Allies shared the blame for it.

Throughout their campaigns in Sicily and Italy the Allies made poor use of sea power. Patton was the exception, several times using landing craft to outflank German defenses in Sicily. His example had little effect on other Allied commanders. British military historian General J. F. C. Fuller tellingly summed things up. "The fact remains that the most economical solution was seaborne attack, because in coastal operations he who commands the sea can nearly always find an open flank leading to the enemy's rear—the decisive point in every battle. This was *the* lesson in the Sicilian campaign, and it was not learnt."[6]

Politically and strategically the results were even grimmer. On July 17 General Eisenhower decided to invade Italy as soon as the Sicilian campaign was over. This step was almost inevitable once the Army abandoned Roundup. Any chance of reviving Roundup was foreclosed by the leisurely Sicilian campaign, which ended too late in the year to organize an invasion of France, while leaving substantial military resources assembled in the Mediterranean. The temptation to use them was strong, and, like the British, though less intensely, Americans also wanted to "knock Italy out of the war." The appeal of this robust phrase was such that little thought had been given by Roosevelt and Churchill as to what would result from a peninsular invasion.

On July 25 Mussolini was discharged as Premier by King Victor Emmanuel III and put under arrest. No Italian came to his aid—evidence of how completely Il Duce had lost support, even among his own Fascists. Mussolini's successor, Marshal Pietro Badoglio, at once announced that Italy would continue fighting as a loyal member of the Axis. This no one believed for a minute, and rightly so, as he wasted little time opening negotiations for an armistice.

Germany did not intend at first to make a stand in Italy. In case of an invasion, the plan had been for the German Army to fall back, across the Alps if necessary. Given Allied air power and amphibious capabilities, German planners considered the peninsula impossible to hold—as it would have been had the Allies not squandered their assets. Mussolini's fall created an opportunity to eliminate Italy almost without a fight, and, had the Allies acted boldly in response to Badoglio's overtures, things might have gone better.

As the Allies dickered with Badoglio, the Germans were building up an army of 18 divisions in Italy, while at the same time Eisenhower's forces were being drawn down by the transfer of men and ships to Britain and the Pacific. On August 18 Eisenhower received instructions from the Combined Chiefs of Staff to demand an unconditional surrender. On September 3, Montgomery's Eighth Army crossed the Strait of Messina. As plans went ahead for an amphibious landing at Salerno and the occupation of Rome by airborne troops, Badoglio learned the full details of the stringent terms being offered and threatened to call everything off. Eisenhower forced Badoglio to announce Italy's surrender over the air by revealing the extent to which he had already committed himself.[7] Eisenhower had, as he said at the time, played poker and won.

On September 9 General Mark Clark's Fifth Army, consisting of four divisions plus rangers and commandos, went ashore at Salerno (codenamed Avalanche), meeting such fierce German resistance that it was almost driven off. The Germans seized control of Rome and most of the country, Badoglio and his associates fleeing south to the protection of Britain's Eighth Army. The Italian Fleet set sail for Allied ports. Italy's soldiers abroad became German prisoners, while those at home were disarmed and released. Eisenhower canceled the Rome assault and dropped some of the transferred paratroopers on Salerno. With heavy fire from naval guns and a maximum air effort, the beachhead was secured. German forces disengaged, and in two weeks Eighth Army arrived, giving the Allies a continuous line across Italy.

Field Marshal Albert Kesselring, who commanded in Southern Italy, was persuaded by the Allies' narrow margin of victory at Salerno that they could be stopped. Hitler required little persuasion to send reinforcements, and the German Army quickly dug in. Instead of an easy takeover, the Allies now found themselves caught up in a grueling war of attrition that had no strategic purpose, but from which they could not escape.

By chance Sicily was cleared while the Allies were having yet another conference, this time in Quebec, which began on August 14 and lasted for 10 days. Quadrant was stormier even than Trident had been, for this time the Americans were set on the invasion of France, now given the codename by which history knows it—Overlord. On several occasions, tempers were so high that the chiefs met alone without their staffs.

No blood was shed in a literal sense, but the rhetorical violence was considerable, because, though the British paid lip service to Overlord, they also kept pressing for a major campaign in Italy that the Americans feared would compromise it. Brooke regarded the Americans as extremely obtuse not to see that a serious Italian effort would benefit Overlord by drawing German divisions from France. He was bitter that, while the Americans were capable of supporting full-scale offensives in both Italy and France, they perversely insisted upon building up their strength in the Pacific instead—where they already had about 90 percent of their landing craft and 13 assault divisions. Americans correctly felt that this argument showed that Britain lacked faith in Overlord. Actually, unbeknownst to them, Churchill was trying to win his Chiefs of Staff over to irrelevant operations against Sumatra and various Aegean islands.

Quadrant's final agreement was that Bolero, the buildup of forces in England, should receive a high priority, that Overlord should be launched on May 1, and that the invasion of Italy should proceed only as far as Rome. For the first time at a major Anglo–American strategy conference it was the British who lost. Though Brooke's basic strategy had been rejected, he had gained too much all the same: Marshall and his colleagues did commit themselves to Allied efforts designed to take Rome, Naples, Sardinia, and Corsica—plus other objectives.

In so committing, the Americans lost sight of their original reason for going into the Italian peninsula, which was to free the Mediterranean and drive Italy out of the war. These goals had been realized when the Armistice took effect, making operations in Italy itself unnecessary and even harmful. By threatening to invade Italy, rather than actually doing so, the Allies could have tied down many German divisions, just as they did in Norway. Gaining control of the

Mediterranean had shortened the route to India, giving the Allies the equivalent of a million tons of shipping. A good part of that would now have to be used to supply Italian civilians, precisely what U.S. Army planners had warned against.

Quadrant therefore wiped out much of what been gained by taking Sicily, and even North Africa. Brooke insisted in his diary that if only America had made a maximum effort in Italy, huge German armies would have been destroyed. This seems doubtful, for in actual fact a German force of 22 or 23 divisions held off up to 30 Allied divisions for the rest of the war. According to this ratio, it would only have required 44 German divisions to neutralize an Allied force of 60, which the Allies could not have provided except by canceling Overlord. Brooke notwithstanding, Italy was the wrong place for a Second Front. Because it was so far from England, fighting there required excessive amounts of shipping as compared to that needed to invade northern France. Too, its mountainous terrain favored the defense. And it was virtually a strategic cipher, so that even if the Allies had won there in 1943 they would have gained little. Italy would have been a liability to the Germans, if the Allies had refused to invade it. By doing so they only succeeded in making it a German asset.

The boot of Italy is 750 miles long, and south of the Po River plain its only flatlands are narrow coastal strips separated by the Apennines—a cruel mountain range with peaks as high as 6,000 feet. For the Germans this was ideal defensive country. There was little room for tanks to maneuver, and the ridges had to be taken by infantry walking, or, as often, crawling, up the rocky pitches. There were few good roads, which the Germans easily obstructed by blowing bridges, planting mines, and shelling exposed sections. Numerous rivers had to be crossed under enemy fire. Whenever, after tremendous effort and heavy casualties, the Allies were on the verge of seizing an enemy front, the Germans would simply fall back on another line of defense. During winter, and 1943's was to be the worst in decades, they would profit from bad weather that nullified the Allies' air superiority and made the roads impassable. As if all this wasn't enough, Germany's buildup in Italy was faster than that of the Allies. In December 1943 there would be only 14 Allied divisions, as against 20 German.

Allied planners decided to capture Rome although the Allies didn't have enough troops to do the job, and they would never have the amphibious capacity to leapfrog up the coast—to find the open flank that led to the enemy's rear, what Kesselring dreaded most. Instead of seaborne assaults behind enemy lines, the Allied forces would grind their way up the Italian peninsula. This proved so torturous that it was finally decided to make an amphibious landing at Anzio, codename Shingle, despite the shortage of landing ships.

To support Shingle both Allied armies launched new offensives beginning on November 20. Both failed, Eighth Army taking a month to advance 15 miles. This put an end to Anzio, so it seemed—except that Churchill, eager to save his Mediterranean strategy, persuaded Roosevelt on December 25 to overrule the military and order that 56 LSTs scheduled to leave the Mediterranean be allowed to participate in Shingle. As a result, there would be sea lift for two divisions, and, while Churchill would have preferred three, he believed that if he had asked for many more LSTs, he would not have gotten any. Thus, the American VI Corps landed at Anzio on January 22, 1944.

The assault was too small and too slow moving inland, which gave the Germans time to recover after their initial surprise. By the time the Americans finally began to move off the beach, Kesselring had assembled elements of eight divisions around it, with more on the way. VI Corps couldn't break out of Anzio, and Fifth Army's effort to link up with the beachhead came to grief. Finally, after months of stalemate, the Allies launched a new offensive that succeeded in taking Rome, after which a new stalemate developed. The peninsula would not be cleared of Germans until 1945.

Italy was the scene of remarkably hard fighting, much of it in country accessible only by foot, where, after his rifle, the mule was a soldier's best friend. Though the campaign itself may have been a mistake, those who fought there suffered as much, and displayed as much courage, as any other soldiers in the war. Major General Leroy Lutes, a trouble-shooter for Somervell who visited nearly every major battlefield, said after the war that the worst conditions experienced by the American Army were the Italian mountains in winter.[8]

The following statement could have been written by many Americans in many parts of the world, but actually came from the hand of a soldier named Sandford Africk, who was badly wounded during the Italian campaign. Shortly after being hit, he wrote a matter-of-fact letter describing his condition. Months later, still in a hospital, he expressed his deepest feelings.

> My whole company was replaced except for a handful of lucky men. All my buddies were killed or wounded. At one place I and my squad leader were the only two that were alive and unwounded after the squad

was caught in a mortar fire trap. That fellow that I wrote you about that used to hunt chickens and rabbits with me was killed lying next to me. My heart almost broke as I looked at him, but what could I do.

So many buddies gone and so many wounded! My lieutenant got off easy with a scratch on his arm. He is the only officer alive except for the company commander who will have a stiff arm for the rest of his life. Oh, darling, it was hell having my friends falling all around me and all we could do was say goodbye with a salute, and kill more Germans. We walked straight into death, not one man flinched or tried to save himself. I am proud to say, darling, that I was one of the brave lost children. We were only children after all. The dead boys were cuddled up, the wounded cried for dead friends. All children, after all."[9]

And yet, of course, warriors too.

Though Quadrant had presumably settled the debate over invading France, Britain continued to stall. The British still did not like Overlord, and were just beginning to worry about postwar relations with Russia. In August, Stalin began communicating with Churchill again, but Russian encouragement of the Free Germany Committee, the Soviet propaganda campaign for a Second Front, and rumors that Russia might make a separate peace, continued to strain relations. During Quadrant the Allies received a particularly harsh message from Stalin, who was annoyed at being excluded from the Italian Armistice. All this, together with Russia's great victory at Kursk in July 1943, which eliminated any possibility of a German recovery in the East, inevitably led to questions about where the Allied armies ought to be positioned at the end of the war.

This question never interested Churchill and Roosevelt to the degree it should have. Britain did argue that by invading the Balkans they could prevent Russia from occupying any large part of Eastern Europe. To U.S. Army planners the Balkans was only a traditional British sphere of interest of no use to America. They continued to feel that, even if getting to Germany ahead of the Soviets was a good idea, it could not be achieved by attacking through the mountainous and easily defended terrain of southeastern Europe. The costly and unproductive Italian campaign only reinforced this point. Further, as Soviet help would be needed in the war with Japan, American planners had no desire to antagonize Russia needlessly.

In a memo dated August 22, 1943, the Research and Analysis Branch of the Office of Strategic Services advised the Joint Chiefs that while Soviet domination of Europe in the postwar appeared likely,

America could not prevent it. There were only two ways to prepare for the new era of Russian dominance. One would be to compromise with the Soviets as much as possible and build upon common interests, the path Roosevelt was actually taking. The other method was to defeat the Germans quickly, and thereby gain a strong postwar bargaining position. Because the Soviets were demanding it, an early and massive invasion of France would advance both strategies at once. Concentrating on Western Europe was "the one move that is best calculated to give the Western Allies, in advance, an effective bargaining position for a compromise settlement with Russia, and a base for participating in such an agreed occupation of Germany by the United States, Britain, and Russia, as will secure the bargain."[10]

Mediterranean operations did not have the desired result of pleasing Stalin. Instead, they aroused his suspicions. On the other hand, Stalin was pleased by the firm commitment to Overlord that had been arrived at in Quebec. During a meeting of Foreign Ministers in Moscow that October the Soviets were happy to sign various agreements drawn up by the State Department. They also were reassuring on the issue of a separate peace, and displayed interest, for the first time, in a summit meeting of the Big Three.

In September 1943 Stalin, who previously had always found a reason not to confer with the Allies, finally agreed to a conference. Probably this was because of Russia's victory at Kursk. Stalin had breathing space now and could not be forced into making unwanted concessions in return for Overlord. To the contrary, Overlord's success would depend on Russia's launching a supporting offensive to prevent Germany from reinforcing France with troops drawn from the Eastern Front. Further, by playing hard to get, Stalin had moved Roosevelt to signal that he might make concessions on the Polish boundary issue and recognize Soviet annexation of the Baltic States. Stalin was gaining the upper hand, and a meeting with the Allied leaders would enable him to exploit it. Roosevelt confirmed this belief by agreeing to Stalin's demand that the meeting be in Teheran, highly convenient for him but not for the ailing President.

Before arriving in Iran, there were meetings for FDR to attend with the British at Cairo. However, instead of using these to prepare for hard bargaining with Stalin, Roosevelt saw to it that most of the time was spent on China—partly because he was still trying to build it up, and partly because he wanted to avoid discussing Teheran with the British. Each of the Big Three had a different agenda. Churchill, to the despair even of British diplomats, was still trying to stop Overlord and promote his Mediterranean strategy. Stalin was determined to have the Second Front, and would not discuss anything else until its main features had been settled. Roosevelt was most interested in the postwar settlement, which he believed depended upon establishing a good relationship between Stalin and himself.

As a result of Churchill's stubbornness, much of the Teheran Conference was given over to wrangling about Overlord. For days the Big Three argued as to when it should take place, who should be in command, and if and when there should be a supporting invasion of southern France. They also haggled over prospective operations in the Mediterranean. At various times both Churchill and Roosevelt attempted to curry favor with Stalin at the other's expense. Stalin, for his part, issued the customary veiled threats to make a separate peace if Overlord were canceled. Churchill gave in finally, as he had to, agreeing that Overlord would take place in May 1944, and that there would be landings on the French Riviera associated with it. There was never any doubt of this once Stalin made clear, as he did almost immediately, that he backed the American position.

The Big Three ended their talks with a flurry of pledges and pronouncements. They issued an ambiguous statement on Iran. They promised to support the Yugoslav Partisans in various ways. Turkey would be encouraged to enter the war. Stalin was to launch an offensive in support of the invasions of France and enter the war against Japan within months of V-E Day. In Europe Russia would gain Konigsberg, half of East Prussia, a third of the Italian Navy, and a free hand with Finland. During a conversation with Stalin FDR revealed that he would not challenge the Soviet annexation of Latvia, Lithuania, and Estonia. In East Asia Darien would be a free port, while Russia would acquire the southern half of the Sakhalin Islands in addition to the Kuriles. Most of all, Russia would move its European boundary west to the so-called Curzon Line, at the expense of Poland—despite the opposition of Poland's government in London. Stalin agreed to join a global collective security organization after the war. He gave his blessing to Roosevelt's plan for partitioning Germany.

Turkey never entered the war, despite heavy British pressure—and lucky for the Turks that they didn't. If an Allied force had been sent to Turkey it would only have provided Stalin with an excuse for following suit. Once in, the Soviets would have been exceedingly difficult to get out. Otherwise, the understandings arrived at in Teheran determined the postwar settlement—the Yalta Conference mainly confirming what had already been agreed upon.

It became evident after the war that Stalin had gained most from the negotiations. At Teheran he had been promised much booty, some of it to be taken from enemies but in Poland from an ally. Further, not only had Stalin been allowed to draw up his own Polish boundary, but nothing was said about the rest of Eastern Europe that would prevent him from having his way there as well. The Big Two contributed to this end, Churchill by wasting so much of the conference on his Mediterranean schemes, Roosevelt by acting as if the Allied bargaining position was as strong as when Russia's survival had been at stake.

Individual shortcomings are not chiefly why the postwar settlement would seem so one-sided. No amount of brilliance, unity, or advanced planning could have generated terms much more favorable to the West. Stalin would get about what the Red Army was taking anyway by force of arms; the Allies could not compel Russia to deal fairly with the nations it was "liberating." Any effort to do so would have jeopardized the Soviet offensive, without which Overlord would be at serious risk. Once the Allies committed themselves to the cross-Channel attack they were at Stalin's mercy to some extent. This was not a good reason for abandoning Overlord, since doing so could have resulted in Soviet troops occupying most of the Continent. But it meant that in order to save Western Europe, the East might have to be sacrificed.

If Roundup had gone forward in 1943 it would have come at a time of greater Soviet need, thus strengthening the Allied position. It might also have enabled the Allies to liberate at least part of what became Russia's European empire. However, what the Allies actually faced at Teheran was a poker game in which Stalin held the high cards. That, and not incompetence or treachery, explains most of what followed.

Why did Roosevelt fail to take out insurance for himself by warning Americans that the peace was not going to be made in heaven? Stalin suggested as much when Roosevelt told him that it would be nice, when Russia reannexed the Baltic States, to offer them some semblance of democracy to appease American opinion. Stalin replied in effect that it would be better still if Washington told Americans the truth and persuaded them to accept it. The source notwithstanding, there was something to this. As the peace would be a letdown in important respects, it might have been prudent to advise people ahead of time so that they would not expect too much from it. A better-prepared public might have gotten less excited after the war, and been less willing to look for scapegoats.

The crucial fact about the peace—one that most Americans utterly failed to understand and that Roosevelt dared not admit—was that eliminating the Axis states would create vacuums of power which the Soviets were going to want to fill whatever America did. Roosevelt's job then, as he apparently saw it, was to prevent the resulting friction between America and Russia from getting out of control. It is a measure of his artfulness that there still remains confusion over how he intended to do this. Roosevelt's last major address, a speech to Congress on March 1, 1945, after his return from Yalta, was pure Wilsonianism, the President announcing "the end of the system of unilateral action, the exclusive alliance, the spheres of influence, the balance of power and all the other expedients that have been tried for centuries."[11] He had spoken in this vein before, but by 1945 Wilsonian rhetoric was meaningless. New power relationships were rapidly forming, and order could be maintained in a turbulent world only by means of those very techniques Roosevelt had ostensibly just discarded.

There is, however, every reason to think Roosevelt was playing a wilier game than might be inferred from his appeals to popular sentiment. Efforts to determine what that was turn on the deal struck at Yalta in February 1945, which nailed down the Tehran understandings. The Crimean meeting of the Big Three was a naked great power summit. Not only were the smaller Allied states excluded as usual, but also France and China, despite Roosevelt's having at times named the latter as one of the policemen who were supposed to maintain world peace.

On the public level agreement was reached at Yalta concerning the occupation zones in Germany and Central Europe; a new provisional government in Poland with free elections in the other liberated states, plus their representation in the United Nations; and a formula for the veto authority to be exercised by the powers. Secretly, Russia promised to enter the war against Japan within two or three months of V-E Day. In return it would gain the Kurile Islands, the southern half of Sakhalin, the restoration of rights and privileges in Manchuria lost during the Russo–Japanese War, and the recognition of its puppet state, Mongolia.

Most historians agree that the Soviets were allowed to take only what they could not have been kept from seizing. The Asian territories thus disposed of, though often regarded as a bribe to obtain help against Japan, were beyond Allied control and ripe for Soviet picking. Since there was no way to keep them out of Russia's grasp, Roosevelt and Churchill made a virtue of necessity, for the sake of cordial relations. In Europe too the settlement was determined by Soviet power. The Allies, having waited so long to invade France, were in no position to demand that the Russians retreat from positions they had won by hard fighting. It was not sympathy for Communism, but the lack of prewar preparedness, aggravated by bad strategy, that were responsible for the Allies' weak hand at Yalta.

By February 1945 it only remained to face the music, which the Big Two did as gracefully as possible at their meeting with Stalin. In the field Allied commanders respected the occupation zones agreed upon earlier, the alternative being to break the Yalta accords and immediately launch the Cold War. Rather than taking a hard line, the Allies bent over backward to accommodate Russia—a popular position at first, even ardent anti-Communists like Herbert Hoover and John Foster Dulles praising the Crimean settlement.

The only mystery about Yalta is what Roosevelt really understood the Declaration on Liberated Europe, a part of the final protocols, to mean. The language is plain enough, the Big Three affirming the Atlantic Charter, and calling for provisional governments in Eastern Europe "broadly representative of all democratic elements in the population and pledged to the earliest possible establishment through free elections of governments responsive to the will of the people."[12] In his history Churchill claimed that it meant exactly what it said. If only Stalin had lived up to it, there would have been no Cold War. Harry Hopkins, who was present at Yalta, took the same view, telling Robert Sherwood "We were absolutely certain that we had won the first great victory of the peace. . . . "[13] For a time historians too accepted the Declaration at face value, though eventually revisionists would argue that the real intent was to install anti-Communist governments in Eastern Europe and make it an American market—yet another example of Open Door imperialism.[14]

As a matter of record, Churchill had conceded Soviet domination of Eastern Europe well before Yalta, specifically at a meeting with Stalin on October 9, 1944. He failed to obtain guarantees for Poland, whose future concerned the Allies most because Britain had gone to war over Poland, and the United States was home to millions of Polish–American voters, otherwise, Stalin was amenable. Churchill tells us that, Stalin consenting, he drew up a list of Balkan nations, specifying the extent to which Britain and Russia would dominate each of them.[15] The exact terms do not matter, since Roosevelt refused to go along, but in effect Churchill had accepted Eastern Europe as a Soviet sphere of influence. There is evidence, despite his repudiation of the Churchill–Stalin understanding, to suggest that, privately, Roosevelt did as well.

Many historians believe that Roosevelt had no intention of antagonizing the Soviets over Eastern Europe for as long as their military support was needed, and perhaps not afterward either. Soviet–American cooperation was the key to a peaceful world, and therefore much more important than Poland's boundaries or anything else in Eastern Europe.[16] Because Roosevelt made every effort to avoid antagonizing Russia, he was later accused of being ingenuous about Stalin and Communism. Roosevelt himself provided fuel for such charges by stressing his good personal relationship with Stalin, and by offering absurd characterizations of the treacherous Soviet leader, as when he told the Polish ambassador that Stalin was a "realist who is neither an imperialist nor a communist."[17] FDR's unrelentingly glib and superficial mode of discourse is easily turned against him by historical prosecutors. If we judge him by his actions, however, a different picture emerges.

Despite much talk about international democracy, the UN structure insisted upon by Roosevelt vested effective power not in the General Assembly, wherein each nation had one vote, but in the Security Council, which could not act without the unanimous consent of a handful of permanent members. It appears that Roosevelt had no faith in a universal system of collective security, favoring instead what has been called "containment by integration."[18] He would make Russia one of the world's policemen, thereby preserving the Grand Alliance.

At the same time, Roosevelt took out insurance against Russian bad faith. He refused to discuss postwar aid to the Soviets with the obvious intent of making it dependent upon their collaboration. He also kept the atomic bomb project a secret—not only the details, but the fact of its existence. That Stalin knew about it anyhow through his spies only reinforced the message. Thus, far from naively caving in to Stalin, as his critics later asserted, Roosevelt was engaged in a delicate balancing act. Even FDR's insistence on personalizing his relationship with Stalin was less shallow than it looked. He understood that because Stalin decided everything, there was no point in talking to anyone else. Later experience would support this view, for every improvement in Soviet–American relations has resulted from personal diplomacy, as between Khrushchev and Eisenhower in the 1950s, and Gorbachev and Reagan in the 1980s.

Many who have studied Roosevelt's policy toward the Soviets

regard it as well-considered, and about as good as possible under the circumstances. This seems also to have been Roosevelt's personal opinion. Upon returning from the Crimea he spoke to A. A. Berle, a foreign policy advisor who wanted to get tough with the Russians. Asked about the Yalta agreement, FDR threw up his hands and replied "I didn't say it was good, Adolf, I said it was the best I could do."[19] There were a host of reasons for this, from the need for Soviet help against Japan to decisions Roosevelt had made years earlier—for example, not to negotiate with the Soviets, as Stalin wanted, over East European boundaries in 1942, a time when Soviet survival was still in doubt and the West had considerable leverage. Roosevelt believed that the public would resent any such deal, as it had the secret agreements made by the Allies with each other during World War I. Even so, it was another lost chance.

An underlying reason for his weak position was Roosevelt's subordination of grand strategy to immediate military needs, and of both to domestic politics. Had Roosevelt from the first made achieving a favorable balance of power after the war his primary goal, he would have taken an entirely different tack, striving for an early entry into the war, full domestic mobilization, a smaller bomber force, and the largest possible Army. He would also have moved heaven and earth to secure an invasion of France in 1943. Had the attack failed it could have been mounted again the following year. If successful, the Allies would not have been on the Elbe when victory came, but farther to the east— perhaps far enough so that there would have been little need to make concessions at Yalta or anywhere else. Stalin might have been more cooperative in that case; but if not, if the Cold War was unavoidable, the West would have been better positioned.

This is not the wisdom of hindsight but rather what was advocated at the time. Writing to FDR in January 1943 William Bullitt pointed out that American influence over Britain and Russia was greater than it would ever be again, so the time was ripe to take steps that would secure the balance of power. "There is only one guarantee that the Red Army will not cross into Europe—the prior arrival of American and British armies in the eastern frontiers of Europe."[20]

The most prominent figure to anticipate trouble was Walter Lippmann, the dean of American political commentators, whose analysis was much the same as Bullitt's, though he favored a softer approach to Russia and accepted the military decisions that Bullitt sought to change. In *U.S. Foreign Policy: Shield of the Republic* (1943), Lippmann pointed out that, in the past, America and Russia had regarded each other as "a potential friend behind potential enemies."[21] However, when peace came their old enemies would be gone, and Russia and the United States—with no buffers between them—might develop conflicts of interest. To avoid or minimize feuds Lippmann would come to favor not a United Nations solution, but rather negotiated spheres of influence. To a friend he wrote that a new League of Nations "directed against everybody in general and nobody in particular, would quickly develop a pro- and anti-Russian alignment." Instead, "I want to find ways of binding together the Allies which are sure to bind them, and I do not believe they will be successfully bound together by any general covenant."[22]

That was what Roosevelt wanted, too, his problem being that enthusiasm for Wilsonian solutions was running high. Wendell Willkie's *One World* (1942), the epitome of "globaloney," had sold a million copies, and in 1944 Sumner Welles's more sophisticated *Time for Decision* was a best seller too, and named by critics as one of the year's best books. In the Presidential campaign Republicans took the UN as an accomplished fact, while Lippmann's *U.S. War Aims* (1944), which in so many words called for spheres of influence, was ignored. As Wilsonian principles were riding high, Lippmann failed to win many converts to the principles of traditional statecraft.

The climate of opinion appears to explain why Roosevelt so often served up Wilsonian platitudes instead of admitting unpleasant truths, speaking in one fashion while acting in another. Thus, though he climbed aboard the UN bandwagon, his remarks about the world policemen and the vesting of UN authority in its Security Council suggest that he really had in mind a concert of powers. In this he resembled Count Metternich rather more than Woodrow Wilson.

Lippmann had nothing to lose, and so could afford to speak plainly about the facts of international life. FDR had to avoid candor since it entailed excessive risk. An electorate accustomed to having foreign affairs discussed in terms of moral and legal abstractions, and which was constantly being warned against the evils of power politics—as if they were a matter of choice—could hardly understand where its true interests lay and resented having them stated. This was true of most experts also, as can be seen from the reaction to Spykman's *America's Strategy in World Power*, which gave offense not because Spykman was wrong but because he was politically incorrect.

Also to be kept in mind were the hard electoral realities that promoted equivocation. Roosevelt could not openly concede Eastern Europe to the Soviets because of the inevitable backlash. He knew that the Soviets would dominate the area, but seems to have hoped for an "open sphere of influence" that would give the locals as free a hand as was consistent with Russian security.[23] Stalin's sardonic advice to the contrary, Roosevelt refused to prepare Americans for the unpleasant realities that peace would bring, preferring to manipulate public opinion rather than challenge it. Probably he had no choice—but even if he did, taking such a risk was a great deal to ask of a dying man with the weight of the world on his shoulders. All the same, no matter how valid his motives, Roosevelt helped to raise expectations, concealing the Hobbesian world of power politics behind a garland of Wilsonian slogans.

In criticizing Roosevelt, one must compare him to other world leaders, none of whom, except de Gaulle, who had little influence, possessed a Clausewitzian grasp of the relationship between military means and political ends. Although Churchill said that Stalin was the greatest bungler of the Second World War, one could as easily nominate Hitler. His failure to prepare in advance for a cross-channel assault enabled Britain to stay in the war. Hitler's invasion of Russia went a long way toward guaranteeing his own defeat. Hitler lacked a grand strategy, making haphazard plans as he went along that were always being overtaken by events. The Japanese were worse, their strategy being to attack the greatest industrial power on earth and hope for a miracle.

Stalin was certainly the greatest bungler in the Grand Alliance, nearly losing his throne and his head by clinging to the Soviet–German Pact when it was obvious to everyone else that Hitler intended to crush him. Even Churchill, justly admired at home and abroad for his indomitable courage, was opportunistic and shortsighted, advancing Mediterranean schemes that would have done little to defeat Germany while leaving the Soviets masters of Europe. His conversion to fear of Russia, so often used as a club with which to beat Roosevelt's Soviet policy, was tardy and ineffective—and, in any case, at odds with his peripheral obsessions. He too had no grand strategy worth the name, despite his unquestioned brilliance.

By this standard, a realistic rather than an ideal one, Roosevelt appears more impressive. His policies brought victory to the United States at a human cost that was low compared to that of others and left America at the end of the war the world's richest and most powerful nation. Partly a matter of luck, this also resulted from a deliberate policy of subordinating postwar considerations to immediate requirements.

Roosevelt had good reasons for avoiding brutal candor, beginning with the fact that he still hoped Stalin was a reasonable man with whom one could do business. Another was that the public's shock upon learning of Stalin's plans for Poland and the Baltic States would weaken Roosevelt politically. It might also weaken civilian morale at a time when American casualties had yet to peak—which would not be until after D-Day. Moreover, revealing Stalin's expansionist plans would be a godsend to Nazi propagandists, damaging the Allied cause in Europe and stiffening German resistance. If not presented in the right way it would antagonize Stalin, too, just when the Allies would need him most on account of Overlord. There is no evidence that Roosevelt considered instructing Americans as to the new balance of power in Europe that they were helping to bring about. If he had, it would not have taken him long to reject the idea. He would trust to luck, as so often before, and to his own abilities.[24]

Though Churchill begrudged Overlord almost up to D-Day, Teheran put an end to the debilitating conflict between Britain and the United States over grand strategy, and not a minute too soon. For Britain the Mediterranean had been a sea of dreams, enabling it to put off the evil day when France would have to be taken. Henceforth the war would become, as it had to, a vicious slugging match.

In view of their losses in the previous war and their immense contribution to winning this one, the British cannot be blamed for arguing as they did. Democratic states, and America was no exception, shrink from campaigns that are sure to incur heavy losses. But, unless the Allies wished to hand Europe over to the Soviets, which Britain certainly did not, there was no alternative to Overlord. The Americans, constrained for a long time by their limited resources, had been patient—too patient, in fact. Yet, though the focus of debate would narrow considerably after France was invaded, Britain would still be able to influence military planning with fateful consequences.

10

The Politics of Sacrifice

Americans were willing to sacrifice so long as the hardships were fairly shared. In a fundamental sense, of course, the sacrifices of war can never be evenly distributed. Nothing that is lost at home can begin to compare with what those in uniform give up. Nevertheless, on the homefront during World War II there seemed no reason why domestic losses should not be more or less equally shared. It was hardly by chance that the term "relative deprivation" came into use at that time, since although doing without was acceptable, doing without more than others was not.[1] When it came to rationing goods this was a simple matter. On the vexed questions of taxes, prices, and especially wages, agreement was hard to reach.

As strikes appeared to be the most dramatic examples of group selfishness in wartime, no domestic issue aroused more passion than the rights of labor unions. To the men in uniform, civilian workers seemed both overpaid and overly endowed with sexual opportunities as it was, but saboteurs of the war effort when they went out on strike. Many people had always regarded unions as un-American, and never more so than in wartime. To unionists themselves the war was a mixed blessing. Although it brought full employment and higher wages, it also threatened a movement that had just recently organized the mass-production industries, a feat accomplished only after enormous efforts

201

and bloody fights with management during the turbulent thirties. The challenge to democracy was to preserve these gains while at the same time achieving maximum production. In a series of steps that pleased virtually no one, FDR squared the circle. One of the greatest success stories of the war, how Roosevelt saved the union movement without compromising productivity, is also among the least-known.

At first no one worried about manpower issues because unemployment remained so high. In 1940 there were 9 million men still out of work, and it was not until 1943 that they were fully absorbed. This enabled Roosevelt to put off thinking about the allocation of human resources for several years. Instead, government manpower policy was devoted to preventing strikes, a problem that could not be avoided or delayed because in 1941 there were 4,228 walkouts involving some 2.4 million men and women, making it the biggest strike year since 1919. These strikes, however valid the reasons behind them, threatened the mobilization effort, and so could not be allowed.

The 1941 walkouts were tricky to handle because of the new mutually beneficial relationship between organized labor and Roosevelt. When he came to power, the trade-union movement was still dominated by the nonpartisan American Federation of Labor (AFL). Then the Congress of Industrial Organizations (CIO) came along and, except for John L. Lewis, most CIO leaders were early and constant supporters of Franklin Roosevelt—in turn being helped by him. In 1935 Roosevelt had thrown his weight behind the Wagner Labor Relations Act, which legitimized collective bargaining and made possible a great union movement. The CIO supported his reelection campaign the following year by contributing half a million dollars, a huge sum for the time, and thousands of volunteers.

FDR had been slow to appreciate the value of organized labor, backing Senator Wagner's bill only near the end, but labor's support was soon essential to the New Deal coalition. The CIO's reward was to have federal and state governments intervene on its behalf, an historic change, or at least remain neutral—which could be historic, too, as when General Motors asked the state of Michigan to call out the National Guard and break the sit-down strikes at its Flint, Michigan plants in January 1937. There was ample precedent for this, but a different political environment made it beside the point. Governor Frank Murphy of Michigan was a Democrat who owed his job to labor and was not about to risk it. An era had ended, in recognition of which GM signed with the autoworkers.[2]

This background explains why Roosevelt's answer to strikes against defense plants would not be essentially punitive. Aware of the dangers of assuming dictatorial power, even to strengthen national defense, Roosevelt sought to obtain labor's support through democratic means. Therefore, he created the 11-member National Defense Mediation Board (later the National War Labor Board), which established a process of mediation that would last the war. The NDMB–NWLB was unique among war agencies in that not only labor and management were represented on it, but the general public as well. For most of its life the board was directed by William H. Davis, a successful patent attorney and Democrat with ties to Sidney Hillman of the CIO and Secretary of Labor Frances Perkins. Under his leadership the Board worked to establish industry-wide wage patterns and labor practices, and to prevent strikes. This last aim was accomplished by pressuring union heads to curb militant locals, as during a pivotal strike against North American Aviation in 1941.

The aircraft industry employed 100,000 people in southern California and was ripe for organization. Although shipyards and some other defense plants were paying a dollar an hour, wages in the aircraft plants were only half as much. The United Automobile Workers (UAW) began to actively recruit members in this fertile field. On May 27, at the urging of Secretary of War Henry Stimson, President Roosevelt issued a "Declaration of Unlimited National Emergency." He compared strikes in defense plants to the "fifth column" activities that were thought to have subverted democratic governments in Europe— implying that strikes were treasonous. On June 3 he asked Congress for legislation to keep threatened plants open. On June 4 the workers at North American struck.

Stimson wanted to make an example of this strike, which was highly unpopular. North American possessed 25 percent of the nation's fighter aircraft manufacturing capacity at a time when fighters were in short supply. Complicating the workers' legitimate demand for higher wages, the UAW local at North American was led by Communists. People like Henry and Dorothy Krause, who had played key roles in the sitdown strike against General Motors, were strongly isolationist at the time because of the Stalin–Hitler Pact. They reinforced FDR's fifth column charge by arguing, in effect, that weakening national defense advanced the cause of peace. Ironically, if the North American local had waited a few more weeks there might have been no strike, since after Germany invaded Russia on June 22 American Communists abandoned their isolationism and stridently called for war. But, walking out when they did, North American strikers opened themselves to accusations of disloyalty.

Though Stimson wanted an immediate show of force, Davis, as head of the Labor Board, persuaded him to wait and see if CIO and UAW leaders themselves could not arrest the strike. Richard Frankensteen, who led the UAW's aircraft organizing drive, went on national radio and demanded an end to the walkout, pointing out that it was unauthorized and blaming the Communist element. When local officers refused to comply, he lifted their charter, suspended the negotiating committee, and fired five UAW International representatives who identified with the strikers. At a mass meeting the workers shouted him down and rejected his call to end the strike. FDR responded quickly, and on June 9 the Army took over North American. Local draft boards were ordered to cancel the deferment of any man who failed to report for work.

These forceful measures broke the strike and served notice to the whole of organized labor that Washington meant business. Roosevelt's close ties to labor would not stand in the way of protecting national defense. As a result, the number of strikes had leveled off by summer's end, and fell sharply thereafter. Roosevelt's combination of public censure and federal power had gotten the message across: Democracy would not tolerate threats to its survival, even if democratically arrived at.

However, in addition to its big stick, the government had a carrot as well. Once North America was turning out fighters again the NDMB ordered it to grant all the union's wage demands, amounting to a 50 percent increase in certain categories. It further required that management institute other practices, such as payroll deductions for union dues, that the UAW had wanted. This quid pro quo strategy was greatly extended after Pearl Harbor, when the NDMB became the War Labor Board. It would battle unceasingly to prevent strikes, but with a minimum of actual force and with incentives designed to secure labor's cooperation.

Despite the government's victory at North American, labor unrest continued to threaten the war effort. From 1942 on the WLB's biggest headache was pay. Since price controls did not become effective until 1943, and then were fixed at wartime levels, union leaders soon found themselves under pressure from the rank and file to negotiate higher wages. But if wages rose, so would prices. In a war economy income exceeds the supply of civilian goods, producing inflation. Ideally, government could have raised taxes, or in other ways locked up all surplus income, thus keeping the supplies of money and goods in balance. Doing so would not only have prevented inflation, but distributed the sacrifices of war more fairly—among civilians as also between them and the armed forces.

These moves might have angered the typical voter, who, government believed, preferred to have any and all financial sacrifices borne by someone else. Consequently, Roosevelt's Administration felt that it had to erect a complicated structure of taxes and controls that would give the impression of being—or at least could plausibly be defended as—both fair and efficacious, while at the same time making the fewest possible demands upon civilians.

Wages, prices, and taxes were all of a piece, and could not be controlled except in relation to each other. In the early war years there were heated debates within the Administration over how to reconcile conflicting imperatives. Raising taxes did limit inflation, and was essential in any case to help finance the war. It cost $304 billion to wage World War II, of which 45 percent was paid for out of current revenues. This was a much higher ratio than in any previous war, and increased the percentage of national income that went to pay federal taxes from 7.1 percent in 1940 to an impressive 24.2 percent in 1945. To avoid inflation altogether it should have been higher still, but Congress ruled that out. Further, government borrowings to finance the 55 percent of war expenditures not paid for by taxes were themselves inflationary.

Had Roosevelt's Administration bridged the gap between its income and its expenses by making the purchase of war bonds obligatory, consumers would have had less money to spend, easing the pressure on prices. Treasury secretary Henry Morgenthau, Jr., insisted that government bonds and notes be sold on a voluntary basis, fearing that, otherwise, Congress would reduce taxes to ease the strain on consumers. Given Congress's aversion to taxes, Morgenthau was probably right. Roosevelt supported him for that reason, and also because he agreed with Morgenthau that bond drives would generate publicity useful to the war effort.

Elaborate public bond drives successfully raised $49 billion, amounting to about one-sixth of the war's cost. The rest of the shortfall was covered by bond sales to corporations, insurance companies, and brokers, and by borrowing from banks—a procedure that increased the money supply but risked boosting inflation. Morgenthau understood this, yet without higher taxes and/or compulsory saving, he saw no other way. He also took comfort from Treasury's successful effort to hold down interest rates on government securities, which action was anti-inflationary then and also reduced the charge on future generations. In his diaries, Morgenthau pointed with pride to the fact that average interest rates on the national debt fell from 2.53 percent in 1939 to 1.94 percent at war's end—a substantial achievement, since during World War I the interest rate had doubled.[3]

Given these constraints, the Administration had no choice except to hold down wages. Since doing so by itself would have been intolerable to labor, other means of ensuring stabilization had to be employed as well. Partly a matter of balancing priorities to achieve the highest efficiency, decisions about wages, prices, and taxes would determine what kind of war effort the nation was to have. Would it be one imposed from the top, or would it be based to some degree on what the people were believed to want? In a democracy there could only be one answer. To work, policies had to have broad support. The question was how to mediate the claims of interest groups in order to find compromises that most Americans could live with.

Many in the Administration supported a freeze on both wages and prices. Some, including Leon Henderson, who headed the Office of Price Administration, wanted higher taxes and compulsory savings also. Roosevelt heeded everyone's advice in his stabilization address of April 27, 1942, which called for a seven point program entailing higher taxes, price controls, and a wage freeze to be worked out by the War Labor Board. The Board finally decided that wages should be pegged at the level existing on January 1, 1941, plus 15 percent. This resulted in average hourly compensation for industrial wages rising by more than a quarter, from 66 cents at the beginning of 1941 to 85 cents as of January 1, 1943, while consumer prices increased by 16.4 percent. In July, 1942 the Board confirmed its policy in a decision affecting the smaller steel producers. What became known as the "Little Steel formula" would determine wage policy for the balance of the war.

The wage freeze—as it was called, despite being less drastic than the term implied—reduced inflation at the expense of industrial unions. After Pearl Harbor most labor leaders had pledged not to strike while the war lasted, on the assumption that unionized workers would be compensated for their restraint. By freezing wages government had eliminated the main reason for joining a union, and in 1942 membership declined—sharply in some cases.

To save organized labor the WLB fell back on the union shop. In return for a no-strike pledge and assurances of union cooperation with government, the WLB insisted that unionized employers include in their labor contracts what was called a "maintenance of membership" clause. As defined in June 1942, it stipulated that workers in organized plants automatically became union members unless they refused to within 15 days of being hired. Thanks to this device, the fall in membership was halted and organized labor grew from a total membership of 8.7 million in 1940 to 14.3 million five years later.[4] While the ruling did wonders for union security and offered leaders some protection against rank and file discontent, it failed to satisfy workers—most of whom joined unions for practical rather than ideological reasons.

Unable to meet worker demands for higher wages, CIO leaders tried to appease them in other ways, as by supporting the War Manpower Commission. The WMC was created by Roosevelt in April 1942 to establish general policy about manpower use, which other agencies were then to execute—a device much favored by Roosevelt because it diluted bureaucratic power. But unlike James Byrnes, who had access to FDR and therefore the authority to make OWM effective, the Manpower Commission lacked strong leadership and was ignored by the military and the War Production Board alike. The military refused to slow its rapid expansion in 1942 and 1943, as Chairman Paul McNutt of the WMC requested to ease the strain on industry. The Pentagon was quite right on this point. If McNutt had gotten his way, the Army would have been too small to invade Europe!

A more valid complaint of the WMC was that, throughout the war, military planners refused to take into account such considerations as manpower and housing when letting contracts. The CIO joined with McNutt in wanting to see plants built or expanded, whenever possible, in areas with ample supplies of housing and plenty of unemployed workers. However, the armed services liked working with familiar suppliers, and acknowledged no other needs but their own. They were not always that good a judge of their own needs either. In many cases the Army and Navy would have gotten better results by building plants where the workers already lived instead of forcing them to move somewhere else, usually a place where vacant housing was either scarce or nonexistent—leading to high rates of turnover in the new plants at the expense of production.

After failing to make the WMC effective, CIO leaders lobbied to have all war agencies assembled in a super department modeled on Britain's Ministry of Supply. Civil servants would replace dollar-a-year men, those executives loaned by business who continued to draw their old salaries. Labor and other groups would have an advisory role. As in Britain, this new agency was not only to oversee production, but also to safeguard labor's interests and plan for reconversion of the war economy. There was considerable support for this idea among New Dealers, small manufacturers who resented the military's sweetheart relationship with a handful of corporate giants, and some congressmen. Harry Truman's Senate Special Committee to Investigate the Defense Program introduced a bill calling for an Office of War Mobilization similar to what the CIO wanted, but this proved a futile gesture given the opposition of the military, big business, and especially President Roosevelt.

Had one been set up, a ministry of supply would have failed to satisfy industrial workers, who wanted pay increases that government could not allow. In point of fact, like almost everyone not in uniform, those employed in manufacturing benefited from the war—their real compensation rising by 22 percent between 1940 and 1944. Even this was not as large an increase as many others enjoyed. Net income per farm doubled between 1941 and 1945. The after-tax profits of corporations had increased by 57 percent in 1943, declining slightly thereafter. The net after-tax assets of corporations nearly doubled. Workers gained less, and so had an absolutely valid complaint. Yet the wage freeze did not apply when a worker moved to a better job or had his job upgraded. Millions received hourly increases in these ways. Many also had their fringe benefits enlarged, which benefited them financially even when pay rates remained stable.

Authorities differ as to how much income increased, but all agree that the main reason why workers earned more was that they spent more time on the job—an average of 45.2 hours per week in 1944 compared with fewer than 38 before the war.[5] As prices had risen as well, however, it appeared to some that they were working harder yet earning less. Though untrue, this perception was hard to shake, especially since workers were gaining less than farmers and corporations. This all led to unhappiness—especially after John L. Lewis broke the no-strike pledge and got away with it.

He did so in 1943, the year of the miners' revolt. Coal miners had the dirtiest, toughest, and most dangerous jobs in America, and the war made them worse. Mobilization stimulated coal production, which rose from 500,000 tons in 1940 to a peak of 684,000 tons in 1944, breaking a record that had stood since 1918. Because little could be done to improve safety at a time of maximum effort, the mines became even more hazardous.[6] Each week some 500 miners were killed or injured, a rate approaching that of combat. As of May 1943, the armed forces had sustained at total of 27,000 casualties, while in the same period 35,000 miners were injured—2,000 fatally. No other group of civilians was exposed to this level of risk, and yet, whereas real wages rose for most industrial workers after Pearl Harbor, inflation caused the income of miners to fall. In the coal pits tempers flared.

Though it resulted from wage discrimination, strike fever was blamed on Lewis, who personified labor's rank-and-file more flamboyantly than anyone else. A miner's son and a former miner himself, Lewis never forgot that it was the miners who had made him. With his great shock of hair, red originally, and then pure white, huge eyebrows, cobalt eyes, and powerful body, he was a favorite target of cartoonists. A splendidly biblical orator, fearless, belligerent, wily, he had mastered the arts of timing and bluff. By 1943 Lewis was an isolated figure. Never popular outside the labor movement, he had broken with FDR in 1937, and opposed his reelection in 1940 (Lewis was an isolationist), so in consequence had been forced to resign as president of the CIO. In 1942 Lewis took his mineworkers out of the labor organization that he had done so much to create. Lewis had once dreamed of occupying the White House. Never plausible, that fantasy was now behind him. Yet, as head of the UMW, he was still a force to be reckoned with.

In reality Lewis, though he ran his union with an iron hand, was far from omnipotent. This became evident late in 1942 when hard coal miners went on strike to protest, not the wage freeze as such, but an increase in union dues. The wildcat strike was a direct challenge to Lewis and he crushed it ruthlessly, driving rebel strike leaders out of the coal fields. The signals were clear even so. Without a wage increase there would be more uprisings and ultimately a new union head. Thus motivated, Lewis determined to break the freeze. Early in 1943 he endorsed the anthracite miners' demand for a 30 percent wage increase, thereby committing himself to do as much for the more numerous soft-coal miners whose contracts would be up in the spring. As that would shatter the Little Steel formula, President Roosevelt and his WLB promised to resist Lewis, encouraging mine owners to stand fast.

Lewis opened the bargaining talks on March 10 by asking for wages and benefits amounting to a 50 percent increase. This figure was for negotiating purposes only. Lewis's core demand, what he really expected to get for his men, was two dollars more a day. His actual proposal was not a straight hike, but a device that would give him the substance of what he wanted while allowing the Administration to save face. Instead of asking for an hourly increase, Lewis called for "portal to portal" wages.

Miners were paid only for the time actually spent digging coal, but the coal seams they worked were far from pit entrances and required journeys of up to an hour each way. These rides were made on dangerous open cars subject to derailments, cave-ins, and other hazards unique to the trade. It was only just, Lewis argued, that men should be paid for making such trips as well as for digging coal. A great outcry went up from editorial writers shocked by this display of greed even as young men died in battle. Lewis despised these charges, since miners were dying, too—and in greater numbers than ever because of the demand for higher production. All they asked in return was pay comparable to that of men in much safer occupations. Justice was on the miners' side, and, more helpfully, leverage as well.

Like a hooked fish, the WLB darted this way and that, but Lewis anticipated every move and slowly reeled it in. If portal-to-portal seemed too outrageous, why not give the miners a sixth working day each week? The proposal made sense, and all the more so as coal operators had already been granted price increases for that very purpose, which most had failed to implement. The Labor Board rejected Lewis's suggestion out of hand. On several occasions Lewis negotiated agreements with Illinois coal operators, who didn't belong to the Northern Bituminous Operators Association and had collaborated with him in the past. The WLB voided these as well. Subtlety having failed, Lewis resorted to force. On May 1 the miners walked out and Roosevelt seized the pits. This act put Secretary Ickes, as solid fuels administrator, in the center of things, and Ickes sympathized with the miners, frequently pointing out that "bayonets cannot mine coal."

The logic here was less apparent to others. Roosevelt threatened to draft miners and local draft boards canceled their occupational deferments—as if somehow fewer men could bring up more coal. Lewis was denounced by everyone including the Communists, formerly his allies during their isolationist period. Chairman Davis of the WLB accused him of giving "aid and comfort to our enemies." *Stars and Stripes*, the Army newspaper, cried out editorially: "John Lewis, damn your coal-black soul."[7] *Life* quoted an Air Force pilot who is supposed to have said: "I'd just as soon shoot down one of those strikers as shoot down Japs—they're doing just as much to lose the war for us."[8] A Gallup poll released at the time found that 87 percent of the public had a negative opinion of Lewis—putting him on about the same level as Hitler and Hirohito.

Two more short walkouts followed in June, leading to the ultimate confrontation. In October Roosevelt returned the mines to their owners, and on the twenty-eighth the WLB rejected still another agreement between Lewis and his friends in Illinois. On November 1, over half a million soft-coal miners walked out. Roosevelt seized the mines again—but this time he authorized Ickes to come to terms with Lewis. The bargain was struck on November 3, coal miners receiving about $1.50 more a day on a portal-to-portal basis. The WLB had to go along and by spring the last holdouts among the coal operators had given in.

The miners won not because they deserved to, though they did, but because the nation still ran on coal. His numerous enemies charged that Lewis, drunk with power, had simply bullied the government into submission. This was only half true. Reason having gotten him nowhere, Lewis did get tough. Had he failed to do so, the miners would have supplanted him or pressed ahead regardless. Many wildcat strikes had broken out during the long tug-of-war between Lewis and his opponents. The miners were not intimidated by government threats to draft them or break their union. Lewis held them in line only by leading where they wished to go. The strike did not weaken national defense. All the walkouts together cost only two weeks' worth of coal production. Reserve stocks more than covered this, and, despite the strikes, 1943 was a record year for coal production.

Lewis had played the game brilliantly, confusing his enemies with a mix of old gambits and fresh proposals cleverly timed to achieve maximum effect. In the war of words, he reviled the Labor Board but never President Roosevelt. His was the higher patriotism, he maintained, which recognized that victory was not a matter just of guns and ships but of productive workers also. He played his high card, the dreaded walkout, only as a last resort. It was mostly bluff anyhow, for Lewis knew very well that an enraged public would have his head if, for lack of coal, the war effort suffered.

The same concern inhibited Roosevelt, too, since he would not escape blame in the event that stubbornness on government's part was even partially responsible for declines in war production. When Congress passed a punitive bill (the Smith–Connally War Labor Disputes Act), Roosevelt vetoed it. When his veto was overridden, the

President failed to apply its sanctions. FDR would not make a martyr of Lewis or put other labor leaders in a position where they had to support him. The President's radio talks were friendly, only hinting at coercive steps Roosevelt had no intention of taking. When in the end he gave way, authorizing Ickes to settle on Lewis's terms and absorb the resultant heat, it was only after a long, bruising fight that enabled him to claim that all realistic alternatives to a disastrous strike had been exhausted. FDR walked with consummate skill the tightrope between angry workers and an irate public. In a no win situation, he lost almost nothing. If not his finest hour, it was at least one of his and democracy's most adroit, ensuring a steady coal supply while preserving the Little Steel formula—despite fears that giving in to Lewis would take the lid off wages.

Not surprisingly, the United Steel Workers tried to capitalize on Lewis's victory by demanding a similar raise, retroactive to December 24, 1943, when their contract expired. They did so because the WLB took so long to arbitrate wage disputes that months, or even years, might go by before a judgment was rendered. The WLB refused to budge, however, and on the day before Christmas the steelworkers walked out. Roosevelt acted quickly this time, overruling his board, accepting retroactivity, and putting an end to the strike. Torturous hearings then ensued, and it was not until February 1945 that the steelworkers were granted a back-pay raise equal to about two cents an hour, finesse and delay having accomplished more than brute force ever could. The Little Steel formula remained in effect until the war was over.

That did not mean an end to strikes. To the contrary, as the wage freeze grew in unpopularity, strikes became more frequent. There were 2,000 walkouts in 1942, 3,700 in 1943, and nearly 5,000 in 1944, of which 41 involved more than 5,000 workers. The proportion of all workers involved in strikes quadrupled after 1942—returning, in effect, to peacetime levels. There were differences all the same. Most strikes were "quickie" stoppages that halted work for a shift or less. CIO leaders remained faithful to the no-strike pledge, cracking down on locals that walked out and giving the Roosevelt Administration more than they received in return. It was a hard war for them, trapped as they were between an irritated membership and a toughening War Labor Board. Life was simpler for the AFL, which had not tied itself to the Democratic party and felt no need to discipline locals for breaking the no-strike pledge. Because this made it more attractive to resentful workers, AFL unions grew, to some degree, at the CIO's expense.

Were it not for the WLB's maintenance of membership policy, the shift would have been even greater.

Perceptions of these events differed markedly. To Lewis and many activists the wildcat strikes were government's just reward for mobilization policies that favored business over labor and within the movement some unions over others. To all-outers and the public at large, strikes during wartime were treasonous and government was at fault for not crushing them at once. After the war, faced with more serious labor unrest, President Harry Truman wrote himself a memo saying, among other things "Lewis ought to have been shot in 1942, but Franklin didn't have the guts to do it."[9] Truman did not mean this literally, but he expressed feelings that had been widely held during the war.[10]

Still, the strikes were almost always brief and did not impair the war effort. The imagery was terrible (workers at home betraying our boys overseas), the reality far less serious. Lewis was right to see wartime manpower management as a hodgepodge dictated by conflicting interest-group demands, vagrant public fancies, and political calculations. Further, in light of Roosevelt's willingness to staff war agencies with businessmen while labor's representatives were few, and given the fact that business and agriculture profited from the war in greater measure than labor, one can see why militants felt that unions were entitled to more.

They were mistaken all the same. If workers had gotten what they asked, the resulting inflation would have canceled out most, if not all, of their pay raises. The CIO's restraint was politically expedient, but it was also patriotic and in the workers' self-interest. Moreover, workers were profiting from the war, even if less than others. Their feelings of inequity were nothing compared to those experienced by GIs, who viewed walkouts as stabs in their backs for the sake of handfuls of silver.

This opinion was unjust, yet strikes more than anything else symbolized for servicemen the unfairness of life in wartime. Despite the deep commitment of Americans to the war effort, it resembled an inverted pyramid. On top, a majority of civilians were living, despite shortages and rationing, as well as or better than ever, while at the bottom a comparative handful of fighting men monopolized the suffering. Further, America was unique among the great powers in that civilians did not share the physical risks. Even Britain, which next to America suffered least, was fighting a war of survival. Some 60,000 British civilians were killed by the enemy, compared to 264,000 men and women in uniform. Death made equality of sacrifice more real in England than here.

To servicemen who complained that civilians were making too much money and who called for more discipline and a complete end to strikes, novelist John Dos Passos had an answer:

> You mustn't forget . . . that the day you get your discharge you will start to profit personally from any gains in higher wages and better working conditions those union leaders you say such hard things of have managed to obtain for wageworkers, or that even in uniform your standard of life is higher than that of the troops of our allies because of the standard that has been set in industry by the demands and general cussedness of generations of American working men. If we let into civilian life too much of the regimentation that is generally admitted to be necessary in the army we will be destroying at home the very liberties you are defending against foreign enemies.[11]

That was the simple truth. Also true, though one can understand why the GIs failed to see it, was that farmers and businessmen had no need to take unpopular steps because they were making so much more money.

These broad policies were essential to the success of America, but they provided only a framework. Ultimately the nation would stand or fall according to how well the job was done on thousands of shop floors. FDR recognized this even before Pearl Harbor. In a fireside chat on December 29, 1940, President Roosevelt said "We must be the great arsenal of democracy." Still, after Pearl Harbor, far from equipping its allies, an ill-prepared United States could not even arm itself, and soon cut Lend-Lease aid to Russia and Great Britain. But within two years the production curve grew so rapidly that shipments were later resumed, and then hugely expanded. A few figures indicate the magnitude of this feat. In 1944 the United States produced over 96,000 aircraft, many with four engines, compared to just under 68,000 planes manufactured by the Axis states, which did not make heavy bombers. During the Battle of the Atlantic the Allies lost 8.3 million tons of shipping, yet the United States by itself produced 9 million tons of merchant shipping to more than wipe out the shortfall.

The amounts manufactured for Lend-Lease alone were staggering. At war's end the Soviet Union possessed 665,000 motor vehicles, 400,000 of them made in America. The United States also supplied 2,000 locomotives, 11,000 freight cars, and 540,000 tons of rail, with which the Soviets laid more track than during the 11 years of ruthlessly enforced industrialization that began in 1928. At the same time, America was providing Great Britain with much of its armament, rising to a peak of 28.7 percent of all British military equipment in 1944.[12]

Many new inventions and discoveries came out of the war. However, though Americans viewed them proprietorially, most came from overseas. The British invented sonar, radar, penicillin, and the proximity fuse, while sulfa and DDT were German products. The theoretical work behind the atomic bomb was done mostly by European scientists. America's genius was for engineering and putting inventions into mass production.

At its peak the United States was building a ship a day and an airplane every five minutes. Between 1941 and 1943 America realized more than an 800 percent increase in military production, the GNP rising in constant dollars from $88.6 billion in 1939 to $135 billion in 1945. By then more than half of all world manufacturing was taking place inside the United States. Much of this output was achieved simply by putting what had been excess plant capacity to use. Many who worked in the wartime factories also had been surplus during the Depression. Although 12.5 million Americans were in uniform in 1945, the work force that year amounted to 65,290,000, up from 56,180,000 five years earlier, even though the birth rate had declined for years before the war.

This miracle of industrial growth, an extraordinary achievement that reflected the American "can do" spirit and its willingness to attempt the impossible, was not without its problems. The explosive growth of war industries affected every part of the country, areas with few or no government contracts losing population to luckier regions. Except for Japanese–Americans, just about everyone benefited from the wartime labor shortage. The number of skilled black workers doubled, and, whereas in 1939 the income of nonwhite male workers had been only 41 percent that of whites, by 1950 it was 61 percent. These gains came at a price. Michigan exemplified the difficulties, receiving 10 percent of the prime contracts let during the war, more than any other state except New York, which had an immensely larger population— 13,479,000 in 1940, compared to Michigan's 5,256,000. Seventy percent of these contracts went to plants in the four-county Detroit Metropolitan Area. What today we call the Rust Belt was then the beating heart of the world's foremost industrial nation. Pittsburgh, Cleveland, Chicago—all were synonyms for industrial strength. Detroit, the smoke-stained Motor City, outdid all the rest.

In 1940 Detroit's greatest years lay ahead of it. The local economy was still depressed and few could have supposed that it was about to enter an age of heroic production. There were 3.717 million automobiles manufactured in America that year, quite an improvement over 1932 when only 1.3 million cars had rolled off the assembly lines. Yet, 1940 did not compare to 1929, when the industry had produced over 5 million motor vehicles. Unemployment remained high, 16.7 percent of black workers and 9 percent of white still being out of work. Both figures were understatements because the Census Bureau reclassified workers as "unemployable" when they had been laid off long enough—even though many were able-bodied and willing to work, as events soon demonstrated.

Since they had so much idle capacity, one might imagine that auto companies would have been fighting for government contracts. In fact, the industry had decided that government work was too uncertain, and, in any case, it wanted to concentrate on the civilian market where sales had increased by 28 percent over 1939. William Knudsen and many other federal mobilization officials came from the auto industry and remained loyal to it, failing to order a modest 20 percent decrease in auto production until August 1941—thereby costing the armed services thousands of vehicles that would soon be desperately needed.[13] Even after Pearl Harbor, conversion went slowly. It was not until October 1942 that the auto industry was fully tooled up for war work.

By November 1943, its best month, the Detroit area's labor force had grown from 396,000 to 867,000 persons. Such was the need that even the physically disadvantaged were wanted. Henry Ford led the way by hiring midgets to work inside the smallest spaces of B-24 Liberators at his Willow Run bomber plant. There was never an acute labor shortage in Detroit-area war plants, thanks to the return of the unemployable and retired, plus a willingness to set aside prejudice to some extent and make use, even if not full use, of the handicapped, teenagers, blacks, and married women.

Better pay was a major incentive behind this growth, even though from 1939 to 1945 hourly wages increased by only 9 percent, the reason being that the work week lengthened by 18 percent. At the same time, premium pay—time and a half for overtime, and double wages for weekend and holiday work—was largely eliminated. A bitter pill for autoworkers who had fought hard for premium pay, it stayed unpalatable even after President Roosevelt restored the premium for the seventh consecutive day of work, since that practice never really caught on.

There was a high level of unrest in the United Autoworkers Union—by 1943 America's largest with over a million members. Shop floor militants, usually veterans of the great labor actions of the 1930s, resented the no-strike pledge and the loss of premium pay, among other wartime concessions, and repeatedly elected men with similar views to head union locals. At UAW conventions ferocious battles raged between two main factions. The Communists, formerly radical unionists who now favored all measures boosting production, including the despised speedup, while the followers of Walter Reuther remained vocal on shop-floor issues. Even so, strikes were infrequent and short, despite the longer work week and the loss of hard won benefits. In the Detroit area, as nationally, labor did more than most civilians to win the war. Patriotism aside, its chief reward for doing so was the opportunity to work long hours for somewhat higher wages.

Full employment brought prosperity to Detroit but also taxed its resources. Between April 1, 1940 and November 1, 1943 some 286,790 newcomers arrived in Michigan, making it one of 12 states to gain population during the war, conscription notwithstanding. Yet little new housing was built. State spending for health and education, adjusted for inflation, actually declined. In Michigan, as elsewhere, federal spending for public improvements directly related to war production did not begin to meet the needs. Thus, while the housing supply in the four-county area, private and public together, rose by 15 percent, the vacancy rate fell to 0.5 percent. There were seven responses to every housing ad in 1943.

Schools were overcrowded too, because Washington would not build classrooms for the children of war workers until their schools were filled to 200 percent of capacity. By 1943, under this formula, only 201 classrooms had been built with federal funds in the four county area, although the marriage rate was going up sharply, leading to a 25 percent increase in the number of youngsters aged five and under. This aggravated the child care crisis, as did the fact that many school systems, burdened by rising enrollments and shrinking faculties, went to half day sessions.

Congress seldom provided medical services because that would be socialistic—but, with so many physicians being in uniform, it agreed to temporarily subsidize public health services. As a result, in Detroit the death rate fell steadily from 1943 to 1945, especially among mothers, thanks to the Emergency Maternal and Infant Care program. Public health was almost the only big success among government-sponsored domestic programs during the war and suggests what could have been done in housing and education had they been given a higher priority.

Like most established industrial centers, Detroit suffered less dislocation than did rural and suburban communities that were awarded war contracts. Only one new war plant was constructed inside the city limits, minimizing the strain on existing facilities. Gas rationing and the swelling work force in older plants led to a 59 percent increase in ridership on Detroit's public transit system. By September 1944 almost 2 million people a day were being crammed into the city's aging buses and trolleys. Yet, however slow and uncomfortable it became, at least Detroit had a public transit system, which was more than could be said of many others areas where new plants were constructed.

The most famous wartime industrial site was Henry Ford's huge bomber plant at Willow Run, Michigan, 27 miles west of Detroit. The scale of the place made it a favorite of journalists, who liked to dwell on such impressive statistics as that the main building occupied 67 acres, the final-assembly line was over a mile in length, the airfield covered 1,434 acres and had six runways, one of which was 7,366 feet long. Enough concrete had been poured to build 115 miles of highway. The "Run" would produce 8,564 B-24 Liberators. At top plant speed, one would roll off the assembly line every 63 minutes.

Seemingly a monument to America's industrial greatness, Willow Run was actually one of the most badly planned and managed of all new industrial plants, a result of the haste and competing pressures of democratic America at war. One federal housing official described conditions there as "the worst mess in the whole United States."[14] The first error was the choice of location. When construction began in April 1941, planners assumed that the workers would commute from Detroit on a state expressway built for that purpose. After Southeast Asia fell to the Japanese, the resulting rubber shortage and gasoline rationing made commuting from Detroit impractical. Before long there was not a vacant room within 15 miles of the plant. Because of the failure to build housing on a large enough scale, Willow Run would never realize its potential.

Thanks to federal inefficiency and local opposition, the first dormitory for single workers did not open until February 1943, the first family units in Willow Village, known also as Bomber City, were not available until July, and there were no shopping services for residents until February 1944. Native Michiganders, who resented and looked down on the out-of-state "hillbillies" (those from Kentucky, Tennessee, and West Virginia in particular, who constituted about half of the work force), blocked or delayed every effort to provide housing and support services. Ultimately the government built housing for only 10 percent of the workers and their dependents, a major reason why the bomber plant at its busiest employed only 42,331 workers instead of the projected 100,000.

Some state and local government policies were well-thought-out and executed. The Michigan Highway Commission built hundreds of miles of roads and expressways in 1942, thereby averting traffic gridlock. The Washtenaw County Health Department did not wait for trouble to arise, but was on guard against water pollution from the start and held immunization campaigns before epidemics could break out. The state police and the sheriff's department were ready also, even though crime never did become a problem. In Willow Lodge, the dormitory complex which housed at any given time between 3,000 to 4,000 workers, and in Willow Village, which was home to between 3,000 and 5,000 families, the crime rates were exceptionally low. In the 40 months between January 1943 and the plant's closing, there were only seven major crimes: one murder, one burglary, two robberies, one case of assault, and two cases of arson—both committed by the same troubled youth. A normal city of this size would expect about 430 criminal acts and cases of juvenile delinquency.

Living conditions for new workers in Washtenaw County remained harsh. Most workers and their families lived in cramped and often squalid quarters, half of them in shacks, tents, and trailers, often miles from the nearest shops, without laundry facilities or even running water. School construction lagged as well, so most of their children were in badly overcrowded classrooms or else on half-day schedules. Two years went by before the first family case worker was assigned to Willow Run. Local churches made few efforts to reach newcomers. Little was done to provide organized entertainment. These deficiencies caused a high level of absenteeism in the plant and an enormous turnover. The daily number of absentees ranged from 8 percent to 17 percent, while 10 percent of the work force quit every month. Over the three and a half years during which Willow Run was operational, Ford hired a total of 114,000 workers to maintain an average strength of 27,400. No one calculated what this churning meant in terms of lost production, but it must have amounted to hundreds, if not thousands, of aircraft.

Sociologists Lowell Carr and James Stermer, from the nearby

University of Michigan, made a study of Willow Run. In one of the angriest monographs ever written, they spread the blame for its failures very widely. Except for the United Autoworkers, nobody seemed to care about the plight of Ford's employees. The federal government "dawdled and bungled." War production was subordinated to selfish local interests. Ford resisted every effort to provide public housing—and so did local businessmen and the county supervisors who wanted to protect real estate values and "keep Washtenaw county safe for the Republicans."[15]

One Ford executive told a protest committee that "Ford Motor Company's business is to build the best bombers in the world, and how our workers live off the job is a community problem, not ours."[16] This callousness infuriated the authors, and, though they neglected to mention it, was particularly offensive in light of Henry Ford's previous record of meddling into the private lives of his workers. Ford's security department, which during the war was still run by a notorious thug named Harry Bennet, who, despite his uncouthness, was a Henry Ford favorite, used to spy on workers constantly, not only to weed out union organizers but to enforce the owner's spartan code of personal morality.

Ultimately, the authors maintained, it all came down to politics. How to adequately care for the needs of workers and their families involved merely technical questions to which there were technical answers. But, for lack of any other system or procedure, each difficulty was treated as a political issue and resolved according to clout. Because few bomber-plant workers were eligible to vote in local elections, politicians could ignore them—and did.

A final irony, of which Carr and Stermer seemed unaware, was that the bomber plant itself wasn't that good and neither were the bombers. As an expert witness we may call Charles Lindbergh, whose deplorable politics did not lessen his skills as pilot and engineer. His campaigns against Roosevelt and intervention made Lindbergh a pariah in wartime Washington, as he quickly learned after Pearl Harbor when he attempted to rejoin the military. Secretary of War Stimson told Lindbergh pointblank that his recent activities had made it impossible to give him command of anything. Assistant Secretary Lovett and General Arnold let him know more gently that there was no place for him in the Air Force. For fear of Roosevelt's displeasure, airline executives and aircraft manufacturers wanted nothing to do with him, either. Only Henry Ford, who was highly eccentric and hated Roosevelt, and who was having problems with his bomber plant, would give Lindbergh a job.

Upon arriving at Willow Run in April 1942, Lindbergh took a test flight in a B-24, which did not impress him. Later, when he had a chance to fly a B-17, he thought it the better plane—as did most bomber pilots. General Arnold had invited the Consolidated Aircraft Company to build what became the Liberator in 1939, hoping that it would be markedly superior to the existing Flying Fortress. It was designed around a newly developed narrow wing, which experienced less drag than the B-17's broad one and gave the Liberator greater range. Otherwise, the B-24 was inferior to the Flying Fortress. It was harder to fly, and consequently harder to keep in formation; it performed less well at high altitudes; it had only three power turrets to the B-17G's four; it couldn't take the same punishment as its rugged peer; and it was the target of choice for German interceptor pilots, who found it easier than the B-17 to set on fire.[17] In addition, crews complained that the B-24 was too cramped forward, difficult to bail out of, and obstructive of their field of vision. Liberators did well in the Pacific, where their longer range was useful and Japanese fighters scarce. They should not have been used against Germany at all—but too many B-24s were manufactured (18,482) and too few (12,731) Flying Fortresses.

If the War Department would have done better to make Ford assemble B-17s instead of B-24s, in Lindbergh's view the Ford Motor Company should not have been building airplanes at all. Lindbergh soon discovered that Ford engineers could not even tell the difference between good and bad construction. The very first delivery from Willow Run was a disassembled B-24 sent to Douglas Aircraft, which Lindbergh, agreeing with Douglas engineers, called "the worst piece of metal aircraft construction I have ever seen."[18] Lindbergh also found that Charles Sorenson, the head of production, who knew nothing about airplanes, would not listen to the experts. This was true of most Ford executives who were detested at Consolidated for their arrogance. Thanks to poor planning and general incompetence, the first assembled B-24 made completely at Willow Run, promised for May, came off the line in September. It was not until 1944 that the plant ran smoothly—or as smoothly as possible, given the enormous turnover—and then only at levels of output far below expectations.

Willow Run embodied just about everything that could go wrong with war plants. In addition to callous management, hostile locals, and terrible planning, it was just too big to be absorbed by a small community. Even well-developed cities had trouble when they doubled in size—as did San Diego, California and Hampton Roads,

Virginia—or even increased by a seemingly far less significant amount ("only" 40 percent), like the San Francisco Bay Area. Because war workers and their families might disappear when the emergency was over, few private or public bodies wanted to make capital investments for needs that were considered temporary. Thus, it was rare to have bonds issued to pay for schools, water, and sewers, and businessmen too were reluctant to expand if growth had to be financed with their own money.

However, it was possible for a local boom to be well-handled. One such case was the village of Seneca, Illinois. In 1942 a town of 1,235 people, it swelled to 6,600 just two years later. Because shipyards on both coasts were working flat-out, the Navy gave contracts for smaller vessels to firms in the Mississippi Valley. So it was that the Chicago Bridge and Iron Company contracted to build Landing Ships Tank. CBI chose Seneca because of its location on the Illinois River, which was part of a water system that led to the Mississippi and ultimately the oceans. Further, the shoreline at Seneca rested on a sandstone formation, making it unnecessary to sink pilings or build elaborate shipways. The region had ample electric power, and it was only 75 miles from Chicago, where the company had its headquarters and from which the shipyard could expect to attract workers.

Despite the rigors of shipbuilding the yard enjoyed a splendid record. Though originally it was expected to employ only 3,500 workers, the work force peaked at 10,600, and this despite temperatures of 130 degrees in the holds during summer and a work week of 54 hours, six more than the wartime standard. During periods of greatest need the yard operated around the clock, the employees putting in 70 hours a week, Sundays included. Absenteeism was considered a problem by the company, but it averaged a mere 4.5 percent—less than half the rate at Willow Run on a good day. Though the first LST took six months and 875,000 man-hours of labor to build, the last required only three months and 270,000 man-hours. All told, the yard produced 157 ships and won five Army–Navy "E's" for excellence in production.

High wages explain part of the yard's success, as the workers earned time and a half for overtime, a rarity in war industries. Also important was the willingness of local politicians to cooperate with the federal government. Unlike in Washtenaw County, there was no opposition to public housing, which was well-managed and provided with recreational facilities—especially for children. Thanks to federal aid, the local schools expanded rapidly and newcomers, when questioned by investigators, usually said they were satisfied with their children's continuing education. A critical difference was that CBI, unlike Ford, took an interest in all matters related to employee welfare.

Compare the following passage from a monograph on Seneca to the experience of Willow Run:

> Problems of health, welfare, and delinquency were dealt with adequately, through a combination of federal government funds, health officials, and cooperation among the leaders of the local community, CBI, and housing management. Crime was kept in check, and health was good. Traditional attitudes about crime, welfare services, and health services were respected. There were no conflicts of policy involved, no strange health services or police practices for people to adjust to; and there was plenty of government money to pay for the services needed."[19]

Another reason for the relatively high morale in Seneca and its shipyard was that CBI made a point of dramatizing its war work, taking advantage of the fact that ships did not roll continuously off an assembly line but rather were finished at modest intervals—usually of three or four days. This allowed each LST to be launched with fanfare, the ceremony featuring a female sponsor who might be the wife or daughter of a company official, a naval or union officer, or even an ordinary worker. In addition to music there were always visitors and speakers who would hail employees for their devotion to the war effort. The biggest ceremony of all was for the launching of the hundredth LST on September 28, 1944, which featured movie actor Cesar Romero, and also an enlisted Coast Guardsman. When the first "E" was awarded, an admiral from Washington and CBI's president were on hand. Workers and townspeople alike enjoyed these festive occasions, so that while Seneca suffered all the usual dislocations, shortages, and inconveniences of wartime, life was good there all the same—marked by colorful events and filled with a sense of purpose. Georgia Gleason, a restaurant cook in Seneca who worked a 10- to 12-hour day, remembered later. "It was fun, being young, with all that excitement."[20] Though only one state away, Seneca was a far cry from Willow Run.

Of the great war industrialists Andrew Jackson Higgins was second to none—except possibly Henry Kaiser. A self-educated boat designer and production genius, Higgins created a complex of war industries in greater New Orleans that ran up an amazing record. A Higgins yard once designed and constructed a 45-foot tank landing craft in 61 hours. Most famous for the "Higgins boat," an open, ramped landing craft that the Navy called an LCVP, as it could carry either troops or vehicles, Higgins Industries built over 20,000 boats of various types during the war, a majority of all small craft employed by the armed forces—in addition to larger vessels and a great variety of other products.

Like Henry Kaiser and CBI, Higgins understood that production records were set by contented workers. He therefore paid his employees, some 20,000 at the peak of production, the highest local wages, while also providing housing, shopping facilities, day care centers, schools and the like. These were good for morale, as were his plant newspaper and frequent ceremonies that marked production achievements. Unlike many employers, especially in the South, Higgins was an early employer of blacks and women, and had as fair a wage system as any industrialist in the country.[21]

Thus, the nation armed itself, and its allies as well, despite the ceaseless complaining that enforced sacrifices aroused. The control of wages, prices, and taxes, and the minimizing of labor strife, was a triumph for Roosevelt. The production miracle, if not always so efficiently achieved as memory would have it, was a triumph for the people. These accomplishments were further proof that, its untidy methods notwithstanding, American democracy could manage even the toughest jobs humanely when it wished to. The hardships, and the tragedies, too, resulted when democrats lacked the will to put their principles into action. This was most true when the issues concerned minorities and women.

11

Minorities and Women

The Democratic Failure

Three important groups—refugees, blacks, and Japanese immigrants and their families—presented challenges that America could not meet during the war years. To a lesser and yet important extent, women also were prevented from reaching their full stature. Prejudice was responsible for each of these failures to live up to the egalitarianism that had always been central to the democratic credo. In no other area was American democracy so underdeveloped, which would prove costly not only to the victimized groups but also to the nation at large. In fairness, it must be remembered that no other great power except the Soviet Union, whose record here was ghastly, had anything like the number and variety of minorities as the United States—and none absorbed so many refugees.

Although the Depression had kept Americans from seeing what immigrants had to offer this country, Hitler's war against the Jews offered the United States a priceless opportunity to acquire highly qualified workers and professionals. However, German Jews were suffering at a time when the bars against entering the United States had been raised to their highest levels. Congress had temporarily restricted immigration after World War I. Then in 1924 it limited the total number of immigrants to 165,000 a year, while also establishing quotas for each nationality. The nativism and xenophobia behind this

225

step increased during the Great Depression and continued through most of the war—the American Legion and Veterans of Foreign Wars going so far as to demand that immigration be ended altogether. Congressmen responded by introducing literally hundreds of wartime bills to restrict or abolish the entry of foreigners.

During the late 1930s, the last years when German Jewry could have been saved, public-opinion polls showed that between 71 percent and 85 percent of the American people were against increasing refugee quotas. In 1939 some 66 percent of respondents were opposed to a one-time quota exemption that would have allowed 10,000 refugee children into the country. Not only did Americans not want the wretched refuse of Europe's teeming shores, they also rejected most of the skilled and educated Jews of Germany.

Unemployment was the alibi for this inhumanity, anti-Semitism the true reason. Poll after poll confirmed that over half of all Americans regarded Jews as greedy and dishonest and that up to 40 percent of the population would have approved of, or at least not resisted, a campaign directed against them. Attitudes toward refugees did not change even after the war brought full employment. Thus, while most German Jews could have been saved, until 1941 it was Nazi policy to drive them out, the decision to commit genocide coming later, the great majority would perish. While less could be done, even if desired, for the rest of European Jewry once the Holocaust began, hundreds of thousands of Jews died as late as 1945 who could have been snatched from the fires.

The 40 months following Anschluss were especially critical. After Austria was absorbed by Germany in March 1938, the persecution of Jews increased sharply. For the first time America accepted refugees up to the quota limits, some 85,000 from all of Eastern Europe including Germany, during the next 18 months. Then the screws began to tighten. The German and Hungarian quotas were filled and entry made more difficult by increasing the financial guarantees required before an immigrant could be admitted.

Beginning in the early summer of 1940 America erected a "paper wall" around Central Europe. Ostensibly to guard against the immigration of subversives, American diplomatic and consular personnel were instructed to withhold visas from aliens about whom they had "any doubt whatsoever," a directive that reduced immigration substantially. In June 1941 Germany's consulates were closed in the United States and the Third Reich retaliated by ordering American consuls out of German territory, making further departures by German

Jews impossible. This was followed by the passage of an even more restrictive immigration law by Congress in July, and the ending of legal emigration from Germany and the occupied territories in October. The fate of European Jewry was thus sealed.

From early 1938 until mid-1942 some Jews were saved. The United States accepted 150,000. Britain allowed 55,000 to enter Palestine. By comparison with the rest of the world, which did nothing, these are impressive figures—but in relation to what could have been accomplished, the numbers are very small. The State Department played an active role in this tragedy by resisting every effort to frame a more humane policy, by obstructing the emergency visa program, and by giving anti-Semitic consuls a free hand in deciding visa cases.[1] President Roosevelt tried to help and did once give asylum to 15,000 refugees who were here on temporary papers. The outcry against this led him to back off. In 1940 he allowed State to virtually end the admission program.

Pearl Harbor did not greatly affect refugees, as Europe was already closed and escape impossible. Limited opportunities remained but were seldom used. After the November elections in 1942 Congress blocked Roosevelt's Third War Powers Bill, which would have allowed him, among other things, to suspend immigration laws—even though no one believed that FDR intended to admit many refugees. In February 1943 the Rumanian government offered to let out 70,000 endangered Jews on receipt of a cash payment. Nothing was done because there was no demand for action except by Jewish organizations. They were not effective because they didn't push very hard and because most Jews already voted Democratic, so Roosevelt had nothing to gain by responding to their appeals but much to lose by offending anti-Semites—especially in the South, whose loyalty to the Democrats could no longer be taken for granted.[2]

In 1943 State issued a new visa application form that was four feet in length and had to be submitted with six copies. Not only was the refugee compelled to have two American sponsors, but each of them had to submit references from two other Americans. As a result of these and other obstructions, between Pearl Harbor and V-E Day only some 21,000 refugees entered the United States, about 10 percent of those eligible under the existing quotas. The remaining 190,000 slots went unfilled, even as Europe's Jews were being exterminated. Nor was this a secret, for, while public indignation failed to develop until the death camps were liberated, news of the Holocaust appeared regularly in American papers—usually on the back pages.[3]

It was not until January 26, 1944 that President Roosevelt created by executive order the War Refugee Board, ordering the State, War, and Treasury Departments to give it all possible aid "consistent with the successful prosecution of the war." Even then it was not too late to save those Jews who had not yet reached the death camps. Mass deportations from Hungary began only in May 1944, by which time the WRB was already working to stop them. President Roosevelt warned that those responsible would be punished, as did Secretary of State Hull and other prominent figures—warnings which were publicized by the Office of War Information and the BBC and in pamphlets dropped from aircraft. Pope Pius XII appealed directly to the Hungarian head of state, Regent Miklos Horthy, and to the International Red Cross, on behalf of this remnant.

In July, after 440,000 Hungarian Jews had already gone to the gas chambers, Horthy offered to allow Jewish children under 10 years of age to emigrate and invited the Red Cross to provide relief services to some 200,000 surviving Jews, most of whom were in Budapest. Germany prevented emigration from taking place, but the Red Cross got in and so did Raoul Wallenberg, the young scion of a distinguished Swedish family, who performed incredible feats of valor. Nominally attached to the Swedish legation in Budapest, he was actually sponsored by the WRB, which contributed much of his funding. Wallenberg provided large numbers of Jews with visas and other life-saving documents, many of them forged, and installed them in "safe houses" protected by the flags of Sweden, Switzerland, Spain, or Portugal. He even snatched victims from trains already bound for the death camps and bluffed and faced down Nazi officers, risking his life again and again in dangerous encounters.

Wallenberg was aided by neutral legations, the Church, the Red Cross, Zionist youth groups, and others, all of whom in turn were inspired by his example to make even greater efforts. When the Red Army arrived in February 1945, some 120,000 Jews were still alive as a result of this extraordinary operation. Wallenberg himself saved 20,000 Jews with Swedish documents and Swedish safe houses, and anywhere up to 30,000 more were kept alive in other legations and safe houses by people Wallenberg had recruited, or who followed his lead. Another 70,000 survived in the Jewish ghetto because Wallenberg blocked its destruction by threatening the SS commander of Budapest with punishment after the war.

Wallenberg, for reasons they never explained, was arrested by the Soviets and apparently executed in 1947, losing his own life as a direct result of having saved so many others. The greatest hero of the war, Wallenberg showed how much more could have been done if rescue efforts had received greater backing. With limited resources, and despite the lack of cooperation from most other government agencies, the War Refugee Board helped save perhaps 200,000 Jews—including those in Budapest. If it had been founded sooner and backed more strongly, the total would have been much higher, for numerous schemes to ransom Jews fell through for lack of support.

As much as anyone else, Assistant Secretary of War John J. McCloy was to blame for the government's callousness. McCloy was born in 1895, the only child to survive of a woman left widowed and penniless when John was six. Somehow she managed to send him to the Peddie School in New Jersey, a rigorous preparatory institute, where he did so well that he was awarded a scholarship by Amherst College, from which he graduated in 1916. After a year at Harvard Law, McCloy became a second lieutenant in the Army, returning to law school after the war. After graduating, he was hired by the Wall Street firm of Cravath Henderson & de Gersdorff, becoming a partner in 1929. He handled a great deal of international work for Cravath, spending much of his time in Europe. His diplomatic skills, tenacity, and talent made him a legend on the Street and brought him into contact with Henry Stimson, who recruited him for the War Department in 1940. There, he worked closely with Robert Lovett, another lawyer—Stimson and all four assistant secretaries were successful attorneys in private life. Lovett called McCloy the greatest negotiator he had ever met.[4]

As Stimson's liaison to the WRB, McCloy was in a position to put the War Department's mighty hand behind any rescue scheme. His indifference was particularly felt on the question of bombing the death camps, which the Air Force could have shut down. Jewish leaders first asked that the rail lines along which the victims moved be cut by air attacks. This was not practical, as by 1944 there was abundant evidence showing that rail lines were too easily repaired to make them suitable bombing targets. Not so the gas chambers and crematoria, which in Auschwitz had taken eight months to build under much easier conditions than obtained in the war's last summer. If destroyed, they could not have been rebuilt, making further mass exterminations virtually impossible.

The means for closing the camps were ready at hand. Allied medium and fighter–bombers had the range to attack Auschwitz from bases in Italy. The magnificent British Mosquito would have been perfect. American B-25s and P-38s also had a demonstrated ability to destroy targets the size of those in Auschwitz, which was poorly defended by comparison with German cities. As a matter of record, on September 13, 1944, 96 Liberators bombed the factory areas of Auschwitz, at a cost of only three aircraft. This was just one of many raids in the neighborhood, the skies of which were swarming with Allied planes. By actual count, between July 7 and November 20, 1944, a total of 2,500 bombers struck targets within a 35-mile radius of Auschwitz.

The War Department refused all requests from Jewish leaders and the WRB to knock out Auschwitz, claiming falsely that it was beyond the range of medium and fighter–bombers. To which McCloy added that targeting Auschwitz would require the "diversion of considerable air support essential to the success of our forces now engaged in decisive operations," another lie.[5] The official Allied position remained that the best way to save Europe's Jews was to conclude the war as early as possible, even though a mere handful of planes could have crippled the death camps, and was beside the point, since by the time the war actually ended, most of Europe's Jews were dead—including those hundreds of thousands who could have been saved at negligible cost by a few bombing attacks.

After the war, as American high commissioner in Germany, McCloy worked on behalf of displaced Jews and helped persuade Konrad Adenauer to increase the reparations being paid to Israel. On the other hand, he also helped cover up the escape of Klaus Barbie, a notorious Gestapo officer, and hired one of Hitler's former intelligence officers, General Reinhard Gehlen, to advise Adenauer on foreign intelligence. McCloy's problem appeared to be that he was too much the lawyer interested in resolving cases, too little the human being. Yet, in later years, McCloy became one of the most influential men in the country.

Even more than the failure to admit refugees before the war, which can be partially attributed to ignorance, the limited efforts to save Europe's remaining Jews is a stain on the nation's honor that cannot be explained away—though there is a possible explanation for it. The Northeastern WASP elite that ran the war effort did an excellent job on the whole. At the same time its racism and anti-Semitism were responsible for America's worst violations of human rights and common decency. McCloy's moral blindness, which led an exasperated Henry Morgenthau to call him an "oppressor of the Jews" at a meeting of Roosevelt's Cabinet, was not unique to McCloy, but pervaded the

WASP establishment.

In contrast, one need only look at Morgenthau—who, despite his inherited wealth, as the only Jew at the highest level of government brought a different perspective to it. Morgenthau moved mountains in the vain effort to save Rumania's Jews, and it was thanks to him more than anyone else that the War Refugee Board came into being. If there had been even a handful of Morgenthaus at the top, many additional lives might have been saved. As it was, in no other area did the narrow social base of America's leadership class produce a more tragic outcome. This is not to suggest that had there been more Jews in government all would have been different. Walter Lippmann, the powerful columnist, did nothing to help. Neither did *The New York Times*, although its owners were Jewish. What government needed was more compassion for Holocaust victims, the likelihood—though not the certainty—of which would have been greater had Morgenthau not been alone.

McCloy also played a major part in the greatest domestic violation of human rights during the war—the mass internment of Japanese–Americans. When war was declared there were 117,000 Americans of Japanese origin or descent on the West Coast, mostly in California. They had been under surveillance by the Office of Naval Intelligence since 1935 and since 1939 by the Federal Bureau of Investigation as well. In 1940 a committee made up of the directors of the FBI, the ONI, and the Army's G-2 division was established to coordinate surveillance efforts, and it compiled a list of suspected alien subversives. Many names on the list resulted from ONI having burglarized the Japanese consulate in Los Angeles. Detaining a Japanese naval officer who had organized an espionage ring yielded additional information.

When America went to war the three agencies were confident that they had identified all potential subversives, the majority of whom they arrested within three weeks of Pearl Harbor. In all, 2,192 Japanese aliens were taken on the mainland and 879 in Hawaii. Most of them were members of the first generation of Japanese–Americans (known as Issei) who had been denied citizenship by Congress and the courts on racial grounds despite, as a rule, long residence. With the completion of these arrests, the FBI and the Justice Department were satisfied that Japanese–Americans no longer posed any threat to national security.

All the same, on February 19, 1942, President Roosevelt signed

Executive Order 9066, directing Secretary of War Stimson to designate
military zones from which anyone could be excluded. Ostensibly this
was a security measure. Lieutenant General John L. DeWitt, chief of
the Western Military Command, had been urging the removal of all
enemy aliens. He also wanted to raid their homes and confiscate
cameras, radios, and weapons that might be used for disloyal purposes.
FBI Director J. Edgar Hoover resisted the idea, saying that such raids
"would not only be most difficult but would also have a very bad effect
on the law-abiding people who were raided."[6] Mass raids took place
anyway, turning up nothing.

Meanwhile, tremendous political pressure was being put on
Roosevelt by Californians and their congressmen to intern all Japanese–
Americans. Journalists took up the cry—the venomous Westbrook
Pegler, of course, but also, on February 12, Walter Lippmann, the most
influential political columnist America has ever had. Lippmann
repeated an argument that was being used privately, writing that the
absence of sabotage proved Japanese–Americans were only waiting
until they could strike with greatest effect—a criterion that would have
justified locking up the entire population of America. Greed and
hysteria were at work, but, in addition, Japanese atrocities in China had
deepened the prejudice against innocent Japanese–Americans, even in
far-off Arkansas. It was intensely anti-Japanese, the state's wartime
history claims, because for years the national and state press had been
depicting "the Chinese as a noble, peace-loving people and the
Japanese as militant aggressors and sex fiends."[7]

Senior officials tried to avoid becoming responsible for mass
internment. Attorney General Francis Biddle would not issue such an
order, passing the buck to Stimson, who attempted to pass it on by
asking Roosevelt if he wanted an evacuation, and, if so, on how large a
scale. Roosevelt passed back, saying Stimson must act according to his
own best judgment. On February 17 Stimson, who disliked the idea
but was being urged by John McCloy to implement it, caved in,
overriding Major General Mark Clark, who argued that internment
would tie up too many soldiers. Biddle crumbled under pressure as
well, the result being Executive Order 9066, essentially a blank check
authorizing DeWitt to act as he pleased. A bill to enforce it sped
through Congress, with Senator Robert Taft of Ohio, who called it the
sloppiest criminal law he had ever seen or heard of, raising the only
objection.

On March 18 FDR signed Executive Order 9102, establishing the
War Relocation Authority, which was to share responsibility with the

War Department for internees. Milton Eisenhower, Ike's brother and a long-time civil servant, became its director. His hope that Japanese–Americans could be employed on sugar beet farms died when western-state governors, who favored concentration camps, insisted upon internment. Most Japanese–Americans were behind barbed wire by June 7, 1942—first in temporary centers and then in more permanent camps, where some 112,000 men, women, and children would be held for an average of 900 days under harsh conditions in rural areas and wastelands. There were 10 major camps: two each in California, Arizona, and Arkansas and one each in Idaho, Wyoming, Utah, and Colorado. All had much more severe climates than the internees were used to, both in winter and summer.

The camp complex at Poston, Arizona was desert country, lacking in shade, whipped by dust and sand. When the internees began arriving in July many were felled by the intense heat. One said later: "People kept falling down. We thought it was Devil's Island."[8] Seven victims of heat stroke died in the first days. Many internees believed this was intentional, Poston in their eyes being a death camp. The Army-style barracks in which they lived offered no shelter from the heat, were overrun with insects, and were impossible to keep clean. Camp Minidoka in Idaho, while hot in summer, experienced temperatures that fell to 25 below zero in winter. Tule Lake in California, despite its pretty name, was a dry lake bed located at an elevation of 4,000 feet. Temperatures in winter there fell to 29 below zero. In all the camps sanitation was poor by civilian standards and the lack of privacy onerous. Overcrowding, boredom, and hard work were the rule.

Camps were established not only in the arid and unpopulated West, but also in Arkansas, which was, like other Southern states, far from unprejudiced. Thousands of internees found themselves in either of two camps where they had been sent to work the rich bottom land of the Mississippi Delta. Hot in summer, the camps were swampy and damp all year round. In addition to numerous insults and some physical maltreatment, the internees were not allowed outside their camps, despite the intense labor shortage gripping Arkansas. The state medical society refused to provide care for the internees. A bill passed the state legislature denying Japanese–Americans the right to buy land in Arkansas. Despite sympathy for the heroic Chinese, another bill passed the state's lower house barring members of the "Mongolian race" from attending white schools. Both state houses unanimously passed a resolution denouncing the War Relocation Authority's policy of allowing internees to attend college in other states.

The general policy of imprisoning and persecuting Japanese–Americans was upheld by the Supreme Court—not only because it never had much respect for civil liberties in wartime but specifically because the government falsely claimed that there was no time to screen Japanese–Americans individually, though in fact such a screening had taken place before Pearl Harbor. At McCloy's orders the government also suppressed all the evidence it had, which was considerable, that undermined the case for internment.

The real reasons for putting Americans in concentration camps were fear, greed, and racism. Immediately after Pearl Harbor many citizens on the West Coast panicked, seeing every Japanese gardener as a potential danger. Japanese–Americans had founded thriving small businesses and grew nearly 40 percent of California's produce, thus building up properties which white Americans coveted. Most were sold at a loss by their owners before their internment. Racism justified all, even California Attorney General Earl Warren claiming that, while methods existed to determine the loyalty of Caucasians, that is, German and Italian–Americans, small numbers of whom were also detained, no such tests existed for the inscrutable Oriental.

Early on men of conscience began working behind the scenes to undo this miscarriage of justice. The first step was to remove General DeWitt, a racist who stood in the way of any return—which was done on September 17, 1943. He was replaced by General Delos C. Emmons, who as Army commander in Hawaii after Pearl Harbor had resisted the pressure for a mass internment of its Japanese–Americans. On December 3, 1943 Attorney General Biddle requested that President Roosevelt institute a liberal release and return program. In February 1944, Harold Ickes, whose Interior Department controlled the WRA, made similar requests. When FDR continued to ignore these Ickes assigned Under Secretary Abe Fortas to work on the problem. Fortas visited the camps and, horrified by their starkness, brought back compelling arguments in favor of early release.

Additional entreaties by Ickes and others met with failure. In June McCloy told General Emmons that Roosevelt did not want to lose any votes in California by releasing Japanese–Americans. Emmons was soon reassigned, presumably for advocating early release. His successor, General Charles H. Bonesteel, also opposed the internment program and lobbied ceaselessly against it—which was probably why he too was reassigned after less than six months in the Presidio.

The tide had turned all the same. At the first Cabinet meeting after Roosevelt's reelection in 1944, Biddle asked Roosevelt to release all internees certified by the Justice Department as loyal. This time, having nothing to lose, FDR agreed. On December 10 the new commanding general issued Public Proclamation No. 21, which was drafted by Bonesteel, rescinding DeWitt's evacuation and exclusion orders and allowing most internees to return to the Coast.

In 1948 Congress passed an Act that doled out $37 million in compensation to Japanese–Americans who, the Federal Reserve Bank estimated, had been deprived of $400 million in property alone, not counting lost income and wages. Recently, Congress passed another Act that may award survivors of the relocation camps $20,000 apiece, the equivalent of about 2,000 wartime dollars, or some $400 less than the average American family's income in a single war year. The symbolism meant more than the money—which, on the one hand, was too little from the standpoint of actual damages and, on the other, not really needed, for after their release, Japanese–Americans as a group went on to become extremely well-educated and successful. If not the best revenge, this must have been at least some consolation.

Biddle regretted having given way on internment, and others too would later wish they had not gone along, or, if their records were clean, that they had fought harder to prevent it. McCloy was unrepentant to the end, telling a presidential commission in 1981 that internment was "retribution for the attack that was made on Pearl Harbor."⁰ In his autobiography, Stimson blandly maintained that Japanese–Americans were imprisoned for their own good as protection against vigilantism. He also patted himself and McCloy on the back for the splendid record of Japanese–American combat units, whose formation they had encouraged.

Premier among these units was the elite 442nd Regimental Combat Team, which, with an average strength of about 3,000, sustained 9,486 casualties and became the most decorated unit in the Army. In all some 33,000 Nisei, second-generation Japanese–Americans, served in the armed forces with great distinction, fighting and dying for the sake of a country which had put their families in prison. The irony seemingly escaped Stimson and McCloy—though not the internees, who had ample time to reflect on it.

Negroes, by far the largest racial minority, were as segregated and discriminated against during the war as before it. But manpower shortages and the President's need for black votes combined to make the picture somewhat brighter than it might have been. The mobilization plan of 1940 called for proportionately half as many blacks as whites to be drafted, and those were to be confined largely to service rather than combat units, excluded entirely from the Army Air Corps and Marines, and from the Navy except as messmen.

Military discrimination became a political issue in that election year, and to hold the Negro vote Roosevelt forced the Army to say that it would become 10 percent black, giving roughly the same ratio of Negroes to whites that obtained among civilians. This did not go far enough, and in response to further pressure the Army announced that it would form a number of black combat units, promote a Negro Colonel to the rank of Brigadier General, and appoint Negro advisors to Secretary Stimson and Selective Service chief Brigadier General Lewis B. Hershey. These actions kept black voters in line, even though Negroes continued to serve in segregated units.

In 1942 they were still underrepresented in the military, a situation not only politically unwise but a waste of manpower. Consequently, Roosevelt ordered the Navy, much against its will, to enlist Negroes for general service. The Army General Staff suggested that racially integrated units be formed. This proved to be too radical a step, despite the added difficulty involved in building segregated training camps. However, except by the Air Force, officer candidate schools were integrated as an economy measure. At the end of 1944 there were more Negro officers than could be placed because of the Army's insistence that only whites command Negro units. Another rule was that no black could be ranked higher than the lowest rated white in any unit, which meant in most cases that Negroes could not rise above first lieutenant. This was justified on the ground that black troops preferred white officers, which was untrue, particularly as so many white officers were Southerners with racist attitudes offensive to Negro troops.

By the same token, white officers seldom wished to be assigned to Negro units. If they were hard on the troops, charges of discrimination resulted; but if they stood up for their men they were often scorned by peers and accused of being "nigger lovers." Commanding Negro soldiers was onerous, too, as 70 percent to 90 percent scored in the lowest Army classification test categories, compared to only 20 percent to 40 percent of whites, so training them took longer and required more patience. To prevent outbreaks of violence by or against them, commissioned whites often had to patrol black housing areas and undertake other duties in addition to their own that commanders would not trust to Negro officers. In the South, white officers of black units were discriminated against socially. Everywhere it was believed that they were made to command black troops as some kind of punishment. Understandably, white officers hated being assigned to Negro units and schemed constantly for transfers.

In addition to suffering from reluctant commanders, segregation, and discrimination, Negro soldiers often were victims of violence, especially in the South, scores being killed or wounded during the war. Often these casualties resulted from fights between black soldiers and white soldiers and civilians, but even minor violations of local racial codes were punishable by death. In March 1942 Sergeant Thomas B. Foster of the black 92nd Engineers Battalion was shot five times and killed by Little Rock, Arkansas police for questioning the methods being employed by MPs in arresting a drunken Negro soldier. There were race riots and fights between black and white servicemen all over the world. The resulting low morale among black troops was attributed by John McCloy to Negro oversensitivity and the fault-finding Negro press. As the pressure did not go away, in 1944 he ordered the desegregation of all facilities on military posts—an edict that was seldom observed or enforced.

As late as the spring of 1943 only 79,000 out of a total of 504,000 Negro soldiers were overseas because commanders did not want black combat units. The Army solution was to begin converting them to service troops, who were accepted—the more menial the work the better. When Representative Hamilton Fish (R-NY), who had commanded black soldiers in World War I, asked Stimson to explain this policy, he was told that Negroes "have been unable to master efficiently the techniques of modern weapons."[10] Stimson also denied that the War Department was trying to keep blacks out of combat, though in fact it was. Thus, only one black division was ever committed to battle, the 92nd Infantry. It did poorly on the Italian front owing to acute morale problems, which the Army's own investigator told the press had been caused by segregation. The Navy, for its part, assigned blacks to labor units after being ordered to expand their role beyond that of messmen. Only after riots broke out did it begin to integrate a handful of auxiliary ships.

There were minor exceptions to the rule that Negroes were seldom allowed to fight, and even more rarely given the means to do so effectively. The black 99th Pursuit Squadron was a great success, as were a small number of black combat units in the Ground Forces. During the Battle of the Bulge Negroes in the Army Service Forces were allowed to volunteer for infantry platoons. Thousands did so and performed well in combat—although many were rushed to the front with little or no training. The tiny Coast Guard, which totaled only 240,000 men compared to the Navy's four million, was outstanding, commissioning 700 Negro officers to the Navy's 58. But, on the whole, blacks were underutilized by the military in World War II—a blunder, given the manpower shortage, as well as an injustice.

Despite everything, the black experience of war had long term benefits beyond their eligibility for the GI Bill of Rights. A recent study suggests that Negro veterans gained a larger view of the world and of their own capabilities.[11] The most obvious evidence of this is that so many did not return to the South, whose caste-like social system closed off most opportunities for advancement. By 1950 more than half of all black veterans were living in a different region from where they had been born, compared to about a third of Negroes in the same age group who had not served in the military. This was important because in 1949 each additional year of age added $75 to the annual income of whites, but only $20 to that of blacks—unless the latter had moved to the North, in which case their rate of increase was the same as for whites. For whites, each year of military service was worth as much to their later earning power as an additional year of education, but for blacks each year of service was worth up to three years of education. It is one of the few happy ironies of the war that the military, which did not want blacks in the first place and did everything possible to make them feel inferior, benefited them all the same.

For black workers World War II opened up opportunities that had never before existed. This too was inadvertent, for, like the armed services, industry had no plans to utilize Negroes. In 1940 there were 5,389,000 employed blacks, of whom 3,582,000 were male, almost none working at well-paid defense jobs. Further, in a survey made by the U.S. Employment Office, more than half of responding defense contractors said they would not hire Negroes in future. This situation outraged A. Philip Randolph, President of the Brotherhood of Sleeping Car Porters, the only black union of any consequence, who called for a Negro march on Washington to protest against job discrimination. As the old AFL unions were for whites only and the CIO unions too new to have many black officers, Randolph was the ranking Negro trade unionist in America and commanded great respect. His call was supported by Walter White of the National Association for the Advancement of Colored People, the leading civil rights organization.

Despite the pleas of Mayor Fiorello LaGuardia of New York and others not to impair the defense effort or embarrass the President, Randolph went forward with his plans and it was expected that 50,000 Negroes would turn out on July 1, 1941. Four days before the scheduled march, FDR invited a group of leaders—including Randolph and White—to meet with him, and the result was Executive Order 8802. It established what became a Fair Employment Practices Commission (FEPC) that would also work on behalf of Jews, aliens, naturalized citizens, Asians, Hispanics, and American Indians. It would enjoy considerable success, aided greatly by labor shortages that forced employers to lower old barriers. By 1944 blacks held 7.5 percent of all jobs in war industries, which was less than their share of the population but still a major improvement.

The industries that resisted hiring blacks, or did so only at the lowest levels, were frequently those dominated by racist labor unions. The Machinists and Boilermakers between them represented 30 percent to 40 percent of airframe workers and over a fifth of shipyard employees, but the Machinists were lily white and the Boilermakers restricted blacks to segregated and voteless locals. Of the 31 national unions that openly discriminated against blacks, 19 were in the railroad industry, most refusing to change their practices despite FEPC orders and court rulings. White workers frequently went on strike to protest the hiring or promotion of Negroes. When the Philadelphia Transit Company was struck to protest the upgrading of eight Negro porters to drivers, it had to be taken over by the Army.

Bad as job discrimination was, it paled alongside racial violence. Attacks on blacks were everyday occurrences in the South, where lynchings continued throughout the war, but they had now become common elsewhere. The year 1943 opened with a series of racial clashes. Fights between white and black gangs in Newark, New Jersey resulted in the death of one Negro. A black soldier was killed in a race riot in Centreville, Mississippi. A riot among soldiers in El Paso, Texas caused two deaths, and at Camp Stewart, Georgia a gun fight between Negro soldiers and military policemen resulted in five casualties—one fatal. When 12 blacks were promoted at a shipyard in Mobile, Alabama, white workers ran wild, seriously injuring 20 Negroes. A race riot in Beaumont, Texas left two blacks dead and 50 injured. Not all the attacks were against Negroes. In California, riot victims were usually Mexican–American youths known as "zooters" or "zoot suiters" because of their colorful apparel, the zoot-suit having a very long jacket, heavily padded shoulders, and balloon trousers with tight cuffs. In June mobs of servicemen, egged on by civilians, began beating zoot suiters and continued doing so until the zoot-suit was no longer seen in public.

On June 15 and 17 there were minor race riots in the Detroit area, where an influx of blacks had worsened an already acute housing shortage. June 20, a Sunday, was unusually warm, with temperatures reaching 90 degrees, leading thousands of people to jam Belle Isle in the Detroit River seeking relief. Fights broke out all day and by 11:00 P.M. had degenerated into mob violence. Downtown a black mob, inflamed by rumors, seems to have rioted first, after which whites retaliated, with police support and approval hunting down and killing blacks. After several days of mob violence, federal troops were called in to restore order—by which time some 35 people, a majority of them black, were dead, over 700 were wounded, and 1,300 were under arrest. Seventeen blacks were shot by the police, who reported in every instance that the victim had been looting. Although whites looted and burned too, none was shot by policemen.

Given the appalling amount of racial violence during the war, some of it to be sure instigated by blacks but more often provoked against them, there was no reason to be optimistic. Yet amid the turmoil momentous changes were developing. In his aptly titled book *New World A-Coming,* one black journalist pointed out some that were already visible in 1943.[12] Negro voters had become politically significant in 17 Northern states with a total of 281 votes out of 531 in the Electoral College. In Harlem, Adam Clayton Powell, Jr. was already a rising star. He would be elected to Congress in 1944, becoming the first Negro to represent an inner city district. Rising wages and an increased political awareness were leading blacks to join the NAACP in unprecedented numbers. It would multiply tenfold during the war, achieving a dues-paying membership of half a million by 1945.

There were some 230 black newspapers with 2 million readers— among them one daily, the influential *Atlanta Daily World*—which were served by the Associated Negro Press of Chicago. The black press was now able to make up for the white media's habit of ignoring news of interest to Negroes. Many small changes were taking place locally that in the aggregate would prove to be important. In Little Rock, after the murder of Sergeant Foster, and despite the opposition of the Policeman's Association, eight Negro officers were hired. Later the Federal Court of Appeals, in an unrelated case, ordered Little Rock to equalize the salaries of white and black school teachers. Small steps, to be sure, but inch by inch the rock of segregation was being chipped away.

Another important element, taken for granted at the time but for Negroes a source of strength that would be greatly missed later, was that a majority of black children were still being raised in two-parent families. Negroes were poor, but they lived in viable communities and had a working family system. These resources, together with wartime gains, did much to make possible the civil rights revolution of the fifties and sixties.

Because a handful of German Jews did reach the United States, and Japanese–Americans and Negroes improved their position later, does not change the shameful record just discussed, which had practical as well as moral implications. Though American production astounded the world, there were barely enough people to do the job and also meet military requirements. Had German Jews been admitted earlier, and Japanese–Americans and blacks fully utilized, the war effort would have benefited proportionately. There is no way of calculating how much prejudice cost the nation in lost workers and soldiers but it had to be very great.

Above and beyond the physical harm was the moral cost to the nation. America represented itself to the world as the land of the free and the home of the brave, but this was only a half-truth. Bravery was commonplace in the war, fairness to minorities infrequent. American democracy, which boasted of providing equal justice to all, failed to make good on its pledge in the one area above all others by which democracy is tested. Later generations would have to redeem the promise of American life.

Though less brutally treated than minorities, working women also suffered from discrimination, a fact which remains astonishing for, in most war plants, however well or badly run, the key problem was the manpower shortgage to which women were the solution. A few figures make this clear. Of the 9 million additional persons who entered the labor force during World War II, some 3.3 million represented natural increase, the balance coming from people who would not otherwise have been employed. Boys and girls left school early to work in factories, or at least to replace those who had moved up to better paying jobs. Old men came out of retirement to fill in for youths who had been drafted. The most numerous new adult workers were married women, despite the prejudice against them. In 1936 a Gallup poll had disclosed that 82 percent of male, and three quarters of the female respondents believed that wives with employed husbands should not work. War did not change these attitudes as much as might be supposed, because American democracy had not yet reached the point where gender was seen as irrelevant to the full exercise of personal rights and capacities.

Fortunately for the war effort, married women joined the labor force anyway. Between 1940 and 1944, the number of employed women rose by half, reaching a high of 19 millon, and, for the first time in American history, married women outnumbered singles. This was not a matter of choice but of need. When the supply of white males and single white females was exhausted, employers had no alternative but to hire married women and blacks. However, unlike today, and despite the fact that the basic allotment for a serviceman's wife was only $50 a month (worth perhaps $500 today), young mothers remained at home. The number of women workers under the age of 35 increased just half a percent more than if there had been no war. The Women's Bureau found that only 32 percent of the married, widowed, or divorced women in the work force had any children under the age of 14—in half of these cases only one.

Women over 35 years of age accounted for 60 percent of the increase. There were several reasons for this. The government did not want young mothers to work, Chairman Paul McNutt of the War Manpower Commission issuing a directive saying "No women responsible for the care of young children should be encouraged or compelled to seek employment which deprives their children of essential care until all other sources of supply are exhausted."[13] Few efforts were made to assist employed mothers of young children. Though some department stores, led by Bloomingdale's of New York, set up defense plant branches, most stores kept the same hours as in peacetime, leaving women coming off the day shift with little or no time to shop for food and other necessities.

Only 130,000 children were served by the Lanham Act, which provided federal subsidies for child care. Part of the reason was that mothers mistrusted, often rightly so, the quality of jury-rigged facilities. In other cases, nursery fees were so high that working women could not afford them. Notable exceptions were the Kaiser Corporation's shipyard care centers, open 24 hours a day and staffed by child development experts. The excellence of these centers and their success in persuading young mothers to use them was, for the most part, an example that persuaded few employers.[14]

Great Britain, where the labor crunch was more severe, showed how much more could have been done. Britain conscripted women between the ages of 19 and 30, offering them a choice between the armed services and essential war work, and, although this was not rigorously enforced, expected most women under the age of 60 to contribute in some way to the war effort. Child care support was provided on a much larger scale than in the United States, stores were required to remain open late, and in other ways the state did a good deal to make motherhood and employment compatible. As a result, it was estimated that eight married women out of 10 between the ages of 18 and 40 were in either the armed services or industry.

Though American support was never this good, the work force changed. In 1940 about half of the 11 million working women held poorly paid clerical, sales, and service jobs. The one-fifth engaged in manufacturing were concentrated at the low end, mostly in textile and clothing factories. Four years later:

> At the peak of women's wartime employment, in 1944, the percentage of the female labor force in clerical, sales and service jobs had declined to 34 percent. Although the entrance of over three million women into manufacturing represented a significant 140 percent increase over the figure for 1940, the 460 percent increase in the number of women employed in production in the "war industries"—metals, chemicals and rubber—that had employed few women before the war, was even more dramatic. Of equal importance, the war offered many women upward occupational mobility. Although 49 percent of the women employed in war industries in March 1944 had not worked before the war, 27 percent had shifted from other occupations."[15]

Officially, the American view was that married women were only working for the duration and would return home when it was over. There were many exceptions to this rule even in 1940, when 15 percent of married women held outside jobs. After that the proportion of married women who joined the labor force increased to one in four in 1950 and then to over half in 1980. The proportion who were active mothers rose as well, so that by 1980 three out of five married women with children aged 6 to 17 were in the work force, and two out of five with children under the age of 6. By June 1987 more than half of all women, 51 percent, to be exact, who had given birth during the previous year were gainfully employed. Thus, while the prominent role played by married women in wartime was seen as a temporary expedient, it marked an historic change from a relatively small female work force dominated by young singles, to an immense force comprised for the most part of older, married, or formerly married women.

The experience of women in the auto industry typified how this transition was effected. As conversion to defense work picked up, the United Automobile Workers (UAW) union, though among the most progressive in the country, shared the common concern over getting unemployed men back to work. Its annual convention in August 1941 resolved to oppose "any attempt to train women to take the place of men on skilled jobs until such time as all the unemployed men have been put back to work."[16]

However, to keep wage rates up in case worse came to worse, the delegates also declared that women should receive equal pay with men if they held identical jobs. That the UAW meant to protect men anyway became clear in October, when it filed a strike notice against the Kelsey Hayes Wheel Company in Detroit, demanding "the removal of all girl employees from machine work"—which was, in the union's view, "a man's job." When two more women were hired, male workers staged a walkout, forcing the company to remove women workers from skilled jobs and limiting them to 25 percent of the local work force.

So long as men remained unemployed, the UAW was determined to keep women out of its plants. It was also determined in practice, as at Kelsey Hayes, to see that men earned more than women for doing the same work. Because employers seldom wished to fight the union on this issue, most new hires were male. Thus, the female proportion of the auto industry's work force steadily declined between 1939 and 1941. When the auto industry began to convert to war production after Pearl Harbor, there were massive temporary layoffs. As employment began to rise again, men were rehired at a much greater rate than women.

When the supply of unemployed men disappeared prejudice had to weaken. By November 1943, when their numbers peaked, there were 203,300 women in auto factories, constituting 26 percent of the labor force. In some plants the rise was far more dramatic, rising from zero women in Ford's River Rouge complex in 1942 to 5,000 one year later. Wage rates, however, remained unequal, the UAW, contrary to its prewar stand, insisting on differential wages for what were defined as "male" and "female" jobs. Seeds of change were planted just the same. Even before V-J Day, the UAW International Executive Board recommended eliminating job classifications by sex. When women were laid off at the end of the war in favor of inexperienced men, they did not go quietly. At Ford's Highland Park plant, 200 women picketed the employment office, bearing signs reading "Stop Discrimination Because of Sex" and "The Hand that Rocks the Cradle Can Build Tractors, Too." In the short run they lost—but today women do work on assembly lines, just as they did during World War II.

For American industry as a whole, practices varied widely. In Detroit women held 20 percent of the jobs in aircraft factories, while at Boeing's facilities in Seattle they made up 47 percent of the work force. In Seattle women held 1.8 percent of the jobs at one shipyard, 21 percent at another. Despite regional differences, the total number of women in war industries soared, in Detroit alone the figure rising from 46,800 to a high of 215,000 female industrial workers. Apart from patriotism, the chief reason why women poured into factories—dirt, noise, and danger notwithstanding—was money. Even without wage parity, women earned more as factory workers than in their previous jobs. By 1945 at Willow Run, one-third of the women workers had experienced pay raises of 100 percent since the war began, compared to one-ninth of the men.

Though the prejudice against working women declined, or rather was suspended for the duration, one thing that did not change was the refusal to take full advantage of women's potential. Black women were discriminated against in war plants even more than white women, not only by employers but by workers. During one two-week period in Detroit there were five "hate" strikes occasioned by the employment of black women. Yet black women were more eager than whites to work. While the participation rate of all women in the Detroit work force rose from 29.5 percent in 1940 to 39.7 percent in 1944, the rate for nonwhite women went from 31.6 percent to 48.8 percent. By 1945 the percentage of employed black women who were in private household service had declined from 60 to 45. As a woman later said: "Hitler was the one that got us out of the white folks' kitchen."[17] They would not go back.

Even when labor was in shortest supply, little was done to relieve women of domestic duties that impaired their job effectiveness. In Seattle's war industries during 1943 women workers were more than twice as likely to be absent from work as men. The War Manpower Commission believed that 100,000 worker hours were lost per month in Detroit because women took days off to do their laundry. In Baltimore the quit rate for women workers was 6.16 percent, compared to 4.78 for men. If shopping and laundry services, hot take-out meals, and more and better nurseries had been more widely available, all these losses could have been cut. It would probably have made some difference too if women workers had been promoted and paid equally with men. In 1944 the average wage for working women was $31.21 per week compared to $54.65 for men. Even the high degree of unionization during wartime had no effect, union leaders developing little interest in the special problems of women.

When efforts were made to deal with women's entry into the industrial work force too often their quality was poor. Some factories hired female counselors, but in the absence of supporting services what they could do was painfully limited. Susan Laughlin, a counselor who had no special qualifications for the job except a sympathetic personality, recalled that she once arranged an abortion for a married woman who had been raped after passing out at an office party. More often she was called upon to deal with such problems as when "a girl had come in a bare midriff, and all the men were hitting themselves with hammers."[18] Mostly, however, counselors or "plant matrons" were expected to prevent women from having sex on company time.

On the other hand, there was some concern for safety problems peculiar to women workers—at least on the publicity level. In 1943 the War Production Board asked Veronica Lake, a popular movie star whose trademark long blonde hair fell over part of her face, to adopt a more conservative style. The problem, officialdom reported, was that 20,000 Lake imitators in defense plants were at risk of being caught by the hair in machinery. Miss Lake was cooperative, saying that she wore her hair up most of the time anyway, to keep it out of electric fans, the buttons of friendly men, revolving doors, and other hazards. "This request from the Government is not only a pleasure, it's a relief," she insisted patriotically.[19]

Given the stereotyping and the misogyny, and the mass media's habit of trivializing what they did, what is remarkable is that so many women did find jobs in defense plants. They were essential to the war effort—yet, like minorities, they could have contributed even more but for the prejudices against them. Here as well, American democracy had far to go and much to learn.

12

The Transformation of Everyday Life

The war changed everything except human needs and desires. Many once ordinary tasks became fiendishly difficult to perform. Numerous goods previously taken for granted all but disappeared, were replaced by inferior substitutes, or disappeared altogether. People got by as best they could and some discovered in the war a welcome degree of excitement. Most found it possible, despite shortages and censorship, to amuse themselves, taking their pleasure in ways that tell us much about the American people and what they considered important.

It seems fair to say that life on the homefront was most difficult for married women. A 48-hour week and long commutes were the rule for all workers, regardless of gender. Because so many goods and services—including household appliances and supplies, certain foodstuffs, domestic help, and medical care—were in short supply, wives and mothers, whether employed or not, had to devote more time to such activities as housework and getting their children to doctors. Shopping was further complicated by ration books and the need to go from store to store looking for scarce products.

Like their husbands, service wives could "take it" and did not let fear for their absent loved ones keep them from shouldering what often were heavy burdens. One Illinois mother was left to care for three small boys when her husband went overseas. She worked eight hours a day in a local canning factory, yet managed to run a Cub Scout troop, keep a victory garden, and put a hot meal on the table every night—if only tunafish casserole. When the fare prompted complaints she serenely replied, as every mother did in those years, "Think of the poor, starving children in Europe."[1]

Consumers had to return used toothpaste tubes in order to buy new ones, while tinfoil and cellophane simply disappeared—as did bobby pins, which were replaced by wooden toothpicks and thread. Mostly a drain, shopping could be adventuresome if you had the right kind of luck. In April 1945, Audrey Davis triumphantly wrote to her husband at sea:

> Honey, I'm a success. I got sheets! Such a time—went to four of the biggest stores first and was turned down cold. Finally ended up in the basement of J. C. Penney's . . . and saw some bedding so on the off-chance, I asked. The girl said, shhh, and sneaked into a back room and brought out some carefully wrapped—didn't even know what I had bought, until I got home. I felt like someone buying hooch during Prohibition.[2]

New clothes were devoid of elastic thread and webbing, metal buttons, zippers, hooks and eyes, silk, nylon, canvas, duck, and sometimes leather. Coats could not have pleats, gussets, bellows, yokes. A "victory suit," which carried economy to the point of eliminating lapels, was ruled out. To save wool, double-breasted suits could not be vested, and no suit could come with more than one pair of pants. Cloth could not go over cloth, eliminating trouser cuffs and patch pockets. Women's skirts were limited in length and circumference and certain dyes, especially greens and browns, were sometimes unavailable. Girdles, still everyday wear for women, had to be made of bone or piano wire instead of rubber. Shoes, when you could get them, came in six colors only, three of them shades of brown. Almost anything from coffee to canned goods, half the 1943 production went overseas, could run out without notice, cigarette shortages being a particular trial for a nation of smokers.

Irritation over rationing was continuous and so sharp that in 1943 Leon Henderson, one of the most brilliant New Dealers, had to resign as head of the Office of Price Administration even though he was, according to economist Kenneth Galbraith (who worked for him) one of the "unsung heroes of World War II" and a greater organizer than Albert Speer.[3] Urban Americans grew used to queuing up. Not only were food and clothing rationed, but the number of ration "points" required for specific items fluctuated, obliging every housewife to update her calculations on a weekly, or even daily, basis. Black-marketeering, especially in meat, aggravated shortages. For some, getting meat was a major preoccupation. One mother seems never to have written her son abroad without addressing the problem, although in the mandatory positive voice, as when she told him of her discovery that "Spam fried in butter makes a very tasty Easter dinner."[4]

A striking feature of the war effort, and a source of many problems, was the enormous increase in physical mobility. Including service personnel, 27.3 million people moved from their original county of residence. In the period 1935–40, an unusually active one, total civilian mobility had amounted to 2.8 million persons a year, but during each of the peak war years it averaged 4.7 million. With automobile use restricted, most long-distance travel was by train, putting enormous stress on the rail system and also the passengers—jammed into overcrowded and poorly maintained cars which were slow and often late due to breakdowns or from having been sidetracked for high-priority troop trains.

Difficult as travel became, starting over in strange places was worse. Adolescents were particularly affected, not only because relocation is emotionally most difficult at that age, but also because so many were going to work full-time or entering the services. In 1940 the number of employed persons between the ages of 14 and 17 was 1.7 million, whereas in 1944 it came to 4.61 million, of whom 1.43 million were part-time students. During World War II the decline in child labor was temporarily reversed, as also the trend toward longer periods of education. Total school attendance for the 14–19 age group in 1940 came to 9.159 million persons, whereas by 1944 it had fallen to 7.93 million. The number of boys and girls aged 14 to 18 who were employed rose from 1 million in 1940 to 2.9 million—the number of mill girls alone rising from 271,000 to 950,000.

By May 1943 some 1.8 million boys and girls under the age of 18 were employed by farms and factories. One Lockheed plant had 1,500 boys laboring as riveters and electricians and in metal fabrication and assembly work. According to the firm, two boys in four hours could accomplish more than an adult worker during a regular eight-hour shift.[5] For those children who remained in school full-time, life was harder, too, as teacher quality declined and class sizes went up. In Arkansas by the 1945–46 school year half the prewar teachers were gone and 72 percent of their replacements had completed less than a semester of college. During 1942–43, out of 170,000 Arkansas youngsters between the ages of 13 and 18 about 100,000 failed to attend school, some taking jobs but many because teachers were not available.

As might be expected, crime rates were strongly influenced by the physical and social changes affecting such a large number of people. Since so many young males, the principal crime-committing group, were in uniform, most crimes declined—except possibly rapes, though as they were seldom reported, the statistics are not very useful. But the number of murders, a more reliable figure, fell from 8,329 in 1940 to a low of 6,675 in 1944. Auto thefts went up in 1942 when new cars became unavailable, but the total number of reported crimes followed the same curve as murders, falling after 1940 and rising again only in 1945 when veterans began reentering civilian life. Suicides declined by a third, from about 19,000 in 1940 to some 13,000 four years later. It is an all too human irony that life seemed more worth living in wartime, the suicide rate showing this even more than the rising birthrate.

All these figures are evidence that—not to make light of its hardships—the war was more interesting than the peace had been. The war put an end to Depression America and gave meaning to ordinary lives, since all citizens were to some degree participants in the national effort. Everything changed, not always for the better, to be sure, but change of itself was often welcome after the monotonous years of austerity that followed the stock market crash of 1929. Many people were given jobs they never expected to get, saw places they would otherwise not have known, and lived richer lives.

People needed information and craved entertainment, making the mass media more important than in peacetime. Government's first worry was that the communication and entertainment media not interfere with the war effort. Thus, on December 16, 1941 FDR unveiled an Office of Censorship, headed by Byron Price of the Associated Press. Eventually 15,000 people would work under Price, even though there were no restrictions on news unrelated to the war effort. Much of their work involved monitoring the flood of messages pouring out of the country, which averaged 350,000 cables and telegrams and 25,000 telephone calls a week. News from the war zones was censored by the military, whose policies varied greatly from place to place as also over time. The Navy was most restrictive because of

Admiral King's notorious antipathy to giving out information. It was OWI's view that if King had his way, the only statement issued by the Navy Department would be the one announcing victory. In this spirit the Navy kept its losses at Pearl Harbor secret from the public, leading one journalist to write later that "Seven of the two ships sunk at Pearl Harbor have now rejoined the fleet."[6]

Censorship this extreme, together with press releases that distorted, or even falsified, actual conditions, could not fail to mislead the public. Where the Pacific was concerned, especially during the first two years, people were never prepared for American defeats owing to a steady flow of groundless official optimism. General MacArthur's communiqués were infamous throughout the Southwest Pacific for their self-serving falsehoods. Naval press releases, terrible at first, improved in 1944 when James Forrestal became secretary—for he feared, and quite rightly, that the Navy was losing its public relations battle with the Army and the Air Force. The Navy continued to suppress bad news as long as possible, while MacArthur never was weaned from his habit of treating the press release as a work of fiction. By contrast, while the news from Europe was censored and manipulated also, it was often both speedy and accurate. By 1943 the AAF in Europe was giving out the exact numbers of bombers lost, sometimes only hours after a raid and even when the losses were horrendous.

While the censors frequently exasperated newsmen, public complaints were rare. The media did not have an adversarial relationship with the armed forces. Reporters wanted to portray the war effort in a favorable light. When someone violated a guideline it was not usually for political reasons but out of an inability to resist a scoop. This blend of official censorship and self-censorship meant that the public's view of the war was shaped to fit the government's requirements. Even in 1942, when the military were experiencing their worst defeats, polls showed that the American people had great confidence in the Army and Navy. The distinguished historian Allan Nevins put it this way at the time. "Never had the American high command, in a long, arduous, and costly war, been less criticized."[7]

Since journalists were so restricted, the best war reporting was based not on press conferences and handouts, but on newsmen telling about their own experiences, or what they had learned from interviews. Ernie Pyle was the master of this form, which emphasized individuals and small groups. John Steinbeck claimed that Pyle's hold on public opinion made him more important than many generals. Still, there were limits of taste beyond which no one cared to go. The horrors of battle, the suffering of the wounded, were indescribable and, anyhow, not fit to print. These limitations did not result in Americans turning away from the press. Instead, the daily circulation of American newspapers rose from 42 million daily in 1941 to 46 million in 1944, despite a cut in newsprint. To meet the appetite for war news there were somewhere between 500 and 700 war correspondents, compared to about 100 in the previous war. *The New York Times* alone received 500,000 words of news a day, of which it published only about 125,000.

Much that appeared was not really news at all but rather efforts at boosting morale. Profiles of notable individuals fell into this category— usually general officers, but sometimes lower ranking men who had attracted public attention. An example of this was a long article on Lieutenant Colonel Philip J. Cochran, who was famous as the real life model of a cartoon character, "Flip Corkin" in "Terry and the Pirates," a popular strip drawn by Milton Caniff. If *Life* is to be believed, one can see why. A fighter squadron commander in North Africa, Cochran had 11 citations and 5 medals, and was therefore a genuine hero.

Cochran was a professional Irishman who wore a shamrock on his flying helmet and named all his planes "Shilalah." He was given to colorful speech as well. When asked if he dated nurses, he said that he preferred "hat-check chicks and show girls," which was not entirely true since he had an affair with the glamorous photographer Margaret Bourke-White (one of whose pictures of him appeared in *Life*). When asked after a visit to New York about his dates, he reported: "Most of the chicks I knew have gone to be welders."[8] His favorite songs were reported to be ditties popular in North Africa, such as "Dirty Gertie from Bizerte," "Stella the Belle of Fidella," and "I'm Dreaming of a White Mistress." While in training his squadron had mock air battles with another unit, which Cochran's charges always won because he had a "spotter chick" living near the other squadron's base who telephoned him whenever it took off. Despite heavy fighting and much heroism in North Africa, he had lost only two pilots. There was a lot more to the story than this, but the idea is clear enough. War could be fun as well as hell.

Radio was censored and limited in much the same way as newspapers, and thus, unlike the Vietnam War, World War II was experienced by the public at a distance and through filters of discretion and censorship. This is the view of hindsight, however, for at the time, radio enabled people to feel involved with current events as never before. Radio newsmen became highly professional, giving fewer facts than newspapers but with an immediacy that print could not rival. This was especially true of CBS, where Edward R. Murrow had put together the most brilliant team of broadcast journalists ever assembled. They had their work cut out for them because between Pearl Harbor and V-E Day about a third of network air time was given over to news.

Radio maintained high, even absurd, standards, perhaps because as the newest medium it felt insecure. NBC refused commercials for beer, wine, liquor, deodorants, depilatories, undertakers, and cemeteries. It insisted that anyone broadcasting after 6:00 P.M. wear evening clothes. That was only silly. More damaging was radio's rule that nothing could be prerecorded. This greatly handicapped broadcast journalists, since many events could not be aired as they happened because of time zone differences and because the technology did not yet exist for live transmissions from the field.

Newsreels, film documentaries, and to a lesser extent picture magazines such as *Life* and *Look* illustrated the war vividly. This, together with the huge amount of war reporting by journalists and broadcasters, made the public feel it was well-informed, which was certainly true compared to its experience in any previous war. Events on the homefront, from race riots to production bottlenecks, were fully covered by the press—so much so that, while American intelligence officers often had to guess about what was happening in Germany and Japan, the enemy could find out all it needed to know about American production by reading *Fortune* and *Business Week*. The public knew less about military operations, partly by reason of censorship but mostly because the press usually followed lines laid down by public relations officers. Yet even the Pentagon had its critics, and there were few aspects of the war that did not receive at least a few searching treatments. All this coverage helped make World War II the most absorbing of any twentieth century conflict.

The lack of official direction following OWI's cutback in 1943 posed no problems for the advertising industry, which had already adjusted to wartime conditions. In 1942 it formed the War Advertising Council, consisting of representatives of major ad agencies, large advertisers, and the media, all of which were already working with the OWI and other government agencies. By V-J Day the Council would have conducted more than 100 campaigns to sell war bonds, secure blood donations, conserve food, and inspire enlistments. The Council did not have to scratch for sponsors, because the Treasury ruled that corporations could deduct advertising costs from their taxable incomes, whether they had anything to sell or not. At the current rates this meant that government was actually footing up to 80 percent of the advertising bill, making the cost of keeping corporate names before the public negligible. It also enabled companies to promote the virtues of free enterprise and private ownership at the taxpayer's expense. This was in no sense controversial. Though liberals grumbled that the war was being sold like toothpaste, most Americans took war advertising for granted.

To progressives, leaving war information in private hands meant reaching down to the lowest common denominator. Yet the industry was probably right in saying that without its War Advertising Council things would have been even worse. It strove to reduce "brag" advertising in which a corporation praised itself excessively, political advertising, and advertising that was overly optimistic about the postwar world. This did not keep offensive ads from appearing. One, headed "Who's Afraid of the Big Focke–Wulf?" (a reference to Germany's best propeller-driven fighter plane), so antagonized American bomber crews that one group returned a copy to the offending corporation with the legend "I am" and their signatures inscribed on it. Also dubious were such ads as those of air-conditioning manufacturers who took credit for sulfa drugs and naval periscopes because they were made in air-conditioned facilities. Such ads were most prominent during the war's first year, declining thereafter, the War Advertising Council maintained, partly through its efforts.

Yet, however discreet ads might have been, and much advertising wasn't, there was something undignified about marketing the war effort. This being America, however, hopes for a tasteful and politically edifying call to arms were unrealistic. The United States was not inhabited chiefly by exemplary minorities, class conscious proletarians, and virtuous sons of the soil, as one might suppose from listening to politically motivated folk singers. Real Americans had conventional beliefs, few political ideas, and strong prejudices. They were delighted by commercial songs, movies, and radio programs—and the more sentimental, melodramatic, action-oriented, or comic they were, the better. Americans as a whole were not particularly sophisticated, but they were not fools either, so the war was fought in a commonsense and conventional way rather than according to right or left wing agendas.

This is not to acclaim the popular culture, which was as superficial—though not so vulgar—as it is today. But mass-produced, mass merchandised, commercialized entertainment was central to American life. Any great national enterprise had to accept this. The business of America was show business even then, so the war effort would be defined to a considerable extent by advertisers and merchandisers. There was no conspiracy to this end nor any failure of leadership. President Roosevelt stood on absolutely solid ground in believing that drumming up support for the emergency was best left to drummers. Their success in campaign after campaign was proof of that. So too was the popular demand for advertisements.

A magazine that offered uniformed subscribers abroad a choice between its regular edition, and a special one printed on light paper and containing no advertisements, received many letters specifically requesting the ads. "A survey in the South Pacific in the spring of '45 reported that advertising was among the most popular off duty reading wherever it was obtainable."[9] This reflected an essential truth: Advertising is the stuff of dreams for Americans, and never more so than in wartime.

The unofficial policy of business as usual made sense, within broad limits. Allowing the entertainment industry to carry on as before served valid purposes. As workers had fatter paychecks but could find less to buy, it was good for morale to allow them to patronize clubs and bars and movie theaters. Hollywood was rightly regarded as an essential industry, not only at home but on the fighting fronts to which new films were rushed immediately upon release. The pointlessness of enforcing austerity for its own sake became apparent in 1945 when James Byrnes banned horse racing, imposed an urban curfew, and took other steps to remind people that there was still a war on. The slight practical advantages resulting from such measures were far outweighed by the resulting backlash. In any case, shortages and inconveniences were sufficiently numerous to eliminate any chance that the war might slip from mind.

Though liberal activists failed to get the massive indoctrination campaign they wanted, government did make a limited number of propaganda movies, with instructive results. The best known propaganda films were created for the War Department by Frank

Capra, a successful Hollywood director remembered today for his fable *It's a Wonderful Life* starring Jimmy Stewart and Donna Reed. Capra's seven-picture series, called *Why We Fight*, was required viewing for every soldier who went overseas. The Army was so pleased with these films that it wanted to release them theatrically—thus taking over from Hollywood responsibility for illustrating the war. President Roosevelt, a Capra fan, liked the idea, but others responded coolly.

The film industry did not want the Army to go into competition with it. More importantly, the Office of War Information had an arm, called the Bureau of Motion Pictures, with a highly political agenda which *Why We Fight* disregarded. The BMP's Lowell Mellet told Roosevelt that Capra's first effort, *Prelude to War*, would induce "nervous hysteria" and leave audiences "bewildered rather than fired to a clear purpose."[10] The struggle raged from October 1942 until the following March, when OWI caved in after heavy pounding by Under Secretary of War Robert Patterson and other big guns. With a trailer calling it "the greatest gangster picture ever made," *Prelude to War* went into general distribution. Even though it won the 1942 Academy Award, *Prelude* failed at the box office, saving exhibitors from having to show the others.

This commercial flop was a popular referendum on government sponsored entertainment. Whereas in his own milieu Capra was noted for delightful comedies, like *It Happened One Night*, and dramas showing the little guy taking on the system, notably *Mr. Smith Goes to Washington*, his propaganda films were heavy handed and at times incomprehensible. The least coherent was *The Battle of China*, which begins with an historical sketch featuring such statements as that in their 4,000-year history, the Chinese "never waged a war of conquest." Much of the film's pseudohistory turns on a supposed Japanese blueprint for world conquest called the Tanaka Memorial, which is today regarded as an anti-Japanese hoax.[11] The whole narration is garbled at best, and, at worst, which is much of the time, it alternates between idealized portraits of the Chinese and scenes featuring what the narrator calls "blood-crazed Japs."

The Battle of Russia, regarded by some critics as the best in the series, committed similar crimes against history. Its opening scenes omit not only the Russian Revolution, but the Stalin–Hitler Pact, without which no account of the war in Europe made sense. Russia's catastrophic early defeats—in the first 13 months the Red Army sustained enormous casualties and had 4 million men taken prisoner—

are attributed to ingenious Soviet advance planning. The film's theory is that Nazi (always pronounced "gnatzi") forces were deliberately lured far into Russia so as to meet ever-thickening lines of resistance—which, if true, would certainly have made it the most self-punishing strategic defense ever conceived of in peacetime. Actually, Soviet planners had assumed that the first German attacks would fail, and be succeeded at once by a victorious Russian counteroffensive. The war of attrition was forced on them, not something they dreamed up in advance. *The Battle of Russia* has two parts, the second claiming to show that "there are no invincible armies against the determined will of free and united people." Except for the absence of references to Communism, which Capra loathed, his picture could have been made by the Soviets themselves—and did depend to a large degree on footage supplied by them.

Why We Fight illustrates what can happen when otherwise gifted individuals are assigned to make propaganda. The series is strident, cliché ridden, filled with slogans and heroic posturing. Despite some remarkably vivid combat footage, it now seems about as inspirational as a comic strip. To appreciate its lack of merit, one has only to contrast *Why We Fight* with the outstanding Hollywood propaganda film of the war, *Casablanca*, which succeeded, and still works today, because of not being overtly political. It has an anti-Nazi message to be sure, but one that is understated and woven skillfully into the plot. Touching at some points, stirring at others, *Casablanca* promoted the war effort by refusing to club its audience over the head. Typically, OWI could not see this, and kept *Casablanca* from being shown in North Africa, for fear of offending recently collaborationist Frenchmen.

Since *Casablanca* is unique, it cannot be held up as the model to which American moviemakers should have aspired. But a number of documentaries are evidence that well-presented information by itself could have a strong effect. William Wyler's *The Memphis Belle*, a film produced by OWI about the first B-17 to complete a tour of duty over Europe, falls into this category. Most of the combat documentaries were made by the armed forces themselves, aided by Hollywood directors and technical personnel. These include Commander John Ford's *The Battle of Midway*, *The Fighting Lady* (a carrier film that did well at the box office), and *To the Shores of Iwo Jima*.

The outstanding example is *The Battle of San Pietro*, directed and narrated by John Huston. Though its sound track, featuring the Army Air Forces Orchestra, The Mormon Tabernacle Choir, and the St. Brendan's Boys Choir, is excessive, *The Battle of San Pietro* matter-offactly describes the reasons for, and shows highlights of, a long fight to take a single village in Italy. Its cameramen went in with the troops, shooting scenes that are, in turn, spectacular and intimate. The narrator recites the chilling facts, which included the virtual destruction of a tank company and a casualty toll that was staggering in relation to the number of men committed—amounting in one regiment to a loss rate (1100) equal to its entire complement of riflemen. There are chilling sights as well, including rare shots of dead GIs being wrapped in mattress covers. Some officers did not want *The Battle of San Pietro* shown to troops in training for fear it would injure morale. General Marshall overruled them on the ground that knowing what awaited them could only lead the men to take their training more seriously. Whether it did or not, the film testifies to what could be accomplished when talent was given free rein.

Most of the 2,500 motion pictures that Hollywood turned out during World War II were simple entertainments. Hollywood never stopped making comedies and musicals. After Pearl Harbor war films increased in number, 1943 being the peak year, but by 1944 service pictures were becoming fewer and better. The early war films were often absurd. *Air Force*, a representative moral and artistic disaster, chronicled the adventures of an ethnically balanced B-17 crew that arrived in Hawaii just as the Japanese bombed Pearl Harbor. *Air Force* refers to numerous incidents of sabotage and treachery by Japanese–Americans, even though in real life none had taken place. A new low in cinema was reached when, after destroying an enemy aircraft, a gunner cried out "Fried Jap going down!"[12] The historical facts were all wrong, too, as when Army bombers won what appeared to be the Battle of Midway—an engagement during which, so far as is known, not a single bomb from a Flying Fortress struck an enemy ship.

Except for *Casablanca*, most of the contemporary war films still worth seeing were produced in 1944 and 1945. *Lifeboat*, a political allegory by Alfred Hitchcock about survivors of an engagement at sea who first rescue, and then are forced to kill, a U-boat commander, aroused controversy since, as Bosley Crowther of *The New York Times* put it, Hitchcock "made the Nazi out to be a champion and the democrats a bunch of bungling dopes."[13] Crowther, an exceptionally literal-minded person, as usual missed the point, which was to show both the strengths and weaknesses of democracy when faced with Nazism. The most realistic and moving film was *The Story of G.I. Joe*. Based on a column by Ernie Pyle, it vividly portrayed the infantryman's way of life and death. However, most of the best films about World War II were produced afterward—long afterward in the case of *Patton* and *A Bridge Too Far*, which are among the few that seem likely to last.

Most of the wartime films that people still enjoy are not about the war. They include *The Man Who Came to Dinner*; such Preston Sturgis satires as *Sullivan's Travels* and *The Miracle of Morgan's Creek*; *National Velvet* in which a very young and very beautiful Elizabeth Taylor loves a horse, Bing Crosby's *Going My Way*, and *Yankee Doodle Dandy*, marked by James Cagney's exuberant portrayal of George M. Cohan. They are films that people greatly enjoyed at the time as well, showing a certain consistency of taste.

Because of its great impact, there was never any question of leaving Hollywood entirely to its own devices during the war. While attempts to make propaganda movies failed, liberals did manage to influence the content of feature films all the same. Their efforts give some idea of what a massive propaganda effort would have been like. OWI's "Government Information Manual for the Motion Picture Industry" shows that it had enlisted in the people's war. Because this was a war for democracy, Soviet despotism had to be overlooked. The official line was that when peace came it would be built on the Four Freedoms— freedom of speech and religion, freedom from want and fear. In this struggle all races, like all anti-fascist nations, were of course equal. The facts notwithstanding, OWI's Bureau of Motion Pictures wanted movies to portray the services as if they were racially integrated. Hollywood's job, in short, was to promote mild reforms and an internationalist foreign policy by painting the world not in its true colors but as OWI would have it.

BMP thus created a second code alongside that of the existing Production Code Administration, which governed sex, violence, and language in films. Whereas PCA sought to keep forbidden sights and themes out of movies, BMP wanted to put uplift in while also changing films that might send out politically incorrect messages. It tried to block the showing of *Little Tokyo, U.S.A.* for portraying Japanese–Americans as potentially disloyal—even though this was the government's rationale for imprisoning them. After failing to change *Little Tokyo, U.S.A.* or limit its distribution, BMP sought to influence films before they went into production. The studios accused it of practicing censorship, but at first BMP was not a very effective censor. It lacked power, and it was up against long-standing relationships between the military and the studios. Hollywood had always needed the armed forces' help in producing service pictures and was not averse to representing them on their own terms by way of compensation

Congress unwittingly gave OWI a hold over the movie industry. When funding for OWI's Domestic Branch was slashed in 1943, BMP was transferred to the Foreign Branch. There it awarded export licenses to American pictures, a right no one disputed as America's image overseas was important to the war effort. Even before Pearl Harbor, and more so as growing numbers of people were liberated from Axis rule, foreign markets mattered. Frequently overseas ticket sales provided a film's margin of profit. By threatening to deny Hollywood the privilege of exporting a film, OWI liberals acquired the means of shaping it, within certain limits. An early example of this was King Vidor's *An American Romance*, which started out as a tribute to rugged individualism in the steel industry. After the BMP was finished it became a hymn of praise to labor–management cooperation.

Virtually all the films that BMP liked had the same didactic character. The ones they loved most tended to be both preachy and awful. China was caricatured in such films as *Dragon Seed*, believed by OWI to show the truth about Chinese democracy and the people's war. Even James Agee, a writer and critic with leftist tendencies, described it as "unimaginably bad." However, the premier example of government interference was *Mission to Moscow*, based on the memoir by former Ambassador Joseph Davies. Even more than his book, the film whitewashed the great terror of the 1930s during which Stalin put to death literally millions of Soviet citizens, glorified the great butcher himself, distorted Soviet history, and committed numerous other assaults upon truth, decency, and, for that matter, common knowledge.

The primary responsibility for this fraud is suspected to be President Roosevelt, whose political aims it furthered and who authorized Davies to show it to Stalin, who in turn selected it as one of only 24 American pictures to be shown in Russia during the war, and no wonder. Though Jack Warner filmed *Mission to Moscow*, it so perfectly embodied OWI's view of the people's war that it could have been made in-house. The great philosopher John Dewey called it "the first instance in our country of totalitarian propaganda for mass consumption," which may have invested the film with more dignity than it warranted but definitely captured its spirit. Luckily, *Mission to Moscow* failed at the box office, and the government never tried as hard again to determine the content of a feature film.[14]

On the credit side, BMP tried to get Hollywood to represent the enemy as something less than a monolith of evil, having some success where Germans were concerned. But the national hatred of Japan was so great that filmmakers refused to portray Japanese characters as anything other than subhuman. BMP also failed to change Hollywood's depiction of blacks. A study made in 1945 found that, of 100 black performances in movies, 75 reflected the usual stereotypes, 13 were neutral, and only 12 showed black characters in a new and more positive light.

The interaction between Hollywood's pursuit of gain and OWI liberalism did not have fruitful consequences. War presented the studios with a large captive market, which they exploited by cranking out product as usual. BMP enjoyed, in the end, only modest success. It could not force the studios to make many progressive films. Those it influenced most were not only bad as a rule but often failed at the box office. Like *Why We Fight*, they showed that the wisest course was to avoid propaganda, however well-intentioned.

With few exceptions, government made little effort to control the vast popular music industry to whose sounds the war was often fought. Aboard ship, behind the front, and everywhere at home, radio and the 78 RPM record player were ubiquitous, despite a shortage of shellac, from which phonograph records were made, and the banning of recorded music for public performances in 1942 by the hated James C. Petrillo of the American Federation of Musicians. His was a vain effort to save the studio band from the technology that was destroying it. While studio bands were already in trouble, the great "Big Bands," such as those led by Benny Goodman, the Dorsey brothers, Glenn Miller, and Harry James, still flourished. Most had been formed during the "swing era" of the 1930s and brought the art of popular music to its highest level—a pinnacle never since reached.

While before the war a hit song might sell 400,000 copies of sheet music, during it sales of 600,000 copies became usual. In 1944, sheet music sales were up 25 percent from the previous year. Though this was still the golden age of popular music, to which composers like George Gershwin and Cole Porter had made superb contributions, most hits reflected considerably lower tastes. Not many survived the era, war songs being among the most forgettable. Who wishes to remember "Goodbye, Mamma, I'm Off to Yokohama," "The Japs Haven't Got a Chinaman's Chance," or "When Those Little Yellow Bellies Meet the Cohens and the Kelleys"?

In the same vein was the "Remember Pearl Harbor March" performed by Sammy Kaye. But Frank Loesser had a much greater success with "Praise the Lord and Pass the Ammunition," based on an incident during the attack on Pearl Harbor when a chaplain ("sky pilot") supposedly manned an antiaircraft gun. In reality, Captain William A. McGuire didn't remember speaking the immortal words, and had been passing ammunition himself rather than manning the gun. Never mind, OWI loved it, going so far as to ask radio stations not to overplay the song and thereby shorten its life. The most popular war song, "Der Führer's Face," was kept off radio for a time because censors judged it to be scatological, owing to sound effects that suggested what should be done in Hitler's face.

Later songs became more sentimental, an example being Irving Berlin's "I Left My Heart at the Stage Door Canteen." The most played song composed during the war was Berlin's 1942 "White Christmas," introduced by Bing Crosby in the movie *Holiday Inn*. It was the first song in a decade to sell more than 1 million copies of sheet music and led the Hit Parade—music's equivalent of a Nielson rating—nine times, rebounding again during the Christmases of 1943 and 1944. Songs like this meant much to battle worn troops, as well as to the folks back home. One of the strongest collective memories of Company K of the 84th Infantry Division is associated with this song. Just before the Christmas season of 1944, K Company had nearly been wiped out. During a brief period off the line, the survivors found a piano in a deserted German village. It was brought out into the street, and a company pianist played "White Christmas," bringing tears to eyes that had seen too much.

Apart from fear itself, nostalgia—if one includes in this the separation of young lovers—seems to have been the nation's strongest emotion during World War II and produced the best music. The most popular song of 1944 was the touching "I'll Be Seeing You," and that same year "I'll Be Home for Christmas" (with its melancholy coda, "if only in my dreams") was a hit also. Even novelty songs could elicit a somber mood. Forty-six years later, a writer recalled that on his first crossing of the North Atlantic in 1943, at the height of the submarine war, another young sailor played "Juke Box Saturday Night" over and over on his phonograph. Though it is a bouncy number, being at sea in a dangerous time gave it a "dirge-like quality" to that listener.[15] This must have been a common experience.

Casablanca notwithstanding, Hollywood made its greatest contribution to the war effort simply by continuing to make films as usual. In addition, some stars visited the troops—notably the comedian Bob Hope, who went everywhere, year after year, accumulating more travel time than any other performer. When he was not abroad, Hope performed at training camps and other military installations, broadcasting his radio show from a studio only a handful of times. By one calculation, 3,865 performers made 47,330 appearances in 6,810 events staged for servicemen. The heaviest load was borne by 138 artists who collectively played 9,187 days overseas.

A handful of male leads served even more directly by entering the armed forces, joining the one-fourth of all male studio employees who went to war. Colonel Jimmy Stewart, who had enlisted as a private, led a squadron of heavy bombers—the most important combat position held by anyone from Hollywood. Still, with all due respect to Stewart, a genuine hero, there was much to be said for keeping the stars in show business. It was rightly argued at the time that their contribution to national morale was more valuable than anything they could do as soldiers—unless, like Captain Ronald Reagan, they continued to make movies even though technically in the service.

At that time, movies were still the most important form of entertainment and had a greater hold on the public than can be imagined today. Television fills up many more hours on a daily basis than movies ever did. Partly because of that, viewing TV is a very different experience from what going to the movies once was. Being so much a part of everyday life makes TV ordinary, too—video performers coming to seem almost like family members. Thanks to talk shows, movie actors now enter our living rooms, too. But before TV, movie stars were larger than life, distant images on a silver screen, icons, idols, seen at most three or four times a year, having no real competition for the hearts and minds of the public. Hollywood was, in Hortense Powdermaker's memorable phrase, "the dream factory," and shaped the national imagination as no other medium could.

The war forced many changes in habits and mores, affecting everything from drinking patterns to sex. Bootleggers and hijackers prospered as a result of alcohol shortages. Canned beer disappeared, and even bottled beer was not always available. In 1944 whiskey, then the most popular hard liquor, practically vanished. Distillers thought they had a five-year supply of whiskey on hand when they converted to making industrial alcohol, not knowing that consumption would rise from 140 million gallons in 1941 to 190 million gallons in 1942. The gap was filled, in part at least, by scotch whiskey, which the British filled returning Lend-Lease cargo ships with to ease their balance of payments problem. This vast swilling only partially includes what was consumed by Americans overseas—who, it is said, rarely passed up a chance to get drunk and frequently carried liquor into battle. In 1917, many states were already dry and national prohibition soon followed, but in the Second World War America floated to victory on a tidal wave of booze.

Inevitably, the war affected sexual behavior. One study made soon afterward concluded that it was marked by an increase in promiscuity and a concurrent decline in prostitution.[16] On the basis of very incomplete reports, the Children's Bureau found that of some 23,965 girls processed by courts, 22 percent had been accused of running away from home, another 22 percent of being "ungovernable," and 17 percent of having committed sex offenses. The double standard being alive and well, the rates for boys were 6 percent, 5 percent, and 3 percent respectively. Many communities, especially those near training camps and military bases, made strenuous efforts to reduce prostitution. A large number, some 650, claimed to have closed down their red-light districts. On the basis of nearly 2,000 investigations, the American Social Hygiene Association concurred, finding that the percentage of communities in which prostitution was blatant or obvious declined during the war from 32.9 percent to 3.8 percent. Considering all the fuss and the enormous concentration of single men in training camps, the number of arrests for prostitution went up only slightly, from 2,494 men and 6,493 women in 1940 to 3,138 men and 7,821 women in 1945.

The venereal disease rate among men in uniform was much lower than during World War I. Observers believed that, again unlike in World War I, most social diseases were spread less by prostitutes than by enthusiastic amateurs. This was the impression of Army doctors, and of journalists too, who blamed teenage "victory girls," "khaki-wackies," and "cuddle bunnies" for infecting servicemen. On that basis the Army campaigned against the "promiscuous girl," male promiscuity being, as usual, taken for granted.

The above generalizations and the figures used to support them proved mostly fictitious. It is unlikely that prostitution declined much, if at all, simply because brothels were closed. There is little evidence to suggest that hookers took up war work. Most probably relocated to streets, cars, and other less formal places of business. The distinction always made at the time between victory girls and prostitutes was largely bogus, since most prostitutes were youthful. Of the first 100 arrested under the May Act, a federal statute banning prostitution near military sites, two-thirds were 26 years of age or younger. Given the May Act, it made sense for prostitutes to dress like other young women. Infected soldiers could expect at least a little more sympathy if they claimed that mutual attraction, rather than commercialized lust, had guided their offending members. As the sexual revolution had not taken place, chances were, to most soldiers' regret, that the victory girl was often a prostitute. Paul Fussell's chapter title sums things up: "Drinking Far Too Much, Copulating Too Little."[17]

Official confusion, prudery, and sexism notwithstanding, venereal disease, or "VD," remained a problem for most of the war, as penicillin did not become widely available until 1944. This forced the military to fall back on such time-tested methods as propaganda campaigns designed to create "syphilophobia," thereby frightening men into abstinence. Except for providing the troops with innocent merriment, such efforts accomplished little, for, as one medical officer pointed out, "The sex act cannot be made unpopular."[18] On the subject of chastity, which he tried to encourage, former boxing champion Gene Tunney remarked dryly "Men don't get medals for practicing it."[19] The simple truth was that troops facing death in battle could not be made to fear a curable social disease.

Rejecting inductees found to be suffering from syphilis was not workable either, for, of the first 2 million men inducted, 48 in every 1,000 had it. Among blacks the rate was 272 per thousand. Most black inductees were from the South, and Southern males had a VD rate four times that of Northerners. Early in 1942, the Army began treating infected men instead of declaring them 4-F (physically unfit for induction). By 1945, 170,000 inductees had been cured of syphilis, a process individually taking about 10 days before antibiotics became available. Prophylaxis was effective, too. Once the military conceded that enlisted men could not be scared away from sex, hundreds of prophylactic stations were established in the United States to chemically treat men after intercourse. Large quantities of condoms were passed out as well, some 50 million a month, and were so popular that by the end of the war demand outstripped supply.

Although the common sense approach to social disease offended religious groups, the military could not afford to give it up. Thus, while in 1940 the VD rate for the Army was 42.5 cases for every thousand men, by 1943 it had fallen to 24. For the entire war it came to 37 per thousand, about the same rate as among civilians. In 1940, for every

1,000 soldiers, 1,278 days a year were lost on account of VD but by 1943 only 368. This was a public-health victory whatever its spiritual defects.

The claims of morality were not wholly ignored. Chaplains overseas monitored USO shows and unhesitatingly protested to the War Department if female entertainers exposed too much skin. Carole Landis was criticized for kissing too many GIs in her 1944 Pacific tour. Comedians were faulted for telling blue jokes. Such censorship did nothing for troop morale, however uplifting to moralists.

Marriage was far and away the most important solution young men and women found to the sexual problems of wartime. After Pearl Harbor the marriage rate jumped by 20 percent and by V-J Day one serviceman in three was married. Most of these marriages lasted, too. After peaking in 1946, the divorce rate steadily declined until the postwar divorce rate was considerably below that of the thirties. The war generation partied when it could, sometimes with abandon. But, in the end, what men and women alike wanted was home, marriage, family. In the postwar world their dreams would come true.

Compared to the other warring nations, America had it easy, yet such things are relative. By comparison with peacetime, war brought hardships to Americans in their roles as workers, commuters, consumers, and travelers. These were accepted with many complaints, that being the American way. The right to complain was in fact part of what Americans fought for. Far from hindering the war effort, grousing made its unpleasant aspects easier to bear. So did the vast amount of commercial entertainment, harmless enough in ordinary times but a blessing during the war.

The flood of information, most of it true so far as it went, which involved people in far-off events and reminded them of why they were doing without many familiar items, was especially valuable. That this was accompanied by much commercial hype made little difference. That war propaganda was reasonably accurate and not too heavy-handed mattered a lot. America stayed democratic during the war, one of its great achievements. For this the media deserves a share of the credit.

13

Two Wars in the Pacific

Guadalcanal to Luzon

The war against Japan was far more political than that against Germany. Until near the end, when Eisenhower caught up to him, Douglas MacArthur was the only commander to be labeled a presidential contender. More momentously, and unlike in Europe where they got along well enough, Pacific issues intensified the Army–Navy competition. That was political, too, as each service had allies in Congress and sought public support for its plans. The question was, therefore, whether America should allow strategy to be determined by politics. To that question the answer was yes. President Roosevelt would not make hard choices in the Pacific, and no one else could. This failure of American democracy must be laid at the President's door. He was the commander in chief, and on many occasions did not hesitate to exercise his authority. Yet, most of the important issues of the Pacific War would be decided not on their merits but as a result of interservice bargaining.

The most important failure to result from this unhappy arrangement concerned the issue of supreme command, which Roosevelt had allowed the services to evade altogether by splitting up the Pacific between them. No critic has written more scathingly of this decision than General MacArthur, who in his memoirs said it "resulted in divided effort ... waste, diffusion, duplication of force, and the

The Southwest Pacific Campaign, August 1942

All dates are 1943 unless otherwise stated

Miles
0   200

SOLOMON ISLANDS

MALAITA
Florida
7 Aug '42
SANTA ISABEL
GUADALCANAL
21 Feb '43
Russell Islands
CHOISEUL
15 Aug
New Georgia
30 June
Rendova
2 July
BOUGAINVILLE
27 Oct
Vella Lavella
Treasury Islands
Empress Augusta Bay
1 Nov '43
SOLOMON SEA

NEW IRELAND
GREEN
15 Feb '44

Kavieng
St Matthias Islands
20 Mar '44

Rabaul
NEW BRITAIN
C. Gloucester
15 Dec

Woodlark
Trobriand Islands
Occupied
30 June '43

MANUS
15 Mar '44
Los Negros
29 Feb '44

Long
26 Dec '43
Arawe
22 Sep
Finschhafen
4 Sep
Lae
30 June '43
Salamaua

Nov '42
Goodenough
Buna
22 Jan '43
Gona

NORTHEAST NEW GUINEA
Wewak

PAPUA
Port Moresby
6 Aug '42
GULF OF PAPUA

CORAL SEA

consequent extension of the war, with added casualties and cost." Lest the point be missed, he noted that in consequence "Many a man lies in his grave today who could have been saved."[1] This was, as usual, self-serving, for MacArthur believed that he should have been the supreme commander and his strategy adopted. But that MacArthur was always subjective does not mean he was always wrong. Few outsiders believed that separating command in the Pacific between MacArthur and Nimitz was a sound military decision.

Once MacArthur became a national hero Roosevelt had to give him a major assignment. But to make him commander of the entire Pacific War entailed running severe political risks. It would automatically improve MacArthur's chances of becoming a presidential candidate. It would infuriate the Navy and its backers. Conversely, because of his seniority and status as the number one national hero, it was unthinkable that MacArthur take orders from an unknown youngster like Nimitz (55 years of age in 1942, five years younger than MacArthur). Given these constraints, a theater of his own was the politically perfect solution. MacArthur would be supreme in his corner of the world, while the rest of the broad Pacific would be a playground for the Navy.

What made this decision dubious was less its cynicism than that MacArthur's theater was the best place for a counteroffensive. King had seen this at once, proposing as early as March 2, 1942 "a step-by-step general advance . . . through the New Hebrides, Solomons and Bismarcks."[2] Though he was not yet looking that far ahead, such an advance would logically include moving up New Guinea's coast and on to the Philippines—the path MacArthur ultimately followed. After these tempting targets were assigned to the Southwest Pacific Area (SWPA), the Navy had to come up with a separate strategy to justify both the division of command and the big ships it had on order. This would seem to explain the Central Pacific drive to which the Navy devoted most of its assets.

As MacArthur already had troops fighting in New Guinea, the Navy needed a stopgap to keep it in the public eye while it geared up for its major offensives. This explains Guadalcanal and the Solomons. Since little escaped his watchful eye, one has to assume that Roosevelt understood the basis on which these plans were being laid. Politically the outcome worked to his advantage, one reason for not intervening. But these campaigns would be so wastefully managed that it is hard to avoid the conclusion that, at bottom, Roosevelt did not care about the Pacific War so long as it didn't threaten the fighting in Europe.

Because it never quite did, Roosevelt never felt compelled to make the services come together.

Events sometimes forced America's hand, particularly at first. The Battle of the Coral Sea in May 1942 had not put an end to Japan's activity in the South and Southwest Pacific Areas. Japan's Navy was consolidating its hold on the Solomon Islands even as Army leaders were contemplating further moves in New Guinea, where they were dug in on the north shore of the Papuan Peninsula. Japan was overextended and probably lacked the means to invade Australia. But the Allies could not be sure of this, and Australia's strategic importance meant that it had to be protected—the question being by which armed service. Most Japanese installations fell within MacArthur's Southwest Pacific Area, but to seize or neutralize these bases would require naval support and Admiral King would not allow the Army to control his fast carriers.

The Joint Chiefs struggled over this until they arrived at an ingenious compromise. The effort to protect Australia was divided into three parts or "tasks." Task One was to establish a position in the southern Solomons. As this would require an amphibious landing which, at that time, only the Navy could mount, its South Pacific Area was moved one degree west to include these islands. Task Two would be an Army advance along the northeast coast of New Guinea, concurrent with a naval drive up the Solomons. Task Three was to be an assault on Rabaul, Japan's great air and naval base on New Britain from which it controlled the Solomons and the Bismarck Archipelago. Tasks Two and Three would be under MacArthur's command, with the JCS determining force composition and timing.

Turf having been staked out and honor preserved, King was eager to seize Guadalcanal (codenamed Cactus) in the Solomons, where a Japanese airfield was under construction. MacArthur favored doing so as well, for operations in the Navy's South Pacific Area supported his own, unlike those in the subsequent Central Pacific campaigns which were too far away to help him. The War Department reluctantly went along, despite its suspicion that the Navy was too weak to mount such an offensive and would soon be calling for assistance. The JCS ordered Operation Watchtower, assaults on Tulagi and Guadalcanal Islands, to commence in early August 1942. Just as the Army feared, King was barely able to patch together an expeditionary force.

Operation Shoestring, as participants called it, consisted of three

The Pacific Campaign: The Advances Across the Pacific, November 1943–May 1944

CHINA

BURMA

SIAM

FRENCH INDOCHINA

Singapore

BORNEO

Philippine Islands

JAPAN

PACIFIC OCEAN

Caroline Islands

☩ Truk

Gilbert Islands

Makin

21 Nov '43 Tarawa

Marshall Islands

31 Jan '44

Kwajalein

17 Feb '44

Enwetok

Solomon Islands

15 Feb '44

Green

Rabaul

20 Mar

St Matthias Is

2 Jan '44

Admiralty Is

New Britain

29 Feb

Saidor

Madang

NORTHEAST NEW GUINEA

PAPUA

Guadalcanal

27 April

17 May

Sarmi

NETHERLANDS NEW GUINEA

27 May

Biak

DUTCH EAST INDIES

AUSTRALIA

CORAL SEA

INDIAN OCEAN

Miles

0   800

elements. Its landing party was built around the First Marine Division, which was not yet fully trained, or combat-loaded. The invasion fleet included three of the Navy's four remaining carriers, under the command of Admiral Frank Jack Fletcher, who had let the Marines down at Wake and would do so again in the Solomons. Amphibious Force South Pacific, the vessels transporting the First Marines and their gear, was commanded by Rear Admiral Richmond Kelly Turner, formerly a planner on King's staff and an alcoholic who was known as "terrible" Turner because of his ferocious temper and abusive language. Widely feared and despised as an individual, he would nevertheless become the Navy's leading expert on amphibious operations.

Watchtower nearly failed at the start because of Fletcher's lack of faith in it and his fear of losing carriers, which led him to sail away 36 hours after the Marines had landed and before they were half unloaded. He left only cruisers and destroyers to defend the invasion force. Fletcher's career never recovered from this, because, even as he fled, Japanese heavy cruisers were storming down the "Slot" formed by the Solomon Islands. At 1:30 A.M. on August 9 they took the Allied cruisers by surprise, destroying four—three American and one Australian. The Battle of Savo Island was the U.S. Navy's worst defeat at sea and did much to make the Guadalcanal campaign a prolonged nightmare. Since Turner now had no air cover, Amphibious Force South Pacific weighed anchor at noon, leaving the Marines stranded.

As the Allies were stretched so thin, Watchtower might have ended disastrously but for a stroke of luck. The Japanese had nearly finished their airfield on Guadalcanal, which on August 20 received 19 American fighters and 12 dive bombers, the beginnings of the "Cactus Air Force." Its planes controlled the air and sea by day, confining the enemy to night attacks and limited, high-speed, nocturnal supply runs. This "Tokyo Express" enabled Japanese troops to keep fighting on Guadalcanal, but in the race to build up their respective forces Japan would be the loser.

Watchtower was a mistake all the same, for if King believed that by forcing the operation on Marshall he had a guarantee of boundless support, he was seriously mistaken. Watchtower had to compete not only with MacArthur's theater but with the North African campaign as well. Guadalcanal might have been lost if Japan had made a maximum effort, but instead the Japanese reinforced piecemeal, frittering away their troops. Even so, as a direct result of Watchtower, the Navy was reduced at one point to a single carrier in the Pacific. King won his gamble in the end, thus retaining his job—to the despair of many. Even naval officers frequently were of the same opinion as Brigadier General Dwight D. Eisenhower, who as Marshall's chief planner had frequent contacts with King. In his diary Eisenhower wrote "One thing that might help win this war is to get someone to shoot King."[3]

To compound the Allies' problems, on July 22, at the same time as the Navy was preparing to invade Guadalcanal, 16,000 Japanese troops landed at Buna on the north coast of Papua, threatening Australia. Their objective was Port Moresby, which had been denied Japan by the Battle of the Coral Sea. If the Papuan Peninsula were level, it would have been easy to take, for only a handful of Australian soldiers stood between the Japanese and Port Moresby. What made its defense possible were the Owen Stanley Mountains, which rise to a height of 13,000 feet from their roots in the steaming jungle. The Kokoda Trail over the mountains was only a path, adequate for barefoot natives but not for armed soldiers. Japanese troops who landed at Gona and Buna on the Solomon Sea were obliged to march from tropical heat and filth to freezing mountain passes. For Australians, the Kokoda Trail was a calvary, too, but they stubbornly defended it yard by yard despite appalling hardships.

All who fought in New Guinea were tormented by its horrors, the perils of the jungle being outweighed by "jungle rot," dreadful ulcers that formed all over their bodies, clouds of insects whose bites quickly became festering sores, leeches that attached themselves to genitals and rectums, and such diseases as malaria and dysentery, which struck down five men for every one wounded. But the Australians hung on, and their gallantry and sacrifice paid off. They occupied Milne Bay at the tip of Papua and held it, preventing Japanese flanking movements. They slowed the Japanese drive on Port Moresby as well, which became weaker as it advanced because the enemy could not bring up enough supplies over the terrible mountains. Meanwhile, the Australians had a shortening tail, and as more men and supplies were fed into it they became progressively stronger. The enemy was stopped 25 miles from Port Moresby, then gradually driven back upon supply lines so slim that by October Japanese soldiers on the Kokoda Trail had been reduced to cannibalism.

These two campaigns distorted the entire Pacific War. Guadalcanal had the greatest effect, because Australia supplied men and munitions to MacArthur and so was a logistical as well as a strategic asset. However, everything required in the Solomons had to be sent from home at incredible expense in shipping. This drain was all the more exasperating because, unlike the threat in New Guinea, enemy operations in the Solomons did not endanger Australia and could have been postponed, or avoided altogether. Japan's generals had not even known at first that the Imperial Japanese Navy was building an airfield on Guadalcanal, and resented having to send troops there when it came under attack.

The U.S. Army was similarly dismayed because Admiral King was soon making extravagant demands upon it. He had forced the operation on Marshall by threatening to seize Tulagi, at first considered more important than Guadalcanal, with naval power alone if the Army did not assist him. However, when the fighting started, he immediately began calling for land-based air support. King later said that the Battle of Savo Island was the blackest day of the war for him. After Savo, which showed that the Navy had overreached itself, King's demands became relentless. To hold this island would cost America 24 ships and make the waters between it and Savo and the Florida Islands ("Ironbottom Sound" to Allied sailors) the largest naval graveyard of the war.

Though Marshall refused to be bullied, he understood that having committed itself in the Solomons, America could not back out. While less important than New Guinea, Guadalcanal became more urgent precisely because the Navy was so close to defeat. Whatever it took to hold on would have to be provided, for the time being at MacArthur's expense, over the long run at Eisenhower's. At the end of 1942 there would be more American troops in the Pacific than in North Africa and Britain combined, 460,000 compared with 380,000, in addition to 19 of 66 overseas air groups.

The fight to secure Guadalcanal would last for six months and involve six major naval engagements, the loss of six Allied heavy cruisers and two fleet carriers, and the commitment of 60,000 soldiers and Marines. For four of those months the Marines would be partially isolated, dependent upon a handful of pilots and a few blockade-runners. The Marines hung on by their fingertips, inspiring James Michener to compare the Canal to Valley Forge and Shiloh. When the battle was over, America would be firmly committed to an offensive strategy against Japan that would occupy millions of men and leave Eisenhower with barely enough troops to maintain the Western Front.

The Navy's alternative to inventing a new strategy was regaining control of the old one. Thus, when Marshall began pressing the Navy to honor its July agreement according to which MacArthur would command Tasks Two and Three, its response was to propose that strategic command for the entire Pacific be vested in Admiral Nimitz. The ensuing debate lasted four months and ended in the usual stalemate. King then gave up and secured permission for a Central Pacific offensive. In April the Joint U.S. Strategic Committee (the planning arm of the JCS) recommended that Japan be invaded after an advance across Micronesia, which would make the Navy the premier service with first claim upon scarce resources. The proposal was accepted by the JCS in May and forced upon Britain at the Trident conference in Washington.

But Australia could not be abandoned, nor MacArthur's men left to rot. Thus, at the same time as Nimitz was authorized to take the Gilbert Islands, Operation Cartwheel started up. It was to implement Task One by taking a series of steps up the Solomons and toward the Bismarcks, isolating heavily fortified Rabaul. Task Three, the plan to storm Rabaul, now began to fade away as planners considered blockading and neutralizing it from the air, a tactic which would free up resources for the Gilberts.

MacArthur was predictably furious. He had been denied supreme command, and his plan to liberate the Philippines was now to be delayed—perhaps even forestalled—by the Navy's Central Pacific operations. He was not going to be able to assault Rabaul, either, a fixation with him for a long time, though later he decided that bypassing Rabaul was a great idea and took credit for it. Adding injury to injury, he was also to be denied the use of at least one Marine division, and possibly two, the only American infantry trained to assault enemy beaches. He would be last in line when the Navy distributed the specialized landing vessels that were critical to amphibious attacks. The order of priority for the all important Landing Ships Tank would be Central Pacific first, Admiral Halsey's South Pacific Area second, and SWPA a distant last.

Not only would MacArthur's campaigns be impaired, but the South Pacific Area, which belonged to the Navy and had already cost many lives, would be shortchanged also. This was vividly pointed up by the fall carrier raids on Rabaul. As part of Operation Cartwheel (the multiple advances on the Bismarcks), Bougainville in the Solomons was invaded by Halsey's forces on November 1, 1943. The Japanese first sought to prevent the landings by attacking the invasion fleet with four cruisers and six destroyers. They were driven off by an American task force composed of four new light cruisers and eight destroyers. The Japanese then sent down a large force from its main fleet anchorage in Truk. Codebreakers in Hawaii decrypted the order, warning Halsey that seven heavy and one light cruisers, plus four destroyers, were making for Rabaul, which would put them within easy striking distance of his landing site in Empress Augusta Bay.

Halsey had no battleships or heavy cruisers with which to protect his invasion force, as every available capital ship had been assigned to the Gilberts operation. What he did have on temporary loan were the fast carriers *Saratoga* and *Princeton*. Carrier planes had never attacked a Japanese base as strong as Rabaul, which was believed to have 150 aircraft besides the newly arrived cruisers. But the situation was so desperate that Halsey ordered Rear Admiral Frederick C. Sherman to throw every plane he had against it. Halsey feared that Sherman's air groups would be cut to pieces, yet the losses must be borne if necessary to save the Bougainville beachhead. Sherman launched two strikes on Rabaul that left the Japanese commander with only half his carrier planes, which for their safety he had to send back to Truk along with the cruisers. The threat to Bougainville was over.

These carrier actions were so successful that they diverted attention from the crucial facts, which Ronald H. Spector has pointed out:

> Halsey's entire operation on Bougainville could be threatened by a force of only eight Japanese cruisers because Halsey lacked large ships of his own (except the two carriers which were in the right location largely by chance). The reason for this lack was that almost all major U.S. warships were preparing for a new offensive, soon to open in the Central Pacific. The dangers of a two-pronged advance—one in the southwest and one in the Central Pacific—had thus been graphically illustrated even before the latter was well underway.[4]

If the Japanese had been more skillful and lucky, and the Americans less so, the first carrier strike could have ended disastrously.

Halsey won his gamble, but he should not have had to take it because the Pacific Fleet had grown enormously in 1943 and was capable of providing him with all the support he needed. At the time he was risking two air groups on one throw of the dice there were five new *Essex*-class carriers (CVs) in Pearl Harbor, each with 90 or more aircraft. Also there, or on the way, were five more *Independence*-class light carriers (CVLs), sister ships of *Princeton*. They were built on cruiser hulls and had fewer planes than the CVs but could steam as fast. The *Essex*-class carriers were swifter and nimbler than previous types, more heavily armed, and fired a new type of 5-inch AA shell with a proximity fuse that exploded when merely in the neighborhood of enemy aircraft, greatly increasing the kill rate. Both types of carriers were equipped with a superb new naval fighter, the F6F Hellcat, which could outclimb and outdive the Japanese Zero and was 30 MPH faster, despite being better armed and armored.

Even part of this great force would have taken all the risk out of Halsey's operations. If the bulk of it had been committed to the Southwest Pacific, progress there would have been rapid. MacArthur's advance was covered mostly by land-based aircraft, which limited his speed and alternatives. But with the matchless power of the Pacific Fleet behind him he could have gone anywhere.[5] Even without the big CVs, which the Navy claimed were too vulnerable in shallow waters, he could have gone faster if Kinkaid had been allotted escort carriers, which were small and cheap yet could hold up to 30 aircraft. The Navy hoarded them, too, which suggests that King didn't want to share with MacArthur under any circumstances.

MacArthur's men complained frequently that the Navy consistently denied support to them in favor of the Central Pacific. This was true, and true also of Halsey's fleet, which was not only too small but frequently on short rations. One of the more interesting human documents to come out of the South Pacific is the war diary of James J. Fahey of Waltham, Massachusetts, who enlisted in the USN on October 3, 1942. He spent most of the Pacific War on the light cruiser *Montpelier*, which after being commissioned was sent to the Solomons. GIs in SWPA regarded naval life as soft. It was, but only by comparison with the hell of jungle fighting.

By July 1943 *Montpelier* had been in the Solomons for six months. The men had spent so much time at action stations that they were beginning to black out on their feet. The heat and humidity afflicted them just as it did those on land, and all were covered with sores and rashes. They were starved for decent rations. Even their bread had insects in it from the weevily flour. The supply ships always seemed to be late, and Fahey was grateful when they got two more or less solid meals a day. On a typical day the first consisted of hash, rice, and half a pear, the second of rice, baloney, bread, jelly, and a cookie. To men in foxholes eating C-rations this might have seemed pretty good, but by Central Pacific standards it was poor fare. As late as November Fahey's diary notes "We are always hungry."[6] They were always tired, too, because the shortage of ships in the South Pacific meant there was little relief, the men living in their gun tubs for days upon end. His happiest time at sea—and the ship was always at sea—came when he was assigned to mess duty for three months, which led not only to better food but more sleep than usual as he did not have to man a battle station.

Fahey was no whiner. His diary is remarkably upbeat, full of affection for his shipmates and admiration for most of his officers. He was immensely proud of *Montpelier*, which by war's end had traveled 200,000 miles and had participated in 26 invasions, 42 operations, and 30 campaigns. In the course of these activities it fired a total of over 100,000 rounds of 5- and 6-inch warheads. Ordinary seamen like Fahey made the Navy great. It would have been just as great, and certainly more effective, had it supported a single strategy.

However, instead of aiding MacArthur, the largest fleet in the world was poised to strike at Tarawa and Makin Atolls in the Gilberts. On November 21, 1943, after a brief bombardment, Marines assaulted Tarawa's Betio Island.The result was a blood bath. In three days of fighting on Betio, where the Japanese had dug in, the Marines suffered 3,000 casualties including 1,000 dead, while Japan lost 4,500 men—all on an island of less than 3 square miles.

While many Marines died on Betio because the Navy was in a rush, many sailors died off Makin because the Army wasn't. Since Makin was lightly defended, the assault force of 6,500 men consisted mostly of soldiers, who were opposed, it turned out, by only some 800 Japanese and conscripted Korean laborers. Though the Americans prevailed in the end by sheer force of numbers, it took them four days to secure Makin. On the fourth, escort carrier *Liscomb Bay* was sunk by an enemy sub, at a cost of over 600 lives. Naval officers were not slow to point out that, had Marines been sent to Makin, they would have taken it by storm and *Liscomb Bay* would have been safely at sea when the Japanese sub arrived. This was probably unfair criticism, since Makin was taken according to a timetable agreed to by the Navy.

There is no way to resolve the old Army–Marine controversy over speed and safety, history offering examples to support each argument. However, one thing is certain. The possession of an elite assault force enabled the Navy to stage operations which the Army could not. At Tarawa 40 percent of the combat troops became casualties. In other island assaults Marine regiments would lose even more, up to a peak of 81 percent sustained by the Twenty-ninth Marines on Okinawa. In every case the carnage was to some extent optional, since unlike Bataan, or the Battle of the Bulge, where soldiers had to stand and fight, the island assaults of the Central Pacific were selected from among a range of choices. It is doubtful they would have been made at all had there been no Marine Corps. It was this prodigal waste of lives that finally disenchanted William Manchester, once a proud Marine. Military training has always been designed to make a man rise above his survival instinct. Because the Marines did it exceptionally well, their casualties were the highest. One wonders how many besides Manchester finally came to resent this.[7] Lessons were learned at Tarawa and applied to subsequent landings. The fact remained that assaulting fortified strong points would always be bloody work, no matter how well-supported. Such attacks would become routine in the Central Pacific, but not in MacArthur's theater, where geography and lack of means inspired more creative solutions.

American democracy was poorly equipped to deal with the issue of which way to go in the Pacific. Tarawa horrified people at home, but since the services insisted that two separate campaigns made more sense than one, it was difficult to complain about casualties without calling the entire strategy into question. Few laymen had the confidence or competence to do this, and though Roosevelt did, he had already made his decision not to intervene. Having a civilian Commander in Chief offered many benefits to the United States. The drawback of concentrating power in the President's hands was that if he chose not to exercise it, critics had nowhere to turn. To this dilemma there would be no solution.

MacArthur's counteroffensive did not get off to a brilliant start. For the reconquest of Papua MacArthur had only two American divisions, both National Guard outfits that had not gone through the Army's new training program and were completely unready to fight. Experience would show that, unlike the Army's regular divisions, which had officers promoted on merit and no bad habits to unlearn, National Guard divisions required extra training. But, as they were all he had, MacArthur had to use them. Of his two Guard units, the 32nd Infantry Division was considered least unfit. On September 15 MacArthur's air officer, Major General George Kenney, began flying it to Papua—the first large-scale airlift undertaken by the U.S. Army.

The 126th Infantry Regiment led the way, and its 2nd Battalion was ordered to cross the fearsome Owen Stanleys via the Kappa Kappa Trail, which was even worse than the Kokoda. Led by Company E, half of whose men came from the small town of Big Rapids, Michigan, the 2nd Battalion hacked its way through some of the worst jungle in the world. All supplies, such as they were, had to be parachuted in. Because to fall behind was to die, the men discarded their equipment. They climbed 9,000 feet, taking seven hours to crawl on their hands and knees the last 2,000 feet to the crest of the Owen Stanleys. The 2nd Battalion spent 49 days crossing Papua on foot, a distance the rest of the division covered in 45 minutes by air.

Few men actually died on the trail, but they were so emaciated—Lieutenant Paul R. Lutjens, who weighed 184 pounds when they started, could encircle his waist with his hands at the end—that when thrown into the battle of Buna their casualties were enormous, owing also to criminally bad plans of attack. Of the 172 men in Company E who arrived in Port Moresby on September 15, 1942, only seven remained on their feet four and a half months later when the company was finally relieved. Fifteen men from Big Rapids alone were killed. Six men from the company, including Lutjens, received the Distinguished Service Cross, two posthumously.[8]

This was the price Big Rapids paid for being the home of a rifle company. Many other towns suffered similarly in the war, exposing a cherished democratic myth. Americans believed that security could best be maintained by having a small standing Army backed by a local militia. Good enough in colonial times, modern war required trained troops, which the National Guard could not provide. The Guard was political, not a military institution, maintained for reasons of local pride and because it brought federal payments to the community. Undertrained and underequipped men were no substitute for regular Army divisions, even though used as such. Thanks to the Guard, Pacific islands would become the graves of many brave men who deserved better from their country.

Buna-Gona was one of the worst directed American battles of the war for MacArthur had little understanding as yet of the new Army that Marshall had built. The triangular division was an infantry–artillery team which, with its attached tank battalion, had tremendous firepower. MacArthur broke up the 32nd and sent it to Papua without heavy artillery or tank support. Its luckless commander, Major General Edwin Forrest Harding, was obliged to separate the division into undergunned task forces and throw them against defenses that were virtually impregnable. In the Buna-Gona area MacArthur repeatedly ordered costly frontal attacks that had no chance of success. His Chief of Staff, the much hated Major General Richard K.

Sutherland, inspected the battle area and reported back that not guns but leadership was needed, reversing the actual truth. MacArthur therefore relieved Harding and put Lieutenant General Robert L. Eichelberger in command, saying "I want you to take Buna, or not to come back alive."[9]

Buna fell on January 22, 1943, the first time Japan had sustained a permanent defeat on land. Victory in Papua was won at a heavy cost, which MacArthur refused to admit, saying instead that the "utmost care was taken for the conservation of our forces, with the result that probably no campaign in history against a thoroughly prepared and trained Army produced such complete and decisive results with so low an expenditure of life and resources."[10] His biographer, Clayton James, calls this boast "fantastic," noting that on hotly contested Guadalcanal a total of 60,000 soldiers and Marines sustained 5,845 casualties, of which 1,600 were fatal. In Papua some 40,000 Allied troops were committed, and they suffered 8,546 casualties, including 3,095 killed–a death rate more than triple that sustained on Guadalcanal. The 126th Infantry was completely wiped out, whole battalions being reduced by disease and casualties to a tenth of their normal strength. The official U.S. Army history would later describe the Papuan campaign as one of the bloodiest of the war. Only MacArthur had the audacity to stand these facts on their head.[11]

Yet, MacArthur was learning fast, and the experience would not be wasted. After the Papuan campaign he made a promise—which he kept—that there would be "No More Bunas." Over the next two years, his troops would suffer fewer than 20,000 casualties in the course of many operations, partly because of tactical lessons learned in Papua that would make later campaigns more efficient. He was picking up on the many uses of aircraft, whose value he had previously sneered at. His understanding of sea power was expanding, too. MacArthur's need for sea lift was glaringly exposed at Buna, as he had almost no ships and thus could not stage landings to outflank or isolate enemy fortifications. His complaints led the Navy to assign him a specialist, Rear Admiral Daniel E. Barbey, whose VII Amphibious Force would conduct 56 operations in the Southwest Pacific Area. MacArthur also learned how to exploit the decrypted enemy radio messages provided by Army and Navy intelligence. These would play a key part in future operations by helping to determine which enemy strongholds could be bypassed.

MacArthur still did not have enough of anything. During the first year of campaigning in Italy, the United States shipped 2.3 million long tons of provisions to the Italian people alone, which roughly equalled the volume of supplies provided to MacArthur's entire theater. The Australians made up some of the difference, but his command would never be supplied as well as American troops in Europe, and he would never have enough warships. MacArthur worked wonders just the same.

In 1943 SWPA concentrated on the advance to Rabaul. MacArthur was disappointed when the JCS cancelled his assault on the fortress. However, a series of amphibious and air attacks isolated it and laid the basis for MacArthur's brilliant bypassing strategy. Operation Cartwheel required him to attack west along the coast of New Guinea, north to the Admiralty Islands, and east into New Britain, while Halsey's forces worked their way up the Solomons. Some at home were discouraged by the slow progress to date. In August 1943, *Life* noted sourly that it had a taken a year of fighting to advance from Guadalcanal to the tip of New Georgia, a distance of 200 miles. At that rate the United States would invade Japan sometime in 1957.[12]

These early efforts were shoestring affairs. As American power built up the pace accelerated. In February 1944 a daring surprise attack put MacArthur in the Admiralties, literally, as he accompanied the troops, a rare event, and they were secured a month later. This completed the investment of Rabaul and ensured Japan's defeat. The United States now had air control over a vast region, which the Japanese futilely contested until their air strength was virtually gone. Reflecting on Japan's mindless refusal to stop the war at this point, William J. Dunn, a reporter for CBS News, remarked later that if Helen of Troy's face had launched a thousand ships, "Certainly 'face' launched the death warrants of probably a million Japanese in the last two years of the Pacific War."[13]

The key to MacArthur's success was his use of tactical air, which was more important in SWPA than in perhaps any other theater. The Southwest Pacific is thick with islands which provided numerous sites for airfields. Unlike in Europe, the enemy's air defenses were weak, enabling even heavy bombers to make precise low-level attacks. MacArthur also had two outstanding air commanders in General George C. Kenney and Lieutenant General Ennis C. Whitehead. Kenney taught MacArthur what planes could do, starting with the airlift to Buna that had encountered much skepticism. Gradually they worked out the strategy of blockading enemy strongpoints from the air, and covering and assisting Allied ground troops while, by advancing their forward bases, bringing more and more Japanese targets within bombing range—what was commonly called "the bomb line."

By 1944 MacArthur had the means for his most daring effort yet, a long leap up the New Guinea coast that would carry his forces 580 miles beyond their lines and into the enemy's rear. This campaign would become widely admired as one of the most beautifully planned and executed of the war. The conventional wisdom in April 1944, both Japanese and American, was that Wewak or Hansa Bay in Northeast New Guinea must be the next target. They were inside the bomb line, and the Japanese occupation force of 55,000 men had to be destroyed, according to orthodox doctrine, before American forces could move farther along the coast. The idea of bypassing Wewak developed after bombing attacks on airfields in and around Hollandia destroyed the Japanese air cover. Intelligence reported that, unlike Wewak, Hollandia was lightly defended. When one of MacArthur's planners brought this to his attention, MacArthur decided to cancel the planned attack on Hansa Bay and vault over it to Hollandia.

All went according to plan. Fifth Air Force did so well that the Japanese were left with only 25 planes in the whole of New Guinea. Admiral Barbey's amphibious force, the largest yet seen in SWPA, consisted of 217 vessels carrying 80,000 troops brought together from three different staging areas located up to 1,000 miles away. Air and naval attacks on Wewak and Hansa Bay convinced the enemy that they were MacArthur's targets, and when on April 22 his fleet changed course, the element of surprise was total. As one Japanese commander put it later, "The morning that we found out that the Allies were coming to Hollandia they were already in the harbor."[14] This operation hastened the liberation of New Guinea by several months and provided the Allies with a magnificent harbor that became one of their most important bases. All this was gained at an initial cost of 159 American dead to 3,300 enemy, while, of 7,000 Japanese who escaped into the jungle, barely 1,000 survived.

Flushed with success, MacArthur's forces now moved nimbly forward, seizing one island or coastal base after another. Only on Biak, where the Japanese were strongly dug in and did not charge the beaches and expose themselves to naval gunfire, were there problems. All the same, on August 20, at a cost of 600 American casualties, Biak was secured. In under two years, MacArthur had advanced almost 2,000 miles, 1,100 in the last two months. To this splendid achievement there was only one drawback. Many bypassed Japanese garrisons still had to be taken. Thus, while American forces went on to bigger things, the Australian Army spent the rest of the war mopping up the Japanese in New Guinea—an unglamorous task that cost many casualties. Characteristically, MacArthur gave the Australians no credit for this, and consistently sought to keep even his own commanders from being hailed by the American press.

Yet, though his morals did not change, after his shaky first 14 months MacArthur developed into a commander worthy of his own reputation. The deftness and timing of his operations, the close coordination of land, sea, and air; the boldness and success of his bypassing strategy, have justly been admired ever since. Curiously, though MacArthur has not been forgotten, the victories on which his reputation was built are little known today. The battle for Normandy is famous still, while hardly anyone remembers New Guinea.

In another sense, the surprising thing is that MacArthur's reputation has survived at all, considering how he was loathed by his troops. Their attitude was so pronounced that in 1944, when Republican leaders were running a "MacArthur for President" boomlet, some of them wondered if Roosevelt had not devised a system according to which only MacArthur's enemies were sent back to the States. Nonetheless, while American troops, so intolerant of humbug, exhibitionism, and cant, were naturally put off by MacArthur, many came home who would have died under a less skillful leader. If politics was one reason why Roosevelt backed MacArthur again and again, another was that FDR, and Marshall too, appreciated how much he was doing with how little.

Support for the Central Pacific effort was most marked at the top, thanks to King's driving force and his willingness to make deals. It was a source of great annoyance to him that senior naval officers in the POA did not share his enthusiasm for Central Pacific operations. But King had the final say and persuaded the Joint Chiefs to back him. In November 1943, the CCS approved an "Overall Plan for the Defeat of Japan" that authorized Nimitz to take the Marshalls in January, the Carolines and Truk in July, and the Marianas in October.

This course was agreed to over the objections not only of MacArthur, but also of Admiral Nimitz, plus his second in command, chief of staff, and head planner, all of whom preferred the Southwest Pacific. They met with representatives of Halsey and MacArthur at Pearl Harbor in January 1944 and agreed that the Central Pacific was the wrong area for a major offensive. They especially did not want to take the Marianas, which had no good harbors, were within the range of Japanese land-based aircraft but beyond the American bomb line, and had no military value except as B-29 bases. Instead of continuing westward, Nimitz seems to have favored the conference proposal to turn south, take the Palaus and Truk, and join up with MacArthur for an assault on Mindanao, the nearest Philippine island. This meant having, if not a unified command in the Pacific, at least unity of action, so that the whole of America's increasing might in the Pacific could be applied to a single purpose.

Defenders of the Central Pacific campaigns argue that the two drives were mutually supporting, yet this was seldom the case. They required two entirely separate lines of communication with much duplication of effort, and they competed with each other for scarce resources—notably landing ships and service personnel. SWPA never had enough service troops, engineers in particular, and the Marianas made things worse, as the great bomber bases established there required large numbers of engineers to build and maintain them. The plan suggested at Pearl would have put the Navy's main effort on MacArthur's flank, required only one line of communications to serve both campaigns, and enabled landing ships and carriers to shuttle between the two theaters as needed. These campaigns would have been mutually supporting in fact as well as in theory.

There would also have been no more Tarawas, for in the Southwest Pacific enemy strongholds could usually be bypassed and contained with land-based air—like Rabaul, where 100,000 Japanese troops were dug in behind fearsome defenses. To take Rabaul by storm would have cost more American lives than were expended on Iwo Jima. Instead, it was simply neutralized for the balance of the war. If Iwo Jima and the Marianas had been treated similarly, thousands of lives would have been saved. Between April and October of 1944, MacArthur's forces advanced 1,000 miles from Hollandia to Morotai, destroying nine Japanese divisions at a cost of 10,000 American casualties—including 1,648 dead. Yet, in the Marianas alone that summer, the United States would sustain nearly 23,000 casualties in the process of destroying at most three Japanese divisions.

Unhappily for many Marines, Nimitz did not run the Navy. When King, who did, saw the joint report drawn up at the Pearl Harbor conference in January, he exploded, leaving Nimitz no choice but to obey orders. It was on to the Marianas and their principal islands, Guam, Tinian, and especially Saipan, a name that the Marine Corps will never forget. These were substantial islands, unlike the tiny Gilbert and Marshall atolls, and on Saipan there were 32,000 Japanese troops, about twice the number expected. On June 15 the Americans went ashore and by nightfall 20,000 had landed, despite the usual fierce resistance. By the next day, Spruance had learned that the Japanese Navy was going to make an all-out effort to destroy Fifth Fleet. The IJN had assembled a great armada, including nine new carriers, in hopes of gaining a decisive victory.

Vice Admiral Jisaburo Ozawa knew his force to be weaker than Fifth Fleet, but he counted on two advantages. Because they lacked armor and self-sealing tanks, his planes had more range, enabling them to attack at 300 miles compared to 200 for the Americans. In addition, he thought he would have the assistance of about 200 aircraft based on Guam and Tinian. What he did not know, because their commander misled him, was that American carrier planes had wiped out the airfields he was depending upon for support.

What no one fully appreciated yet was how great the qualitative difference between Japanese and American airmen had become. At Midway Japan's pilots had been the best. This was no longer true, most of Japan's veterans having been killed in action. Along with superior firepower, superior skill, including that of the carrier crews, gave the USN an increasing advantage. At Midway the launch had been so slow that Spruance's attack was late and staggered. Now, at a time when radar gave it 45 minutes' notice, Task Force 58 could launch 300 fighters in under half an hour. Since a Hellcat could climb 20,000 feet in seven minutes, the last ones off would be at altitude before the first Japanese arrived.

Japan's search planes discovered Fifth Fleet late on June 18, 1944, and Ozawa ordered a full attack. The American response was overwhelming. Fewer than 100 of 373 Japanese planes which sortied made it back to their carriers, three of which were sunk and one badly damaged. The Americans lost only 29 aircraft in what was named "the Great Marianas Turkey Shoot" or, officially, the Battle of the Philippine Sea.

Though Saipan made the great Philippine Sea victory possible, it was the biggest bloodbath yet in the Central Pacific, dwarfing Betio because Saipan was a much bigger island. When the battle ended on July 9, 1944, there were 14,000 American casualties and 30,000 Japanese dead. As the Japanese no longer tried to defend beaches, much of the fighting consisted of rooting them out of, or destroying clusters of them in, underground bunkers and tunnels. At Stalingrad

Germans had called their underground battle a "Rattenkrieg," or war of the rats, which precisely described Saipan.

Apart from the high cost of taking it, Saipan was notable for being the first conquered island with a large Japanese civilian population. Of its 12,000 noncombatants (or 18,000 or 30,000, different accounts offering different numbers), most of them women and children, about two-thirds committed suicide, either because honor demanded it or because they had been indoctrinated to believe that their captors would treat them atrociously.[15] It sickened GIs to see whole families jump off cliffs or blow themselves up with grenades. It was also a chilling foretaste of what the invasion of Japan could bring.

On July 26, 1944, as the Marines fought to clear Guam, Franklin Delano Roosevelt sailed into Pearl Harbor. He was running for office again and wished to impress the electorate by showing his flag as commander in chief—an effective gambit, according to Isaiah Berlin.[16] He also had real work to do as the time for a final decision on Pacific strategy was fast approaching. Events had overtaken the old plan approved in 1943. At that time the goal was to reach the South China coast and establish bomber bases from which to reduce Japan. Since then the Japanese had seized more of China, and the AAF was preparing to launch its B-29 Superfortress bombers from the Marianas. What to do next was becoming the subject of heated debate, with King wanting to invade Formosa and forget about the Philippines.

General MacArthur was still insisting that the whole archipelago had to be liberated, for political as well as military reasons. The United States would lose face abroad if it allowed the loyal Filipinos to needlessly languish. The voters at home would be unhappy also. Not only MacArthur, whose motives were transparently selfish, argued that bases in the Philippines should be established before conducting further operations. Nimitz thought so, too, as did also most of his senior commanders, differing mainly in that naval officers did not agree with MacArthur on the need to liberate the entire archipelago. The northernmost island was essential, however, since aircraft based on Luzon could cover the South China Sea and cut off Japan from Southeast Asia. In addition, Manila Bay was far superior as a fleet anchorage to the Marianas.

In Hawaii Nimitz loyally presented King's argument for the invasion of Formosa as the fastest way to Japan. MacArthur eloquently made the case for Luzon being slower but surer. MacArthur may well have arrived at a tacit agreement with Roosevelt by which the President would support MacArthur's plan while the General would issue glowing communiqués from his theater in time for the November elections. Whether that is so or not, FDR did go for the plan. Admiral Leahy favored it, too, and within six weeks of their conference Nimitz, who required little persuasion, had fallen into line.

Roosevelt's trip to Hawaii was the one time when he actively intervened to shape strategy in the Pacific. The success of his efforts suggest what might have been accomplished if he had devoted more time at critical moments to influencing naval strategy. If FDR's voyage to Hawaii was also political grandstanding, as his critics charged, the pity is that he did not do more of it.

There was solid military logic to MacArthur's arguments, but it would be nice to think that sentiment figured in, too. Even though the United States had let them down, most of the 17 million Filipinos were eagerly awaiting MacArthur. Outside of China, no people had suffered as much from Japan's brutal occupation. Except for the Chinese again, none had created such a strong resistance. There were at least 250,000 guerrillas in the archipelago, controlling large parts of it and providing MacArthur with valuable intelligence—3,700 messages a month at the end. Such people deserved all the help America could give them.

It was Admiral Halsey who forced the actual decision. After his South Pacific Area command was dissolved, Halsey alternated with Spruance as the leader of Nimitz's striking force, it being known as Third Fleet when Halsey commanded and Fifth Fleet under Spruance. Only the commanders and their staffs changed when the designation did, all others remaining in place, Vice Admiral Marc A. Mitscher continuing to command the fast carriers. In September 1944 Halsey raided the Philippines and encountered little resistance. He therefore advised Nimitz that Mindanao be bypassed and the central Philippines invaded.

The Joint Chiefs, then in Quebec for the Octagon Conference, promptly directed that operations planned for the Talauds, Mindanao, and Yap be canceled and everything thrown at Leyte—except for a small force that was to take the Palau Islands. Securing the main island of Peleliu would cost American forces some 10,000 casualties to no real purpose, even Admiral Morison agreeing that it ought to have been canceled. Leyte was about to be assaulted by the greatest naval strength ever assembled, for Seventh and Third Fleets together deployed some 17 fast and 18 escort carriers, 12 battleships, 28 cruisers, 150 destroyers, and hundreds of other vessels.

Once the United States was committed to Leyte, momentum quickly developed in favor of Luzon over Formosa. MacArthur informed the JCS that seizing Leyte would enable him to invade Luzon two months ahead of schedule. Formosa could not be attacked that soon, and, before long, planners decided that Formosa could not be invaded at all until after victory in Europe as Nimitz would require up to 200,000 Army service troops for the operation, and they were not available. There were enough troops for the Philippines, whose friendly inhabitants would provide much of the needed labor, and for Okinawa also. Meanwhile, in China the advancing Japanese were seizing more and more American air bases. This ruled out the possibility of land-based air support from China for an assault on Formosa. It also eliminated the value of Formosa as a staging area for landings on the China coast, as these were now out of the question. In the end almost no one except King liked Formosa, and on October 3 he finally gave in. The JCS then directed MacArthur to assault Luzon in December.

Although the Navy provided more help to MacArthur in the Philippines than ever before, command remained divided with results that were nearly disastrous. The IJN knew that losing the Philippines would doom Japan to defeat, if indeed its fate was not already sealed. Since there was no point in holding back, the Japanese Navy determined on a maximum effort. It still had nine battleships, including the world's largest, *Yamato* and *Musashi*, together with a dozen heavy cruisers. It also had four fast carriers, but they could launch only about 100 planes manned by novice pilots. As usual, Japan developed a battle plan of extreme complexity. Its key feature was that the carriers were to act as decoys, luring away Third Fleet, while two surface units converged in Leyte Gulf to annihilate the invasion force. A very long shot, given the USN's overwhelming superiority, it nearly scored, owing to faulty communications between the headquarters of Nimitz and MacArthur.

At about 1:00 A.M. on October 23, 1944, two American submarines sighted a strong Japanese fleet. Under the command of Vice Admiral Takeo Kurita, it consisted of five battleships, including *Yamato* and *Musashi*, plus 10 heavy and two light cruisers and over a dozen destroyers. Prompt air and submarine attacks forced this armada to turn back. In the meantime, a second force, under Vice Admiral Shoji Nishimura, including two battleships, a cruiser, and four destroyers, was detected making for the Surigao Strait at the southern end of

Leyte. Halsey and Admiral Thomas C. Kinkaid, who commanded MacArthur's Seventh Fleet, were awaiting news of the Japanese carriers before committing themselves. At about 5 in the afternoon, Ozawa's carriers were sighted far to the north of Leyte Gulf. Halsey now took the bait. He, and Kinkaid also, not knowing that the carriers had few planes and pilots, took it for granted that this was the Japanese main force.

The mistake was significant because, earlier, Halsey had radioed a battle plan to Mitscher which entailed leaving four fast battleships, five cruisers, and 14 destroyers, to be designated Task Force 34 in Leyte Gulf. Admiral Kinkaid, relieved to know that the beaches would be protected by Third Fleet, deployed his big ships to meet Nishimura in the Surigao Strait, where they would destroy him. Upon hearing the false report that enemy carriers were accompanied by battlewagons, Halsey forgot about forming Task Force 34 and drove north with all his fast carriers and capital ships. Meanwhile, Kurita, who had doubled back, was passing through the San Bernardino Strait undetected.

The brunt of his assault was borne by Taffy 3, one of three groups of escort carriers supporting the Leyte operation. It was laying off Samar in the path of Kurita's Fleet. Taffy 3 consisted of five escort carriers whose planes were armed and their crews trained for ground support and antisubmarine operations. The little CVEs had no armor only a single 5-inch gun apiece. With a top speed of 17 knots they could not outrun a Japanese submarine, much less a battleship. In addition to these, Rear Admiral Clifton T. Sprague commanded only three destroyers and four destroyer escorts. Despite his hopeless position, however, Sprague, in a series of clever maneuvers, launched his aircraft, and in a running battle worked his way in the direction of Taffy 2, which was 60 miles to the south but making its best speed toward him.

Sprague's aircraft had few torpedoes and no armor-piercing ordnance. When their torpedoes and bombs were gone they dropped depth charges and whatever else was to hand. When all was expended, Sprague's pilots made dummy runs on Japanese ships to throw off their gunners and helmsmen. Meanwhile, his destroyers and DE's made smoke to screen the carriers, and repeatedly charged enemy ships, firing their guns and torpedoes—the last torpedo attacks ever executed by destroyers. Taffy 2 joined the battle as well, sending torpedo planes that helped destroy three enemy cruisers.

So furious was the American response that Admiral Kurita lost his nerve. Even though Sprague had only one destroyer left, and the jeep carrier *Gambier Bay* was in flames and sinking, Kurita failed to recognize that he was battling escorts and not Mitscher's fast carriers. Fearful of additional losses, and believing that the American carriers were outrunning him, Kurita broke off the engagement at 9:30 A.M. and swiftly retired. In contrast to that of the Japanese, American morale was such that at this unexpected development a sailor in Sprague's flagship is said to have cried out "My God, Admiral, they're going to get away."

The fight had been one of the most astonishing in naval annals, since Taffy 3, hopelessly outgunned and outnumbered, did not on the face of it have a chance of survival. If Kurita had kept his ships together and driven for the beaches, he could have sunk the invasion fleet and mopped up Taffy 3 later. The Battle of Leyte Gulf showed again how far the Imperial Japanese Navy had declined and how much better the Americans had gotten. Sprague himself summed it up nicely, attributing the result to "our successful smoke screen, our torpedo counterattack, continuous harassment of the enemy by bomb, torpedo and strafing air attacks, timely maneuvers, and the definite partiality of Almighty God."[17] Luck played a part, but courage, proficiency, and leadership were what saved the beachhead. Yet, such extraordinary heroism and self-sacrifice ought not to have been needed. Third Fleet was huge, big enough to have guarded the beaches and at the same time pursued Ozawa. Conversely, if Seventh Fleet had been assigned some fast battleships and/or fleet carriers of its own, it would have been able to protect the beaches as well as fight in the Surigao Strait.

This three-day engagement, know as the Battle of Leyte Gulf, was marked by four separate actions and is considered the biggest naval battle of all time. It was a smashing American victory, and probably would have been about as great even if Ozawa's air groups had been at full strength. America lost the light carrier *Princeton*, two escort carriers, two destroyers, one destroyer escort, and fewer than 3,000 men. The Japanese were deprived of four fast carriers, three battleships, including the mighty *Musashi*, six heavy cruisers, four light cruisers, nine destroyers, and some 10,000 men. In Leyte Gulf the Imperial Japanese Navy came to an end, and the "Divine Wind," the suicide attacks that were now Japan's only hope, had their beginning.

Though the USN emerged from the battle wreathed in clouds of well-earned glory, divided command had almost produced a fiasco. A

Japanese triumph in Leyte Gulf could not have changed the war's outcome, but America would have needlessly lost many men and ships. As it was, Japan's deception plan succeeded, and only the skill and gallantry of Sprague's sailors and airmen, plus timely help from Taffy 2, saved the invasion fleet. Had there been a supreme commander for the entire Pacific, deploying his resources according to need, Seventh Fleet would have been able to protect itself, or, if not, everyone would have known for sure who was supposed to cover the landings. It is true that Halsey blundered by disregarding numerous requests and warnings over a period of many hours, for which a less popular officer might well have been sacked. Even so, his mistakes would not have taken place had there been a rational command structure.

Although some in SWPA blamed Halsey for putting them in danger, MacArthur never did, springing to Halsey's defense and remarking later:

> I have never ascribed the unfortunate incidents of this naval battle to faulty judgments on the part of any of the commanders involved. The near disaster can be placed squarely at the door of Washington. In the naval action, two key American commanders were independent of each other, one under me, and the other under Admiral Nimitz 5,000 miles away, both operating in the same waters and in the same battle."[18]

Leyte proved a much tougher nut to crack than expected because of weather conditions which deprived the troops of land-based air cover and allowed the Japanese to reinforce their garrison. This forced a delay in attacking Luzon, but on January 9, when MacArthur's troops went ashore at Lingayen Gulf, it was in the greatest strength yet, amounting to 10 divisions, five regimental combat teams (augmented regiments comparable to brigades), and various other units—more American troops than would fight together anywhere else in the war except on the Western Front. So many Japanese troops and weapons had been lost defending Leyte that General Tomoyuki Yamashita, famed as the conqueror of Malaya, had decided not to defend Lingayen and the landings were no problem. Getting there was the hard part, for some 200 Japanese suicide planes took a heavy toll of the invasion fleet, sinking 24 ships, seriously damaging 27 more, and inflicting over 2,100 casualties, of whom 738 were killed. Seventh Fleet's little escort carriers did not have the fighter strength to break up these kamikaze attacks, and the mighty CVs of Task Force 38 were not there to do it for them. Once again, divided command resulted in extra losses, though, as there were no local replacements, after the original 200 Japanese suicide planes went down, the Divine Wind ceased blowing.

On February 3, flying columns of the 1st Cavalry Division were in Manila's northern suburbs, liberating Santo Tomas University and nearly 4,000 Allied internees. Because the Japanese commander put up a ferocious and unauthorized defense, it took a month to secure Manila, during which time 70 percent of the city's factories were destroyed, 80 percent of the southern residential area and 100 percent of the business district. There were 100,000 civilian casualties. Among Allied cities only Warsaw and Stalingrad were believed to have sustained more damage.

During this time MacArthur sent Eichelberger to liberate the rest of the archipelago, a campaign that made little military sense, ran contrary to JCS expectations, but delivered many Filipinos from enemy hands and was a masterpiece of dash and daring. Eichelberger's Eighth Army, Barbey's VII Amphibious Force, and Lieutenant General Paul B. Wurtsmith's Thirteenth Air Force combined to pull off 14 major and 24 minor amphibious landings in 44 days, freeing most of the islands.

However, partly because these actions drained troops away from Krueger's Sixth Army, operations did not go so well in northern Luzon, where Yamashita's troops had withdrawn to the mountains. The fighting there was bitter and went on for the rest of the war, some 50,000 Japanese holding out until V-J Day. Some have criticized MacArthur for not beefing up Sixth Army and then crushing Yamashita. Yet the slow approach saved many lives in a situation where haste was unnecessary. Even on this reduced scale, Luzon was the biggest campaign in the Southwest Pacific Area, 8,300 Americans, 1,100 Filipino guerrillas, and 205,000 Japanese dying in the course of it.

Liberating the entire archipelago cost the United States some 48,000 wounded and 14,000 deaths, the great majority being sustained on Leyte and Luzon. Nevertheless, considering the scale of the fighting, casualties were actually moderate. The enemy lost 350,000 troops in the archipelago, making it far and away the most crushing defeat Japan would sustain in the Pacific. On Okinawa, by comparison, 7,000 U.S. troops would be killed fighting an enemy force less than a third the size of Japan's Philippine garrison. Had MacArthur assaulted Yamashita in the headlong Central Pacific style, his losses might well have been similar.

Despite near disaster at Leyte Gulf and heavier fighting than expected on Leyte and Luzon, the Philippine campaign vindicated

MacArthur's course of action. If the Navy had not been allowed to conduct a separate war, this victory would have come even sooner and at a lesser cost. Though the defeat of Japan was inevitable now, America was paying a bloody price for lack of a supreme commander. So also were the servicemen whose dedication and spirit redeemed every mistake. As the lesson of Leyte Gulf was not heeded, they would have to go on doing so. For this reason, among others, the invasion of Japan was a nightmare that seemed likely to become the worst reality of America's war.

The decision to attack Luzon instead of Formosa made China irrelevant, which was all to the good, for nowhere else did American policy fail so utterly, even though it was for China's sake that the United States had gone to war. Had Roosevelt not made Japan's withdrawal from China an essential condition for lifting sanctions in 1941, there probably would have been a *modus vivendi* instead of the attack on Pearl Harbor. To knowingly risk war on its behalf is the most any nation can do for another, yet Americans, including the President, knew almost nothing about the country they were trying to save. Despite this lack of knowledge there was a large body of support in the United States for China, especially after it was invaded by Japan. Following Pearl Harbor China became, as Barbara Tuchman wrote, America's favorite ally. Most Americans seem to have been, if not card-carriers, at least honorary members of what would later be called the China Lobby.

Even though China had been America's reason for entering the Pacific War, Washington could do little to help it during the dark days after Pearl Harbor—beyond maintaining a volunteer American fighter group known as the Flying Tigers that had been established there in 1941. America had few weapons to spare. China could not be easily supplied because Japan controlled all the convenient ports and the Burma Road to India. Nevertheless, Roosevelt was determined to build up Generalissimo Chiang Kai-shek's government, as a base from which to invade Japan, and so that China could serve as a useful ally in the postwar era.[19] Much bitterness would result from this unfortunate decision.

The truth about China was that it would never be able to offer much help, which Brigadier General John Magruder, who commanded the American military mission to China in 1941–42, made clear in his reports. As a strong China was considered essential, truth could not be allowed to stand in the way of policy, neither could the fact that

Washington and Chungking, where Chiang established his wartime capitol, had radically different agendas. Whereas Roosevelt meant to strengthen Chiang's government as a weapon against Japan, Chiang was primarily interested in destroying the Chinese Communist Party. After Pearl Harbor his policy was to let America beat the Japanese while he prepared for his subsequent war with the CCP. Under intense pressure, Chiang would cooperate militarily with the United States but on the smallest scale possible.

Despite a stream of negative reports from American diplomatic and military personnel attesting to the incompetence and unpopularity of Chiang's regime, Roosevelt refused to admit that his China policy was hopeless. He would not accept the view of his ambassador in Chungking, Clarence Gauss, that the country could never be more than a "minor asset" to the United States and had the potential to become a "major liability." Chiang had skillful representation in the United States and was the China Lobby's favorite. Roosevelt could not turn his back on Chiang for political reasons, and the military saw China as the logical springboard from which to invade Japan. Roosevelt also wanted China to be one of his Four Policeman after the war was over. Necessity thus became the mother of self-deception.

In 1942 Marshall sent Lieutenant General Joseph W. "Vinegar Joe" Stilwell, an expert on China where he had served for many years, to command the China–Burma–India Theater of Operations. Stilwell had been military attaché to the American embassy in Peiking when Japan attacked in 1937 and sympathized with the Chinese. He was also an outstanding field commander, having distinguished himself in prewar maneuvers by his flair and imagination. In addition to his theater command, Chiang named him chief of staff of the Chinese Army, an empty gesture as Chiang had no intention of allowing an American to command his troops. They would not be of much use anyway, for the three million strong National Army of the Republic of China looked impressive only on paper. Most of its three hundred divisions were ill-trained, malnourished, disease-ridden, horribly led, and, for the most part, outside Chiang's jurisdiction. Warlords ran most of these divisions, Chiang commanding no more than 30. What few resources he had available went to the 400,000 men who stood guard against the CCP in North China, leaving little for the fight against Japan.

Stilwell reached China in March 1942 just as the Japanese invaded Burma, where the British fought badly and the Chinese worse. Chiang gave Stilwell nominal command of his troops in Burma, but Vinegar Joe discovered that he had no real authority over them. In lightning attacks the Japanese destroyed the Allied front, Stilwell personally leading a column of 114 survivors out of the jungle to India, the only group of escapees to make it without loss of life. Throughout the campaign U.S. journalists had published evasive reports. Upon reaching India Stilwell put things right at a press conference with the blunt statement "I claim we took a hell of a beating. We got run out of Burma and it is humiliating as hell. I think we ought to find out what caused it, go back and retake it."[20] These remarks made him famous.

Stilwell would spend the next two and a half years trying to build up a Chinese force of 30 divisions able to retake north Burma and defend a new land route from India in place of the old Burma Road. Until then, China could only be supplied by air over the treacherous Himalayas—called by fliers "The Hump"—an extraordinarily dangerous route that claimed the lives of many. This trickle of supplies, when a torrent was needed, ruled out major operations. In his effort to open Burma Stilwell's greatest enemy was Generalissimo Chiang Kai-shek, whom he privately called "Peanut," and his next greatest Claire Chennault, who led the Flying Tigers and their successor Fourteenth Air Force. Chennault, wanting to be independent of Stilwell, was making absurd promises to defeat Japan if provided with 147 aircraft. The actual situation, Stilwell pointed out, was that if Chennault annoyed the Japanese too much they would simply take his airfields. The correct strategy was to secure a land route to India first and then undertake more ambitious land and air operations. However, Roosevelt favored Chennault's idea, because Chiang did, and also because it would be easier to supply a small air force than a large ground army. As so often, the Trident conference in May 1943 produced a compromise, dividing the supplies sent to China between Stilwell and Chennault, though Chennault had the higher priority.

In March 1944 Japan launched two major offensives that prompted important changes. One drive along the Burma–India frontier threatened the Chinese "X-Force" operating in Burma under Stilwell's command. This finally led Washington to warn Chiang that all American aid to him would be cut off unless he put the companion "Y-Force" under Stilwell's orders also. Chiang had been accepting aid but keeping most of his troops out of battle, which could no longer be tolerated. Chiang complied, permitting a Sino–Anglo–American offensive to take place in Burma that was ultimately successful. It lost its strategic purpose, however, once the JCS decided not to use China as the staging area from which to invade Japan. This decision came too late to call off the Burma campaign, fully justifying Britain's persistent lack of enthusiasm for it. Japan's new offensive in southeastern China, which overran many of Chennault's airfields, produced a similar result. Constructed and supplied at enormous cost, in the end they accomplished nothing.

Japan's offensive proved Stilwell to have been right about Chennault's bases being indefensible. It also gave Roosevelt an interest in utilizing the Chinese Communists, a step Chiang feared and which he had thus far prevented. On July 6, 1944, at Marshall's urging, FDR cabled Chiang that the crisis made it imperative for Stilwell to take "command of all Chinese and American forces . . . including the Communist forces."[21] Apart from the military advantages, Roosevelt apparently hoped a unified command might enable the KMT and the CCP to settle their differences. Chiang agreed in principle, but took no other action. In September Washington said there would be no more aid unless Stilwell was empowered at once. Vinegar Joe delivered the message to Chiang personally and with great relish, writing doggerel verses afterward to celebrate having kicked Peanut in the pants.

Stilwell's elation was premature, for Roosevelt had sent another personal emissary to China who, though the situation seemed as bad as it could get, would manage to make things worse. Major General Patrick J. Hurley, in private life a wealthy corporation attorney, and formerly Hoover's Secretary of War, was supposed to be impartial. Instead he sided with Chennault, Joseph Alsop, an influential aide to Chennault, and other members of the anti-Stilwell faction who supported Chiang 100 percent and wanted Vinegar Joe sent home. Hurley encouraged Chiang to press Roosevelt for Stilwell's dismissal and was supported in this by Donald Nelson, who after being forced out as mobilization czar had gone to China with Hurley and returned to Washington singing Chiang's praises. Instead of giving in to official American pressure, therefore, Chiang forced FDR to choose between him and Stilwell. By this time American military leaders had lost faith in China and, with things going so well in the Pacific, no longer saw it as essential to Japan's defeat. Ironically, because the CBI no longer mattered, it was unnecessary to keep Stilwell as theater commander. His special abilities would not be required for what was now a routine assignment. Accordingly, on October 18, 1944, Roosevelt recalled Stilwell and replaced him with Lieutenant General Albert C. Wedemeyer. This pleased the Generalissimo, who failed to understand why the change had come about.

Stilwell's recall led to a flood of stories at home detailing, almost for the first time, the manifold shortcomings of Chiang and the ruling

Kuomintang Party. Though the China Lobby would continue to exercise great influence, the American love affair with China was over. From his post in the British Embassy, Isaiah Berlin marveled yet again at the fickleness of the American public. "The pendulum seems now to have swung as excessively against the Chinese as a year or two ago it had swung in their favor. Shrewd observers did indeed predict at that time that this was the only possible result of unreal heights of mystical adoration which were then being lavished upon China in this country. Rise and fall of this extraordinary political romance offers most strikingly instructive exhibition to date of astonishing instability of American popular emotion."[22]

Thereafter Hurley, who had been named Ambassador to China, made certain that there would be no aid to the CCP and no political concessions. American aid to Chiang and the Kuomintang increased substantially in 1945, even though the KMT made little effort to combat the Japanese. The Reds, too, were husbanding their strength for the coming civil war. Momentum accounts for much of this, also the opening of the Ledo Road, renamed the Stilwell Road, to India. After VJ-Day Wedemeyer commenced a vast airlift that moved entire KMT armies into sectors of China previously occupied by Japan and now threatened by the Communists. On September 30, 1945, Marines landed at Tientsin, where the Japanese garrison was fighting a pitched battle against encircling Chinese Communists. The Marines helped break the siege, fighting alongside what only six weeks earlier had been their hated enemy. In Tsingtao a month later Marines also went into action against CCP units. Soon there were 53,000 Marines in North China and some 100,000 American troops in the country as a whole.

But there was little desire in Washington to fight Chiang's war for him. Even Wedemeyer, despite his narrow partisanship, believed the Generalissimo was failing to make reforms that were crucial to his survival. In November Wedemeyer cabled Washington that Chiang remained tied to the warlords and corrupt officials whose deplorable habits had done so much to make the Communists popular. "Consequently, even though they are unscrupulous and/or incompetent, he appoints them to responsible positions in the Government. They exploit the opportunities presented. Further they appoint worthless subordinates in lesser positions."[23] This made it impossible for Wedemeyer, much though he hated Communism, to recommend that America intervene directly in the civil war. Instead he advised continuing to support Chiang's forces without joining them in battle. After considerable agonizing and soul-searching, that is what the Truman administration did. It had very little choice. Americans were sick of war and would not tolerate another bloody campaign in Asia. On the other hand, to abandon Chiang altogether would bring the China Lobby down on Truman's head. It fell on him anyway, especially after Chiang was driven off the mainland by Mao's forces in 1949.

Though reviled by the right wing for "losing" China, Roosevelt and Truman have been criticized by most historians in this field for supporting Chiang exclusively and failing to establish a solid relationship with the CCP. The Communists were extremely eager for recognition, the foreign service officers in China preferred them to Chiang, and so did the United States Army Observation Group, known as the Dixie Mission (because of its location in rebel territory), which went to Yenan in July 1944. Aid for Mao would have resulted in more military pressure on Japanese troops during the war, and, possibly, better relations with the People's Republic of China later. But there was never any chance of reversing American policy, for even after the Stilwell affair Chiang enjoyed too much support in the United States and Mao far too little. Moreover, as events would show, the Communists too had grievous faults. Superior to the KMT as fighters and administrators, they were, at the same time, real Communists, not merely agricultural reformers—as some of their American friends tried to make them seem. Once in power Mao would prove to be much more effective than Chiang, and, because of that, capable of greater evil. For the long-suffering Chinese, Communism would prove to be just one more affliction.

Roosevelt erred in trying to build up China as a future world policeman. Even the more modest aim of helping Chiang in the war against Japan was unrealistic, given his political goals and numerous liabilities. Not counting that portion assigned to the troops who fought in Burma, the military aid sent to China was largely hoarded or wasted. Apart from tying down a Japanese occupation force of twenty-four divisions, China added little to the war effort and was hugely expensive in terms of what it accomplished. The War Department came to deeply resent such costs, particularly those incurred supplying Chennault's fruitless efforts at a time when more airlift was desperately needed in Europe. Yet, though Roosevelt deserves low marks for his shallow and mistaken view of China, the sad truth is that even if he had known better the end would have been little different. Given Chiang's incompetence, his political influence in Washington, and because the Communists were the only real alternative, to America's China problem there was no good solution.

14

Air Power

The Democratic Delusion

U nlike the heads of totalitarian states, democratic leaders had to worry about the cost in lives of every operation. As most casualties were sustained by the ground forces, it was far from coincidental that both Britain and the United States were eager to find alternatives to bloody land campaigns. In the event, they did not. But, in pursuing the dream of a high-tech and low-casualty offensive, both nations inevitably turned to the air marshals and generals, who held out false hopes of there being a relatively bloodless path to victory. This would lead the United States, at bottom a humane nation, to commit its only real crimes of the war.

To compound the tragedy, aerial bombardment not only failed to win the war but cost the lives of many fliers. On the one hand, advanced technology produced remarkable aircraft crewed by the flower of American youth, volunteers all, who were younger than the Army Ground Forces and much better educated. On the other, these brave and gifted young men flew their superb machines in a moral and strategic vacuum. No aspect of America's war remains harder to defend.

The Allied air forces arrived at their common destiny by different means and from different starting points. Unlike the Royal Air Force, which had been independent since 1918, that of the United States remained a branch of the Army throughout World War II. But it yearned to be a separate service and as early as 1935 had embraced an idea designed to bring that about, the doctrine of strategic bombardment. According to this theory, an enemy could be bombed into submission by attacks on its industrial base. Victory through air power was advanced by Air Marshal Hugh Trenchard, founder of the RAF, and by Italy's General Giulio Douhet. It was promoted ardently by Brigadier General William Mitchell of the United States, who resigned his commission after being court martialed in 1925 for going outside of official channels. Despite Mitchell's punishment, air officers kept the faith.

In 1921 Mitchell had demonstrated that even flimsy World War I aircraft could sink battleships at anchor. Air officers used his demonstration to support the thesis that an enemy would have to surrender as a result of attacks on its factories, power plants, infrastructure, and the like, even if its armed forces remained intact. The enemy's industrial facilities were called "strategic" targets, to distinguish them from the "tactical" objectives of aircraft operating in direct support of ground actions. Politics was the main reason for championing strategic bombardment—which, given the differences between a great industrial state and a handful of undefended warships, Mitchell's demonstration had done little to prove. In order to become independent, or so it was thought, the air arm had to have a war winning capability that would make it equal to, or perhaps even greater than, the older services. Thus, the doctrine of victory through strategic bombing came first, the means to achieve it later.

It seemed absurd at first for the tiny Army Air Corps to represent itself as a potentially war winning service. As late as 1939 it had just 1,600 officers, 18,000 enlisted men, and 1,700 aircraft, most of them obsolete. Yet, despite its minute resources, the Air Corps had already ordered heavy bombers and since 1937 had been receiving the four-engine B-17 Boeing Flying Fortress. It had contracts out for the B-24 Liberator and also the ultimate heavy of the war, the Boeing B-29 Superfortress. This put it ahead of the RAF, which, though a larger service when war broke out, and equally committed to strategic bombardment, did not yet have a true heavy bomber. Thus, when the great expansion took place that it counted on and had planned for, the Air Corps would be able to deploy the world's greatest bomber force.

In 1940 when President Roosevelt stunned everyone by calling for an annual production of 50,000 aircraft, he intended 73 percent of them to be Air Corps models. In September 1941 the Joint Board Estimate of United States Over-All Production Requirements recommended that the newly renamed Army Air Forces should rise to a strength of 2.165 million men and 60,000 aircraft. The primary mission of these machines, according to Air Staff plans, would be to destroy the German economy with precision bombing attacks. The official Air Force history compliments this plan, saying "Viewed solely as a program for the strategic bombardment of Germany, AWPD/1 was on the whole a remarkable document."[1] "Remarkable" is not quite right, unless the irony was deliberate, for the authors' own evidence shows that AWPD/1 erred in just about every respect. It allotted too many aircraft for hemispheric defense, too few for defending the Pacific and supporting the invasion of Europe, while exaggerating the ability of aircraft to bring about a German defeat. About the only thing that AWPD/1 seems to have gotten right was its choice of targets— which, when the time came to bomb Germany, the Air Force would ignore.

Moreover, though AWPD/1 was not at fault here, in pursuing their hypothetical war winning mission the air generals had ordered too many of the wrong kind of aircraft. On December 7, 1941, the Hawaiian Air Force consisted of 231 planes, half of them obsolete. The remainder included 12 B-17s, which were useless against warships, and just 99 P-40s, at that time the Army's best fighter plane. In the Philippines the Far East Air Force had fewer than 150 combat aircraft, of which 35 were heavy bombers (not quite as useless here as in Hawaii since they had the range to attack Japanese bases in Formosa, though when war came, they didn't), and another 107 P-40s. Even if the enemy had not destroyed these two air forces in his first attacks, they would still have been overwhelmed because the all important fighters were outnumbered and out of date.

At the Battle of Midway the AAF's contribution was embarrassingly small, despite its subsequent attempt to take credit for ships actually sunk by naval aircraft. The Army had 17 Flying Fortresses and four B-26 medium bombers on the island. The B-17s making 55 sorties (a sortie being one mission by one aircraft) and the B-26s four torpedo attacks, without, so far as is known, hitting a single ship. Despite its uselessness against warships, and despite the Navy's desperate need for land-based, long-range search planes, the AAF would not allow Admiral King to have any B-17s. Until he could get some heavies of his own, the Navy would have to make do with its vulnerable PBY seaplanes. This was par for the course, interservice politics continuing even during wartime. Later on King would return the favor, holding back VLR Liberators desperately needed in the Atlantic.

The AAF's relatively defenseless status when war broke out was no accident. Through the lean years air officers had neglected fighter aircraft on the basis of an untested theory that a heavily armed bomber could defend itself against enemy interceptors. The airmen's desire for heavy bombers had been frustrated at first by the Army General Staff, which was interested in aerial reconnaissance and direct support of ground troops. The Navy had resisted it, too, viewing long-range aircraft primarily as the "eyes and ears of the Fleet." If prewar military leaders had gotten their way, few if any heavy bombers would have been built.

In the cash-short thirties almost everyone except the future "bomber barons" thought it senseless to purchase B-17s when the same money would buy two or three times as many smaller aircraft. Secretary of War Woodring agreed with the Army and Navy brass, but the B-17 was saved after a visit to Assistant Secretary Louis Johnson by a delegation of air officers. Years later General Ira C. Eaker said of Johnson "He caught the vision that we hoped to inspire in him, and he went personally to see Mr. Roosevelt and had them [B-17s] put back in the budget."[2] This did not end the struggle. Only when George C. Marshall became Army Chief of Staff in 1939 could the Air Corps relax. Marshall believed in strategic bombardment, though as a valuable supplement rather than a war winning strategy. So did Harry Hopkins, who was a friend of General Henry H. "Hap" Arnold, Marshall's choice to head the Air Corps.

Thus, on May 16, 1940, when Roosevelt asked Congress for 50,000 aircraft, heavy bombers included, it was against the will of most generals and admirals, but with the support of key civilians. This was one of those rare cases when laymen determined strategy to a large extent and reflected both the public's affection for air power, the term usually given to strategic bombardment, and its fear of heavy casualties. The polls made this clear, survey after survey showing that the bomber was America's favorite weapon. Indeed, to the degree that such a thing is possible, the vast expansion of the heavy bomber force was democratically arrived at.

When Henry Stimson became Secretary of War a few weeks later, yet another voice was added to the chorus of believers in air power. From that time on there was no doubt that the United States would have a heavy bomber force, and, many assurances about it being for coastal defense to the contrary, it would be used as a strategic weapon. Roosevelt's motives, as so often, are not entirely clear. At the time he asked for 50,000 aircraft he seems to have viewed them mainly as a deterrent, telling congressional leaders that there would have been no Munich if the British and French air forces had been larger. Whether he was thinking ahead to it or not, his huge investment in heavy bombers guaranteed that strategic bombardment would be employed by America during the war.[3]

On August 17, 1942, the AAF launched its first European strategic bombardment mission, a force of 12 B-17s attacking a rail yard in Rouen, France. About half the bombs landed on target, which was a big one, and no planes were lost. Brigadier General Eaker, who commanded Eighth Air Force's VIII Bomber Command and had flown the mission, declared it a success, as well he might, considering how hard a road had been traveled to get there. First came the fight to save the B-17, then countless operational difficulties, delays in ferrying over the aircraft, shortages of trained men, and too few British airfields. Worse still had been the widespread lack of faith among military experts in daylight precision bombing.

There were excellent reasons for a negative view of the concept. Germany had attempted it during the Battle of Britain, but suffered unsustainable losses and went over to bombing at night, which, given the technology of the time, made accuracy impossible. The British fared no better. In the twenties and thirties the RAF had been even more fanatical about strategic bombardment than was the Army Air Corps. It also had spent most of its scarce funds on bombers while scrimping on fighter aircraft. Like the Army Air Corps, it had made no effort to develop a long-range fighter, both services believing that since "The bomber will always get through," there was no need for escorts.

RAF attempts at daylight precision bombing under combat conditions were miserable failures. In September and December 1939 it attacked German naval targets with 159 bombers, losing 29. A loss rate of almost 19 percent was intolerable, and thus, when the RAF began subjecting Germany to strategic bombardment, it had to do so by night when the enemy's fighter force was less effective. From May 1940 until the end of 1941 Britain attacked strategic targets in Germany with negligible results. The War Cabinet commissioned a study which discovered that only one in four air crews who claimed to have hit their target had actually dropped their bombs within five miles of it. The RAF's own casualties were higher than those it inflicted upon enemy civilians.

On November 13, 1941 the RAF's Bomber Command was ordered to halt its long range operations. A critical moment of truth had arrived, but HMG declined suggestions that heavy bombers be sent primarily on tactical and reconnaissance missions. Instead, it decided to renew the bomber offensive, only this time not against German strategic targets but rather against the urban population, because with practice the RAF would learn how to hit the target. By the same token, however, as a city was the smallest target it could find at night, Bomber Command could do little more than kill civilians. In February 1942, under a new commander, Air Marshal Arthur Harris, known to his men as "Butch" (short for butcher), Bomber Command began to attack German cities. Its purpose was what Lord Cherwell, the Prime Minister's science advisor, tactfully called "de-housing the workers," meaning in reality to destroy German morale by destroying German civilians.

Britain made this decision, one of its worst, for political reasons. Russia was demanding a Second Front. Since the British were in no position to invade France, a bomber offensive could be represented as the aerial equivalent. It would also meet the British people's demand for a more aggressive war effort, and, if successful in ruining German morale, it might make a real Second Front unnecessary and save Britain from suffering heavy casualties if Europe had to be invaded. Britain would eventually devote up to one-third of its entire war effort to Bomber Command and destroy an immense number of Germans— many more than half of the 600,000 German civilians killed in bombing attacks. It would also lose over 4,000 bombers and 55,000 crewmen.[4]

All this was not yet apparent in 1942 when Eighth Air Force dropped its first bombs on Europe, but several facts were already alarmingly clear. Germany's air attack on Britain had failed and so had the RAF's attempts to destroy strategic targets in Germany. Further, Britain was engaged in a program of area bombing that was extremely expensive in men and machines, yet seemed to have little effect on German war production. Despite Eaker's attempt to play up the attack on Rouen, it only underscored the problems faced by VIII Bomber Command. Dropping 10 or 15 tons of explosives on a large target accomplished practically nothing. No B-17s were lost because Britain's Fighter Command had provided a strong escort—which it could not do over Germany. Knowing the risks involved in daylight bombing, Churchill wanted the AAF to use its bombers in the war at sea, to support the invasion of North Africa, and to join in the night attacks on German cities. The first two were the best uses to which B-17s could have been put, but they were not why the planes had been sent to England.

American generals argued that the experience of other air forces was not relevant because only B-17s and B-24s had been designed for daylight precision bombing. Both types were heavily armed and armored, payload being sacrificed to defensive capability. Thus, while Bomber Command's splendid Avro Lancaster carried immense 10-ton "blockbusters," the American heavies could drop only two or three tons of ordnance on distant targets. However, Lancasters had but five puny .303-caliber machine guns, while the B-17Es that attacked Rouen were armed with a dozen .50-caliber guns, three pairs being mounted in power turrets. The later G model added yet another power turret with two more guns under the nose. By flying in close formations that provided overlapping fields of fire, the American heavies were supposed to be capable of fighting their way across Germany and back again. In any case, there was no point in adding American bombers to the RAF's night attacks because their small payloads made them unsuitable for area bombing. As bombers, the 17s and 24s could only be effectively used for daylight precision attacks. In the Pacific, where the lack of enemy resistance made accurate low-level sorties feasible, heavy bombers were effective. Against well-defended European targets, it would be a different story.

The theory of strategic bombardment by self-defending forces was not put to the test in 1942 because of the need for heavy bombers in the Mediterranean, where they proved useful against enemy ports and other tactical targets. American heavies in England were ordered to attack submarine pens as the Battle of the Atlantic worsened, which they did with no success as their 500-pound bombs could not penetrate the enemy's concrete shielding. At Casablanca, Churchill finally gave up trying to dictate American air strategy and agreed to the Combined Bomber Offensive, which meant that the RAF would go on bombing at night while the AAF attacked by day. However, because heavy bombers were still being diverted to other theaters, Eighth Air Force grew slowly.

It was not until June 10, 1943 that the order was given to attack German targets, with VIII Bomber Command concentrating especially on the Luftwaffe and its supporting aircraft industry. Despite efforts to provide fighter planes with extra fuel capacity, on their deep penetration raids the bombers still had to go it alone, resulting in terrible casualties. A climax was reached on August 17 when two separate divisions attacked Regensburg and Schweinfurt. Of the 315 heavies that reached their respective targets, 60 went down, a loss rate of 19 percent.

One of the navigators in the main force that went to Schweinfurt was Elmer Bendiner, who later composed a powerful memoir of the bomber offensive. When his combat wing wheeled homeward after dropping its load, Bendiner was appalled to see before him pillars of smoke at intervals as far as the eye could see, each marking the funeral pyre of an American bomber. In *The Fall of Fortresses*, Bendiner wrote "All across Germany, Holland and Belgium the terrible landscape of burning planes unrolled beneath us. It seemed that we were littering Europe with our dead."[5] During a flight that lasted about nine hours his ship was in continuous battle for six. He and the bombardier, standing to their nose guns, were ankle-deep in empty shell casings.

After the attack, 552 men were missing, half of them probably dead. The planes that made it back carried with them another eight dead and 17 wounded. At least 17 of the returning aircraft had to be scrapped, the incredible Fortresses having brought their crews home despite terminal damage. The AAF sought to minimize its losses by claiming that the Luftwaffe had suffered even more, 288 enemy fighters being destroyed according to the press release, though, as usual, Germany had lost far fewer aircraft than the Eighth. What the August 17 attacks proved conclusively was that without fighter support even the stalwart Flying Fortress could not always survive over Germany in daylight.

Eighth Air Force continued to make unescorted attacks. On October 14 it bombed Schweinfurt again and lost another 60 aircraft out of 291 that sortied. This was the fourth such attack mounted since October 8 and raised the total of bombers lost to 148 for the period as a whole. "Black Week," as the airmen called it, stopped Eighth Air Force in its tracks. Bendiner, who participated in this raid, says losses were already so great that of the 18 crews his bomb group sent up only four had been in First Schweinfurt. Only 12 returned from the Second, which was, to his mind, a modern version of the Charge of the Light Brigade. He is bitter about these attacks, having learned after the war that they were continued partly out of fear that if Eighth Air Force did not use its heavies they would be transferred to the Pacific:

> We were sent on a hazardous mission to destroy in a single day an
> objective that was vulnerable only to repeated assaults for which we had

(TOP) Casualties of the 16th Infantry Regiment on Omaha Beach, Normandy, scene of some of the hardest fighting on D-Day. Owing to the military manpower shortage, a rifleman was in the front line, with little rest and no rotation, until he was killed, wounded, captured, or the war came to an end. The Army was too small in part because Congress did not believe—public opinion polls to the contrary—that the American people were willing to accept a labor draft. *(Taylor—Army)*

(BOTTOM) Soldiers of the 60th Infantry Regiment advancing through Belgium in the lee of a Sherman Tank. Often a death trap for the men inside because of its outdated design and the superiority of German armor, the Sherman was still a welcome sight to infantry under fire. That America could build the world's best aircraft, and yet fail to provide its fighting men with a decent tank, was a major paradox of the U.S. war effort. *(Spangle—Army)*

(OPPOSITE, TOP) December 1944. Infantry of the 4th Armored Division move to relieve forces at Bastogne, Belgium, executing one of Patton's most brilliant strokes. Though his race through France had been halted when Eisenhower deprived him of fuel, Patton remained the best Allied army commander, working his magic again here during the Battle of the Bulge. (*Ornitz—Army*)

(OPPOSITE, BOTTOM) With the end in sight, men of the 55th Armored Infantry Battalion and the 22nd Tank Battalion attack Wernberg, Germany, April 22, 1945. Generals engineer battles, but it is the ground soldiers who win them. (*Scrippens—Army*)

(ABOVE) Triumphant Yank infantrymen display a captured swastika in front of a wrecked German tank in Chambois, France, August 20, 1944. The U.S. Army had proven to be the best in the world, because of improved tactics, weaponry, and leadership to be sure, but also because America had produced the best educated generation of any warring nation. It was a democratic triumph. (*Tomko—Army*)

(OPPOSITE, TOP) Lunebach, Germany, 1945, after the U.S. Army had fought through the town. Not only was every large city burned out, but thousands of German villages and hamlets like this were wrecked by the Allied armies. (Army—OWI)

(OPPOSITE, BOTTOM) Citizens of Ludwigslust, Germany, receive a lesson from the 82nd Airborne Division, which ordered them to view the bodies of Nazi torture victims. (Clemmer—Army)

(ABOVE) Red Beach, Tarawa, November 1943, a victory for the U.S. Marines that cost an enormous number of lives in relation to the number of men engaged and the value of what they won. Yet, worse lay ahead, for the Navy had settled upon a policy of assaulting fortified islands in the Central Pacific that would cost the Marines dearly. (Navy)

(ABOVE) Task Group 38.8 enters Ulithi anchorage, 1944. This powerful force, two carriers, three fast battleships and four cruisers, was only one of many at Admiral Nimitz's disposal. Had his mighty fleet been used to support MacArthur, as Nimitz himself preferred, the war against Japan would probably have been won more cheaply. *(Navy)*

(BELOW) The conquerors. Marines take a break off Eniwetok Atoll, February 1944. In the end it was always infantrymen who did the hardest and dirtiest work. Due to the Navy Department's unwise enthusiasm for assaulting Japanese fortresses, they had the lion's share of casualties. *(Platnick—Coast Guard)*

(ABOVE) Scenting victory, General MacArthur, President Roosevelt, and Admirals Leahy and Nimitz confer at Pearl Harbor, July 1944. Although the problem of divided leadership and competing strategies that hobbled the Pacific War was never fully resolved, here wheels were set in motion that would take MacArthur to the Philippines and bring the Army and Navy into closer alignment. (Navy)

(BELOW, LEFT) Christmas eve on Leyte, PI, 1944. During Midnight Mass, First Lieutenant Phyllis Hocking checks the glucose bottle of a wounded GI in the 36th Evacuation Hospital, which had set up in a Catholic church. (Army Staff)

(BELOW, RIGHT) Also on Leyte, a Filipino boy salutes an American combat photographer. Except for the Chinese, no people suffered more at Japanese hands than the Filipinos. Yet despite having been conquered by Americans and ruled as an occupied colony since the turn of the century, the Filipinos remained loyal to the United States and contributed much to their own liberation. (Coast Guard)

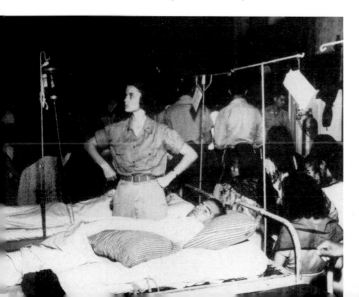

(TOP) Iwo, Jima, February 23, 1945. Joe Rosenthal's renowned photograph became the most famous American combat shot of the war, and continues to be a compelling symbol of the United States Marine Corps, although the flag raising was a staged event, the real one having taken place earlier by the men who captured the summit of Mount Suribachi. Half of the Corps' six divisions were destroyed on Iwo, for the sake of an island that was of little value afterward. (Navy)

(BOTTOM) V-J Day in Times Square, August 15, 1945. Americans had earned the right to celebrate, through their sacrifices and fervent pursuit of honorable objectives. A democratic America which had begun the war slowly, fought it fully to the end. (Kenny—Army)

not the strength. Those objectives could not wait for the arrival of more bombers and long range fighters "because we had to dramatize the importance of air power in the European Theater for the benefit of the public and the Navy."[6]

The aircrews' extraordinary losses destroyed a key rationale for air power, that it would limit casualties on the ground by substituting aircraft for men. In practice this was not borne out. The AAF, with about one-fourth of the Army's manpower, did take only one-ninth of its battle casualties. However, the comparison is misleading because it includes wounded men, of which the Army Ground Forces had many and the Air Forces relatively few. When an American bomber went down, usually half its crew perished and the other half became POWs.

Out of 291,557 American battle deaths in World War II, 52,173 were Army airmen, an enormous number considering that bomber crews made up a small part of the military as a whole. Further, their nonbattle death rate was higher as well because of the hazardous nature of air operations. A total of 35,946 airmen were killed accidentally, 43 percent of all such deaths in the Army. During the worst months of the air war in Europe, medical statisticians followed 2,051 airmen through their duty tour of 25 missions and only 559, or 26.8 percent, completed it—1,195 being killed or missing in action. The odds improved somewhat for American airmen once the Luftwaffe was beaten as a daytime force, though not for Bomber Command, as German night-fighters remained active to the end. Still, bombing Germany was never safe, and overall a high price was paid by American youth to support the AAF's faith in daylight precision bombardment.

Aircrew were given all kinds of special favors, quick promotions, numerous decorations, and freedom from menial duties. Unlike ground soldiers, their tour was limited to 25, later 30, missions involving at most a few hundred hours of combat, although longer tours became more common later. Yet the emotional strain on them was enormous. Some B-29 crews in training, many of whom had fought in the European air war, were given the Neuropsychiatric Screening Adjunct Test, low scores correlating with psychoneurotic tendencies. Officers with combat experience scored lower than those with none. Enlisted veterans scored lower still. Another study of 150 heavy bomber crews found that 95 percent had developed "operational fatigue," marked by tenseness, irritability, hyperaggressiveness, impairment of motor dexterity due to fine or gross tremors, depression, and slowed mental processes. They also showed a big increase in such physical symptoms as nausea, weight loss, dizziness, rapid heart beat, muscle weakness, and the like. During tours of duty airmen suppressed or masked these symptoms, so as not to be separated from their crews. It was only after a tour was finished that the sick call rate rose sharply. Soldiers regarded airmen as the pampered darlings of the Army. This was true in its way, yet deceptive. They had a more comfortable life than the ground forces, yet ran a greater risk of being killed.

After Black Week it was clear that Eighth Air Force had been beaten. There were no more deep-penetration raids into Germany during 1943. Eaker, who had risen to command the entire Eighth, conceded nothing, always insisting afterward that further raids would have been launched except for bad weather. It would have been nice to have had long-range fighter escorts in 1943, but even without them the Eighth had lost "only" an average of 5.2 percent of its bombers per mission, which was entirely acceptable—though not, of course, to the aircrew, none of whom, if losses had been evenly distributed, would have completed their tours of duty.[7]

Eaker's cheery view of the air offensive was not shared by General Arnold, whose nickname "Hap" belied his impatience, hot temper, and ruthlessness. In December he replaced Eaker with General James H. "Jimmy" Doolittle, hero of the first bombing raid on Tokyo in 1942. This was part of a general reorganization according to which VIII Bomber Command was dissolved and its headquarters given to Eighth Air Force. Eighth Air Force HQ in turn became the headquarters of a new entity, the U.S. Strategic Air Forces in Europe, comprising the Eighth and Fifteenth Air Forces—the latter a newly activated command operating from Mediterranean bases. General Carl "Tooey" Spaatz was made chief of the USSTAF, with Eaker taking over all Allied air forces in the Mediterranean, a promotion in theory, though he resented being transferred with its implication of failure.

A more important development was the arrival of the desperately needed long-range P-51 Mustang, the last and greatest propeller driven fighter. It was originally built by North American Aviation for service with the RAF, which upon delivery found it to be underpowered. The British then fitted it with their own superb aeroengine, the legendary Merlin. Thus equipped it could outperform any other propeller-driven fighter. But it still lacked the range to accompany deep attacks. The solution to this problem resulted from an intervention by Robert A. Lovett, Assistant Secretary of War for Air.

As a rule, high-ranking civilians in the War and Navy Departments displayed little independence, believing it their duty to support the brass. However, Lovett had visited Eaker in Britain, and, horrified by its casualty rate, came back determined to see the Eighth equipped with a long-range fighter. Unlike Arnold, whose "hands were tied by his mouth," as Lovett said later, he was not inhibited by having previously championed the idea of a self-defending bomber.[8] He demanded results from Arnold, who dropped the problem on his new chief of staff, Major General Barney M. Giles. The decisive Giles flew at once to California and met with J. H. Kindelberger, president of North American, still the Mustang's only maker. Giles proposed that North American take out a big radio from behind the pilot's seat and replace it with a 100-gallon fuel tank, while also installing bulletproof tanks in the wings. Kindelberger feared that 300 additional gallons of fuel would be more than the wings and landing gear could support, but a test showed that the rugged little Mustang could take it. Thanks to Lovett and Giles, bomber crews would now have a reasonable chance of survival.

By February 1944, reorganized, reinforced, and defended by a large number of fighter groups, the strategic air forces were ready to take on the Luftwaffe once more in Operation Pointblank. On February 20, when bad weather over Germany finally lifted, "Big Week" began. The Eighth put up sixteen combat wings, a battle formation comprised of sixty-three heavies, a thousand bombers in all, and seventeen fighter groups, most equipped with P-47 Thunderbolts and P-38 Lightnings whose range had been extended with belly and wing tanks. These had varying combat ranges, but two groups were flying Mustangs and could go most, and soon all, of the distance to target.[9] In addition, the RAF's fighter command threw in sixteen squadrons of Spitfires and Mustangs. The targets of this immense force were aircraft and ball bearing factories in the Reich, most of which were struck at a cost of twenty-five American bombers and four fighters, the bomber loss rate being just 2.5 percent—a far cry indeed from the attacks on Schweinfurt. Fighter-bomber attacks on German airfields were highly effective as well.

Eighth Air Force was joined on some days by the smaller Fifteenth's Liberators. The RAF's Bomber Command also made five night attacks on Pointblank targets. By the time Big Week was over, the Eighth had made 3,300 bomber sorties and the Fifteenth more than 500. They dropped 10,000 tons of ordnance, more than the Eighth had delivered in its first full year of combat operations. Together VIII and XV Fighter Commands and Ninth Tactical Air Force made 3,773 sorties. The cost was heavy, 2,600 airmen being killed, wounded, or missing, but for the first time something important was gained.

German aircraft production was reduced less than expected because factories had been widely dispersed since 1943. The factories recovered faster as well, so that only about two months' worth of production was lost, compared to three months' as a result of the attacks made in August and October. However, the German fighter force suffered a blow from which it never recovered, losing 600 aircraft and perhaps half that many pilots. The planes were easily replaced but not the men. By March the Luftwaffe was usually avoiding escorted bombers altogether. On April 1 the Combined Bomber Offensive reached its official end. On the twenty-fourth, control of the USSTAF passed to General Eisenhower in preparation for Overlord.

By this time the problem was no longer how to win the air battle, but how best to use the freedom of action that victory had produced. Eisenhower and his ground commanders were fed up with the bomber barons, who had repeatedly failed to make good on their boasts. Harris was the worst offender, telling the Air Ministry on December 7, 1943, as an instance, that if he was given enough planes, "The Lancaster force alone should be sufficient . . . to produce in Germany by 1 April 1944 a state of devastation in which surrender is inevitable."[10] Harris got his aircraft. Germany failed to surrender. So far as Eisenhower could see, and in this he was correct, neither area- nor precision bombing had done much, apart from gaining control of the skies, to prepare the way for Overlord. A fierce struggle over targeting now took place between the air generals and Supreme Headquarters Allied Expeditionary Forces (SHAEF).

Spaatz was committed to the Oil Plan, a proposal for eliminating Germany's sources and supplies of petroleum. Competing with it was the Transportation Plan created by Solly Zuckerman, a British scientist who advised Air Chief Marshal Sir Arthur Tedder, Ike's deputy for air. Zuckerman had discovered that the rail system by which enemy forces in Sicily and Africa moved their troops and supplies had been paralyzed before the invasion of Sicily by bombing only six rail centers. He wanted to repeat this operation on a much larger scale in France. Zuckerman's advice was accepted, a rare event in the air war during which, as Anthony Verrier, a British historian, puts it, "Scientific advisors played a role comparable to court magicians, wizards, or astrologers; if their advice was objective, dispassionate, independent or critical, they were removed."[11]

Although German Air Force installations and aircraft factories retained first priority, the Transportation Plan called for tactical raids on rail yards and similar targets. Heavy bombers also were required by SHAEF to attack V-1 flying-bomb sites on the North Sea coasts, even though Doolittle argued correctly that heavies were not accurate enough to hit the small and easily camouflaged launching ramps.[12] These should have been assigned to the speedy two-engine British Mosquito, which carried a larger bomb load than a B-17 but was as fast as a fighter and so could attack at any altitude with little fear of interception.[13] Another diversion of Fifteenth Air Force heavies to terror attacks on Balkan capitals was equally wasteful. Spaatz was allowed to proceed with his Oil Plan only on a "forces available" basis, but did not have planes enough to do both jobs.

The Transportation Plan worked brilliantly—not so much because of daylight precision bombing attacks by the heavies, but because the fighter–bomber had now come into its own. The wide-ranging tactical air forces were able to cut bridges, and keep them cut, over a very broad area. With the Allies enjoying complete command of the air, they could shoot everything that moved in daylight. Medium bombers also proved highly effective as bridgebusters. Bomber Command showed that it could wipe out tactical targets, both by night, using its improved methods and in low-level day attacks under fighter protection. This was a happy time for Bomber Command, which lost on average only about 1.5 percent of each attacking force and produced excellent results—showing what it could have done save for Harris's area bombing obsession. Instead, when control of Bomber Command reverted to Harris, he went back to area bombing, despite requests by Portal, his nominal superior, to concentrate on strategic targets. For this he should have been sacked, but Portal lacked the nerve.[14]

Because of the Transportation Plan, rail traffic to the invasion area, using an index of 100 for January and February 1944, fell to 69 on May 19, to 38 on June 9, and to 23 by mid-July—despite frantic efforts by Germany to keeps its lines of communication open. Thus, the Allied buildup in Normandy proceeded more rapidly than the German, a vital factor in Overlord's success, as was the Allies' command of the air, to the point where on D-Day the German Air Force made just 319 sorties, compared to 14,700 by the Allies.

Spaatz bootlegged the Oil Plan throughout this period, making attacks nominally in support of the Transportation Plan against petroleum targets. USSTAF had estimated that 90 percent of Germany's liquid fuel and lubricants was produced by 54 oil refineries and synthetic-petroleum plants, of which 27 were especially important. On June 10, 1944, when he regained his independence, Spaatz announced that henceforth oil would have first priority. USSTAF then began attacking targets in the Ruhr and around Ploesti in Rumania. These targets were fiercely defended and thus had the virtue, so to speak, of putting more pressure on the German fighter force, which was now desperately short of pilots.

Though not as costly as in 1943, these attacks were hardly cheap, especially for Fifteenth Air Force since Ploesti was the third best defended target in Europe. The Fifteenth also attacked Vienna, which had the second best air defense. Accordingly, its losses were higher than those of Eighth Air Force and also of Bomber Command, amounting to 318 heavies in July—the Fifteenth's worst month. During August it actually lost more men than did the Allied armies in Italy. When the Red Army reached Ploesti a month later, it found that oil was no longer being produced, an exploit that had cost Fifteenth Air Force 350 bombers.

By September, Germany's petroleum output was reduced to 23 percent of pre–Oil Plan levels, ending German tank training altogether and drastically reducing the training time of Luftwaffe pilots. At the end of 1944 Germany had only four crude-oil refineries in operation, and five or six synthetic plants. By February air attacks on Germany's factories and transportation system had effectively brought industry to a halt. On April 7 the RAF discontinued area bombing, and on the sixteenth Spaatz informed his commanders that the bomber offensive was over. Except for tactical targets there was nothing left to attack.

British air historians, embarrassed by the record of Bomber Command, tend to hold up the AAF as the model which ought to have been copied. Undeniably, for sheer mindless violence, Bomber Command took first place. It commenced terror bombing because it could not attack Germany in any other way. Under Harris it went on raiding German cities long after it was capable of bombing real strategic targets. It committed the two worst crimes of the European air war, the bombing of Hamburg in 1943 and of Dresden in 1945.[15] Both attacks, the second deliberately, created huge firestorms that consumed oxygen faster than it could be replaced, carbon monoxide poisoning killing thousands of people who were untouched by flame or blast. Further,

Dresden had no strategic value, and the war was nearly over. The AAF, in contrast, made serious efforts to bomb precisely and killed far fewer German civilians.

The differences between the two air forces were greater in theory than in practice. More than half of all American attacks ended up with the bombs being dropped through undercast, which was area bombing whatever the military called it. In time, Americans also employed terror bombing intentionally. One series of attacks on February 22 and 23, 1945, codenamed "Clarion," was aimed at small cities and towns that had little or no military importance. The "Thunderclap" bombing of Berlin on February 3, purely a terror raid, killed up to 25,000 civilians. Four other attacks on Berlin were similar in character.

The USSTAF also supported Britain's attack on Dresden in February and, when criticism of area bombing developed, issued a statement saying that there had been no change in policy—an outright lie. Ultimately, American air killed fewer Germans than the British mainly because it dropped smaller bombloads. A touch of moral superiority over the RAF may remain after noting these exceptions, but hardly enough to celebrate.

A crime, the air war was also a blunder. Even the official historians of the AAF admit that daylight attacks on Germany should not have been undertaken before February 1944. Further, though they don't admit this, the constantly shifting rationales of the bomber barons gave their game away. Strategic bombing was supposed to defeat the German nation, but in actual practice the bomber campaign became a war of attrition between the Allied air forces and the Luftwaffe. Control of the skies was supposed to be won by destroying Germany's aircraft industry. As this proved impossible, it was actually won by raids whose principal function was to attract German fighters, the supposedly war-winning heavy bombers serving as bait.

The British and Americans went their own way, seldom coordinating their attacks, which would have made them much more effective.[16] In the same spirit, when it became clear that the American heavies could not perform the mission for which they had been designed, the AAF continued to launch unescorted daylight attacks on the ground that the planes' design ruled out any other uses. The bombing of Japan would take place in a similar strategic void, cities being firebombed because it was what the B-29s could do rather than because doing so made sense.

There was a moral emptiness as well. Alexander P. De Seversky, a founder of Republic Aviation, was the leading publicist of strategic bombing. His best selling *Victory Through Air Power* (1942) was made into an animated movie by Walt Disney. It was a highly appropriate vehicle for De Seversky's fantasies, including his prediction that in three years the AAF would be able to attack Japan from bases in North America. He also firmly asserted that bombers were already capable of "brushing off" enemy fighters, and, though he paid lip service to the original rationale for strategic bombing as being economical and precise, also called for a "war of elimination," which is to say genocide, or something much like it.

Allan A. Michie, a contemporary journalist, was much better informed than De Seversky, whom he rightly called an "air extremist." Michie had been captivated by Arthur Harris, and in 1943 wrote a book advocating that the United States join the RAF's campaign of terror bombing, which he greatly admired, writing that: "About 10,000,000 Germans have been killed, injured, knocked out of their homes, or deprived of their belongings, their clothes, their relatives, their places of employment, or have had their health impaired by the R.A.F. raids."[17] Good as this was, what the Allies really needed to do was destroy Germany's 50 biggest cities, an easy task he was certain. Michie understood that B-17s and B-24s lacked the payload for area bombing. Therefore, he called upon the United States to start building Lancasters on license. So much for air moderation.

Eaker regarded this book as enough of a threat to issue a statement in defense of the Combined Bomber Offensive, receiving a rebuke from *Newsweek* magazine on February 22, 1943 for having failed to address the technical issues. Few Americans complained about the essential barbarity of strategic bombing, which would cause many civilian deaths no matter how skillfully executed. In any case, the AAF would go on to employ terror bombing deliberately, taking a leaf from Britain's book.

There appears to have been only one significant protest against the bomber offensive. The March 1944 issue of *Fellowship*, an American religious publication, carried an article by English pacifist Vera Brittain, criticizing area bombing. It was accompanied by a statement issued over the signatures of 28 clergymen and pacifists declaring "Christian people should be moved to examine themselves concerning their participation in this carnival of death."[18] Their protest was widely publicized but had no effect beyond inspiring General Arnold to demand that his public relations officers generate more favorable press coverage. Because there were no further public protests only news stories in which the word "terror" was used to describe American bombing raids, he was under little pressure to change.

The high degree of independence Arnold enjoyed, and Harris's even greater freedom, underscored a central weakness of the air campaigns which Michael Sherry has pointed out. Not only did the bomber barons themselves have no coherent strategy after the failure of daylight precision bombing, but air power did not figure in the strategy of the Allied high command. Roosevelt, Churchill, and the Combined Chiefs of Staff, despite their huge investment in it, gave little thought to strategic bombing, only now and then insisting on particular missions.[19] Otherwise, it had a life of its own unrelated to the larger war effort.

After victory in Europe a United States Strategic Bombing Survey was commissioned by the AAF. It did not make moral judgments, nor did it seek to criticize the fundamental decisions that had shaped the bomber offensive. Yet, though the USSBS's report was narrow, one may draw from it conclusions that undermine much, if not all, of the thinking behind strategic bombardment. The USSBS was very interested in target selection and discovered that it had been faulty. There should have been more raids on aeroengine plants rather than on airframe assembly targets. The attacks on ball bearing plants did not justify the effort. The Oil Plan was too late and too little, likewise the attacks on rail facilities, which could have been highly effective if begun earlier, since the German economy ran chiefly on coal. When the rail system finally collapsed, German industry did also.[20] The electric power system was highly vulnerable and ought not to have been neglected. These were mainly failures of air intelligence that did not get to the essentials.

Far more telling was the USSBS's discovery that the strength of German industry had been grossly underestimated, as also the number of attacks required to put a given target out of business. Accuracy as a whole was terrible, only 3 percent of all bombs dropped actually striking damageable targets. The bombs themselves were too small, and too many of them were duds. RAF raids often were more effective because they employed much larger bombs and more incendiaries, and kept planes over the target longer, preventing fire fighters from doing their work. In short, though it did not say so, what the USSBS discovered was that the Air Force had used the wrong bombers. Allan Michie was right about one thing after all. What the USSTAF really required were Lancasters, which, when escorted by Mustangs, would have made daylight bombing more effective by increasing the tonnage dropped. Strategic bombing would still have been morally wrong, but with the consolation at least of producing useful results.[21]

The very best course would have been not to send heavies against German targets at all. Doing so was inhumane, since the technology of the time did not permit bombers at high altitudes to discriminate between strategic and residential targets. It was too costly, in that the men and machines were more valuable than the damage they inflicted. The usual estimate is that strategic bombing reduced German war production by about 9 percent. To achieve this, the United States devoted 9 percent of its much larger war effort to bombing Germany, and Britain more than 25 percent. Though fewer American than British aircrew died, the losses were still very heavy. The U.S. Eighth and Fifteenth Air Forces had 73,000 casualties, 29,000 of them fatal. By comparison, the US Navy had a total for the entire war of 69,000 casualties—including 16,000 fatalities. A selective bombing campaign using strongly escorted bombers, and the magnificent Mosquito which required no escort, would have produced good results at a much lower cost.

Strategic bombing did have marginal benefits. It gave the Allies command of the air over Europe. Because of this many German resources needed on the battlefield were diverted to air defense. But the immense Allied superiority in fighters would have given them air supremacy anyhow, and the men and materials employed to defend Germany against air attack could have been destroyed more cheaply in other ways. Further, if Britain and the United States had not invested so much in heavy bombers, they would have fielded larger and better armies and it was the ground forces, supported by tactical air, that were decisive in Europe. The German economy was destroyed too late to make much difference while Eisenhower's armies were slowed down by manpower and supply shortages caused in part by the excessive size of the heavy bomber force—including its enormous ground-support staff.

A few facts and figures will give some idea of the resources committed to strategic bombing. In 1943, a typical bomb group, of which there were 25, provided about 20 heavies for a given mission. The base from which the 200 aircrew took off housed 1,600 men, had required 1.5 million man-hours to build, and consumed 640,000 square yards of concrete—the equivalent of a road 18 feet wide and 60 miles long. Mounting a 500-plane attack took the efforts of 5,000 aircrew, 30,000 groundcrew, and 32,500 other base personnel, not counting the men and women in Air Service Command, who supplied and supported the bases. By the end of 1944 Eighth Air Force alone would be staging 2,000-plane raids. If devoted to the ground war, the same number of men and amount of materials would have given Eisenhower the equivalent of another army in France, something he badly needed. The entire war in Western Europe was jeopardized by this misallocation of strength, as became clear when Allied planners turned their minds to Overlord.

More than any other Allied effort, the air war showed that, while democracy is the best form of government, it is far from perfect. In peacetime Americans had agreed that bombing civilians was murder. When war came almost no one complained about it, even when newspapers reported that the United States was staging terror raids. Some coarsening of its moral fiber must be expected of a nation fighting a terrible foe. But the United States had never previously made war against women and children, and should not have done so then. Even a war for democracy must have limits.

15

The GI

Of the approximately 16 million Americans who served in World War II, some 10 million were in the Army Ground Forces. Unlike sailors and airmen, most soldiers were draftees, and the Army's makeup was heavily influenced by Selective Service priorities. An initial problem was that Americans did not think fathers should be drafted, as a result of which the average age of soldiers in 1944 was 26, while it was 23 for sailors and 22 for Marines. The Army found itself drafting single men in their forties while sparing married men half their age. This had to change as casualties mounted. Thus, although fathers made up only 6 percent of those drafted in October 1943, by the following April they constituted over half.

Another change as the war developed was the process of "skimming," whereby the Army Service Forces got most men with technical skills and the Army Air Force the pick of those who scored highest in qualification tests. As a result, combat soldiers were less educated than other military personnel, having a year of high school on average, and were also shorter and lighter. In 1943 the AAF lost its skimming privileges. In 1944 General Marshall closed down the Army's specialist academic programs, and the training of air cadets as well. The transfer of personnel—some 30,000 air cadets alone—to the infantry was one reason why American divisions improved with time while everyone else's deteriorated.

Most American soldiers saw little or no combat because they played supporting roles to the men who actually fought. In part this was because American soldiers enjoyed a higher standard of living than troops of other nations, also because the Army was so far from its bases at home, and had to devote more of its resources to transportation and logistics. All told, the Army sustained 949,000 casualties, of which 175,000 were killed in action. Thus, the chance of being hit was less than 1 in 10, and of being killed less than 1 in 50. In a combat unit the odds underwent a radical shift, the infantry suffering 264 casualties per 1,000 men per year, and the armor 228. Combat engineers, medics, and tank destroyer units had similar casualty rates.

Even this understates the risk, because casualties were not spread throughout an infantry division but were concentrated in its rifle companies. Additionally, these figures are for the entire war, while the heaviest ground fighting took place between June 1944 and June 1945. For the last six months of 1944, between 12,000 and 18,000 GIs were being killed each month and 40,000 to 60,000 wounded. In a typical rifle company combat losses would ultimately surpass by as much as 50 percent the number of men originally assigned to it. Few riflemen escaped unscathed.

While the greatest number of casualties were sustained in Europe, men preferred it to the Pacific. Overall casualty rates were lower in the Pacific chiefly because 60 percent of all casualties were caused by artillery rounds, and the Japanese had inferior munitions. There were actual cases of Japanese wounded attempting to commit suicide with hand grenades and only bruising themselves. In Europe the "lethality" rate for shrapnel wounds was one in four, in the Pacific only 16 percent. However, the Pacific was much less healthy than Europe, which resembled home to some extent and had towns and liquor and women. Except for beer and illegally distilled spirits, the Pacific had little to offer. Most fighting took place in jungles where heat and humidity were high and the disease rate enormous. Malaria was everywhere, and also dengue fever, parasites, scrub typhus, diarrhea, swimmers itch, tree sap dermatitis, and every other skin ailment known to man, plus a mysterious disease called "blue nail," which the doctors never did figure out.

In consequence, the rates of combat fatigue, what the Army called "neuropsychiatric" or NP cases, were much higher in the Pacific. After three months of fighting on New Georgia a force of 30,000 men had

13,000 hospital admissions for illness and injury. Of these, 27 percent were wounded in action, 11 percent were otherwise injured, 21 percent had malaria, 18 percent suffered from diarrheal diseases, and 19 percent were neuropsychiatric.[1] The incidence of NP cases on New Georgia was not exceptional by World War II standards, since it was a rule of thumb that the longer an action lasted, the more NPs there would be, regardless of other conditions. In Europe the Army would experience 110,000 NP cases as a whole, but they were highly concentrated. During one 44-day period of intense combat on the Gothic Line in Italy, 54 percent of all casualties were neuropsychiatric.

The high incidence of NPs caught both psychiatrists and Army leaders by surprise, despite the relatively large number of mentally damaged soldiers that World War I had produced. These were so many and so serious that as late as 1942 some 58 percent of all patients in Veterans Administration hospitals were World War I "shell shock" victims. World War II psychiatrists believed they had developed a screening process that would keep most men liable to become NP cases out of the Army. Their confidence was such that of 5.2 million men who appeared at Army recruiting stations, 1.6 million were rejected for "mental deficiencies." Yet, psychiatric discharges from the Army would be 2.5 times as common as in the previous war.[2]

By mid-1944 it was clear that experience did not support previous theories about the relation between combat and mental illness. Upon returning from Italy, where he had studied the problem first-hand, John W. Appel wrote a report giving the military new guidelines for dealing with neuropsychiatric problems. Their primary cause, he argued, was not individual weakness but that American soldiers remained in combat for longer periods than their nerves could tolerate. This personal observation was correct. It was Army policy to keep combat units on line for long periods, replacing losses individually rather than by units. Thus, as Stephen Ambrose says, "The veteran could look forward to a release from the dangers threatening him only through death or serious wound. This created a situation of endlessness and hopelessness" that made for a heavy NP caseload.[3]

Combat officers had also noticed that men reached their peak of efficiency after about 90 days on the line. Then they all started to deteriorate, regardless of individual strength or courage. A survey of platoon leaders in two veteran infantry divisions by the Army Research Bureau revealed that when asked which soldiers they would most hate to lose, the greatest concentration among enlisted men were those with four to five months of experience, including days spent in rear areas, and among NCOs those with six to eight months. Both groups reached their highest level of performance between their third and seventh months, while after eight months they were less effective than men with shorter combat records. Contrary to the earlier view that some men were predisposed to break down, it was found that after enough time in battle, 200 days being about the maximum, somewhere between 140 and 180 the average, everyone broke.

Appel was right, therefore, when he urged the Army to take men out of the line at regular intervals and to rotate them back home after a fixed period of duty. He also stressed the importance of keeping the troops together, since unit cohesion was an important factor supporting mental health. As a result, the Army in Europe did introduce reforms, even though, for lack of replacements, too late and on too small a scale. Unlike his British and even German counterparts, the American combat soldier was doomed to fight on without adequate rest or relief until the war was over.

Though the Army did not change, psychiatrists did, introducing more aggressive therapies. North African NP casualties had been sent to hospitals hundreds of miles to the rear, from which fewer than 10 percent returned to duty. Later, a series of psychiatric care levels was established that started with battalion surgeons operating close to the front. They provided psychiatric first aid, consisting mostly of mild sedation, a good night's sleep, and hot food. More serious cases went to division clearing stations two to five miles farther back, where they were sedated longer and allowed to bathe. For tough cases the next level of treatment was at "exhaustion centers" where patients might actually receive psychiatric treatment. After a week or 10 days, if all else had failed, the most seriously disturbed went into neuropsychiatric hospitals, from which they seldom returned to combat.

This graduated approach produced impressive results, about 60 percent of NPs returning to their outfits within five days, while 70 percent of those hospitalized were later given noncombat assignments in which they replaced men fit for battle.[4] By revolutionizing neuropsychiatric care, American doctors made their biggest contribution to victory. Conventional medicine improved as well, thanks to sulfa drugs, penicillin, blood plasma, and other medications and treatments. However, they were offset to a large degree by developments in weaponry and munitions. Thus, despite the fact that medical care had progressed enormously since the 1860s, battlefield death rates remained similar to those of the Civil War. It was only in psychiatry that doctors got ahead of the game. This breakthrough would prove critically important after Overlord, when every man was needed.

If the Army failed its combat soldiers in many ways, at least it did succeed in establishing a healthy attitude toward combat fatigue. GIs were tolerant of fright as long as a man struggled against it and were understanding of those disabled by fear, knowing they could not help themselves. Only those who asked for relief were regarded as cowardly. The Army's permissive attitude toward fear probably cut the number of NP cases and definitely reduced certain neurotic reactions that had been common in World War I. Notable among these was "conversion hysteria," in which repressed fear led to physical impairment. This was not true of paratroopers, however, whose code of toughness prevented them from acknowledging fear, and who were therefore the only group of soldiers to get such conversion symptoms as paralysis of the legs. Thus, in spite of officers like George S. Patton, Jr., who detested NPs, combat soldiers gained from the Army's sophisticated approach to the stress of battle and were more effective because of it.

Easily the most striking thing about the GI was how well he fought, considering his truly remarkable lack of abstract motivation. Thanks to extensive studies made at the time by social scientists, we know more about the GIs (the letters "GI" standing for Government Issue, the legend inscribed on their belongings) than we do about the soldiers of any other war. These examinations, which were summed up in two fat volumes entitled *The American Soldier*, make abundantly clear that most GIs had little interest in war aims and cared only about getting it over with. Investigators found that fewer than a tenth of the men viewed the war "from a consistent and favorable intellectual position," which is to say, understood the issues and supported the war effort on its merits.[5]

Nearly all accepted that having been attacked the United States must defend itself and that they owed the nation a duty. However, for most, winning the war was not the primary goal but rather a means to their real end, to be discharged from the Army. Thus, when soldiers were asked to name the Four Freedoms for which they were ostensibly at war, only 13 percent could remember as many as three. This low level of interest in the war's purpose might seem odd today, considering that it is remembered as the one all Americans believed in. Yet, it could not have been otherwise, given the strength of isolationism earlier and the fact that America seemed to have so little at stake as far as most citizens were concerned.

In some ways the soldiers' lack of political conviction was one of the biggest nonissues of the war, not just among liberals but in the mass media, too. *Life* was forever lamenting the GI's failure to take an interest in world affairs. This theme was developed extensively by Hanson W. Baldwin, a leading military correspondent for *The New York Times*, who argued that the GI had to achieve moral as well as technical excellence. "He could be a better soldier if his curiosity and eagerness for knowledge and discussion were satisfied adequately; if he developed a political consciousness as well as combat proficiency, and if the Army tried to inculcate in him ideals of character and standards of self-discipline as well as efficiency in battle."[6]

Baldwin seemed unaware that the Army did try to fire men up, with little success. Making them watch Frank Capra's "Why We Fight" series improved their knowledge of the issues but had no effect on attitudes. Orientation courses given by the Army's Information and Education Division also had little effect. Among other things, the orientation lecture was an official activity, "which meant that there was a tendency for the men to regard it with the same hostility and distrust that they had for the Army as a whole."[7] There was also the fact that, after being lectured about democracy and individualism the soldier returned to an environment where there was no democracy and little respect for the individual.

To the GI, all efforts at official uplift were "bullshit," like practically everything else in the Army. On the other hand, these lectures, though they had no effect on attitudes, were useful when well done because the soldiers enjoyed them. Often the topics interested GIs. Moreover, these were the only times when soldiers were asked to express an opinion. The lesson here, which good commanders knew anyway, was that while you could not motivate GIs to fight by invoking lofty principles, you could raise morale—morale being, in fact, the American substitute for ideological or nationalistic commitment.

A variety of factors, beyond such obvious ones as training and leadership, combined to make individuals good fighters. The Army Research Branch used the ratio of nonbattle to battle casualties as a measure of combat effectiveness, since it was axiomatic that companies with more nonbattle casualties, usually self inflicted, would send fewer men to the front. In actual practice it found that units with high rates of nonbattle casualties were unusually reluctant to go into battle and lacked self-confidence.

A regiment of the 70th Infantry Division, which reached France just in time for the Battle of the Bulge, was found by Research Branch investigators to have 33 percent of its men above average in combat effectiveness, 39 percent average, and 28 percent below average. However, when education, Army test scores, age, and marital status were factored in, quite different results emerged. Of the men who were high school graduates, scored well on tests, displayed mechanical aptitude, were married, and over the age of 24, 58 percent were rated above average in combat and only 6 percent below. Conversely, of unmarried grade school graduates under the age of 24 with low test scores, only 22 percent rated above average, and 40 percent below. This was striking evidence that the Army's original policies of exempting married men and skimming those drafted had been harmful to battle readiness. The preference of every armed service for men in the youngest age groups, which did not change, was probably mistaken as well.

Severe punishments were of little or no value in getting men to fight. Soldiers did not fear being executed for cowardice since this happened only once. They were unafraid of long stockade sentences also, believing that terms of imprisonment would be revised downward after the war. They did fear loss of pay and family allotments if courtmartialed, of being disgraced in the eyes of family and friends, and experiencing shame or guilt. If an officer was respected by his men, these pressures worked in his favor. If he was disliked, on the other hand, punishments alone would not make his unit effective. Veterans admired and had greatest confidence in officers who took a personal interest in them, showed courage, and led from the front. Company-grade officers knew and practiced this, which contributed to their astronomical casualty rates.

The Army Ground Forces did not do all that it could have to raise morale, especially by comparison with the Army Air Force, which gave aircrew special privileges, high rank, promotions, and numerous awards and decorations. One survey of men in the European Theater of Operations (ETO) found that while combat aircrews wore the same number of campaign stars as combat soldiers, they had 530 awards and decorations for every 100 men, whereas ground troops averaged only 39. Worse still, a large share of ground Army medals were given out to headquarters personnel rather than to fighting men.

The 84th Infantry Division's K Company, which suffered over 100 percent casualties among its riflemen, received six Silver Stars, two posthumously, 15 Bronze Stars, and one Belgian decoration. The 58 officers in division headquarters received four times as many medals and the enlisted men in headquarters twice as many, even though K Company sustained more casualties in its worst hour on the line than the total number experienced by these rear-echelon troops during their entire time in Europe. E Company of the 101st Airborne had a similar experience. A unit of 140 men that suffered over 150 percent casualties had received by V-E Day just three or four Silver Stars and a dozen Bronze Stars. Purple Hearts aside, most men had nothing beyond the four battle stars, which were awarded to everyone, clerks and riflemen alike, on their ETO ribbon. The unfairness of this generated much ill will among the troops.

Medals were not merely symbolic, for each decoration added five points to the total that determined when a man would be discharged from the Army. In recognition of this, after V-E Day Major General Maxwell D. Taylor, who commanded the 101st, gave every combat veteran a Bronze Star to speed him homeward. Mostly, however, combat soldiers not only got few rewards but were actually discriminated against. In contrast, aircrews on short leaves or weekend passes had superior quarters and facilities available to them. Their rapid promotion was a staple of GI humor.

The ground forces could have done these things, too, but seldom made the effort. When on leave, combat soldiers had either the same comforts and entertainments as men stationed in the rear or even fewer. By the time supplies of food and clothing reached the front, all the best items had been siphoned off. While in aircrews all enlisted men were NCOs, men who entered the ground forces after July 1, 1943 had little chance of making sergeant unless their superiors were killed or wounded. The one advantage of being a combat soldier is that this happened very often. Otherwise, it remained the rule for combat troops that those who ran the greatest risk got the worst of everything.

Also self-defeating, as well as unfair, was the military's treatment of homosexuals. Ever since the Kinsey report on male sexual behavior came out in 1948, it has been a truism, though not necessarily true, that about 10 percent of males are homosexual. Whatever the exact percentage, there were a large number of gay men in the services about whom little was known until recently. Now, thanks to the work of Allan Bérubé, it is possible to make some generalizations.[8] An important one concerns the decision to have a military policy on homosexuals. Before World War II, while homosexual acts were forbidden, no effort was made to weed gays out of the armed forces. This became official policy only in 1941, when homosexuality was listed for the first time as a disqualification for military service.

In practice, the ban was not widely enforced, since it would have quite literally decimated the armed forces. There was no practical reason for excluding gays, since it has never been shown that homosexuals are inferior fighters or harmful to unit efficiency. But it was, and remains, a Pentagon article of faith that homosexuality in some undefined way makes men and women less soldierly. However, the screening process was so crude that of about 18 million men examined for service, only between 4,000 and 5,000 were rejected on the basis of sexual orientation.

A more important change was the military's decision to discharge gays, not just for committing a homosexual act, but simply for being homosexual—a loosely defined category that was subject to much abuse. Under this new regime, thousands of soldiers and sailors were discharged, compared with only a few hundred men who had been convicted of sodomy—a penal offense—between 1900 and the beginning of World War II. Represented as the humane alternative to prison, undesirable discharges nevertheless had severe consequences for many who were returned to civilian life. In March 1945 Secretary Stimson, deciding that the Army could no longer afford this prejudice, ordered that all cases of discharged self-confessed homosexuals be reviewed with an eye toward reinducting as many as possible. Many gays had become combat medics, or chaplain's assistants who sometimes also performed medical duties. Given the high casualty rate among medics, the need here was especially great.

On the other hand, despite the turn away from punishment to discharge, there were numerous episodes of antigay witch hunts and purges, usually depending on the whims of individual officers. The victims were confined in makeshift prisons called "queer stockades," "queer brigs," and "pink cells" by the troops. Though the figures remain secret, many gays were imprisoned in this way, some to be sent home on "queer ships." Tens of thousands were given so-called blue discharges which, among other penalties, denied the holder any rights under the GI Bill, regardless of length or quality of service. Although for a brief period after the war some blue discharges were reclassified, in 1947 the military resumed its policy of stigmatizing homosexuals. It still remained easier to be gay than black, since all Negroes were discriminated against, while only the small proportion of gays who were identified as such became subject to penalties and punishment. Yet, it is not much of a defense that antigay military policies could have been even worse.

The principal reason for the Army's manpower shortage, which became acute after D-Day, was its inability to use women on a large enough scale. The War Department was not to blame for this. Marshall and Stimson were early and enthusiastic backers of the effort to recruit women. In 1941 when Eleanor Roosevelt and Representative Edith Nourse Rogers (R–MA) urged that women be enlisted, the Army drew up a bill establishing the Women's Army Auxiliary Corps, which Mrs. Rogers introduced in Congress. Opposition to having women in the military was immediate and worsened as time went on. Some thought the WAAC would be too expensive, others that it would hurt discipline. As finally enacted, the bill discriminated against women soldiers by making their pay structure lower than that of men.

A War Department study established that fully half of the Army's jobs could be performed by women, for behind the front was a huge weaponless army of uniformed clerks and laborers whose work was not gender-specific. The Navy, hostile to having women at first, came to similar conclusions. It then outdid the Army by creating its own Waves, who made twice as much money as Waacs, and had a smarter uniform. This latter judgment is not a matter of personal opinion, since on January 29, 1944, Dr. Gallup released a poll showing that a large plurality of Americans believed the Waves and Spars (Coast Guard) had the best looking uniforms, with the female Marines being a distant second and Army women dead last.

In addition to pay inequities, the WAAC was put into General Brehon Somervell's Army Service Forces, which made every mistake possible in recruiting, training, and deploying women. In 1943 a new Women's Army Corps (WAC) came into being, to which most Waacs transferred. It was placed directly under the General Staff, after which conditions improved. What could not be improved, however, was the widespread contempt for female soldiers, which resulted in endless amounts of bad publicity and slanderous whispering campaigns.

Wacs were said to be promiscuous, indeed, to have volunteered for predatory sexual purposes. A classic headline that appeared in the *Washington Times–Herald* read "Stork Pays Visit to Waac Nine Days After Enlistment." Army and civilian newspapers ran many cartoons making fun of women in uniform. Surveys found that many soldiers were convinced that 90 percent of Wacs were prostitutes, even though their VD rate was minimal compared to that of male soldiers, and pregnancies in the WAC were one-fifth those of single civilian women in the same age group. Yet servicemen continued to warn their girlfriends against joining up on the ground that Wacs were whores— or, alternatively, lesbians, and in either case unfit associates.

The War Department racked its collective brain to counter this negative propaganda. An early recruiting campaign with the theme "Release a Man for Combat" backfired, as it implied that women who enlisted could be condemning their loved ones to death. Some believe the WAC never recovered from this. In any case, the whispering campaign was so salacious and widespread that it could easily have been fatal by itself. The result was that while Marshall hoped for a WAC of 500,000 women, it never exceeded 100,000.

If Congress had been willing there was an easy solution to this problem, for Gallup polls taken throughout the war showed that a majority of women aged 21 to 35 supported the idea of a female military draft. Conscription would have put the morality issue to rest, for conscripted women, like male soldiers, would have the same sexual tastes as civilians. In light of the double standard, according to which men who joined up freely were patriotic but women who did so were sluts, the draft was just as important for the WAC as for the regular Army.

Congress's failure to enact a female draft was a serious blow to the war effort. The limited number of women who braved public scorn to volunteer released the equivalent of seven divisions of men for active service. The Army Ground Forces did not make the best use of its women. Too many Wacs were employed at clerical tasks that could as easily have been done by civilians. But some were used as decontamination experts in the Ordnance Corps, as photographers and cryptoanalysts, and in other specialized jobs. The Army Air Forces, which enlisted half of all Wacs, employed them to the fullest. General Arnold opened every noncombat assignment and school to Wacs, who performed superbly.

Ultimately 10,000 Wacs served in the ETO and 6,000 in the Southwest Pacific, where they quickly proved their worth. Eisenhower could not get enough of them. MacArthur called Wacs "my best soldiers." Women nurses, who encountered little resistance, served nobly in all theaters, and intrepid civilian women ferried military aircraft across some of the most dangerous transoceanic routes. Thus, long before the war in the Persian Gulf, women proved that they belonged in uniform. If only the War Department could have overcome prejudice and congressional opposition, women soldiers would have solved the military manpower problem.[9] Perhaps even more than overt discrimination, the failure of democracy to recognize women as equals jeopardized the war effort.

As the war in Europe progressed GIs became better fighters, but they never lost the qualities that made them civilian at heart, their contempt for bullshit and for "chickenshit," too, which was rampant in the Army, as well as their compassion. Though some GIs committed crimes or, ground down by combat, were cruel to prisoners and even civilians, the majority retained the values they had brought with them into the Army. Usually the earliest contacts between liberators and the liberated was made by GIs passing out food and treats. For many in France the first signs of freedom were showers of candy and gum pouring from the open hatches of rolling American tanks. As conquerors they would act much the same, defeating the Army's efforts to keep them from fraternizing with Germans.

Liberals wanted GIs to be high-minded and political. Generals would have liked to see more military polish and snap. What they got was an Army of homesick, wisecracking skeptics who were at the same time soft touches for a hungry child or a pretty face. These habits did not prevent them from becoming outstanding soldiers, while their retention of civilian values was proof that, for all its failings, American democracy worked.

16

Overlord

In 1944 the U.S. Army would meet its supreme test by invading occupied Europe. When they grappled with the mighty Wehrmacht, America's young men would be led by two of the greatest commanders their country ever produced—Dwight David Eisenhower and George S Patton, Jr. Though products of the same democracy, they could hardly have been more dissimilar. Between them stretched the entire range of personality types that characterized American commanders. Eisenhower was friendly, unpretentious, efficient, in many ways the national ideal of a military leader, and celebrated as such. Patton was at the opposite extreme, the epitome of arrogance and theatricality, yet he was admired also. The American military, like the nation itself, was a coat of many colors.

Eisenhower was born on October 14, 1890, the third son of industrious, devout, German–American parents of modest means but remarkable talents, judging by their successful children. He grew up in Abilene, Kansas, once a famous cowtown but in Eisenhower's youth just another drab Midwestern village with no claims to distinction. It also lacked diversity, the citizens being WASP Republicans with similar ideas about everything. Eisenhower always regarded it as an ideal hometown just the same, because class lines were not sharply drawn and there was a strong emphasis upon democracy, morality,

North Sea

ENGLAND

London

English Channel

THE NETHERLANDS

Amsterdam

Rotterdam

Neder R.

Arnhem

Ems R.

Waal R.

Nijmegen

Maas R.

Rhine R.

Wesel

Dortmund

Eindhoven

Essen

Ruhr R.

Scheldt Estuary

Antwerp

Dusseldorf

BELGIUM

Roer R.

Cologne

Brussels

Aachen

Duren

Bonn

Scheldt R.

Liège

HUERTGEN FOREST

Namur

Malmédy

Monshau

Remagen

Dinant

Trois Ponts

St.Vith

Coblenz

Houffalize

Frankfurt

Bastogne

Our R.

Main R.

Echternach

LUX.

Moselle R.

Mainz

Sedan

Luxembourg

Saarbrücken

Verdun

Metz

Moder R.

Seine R.

Meuse R.

Nancy

Paris

Strasbourg

FRANCE

BLACK FOREST

Colmar

Loire R.

Belfort

Kms
0   100

0   100
Miles

Saone R.

SWITZERLAND

Zurich

Bern

Baltic Sea

● Hamburg

Elbe R.

Aller R.

Leine R.

...eser R.

Potsdam ● ◎Berlin

G E R M A N Y

● Kassel

Saale R.

Mulde R.

● Torgau

Leipzig ●

Dresden ●

Neisse R.

P O L A N D

Oder R.

◎ Prague

C Z E C H O S L O V A K I A

● Bayreuth

Pilsen ●

● Nuremberg

Regensburg ●

Stuttgart

Danube R.

● Augsberg

● Munich

A U S T R I A

Vienna ◎

● Berchtesgaden

● Innsbruck

© A·Karl/J·Kemp, 1991

achievement, and hard work. Much as he resembled them in other ways, Eisenhower was different from small town Americans of his generation in being relatively unprejudiced and having a knack for dealing with all kinds of people. These gifts would help make him the outstanding leader of coalition forces in World War II.

Eisenhower attended West Point for the free education rather than from dreams of martial glory. His early career was accordingly undistinguished. When Eisenhower graduated in 1915, he ranked sixty-first in a class of 164. In 1922 he was assigned to the Canal Zone as executive officer to General Fox Connor, who changed his life. Connor, a student of military science and history, became Eisenhower's mentor, leading the young officer through a program of study with a particular aim in mind. Connor believed that there was going to be another world war in which American generals would lead allied forces. He wanted Eisenhower to be one of these favored commanders. After Eisenhower's three-year tour in Panama was up, Connor pulled strings to get him into the Command and General Staff School at Leavenworth, an essential requirement for promotion to the highest ranks. After a year of study Eisenhower graduated at the top of a class of 275 officers, all selected for their promise.

Because peacetime Army promotion was glacially slow, this achievement, while it made him known to superiors, did not bring immediate benefits. However, in 1933 Eisenhower became an aide to General Douglas MacArthur, then Army chief of staff, whom he served under in Manila as well after MacArthur took command of the Philippine armed forces. In 1940, only a lieutenant colonel after 25 years of service which had earned him the highest praise from MacArthur as well as Connor, Eisenhower became a regimental executive and battalion commander in the 3rd Infantry Division. The Army was now on the verge of tremendous growth, and Eisenhower would rise with it. In January 1941 he was made chief of staff to General Walter Krueger's Third Army, receiving much of the credit when Third Army defeated Second Army in the big Louisiana maneuvers of August and September. Five days after Pearl Harbor, General Marshall summoned him to the War Department, where by April Eisenhower was a major general in charge of planning. On June 11, 1942, he was appointed to command the new European Theater of Operations—which brought him a third star and eventually five.

By the end of 1943 Eisenhower had behind him not only a meteoric rise, even by wartime standards, but the experience of successfully commanding three amphibious invasions. This made him the logical

Normandy and the Anglo–American Advance to the Seine, June–August 1944

ENGLISH CHANNEL

Cherbourg

Le Havre

Rouen

Somme

Oise

Seine

Paris

Soissons

Marne

Orleans

Loire

Rennes

St. Malo

Brest

Lorient

St Nazaire

Caen

1 Can

2 UK

1 US

3 US

5

15

1

Front line, 31 July
Front line, 14 August
Front line, 23 August
Allied movements
Fortified area

Miles

0   80

The German Defeat in the West, August–September 1944

Legend:
- Front line, 26 August
- Front line, 3 September
- Front line, 14 September
- Allied movements

0   Miles   100

person to take charge of Overlord, which would be the greatest such operation in history. Yet, at the time people took it for granted that General Marshall would command the invasion, Eisenhower replacing him as chief of staff. Admiral King, shortly before the Teheran Conference, told Eisenhower that this would be his next job. On December 5, 1943, after a good deal of beating around the bush, according to Marshall, Roosevelt asked the Chief of Staff what position he wished to have next. Marshall wanted to command Overlord but, good soldier that he was, told the President that he would cheerfully do whatever he was asked. Roosevelt then said "Well, I don't feel I could sleep at ease if you were out of Washington."[1] So it was that Eisenhower won the prize assignment.

FDR's decision was among his most important. Apart from

Marshall's gifts as a leader and military executive, the main argument for giving Overlord to him was sentimental. If Overlord resulted in victory, its commander would be seen, both at the time and by posterity, as the preeminent American general of the war. After building up the American Army from scratch, Marshall had earned the right to lead it in its greatest battles and enjoy the resulting glory. Otherwise, trading Marshall for Eisenhower had nothing to recommend it. Each would have to learn a new and radically different job. Each would lack the experience that had helped make the other successful.

Commanding an Allied force called not only for leadership but diplomatic talents and the right kind of temperament. Marshall, distant and austere, seldom established the warm personal relationships that made Eisenhower so popular with foreigners. In February 1944 British officers who had served under Eisenhower in the Mediterranean presented him with a silver tray upon which their signatures had been engraved. Admiral Sir Andrew B. Cunningham, in making the presentation, said that when many of those present began working for Eisenhower, they quickly discovered him to be "a man of outstanding integrity, transparent honesty and frank almost to an embarrassing degree. . . . No one will dispute it when I say that no one man has done more to advance the Allied cause."[2] "Ike," as everyone called him, had the ability to establish close working relations with a remarkable range of people, up to and including such incredibly difficult figures as MacArthur and de Gaulle. This quality had much to do with his success as supreme commander.

A further question, and a purely professional one, is whether Marshall would have been able to make command decisions of the same high order as Eisenhower's. Some of Eisenhower's subordinates liked to represent him as a politician, while they, of course, were the real soldiers, unjustly required to obey him. Even Omar Bradley, Eisenhower's favorite, at times took this view. In one of his two memoirs, Bradley wrote "Ike was a political general of rare and valuable gifts, but as his African record clearly demonstrated, he did not know how to manage a battlefield."[3]

It is true, as Eisenhower admitted, that Torch was a shambles, though the blame for this was widely shared. But by the time he was given Overlord Eisenhower had matured as a commander and was still getting better. Without taking back his earlier slight, Bradley conceded as much later on in his book, which shows Eisenhower taking charge of the land war and skillfully directing it. Many men had died to qualify Eisenhower for supreme command. To put someone else in his place would have been stupid. Roosevelt had put the right men in the right jobs and wisely kept them there.

Notwithstanding the efforts to portray Eisenhower as a politician in uniform, he was a gifted commander. He made the decision to attack Salerno despite the shortage of landing craft and ground-based air support, and he also made the tactical dispositions that enabled him to win his gamble. He alone would decide to invade France on June 6, 1944, betting that bad weather would clear long enough to put his expeditionary force ashore—thereby winning the biggest gamble of all. During the Battle of the Bulge, he personally made the tactical arrangements that turned defeat into victory. Eisenhower lacked the flamboyance of MacArthur and Patton, but, like his great predecessor, Ulysses S. Grant, he had both strategic foresight and the stamina to fight a war of attrition. That he was more charming than Grant did not mean that he was less able or possessed inferior grit. A fine diplomat and publicist to be sure, Eisenhower had brains and courage as well, which is why he was the foremost Allied commander.

George S. Patton, Jr. was born in 1885 to a wealthy family and married into a richer one. Even as a child he dreamed of becoming a soldier. In 1909 he graduated from West Point and during World War I trained and commanded the first brigade of American armor to fight in France. Though tanks were still primitive and unreliable, Colonel Patton quickly grasped the importance of this new weapon. He became, along with Major Eisenhower, an early proponent of armored warfare. Both were silenced by the Army brass, which favored horses, and Patton spent the next 20 years serving in cavalry units. The time was not wasted, however, for, contrary to his image as a roughneck, which he carefully cultivated, Patton was a scholarly and intelligent officer, an expert on military history and tactics, and a superbly qualified soldier who graduated with distinction from the Cavalry School, the Command and General Staff College, and the Army War College. His professional experience was immensely broad. By 1944 Patton had served at every level of command from platoon to field army and had also been a divisional, corps, and War Department staff officer.[4]

Patton rose rapidly once the Army committed itself to tank warfare, becoming commander of the newly formed 2nd Armored Division. In peacetime maneuvers during 1941 it ran wild, establishing Patton as the Army's preeminent tanker, which led to his being given a corps in

Operation Torch. Brilliant performances in North Africa and Sicily showed that he was fit to command at the highest level.

Though it was Marshall who gave him his first big chance, Patton owed his fame to Eisenhower.[5] During the Sicilian campaign Patton had, on two different occasions, slapped GIs who were suffering from combat fatigue—a malady that he interpreted as cowardice. Eisenhower was furious when he found out about the incidents and reprimanded Patton severely, forcing him to make public apologies to the men and women of Seventh Army. Yet, Eisenhower also took great pains to keep the episodes secret. They were not reported until the muckraking columnist Drew Pearson broke the story in November 1943. Eisenhower then waged a campaign to save Patton's career, persuading Marshall that he could not get along without his most aggressive combat leader. Eisenhower literally sang Patton's praises. Writing to a friend, Eisenhower said "He is a gorgeous commander when the going is tough. He has more 'drive' on the battlefield than any other man I know."[6]

Eisenhower handled Patton deftly, getting the best out of this impulsive, foul-mouthed, and reactionary soldier, while keeping his worst tendencies in check. After saving Patton, Eisenhower gave him no role in Overlord except the command of a nonexistent army group in southeastern England. In doing so he helped mislead Hitler into thinking the invasion would take place at the Pas de Calais instead of Normandy—since it was self-evident that Eisenhower would not leave what the Germans regarded as his best general on the sidelines. At the same time, keeping Patton out of the invasion was a way of reminding him of his probationary status. As a result, Hitler was completely deceived, while Patton, once taken off the bench, scored many touchdowns. Without Eisenhower, who not only got Patton through the slapping incidents but a freak incident in Britain when, during a speech to English ladies, he allegedly slighted Russia, Patton would never have gotten Third Army. As its commander Patton would repay Eisenhower many times over.

Patton was nowhere near as decent a man as Eisenhower—or Bradley, for that matter. He abused officers who displeased him and was a martinet who carried discipline to absurd lengths from the soldier's point of view, by, for example, forcing his troops to wear neckties except during actual combat. His absolute lack of perspective in these matters was demonstrated when the famous soldier–cartoonist Bill Mauldin chanced to visit Third Army. Patton called Mauldin in and chewed him out for weakening discipline with his irreverent cartoons, completely missing their value in an Army that was hopelessly civilian at heart.[7]

For these and other eccentricities Patton was, in some ways, one of the generals GIs disliked most. He genuinely cared about the welfare of his troops. He hated to take casualties and almost always succeeded in minimizing them. He frequently visited hospitals, too frequently, his aides thought, as the suffering of wounded men upset him and caused the slapping incidents. Above all, because he made his soldiers victorious, it later became a point of pride to have served under Patton.

Patton was the best American field general not because of his swaggering and showmanship, his immaculate uniforms and ivory-handled pistols, or his profane orations to the troops, which were wonderfully rendered by George C. Scott in the movie *Patton*, but because he was a superb professional and a master at combining all arms so as to achieve maximum force. Among the Allied commanders in Europe, Patton was the only one who understood strategic maneuver, by means of which one could outflank an army and totally destroy it. Most other Allied commanders were concerned with limiting their risks, which also meant limiting their gains.

Had it not been for the slappings Patton might have become commander of 12th Army Group instead of Omar Bradley, who was junior to him and lacked Patton's brilliance. Patton was crushed when Eisenhower passed him over, though he understood the reason why, and was lucky to keep Third Army. Bradley could be counted on not to embarrass Eisenhower or antagonize the British, while Patton was likely to do both. It was his unstable personality and big mouth that cost Patton an army group, failings that were hurtful to him but even more to the U.S. Army.

Eisenhower and Patton were the odd couple of the ETO. Eisenhower was democratic to the bone, and, though an excellent soldier, a student also of the political arts. Patton was a natural autocrat who loved his country but never troubled to learn the political skills, which, if united with his genius for war, would have qualified him to be Ike's right-hand man. They might have been the greatest team in American military history, eclipsing even Grant and Sherman. It was not to be, yet they would accomplish much and, in their different ways, reflect great credit on the land that had raised them.

Because Overlord succeeded, it is easy to get the idea that victory was a foregone conclusion. The Allies had overwhelming sea and air superiority by June 6, 1944, which enabled them to cover the Channel with ships and the skies with fleets of aircraft. To see the films of this immense force, staggeringly large even by World War II standards, is to marvel that Germany ever supposed it could defeat the Grand Alliance. Of the five invasion beaches, only one proved difficult to take, but even Omaha Beach, which General Bradley called a "nightmare," was secure by nightfall. With 156,000 men ashore, protected by naval gunfire and unlimited air support, the Allies were safely dug in.

These appearances deceived, for Overlord was actually a high risk operation. At Teheran Churchill had told Stalin that if the Germans deployed 40 to 50 divisions in France "I did not think the force we were going to put across the Channel could hold on."[8] As it happened, Germany had some 55 divisions defending France on D-Day, while the Allies, who had expected to field 48 for Roundup, could muster only 35. The rule of thumb was that an attacking force had to outnumber defenders by at least 2 to 1, so, on the face of it, there was no reason to suppose that France could be successfully invaded, despite the Allied superiority in air and naval power.

The Allies had certain advantages that, properly handled, might offset their shortage of troops. For one, Germany could not deploy all its forces on the Channel because the rest of France had to be garrisoned as well, especially the Mediterranean coast. For another, Russia had agreed to launch an offensive at the same time as Overlord, to prevent Germany from reinforcing in the West with troops brought from the Eastern Front. Third, the Allies had broken Germany's military codes and could read its radio traffic. Ultra, as this information was called, had been most useful in Africa, where radio was the principal medium of communications. It would be of less value on the Continent, where secure land-lines and telex reduced German radio use. Even so, the Allies would usually know the enemy's strength, what in military language is called "the order of battle," a not inconsiderable edge.

However, because Germany had been given such a long time to fortify its "Atlantic Wall", a hollow term in 1943 but real enough a year later after Rommel had built it up, the Allies had to call upon all their ingenuity. To prevent the Wehrmacht from reinforcing its beach defenses the Allies devised the Transportation Plan. As propounded by British scientists and articulated by Air Chief Marshal Leigh-Mallory, head of the Allied Expeditionary Air Force, it aimed at paralyzing the French rail system with heavy bomber raids on the marshaling yards.

As General Spaatz had predicted, these attacks on rail yards contributed little to Overlord's success, for the Germans simply canceled French civilian traffic. Such capacity as remained after the bombings was adequate for military purposes. Air supremacy was critical all the same, for while the Transportation Plan was falling short, medium and fighter–bombers isolated Normandy. Even though the greater part of the American air production effort had gone into heavy bombers, Major General Lewis H. Brereton's Ninth Air Force had by D-Day 11 medium bomber groups, each comprising 64 aircraft, and 18 fighter groups with 75 planes each. At first they supported the Transportation Plan, but experience in Italy had suggested that concentrating on railroad bridges would yield the greatest rewards. Advocates of the Transportation Plan charged that it would take 1,200 tons of bombs to destroy a single bridge across the Seine. On May 10, 1944, a flight of Brereton's P-47 Thunderbolts dropped just two 1,000-pound bombs on a rail bridge, completely destroying it.

Supreme Headquarters Allied Expeditionary Forces (SHAEF), then drew up a plan for bridge-busting attacks all over Northern France that would isolate not only the Normandy beaches but also the Pas de Calais. The campaign began on May 24, and by D-Day the U.S. Ninth and the RAF's Second Tactical Air Forces had destroyed all nine Seine railroad crossings and a dozen highway bridges. Further, Allied air kept the crossings closed by bombing repaired structures, boats that the Germans pressed into service, and temporary bridges. These attacks severely limited Germany's ability to move troops and supplies.

Equally important were the deception plans that kept Hitler, who made the key decisions, from concentrating his troops in Normandy. There were six principal plans, all told, plus 36 secondary ones, entailing leaked information, guerrilla raids by resistance forces, Allied military actions, and a host of other activities that misled Germany and kept its troops dispersed. One of the two most important was Fortitude North, a cost-efficient scheme that required only a handful of men and women. They created a fictitious British Fourth Army in Edinburgh Castle and, by pouring out radio messages, convinced German intelligence that Norway was about to be invaded. In consequence, all 13 German divisions in Norway remained there instead of defending France.

The most important deception plan, codenamed Fortitude South, had two parts: to persuade Germany that the main Allied effort would be at the Pas de Calais, where the Channel was narrowest; and then after D-Day to suggest that the Normandy landings were only a feint, the real target still being Calais. In a counterintelligence triumph, the British "turned" an entire German spy network which provided the Reich with a flood of misinformation. The centerpiece of this massive deception effort was a fake army group, supposedly consisting of 50 divisions and a million men in the southwest of England, commanded by Patton. To support the illusion, mock landing craft were moored in rivers. What seemed to be ammunition dumps, hospitals, field kitchens, and weaponry of all kinds, including a brigade of rubber tanks, were scattered over the countryside. So authentic were the means employed that German intelligence became convinced that the First U.S. Army Group (FUSAG) did exist and was going ashore at Calais. The Germans braced themselves for an assault by upwards of 90 divisions instead of the mere 35 that were actually deployed.

While German intelligence was being misled, the Allies had available to them a mountain of data gathered by agents in France, the French resistance, aerial reconnaissance, radio intercepts, frogmen, and commandos. On the basis of this information plans could be laid and troops trained with a high degree of precision. Further, the British had developed a variety of special armored weapons: amphibious tanks, tanks that could blow up minefields by beating them with flails, flame-throwing tanks, mortar-firing tanks, bridge laying tanks, and more. Overlord was the best planned Allied operation of the war, and the extent and complexity of its arrangements have often been cited to demonstrate that 1944 was the earliest possible time when France could have been assaulted. The obvious reply is that had the invasion taken place a year earlier, against an inferior and poorly emplaced German force, all this would not have been needed.

Even so, despite vast and meticulous preparations, Overlord remained chancy. Everything had to go right, particularly the deception plans. The Allies needed luck and the weather, always the greatest problem for a seaborne assault. There were only three days in each two-week period in June when low tide and first light came together, an essential condition as Rommel's defenses were concentrated on the tidal flats. The massive parachute drops that would begin the attack needed at least a half-moon, reducing the available days to three a month. Further, on these three days, onshore winds ought not to exceed 12 MPH and offshore winds 18 MPH. Visibility had to be at least three miles for naval gunfire to be accurate and the cloud base no lower than 3,000 feet for fighter–bomber support.

By one calculation the odds against all the required conditions prevailing in early summer were 50 or 60 to one. Little wonder that Churchill was fearful, committing himself only in May, when, after lunching with Eisenhower, he said "I am in this thing with you to the end, and if it fails we will go down together."[9] No doubt Eisenhower would have preferred a more hopeful pledge, but the die was already cast, and he had enough confidence for both of them.

He had enough nerve, too, and was called upon to display it. In the entire war no Allied commander had a tougher decision to make than Eisenhower did on the evening of June 4, 1944. Overlord had been scheduled for June 5. The assault troops were already embarked when a Channel storm brought six-foot waves, far too high for landing craft, and grounded the all important air support. At 4:30 A.M. on the fourth, Eisenhower ordered a postponement, meeting again that night with his commanders at invasion headquarters, Southwick, a fine country house near Portsmouth. He had to decide whether to go ahead on Tuesday the sixth or stand his forces down until June 19, the next date when low tide and first light would coincide. It was raining hard at the time, but RAF Group Captain J. M. Stagg, SHAEF's chief weatherman, reported that a bubble of decent weather had formed and would shortly provide 36 hours of reasonable visibility over the Channel. Forecasting depended more on guesswork in 1944 than today, but the good weather did exist and was being tracked by Allied planes and radar. At 9:45 P.M., with rain still pouring down, Eisenhower ordered the first ship movements to begin. Early next day, the fifth, with just enough time remaining for the attack to be called off, Ike set the wheels in motion.

Eisenhower knew the risk he was taking, since if bad weather continued, Overlord would fail. In that event, if the losses were heavy, there might not be time to mount another assault on France in 1944. After issuing his final order and meeting with reporters, Eisenhower sat down and wrote two statements, the one he actually delivered and another for use in case of failure. Three sentences in the latter statement are especially revealing. "My decision to attack at this time and place was based upon the best information available. The troops, the air and the Navy did all that bravery and devotion to duty could do. If any blame or fault attaches to the attempt it is mine alone."[10] Those few sentences defined his stature as a man.

Despite the odds, Overlord succeeded. High winds and nervous pilots caused many paratroopers to drop outside their landing zones, resulting in heavy casualties. High waves sank dozens of amphibious tanks whose inflatable canvas covers were never designed for rough water. The casualties at Omaha Beach ran to several thousand. Of 225 men from the 2nd Ranger Battalion who climbed the sheer cliffs of Pointe du Hoc under heavy fire, only 90 were still standing by nightfall. But Fortitude worked, the landings succeeded, and subsequent efforts to reinforce the defenders were smothered by Allied air power and delayed by French resistance forces, who blew bridges, cut telephone lines, and attacked road convoys.

On D-Day alone French railways were cut 950 times, and thereafter every train leaving Marseilles for the north derailed at least once. Air attacks on the 2nd SS Panzer Division kept it from entraining its tanks in Toulouse for 11 days. French resistance units are thought to have immobilized 1,800 locomotives and 6,000 railway cars. The Germans were reduced to moving only at night, making speedy reinforcement of Normandy impossible. On June 19, the fallback date if Eisenhower had postponed his attack, the worst storm in 20 years struck the Channel, inflicting more damage than the Allies had suffered from German resistance on D-Day. If he had not chosen to attack on June 6, Overlord would have failed on the nineteenth with momentous consequences. Fortune favors the brave, it is said, but never more so than on D-Day.

At sunset on June 6, 1944, the European Theater of Operations, U.S. Army (ETO), at last included the Continent. Its failure to prevent the Allies from securing their beachhead was a strategic defeat for Germany that would ultimately prove fatal. This was apparent to Rommel and many other German commanders. When Hitler refused to face the facts, the plot to overthrow him and negotiate a surrender thickened. On July 20, 1944, the dissidents struck, but this time fortune did not favor the brave. Hitler survived the bomb that was supposed to destroy him, so the killing continued.

Despite all that had gone right on D-Day, the Allied attack soon bogged down. There were two sets of causes for this. Among the tactical reasons was that Montgomery's troops failed to take the key city of Caen. At the last briefing before June 6, which took place in a London school, Montgomery had boasted that he would seize Caen on the first day, and his armor would soon be "knocking about" in the open country beyond it. He launched one airborne and three infantry divisions against Caen, which was lightly held. Instead of storming it the British proceeded so leisurely that the enemy was able to reinforce Caen, ending the dream of a breakthrough. As Bradley remarked acidly in his memoirs, "The 'new' bold Monty of the St. Paul's schoolroom was gone. The old cautious, methodical Monty was back."[11]

Undoubtedly the war would have gone better if someone else had commanded 21st Army Group. Montgomery was a good soldier and an outstanding trainer of troops, but he also had serious faults. He was, as Bradley said, too cautious. This had paid off in North Africa, where he refused to attack Rommel at El Alamein until he had an overwhelming advantage in men and weaponry. Thus, after Rommel had beaten a series of commanders, Montgomery gave the British their first great victory of the war and became a national hero. In Europe, however, as before Caen, he would invariably take too long to act in rapidly developing tactical situations. To add insult to injury, Montgomery would claim afterward that the stalemate before Caen had been part of his master plan to tie down large German forces and make possible the subsequent American breakout. This was only his first display of that boastfulness and tendency to take credit for the achievements of others that Americans so detested.

Another Allied problem was that intelligence had failed to grasp how difficult it would be to penetrate the hedgerows that lined Norman roads. These were not simple strips of brush but earthen dikes knit together by root systems that made them highly resistant to shot and shell and impenetrable to armor. They lined the countryside in ranks, so when a hedgerow was about to be taken the Germans would simply fall back on the next. Fighting in the "Bocage," as this country is called, would cost the Americans dearly. If Montgomery had seized Caen the hedgerows would not have mattered, since the axis of the Allied advance would have been through a rolling plain. The result instead was a grueling infantry campaign that produced enormous losses. The U.S. 90th Division sustained 100 percent casualties among its riflemen in Normandy, 150 percent among their officers. In a single attack, Britain's 15th Highlanders lost half their frontline strength. For lack of replacements, Montgomery was soon cannibalizing his own divisions.

The Western Front, as all had feared, was going to make earlier Allied operations look exactly like what they had been, preliminaries to the main event. It was also going to underline Allied deficiencies in weapons and training, another set of reasons that explain the stalemate. Germany's tenacious defense of Normandy was a function not only of the Bocage but of German excellence in fighting skills and weaponry.

The German Army was not what it had been. The units that fought in France were understrength, made up to some extent of garrison troops, and fleshed out with volunteers and conscripts from all over occupied Europe. Yet German soldiers remained aggressive and willing to make the extra effort. Even after taking heavy punishment, fragments of shattered German outfits would be assembled in "kampfengruppen" (battlegroups) and continue to fight.

There were several explanations for German combat efficiency. For one, as citizens of a totalitarian state that was heir to a strong militaristic tradition, Germans were good at taking orders. Yet, paradoxically, they also displayed great initiative. American propagandists maintained that, owing to their individualism, Yanks were more effective in battle than the enemy, whose men were supposedly automatons who could not think for themselves. There was little truth to this. German soldiers were often more flexible than Allied troops, sometimes quicker to exploit opportunities and able, even on the lowest levels, to act without instructions. Their training of NCOs was the best and emphasized adaptability and independent decision making. They also excelled at integrating infantry, artillery, and armor into a smoothly operating force.[12] The Germans were masters of small-unit combat, a great asset at any time but especially in the Bocage, where all fighting was local.

Another benefit, perhaps the greatest, was that German troops fought on the defensive, with all the advantages that gave them. Well dug in, unreachable for the most part by Allied air, they could pour fire from protected positions upon GIs who had to advance in the open. Unlike American troops, most of whom were new to combat, German units included many veterans who capitalized upon their attackers' inexperience.

However, these enemy advantages would erode with time, not only because Germany was running out of good troops, but because the Americans would get better. On D-Day the most effective soldiers were rangers and paratroopers, hand-picked men who had been gruelingly trained. The 506th Parachute Infantry Regiment of the 101st Airborne went through a screening process so rigorous that it took 500 officer volunteers to produce 148 graduates and 5,300 enlisted men to produce 1,800 troopers. This assured that on D-Day the parachutists would take their objectives. Men trained less exactingly would need tempering in combat to acquire this fine edge. Eventually Americans so perfected their techniques that their all-arms cooperation would surpass even that of the Germans. Further, the men would improve, too, as ex-students were fed into the ground forces from AAF cadet programs and Army specialty schools.

Americans, with their antimilitary heritage and late entry into the war, could be expected to lag behind the Germans in combat effectiveness. There was no excuse for inferior weaponry. Nothing hurt the ground troops more than the lack of decent armor. America's main battle tank was the 32 ton Sherman. Designed in 1941, the Sherman was obsolete. Army ordnance officers had praised it to the skies, telling the press "We're so far ahead of the Heinie in tank design and production that he's never going to catch us."[13] By 1944 that boast was a grim joke. Germany's best tanks greatly outclassed the Sherman, which was underarmored and when hit tended to go up in flames, hence its nickname, the "Ronson." Most Shermans lacked firepower also, generally being armed with 75-mm or 76-mm guns whose rounds could not penetrate the frontal armor of German tanks. By 1944, the Army would have been better off to scrap the Sherman and copy the Russian T-34, which had an 85-mm gun and was comparable to the German Panther.

The Sherman's weaknesses might have been offset to a degree if the Army had possessed an antitank gun as good as the German 88-mm. What it had instead was the tank destroyer, a partially armored vehicle that was supposed to relieve Shermans of the need to take on enemy tanks but in practice couldn't do so. The basic tank destroyer was only a half-track with a 75-mm gun that made it topheavy and unstable. "TDs" were vulnerable to enemy fire and no match for German armor. At great risk when sent up against enemy tanks, they were most effective when used as assault guns providing close support for the infantry, which became their primary job in combat.[14]

In Normandy the Sherman would come up against the fearsome Tiger tank, a 56-ton monster armed with the legendary "88." It could penetrate 4 inches of armor at 1,000 yards and was notably accurate. Though slow, the Tiger was so heavily armored as to be nearly invulnerable. A striking demonstration of this was provided on June 13, 1944, when the British 7th Armored Division attacked with over 200 Sherman and Cromwell tanks. They were thrown back by six Tigers, Obersturmführer (First Lieutenant) Michael Wittmann, Germany's leading tank ace, alone destroying or disabling 25 tanks and 28 other vehicles. Germany also deployed the Panther in Normandy, a medium tank that was lighter and faster than the Tiger, but also hard to destroy. A rule of thumb was that it took five Shermans to kill a

Panther. Even the venerable Pz IV, originally designed in 1937 and the most common enemy tank, had been upgraded and was at least a match for Shermans.

The Army knew the Sherman had seen better days, but, instead of rushing production of a new tank, manufactured more Shermans instead. Almost 50,000 Shermans in various configurations would be built, compared to 1,350 Tigers. Normandy, where one Tiger with hedgerows on its flanks could stop an entire armored column, showed the folly of relying on superior numbers alone. The British fit their Shermans with a 17-pound gun that was much more effective than the American 75 and better also than the 76-mm gun that was the 75's replacement. The U.S. Army refused to utilize 17-pounders, instead designing a whole new tank, called the Pershing, around a 90–mm gun—although a limited number of Shermans were also armed with it. Because of snags in development, only 20 Pershings saw combat in Europe, while thousands of Shermans were being destroyed for want of an adequate gun. Heads should have rolled for this.

Brendan Phibbs, then a combat surgeon attached to the 12th Armored Division, tells how critics of the Sherman ran into a stone wall. "To suggest that the M4A3 Sherman tank was a ridiculous thin-walled undergunned piece of shit—and we often did—was to bring down savage attacks that questioned one's fitness to be an officer or even one's patriotism."[15] The Army defended the Sherman instead of upgrading it, which could easily have been done. When the Israelis acquired Shermans after the war, they added more armor, a diesel engine, and a bigger gun. Thus refitted it held its own against Arab T-34s. The U.S. Army could have done this, too, and saved many lives.

The case for the Sherman boils down to this. As a medium tank designed for speed it proved its worth in the breakout from Normandy, the race across France that followed, and the slashing attacks that cut Germany to pieces during the final weeks of the war. True, so far as it goes, the case fails to address several issues. One is that Shermans would have been just as fast, and much more deadly, if all had been fitted with 90-mm guns. For another, most of the fighting in Western Europe involved limited attacks against enemy positions in which speed was not a factor. These assaults should have been undertaken by heavy tanks—Pershings or upgraded Shermans—leaving the medium tanks to roll in hot pursuit, the job for which they had been designed.

German tank superiority was most costly to the Allies, but other German weapons were better, too. The semiautomatic American M-1 Garand rifle and the British Lee-Enfield were more accurate than the bolt-operated German Mauser. But rate of fire counted most in combat, and here the Germans were far ahead. Their MG 42 could fire 1,200 rounds a minute, while the American .30- and .50-caliber machine guns, the U.S. Browning Automatic Rifle, and the British Bren, fired about 500 rounds a minute. German units had more automatic weapons per company, 16 machine guns compared to 11 American and 9 British. All German small-arms ammunition produced less flash and smoke than that of the Allies.

Enemy mortars were better, too, and the Germans concentrated their fire more effectively. The Panzerfaust (tank fist) was the best hand-held antitank weapon of the war. Light and easy to use, it could penetrate 8 inches of armor at 240 feet. The U.S. Bazooka was heavy, awkward to handle, and could penetrate only the side armor of German tanks. It was most useful to the infantry for rocketing enemy positions. The British PIAT weighed twice as much as the Panzerfaust, and was accurate only within 100 feet, giving the operator little chance of survival.

The United States Army had no good antitank gun, the standard weapon in 1944 being a 57-mm piece that could not penetrate German armor. Like much of the Army's munitions, it reflected the views of Lieutenant General Lesley J. McNair, commander of the Army Ground Forces, whose lack of battle experience did not inhibit his self-confidence.[16] McNair wanted the Army to be lean and mobile, like cavalrymen of old, thereby sacrificing the armor plate and firepower that were needed in Europe. To a large extent this seems to explain why the Army did not have an adequate tank, and also why, though combat established that the best antitank weapon was another tank, it had so many tank destroyers. Meanwhile, Germany had the superb 88, the most deadly antitank gun of the war as well as the best tank cannon.

Several reasons explain why Germany was beaten in the West, its numerous advantages notwithstanding. Its superweapons, such as its jet aircraft and most advanced missiles, became operational too late— though if the war had lasted another year they might have made a great difference. For most of the war Russia tied down Germany's largest armies in the East, making a Western Front possible. Overwhelming Allied air strength curtailed German mobility. None of these things would have mattered if the infantry had been no good. But Marshall's new divisions were well-trained and well-supplied with guns, artillery being the American infantry division's strongest suit. Although the U.S.

Army did not have a mobile close support weapon like the German 75-mm gun, most divisions were provided with an attached tank battalion that made up the difference. It was in the divisional artillery batteries, with their concentrations of splendid 105-mm and 155-mm guns, that the real power lay. American gunners excelled at their technical art, guided by forward spotters who flitted about in tiny Piper or Stinson aircraft. Their specialty was the "TOT" or time on target concentration, during which all available guns would commence firing upon specific coordinates for a designated period—the first round of every gun timed to impact at the same moment. The resulting storm of fire that broke without warning was the American tactic that German soldiers feared most.

As with infantry tactics and divisional design, the principles that made U.S. artillery so formidable had been developed before the war, though the Army then had almost none of the equipment it would need to make them work. Lacking modern guns, vehicles to move them with, bore-safe fuses, reliable communications, and much else, artillery officers planned as if all would be available when needed. Thus, they invented the principles and techniques that helped make the American division an artillery-infantry team of enormous power, though it would have been more powerful still if equipped with better armor and infantry weapons.

The American Army, which had been designed for high mobility with its medium tanks and numerous vehicles, seldom found itself in circumstances where its mobility could be exploited. In the jungles and volcanic islands of the Pacific, speed was impossible. In Normandy, as in Italy, the Army fought a sluggish war of attrition. Yet, the potential remained. Unlike in other armies, most American vehicles had four-wheel drive, enabling them to function in all weather and on extremely poor surfaces. At most, a few extra truck companies were all that was needed for an entire division to move out. The Army had previously distinguished between infantry and motorized infantry divisions, but regular divisions proved in practice to be so mobile that the distinction was dropped. Ease of movement and the power given a U.S. infantry division by its artillery and attached tank battalion made it a mighty instrument of war—though this was not apparent at first.

After six weeks of fighting in Normandy, the Allies were still confined to a bridgehead 50 miles wide and from five to 15 miles deep. However, as the slogging match wore on, America kept building up its strength while Germany could not, a fact well known to Allied commanders thanks to Ultra intercepts. To break the stalemate Omar Bradley and his British counterpart, General Miles Dempsey, developed separate plans for breaching the enemy's lines, Bradley's being codenamed Cobra and Dempsey's Goodwood. The British jumped off first on July 18, three divisions attacking in the Caen region six hours after the Germans had been softened up by RAF heavy bombers. After initial gains, bad weather and a German counterattack stopped the British cold.

This left Operation Cobra, the brainchild of Bradley and VII Corps commander Major General J. Lawton "Lightning Joe" Collins. The American front was less desirable from the attackers' standpoint than the Caen sector, as it was swampier and deep inside the Bocage. In order to reach dryer ground, First Army took 40,000 casualties in a two-week period while gaining only seven miles—the worst rate of loss the U.S. Army would ever sustain on the Western Front. However, in addition to better ground, the Americans now had napalm and a new device invented by Sergeant Curtis G. Culin. The "Rhino" was a set of heavy steel prongs welded to a Sherman. Thus equipped when it encountered a hedgerow the tank, instead of rolling up and stalling, could spear into the base and power through. American armor was no longer confined to narrow lanes but could burst out of hedgerows into the enemy's flanks.

Cobra was preceded by a massive aerial bombardment involving heavy, medium, and fighter–bombers in various combinations. On July 24 the bombing began, then was called off by bad weather after many planes had already sortied. A flight of 16 heavies dropped short, killing 25 and wounding 131 American soldiers. On the twenty-fifth the bombers came back in force and some bombed short again, killing 111 Americans and wounding 490. Among the dead was an important visitor, Lieutenant General Lesley J. McNair, commander of the Army Ground Forces, who became the highest ranking American officer to be killed in Europe. Despite having been heavily bombed, the Germans recovered quickly as usual, on the first day holding three U.S. infantry divisions to a two-kilometer advance. Collins then decided to throw in his three armored divisions, which were being held back to exploit a breakthrough that now seemed unlikely to happen. When they hit the German line it started to collapse.

Cobra stipulated a careful advance into Brittany in order to secure Brest and other needed ports, after which there was to be another methodical advance toward the Seine. But the planned breakthrough was turning into a breakout as armored units crashed through enemy positions. On July 30 the 4th Armored Division seized Avranches at the base of the Cotentin Peninsula, opening up not just Brittany but southern Normandy as well. American pressure forced the Germans out of cover during daylight, exposing them to rampaging fighter–bombers.

Under the leadership of Major General Elwood R. "Pete" Quesada, IX Tactical Air Command pilots were becoming the leading tank killers of the war. Quesada had offended RAF officers by hanging ordnance on their elegant Spitfire, making it a "lowly" fighter–bomber, but it was effective in that role. The British in turn showed Americans how to mount rockets on rails under their wings, to produce an enormous rise in firepower. Tightly vectored by air-support parties riding the lead tanks of American columns, packing two 1,000-pound bombs, or batteries of 10 5-inch rockets, Lightnings, Mustangs, and Thunderbolts blasted their way across France, attacking as close as 100 yards ahead of American troops.

"This man Quesada is a jewel," Bradley informed Hap Arnold. He was willing to try anything and so inspired his pilots that they "now do almost the impossible whenever they think we need help. In my opinion, our close cooperation is better than the Germans ever had in their best days."[17] There would be no great massing of German armor on the Western Front after the Battle for France, except in foul weather. Tanks remained a formidable German asset, but they had to be dispersed and concealed and could operate at will only when planes were grounded. Tactical air evened the odds, making up for America's inferior tanks and lack of manpower.

Third Army headquarters was soon to be activated, but Bradley grew impatient and on July 27 ordered Patton to take immediate command of Major General Troy H. Middleton's VIII Corps, the rest of Third Army to join him on August 1. All things now became possible. On July 28, as the German front began to unravel, Patton ordered his 4th and 6th Armored Divisions to lead VIII Corps' advance. He was throwing into battle divisions that had trained under him in England and had absorbed his doctrine of mobile warfare. The 4th Armored had served as a test division for the development of Patton's theories of tank–infantry cooperation. In both divisions he had instilled his belief that armor should strike swiftly and go deep, flowing around enemy strongpoints to plunge into vulnerable rear areas.

Although essential to it, mobility is not the same as maneuver, and the American Army's dedication to mobility had failed to develop in most commanders a corresponding enthusiasm for strategic maneuver. Though the troops could move far and fast, American planning was too cautious and unimaginative to exploit this capability. The holding attack may have been doctrine at the Infantry School at Fort Benning, but, in practice, when the going got tough, American generals often fell back on Army tradition. In this sense the Army remained tied to its Civil War experience, when victory had resulted from cornering the enemy and battering him to pieces—a costly way of fighting, for winners and losers alike. The German Army, by contrast, was dedicated to maneuver, and remembered the words of its great nineteenth century leader, Helmuth von Moltke "The only strategic maneuver which lends itself to producing a battle of annihilation is the wide envelopment."[18] Patton knew this, too, and unlike most American generals believed that the point was not just to hit hard and fast, but also where you were not expected, and to outrun and outflank the enemy and mislead through indirection. Further, Patton had the ability to "read" a battle, that is, to anticipate enemy moves, and recognize an opportunity before it became obvious.

Such an opening was created by the breakout from Normandy, as Major General John Wood, the commander of 4th Armored, was first to see. The outstanding armored division commander on the Allied side, the "American Rommel" to Germans, Wood took an even more radical view of armored attack than Patton, with whom he often clashed.[19] Once through Avranches, Wood was eager to turn east, get into the Germans' rear, and envelop the bulk of their forces. Bradley's newly activated 12th Army Group still had its heart set on the original aim of seizing Breton ports. In only 72 hours Patton poured seven divisions through the narrow Avranches bottleneck. The lack of enemy resistance, and Wood's prodding, inspired him to ask permission to begin sending part of Third Army eastward, around and behind the enemy's front. Bradley approved, and though there would still be a wasteful sideshow in Brittany, before long Patton had moved 200,000 men and 40,000 vehicles

"through what amounted to a straw. Every manual on road movement was ground into the dust. He and his staff did what the whole world knew couldn't be done: it was flat impossible to put a whole army out on a narrow two-lane road and move it at high speed. Everything was going to come to a screeching halt. He even intermingled units. Yet out the other end of the straw came divisions, intact and ready to fight. If anybody else could have done it, no one ever got that man's name."[20]

When Third Army reached open ground, Patton ordered Major General Wade Hampton Haislip's XV Corps to drive on Le Mans, headquarters of the German Seventh Army, 42 miles away. While doing so would expose Haislip's flanks to counterattacks, Patton sensed that the German left wing was too disorganized to mount them. XV Corps stormed up the Norman roads, making 75 miles in three days and bagging thousands of Germans. Collins' VII Corps was moving, too—but not the rest of First Army, because the German right wing still held fast. This made Bradley cautious, as did the knowledge gained from Ultra intercepts that a German counteroffensive was in the works.

As the German left wing fell apart, Hitler and his high command were faced with two choices. One was a hasty withdrawal to the Seine, and probably back to the West Wall. This would put the Allies within striking distance of the Ruhr industries, which, if taken, would force Germany to its knees. Thus, while the Red Army was still grinding its way through Poland, the Allies had a chance to win the war, so radically had their invasion of France changed the strategic equation. For this reason Hitler ordered Field Marshal Hans Gunther von Kluge, OB (Commander in Chief) West, to attack toward the Avranches gap and cut Patton's lines of communication and supply.

At midnight on August 6 the newly formed 47th Panzer Corps attacked Mortain and the U.S. 30th Infantry Division, which reeled but did not break. While the 30th held its ground, the RAF's 2nd Tactical Air Force and the U.S. IX TAC were filling the skies with tank killers. The Germans came within 15 miles of Avranches, where the lines of communication for a dozen U.S. divisions crossed, then ground to a halt. That failure created an opportunity for the Allies to encircle and destroy two German field armies. Patton was the first to see it. With Bradley's approval he turned XV Corps at Le Mans and drove on Argentan, a move that came to be known as the short hook. At the same time, Montgomery ordered the First Canadian Army, scheduled to attack from Caen toward the Seine, to aim for Falaise instead, to complete an historic double envelopment—the rarest but most decisive maneuver in warfare.

On August 13, Hitler finally allowed his threatened armies to halt the attack on Mortain and shoot their way out of the closing circle. At that absolutely vital point the Allied leadership went dormant. There seems to have been no communication between Montgomery and Bradley for three critical days.[21] Montgomery's lead divisions, the Canadian 4th Armored and the Polish 1st Armored, were green and made mistakes, such as stopping to reduce German strong points. Montgomery failed to reinforce them, allowing the attack to stall, apparently because he was still tied to the original plan and couldn't adapt to good fortune.

Patton begged for permission to close the gap himself by sending XV Corps into the area assigned to Montgomery's 21st Army Group, pressing Bradley to the point where he refused to take Patton's calls. Whether Patton could have succeeded is uncertain, since Haislip needed more divisions than he had in order to keep the Germans from bursting through his lines once he closed the pocket. The point is academic, because Bradley ordered Haislip to stop at Argentan, despite Patton's frantic efforts to persuade 12th Army Group HQ to let XV Corps drive forward. Bradley reverted instead to the original plan for a long envelopment that was supposed to trap the retreating Germans near the Seine, depleting XV Corps for that purpose. Then, on the sixteenth, with numerous Germans still inside, the two Allied army group commanders decided once again to close the gap. This was achieved by August 21.

None of Bradley's decisions has been so thoroughly scrutinized as his cancellation of Patton's short hook, a move which continues to have both critics and defenders. There is evidence to support both sides, but, as the possible rewards were so great, it seems incredible that Patton was not given his head on August 13 when he pleaded for permission to close the gap. Bradley's caution was inspired by fears of antagonizing the British by invading their space; of undermining the confidence of the Canadian Army; that Patton's troops would be attacked by the two Allied tactical air forces, whose bomb lines were converging; and of added casualties if the Germans smashed through XV Corps. These concerns do not, in retrospect, seem all that compelling, since if Patton had succeeded, Germany's entire position in the West would have been destroyed. For such a prize a considerable amount of risk ought to have been worth running. Bradley never thought so, writing in his memoirs: "I much preferred a solid shoulder at Argentan to the possibility of a broken neck at Falaise."[22] Had Patton commanded the ground forces instead of

Bradley, the short hook would have been thrown, and the war might well have come to a speedy conclusion.

As a result of Bradley's hesitation, and despite fearful losses, the Wehrmacht pulled the largest part of its forces out, including most higher headquarters and 12 of 15 divisional and four of five corps commanders, together with staffs, cadres, and numerous support units. This made it possible for the German Army to effect the seemingly impossible again by rebuilding its Western Front. Heavy casualties made doing so difficult, but not hopeless, which it would have been if these indispensable leaders and specialists had been lost. Had the bulk of their troops been lost too, Germany would have been finished.

Even so, wiping out the Falaise pocket climaxed a great Allied victory. At a guess, the Allies took 50,000 German prisoners and killed 10,000 more. A partial count of wrecked or captured German equipment ran to 220 tanks, 160 assault guns, 700 towed pieces, 130 antiaircraft guns, over 5,000 motor vehicles, 2,000 wagons, and 1,800 horses—an oddity of the German war effort being that regular infantry divisions continued to depend on animals for transport. The last days of the pocket were harrowing. As early as August 14, morale had sunk to the point where a large number of Germans caught on a road broke out white flags and surrendered to the U.S. 405th Fighter-Bomber Group, whose swirling Thunderbolts formed the POWs into columns and escorted them to the nearest Americans. By August 17 the gap had narrowed so much that bomb lines no longer existed.

When Eisenhower toured the battlefield he said that it "could be described only by Dante. It was literally possible to walk for hundreds of yards at a time, stepping on nothing but dead and decaying flesh."[23] Among the casualties was Field Marshal von Kluge, who had tried to get the counteroffensive called off—and who, as it turned out, was implicated in the July 20 plot to kill Hitler. He committed suicide on being relieved as OB West, sparing himself from being strangled to death by a loop of piano wire, the fate of his apprehended co-conspirators.

The U.S. Army's experience in France by summer's end pointed in two directions. One route was to give Patton his head, capitalizing on American mobility and the cover provided fast-moving divisions by their tactical air support. The other was to respect British pride by giving Montgomery every chance, pay strict attention to logistical difficulties, which were growing more severe as Patton advanced, and guard against German flank attacks on Patton's extended columns. One way held out hope of a quick end to the war, the other of avoiding a German counteroffensive that would undo what had been accomplished. In retrospect, the answer would seem obvious. At the time, flushed with success and scenting victory in the air, the second course—which was both more prudent and more acceptable to the British—made the most sense to Eisenhower. He would have it both ways, the theory ran, which was to cost the Allies dearly.

17

Victory in Europe

Two problems above all others complicated the American march toward victory over Hitler. The first was Great Britain's insistence on giving Field Marshal Montgomery and his 21st Army Group pride of place in the Allied advance. Secondly, the U.S. Army was not strong enough for Eisenhower to override Montgomery until very late in the war. America had every reason to be grateful to the British. Their lonely stand against Hitler in 1940 was the key to Germany's defeat. They fought longer and suffered more than Americans did to bring that triumph about. Yet, everything following D-Day showed that Britain was past its peak. A small country with limited means, it was fast nearing exhaustion. After the breakout from Normandy, Britain should have allowed America's growing armies to spearhead the Allied attack. They would do so in the end, but they could have brought the war to a swifter conclusion had British pride not stood in the way. As it was, for Bradley and his commanders the battle with Montgomery was an integral part of their fight against Hitler.

American manpower and logistical shortfalls were the other reason why victory proved elusive. What made British stubbornness such a serious thing was that, despite their size, the American armies were never quite large enough or well enough supplied for Eisenhower to disregard British pressure. The greatest failure of the American nation in this respect was to calculate its military needs in Europe too closely. Eventually there would be enough men and munitions for the U.S. Army to prevail over British caution, but not in 1944. Patton would win many victories. The biggest one of all, which was within his grasp that fateful summer, would be twice denied him—at the Falaise Gap, and again shortly afterward.

The lack of cooperation between Bradley and Montgomery made it essential for Eisenhower to take personal control of the ground war. Unity of command became all the more urgent on August 15, when Truscott's VI Corps landed on the coast of southern France. This effort, formerly codenamed Anvil but now Dragoon, to signify Churchill's displeasure, had caused more inter-Allied friction than any operation since Torch. It had been laid on in the first place as much to please Stalin as for its merits. At Teheran he argued strongly that invading the Riviera would draw off German forces from the Channel, permitting the Allies to envelop all the Germans in France. For maximum effectiveness, he suggested, Anvil ought to take place before Overlord. Churchill violently opposed Anvil from the start, partly for the same reasons he resisted Overlord, but especially because Anvil would be made by troops withdrawn from Italy, dooming his hopes for a speedy end to the Italian campaign and for new operations in the Balkans.

The landing-ship shortage ultimately made it impossible for Anvil–Dragoon to precede, or even coincide with, Overlord, hence the postponement to August, when LSTs could be released to it from the English Channel. This delay eliminated the strategic purpose of Anvil and, it has been argued, may even have forced German units out of France that otherwise would have been trapped after the breakout from Normandy. To Eisenhower Dragoon still made sense, as it would engage substantial German forces and secure desperately needed port facilities on the Mediterranean coast. Churchill, after making a last emotional effort on August 9 to block it, flew out to observe Dragoon first-hand from the deck of a British destroyer. In a letter to his wife on the seventeenth he described it as a "well-conducted but irrelevant and unrelated operation."[1]

Though his pique was understandable, Churchill did Dragoon an injustice. Truscott failed to bag the German Nineteenth Army because he only had three infantry divisions in pursuit and they were always outrunning their supply lines. Yet the Allies captured 57,000 Germans in two weeks, and, at the same time, France's II Corps liberated the vital Mediterranean ports. A month after Truscott went ashore, the docks of Marseilles were in operation. By war's end, over 900,000 American troops had landed in Marseilles, Toulon, and Port de Bouc. These invaluable facilities were soon handling over a third of all American supplies to Europe. Dragoon made possible the creation of 6th Army Group, under Lieutenant General Jacob M. Devers, consisting of the French First and U.S. Seventh Armies. It would soon take its place on the line next to Bradley's 12th.

Meanwhile, Patton was driving ahead with three corps in pursuit of the retreating Germans. To keep track of his fast-moving columns, he formed a personal reconnaissance force known as "Patton's Household Cavalry," its platoons bypassing the formal chains of command and communication to keep Third Army up-to-date. He had his own air force as well, Brigadier General Otto P. Weyland's XIX TAC, which was headquartered next to Patton. By August 26 Third Army was across the Seine, having advanced almost 400 miles from its jumpoff point, employing to the fullest that mobility for which the U.S. Army had been designed but, until recently, had never been able to exhibit.

Eisenhower and Bradley hoped to postpone the liberation of Paris, the freeing of which would slow 12th Army Group and require the Allies to provide 4,000 tons of supplies a day to the hungry Parisians. But de Gaulle was pressing SHAEF very hard because Hitler had ordered the city destroyed and French Resistance fighters were already in the streets. Paris could not be bypassed while it was in such danger, and the honor of liberating it was given to General Philippe Leclerc's 2nd Armored, supported by the U.S. 4th Infantry Division, which had to be held up so Leclerc could get there first. After an exciting march of triumph, American troops passed through the city and resumed their pursuit. Of course, as always in war, it was the fighting men who went ahead while the rear echelons, various headquarters and supply and technical units, enjoyed the liberation.

Victory in the West now seemed tantalizing close at hand. The long envelopment had failed to catch many escaping Germans, but they were still on the run with Patton close behind. Although Montgomery was working hard on SHAEF to have the main axis of the Allied attack run through the Low Countries, Patton believed that, with sufficient support, he could smash into the West Wall before Germany manned it. The Germans had already lost nearly 300,000 men to death, wounds, or captivity on the Western Front. During the same months (June, July, and August), the Wehrmact had sustained another 900,000 casualties on the Eastern Front, losing also the Ploesti oil fields, Germany's last source of natural petroleum. Obviously the Third Reich had to be running out of options.

Contrary to reason, however, Germany was not yet finished. Hitler had already launched a massive rebuilding program that would create new divisions, seemingly out of thin air. A hundred garrison battalions were sent to the fronts, 25 Volksgrenadier (people's) divisions were raised, and 10 new panzer brigades were assembled from remnants of old ones. The lessening of Allied pressure in Italy enabled two veteran panzer grenadier divisions to be transferred to the West. As the Allies drove the German Army back upon its lines of supply, German logistical problems eased while the Allies' became more serious. These elements were responsible for what in Germany would be called the Miracle of the West.

Eisenhower made the precipitating decision on August 23, when he ruled that what the Allies needed more than anything else was Antwerp, which was capable of handling 60 million tons of cargo a year and would solve the supply problem. As there was not enough fuel for two operations, Eisenhower decreed that the bulk of 12th Army Group's gasoline would henceforth go to the British. This meant that Patton's tanks would run out of gas in a week. To Bradley, giving Montgomery his head was tantamount to embracing his grandiose "single thrust" conception, according to which most Allied divisions should be given to him for a drive across the Low Countries to the Ruhr and then Berlin.

Though Bradley was not a raving Anglophobe like Patton, by now he hated Montgomery as much as any other American did. He wanted Eisenhower to stick with the "broad front" concept formulated before Overlord, according to which the British would advance north of the Ardennes, the Americans and French to the south. Bradley did not rule out a British advance. He wanted Antwerp also and knew it was politically important to overrun the V-weapon launching sites from which Hitler was harassing England. But with victory so near, it seemed madness to rein in Patton.

Soon Third Army was across the Meuse and its patrols had reached the Moselle. From there it was only 45 miles to the West Wall, twice that to the Rhine. Then, on August 30, Patton's army ran out of gas— both its own and that captured from the Germans. It had been consuming 350,000 to 400,000 gallons a day, but now was issued only half that much, and finally just a trickle. There was nothing Patton would not do to augment his supply, and Third Army became notorious for its scavaging methods. "Roving foraging parties impersonated members of other units, trains and convoys were diverted or hijacked, transportation companies were robbed of the fuel they needed for the return journey, and spotter planes were sent hundreds of miles to the rear to discover fuel shipments."[2] All the same, when Patton's official rations were gone, Third Army could not steal enough to make up the difference. However, in a meeting with Bradley and Patton on the second, Eisenhower agreed to step up deliveries. He could not do so for long, though, as the Red Ball Express was wearing out.

Begun on August 25, the Red Ball was a chain of trucks stretching from the Channel to depots near the front and back again on parallel one-way roads. Patton's rush across France had been unexpected and, as trucks were in short supply, they had to be used continuously and without regular maintenance. There was no time to maintain tanks, either, so by mid-September both the Red Ball and Third Army were running out of usable vehicles. Further, the logistics experts at SHAEF calculated that even if all supplies and equipment were diverted to Patton for a dash to the Rhine, he would arrive there without having destroyed the German main force, and would have an exposed northern flank as much as 300 miles long. On the other hand, if priority shifted back once again to 21st Army Group, which was closer to the Channel ports, existing resources could be stretched somewhat further.

This analysis, which may have been wrong, because logistical officers tended to be over cautious, led Eisenhower, after a stormy meeting with Montgomery on September 10, to make another strategic shift in favor of the British. The promise of more fuel, in turn, led Montgomery to advance the date for Operation Market-Garden to September 17. It was an extremely daring plan, out of character for Montgomery and unlike anything the Allies had attempted before. It entailed dropping a carpet of three Allied airborne divisions up to 60 miles ahead of the closest British ground units, the farthest objective being the Dutch city of Arnhem, which, if seized and held, would put 21st Army Group across the last water barrier to Germany. From that position it would be easy to flank the West Wall and collapse Germany's line. The alternative was for Dempsey's Second Army to fight across eight water obstacles that lay between it and the north bank of the Neder Rijn at Arnhem, which could take months. Desirable in its own right, taking Arnhem was all the more compelling by the seventeenth, when the U.S. First and Third Armies had stalled for want of gasoline. All hopes of a quick victory now depended upon the U.S. 82nd and 101st Airborne Divisions, and particularly the British 1st Airborne, which was assigned to take Arnhem.

Though a handful of British paratroopers under Lieutenant Colonel J. D. Frost seized one end of the highway bridge in Arnhem and held it for three days against several panzer divisions in one of the most memorable actions of the war, Market-Garden failed. British commanders had ignored intelligence reports that a Panzer division was near Arnhem, when in fact there were two. Whatever chance of success remained was thrown away by lack of aggressiveness. The British airborne troops were dropped too far from their target and moved too slowly afterwards, so that the bridgehead was held by a scratch battalion instead of the whole division. Britain's XXX Corps, which was supposed to relieve the paratroopers, did not drive hard enough, allowing the Germans sufficient time to redeploy. After Market-Garden the Allies were forced once more to fight a war of attrition, as in Normandy, but with worse supply problems.

All of this was particularly exasperating because on September 4 the British 11th Armored Division had taken Antwerp with its docking facilities intact. Then, unaccountably, the British took two days off from the war before resuming their advance. By then, German troops had dug in on both sides of the 60-mile-long Scheldt Estuary, which links Antwerp to the sea, rendering the port facilities useless. It would not be until November 28 that the first Allied ship reached Antwerp, 85 days having been lost. All might have been different if positions had been reversed, with Bradley's more numerous and powerful divisions anchoring the Allied left and Montgomery holding down the middle. Their places had been determined by Overlord, the U.S. attacking on the right because Britain's most westerly ports were handling the American buildup, and it was much too late, and politically impossible, to change places.

The upshot was that, for the sake of a high-risk British plan that failed, Patton had been denied the men and supplies he needed to complete a strategic maneuver with war-winning potential. There would be no more such opportunities until the following spring.

After the war of attrition resumed, the fundamental problem was not just that Montgomery had too few divisions but also that Germany, despite its losses, had too many. By mid-September Eisenhower commanded 55 divisions, 40 infantry and airborne and 15 armored, but Field Marshal Gerd von Runstedt, Hitler's new OB West, could dispose of 48 infantry and 15 panzer and panzer grenadier divisions. They were understrength to be sure, lacking air support and outnumbered in tanks by something like 10 to one. Yet the Germans had lost none of their cunning or their ability to turn raw recruits and battered veterans into effective units seemingly overnight. In addition, they would be fighting defensively from prepared positions, with all the advantages that implied. Under these conditions, American mobility and firepower would count for less, the American manpower shortage for more.

The War Department had planned on infantry casualties amounting to three-quarters of the European total. In Normandy and thereafter the infantry actually absorbed about 85 percent of American casualties, and not the entire infantry, either, for 95 percent of infantry casualties were taken by the rifle companies, which at full strength amounted to only 3,240 out of a total of 15,514 men per division. In practice, therefore, when the U.S. 28th Infantry Division sustained 6,104 casualties attacking the Huertgen Forest, its entire frontline combat strength had been wiped out not once but twice. Losses on this scale were horrifying in the extreme, mute testimony to the agonies of the combat riflemen. They were also unaffordable.

Huertgen should never have been attacked. The forest itself was worthless even though heavily defended by a network of bunkers with overlapping fields of fire. Because of the trees, American air power and armor could not be employed. Yet, beginning on September 19, division after division was fed into the meat grinder: the 9th Infantry to begin with, then the 28th, the 4th, the 8th, the 83rd, and a combat command of the 5th Armored Division, all being destroyed in their turn. When Major General James M. Gavin, commander of the 82nd Airborne, arrived at the Huertgen in February he was appalled to find the ground still littered with American corpses. Of the battle he said simply "It had been our Passchendaele."[3]

Huertgen greatly intensified the combat manpower crisis. On D-Day only 52 percent of replacements in the ETO were infantry. By September 1, just 42,000 infantry replacements were on hand though 55,000 were needed. Worse still, a mere 15,000 of these had been trained as riflemen. The War Department badgered SHAEF for not using its manpower efficiently, and with some justice, though the fault lay with decisions made or approved by the War Department. Apart from having too big an administrative tail, the American forces in Europe had too many men in units that experience would show could be cut, such as antiaircraft and tank destroyer battalions, and too few men in foxholes. Retraining put some men from these units at the front but not enough to make up the shortfall.

For the three months following D-Day the casualties broke down as follows. About 30 percent of total casualties were killed, captured, or missing, and thus lost for good, and around 70 percent wounded. Of the wounded, 45 percent recovered and went back to the front, while another 11 percent could be used in limited assignments. Forty-six percent of the wounded were available for some kind of duty within 120 days, and therefore constituted an essential source of reinforcement for the combat divisions. Much of this potential was lost because of red tape and absurd Army regulations which kept soldiers wishing to return to their outfits idling away in replacement depots. It was not until January 1945 that General Devers persuaded SHAEF to allow recovered 6th Army Group enlisted men to return immediately to their units, after which this practice was applied to 12th Army Group also. In March company-grade officer "casuals" were given the same permission, and finally all restrictions were lifted.[4]

These changes were too late and too little. They also did not address the more serious problem of how to keep units in combat at the highest level of effectiveness. Not only could the troops not be rotated home, but, for lack of men, the U.S. Army did not even have a system that would allow divisions to be transferred out of the line periodically to rest and refit. Then, too, because replacements were supplied on an individual basis rather than as units, they seldom had time to become oriented or receive additional training before going into battle. Accordingly, casualties among new men tended to be much higher than for veterans.

These policies, wasteful to begin with, were compounded by the lack of infantry-trained replacements. From May through July, the percentage of replacements who could fight on the line ranged from 35 percent to 58 percent. There was much wrangling over this between the War Department and SHAEF, Washington pointing out repeatedly that the ETO was overstrength in almost every military occupation except that of rifleman. SHAEF pointed out, in turn, that many of these specialists were doing essential work, for example as drivers in the Red Ball Express.

A great variety of expedients were used to ease the deficit. General Marshall had already cut back the Army Specialized Training and air cadet programs drastically, most transferees going to the ground forces. Draft standards were reduced, and the deactivation of antiaircraft and tank destroyer units hastened to provide additional replacements. By the end of the year, even the belief that black soldiers could not, or should not, fight had to be set aside.The main solution was to speed up the movement of divisions overseas. This increased the already very great logistical problems of the Communications Zone (COMZ), which comprised the Army's rear echelons, and many divisions had to be held in Britain for lack of transportation.

Accelerating the pipeline also had limits, owing to the decision made in 1943 to settle for a 90-division Army. The War Department's Victory Program of 1941, conceived mainly by Major Albert Wedemeyer, had called for an Army of 215 divisions, a sufficient number to do the job even if Russia were defeated—or so it was hoped. In 1943, with Russia no longer at risk of being put out of the war, Marshall decided on a 90 division ceiling for the Army. Secretary Stimson had strongly opposed this cap, and journalists did as well. *Life* ran two editorials on the subject, pointing out that at most the United States was going to have only 100 divisions at a time when the Axis powers had 483 divisions in Europe and Africa alone. Perhaps that would be enough, *Life* warned, but the margin looked awfully thin. Why, it wondered, if Great Britain had 10 percent of its population under arms, was the United States only planning to put 8 percent into uniform?[5]

To this excellent question there appear to have been several answers. One was that General Marshall believed that it was best to have a relatively small number of divisions maintained at full strength by a constant stream of replacements, rather than, like most other armies, feeding in fresh divisions as those on the line shrank. In principle there was much to be said for this, since each new division brought along not only its fighting men but its administrative and support people too, so that the ratio of "tail" to fighting front expanded at a rapid rate. Yet, however excellent in theory, it depended on a greater stream of individual replacements than the Army proved able to supply.

Another reason, more of a subtext than a matter of public declaration, was that Congress would not expand the draft to build an Army of the size Stimson wanted. Despite numerous polls showing that a majority of the public were willing to support both a labor draft and the conscription of young single women into the Women's Army Corps, Congress refused to do either. In 1944 when FDR proposed a national service bill that would have put civilian labor under tighter control and made Selective Service more productive, Congress rejected it out-of-hand. It also refused to expand the military draft when that was requested. Thus, while Marshall may have been mistaken about the divisional strength of the Army, the political realities were such that, even if he wanted them, he was not going to get more people.

Stimson attempted on three different occasions to persuade Marshall to expand the Army Ground Forces, the last during the Battle of the Bulge when it was too late to make any difference. Stimson was on the mark as far as battlefield requirements were concerned. Later he would generously declare that, as the war in Europe had been won, Marshall was clearly right about the size of the Army. This did not take into account the time lost in 1944, when a larger force might very well have won the war, or the terrible cost to the riflemen, or that Eisenhower lacked a strategic reserve which could have made a great difference. In this sense Marshall was wrong. Having substantially more divisions in France might well have shortened the war considerably if Congress had made that possible. Since it didn't, there was nothing to do by 1944 except accelerate the pipeline.

The stalemate that followed Market-Garden did not mean that serious fighting came to end. The broad front strategy required that pressure on the Germans be maintained, and so as new divisions arrived from the states they were put on a line that was pressing relentlessly forward—at heavy cost to the Germans, and to the Americans as well. The experiences of the 12th Armored and 84th Infantry Divisions were representative.

In the fall of 1944, young Brendan Phibbs was the chief surgeon of Combat Command B of the U.S. 12th Armored Division. Every division of armor had three such commands, the other two designated A and R. A combat command was made up of three battalions, one each of tanks, armored infantry, and self-propelled guns, plus various specialized units such as Phibbs' medical company. Like most fresh divisions in 1944, the 12th Armored had trained for two years in the States before being sent to France. Gunnery received particular attention because the feeble 76-mm cannons of their Sherman tanks were known to be nearly useless against Germany's heavily armored new models.

On November 17, 1944, a day before their first battle, officers of the 12th gathered in a schoolhouse on the Lorraine front for a briefing. Phibbs was there because of his fluent German, which made him an unofficial translator between division HQ and the German-speaking Alsatian resistance forces. The 12th was taking over a sector from the 4th Armored Division, Major General John Wood's crack outfit which was much feared by the Germans. Indeed, German soldiers were told that membership in the 4th was limited to men who had been professional killers in civilian life. The 12th's briefer was Creighton Abrams, a future Army chief of staff but then a rugged, cigar-smoking tank battalion commander, renowned at the front for his ingenuity and dash. Better known to the Germans at this time than he was to the public, Abrams was the leading American tank commander below the rank of general. He would go on adding to his laurels. By V-E Day he would have worn out six tanks, all named Thunderbolt, without losing one to enemy action or being wounded himself. Supposedly he liked to be "way out on the goddam point of the attack, where there's nothing but me and the goddam Germans and we can fight by ourselves without stopping to report back to Headquarters."[6]

Colonel Abrams had two points he wished to impress upon the 12th's green officers. His first was to remind them that, because their main battle tank was so feeble, if they attacked the enemy head-on they would be cut to pieces. The second was that they could win anyway by moving faster than the German, hitting him where they weren't expected, and making him cut and run. Creighton described how to do this in some detail, the assembled officers hanging on every word. They are, Phibbs recalled, "crouched around sudden death and they know it and feel it, right to the edge of dread."[7] The exception was General George Beaky, commander of the 12th, who was paying little attention. As Phibbs recalled it, the briefer's final remarks were: "'Brains and speed, that's how you survive.' Creighton faces Beaky and exhales a sigh full of smoke. 'Speed and,' he pauses and almost shakes his head, 'brains.' The word echoes tragically: the hero seems to shrug as he turns and walks quickly through the blackout curtain."[8]

General Beaky, as Phibbs calls him, was new to the 12th, having replaced the officer it trained under only a few months earlier. Like many inexperienced commanders before him, Beaky was certain that he knew more than the experts, especially those lower in rank. His division's first assignment was to oust a formation of German armor sheltered behind pillboxes of the Maginot Line, whereupon he ordered a frontal attack—the last resort of a desperate commander and the first of a witless one. Phibbs' friend Mike, who would lead the attack, tried to sell Beaky on a flanking maneuver, as the German position was narrow and would be easy to turn.

Finally the General issued a direct order, and Mike gave up. He turned to a friend and said "This is it, Coop. Good-bye."[9] Since he would be in the vanguard of the doomed assault, he had little hope of survival.

Beaky's instructions were for the tank battalion to cross 1,000 yards of bare ground and attack German armor dug in behind 20 feet of concrete. As their radios had failed, Mike directed the charge with hand signals from a standing position in the open hatch of his Sherman amid withering German fire. Mike was an early casualty, his head torn from his body by one of their opening shots. The Americans tried to return fire, but, even when they scored clean hits, their shells glanced off the impenetrable German hulls. Many Shermans burned and the rest fell back. It was a bloody fiasco, just what Abrams had said would result if thin-skinned tanks made frontal assaults on an enemy fortification.

Despite three years of combat experience, the world's foremost industrial nation sent its tankers into battle armed with inferior weapons. Their commander employed a tactic that had been obsolete for a hundred years and which he had been specifically warned against. Yet, despite this unpromising start, the 12th Armored got better and better, its men learning fast the tricks of their deadly trade. Like the 4th, it became an ace division, beating the masters of armored warfare at the game they had invented. But the cost of this education was heavy.

Two officers who served in K Company, Third Battalion of the 84th Infantry Division's 333rd Regiment have written a vivid account of their introduction to combat, which was similar to that of the 12th Armored. K Company began with 200 men and sustained 200 casualties during its 100 days on the line. This 100 percent casualty rate, even more than that among riflemen, was about average for a line company. K was a typical infantry company with three rifle platoons and one weapons platoon, the rifle platoons having three squads of 12 men each, the balance consisting of cooks, clerks, and others who normally did not see combat. The 84th was one of the fully trained new triangular divisions with all the advantages of firepower and mobility which that designation entailed. But it was thrown into battle without any of its assets being deployed except the raw courage of the foot soldier.

Upon arriving in Europe the 84th was assigned to attack the Geilenkirchen Salient north of Aachen, Germany, a part of the Siegfried line, which was manned by two veteran SS panzer divisions. Supported by tanks of the Sherwood Rangers Yeomanry, its 333rd and 334th Regiments jumped off on November 21, 1944. By the end of the day a majority of the attacking companies had sustained heavy losses. Instead of regrouping or being reinforced, the regiments were ordered to attack again and on the twenty-second were stopped once more, K Company having been reduced to 70 men. On the third day the survivors were ordered back to their starting point.

Lieutenant General Brian Horrocks, who commanded the British XXX Corps to which the 84th had been attached for this operation, was impressed by the fighting men of the 84th but appalled by their leaders. American commanders made no effort to see that the men on the line received hot meals during the fighting. No American senior officer, not even a battalion commander, visited the front during the battle, while Horrocks himself came forward to confer with his tank leaders. He thought this fight was one of the hardest small unit engagements of the war: "I was filled with admiration for the extreme gallantry displayed by the raw GIs of the 84th Division. If only their administration and staff arrangements had been up to the level of their courage, the veteran German troops might well have had a bloody nose."[10]

The report of Captain John J. O'Grady of the Ninth Army's historical section, who followed the battle from the Third Battalion's command post was even more scathing. To his mind, the assault was doomed from the start. The 333rd had been made to attack up a narrow river valley under circumstances which ruled out maneuver against a strongly entrenched enemy. The rifle companies lost half their men on the first day, the survivors another half on the second. Higher headquarters provided nothing for the men except orders to keep on moving.

> Tactics and maneuver on battalion or regimental scale were conspicuous by their absence. It never seemed to occur to anyone that the plan might be wrong; but rather the indictment was placed on the small unit commanders and the men who were doing the fighting. The companies went into battle against the formidable Siegfried Line with their T/O weapons and nothing more. Hand grenades and rifle bullets against pillboxes. The 84th Division walked into the most touted defensive line in modern warfare without so much as the benefit of a briefing by combat officers who had been fighting the problem for some months and had found workable solutions.[11]

It was the experience of the 12th Armored all over again. The Army could build great divisions, but all too often their new commanders did not know how to use them. As always, it was the fighting men who would pay for this.

In less than a week the 333rd and 334th had suffered 2,000 casualties—169 men killed, 742 missing, most presumed dead, and over 1,000 wounded—plus 500 nonbattle casualties, most resulting from trenchfoot. Between November 19 and the twenty-fourth, K Company's four platoons had 11 men KIA, 2 MIA, 42 wounded, and 18 nonbattle casualties. Half the sergeants and the company commander were gone. When the company left Geilenkirchen on November 29, barely a week after going into battle, more than half its combat strength consisted of replacements. Sixteen survivors had been promoted, 10 of them ASTP transfers. The 84th had received 2,800 of these men, young Henry Kissinger among them, who had been sent to the infantry when their training programs were cancelled.[13] In K Company, as in many others, they would provide more than their share of leadership. From that time on, having lost all confidence in the brass, K Company would live by its wits.

Bradley's 12th Army Group would meet its supreme test in the Ardennes Forest. The Battle of the Bulge was the greatest clash on the Western Front and the biggest engagement America has ever fought. Some 600,000 American soldiers were involved and took proportionate casualties—20,000 killed, 20,000 captured, and 40,000 wounded. Two U.S. infantry divisions were all but wiped out and 800 tanks destroyed. However, harrowing though these losses seemed, Germany's were worse, totaling perhaps 100,000, a third of the attacking force. At the Bulge Hitler used up his manpower reserves, hastening Germany's defeat.

Hitler began planning his counteroffensive in late July, at a time when he had just lost 25 divisions on the Eastern Front, and the Allies were busting out of Normandy and had already taken Rome. The 25 Volksgrenadier divisions he raised during the fall consisted largely of teenagers and Hitler Youth who were poorly trained but high on motivation. The ten panzer brigades he assembled, each with 40 new tanks, included many Tigers and Panthers. In its final form the attacking force would consist of three armies, amounting to some 300,000 men, 1,900 artillery pieces, and 970 tanks and armored assault guns. In the East these armies would have been swallowed up. On the smaller Western Front they might make a difference. Probably they wouldn't, but, Hitler had nothing to lose by trying, for if the Ruhr fell the war was as good as over.

Germany knew about inter-Allied friction from reading British and

American newspapers and hoped to exploit these tensions by driving a wedge between the American 12th and British 21st Army Groups where their fronts joined in Belgium. The plan was for his main strike force, SS General Josef "Sepp" Dietrich's Sixth SS Panzer Army, to drive through the Ardennes Forest, cross the Meuse, as the Germans had done in 1940, and wheel north to Antwerp. Supporting it on the left would be the Fifth Panzer Army, while the Seventh Army would hold open the southern shoulder of the breach against Patton's counterattack. Bad weather would ground the Allied fighter–bombers, unleashing Germany's armor.

When Germany struck the U.S. Army would have only a cavalry group, one armored division, and four of infantry holding the Ardennes front. Two of the infantry divisions were green and two exhausted by the savage fighting in Huertgen Forest, which had cost First Army 34,000 casualties. The Germans expected to overrun these raw and worn divisions. In the ensuing rout, American morale would collapse, Allied bickering reach new heights, and the Grand Alliance fall apart. Whether anyone actually believed this fantasy is hard to say, but, because Hitler would not surrender and could not be replaced, the Wehrmacht had to obey orders.

Though the strategy behind this attack was pathetic, tactics and logistics were up to the usual German standards. Three armies were assembled in the Eifel Mountains of Germany without Allied intelligence's knowledge, a remarkable feat considering that the men and supplies had to be brought from as far away as Austria and Denmark. To conceal their intent, the Germans put together an effective deception plan, "Watch on the Rhine," beating the Allies at their own game. Thanks to this intelligence coup, when the German counteroffensive began on December 16, it completely surprised most Americans.

Major General Troy H. Middleton, who commanded First Army's VIII Corps front, which included the southern Ardennes, was anxious about his vulnerable position, though Bradley felt he was in no danger. Eisenhower knew that the Ardennes sector was weak, but he could not reinforce it except at the expense of limited offensives taking place elsewhere as part of his broad front strategy, which was being executed with too few troops to provide a margin of safety.[13] On December 16, the entire American reserve consisted of the 82nd and 101st Airborne Divisions, both being refitted after suffering heavy losses during Market-Garden. Though they would play important roles in the Bulge, a reserve that consisted of two undermanned divisions, which even at full strength had only 10,000 men apiece, no armor, and few guns, was close to having no reserve at all.

After a short artillery barrage, the Germans attacked on the sixteenth along an 85-mile front, taking SHAEF by surprise. What should have been easy for the Wehrmacht became terribly difficult, thanks to the heroism and gallantry of greatly outnumbered Americans. Most remarkable was the defense put up by the 99th Infantry Division, a new outfit that had seen little action. Like other divisions in the Ardennes, it occupied a stretch of line that ought to have been held by a corps. Though caught off guard, the men of the 99th fought back furiously, to the point of calling artillery fire down on their own positions.

The 99th was the northernmost division to be attacked. Behind it lay Elsenborn Ridge, high ground covering two critical road junctions without which the Sixth SS Panzer Army could not advance. Though Dietrich did not know it, quite by chance the veteran U.S. 2nd Infantry Division was attacking just above him. As the 99th's situation worsened, Major General Leonard T. Gerow of V Corps, which was responsible for the northern Ardennes, put the 2nd Division's reserve regiment in front of Elsenborn Ridge.

On the seventeenth Lieutenant General Courtney H. Hodges of First Army gave Gerow a free hand. He immediately ordered the 2nd to break off its attack and join its 23nd Infantry Regiment at Elsenborn. Hodges also ordered up the famed 1st Infantry Division, "the Big Red One," from Aachen where it was resting. The 2nd Division executed a tricky maneuver, known as "skinning the cat," which involved disengaging battalions from combat, passing them through a defensive line, having them set up another line farther back through which the battalions now in front would themselves pass in turn, and so on for 7.5 miles to Elsenborn Ridge. Despite the miserable weather and general confusion, this difficult operation went smoothly, evidence of how good the Army had gotten since it came ashore in France.

Meanwhile, the 99th's battered components disengaged and passed through the 23d Infantry to regroup and dig in on Elsenborn Ridge, where the 2nd Division would join them. By December 18 Elsenborn was proving its worth. American artillery laid down murderous barrages from the ridge. Protected by fog and darkness, American tanks and guns were lying in wait along narrow roads, striking from the side and rear, where even the Tigers were vulnerable. On the eighteenth, Dietrich attempted to bypass Elsenborn, but his attacking force was prevented from reaching the strategic Malmedy road by elements of the Big Red One, which had gotten there just in time.

The defenders of Elsenborn Ridge were then joined by the 9th Infantry Division. Together these four divisions, the 2nd and 99th in the center and the 9th and 1st on their flanks, had created an unbreakable line by December 20. As a result of their inspired stand, the German counteroffensive was spoiled after only five days of battle. Dietrich realized this and wanted to settle for limited gains, but Hitler insisted on continuing the attack even though Elsenborn Ridge barred the Sixth Panzer Army from Antwerp. This was sheer mulishness on his part as the operation now lacked any strategic purpose.

Most accounts of the fighting turn on the 101st Airborne and its defense of Bastogne, which was indeed remarkable. But the key position was Elsenborn Ridge. The holding of it by the 2nd and 99th Infantry Divisions, the latter often fighting in small units out of touch with higher command, against attackers who outnumbered them 5 or more to 1, was the outstanding achievement of the battle. In the critical early days, these two divisions repelled an entire German corps, the elite I SS Panzers.

At the southern end of the front the enemy was also in trouble. While Germany's Seventh Army greatly outnumbered the veteran U.S. 4th Infantry Division, which had taken 6,000 casualties in the Huertgen Forest and was still recovering, it put up a tremendous defense, slowing down the German advance and gaining time for reinforcements to move up. As a result, another unbreakable line was established which forced the Germans to narrow their attack to the central Ardennes, in which there was little room for maneuver.

The Fifth Panzer Army was now playing the part originally assigned to the Sixth. Things were going much better for Germany in the central Ardennes because of outstanding leadership by Lieutenant General Hasso von Manteuffel. His plan of attack did not rely on brute force but was marked by stealth and speed, deep-penetration units racing through American lines without benefit of artillery support. These and other enterprising methods drove the veteran American 28th Infantry Division back and wiped out the 106th. It had just arrived in the Ardennes and was a scratch outfit, having been cannibalized and then rebuilt. A majority of its enlisted men had not trained together. It occupied positions that were easy to outflank but hard to retreat from. As a result it was cut to pieces. In addition to heavy casualties, at least 7,000 men became prisoners—

the largest number of American POWs ever taken by Germany in a single action.

However, while Manteuffel effectively destroyed two divisions, it had taken him longer than he could afford. Before the 28th and 106th went under they fought hard, the time they won enabling Eisenhower to rush support to the pivotal crossroad villages of St. Vith and Bastogne. Manteuffel did eventually take St. Vith, but the 7th Armored Division defending it held up an entire German corps for three days, ruining Manteuffel's schedule and giving American generals time to gain control of the battle. When the 7th was allowed to withdraw, Montgomery said "They can come back with honor. They put on a wonderful show."[14] During this critical period Eisenhower was drawing men and supplies from other sectors of the front and pouring them into the Ardennes, 250,000 men and 50,000 vehicles in the first week, a performance no other army in history has ever equaled.

Though surrounded Bastogne remained in American hands, thanks to the 101st Airborne, Combat Command B of the 10th Armored, and the crack 705th Tank Destroyer Battalion—plus a group of some 500 men, a ragtag collection of individuals and small units, who were organized into a reserve, named, with characteristic GI humor, Team SNAFU. With the aid of breaks in the weather that permitted air support and resupply, this mixed force held out until Patton's relief column reached it on December 27. That same day, survivors of the 2nd Panzer Division gave themselves up, having almost reached the Meuse before being blocked by the U.S. 2nd Armored Division. It was as far as the Germans would get.

A great American victory, the Battle of the Bulge might have been greater still. Eisenhower had reacted quickly to the German attack, sending two armored divisions to Middleton's sector on the sixteenth despite Bradley's reservations. Hitler had told his Generals that it would take at least two days for Eisenhower to realize the trouble he was in, and two or three more to get permission from Roosevelt and Churchill to call off his offensives and reinforce the Ardennes. By then the Germans would be across the Meuse and on their way to Antwerp. Hitler assumed that Allied commanders were as tightly controlled as his own, and did not understand that Eisenhower had real authority— even over British troops, although Montgomery did all he could to limit it.

On the seventeenth, Eisenhower sent more men to the Ardennes and put a stop to American offensives elsewhere in preparation for his retaliatory strokes. On the eighteenth he met with his top commanders and told them to view the Bulge as an opportunity, not a problem. When the Germans were further extended he wanted to attack both their flanks and bag the lot. By the nineteenth, preparations for this double envelopment were underway, and Patton was beginning the intricate process of pulling three divisions out of his front and advancing them to the north at right angles across his own lines of communication. Even more than the 2nd Infantry Division's skinning of the cat, this was a devilishly complex maneuver. Pulling it off in three days was one of Patton's masterpieces.

He moved so fast partly as a result of advance planning based on Patton's concern about the inactivity of VIII Corps, which he believed invited a German attack. He wrote about this in his diary as early as November 25. On December 12, four days before the German counteroffensive, he ordered his staff to make plans for a Third Army response in the event of an enemy breakthrough on the VIII Corps front. On the sixteenth German radio silence led Patton to order plans for ending Third Army's offensive and turning it at right angles for an attack into Luxembourg. Thus, when on the nineteenth Eisenhower asked him how long it would take for Third Army to attack to the north, Patton surprised everyone by saying he could launch three divisions in 72 hours. Eisenhower wanted six divisions, as would indeed have been better, but Patton argued that speed was more important than mass.

To Bradley, who disliked him, this was Patton's finest hour. When he attacked on the twenty-second across his own axis of advance, Patton's generalship, Bradley says, "was magnificent, one of the most brilliant performances by any commander on either side in World War II."[15] Many other professional soldiers agreed. Major General Gavin, whose 82nd Airborne fought in the Bulge under First Army, described the feat in these words. Patton "had disengaged three divisions actually in combat and launched them over one hundred miles of icy roads straight into the German offensive. The rapidity and violence of his attack took the Germans by surprise and completely upset their time table. Of all the army commanders, only Patton could have carried out such an operation."[16]

On the twentieth, with Bradley separated from his First and Ninth Armies by the German penetration, Eisenhower gave temporary command of them to Montgomery, leaving Bradley with only Third Army under his immediate control. This decision, a result of Bradley's comparative isolation in Luxembourg, was Eisenhower's major mistake and would have serious consequences. For one, though Eisenhower was eager to begin enveloping the Bulge, Montgomery, as always, dragged his feet. Further, when he did attack, he wanted to push the Bulge back into Germany rather than cut it off. After a meeting on the twenty-eighth, Eisenhower believed that he had gotten Montgomery's promise to attack on January 1. Then, on the thirtieth, Major General Francis de Guingand, Montgomery's likable Chief of Staff, notified Eisenhower that Montgomery would not jump off until January 3—or later.

Eisenhower was furious with Montgomery, forcing De Guingand to shuttle back and forth between SHAEF and 21st Army Group. While the debate was raging over what Montgomery had promised to do, he sent Eisenhower a letter demanding to be put in complete charge of the land battle, which under his direction would feature a single thrust to Berlin—a blatant attempt to take advantage of the crisis and impose his theater strategy upon Eisenhower. Instead, Eisenhower returned First Army to Bradley, with orders to pinch off the Bulge, and prepared for a showdown with Monty. Contrite now, for Eisenhower had almost sacked him, Montgomery did advance on January 3, though not as strongly as Eisenhower wanted and not in the right direction. So passed the opportunity to destroy three German armies, a result of Montgomery's obsession with his single front strategy. Under pressure from both ends, the Germans withdrew slowly in good order, inflicting maximum damage. The Battle of the Bulge was declared at an end on January 28, though the old lines were not restored until February 7.[17]

The Battle had many unique features. To sow confusion behind American lines, the Germans sent in commando teams under Obersturmmbannführer (Lieutenant Colonel) Otto Skorzeny, famous for his daring rescue of Mussolini from a mountain top in 1943. Posing as American soldiers, the commandos generated much confusion, mostly by leading American guards to question all officers at great length to determine their authenticity. Generals were a favorite target, one being held prisoner for hours after putting the Chicago Cubs in the wrong baseball league. At another roadblock a soldier insisted that Omar Bradley had erred in naming Springfield as the capitol of Illinois. When stopped again, Bradley failed to name the third husband of movie star Betty Grable (Harry James, a band leader). It was beginning to look as if Bradley would have to take time off from the war to bone up on popular culture.

The Bulge was the first battle in which Negro troops played an important part. Desperate for replacements, Eisenhower accepted thousands of black volunteers from the service forces, many taking reductions in rank because only privates and PFCs were wanted. They performed well enough so that some officers decided the Army was wrong to keep 10 percent of its enlisted men out of combat because of racial prejudice. Thereafter, more blacks saw action, and, though they were still "Jim Crowed," a process had begun that would lead to full integration after the war.

As a rule, all forces in Western Europe observed the Geneva Convention, which specified how prisoners should be treated despite isolated instances on both sides of soldiers being murdered after having laid down their arms. The worst atrocities took place in the Bulge, most of them committed by Taskforce Peiper, a reinforced regiment of the 1st SS Panzer Division under Oberstummmbannführer Joachim Peiper. It led the northern assault and begin shooting American POWs almost at once, along with many Belgian civilians. The most brutal assault on POWs, known as the Malmedy Massacre, resulted in the death of some 86 American prisoners.

What gives the Battle of the Bulge a special place in American military history is the remarkable skill and courage displayed by ordinary soldiers. The German counteroffensive was blighted at the start by heroic defensive actions at each end of the front. That the 4th Division fought well was, perhaps, not surprising in view of its record. But the magnificent stand of the 99th violated the rule of thumb that raw divisions needed seasoning in order to become effective. However, it was no accident that the green youngsters of the 99th fought splendidly, but rather the result of the more realistic Army training that most of the newest divisions had received, and also because they benefited from the infusion of former air cadets and ASTP students. The stellar performance of these new divisions further discredited the Army's old practice of using the infantry as a dumping ground for its least capable soldiers. The veteran divisions, too, purged of incompetent officers and gaining from experience and higher quality replacements, were fighting extremely well. It was all coming together for the American Army in Europe. Eisenhower would always be short of divisions, but those he now had were choice.

This was apparent to the Germans, too, who had counted on qualitative superiority making up for their being outgunned. The Bulge was the graveyard of this illusion, a German report dated January 20, 1945 calling the American soldier a "first-rate, well trained, and often physically superior opponent." He had been undaunted by the bitter cold and harsh weather, for which he was in many cases not properly dressed. Surrounded American units had in a number of cases fought to the last man. On the attack, American soldiers had proved to be "tough fighters in close quarters," even when lacking air and armor support.[18]

America's success in the Bulge was scarcely marred by Montgomery's effort to take credit for it. On January 7, with the outcome no longer in doubt, Montgomery, who had done very little besides spoiling Eisenhower's double envelopment, held a press conference to discuss his superb leadership. Even Churchill was embarrassed by Montgomery's falsehoods. On January 18, 1945, he pointed out in the House of Commons that American troops had done almost all the fighting and suffered almost all the losses. "Care must be taken not to claim for the British Army an undue share of what is undoubtedly the greatest American battle of the War, and will, I believe, be regarded as an ever-famous American victory."[19]

Though Montgomery, complacent as ever, was satisfied with a tactical success in the Ardennes, American commanders were not. They knew a great opportunity had been lost, and not only on account of Montgomery but because they were so short-handed—Patton complaining to Secretary Stimson of this after the battle. In January, 73 Allied divisions were facing 70 German. Yet, if the Bulge showed how dangerous it was to fight Germany with such a narrow to nonexistent margin, it also marked Eisenhower's coming of age as a battlefield commander. Many senior officers believed that it was a mistake to put Eisenhower in charge of the ground war while at the same time he remained supreme commander of the Allied Expeditionary Force. No doubt the two jobs should have been held by different men, but the existing arrangement was politically essential. Montgomery would not serve under any other American general, and it was impossible to put Montgomery in command of the Americans, whom he had so thoroughly alienated.

Thus, only Eisenhower could direct the Allied Army groups, and, as the Bulge showed, he was becoming good at it. Apart from giving Montgomery command of two American armies, a very big mistake to be sure, Eisenhower performed faultlessly. He sensed the danger before any of his leading commanders except Patton, started sending reinforcements on the first day Germany attacked, and completely redesigned the Army's existing campaigns—not only to avert disaster but to exploit the opportunity. After the Bulge, there could be no question about Eisenhower's competence. Even Bradley, who deeply resented what he saw as Ike's habit of deferring to the British, and who regarded himself as the better soldier, dropped his reservations. "Ike was more forceful and commanding than I had ever seen him. 'Calamity acted on Eisenhower like a restorative,' Alan Brook wrote, 'and brought out all the greatness in his character.' This was true and the change was remarkable. I soon saw that Ike was not going to rubber-stamp my plans as he had so often done in the past. From now on, Ike would run the war."[20]

In other ways the Bulge was a soldier's battle. The American Army in Europe had failed utterly to anticipate the German counter-offensive. Patton excepted, it had made no preparations for such a turn of events, did not detect the German buildup, and gave the troops no warning. When the Germans fell on them, it was with overwhelming local superiority in manpower and materiel. Further, the Germans not only had better tanks but, for a change, more of them. Air power, the Allied equalizer, was grounded by bad weather for almost a week. The Germans should have swept through the Ardennes in a couple of days and ravaged COMZ. It was ordinary GIs who prevented this. Despite being outnumbered and outgunned, they fought as if possessed and bought the time that gave America victory. The Army of the United States never had a prouder moment.

After the Bulge, Eisenhower still faced the same problem, how to advance on several fronts when he only had the means for one. Further, despite having suffered heavy losses, it appeared as if Germany might actually achieve numerical superiority on the Western Front. Eisenhower expected to have 85 divisions in the late spring or early summer, but the pipeline would then be empty, and with the British already cannibalizing their units, the Allied Expeditionary Force would gradually diminish. Meanwhile, Hitler had the capacity to substantially increase his strength on the Western Front. Armaments were still pouring off the assembly lines, German fighter production alone having risen from about 1,000 a month to 3,000 at year's end (4,000 in September), including hundreds of jet planes against which there was no real defense. Germany had over 70 divisions facing the Allies, plus another 24 in Italy, 17 in Norway, and 10 in Yugoslavia. By pulling out of Scandinavia and the Balkans, Hitler could have put a hundred divisions on his West Wall, already an imposing bulwark. Under those circumstances, any strategy adopted by Eisenhower would be unlikely to enjoy quick success.

But Germany's strength on the Western Front in 1945, though real, was also misleading, for Hitler had ruthlessly stripped his eastern armies. At the time of the Bulge, a mere 133 German divisions were fighting Russia, surviving only because the Red Army had not yet launched its winter offensive. Most of the new Volksgrenadier divisions had been sent to the West, and most of the new fighter planes, tanks, and assault guns as well. To Albert Speer and others in the Reich, Hitler's strategy seemed ridiculous in light of the Soviet threat. But the Red Army, which in December was still advancing through agricultural regions of little strategic value, was far from Germany's industrial heart, which the Allies were close to seizing. In robbing Peter to pay Paul, Hitler was making the best of his extremely limited options.

It remained true that only time could be won on the Eastern Front, while in the West there remained a tiny chance of victory. As nothing less could save him, Hitler had no use for caution and no concern for what might happen to Germany if he failed. He made this clear when the end came by blaming the German people for letting him down, thereby forfeiting their right to exist. One of the many German delusions had been that Hitler was a great patriot, when in fact he was a monster of selfishness, an error for which Germany had already suffered much and would suffer more in future.

On January 12 the Soviets kicked off their long awaited offensive and the Eastern Front promptly collapsed. On January 30, by chance the twelfth anniversary of Hitler's accession to power, Speer sent him a memo stating that, because of the loss of manufacturing capacity and shortages of raw material, armaments production was about to collapse also, a report which Hitler suppressed. According to Speer, German morale was ruined, too, even that of Nazi leaders. Yet, with Germany on its last legs, the cities burned out, the noose around it tightening, the magnificent German Army fought on without either hope or purpose. Some veterans would later argue that, by continuing the war, they attempted to save as much of Germany as they could from being overrun by the Soviets. This excuse would be plausible if resistance on the Western Front had stopped. Instead, right up to its last days, the German Army was still fighting hard in the West, blowing bridges and doing all it could to delay the Allied advance.

While those on the inside could see that Germany was finished, the Allies did not. The Bulge seemed to show that Germany could still take the offensive. It was known that German industry was still producing fighter planes in quantity, despite all the bombing attacks. While Spaatz's oil plan had sharply limited the production of aviation fuel, which kept Luftwaffe pilots from getting enough training, they had plenty of aircraft, and increasingly these were jets, whereas the first American jet was not expected to become operational before October.

In addition, Bradley's "hurry-up" offensive, which he launched to take advantage of Germany's retreat from the Bulge, foundered. On February 1 he was up against the West Wall and going nowhere fast. At the same time, losses were continuing to mount. The Army's casualties, including those resulting from illness or injury, totaled 134,400 in December, 136,700 in February, and would come to 101,000 in March. Meanwhile, on March 3, the last American divisions arrived in Europe. Except for individual replacements, there were no troops left in the States, forcing Eisenhower to consider cannibalizing his newest armored divisions. By late January he was short 82,000 infantrymen, and the deficit was growing.

Fortunately for all concerned, the war was nearly over. At Malta, en route to the Crimea, American and British chiefs met to plan their final offensives. A last British effort to get Montgomery 16 American divisions for a single thrust, plus command of all land forces, was quashed for good by Marshall. While Britain cited the Bulge as evidence that the Allies were too weak for more than one offensive, Eisenhower had drawn the opposite conclusion. The Allies needed to launch more than one attack in order to keep Germany from concentrating all available forces against it. Montgomery would get 12 U.S. divisions, and his Veritable and Grenade offensives would be strongly supported.

Even though Britain wanted the remaining American armies to go over to the defensive, Bradley would be allowed to mount a secondary advance on Frankfurt–Kassel. He was content with this, knowing that Montgomery would attack too late and move too slowly. Moreover, although this was unclear as yet, retraining programs, dragooning men from the Air Force and COMZ, together with Germany's increasing weakness, would provide sufficient riflemen for a big American push. Although it was too late in the war to alter its course, Bradley at last had the means to make Montgomery irrelevant.

The British commenced Operation Veritable on February 8, and during the next two weeks covered only 17 miles. Meanwhile, Patton, who had been ordered to conduct an "active defense," had broken through the West Wall on a 40-mile front. Simpson's Ninth Army, as part of 21st Army Group, jumped off on February 23 and made the long awaited breakthrough, advancing 53 miles in two weeks, capturing 30,000 German troops and clearing 34 miles of the Rhine's west bank. While it raced forward, Bradley was working with Hodges and Patton on a plan of attack that would put them on the Rhine as well. This went beyond the nominal role of "aggressive defense" that the official plan assigned to First and Third Armies and would enable them to cross before Montgomery if he failed to accelerate. On March 7 both armies reached the Rhine.

SHAEF's plan was for Montgomery to cross on March 24 with 32 divisions. It was Bradley's intention to take advantage of the room Eisenhower was giving him to merge the Third and Seventh Armies, plus the French First, for a massive sweep to Frankfurt. This in turn would enable First Army to cross the Rhine, and the combined Franco–American force of 40 divisions would drive on Kassel. Plunder, the British operation, was supposed to be the main event, making Bradley's Undertow a secondary operation. If all worked as Bradley expected, however, the American drive would change that.

On the evening of March 7 Bradley's plan was nearly torpedoed when he received an order from SHAEF to put 10 divisions of First Army in reserve for Operation Plunder. Bradley hit the roof, for he considered the First to be his best Army, a view many failed to share, as Hodges was not a highly esteemed commander. In any case, it was crucial to Undertow's success. Luckily, as he was arguing with Eisenhower's representative, Major General Harold R. Bull, known to intimates as "Pink," Bradley received a call from Hodges saying that his 9th Armored had just captured the Ludendorff railway bridge at Remagen, the Germans having failed to blow it. Bradley ordered Hodges to cross in strength and hold the bridge at all costs.

Though Bull made light of this gift from the gods, Bradley was, to use his own phrase, "engulfed in euphoria." Now he had the opportunity to launch an offensive that would rival, and perhaps supplant, Montgomery's, which was not to take place for two weeks. Eisenhower was also excited, and gave him permission to put four divisions across. On March 13 Eisenhower instructed Bradley to secure the bridgehead at Remagen and attack toward Frankfurt, junking Undertow. He also approved Bradley's "right-hook plan," knowing full well, Bradley believed, that while Plunder was still nominally the major operation, the American attack would supersede it. Hitler too recognized the importance of the Ludendorff bridge. Officers held to be responsible for its loss were summarily shot, Rundstedt was relieved as OB West and replaced by Kesselring.

On March 13 Patton jumped off, followed by Seventh Army. After hard initial fighting they began to roll, capturing 90,000 Germans between them—the biggest bag of prisoners since the Germans lost North Africa. On the twenty-third, Patton called Bradley to say he was over the Rhine, having crossed on the fly without even an artillery barrage. He was exuberant over beating Montgomery, who had spent too much time as usual perfecting his arrangements. Montgomery made his crossing easily on the twenty-fourth, as scheduled. Meanwhile, American troops were pouring across the Rhine in boats and over pontoon bridges. Their effort to contain the U.S. Army having failed, the British had no choice but to accept a revised plan which had American forces driving for the Elbe—where the Allies and the Soviets would meet—while Montgomery protected their northern flank. If any doubts remained, their numerous successful crossings demonstrated that the Americans were far better than the British at improvisation and rapid advance. On April 4 Eisenhower returned Simpson to Bradley, who now commanded four U.S. armies with 48 divisions and 1.3 million men, the largest U.S. ground force ever commanded by an American general. With it he would promptly win the war in the West.

Though John Wood had been sent home and was not there to see them, the final attacks were straight from the 4th Armored textbook. They involved "sending large armored formations into Germany to execute a series of deep, bold penetrations and encirclements. These culminated in the dramatic sweep to the Elbe River, a campaign after Wood's own heart."[21] It was after Patton's heart as well—and finally that of the entire Army in Europe.

The destruction of Nazi Germany was the most splendid feat of arms in modern history. Though the Soviet Union bore the greatest burden, America's contribution—in men as well as supplies—was decisive. While there was glory enough for all who shared in this triumph, Eisenhower was to gain the most. Paradoxically, he would also become the most criticized American commander in Europe because of his decision to let the Soviets take Berlin.

Originally Americans, like the British, saw Berlin as the great prize toward which their efforts should be directed. But at Yalta, with the single thrust strategy having been permanently quashed, and with Roosevelt visibly failing, Britain took the lead in agreeing to occupation boundaries that put Berlin well within what would become the Soviet zone, though the city itself was to be divided among the victors. In late March, with German resistance crumbling, it suddenly became possible for 12th Army Group to drive straight for Berlin. All knew that whoever attacked Berlin would take heavy losses. It is believed that the Soviets sustained 100,000 casualties in their assault, a conservative estimate. Any responsible American commander was bound to shrink from the idea of losing so many men for territory which would have to be relinquished and which, unlike the Rhine/Ruhr, had no strategic value. Thus, at the end of March, on his own initiative Eisenhower notified Stalin that he anticipated meeting Soviet forces roughly along the lines established at Yalta. Over British protests, the Joint Chiefs backed him up.

There would be no race to Berlin. Instead, part of the Allied force drove southward toward what the Nazis were calling the National Redoubt, the supposed site of their last stand. Although it did not exist, this does not invalidate the decision to stop short of Germany's capital. The Americans were wrong about the National Redoubt. They may have been wrong, though this is doubtful, considering the Soviet experience, in believing that Berlin would be tough to conquer. They were right in not wanting to spend lives to take territory they could not keep. Anyway, beating out the Soviets would have been virtually impossible, since they were closer to Berlin than the U.S. Army and in much greater strength.[22] Eisenhower took the safest course, which here was also the best.

The war ended abruptly. Ninth Army reached the Elbe on April 11, after traveling 226 miles in 19 days. On the sixteenth, Soviet forces attacked Berlin. Two days later, enemy resistance in the Ruhr ended, the Allies taking 317,000 prisoners. While Montgomery moved sedately across northern Germany, more Americans reached the Elbe, and Patton drove into Czechoslovakia. The German retreat quickly became a rout, Ridgway's XVIII Airborne Corps alone capturing 360,000 enemy soldiers. Hitler committed suicide in his Berlin bunker, after giving orders, not obeyed, to destroy all of Germany's remaining physical assets. On May 7 Admiral Karl Doenitz, who had taken command of the Third Reich, surrendered it to Eisenhower at 2:41 A.M. in Reims, France. Since D-Day, Bradley wrote, "586,628 American soldiers had fallen—135,576 to rise no more. The grim figures haunted me. I could hear the cries of the wounded, smell the stench of death. I could not sleep: I closed my eyes and thanked God for victory."[23]

The war in Italy came to an end at almost the same moment. After taking Rome, the Allies had crept forward until halted by the Gothic Line, which ran diagonally across Italy just above Florence. There Kesselring made his last stand, pinning the Allies down for yet another winter. In April 1945, Allied troops broke through and, while another line of defense had been constructed above Venice, the escaping

Germans couldn't reach it. Their flight across the Po Valley was broken up by partisan uprisings, downed bridges, and wide-ranging fighter–bombers. Allied units raced ahead, getting to the Venetian Line beforehand and sealing off the Alpine passes. Mussolini, who had been rescued by German commandos in 1943 and made head of an Italian puppet state, was captured by partisans and shot, along with his mistress, on April 28, 1945. At noon on May 2, the day after Hitler killed himself, the last German forces surrendered—having fought on doggedly long after doing so served any rational purpose.

Victory came too late for most victims of the Holocaust but otherwise just in time, for German scientists were far ahead of the Allies in weapons development. In the V-1 flying bomb, Germany had the first cruise missile, and in the V-2 a surface-to-surface missile with a range of 200 miles. Before the Peenemunde research site closed down, German scientists were testing elements of what would have been the world's first true ICBM and were planning a sub-launched V-2. They also had the first operational guided surface-to-air missile, the C-2, that was effectively used against Allied bombers in the last days of the war. Another group, these working for the Henschel firm, had nearly completed the radio-guided Hs-117 Butterfly air-to-air missile. Henschel was developing precision missiles, what would later be called a "smart" bomb, and an aerial-guided torpedo. The Wehrmacht actually fielded the Red Ridinghood wire-guided antitank missile.

In addition to the Messerschmitt 262 jet fighter, which Nazi Germany deployed in its last months and against which the Allies had no practical defense, Heinkel built its own jet and Messerschmitt a rocket-powered interceptor, the 163 Komet. The Horton firm had a jet-powered "flying wing" prototype and Junkers the prototype of a six-engine, sweptwing jet bomber.[25] German U-boat models continued to improve as well. At the end, Doenitz sent to sea the first true submarine, a vessel that could cruise underwater for extended periods without having to surface or employ a Dutch breathing mast, the Schnorchel, with which late-model U-boats were equipped. If the war had lasted another year, as might easily have happened, these weapons would have been produced in quantity, with deadly consequences.

The Anglo–American effort has justly been acclaimed as the most successful war coalition in history. But for it to work as it did, compromises were made that exacted a heavy price. The British fought hard in Normandy, making Cobra possible. However, by the time of the breakout, Montgomery's 21st Army Group was too weak for the grandiose single thrust strategy he ceaselessly advocated. Yet, not only Montgomery but the British nation insisted on a level of American support that drained Third Army of vital supplies and stopped Patton at the moment when German disorganization was greatest and victory within his grasp. It would not come until the following spring, and then only because Bradley, discreetly supported by Eisenhower, seized the initiative from Montgomery and turned a secondary offensive into the main event.

British reluctance to face facts was understandable, if shortsighted. America's failure to provide men and supplies in the quantity needed was inexcusable. Harmful to Army operations all the way through and placing too great a strain on American combat soldiers, it also prolonged the war. Many died who would have lived if Britain had given the U.S. armies free rein, or, on the other hand, if the U.S. had been strong enough to disregard British interference. Too much was sacrificed for warm relations with the British and easier conditions in the States. Good politics, as so often before, resulted in bad strategy. But at least, and at last, the war in Europe was over.

18

The War Winds Down
at Home

The shortage of men and supplies in Europe was partly a function of decisions made earlier, partly a result of production cutbacks and slackening zeal. It was a central irony of the American war that, just as the butcher's bill abroad became greatest, everything at home conspired to reduce the voluntary sacrifices and restraints that, in the absence of full mobilization, were so important to the war effort. This resulted not so much from individual loss of commitment as from policies decided on in Washington.

1944 began misleadingly with Roosevelt giving what biographer Burns calls "the most radical speech of his life." In it he called for five tough war measures, including a national service act. He also proposed an economic bill of rights which in the postwar would entitle every American to "a useful and remunerative job," adequate food, clothing, recreation, a decent home, medical care, and education. "Dr. New Deal," replaced at an FDR press conference two years earlier by "Dr. Win-the-War," seemed to have made a comeback.

It was all an illusion. The economic bill of rights was buried in that graveyard to which the reactionary Seventy-eighth Congress consigned everything smacking of social reform. National service, though long overdue, suffered a similar fate. Technically Democratic but dominated by Republicans and Southern conservatives, this

Congress was even less willing to inconvenience civilians than the
Seventy-seventh had been. *Life*, which had supported the Republican
candidates who were holding back the war effort, now agreed with
columnist Walter Winchell that Congress might as well be called "The
House of Reprehensibles."[1]

Many people followed the Congress' example by spending more and
more money on luxuries and recreation. After the racing season began
in December 1943, South Florida boomed. In 1942, most of Miami's
big hotels had been taken over by the Army. Later, when "the Army
turned two-thirds of them back to civilian trade it was as though
someone had called off the war."[2] While the hotels were jammed with
tourists displaying their wealth, local defense plants were shorthanded
because workers could not afford to live in Miami. For the same
reason, wives who had followed their soldier husbands to Florida were
being forced out of the state. Perhaps, *Life* speculated, the "coming
leap into the blood bath" when the Allies invaded France would get
people to thinking harder about the war and its purposes.[3] In fact, it
did not.

Because of the looming military manpower crisis President
Roosevelt ordered Selective Service to review all cases of
occupational deferment. To see how that worked, *Life* visited Draft
Board No. 49 in Detroit, which was responsible for 12,500
registrants aged 18 to 65, of whom 2,350 were already in uniform.
The three members of No. 49 devoted about 20 hours a week to
their unpaid duties, which included a weekly meeting on Tuesday
night to discuss the problems of individual "clients." On this
particular Tuesday, 21 clients met with the Board. One, who would
turn 38 in six months, a freight forwarder for the Ford Motor
Company, was building a house for his wife, baby, father, and invalid
mother. It would be livable in two months, and he wished to be
deferred until then. A barber, aged 36, with a wife and two children,
asked for advice rather than making an appeal. A single lawyer, aged
32, who had been deferred to care for his paralyzed mother,
reported that she had died and he was ready to be put in 1-A, which
would assure his prompt induction. The board gave the freight
forwarder another deferment, held the barber's case over for two
weeks, and reclassified the lawyer 1-A.

Although this meeting showed why Selective Service was widely
regarded as fair, none of these cases justified deferment by the
standards of other fighting nations. The United States had failed to
address the question of what was really essential in wartime and

therefore still had plenty of mink farmers, bartenders, pet veterinarians, florists, and other unessential workers at a time when it was still short of manpower. Efficiency aside, the lack of national service meant that civilians were not carrying their share of the burden. Roosevelt should have asked for national service two years before, when people were more highly motivated, the delay having proven fatal.

In addition to rejecting national service in 1944, and just about everything else Roosevelt asked for, Congress overrode FDR's veto of a tax measure, the first important revenue bill in history to become law over White House opposition. Senators rejected an important proposal, the Murray–Kilgore Bill, that would have strengthened unemployment insurance coverage for war workers during reconversion and extended federal responsibility for unemployment. This line was far from unpopular. In August 1943, and again in April 1945, Gallup asked whether people wanted reforms made after the war, or should the country resume business as usual. Both times a majority said that they wanted no changes, though between the polls support for reform grew from 32 to 39 percent. The New Deal was safe, as time would make clear, its basic policies having become part of the national consensus. But the American people remained conservative at heart, despite depression and war, though less conservative than Congress as the next election would show.

By 1944 everyone smelled victory and saw no need to keep their noses to the grindstone, especially since war production was being cut back. Once government began reducing defense orders, no appeal for voluntary sacrifice could be expected to have any effect. Good harvests reduced the incentive to maintain Victory Gardens. The wheat yield in 1944 would be the largest in history, the corn crop second only to the record harvest of 1942. People responded accordingly. Whereas in 1943 some 21 million families had planted gardens, in 1945 only 17 million would do so. With plenty of money and no durable goods or new housing to buy, consumption of whatever remained was bound to increase. Hence the paradox that, as the war entered its bloodiest phase, at home the good times were rolling.

That September, after the fighting in Normandy had produced enormous casualties, *Life* devoted its entire issue for the week of the twenty-fifth to the homefront, reporting that the dimout was over and the bright lights were back on Broadway. Seats at the hit musical "Oklahoma" were going for as much as $29 (the equivalent of perhaps $250 today), yet a million seats had already been sold. Consumer spending would reach $95 billion in 1944, about as much as the total national income had been in 1941. Business was brisk for sellers of liquor, jewelry, furs, and used furniture. When the soldiers came home they would be delighted to see that barebacked sundresses were all the rage. Beaches had been packed all summer. Yet armaments were pouring off the assembly lines, and the railroads had moved 106 percent as much freight in the first six months of the year as in all of 1939.

In October, with the election near at hand, domestic consumption was surging. Farmers had made $20 billion that year, compared to an average of $8 billion in the late 1930s. Workers would earn $44 billion, as against $13 billion in 1939. Department stores were packed with buyers of luxury goods, despite the shortage of salespeople, restaurants were mobbed, movie and stage theaters teemed, night clubs flourished. Hotels were booked solid for weeks in advance, even though the best rooms cost as much as $105 a day. New records were constantly being set for tickets sold to shows, trains, horse races. Even book purchases were up. All this was a function of national income having reached $150 billion while there was only $95 billion worth of goods and services available for purchase. Flush times were the inevitable result.

Under these circumstances it was hard to get interested in the Presidential election. Yet, there was one going on, and, as usual, lust for office moved opposition candidates to take off their gloves, even though there was little chance of defeating Roosevelt. Unlike in 1940, he made an early announcement of his intention to run, thus sapping the GOP nomination of its worth. Thomas E. Dewey, formerly a mob-busting district attorney and now Governor of New York, accepted it anyway. As Dewey represented Eastern internationalist Republicans, the ticket was balanced by nominating as his running mate the isolationist Governor of Ohio, John Bricker, a darling of the paleolithic right. To Isaiah Berlin's by now expert eye, the GOP platform was a collection of "ancient platitudes, the lowest common denominator of antiNew-Dealism."[4] Berlin understood that political platforms didn't mean much, still, he found it depressing that Republicans believed they could win with such a dreary wish list. However, he soon decided that they didn't expect to win at all and thus lacked any incentive to come up with something fresh.

The Democratic convention proved exciting because, while the presidential nomination was set, the choice of a vice president was open. The incumbent, Henry A. Wallace of Iowa, was popular among liberal Democrats, but Southerners hated him, as did the big city bosses who still had great power. FDR was willing to dump Wallace if that seemed expedient, and, as he ignored his vice presidents anyway, didn't have a strong personal preference. The choice of party leaders was Harry S Truman of Missouri, an obscure U.S. Senator until 1941, when he became chairman of the Senate Special Committee to Investigate the National Defense Program.

Like so many other leaders of the period, Truman came from the small town, Midwestern heartland of America. Born and raised in Independence, Missouri and its environs, he was about as typically American as you could get. Yet, like Eisenhower, his plain vanilla exterior concealed a formidable personality. A poor speaker whose seat in the Senate was his reward for loyalty to a political boss, Truman had previously been best known for his immaculate grooming, "dapper" was the word always used, and self-effacing friendliness. These appearances were deceptive. While he had no education beyond high school, Truman was an inveterate reader of history, biography, and the classics, about which he knew more than most college graduates. A member of the Missouri National Guard, he had been elected captain of an artillery unit in World War I, leading it with distinction. The "boys" of Battery D, mostly Irish–Catholics from Kansas City, would be the core supporters of this rural Baptist when he entered politics, early evidence of his ability to rise above the prejudices of his youth.

Western Missouri was dominated by the T. J. Pendergast machine. Truman would not have had a political career if he failed to go along with it, yet he remained scrupulously honest. He served eight years as presiding judge of Jackson County, an administrative post similar to that of county executive elsewhere, which provided abundant opportunities for graft in the awarding of contracts for roads, bridges, and other public facilities. But when the 50-year-old Truman arrived in Washington in 1935, he was literally broke. After renting a modest apartment for self, wife, and daughter, he had to take out a bank loan to pay for the furnishings.

Truman's failure to enrich himself struck many of his Pendergast colleagues as odd, but if not for his honesty he would never have become President. In 1939, "TJ" went to jail for tax evasion, and the organization collapsed. As no breath of scandal had ever touched Truman, he survived, winning reelection in 1940 on his own, with a little help from the machine's leftover parts. Moreover, though the race was tight and every vote mattered, Truman took a radical stand on race, telling white audiences "I believe in the brotherhood of man; not merely the brotherhood of white men, but the brotherhood of all men before the law. . . . "[5] Truman had bravery as well as character, and was more of a man to reckon with than most people thought when he arrived in Washington as the "Senator from Pendergast."

Popular in the Senate, Truman had been allowed to form his investigating committee out of courtesy more than anything else, few sharing his belief that corruption in defense spending could be dealt with by legislators. The skeptics were wrong. Truman's committee could not detect every scam, but it did a remarkably good and honest job of discovering waste, incompetence, and collusion. This was a direct result of Truman's tenacity, his meticulous nonpartisanship, and his experience in Missouri, which had taught him where to look for the dirt. Within a year his was the congressional committee that citizens respected most— or at all. Newspapers called him the "billion dollar watchdog," a considerable underestimation of what he would save the taxpayers.

Truman, unlike Wallace, was everything party leaders wanted. Well known and admired, he was acceptable to labor and Northern liberals because of his pro–New Deal voting record, and to Southerners because he was, or appeared to be, one of them. Few if any seem to have asked if he was qualified to run the nation, yet in selecting Truman the delegates were also naming the next President. All knew the likelihood of Roosevelt's dying in office was great. All ignored this for the sake of a balanced ticket. It was ever thus, but not since 1864 had the decision been so important.

No thanks to the political process, Truman would prove to be a better than average President. Though historians do not rank him as highly as Roosevelt, whose craftiness and foresight Truman could not match, he was a much nicer man. Those who worked for Truman loved him for his considerate, decisive, straightforward nature. In 1948 George Marshall, by then his Secretary of State, summed Truman up as well as anyone ever has. At the President's birthday party he rose unexpectedly and, his eyes on Truman, said:

> The full stature of this man will only be proven by history, but I want to say here and now that there has never been a decision made under this man's administration, affecting policies beyond our shores, that has not been in the best interest of this country. It is not the courage of these decisions that will live, but the integrity of the man.[6]

Marshall was right.

Given his failing health, it must be asked if FDR was wrong to run again. As the war progressed he gave fewer and fewer press conferences, only 55 in 1944, his last full year in office. They became shorter also, not only to protect military secrets but on account of his diminishing powers.[7] Because of who he was and what he had done for them, and also for patriotic reasons, journalists, far from making an issue of his weakening grasp, did not publicize it. In addition, FDR had a way of bouncing back. Everyone who knew him was struck by the restorative effects of vacations and trips at sea. He summoned up reserves of strength even during his last campaign, when his vital systems were collapsing.

One historian sums up Roosevelt's condition in 1944 with these words. "He experienced intermittent bouts of forgetfulness because of an insufficient blood supply to the brain (the medical phrase is secondary metabolic encephalopathy) caused by a combination of high blood pressure, congestive heart failure, anemia, and congestion in his lungs."[8] Between April and September 1944 his blood pressure was so high as to constitute a medical emergency. Yet his memory lapses, though they become more frequent, were short-lived; there is no evidence that his mental capacity was otherwise impaired, and his enfeebled condition did not keep the President from hitting the campaign trail hard to ensure his reelection.

Roosevelt used one of the first important pollsters, Hadley Cantril, and tailored his campaign according to Cantril's findings. Thus, in the fall, when polls showed that voters had doubts about his health, Roosevelt spoke outdoors in Ebbetts Field, home of the Brooklyn Dodgers, then rode for four hours through pouring rain in an open car, after which he gave a major address to the Foreign Policy Association. He exhibited stamina several more times before the election, defusing charges about his ill health although they were actually true. This was merely deceptive, whereas the reports issued by his personal physician, Vice Admiral Ross T. McIntire, were blatantly false.[9]

Yet, it seems fair to say that if Roosevelt's methods were not entirely pure, his motives for wanting a fourth term were honest. By this time the President had enjoyed all the power and glory that a human being could covet. What remained was to finish the job. Since Germany and Japan were losing the war, it no longer vitally interested him. The great unfinished task was to secure the peace, which he hoped to do by cementing the Grand Alliance of Great Britain, the Soviet Union, and the United States. No other politician, he rightly believed, knew as much about this as he. No one had the experience and skill needed to deal with Churchill and Stalin. Like most great men, Roosevelt considered himself to be indispensable, and in truth, even as his powers declined, he was still better qualified to steer the ship of state through troubled waters than any other American. As long as his lion's heart still beat, the people were right to back him.

The campaign plodded slowly along until Roosevelt's brilliant speech to the Teamsters on September 23, indicting the GOP for telling lies about his pet dog Fala, a speech Berlin described as "a return to the best and most ruthless of his old fighting days."[10] Even *Life*, which supported Dewey, said that Roosevelt had "never been better."[11] This attack stung Dewey, and from then on he and Bricker passed up no chances to throw mud. Roosevelt was said to be a left winger and Truman a Ku Klux Klansman. The CIO's Political Action Committee, which vigorously supported Roosevelt, was labeled a Communist front. According to Bricker, New Dealers had gotten the country into war as a cure for unemployment. Slander did the Republicans no good, however—the President kept on rolling. He climaxed the campaign in Boston by ridiculing Dewey's desperate tactics, quoting from different speeches made on the same day in which Dewey had accused the President of allowing Communists to seize power and also of planning to make himself king. To Berlin it was the "most infectious and sparkling performance of the entire campaign," marked by "flights of virtuosity reminiscent of his greatest days."[12]

Newspapers anticipated an extremely close election, but Harry Hopkins' estimate that FDR would take 30 states proved to be most accurate. Among the pollsters, Gallup had the best forecast, predicting that FDR would get 51.5 percent of the civilian vote (service personnel could not be polled), only .8 percent below the actual figure. Roosevelt led Dewey by 3.6 million ballots and carried 36 states with a total of 432 electoral votes to Dewey's 99. It was his narrowest margin of victory, though a clear one all the same, and carried over into the House of Representatives, where the Democrats returned to power. Many notorious isolationists—Representative Hamilton Fish of New York, Senator Champ Clark of Missouri—went down to defeat at last, easing the path of American entry into the United Nations Organization. Perhaps if the Republicans had come up with a more inspiring candidate, that might have made a difference. However, as Berlin remarked, to Roosevelt's Gladstone there was no Disraeli.

The Battle of the Bulge came as a shock to Americans who were under the impression that Germany had been all but defeated. It provoked a burst of austerity requests and measures and was one reason why, in his January State of the Union message, President Roosevelt asked again for national service, now labeled a "work or fight" bill, and for legislation to utilize the 4 million men rejected by the draft as physically unfit (known as 4-Fs) often for health problems that were no barrier to full-time employment. He also proposed a budget for fiscal 1946 that entailed only small reductions in defense spending.

To put people in the right frame of mind, James Byrnes closed the race tracks, ended the reconversion of war plants to consumer goods production, and placed a midnight curfew on bars and night spots. Supposedly this was to conserve fuel and essential services, but everyone knew the primary purpose was motivational, and it didn't work. Those most affected by the curfew were servicemen on leave, and night shift workers. As Geoffrey Perrett puts it, "Union officials protested. Servicemen protested. Most of the country, in fact, protested, except for its liberal intellectuals who were always eager to make the war on Fascism ascetic if possible."[13] The curfew was so unpopular that it could not be enforced. Late night speakeasies reappeared. Drinking and sex took place outdoors. After three months officials opened the tracks and lifted the curfew.

Though the Pacific War was approaching its climax, the production effort had begun to wind down. Demobilized servicemen were coming home in growing numbers. Halting reconversion deprived people of jobs without adding to the war effort. Moralizers blamed people for being self-indulgent, yet the polls did not support their claim. A Gallup poll released almost nine months before FDR got around to proposing something like it showed that 78 percent of respondents favored drafting 4-Fs into war plants. After the Battle of the Bulge, 56 percent favored a general labor draft, only 36 percent of those questioned objecting. People knew they had it easy. In February 1945 Gallup released a poll in which only 36 percent answered yes to the question "Have you had to make any real sacrifice for the war?" The most common reason for an affirmative answer was having a loved one in the armed forces, not any material deprivation.

There was always more support for a greater war effort than Congress would authorize. You could hardly blame people for letting their Victory Gardens go to seed after years of bumper crops, or for buying whatever they could with the surplus income Congress would not tax, or for holding nonessential jobs in the absence of a labor draft. These were policy issues, not questions of conscience. Moreover, it became public knowledge at the end of February 1945 that the War

Department planned to release between 200,000 and 250,000 servicemen a month after V-E Day, which would end the civilian labor shortage.[14] No wonder appeals for austerity fell upon deaf ears.

Good weather had arrived in Warm Springs, Georgia, on April 12, 1945, and President Roosevelt was planning to attend a late afternoon barbecue at his favorite picnic spot. While friends were preparing it, Roosevelt was in the Little White House with two female cousins, Elizabeth Shoumatoff, who was painting his portrait, and his former mistress, Lucy Mercer Rutherford. Though he had promised Eleanor not to see Lucy again after breaking off the affair, they had begun meeting on the sly after Lucy became a widow in 1941—a conspiracy that was made possible by the support of various relatives, including the President's daughter, Anna Roosevelt Boettiger, who was currently living in the White House.

The President had been sinking fast and at Warm Springs was attended by a young naval heart specialist. Roosevelt took little interest in his health, submitting to various tests but asking no questions about his condition and making few changes in his way of life beyond going on a diet—which gave him the gaunt look we see in his last pictures. While Madame Shoumatoff painted FDR was signing documents, and at 1:00 P.M. announced that he would be through in 15 minutes. The time was almost up when he rubbed the back of his neck and said quietly "I have a terrific headache." They were his last words, the President slumping unconscious in his chair, felled by a massive stroke. He was pronounced dead by his cardiologist at 3:55 P.M.

The nation was shocked. FDR had been President of the United States for 13 years. Young Americans had known no other President. Even many adults had trouble remembering that he had not always been their leader. He had steered America through the Great Depression, the most severe domestic crisis of this century, and then through almost all of its greatest war. The public was sharply divided over his merits. To New Dealers and working people, Roosevelt was the savior of democracy, if not an angel of mercy. Conservatives hated him as a would-be dictator and semisocialist who was bent on making everyone a slave of the welfare state. To isolationists, Roosevelt was a warmonger, while all-outers regarded him as dangerously slow and too satisfied with half measures.

All criticisms of Roosevelt are valid, more or less, reflections of his eclecticism and taste for the expedient. He made mistakes as a result of vanity, overconfidence, laziness, and other unattractive traits. He never took a highway if a back road would do. Yet, whatever his methods, on the big things he was usually right, or, as with de Gaulle, eventually able to see reason. He picked able men to run the war. He maintained close relations with Britain and, to the degree possible, Russia. When he failed, as in China, it was usually because to the problem there was no solution. No other American politician of his time could have done as well. One has only to think of the alternatives—Willkie, Dewey, Taft, Vandenberg, Wallace, Garner, Truman—to appreciate the distance between Roosevelt and the leading contenders. In an age of giants he was the only American on a level with Churchill and Stalin. Harry Truman was a decent man who would do his best, but, with Soviet–American relations coming to a head, Roosevelt was irreplaceable. With his passing went whatever slight chance there was of avoiding the Cold War.

Though it had never supported him, *Life*'s editorial response to Roosevelt's death was apt. It noted that people kept saying they felt as if they had lost a father.

> It was a confession of loving dependence. Even those who opposed Roosevelt, even some who hated him shared the abrupt sense of dizziness, as though a whole wall of the nation had been blown away. At the moment of his death he was the most important man in the world. He was the one American who knew, or seemed to know, where the world was going. The plans were all in his head. Whether one liked this or that policy or not, one knew that he would do what he would do. It was easier to let him worry for the whole country.[15]

This characterization of Roosevelt as America's godfather, true, so far as it went, was not the whole truth. Roosevelt's most lasting memorial was American democracy itself, which, for all his paternalism, he left stronger than he found it.

That FDR would be democracy's foremost champion was already apparent at the end of his first term. Arthur M. Schlesinger, Jr., in his superb appreciation of Roosevelt, says this:

> When Roosevelt was re-elected in 1936, the French Chamber of Deputies passed, without dissent, a resolution of congratulations. "Henceforth democracy has its chief!" said *Paris-Soir*. After his brilliant triumph President Roosevelt has become the statesman on whom every hope is to be pinned if the great liberal and democratic civilization of the west is one day threatened, either by Bolshevism or autocracy.
>
> When he accepted renomination at Franklin Field on June 27, 1936, he seemed also to accept a larger challenge. There were, he said, people

in other lands who had once fought for freedom, but now appeared too weary to carry on the fight, who had "sold their heritage of freedom for the illusion of a living."

"I believe in my heart," Roosevelt said, "that only our success can stir their ancient hope. They begin to know that here in America we are waging a great and successful war. It is not alone a war against want and destitution and economic demoralization. It is more than that: it is a war for the survival of democracy. We are fighting to save a great and precious form of government for ourselves and for the world.

"I accept the commission you have tendered me. I join with you. I am enlisted for the duration of the war."[16]

It was a war that, at the time of his death, Roosevelt knew he had won.

19

The Destruction of Japan

The end of the Pacific War is chiefly remembered for the atomic bomb, which continues to inspire guilt. Popular at first, the decision to employ atomic weapons is now often seen as heartless and unworthy of a democratic nation. Though this critique speaks well for the American conscience, it is taken out of context, since the use of the Bomb cannot be understood except in terms of what preceded and followed it.

As in Europe, the longer the Pacific War lasted the more costly in lives it became. The early battles in Luzon, New Guinea, and Guadalcanal, furious though they were, because they involved relatively small groups of men did not produce heavy losses. As the noose tightened around Japan, however, each victory became more expensive. Even as the war effort at home slackened, Pacific operations became larger and correspondingly more bloody. Despite its hopeless position Japan showed no signs of giving up, raising the prospect of far more hideous casualties in the immediate future. Poorly conducted campaigns, on Iwo Jima and especially Okinawa, lifted these fears to their highest level and guaranteed that the Bomb would be dropped.

Iwo, a small volcanic island, only 4.5 miles by 2.5 miles, was a thorn in the AAF's side, as it lay between B-29 bases in the Marianas and their targets in Japan. Japanese fighters based on Iwo obliged the

The Pacific Campaign: The Advances Across the Pacific, June 1944–July 1945

CHINA

JAPAN

Formosa

Okinawa | 1 April '45

19 Feb '45

PACIFIC OCEAN

Marshall Islands

15 June
Saipan
Guam | 24 July
21 July

☫ Truk

23 Sep
Ulithi

16 Oct

Caroline Islands

Philippine Islands

Ngulu
Palau Islands

17/20 Oct
Leyte

15 Oct
30 July

2 July
Biak
Noemfoor

9 Jan '45
Mindoro

15 Sep
Morotai

Sansapor

Rabaul ✸

NORTH-EAST
NEW GUINEA

Solomon Islands

PAPUA

NETHERLANDS
NEW GUINEA

CORAL SEA

FRENCH INDOCHINA

Saigon

1 May '45

BORNEO

1 July '45

DUTCH EAST INDIES

AUSTRALIA

SIAM
Rangoon

Nov - May '45
BURMA

2 May '45

Various landings in
Central & Southern
Philippines
Feb to July 1945

10 June '45

Singapore

Batavia

INDIAN OCEAN

0   Miles   800

Superfortresses to fly around it, consuming additional fuel at the expense of bombload. Iwo's radar picked them up even so, warning the home islands. In American hands, Iwo would instead provide fighter escorts for the B-29s, and emergency landing strips, which was why the Joint Chiefs authorized its seizure. As it turned out, Iwo was one of the best defended Japanese positions that American troops would ever be called upon to storm. When the Marines came ashore on February 19, 1945, Iwo Jima became a slaughterhouse.

Although by this time American mastery of the art of amphibious warfare was complete, the assault force was poorly supported. Carriers and battleships provided only four days of bombardment, instead of the 10 that Marine planners had requested. This was a serious lapse because, while nothing could reach the enemy's deep bunkers, artillery emplacements near the surface were vulnerable to naval gunfire. All the same, after four days Spruance took off on a big carrier raid into Japanese home waters. Thus, when the Marines hit the beach, many known gun positions remained intact—more so than on any other Pacific island. The casualties would reflect this.

Iwo Jima is best known for the photograph, taken by the Associated Press's Joe Rosenthal, of an American flag whose staff was being forced into the ground by a group of Marines atop Mount Suribachi.[1] That took place early in the battle, which raged on until the end of March and was characterized by savage infantry actions in places like the "Meat Grinder" and "Bloody Gorge." Twenty-seven Marines and naval corpsmen (medics) won the Medal of Honor on Iwo, a measure not only of American gallantry but the savageness of the fighting. When it was over, 6,821 Americans had been killed and almost 20,000 wounded. Most of the enemy were killed, too, in excess of 20,000 men, but for the only time in the Pacific War total Japanese casualties were fewer than those sustained by Americans. Three Marine divisions were used up in this blood bath, half the Corps' total strength. One-third of all Marines killed in the Pacific died on Iwo Jima.

In his riveting account of the battle Bill Ross, an ex-Marine who fought on Iwo, is extremely hostile toward conservative newspapers, what he calls "the Hearst–McCormick–Patterson press." Because the Navy was now giving reporters a much freer hand than earlier, America learned of its casualties before the fighting was over. This prompted certain publishers, notably William Randolph Hearst, to question the wisdom of assaulting such a fortress. Worse still, from the Marine point of view, he exploited the death toll to boost MacArthur. "Why do we not use him more," Hearst asked, "and, indeed, why do

CHINA

RUSSIA

SEA
OF
JAPAN

KOREA

YELLOW
SEA

JAPAN

EAST
CHINA
SEA

PACIFIC
OCEAN

Okinawa

Formosa

Yomitan
Airfield

Kadena
Airfield

SHURI

NAHA
Yonabaru

Mabuni

OKINAWA

• Shimura's position
(bypassed)

Wana Draw

Kochi •   ⌇ *Kunishi Ridge*

*Sugar
Loaf*   *Asa Kawa*

SHURI

NAHA   Castle •

Yonabaru

**OROKU
PENINSULA**

•Haebaru
Hospital

Site of 22nd Regiment tunnel
and Naval Base Force tunnel

SOUTHERN OKINAWA   **CHINEN
PENINSULA**

• Kochinda

Kochi Ridge

*Yoza
Dake*

• Maesato

• Site where Kojo disbanded
the last of his battalion

Macabe•

*Cave of
the Virgins*   Hill 89 ✷

Minatogawa

Mabuni

N

0 1000 2000 3000 4000 5000

Meters

G.W.Ward

we not give him supreme command in the Pacific war, and utilize to the utmost his rare military genius of winning important battles without excessive loss of precious American lives?"[2] Ross thinks this was contemptible of Hearst. So did some 100 Marines who invaded the offices of Hearst's flagship, *The San Francisco Examiner*, demanding a retraction. One need not admire the gutter press, or lack respect for the Corps, to feel that Hearst's question deserved a better answer.

The painful truth is that Iwo Jima should have been bypassed, the failure to do so being rationalized afterward by citing the 2,400 Army bombers that made landings on the island. Since each B-29 carried a crew of 11, it would be argued that taking Iwo saved over 25,000 lives. This is a feeble defense. Many of the landings were nothing more than scheduled refueling stops. Of the crews that were actually in trouble, some would have made it home. Others that went down in the sea would have been picked up by submarines assigned to that duty or by specialized air–sea rescue units. There is no way of proving that the lives lost on Iwo were offset by the number of B-29 crewmen who were saved by landing on it. Even if there was some small net profit in the exchange, B-29s played a smaller role in defeating Japan than did the Marines. Had Japan been invaded on schedule, as Ronald Spector points out, "The wholesale sacrifice of three well-trained and expert assault divisions simply to secure emergency landing fields might have loomed as a gross strategic error."[3] Iwo was a costly blunder at the least, a waste of precious riflemen.

Instead of being regarded as a monument to official bungling, Iwo came to symbolize heroism and devotion to duty. Ironically, it was not the actual valor of Marines that accomplished this so much as Rosenthal's dramatic photograph of the flag raising. Moreover, what he photographed was not the raising that signaled Mount Suribachi had fallen, which occurred earlier and was performed by the men who secured its summit, but a second ceremony laid on because the first flag was too small and shabby. Rosenthal's picture appeared in every newspaper, and made the three surviving flag raisers, the others having died in battle, nationally famous.

The flag photograph provided the logo for America's Seventh Bond Drive ("The Mighty Seventh"), then underway in the States. This was but the first of many uses to which the picture was put. The most powerful representation of the American war effort, it is also the most ironic—not just because the real event took place before the flag was raised, or that Iwo became more famous for Rosenthal's photograph than for the battle itself, but because, after all that had been suffered to take it, the military valued Iwo so little. When Colonel Paul Tibbits flew the first atomic bombing mission, his orders in the event he had to abort were to land on Iwo, or, that failing, to ditch there. As the historians of its iconography rightly say, "Despite the terrible price paid for the island, Iwo Jima was, in the end, expendable."[4]

Two other phases of the Pacific War always figure in arguments over the use of atomic weapons: the undersea campaign and the firebomb raids. Both are cited as reasons why the Bomb need not have been dropped. But, though radically different in their results, neither could solve the problem.

While the fighting raged on various islands, much of Japan was being reduced to ashes and rubble by the AAF's mighty new aircraft, the Boeing B-29 Superfortress. As in Europe, though with even less excuse, the conventional bombing campaign there was both immoral and a military failure. Numerous histories have been written to deplore the atomic bomb, only a few have examined the conventional bombing attacks that killed many more Japanese civilians and accomplished nothing. Once again, brave crews and magnificent aircraft were put to uses unworthy of both them and the American people.

Rushed into production before testing was complete, a decision known as the "three-billion dollar gamble," the B-29 had many bugs, but came into service in four years rather than the usual five. The B-29 was a generation ahead of existing heavy bombers, having a pressurized cabin with remotely controlled power turrets, a service ceiling of 38,000 feet, and a speed of 361 miles an hour. With a 4-ton bombload, twice that of the Flying Fortress, it had a combat range of 3,500 miles. Despite its excellent qualities, however, the B-29's deployment in China was a failure. The bomber bases were hard to supply and too far from most targets in Japan for even this long-legged aircraft. The operations of XX Bomber Command in China were enormously difficult to mount, and impossible to justify, given the meager results. At the end of 1944 it was withdrawn to the Marianas.

Few senior officers outside the Air Force were enthusiastic about strategic bombing by this time, and there was constant pressure to use heavy bombers in direct support of troops. That was why General

Arnold had persuaded the Joint Chiefs of Staff to make B-29s independent of theater commanders in the Pacific. He would personally direct Twentieth Air Force, to which all Superfortresses were assigned, with operations to be run by the heads of its bomber commands. Given the vast resources that had been committed to the B-29, and considering the Navy's skepticism in particular, the AAF had much at stake in its bombardment of Japan. Yet, though the Marianas were far superior to China as a base of operations and Tokyo was only 1,200 miles from Saipan, XXI Bomber Command, the principal striking force, accomplished very little. The B-29 still suffered from technical difficulties, maintenance was poor to begin with, and the long flights to Japan consumed more fuel than expected, leaving little margin for error.

The AAF had not been prepared for the tremendous winds and heavy cloud cover found over Japan. Its very first attack, launched from the Marianas on November 24, 1944, was made by 111 aircraft. Of these, 17 aborted and returned to base, six could not bomb because of mechanical failures, and those that made it to Tokyo could not see the target because of undercast and were swept along by 120-knot winds that made even radar useless. A mere 48 bombs fell on the primary target. Though only one Superfortress was lost to enemy air defenses, 29 ran out of gas and had to ditch in the ocean. This fiasco was followed by others, the problem being that bad visibility and winds as high as 200 knots an hour made accuracy impossible.

Arnold answered the problem by sacking Major General H. S. "Possum" Hansell, the chief of XXI Bomber Command and a believer in precision bombing. His transgression seems to have been not launching firebomb raids against Japanese cities. Hansell failed to realize that the AAF was now committed to area bombing, its prewar theory of strategic bombardment having proved invalid. His replacement, Major General Curtis E. LeMay, formerly the tactical wizard of Eighth Air Force, understood that he was supposed to terrorize Japan.[5]

Once accuracy became unimportant, a battery of new methods could be used to burn out Japanese cities, which were especially vulnerable because of their flimsy construction. Area bombing could take place after dark, as Japan had few night fighters, and at low altitudes where the B-29 consumed less fuel and could carry heavier bombloads. The skies over Japan were more often clear at night, winds at low altitudes were not great, and loran sky waves (long-range radio signals) came in better, making for superior navigation, an important point, since at night, bombers could not fly in formation and it was every plane for itself.

The first firebomb raid took place on the night of March 9–10, 1945, when 334 Superfortresses carrying 6-ton bombloads attacked Tokyo. The resulting devastation consumed almost 16 square miles of the city and one-fourth of its buildings. One million people were made homeless and at least 100,000 killed. General Arnold could not have been more excited, wiring LeMay "Congratulations. This mission shows your crews have got the guts for anything."[6] It was the single most destructive air attack of the war—including the atomic bombings—and was followed by many others. When Japan surrendered, 40 percent of its 66 major cities had been destroyed, perhaps 400,000 people killed, some 9 million forced to move to the country, and 13 million rendered homeless. XXI Bomber Command had given terror bombing an entirely new dimension, far surpassing the RAF's attacks on German cities. Little effort was made to determine the usefulness of firebombing, the policy being simply to smash and burn until Japan gave up.

As with Germany, the bombardment of Japan was both morally wrong and a waste of American resources. It is true that legitimate targets were sometimes destroyed, but most were marginal. The official AAF history is candid about this, admitting it was instead the blockade that destroyed Japan's defense effort. By April 1945 the flow of oil into Japan had been cut off completely. It was only a matter of time, and not much time at that, before the wheels of Japanese industry would stop turning. On June 26 XXI Bomber Command launched an oil plan of its own, similar to that employed with such success against Germany. After the war it was found that Japanese refineries were operating at only 4 percent of capacity when the campaign against them started. Thus, though hugely destructive, firebombing contributed little to the defeat of Japan and of itself would never have produced a surrender.

Japan actually owed its desperate state in 1945 chiefly to American submariners. Few had expected such success, given the service's depressing record of failure in 1942, when the submarine force consisted mostly of small and obsolete boats, many with defective engines. Worse still, the Navy's Mark XIV torpedo had never been tested at sea, and turned out to be riddled with defects. Tactics were defective as well, the boats being assigned to patrol huge areas instead of the Luzon strait and other places where enemy shipping was concentrated. They hunted singly rather than in groups, despite the success Germany was enjoying with its wolf packs.

The USN acted as if U-boats did not exist, neglecting the rich store of knowledge about submarine tactics that had been acquired fighting them in the Atlantic. Further, American skippers were too old and cautious, having acquired command through seniority at a time when conserving torpedoes was an important leadership requirement. Finally, the submarine fleet was divided into three commands, two based in Australia and the largest in Pearl Harbor, an arrangement that encouraged them to compete with each other instead of cooperating.

It soon became clear that the Mark XIV was ineffective, but the Naval Bureau of Ordnance, known as the Gun Club, refused to admit error, insisting month after month that submarine skippers were responsible for the weapon's feeble performance. After many months of unsuccessful torpedo attacks, tests in the field proved conclusively that the Mark XIV was no good. Its magnetic detonator did not work, it ran too deep, and even when a torpedo made a perfect hit at a 90-degree angle, the firing pin crumpled instead of triggering the detonator. Machinists fabricated sturdier pins and at last, after 21 months of war, the submarine force had a reliable weapon. The Gun Club, an enemy second only to Japan, finally went down to defeat.

Together the three submarine commands mounted 520 war patrols in 1944 and sank 603 enemy vessels totaling 5.1 million tons. This was a level of damage that Japan could not hope to survive. In the previous year, Japan had imported 16.4 million tons of bulk commodities, but in 1944 that was reduced to 10 million. In a single year the Japanese merchant fleet, excluding tankers, was cut in half, bringing it down to 2 million tons. Tanker capacity remained constant at 860,000 tons only because Japan built 204 additional ships. Without them, tanker tonnage would have fallen by about two-thirds. Even so, at the end of the year, oil imports were down to 200,000 tons a month, from 700,000 in September. Soon there would be none at all.

The submarine war came to an end in December 1944, when Japanese merchantmen abandoned the open ocean. From then on they kept to the narrow waters of the Sea of Japan or the Yellow Sea, sailing close to shore and anchoring in harbors at night. While this protected Japanese ships against torpedo attacks, it also made them practically useless. During the Okinawa campaign not a single Japanese supply ship reached the island. After the war it was calculated that American submariners had destroyed 1,314 enemy vessels, including one battleship, eight carriers, and 11 cruisers. A force of 16,000 men accounted for 55 percent of all enemy ship losses, driving its merchant fleet from the high seas and putting Japanese industry out of business. In doing so, 3,500 U.S. submariners perished, the highest loss rate of any American combat arm and yet a very low figure compared with the number of Americans being killed on land. Despite almost two years of bungling, and the lack of a torpedo as good as the Japanese Long Lance, and even though American fleet subs were inferior not only to German U-boats but to the best Japanese types, the submarine was far and away America's most effective weapon.[7]

The blockade of Japan, though largely accomplished by submarines, was completed by the Army Air Force. There was considerable irony in this, for XXI Bomber Command's greatest success was forced upon it by the Navy. By 1945 most of Japan's convoy routes had been closed by the U.S. undersea and surface fleets. Much of what traffic remained went through Shimonoseki Strait, gateway to the Inland Sea. The Navy wanted it mined, and experience had shown that heavy bombers could do this best. The AAF agreed, mainly, it seems, because otherwise the Navy would have demanded B-29s to do the job itself. To avert that dreaded prospect, Arnold ordered a mine-laying campaign to begin on April 1, 1945. Mining the Tsushima and Shimonoseki Straits and the ports of Kobe and Osaka proved to be sensationally effective, the tonnage of shipping received in Kobe alone declining from 320,000 tons in March to 44,000 in July. Once LeMay realized this he stepped up the effort, overwhelming Japan's minesweeping force. By this time Japan had given up trying to import anything but foodstuffs, and was failing even at that.

In the last four and a half months of the war, mines accounted for half of all Japanese shipping losses. AAF mining operations played an important role in completing the blockade, a larger one than did the better known firebomb raids. They were also more humane. Only 16 aircraft were lost out of 1,528 sent out to plant mines. While it is not known how many Japanese seamen were killed the number had to be small, as mining was done in shallow waters close to land, giving crews a good chance of survival.

The last bloody scene in the Pacific War took place on Okinawa, a battle that contributed importantly to the decision to employ nuclear weapons. Unlike Iwo Jima, Okinawa, a 60 mile-long island in the Ryukyu chain, was worth having, at least in part. Located only about 350 miles southwest of the home island of Kyushu and 1,000 miles from Tokyo, Okinawa was within easy fighter–bomber range of many targets in Japan. To take it, Nimitz assembled yet another great armada: more than 180,000 troops and 1,200 vessels, including 40 carriers of all sizes and 18 battleships.

To defend the island Lieutenant General Tomohiko Ushijima had some 110,000 troops centered around the ancient castle town of Shuri in south-central Okinawa. In the surrounding mountains the Japanese had built a network of underground strongpoints, the Shuri Line, which bristled with guns and mortars. Ushijima did not intend to contest the landings, a tactic which experience had shown only led to an early defeat, but rather to hold the south end of the island with its airfields and harbor.

After uncontested landings on April 1, the fight for Okinawa turned into a battle of attrition. There were 10 mass kamikaze attacks against the fleet between April 6 and June 22. Hardest hit were the outlying radar picket destroyers, but the big ships took a pounding also. Here the British played an important role, for the only time in the Pacific. Although Royal Australian and Royal New Zealand Navy ships had fought side by side with the USN for years, Admiral King, a notorious Anglophobe, had not wanted Britain to interfere at all in his war and did everything to prevent it. King was forced by Roosevelt to accept the Royal Navy's contribution, which included not only fighting ships but a supply train that made them self-sufficient.

As it turned out Spruance had fewer fleet carriers than at the Battle of the Philippine Sea, so the Royal Navy's Task Force 57, comprising five fast carriers, two fast battleships, five cruisers, and 15 destroyers, proved invaluable. Best of all, the British carriers had strongly armored flight and hangar decks that could withstand kamikaze attacks much better than their thin-skinned American sisters. British armor was carried at a price, slowing the carriers and reducing the size of their air groups. But when a kamikaze struck an American flight deck it was back to Pearl for the carrier, whereas a British flattop would simply be dented.

While the Royal and U.S. Navies fought off kamikaze attacks, the soldiers and Marines ashore were engaged in violent combat. If Iwo Jima was the most pointless American campaign of the Pacific War, Okinawa may have been the worst managed—inexcusably so, given the accumulated power and expertise that was available by 1945. Tenth Army commander Lieutenant General Simon Bolivar Buckner presided over a series of grinding frontal attacks, resisting suggestions that he take advantage of his amphibious capability to land in the enemy's rear. Buckner ought to have been relieved. He was killed by the enemy instead, sharing the fate of the many victims of his incompetence.

Americans were now far and away the world leaders at all arms and interservice cooperation, capable of uniting land, sea, and air power into a smoothly running and irresistible force. The Marines had always been an elite. The regular Army divisions had greatly improved. In the Pacific, as in Europe, they were profiting from the high quality of replacements, many of them transfers from the AAF cadet corps and the Army training schools. According to Geoffrey Perret, "Eichelberger was astounded by the quality of troops who arrived in the Philippines during the campaign on Luzon."[8] On Okinawa, too, they would show their mettle.

Buckner took the marvelously flexible weapon put in his hands and used it as a blunt instrument. The battle did not end until June 21, by which time 7,000 Americans had been killed on land and 4,900 at sea, where 29 ships were put out of action, more than in any previous naval campaign. In addition, 32,000 men were wounded on land, and 4,800 sailors. Twenty percent of all casualties sustained by the U.S. Navy in World War II were taken in the waters off Okinawa. An operation that was supposed to last 45 days took closer to 80, despite the expenditure of 7.5 million howitzer rounds, 60,000 5- to 6-inch naval shells, 20,000 rockets, almost 400,000 grenades, and 30 million small-arms and automatic-weapon rounds.

The Japanese lost 1,465 kamikazes, 150,000 Okinawan civilians, about one-third of the total population, and most of the garrison of 11,000 Japanese soldiers were taken prisoner, by far the largest bag of the war.   General MacArthur severely criticized the land engagement, arguing that after northern Okinawa had been taken, American troops should have dug in and let the enemy come to them. The Navy would not have gotten its fleet anchorage any time soon, but there was plenty of room in the north for air bases. Of course MacArthur was offering a formula for Okinawa somewhat different from his own campaign on Luzon, where, instead of waiting for Yamashita to attack, Sixth Army chewed away at Japanese defenses. Still, though tactless and self-serving as usual, MacArthur was right. In his hands the battle for Okinawa would have been less bloody and more creative.

Instead, men were thrown against nearly impregnable Japanese defenses. It was the First World War all over again, heavy artillery barrages followed by head-on attacks, sometimes across open ground. The casualty rate, 35 percent of all troops involved, was a function of these abysmal tactics. Nonbattle casualties, mostly neuropsychiatric, were extremely high as well, amounting perhaps to 10 percent of all those who fought. At Sugar Loaf, linchpin of the Shuri Line, one-third of Marine casualties were NPs. Fourteen percent of all Marines killed in the war died on Okinawa. One percent of total American casualties in World War II were sustained taking an island of 875 square miles, about 0.6 percent of Japan's total area.[9] This appalling rate of loss would have far-reaching consequences.

The main problem facing American leaders when Roosevelt died in April was how to bring about a Japanese surrender. Although the blockade had sealed its fate, and firebombs were making Japanese cities all but uninhabitable, Japan's leaders still would not concede that further resistance was useless. This stubborn fact undercuts those critics who have argued that blockading and/or bombing Japan made nuclear strikes unnecessary. They rely heavily on the United States Strategic Bombing Survey's postwar *Summary Report*, which concluded that the blockade would have obliged Japan to surrender in 1945, probably before November 1. If the authors were right there had been no need for drastic action because starvation alone would have brought Japan to the peace table.

Certainly that is how Americans would have behaved, but as the Japanese did not think along American lines, the USSBS had no basis for such a judgment. Like American planners before the war, it mistakenly assumed that Japanese leaders would do the sensible thing. The truth in 1945 was that the Japanese military had no intention of giving up. They meant to fight to the last man, woman, and child in the event of an invasion. If the Americans did not come ashore, they were prepared to see everyone starve rather than surrender. The self-destructive course pursued by Japan for years offered little hope that Tokyo would give up within the foreseeable future.

On May 25, 1945 the order was issued to assault Kyushu, the southernmost home island of Japan, on or about November 1. Yet, though the Army and Navy were now fighting the same war, they still refused to name a supreme commander. Instead, a bizarre directive was issued making MacArthur responsible for the invasion of Kyushu "including, in case of exigencies . . . the actual amphibious assault through the appropriate naval commander," while Nimitz was assigned "responsibility for the conduct of naval and amphibious phases" subject to the aforementioned exigencies.[10] Fortunately for all concerned, this formula was never put to the test.

Historians who believe the Bomb should not have been dropped sometimes try to make invading Japan seem a better alternative by projecting improbably low casualty figures. But in the three months since Harry Truman became President the United States had sustained nearly half of all the casualties inflicted upon it by the Japanese in three years of fighting. Okinawa in particular cast a long shadow over the debates on how to bring Japan to its senses.[11]

In one meeting with the Joint Chiefs President Truman expressed his fervent hope that Kyushu would not be as bloody as Okinawa. Admiral Leahy offered no encouragement, saying that of the 767,000 men participating in Operation Olympic 268,000 men would probably be killed or wounded—more casualties than in the entire Pacific War to date. The Japanese thought so, too, for Kyushu was as mountainous as Okinawa and much more heavily defended. Fourteen divisions and five independent brigades were deployed in caves, bunkers, and blockhouses, whereas the Japanese 32nd Army on Okinawa had consisted of only two full divisions plus miscellaneous units. Thousands of kamikazes were being held in reserve. The entire adult civilian population was expected to defend the sacred soil of the motherland with hand-held explosives, wooden pikes, and fingernails if necessary. The casualties on both sides were certain to be appalling, and when the main island Honshu was attacked, worse would follow.

Critics of the atomic bomb never take into account the shock felt by leaders in the United States over the rapidly escalating casualty rates. Marshall, a humane man, had been so upset by the losses on Iwo Jima that he recommended using poison gas on Okinawa, even the thought of which had been taboo until then. American battle casualties on Okinawa amounted to about half those of Japan—not counting the U.S. Tenth Army's heavy nonbattle casualties. Since 2 million Japanese troops were dug in on the home islands MacArthur anticipated that 1 million Americans would be killed or seriously wounded.

In addition to continuing the blockade or invading Japan, a third alternative existed in 1945, negotiating a settlement. Some in Japan desired this, efforts having been made to employ the Soviet Union as a mediator. These overtures were ignored by Stalin, who did not want peace until Russia had entered the war and seized the territories promised to it at Yalta. Thanks to radio intercepts Washington was aware of Tokyo's peace feelers, which fact has led to much criticism of American leaders for not taking advantage of them to open talks with Japan. Washington declined to do so because the

Army still ran Japan and, as the intercepts made clear, it had lost all touch with reality. Despite their hopeless position, Japan's Army leaders continued to insist that there be no occupation of Japan and no change in its political system. Thus to Washington, there was nothing to talk about.

It is against this background that the decision to wage nuclear war on Japan must be seen. The United States had begun work on atomic fission out of fear that Germany was conducting similar research. Germany had the potential to do so, but decided in 1942, just when the Manhattan Project was getting underway, not to make a major investment in nuclear studies. Only America could afford to spend heavily on a weapon that might not work and probably would not be operational before the war was over. In any case, German science and technology were already at full capacity producing the numerous superweapons then under development.

When American scientists finally learned that there had never been an atomic arms race the information was academic, since J. Robert Oppenheimer's team had reached the brink of success. Laboratory tests had already determined that a certain type of atomic bomb, one which employed a gun mechanism to ignite uranium, would work. It remained to be seen if the more efficient plutonium bomb, which was to be set off by an implosion device, would function as theory dictated. On July 16, 1945, at the Alamogordo Air Base in New Mexico, it was tested, producing what one witness called a "foul and awesome display." Oppenheimer found the right words, a line from the Hindu *Bhagavad-Gita* in which Vishnu says "Now I am become Death, the destroyer of worlds."[12] This, the first atomic explosion, was codenamed Trinity—no blasphemy intended.

There had been considerable discussion at the Los Alamos labs about how to exploit the Bomb. Some felt it should not be used at all, since Germany was out of the picture. The fear of Hitler getting a nuclear weapon first had been a tremendous incentive for Manhattan Project scientists. Having the Bomb as a deterrent was one thing, dropping it another. It would have been surprising, even near the end of a long war, if qualms were not felt against using such a dazzling scientific feat to commit mass murder. Then too, anyone with the slightest degree of foresight had to worry about what unleashing this terrifying new weapon would mean in future. Even men as unimaginative as John McCloy and Henry Stimson were worried about the long-term effects. When Stimson briefed President Truman on the atomic bomb project, he argued that the weapon should not be used against Japan without thought being given to its effect upon postwar relationships.

Stimson was concerned about a future atomic arms race, as were many scientists also, Leo Szilard pursuing the question more intensely than anyone else. Szilard, a brilliant refugee scientist, had played a key role in launching the atomic bomb project, now he took the lead in attempting to prevent its use. Writing to James Byrnes, who was soon to become Secretary of State, Szilard argued that the atomic weapon would cancel out America's strongest military asset, its ability to produce more military hardware than any other nation. Once an atom bomb was tested and used, other countries would follow suit, making conventional weapons less important and reducing America's edge. Szilard was also troubled about international control and related issues that bothered Stimson and others as well.

Szilard got nowhere with Byrnes, who had been told by Major General Leslie R. Groves that Russia couldn't build an atomic bomb because it had no uranium. This was wrong, Szilard explained, because while the United States presently enjoyed a monopoly of high-grade ores, Russia had enough low-grade uranium to build all the fission bombs it wanted. Szilard also thought Byrnes was completely mistaken in supposing that the atomic bomb would be of any use in postwar dealings with the Soviets. "I shared Byrnes' concern about Russia's throwing around her weight in the postwar period, but I was completely flabbergasted by the assumption that rattling the bomb might make Russia more manageable," Szilard recalled later.[13] On the other hand, many besides Groves, including even Oppenheimer himself, a former Soviet sympathizer, held that dropping the Bomb on Japan would make Russia more compliant. Later events failed to bear this out. During the years when America monopolized it, Stalin conducted his foreign relations as if the atomic bomb did not exist.

Confusion abounded in the many related discussions at various levels that took place during 1945. Szilard's point about nuclear weapons reducing the value of America's conventional capability seems to have gotten lost. Leaders and experts disagreed on the extent to which having an atomic bomb would impress Russia. Szilard's hope that the atomic device could be kept secret was politically naive, as sooner or later Congress would demand an accounting, and even if it didn't, the project was too big to be hidden for long in an open society. Stimson hated killing civilians and had never faced up to the butchery done by aircraft in Germany. He was distressed by the firebomb raids then being made against Japan, which could not be represented as anything except terror attacks. He successfully insisted that the city of Kyoto, a center of Japanese religion and culture, not be bombed, but otherwise dithered on the issue of target selection.

President Truman was in Potsdam, Germany, attending the last summit conference of the war with his military advisors when Stimson brought him Groves' report on Trinity. Arnold had long argued that conventional air power would force Japan to surrender. Most of the largest cities had already been burned out by mid-July, and Japanese morale showed no sign of crumbling. General Marshall believed that just as air power had failed to defeat Germany, so also would it fail with Japan. After the bloody Okinawa campaign Marshall concluded that if the Bomb was not used, nothing short of invading it would force Japan to surrender. If the Okinawa ratio held, this would mean at least a quarter of a million American deaths. There was also a fear that even if Japan surrendered, its huge armies in Asia might fight on. The Bomb was useful, in this light, not just because it was so powerful but because its shock value offered the hope of making a fundamental change in Japanese thought. With great reluctance, therefore, Marshall concluded that the atomic weapon had to be used.

Not all agreed. When Dwight Eisenhower learned of the Bomb, he recommended against its employment, on the grounds that Japan was going to surrender anyway, and because he did not wish America to set off a nuclear arms race. Since its blockade of Japan was going so well, the Navy too was unenthusiastic. Admiral Leahy strongly opposed using the Bomb, not only for reasons of service loyalty but because it seemed to him immoral, falling into the same category as poison gas and bacteriological weapons. These reservations are evidence that even the national hatred of Japan had not blunted the moral sentiments that Americans were raised to value. But in war the moral choice is not always the right one. Truman and Marshall were decent men, too, but they could not justify sacrificing American lives when a way existed to save them.

On July 26 the Potsdam Declaration setting forth the conditions Japan must accept was issued. In it the United States, Great Britain, and China called upon Japan to surrender unconditionally or face "prompt and utter destruction." The terms of surrender included an end to Japanese militarism, the punishment of war criminals, an occupation of Japan, the evacuation of all territories except the home islands themselves, and complete disarmament. In return the Allies promised to establish a democratic political order, to allow the rebuilding of Japanese industry, and to end the military occupation when Japan acquired a "peacefully inclined and responsible government." On July 28 Japan rejected this offer.

Meanwhile, the 509th Composite Bomb Group under Colonel Paul Tibbets was making its final arrangements. On August 6, 1945 the Superfortress Enola Gay, Tibbets at the controls, rose from its runway on Tinian Island carrying "Little Boy," the first uranium bomb. At 8:16 A.M. (local time), Little Boy detonated at an altitude of 1,900 feet over the city of Hiroshima, turning it to ashes. A mushroom cloud boiled above scenes of horror that exceeded those produced by conventional firestorms. For one thing, the blast effect was immensely greater. For another, radiation would kill many who survived burns, concussion, and the firestorm's deadly gases. It would go on killing survivors for years to come, an especially frightening feature of this terrible new weapon. That fact would come as a surprise to American scientists, who had greatly underestimated the radiation effects. The casualty figures for Hiroshima vary from account to account. Richard Rhodes offers the highest estimate, maintaining that 140,000 people were dead as a result of the nuclear explosion by the end of 1945, with a total of 200,000 deaths having been reached five years later. Most experts cut this estimate in half, which is still an appalling figure.

On August 9, Japan having failed to surrender, "Fat Man," the first plutonium bomb, was dropped on Nagasaki. Some 70,000 more Japanese died as a result of it by the end of the first year, the ultimate death toll for both attacks usually being estimated at around 200,000. On August 10 word was received in Washington that Japan would surrender if the Potsdam Declaration "does not comprise any demand which prejudices the prerogatives of His Majesty as a Sovereign Ruler."[14] Though this offer involved a condition, there seemed no reason to quibble, and just after midnight on August 12, Tokyo learned that its proposal had been accepted, in the nick of time, for Groves was shipping another Fat Man to Tinian on that day or the next. Japan surrendered officially on August 15.

The Bomb was met with wonder and jubilation at first, the soldiers and sailors who were expecting to assault Japan overflowing with emotion. Paul Fussell, later a distinguished literary scholar and essayist, but at the time an infantry platoon leader who had barely survived the war in Europe, has never doubted the wisdom of using nuclear weapons. When he and his fellow GIs who were scheduled to invade Japan learned of the Bomb, "For all the fake manliness of our façades, we cried with relief and joy. We were going to live. We were going to grow up to adulthood after all."[15] The nation as a whole greeted V-J Day ecstatically as the culmination of all its hopes and dreams since the attack upon Pearl Harbor.

It was only later that doubts arose. The first dim note was sounded by John Hersey, then a noted war correspondent, who described the fate of six survivors in *The New Yorker*. Republished as *Hiroshima* (1946), his account made human beings out of the previously hated "Japs." Many books would later be written agreeing with Eisenhower that there had been no need to drop the atomic bombs, as Japan was on the verge of surrender. Much use would be made of the Strategic Bombing Survey of Japan and its determination that the blockade alone would have ended the war in six months. Some would charge that the main reason for employing nuclear weapons had been to impress the Soviets; Hiroshima and Nagaski being sacrificed for this unworthy purpose.[16]

Washington made up its mind too quickly it is true. There never was enough thought given to the problem of how to force a Japanese surrender, a failure characteristic of the entire Pacific war. Without a supreme commander, the Army and Navy arrived at Okinawa out of sheer momentum as much as anything else. With its conquest, the siege of Japan became complete. Land-based aircraft of many types could now freely attack southern Japan. Movement into and out of the home islands had almost completely stopped. So few cities remained unburnt that General LeMay was about to run out of targets.

Yet, as neither blockade nor terror bombing had worked, the only remaining alternative was to invade Japan. Waiting for the blockade to do the job, as some favored at the time and many have wished for since, was not a real option. A protracted siege would have been extremely unpopular in the United States. The Strategic Bombing Survey notwithstanding, there is no way to tell how long it would have taken to force a surrender because, for the Japanese, it was a political rather than a resource problem and cannot be quantified. The American people wanted an end to the war, or at least to wartime restrictions. As the siege progressed, the pressure for a partial demobilization would have been hard for Truman to resist. In time, American forces might have become too weak to invade Japan if the blockade did not force a surrender.

Meanwhile, the Soviets would be enjoying a free hand in both Manchuria and China. In six months or a year, even if Japan finally surrendered, the United States might have achieved a bloodless victory while losing most of East Asia to Communism. Thus, for geopolitical as well as domestic political reasons, the invasion had to go forward. In retrospect, Yalta looks like a bad deal chiefly because Soviet help against Japan was not actually needed. If the war had dragged on, Yalta would have been praised for limiting Soviet gains, assuming Stalin lived up to the agreement. Such are the risks of statecraft.

Finally, if Truman had failed to use the Bomb and invaded Japan instead, the resulting casualties would have destroyed him politically. Truman would never have been forgiven for sending hundreds of thousands of boys to their death when he had the means to spare them. In a democracy the existence of the Bomb compelled its use. An absolute ruler would have enjoyed the luxury of choice; Truman, as a politician who would have to account for his actions, did not. George M. Elsey, then a young naval Lieutenant assigned to the White House Map Room, put it succinctly. "Truman made no decision because there was no decision to be made. He could no more have stopped it than a train moving down a track. It's all well and good to come along later and say the bomb was a horrible thing. The whole goddamn war was a horrible thing."[17]

A final criticism has to do with tactics. There were people who wished to give the Japanese leadership a more specific warning than the vague Potsdam threat. Some also favored a demonstration, perhaps on a vacant island. Even if it was necessary to drop one Bomb, critics have argued, Japan should have been given more time to surrender before being struck again. The idea of a warning was dismissed out of hand, and rightly so, for words had no effect upon the Japanese Army. A demonstration was considered but ruled out, because censorship would have kept the Japanese public from knowing what was at issue; for fear that the bomb might not go off, thus reinforcing Japanese stubbornness; and because atomic bombs were being produced so slowly that it did not seem prudent to waste one. The idea was to give Japan the greatest possible shock, and in doing so to create the impression that America could obliterate the entire country. Events were to justify this reasoning.

There was a peace party in Japan near the war's end whose most important member was Emperor Hirohito. Although different Japanese leaders lost hope at different times, the fall of Germany made it clear that Russia was about to declare war, ensuring Japan's doom.

The Soviets were not helping to find a diplomatic solution. Worse still, the Japanese military insisted that any armistice must leave them in power, which would have ruled out negotiations even if the United States were not still insisting upon unconditional surrender.

Even the atomic bombing of Hiroshima had little effect upon Japan's military leaders. But the destruction of Nagasaki on August 9, together with Russia's declaration of war a day earlier, one week sooner than promised, brought quick results from another source. On the tenth a meeting was held, attended by the Emperor and the Supreme Council for the Direction of the War, which actually ran the country. Of the Big Six, as they were called, War Minister Korechika Anami and Army Chief of Staff General Yoshijiro Umezo were most important. At this time the Big Six were divided over whether or not to surrender, the Army still insisting on terms it was obvious that the Allies would not accept.

The resulting impasse was broken when Prime Minister Admiral Baron Kontaro Suzuki called upon Hirohito to decide. This was the first time in modern history that an Emperor had been asked to make such a decision. Ordinarily, Hirohito did not even speak at official meetings. This time he did, by prearrangement with Foreign Minister Shigenori Togo and Premier Suzuki, ordering his shocked listeners to accept the Potsdam terms. Though in theory the Emperor's opinion was only advisory, his intervention broke the stalemate. Unbeknownst to American leaders, this was the goal toward which the entire Pacific War had been directed.

Left to its own devices the Japanese Army would never have given up. Its leaders, covered with guilt as they were, could not admit to having made a fatal mistake in 1941. Beyond that, they were bound by the same code that had led the overwhelming majority of Japanese fighting men to favor death over dishonor. If failing to submit meant the end of the Japanese nation, that was too bad, in the Army's view, but better than the alternative. In any case, they cherished the hope that they could hold out in the mountains forever, like the Chinese, who had been beaten repeatedly but never conquered.

Civilian leaders, and some naval figures, did not share this illusion, but it was worth their lives to say so, for the assassin's hand would stop the mouth of anyone identified by young officers as a traitor. Hirohito's intervention changed all that. Had Japan not been faced with what seemed to be immediate and total destruction, Hirohito would probably not have succeeded in taking control of the government. But, save for that very fact, he probably would not have tried. Before the events of

August 6–9 his advisors feared that if he came out for peace the military would depose him in favor of some more compliant member of the royal family. Thus, he had stood by while his people were being exterminated. The second Bomb inspired Hirohito to act at last, transforming the political equation. Protected by his imperial decree, it might now be possible for statesmen to make peace and yet live.

Even so, the surrender was a close thing, as subsequent events make clear.[18] Japan's message accepting the Potsdam terms was conditional on the monarchy's being preserved, but Secretary Byrnes equivocated on this point in his response, an ambiguity which the Big Six used to justify continued delay. Individual leaders sent out conflicting signals, for, in addition to their own varying degrees of fanaticism, they were under heavy pressure from the murderous Young Tigers, whose "rule from below" was one of the most toxic features of Japanese politics. To guard against a surrender, junior officers were already conspiring to seize Hirohito and take charge of the government, their rationale being that the Emperor had been misled by evil advisors and must be kidnaped for his own good. Notices appeared in public places naming members of the peace party and calling for their death.

During one Japanese cabinet meeting, Ministers learned that Japanese radio was about to broadcast an order in their name calling for a general offensive against the Allies. Though it was stopped just in time, the fraudulent order had actually been endorsed by the Vice War Minister and the Vice Army Chief of Staff. As discipline collapsed, it was beginning to seem only a matter of time before the Big Six lost control of their own armed forces. The Kampetei, Japan's dreaded Gestapo, was also opposed to surrendering and would support a military rebellion.

On August 14, no further steps having been taken, Hirohito called an Imperial Conference, the first since 1941, when war with the West was agreed upon. At it he once again commanded officials, many of whom wept, to accept the Potsdam terms. It was the most emotional event in the history of Japanese government. Yet, even this was not enough to guarantee obedience. Early on August 15 a handful of rebellious junior officers demanded that the commandant of the Imperial Guards Division, which protected the Emperor, join them in seizing Hirohito and preventing any surrender. When the General refused, they killed him, and, using forged orders, took command of the Guards and sealed off the palace. Troops led by these Young Tigers then searched the Household Ministry for the recording they knew Hirohito had made to inform his people of the surrender. At the same time, other conspirators seized local radio stations and death squads searched for Prime Minister Suzuki and Marquis Koichi Kido, the Emperor's closest advisor, whom the fanatics correctly believed had guided the Emperor's steps, and also the Privy Council President. All survived, thanks to luck and the plotters' incompetence. War Minister Anami, who had encouraged the plotters at first, took his own life.

For the plot to succeed, officers of the highest rank would have had to join in with the Young Tigers, but, thanks to the Emperor's decree, none did. Instead, General Shizuichi Tanaka, who commanded the Eastern Military District, learning of the rebellion, went to the palace grounds, arriving shortly after 4:00 A.M. on the fifteenth. He ordered the troops back to their barracks and informed the conspirators of their duty to commit suicide. Both the Emperor, who was asleep in his bunker throughout, and the recording were saved. It was played over Japanese radio at noon. Yet, though reducing the nation to tears, it did not prevent further acts of defiance. Isolated kamikaze attacks were made against American ships and positions. Several hundred Army trainees seized a Tokyo park for two days, after which the rank and file surrendered while their leaders committed suicide. The conspirators who had tried to murder Kido ended up digging into the summit of a hill near the palace, where they holed up for four days before all 12 killed themselves.

Many attacks were made by diehards on government installations, radio stations, and post offices in the provinces. A conspiracy among naval air officers to keep on fighting was discovered and crushed. Vice Admiral Matome Ugaki led a flight of Japanese planes on a kamikaze attack against the American fleet, all 11 aircraft mysteriously disappearing at sea. On August 16 Hirohito sent three princes to overseas headquarters, so that no one could pretend that the order to surrender was a fake. Later he dispatched two more princes to restrain military zealots in the home islands. Yet more than 1,000 officers, General Tanaka among them, and hundreds of civilians took their own lives. Many did so in a plaza before the ruins of the Imperial Palace, which ran with blood for days after the surrender. Premier Suzuki did not kill himself but remained in hiding for months in order to avoid assassination.

All of these acts of resistance and protest took place after the firebomb raids had done their bloody work, after millions had fled to the countryside, after the Soviets had declared war, after atomic bombs had destroyed Hiroshima and Nagasaki, and after the Emperor had twice ordered the government to surrender. Many of them came after Japan had actually surrendered, the Emperor had so informed the nation, and an imperial rescript had been sent to all Japanese commands mandating their obedience.

This level of resistance strongly suggests that if the Bombs had not forced the Emperor's hand, there would have been no surrender, not in August, and perhaps not by November when the invasion was to begin. It also suggests that timing was important as well, for by dropping the two Bombs close together, the United States forced Hirohito and the High Command to move so fast that plotters and potential rebels were unable to put together an effective conspiracy. Even a week or two of delay might, in that charged environment, have made a crucial difference. Terrible as they were, by forcing a quick and favorable outcome, the atomic weapons saved many more lives than they took. As George Feifer puts it "The nation in trance did not care about the odds against her. Something was needed to free her from her spell." Where conventional weapons had failed, the atomic bomb succeeded because it "was another order of force, greater and more authoritative. The miraculous apparition presented a way out for the land of the Rising Sun."[19]

If the atomic bomb had not redrawn the political and psychological map, Japan would have been invaded, with horrible consequences, for the people most of all. During the Okinawa campaign one-third of the civilian population died. Bombarded day and night; hiding out, sometimes for months, in caves filled with casualties and excrement; starving; thirsty; often being raped and murdered by Japanese soldiers, their suffering was indescribable. On the home islands, so much more strongly defended and with a vastly larger population, the agony and the deaths would have been beyond imagining. Even if the Okinawa precedent had not been duplicated exactly, millions of Japanese civilians would have died, in addition to the fighting men on both sides. For this reason, unlike the enemy civilians killed by ordinary bombs, the victims of Hiroshima and Nagasaki did not die in vain.

The American conscience would be more clear if Washington had not insisted upon unconditional surrender until the last minute, though doing so probably did not lengthen the war. Military fanaticism was such that diplomatic approaches were unlikely to have accomplished anything. Still, upon receiving the intercepts in July that showed Japan to be extending peace feelers through Russia, Washington ought to have signaled that the Emperor had nothing to fear. He would have to be retained in any case, if only because without his support the occupation was sure to be difficult. To have given the Japanese assurances as to his safety would only have been to admit the inevitable. If granting this condition had not shortened the war, it might have made the actual surrender less difficult for Japan. Yet, even if Washington had been more thoughtful, considering what we know about Japanese politics at the time, it still appears that nothing less than atomic destruction would have forced an early surrender. That was the lesson of Okinawa, and its legacy.

Although no nation can come out of a long and brutal war with an unblemished record, Americans had little reason to feel ashamed. Except for the terror bombing of Germany and Japan, a big exception of course, America waged as humane a war as it could. And if its hands were not perfectly clean, one need only look at those of Germany and Japan and Russia to restore perspective. Fighting for their lives against cruel foes, Americans did what they had to do. For this the entire world, including the enemy peoples whose own freedom was thereby gained, remains in their debt. Americans spread democracy in the most unlikely places, where it remains a monument to their effort and their sacrifice.

20

The Reckoning

A disaster for everyone else, World War II was experienced differently by the United States. Its worse feature, the 405,000 servicemen who died of all causes, was more than offset by population growth, the total number of Americans rising from 133.4 million in 1941 to 140 million in 1945, mainly through natural increase. Sixteen babies were born for every man who died in uniform. Further, they were born into a country whose people had gained much from military spending, mean family income rising by over 25 percent in constant dollars between 1941 and 1944, a remarkable accomplishment for a nation at war.

This is not to minimize the sorrow. For those deprived of a loved one, no amount of prosperity could serve as compensation. Many individuals suffered such devastating losses, and many neighborhoods and towns as well. However, most of the boys not only returned, but were better equipped for civilian life than when they left it, tempered by war, older than their years, determined to make up lost ground. Greatly aided by the GI Bill and the surge of postwar prosperity, which they profited from, but to which they also contributed, they would go to school or get jobs, marry, and settle down. A magnificent generation in war, they would be splendid in peacetime also.[1]

Justice, too, would be served by the war. At the time, most

429

Americans felt that victory had vindicated their democratic system and in many ways it had. To remain democratic, to the extent even of holding elections on schedule, while fighting a long and terrible war showed how committed Americans were to safeguarding their political rights. Moreover, American war aims were appropriate to a democracy, the nation asking for no territories, no indemnities, and, in a real sense, no revenge. America fought a generous war, and its benevolence extended afterward to rebuilding the economies of the states it had defeated as well as those of its allies. Americans could be proud of themselves, not only for winning the war but, by and large, for the way in which they won it.

America nevertheless failed to live up to its highest principles in very important ways, discriminating against refugees, Japanese–Americans, and blacks, while denying women full equality on the job and in the armed services. These faults were poorly understood at the time, and, except by the victims, too seldom censured. The experience was not wasted, even so. Blacks lost little time organizing after the war and 15 years later legalized segregation was everywhere under attack, with veterans playing a major part in its destruction. Immigration laws were revised, enabling many refugees to come here after the war ended. Ultimately even racial exclusion practices were struck down, opening the Promised Land to Hispanics and Asians on a scale undreamed of in the 1940s. Japanese–Americans had a long wait before the crime against them was acknowledged, but finally even this injustice was owned up to and restitution ordered by Congress. Women never got their due. When gender discrimination came under assault in the late 1960s it was for reasons unrelated to women's wartime contribution, which has never been sufficiently recognized.

That many wrongs were righted after the war does not excuse their commission. What it does show, however, is that American democracy was evolving. Wartime injustice was produced by the nation that was, not the nation that would be. Those Negroes and Japanese–Americans who fought for the chance to fight for their country were right, because the political system they defended with their lives was not so much an institution as a process. Jim Crow was legal in 1945, but in 20 more years it would be finished. The great thing about democracy is that it self-corrects, and in all these areas did.

Some valuable lessons were learned from the war, others quickly forgotten. The one that made the greatest impression was the danger of being unprepared and alone. When the Cold War developed, America would arm itself to the teeth and form military alliances with dozens of countries. Though moderation would have been better still, this overreaction was certainly preferable to a feeble response. The lesson of the 1930s was learned at last, even if all too well.

The mobilization muddles were not taken to heart, or even remembered for long. Everyone knows the Army was large, but few that it was not large enough, and desperately short of Wacs. The manpower crisis is little remembered, the failure to enact national service not at all. The resulting lack of rotation for combat troops figures only in history books. The cost of fighting two Pacific Wars instead of having a single strategy has never been conceded. There has never been, and never will be, a movie about strategic bombing that shows it didn't work.[2]

The structural weaknesses of American democracy that gave isolationists almost a veto over national security affairs in the prewar era have not changed, either. This has nothing to do with civil rights and liberties, rather, it concerns the way decisions are made in a country where representatives run for office every two years, and in which the executive and legislative branches are frequently deadlocked. Public-opinion polls are more potent than ever. Congress remains reluctant to offend any interest group, or pass measures, however needed, that will cause inconvenience. The short term, even more than before, is what counts in Washington.

One of the more striking aspects of the war was a generosity of spirit that it brought forth. Though government programs often fell short of need, volunteerism and individual effort took up much of the slack. While this side of the war is poorly documented, many remember it as a time when people helped each other out with car pools, block organizations, and simple neighborliness.

Before troops were shipped overseas, their wives often followed them from camp to camp, living in squalid conditions but sustained by each other, and sometimes by the kindness of strangers. Susan Keller, whose husband Dempsey was in Company K of the 84th Infantry Division, followed him to Louisiana, even though she had no car and an infant in arms and another on the way. The only place she could find to live was a single room with a family of five. The parents not only took Susan in but to the hospital when her second child was born, frequently looking after her children in addition to their own.[3] Such experiences were far from rare. Americans were united in a common cause and had a sense of the country as being more than the sum of its interest groups. Whatever their faults, those Americans were, as Stephen Ambrose says, a "we" generation and knew it.

On V-J Day, Marjorie Haselton of Massachusetts wrote to her husband in China:

> You and I were brought up to think cynically of patriotism . . . by the bitter, realistic writers of the twenties and thirties. [But] this war has taught me—I love my country and I'm not ashamed to admit it anymore. . . . I am proud of the men of my generation. Brought up like you and I in false prosperity and then degrading depression, they have overcome these handicaps. And shown the world that America has something the world can never take away from us—a determination to keep our way of life. . . . Call it Yankee ingenuity or whatever you will, it still is the one force that won the war—the thing the enemy never believed we had. That is why, tonight, I am proud to be an American and married to one of its fighting men. . . . You proved that Americans may look soft and easy going, "spoiled" by the highest standard of living in the world, yet when the hour of need came you showed them we could take it—*and* dish it out.[4]

On the same day, Rose McClain of Washington State wrote a less militant but equally heartfelt letter to her husband in the Pacific:

> Today I cried and thanked God for the end of this war and I shall continue to pray that this shall be the end of war for all time. That our children will learn kindness, patience, honesty, and the depth of love and trust we have learned from all of this, with out the tragedy of war. That they shall never know hate, selfishness and death from such as this has been.[5]

Nancy Arnot Harjan was seventeen when the war ended. She had been doing her bit, giving blood, knitting scarves and caps for the servicemen, dancing with sailors at the USO, and bringing them home for dinner. On one level she knew that most of the warriors were boys like those she dated. Yet, on another level, as she later recalled:

> I saw on the news films the Parisian people, with tears streaming down their faces, welcoming our GIs. They were doing what I wanted them to do. When the Holocaust survivors came out, I felt we were liberating them. When the GIs and the Russian soldiers met, they were all knights in shining armor, saving humanity. [Laughs.] I believed in that.[6]

The embarrassed laughter is that of the adult recalling her naive youth, yet, what she remembered thinking then was, if not the entire truth about the war, certainly true enough.

Though an exciting time for girls like Nancy, the war years were hard on women separated from the men they loved. This was true even of college students, who had fewer problems than most. Katherine McReynolds was an undergraduate at the University of Missouri who, after the war had ended and she did not have to keep up a cheerful front, wrote to her future husband overseas:

> [Our housemother] thinks we all seem so mature. Why shouldn't we? Franny's Richard and June Digby's twin brother were killed. Meyer's fiance spent six months in a German prison camp. The rest of us have been worried sick and hopelessly lonesome for years. It's a wonder we aren't old women.[7]

There is no way to factor these elements into a comprehensive equation. How do we balance precious lives lost against those precious new lives brought into the world even as the fighting raged? The sum of human suffering, at home and on the battlefield, cannot be measured against the good times that got better and better even as the casualties rose.

All one can say in the end is that the war was, and remains, well worth the effort and the heartbreak. As evidence, one has only to imagine what kind of world we would live in today if America had remained neutral. Russia might have survived in a shrunken form, and Great Britain for a time also, but the rest of Eurasia would have been enslaved by the Axis powers. The Holocaust would have gone on to its bitter end, and we can be sure that a victorious Hitler, armed soon with atomic weapons and ballistic missiles, would have caused additional havoc—dwarfing that which was actually wreaked. The most to be hoped for in that event would have been the world that George Orwell described in *1984*—at worst, no world at all.

By passing this greatest of all modern tests America also won the right to become a better nation. Though social reform was not why most servicemen took the risks they did, it would be one of the outcomes. Some reforms, like the defeat of racial segregation, would have roots in the war experience. Others would result from the democratic impulse itself that the war had been fought to preserve.

In a host of ways the war brought out, or underlined, the strengths of America that far outweighed its defects. Family values were not just a political slogan but a fact of daily life. Most people married for keeps.

Fathers supported their children. The war years were not an age of innocence—as this book has been at pains to establish. Relations between the Allies were strained, politicians often cynical, and individual selfishness remained about the same. But, more so than now, Americans accepted responsibility for their acts and did not uphold personal gratification as the be all and end all of life. They believed in doing their duty, at home as at the front.

The most pluralistic of democracies, a Trans-National America, as the social critic Randolph Bourne had called it, this country proved that ethnic diversity enriched rather than weakened.[8] Its fighting men met every test. Its leaders may have faltered, but did not fail. The people overcame their enemies, surmounting as well the difficulties presented by allies, a chaotic and divided government, among other faults, to gain what Roosevelt had promised would be "the inevitable triumph." "Sweet land of liberty," the children sang, and so it was, and so it would remain—thanks to a great generation.

Notes

Chapter 1. Day of Infamy

1. Here, as thoughout this book, the figures are proximate, different authorities invariably providing different numbers. As the orders of magnitude seldom vary, these discrepancies should not matter.
2. Quoted in Gordon W. Prange, Donald M. Goldstein, and Katherine V. Dillon, *December 7, 1941: The Day the Japanese Attacked Pearl Harbor* (New York, 1988), p. 232.
3. Walter Lord, *Day of Infamy* (New York, 1957).
4. Quoted in Prange, pp. 278–79.
5. Quoted in Prange, p. 165.
6. Winston S. Churchill, *The Second World War: Volume 3, The Grand Alliance* (Boston, 1950), p. 606.
7. Quoted in Prange, p. 255.

Chapter 2. America in 1941

1. The history and ideal of assimilation are elegantly summed up in Arthur M. Schlesinger, Jr., *The Disuniting of America: Reflections on a Multicultural Society* (Knoxville, TN; 1991).
2. Unless otherwise identified the statistics cited in this book are from U.S. Department of Commerce, Bureau of the Census, *Historical Statistics of the United States: Colonial Times to 1970* (Washington, DC; 1975). On the condition of women see Nancy F. Cott, *The Grounding of Modern Feminism* (New Haven, CT; 1987) and William L. O'Neill, *Feminism in America: A History* (New Brunswick, NJ; 1989). John Hope Franklin, *From Slavery to Freedom: A History of Negro Americans* (New York, 6th Ed.; 1988) is the standard text.

3. Unless otherwise identified the Gallup polls cited throughout this book are taken from George H. Gallup, *The Gallup Poll: Public Opinion, 1935-1971* (New York; 1972).

4. Some historians dislike isolationist as a term, John Gaddis preferring "continentalist," while Warren Kimball suggests that "unilateralist" is most accurate as many Americans were not averse to overseas action so long as the nation remained unaligned. See John Lewis Gaddis, *The Long Peace: Inquiries into the History of the Cold War* (New York; 1987) and Warren F. Kimball, *The Juggler: Franklin Roosevelt as Wartime Statesman* (Princeton, NJ; 1991).

5. The Spanish war was remembered fondly as an easy win, but acquiring the Philippines later came to be seen as a mistake. Many Filipinos had not wanted to pass from Spanish to American hands and the United States was forced to fight a bloody war against the Philippine independence movement. It transpired that the islands were unprofitable to own and impossible to defend. Thus it was decided to give them their independence, an event which was scheduled for July 4, 1945—ironically, against the wishes of Philippine leaders who now preferred dominion status.

6. Nicholas J. Spykman, *America's Strategy in World Politics: The United States and the Balance of Power* (New York; 1942).

7. *Ibid.*, p. 27.

8. *Ibid.*, p. 454.

9. *Ibid.* p. 460. Charles de Gaulle was another who read the future similarly. Upon hearing of the Japanese attack on Pearl Harbor he fell into deep thought and then spoke as follows: "Now the war is certainly won! And the future has two phases for us: the first will be the salvage of Germany by the Allies; as for the second, I am afraid it may turn out to be war between the Russian and Americans and the Americans run a great risk of losing that war if they do not succeed in taking the necessary steps in time." Quoted in Jean Lacouture, *De Gaulle: The Rebel: 1890-1944* (New York; 1990), p. 330.

10. For example see Paul Hutchinson, "America's Strategy in World Politics," *The Christian Century* (April 1, 1942), p. 427. C. J. Friedrich, "America's Strategy in World Politics," *American Historical Review* (October, 1942), p. 155. "America's Strategy in World Politics," *Time* (April 20, 1942). Friedrich, a noted historian, complained of Spykman's "excess of cynicism about the reality of ideals as forces shaping human conduct."

11. Quoted in Robert Dallek, *Franklin D. Roosevelt and American Foreign Policy, 1932-1945* (New York; 1979), p. 164.

12. This was because the public did not believe a strong defense promoted belligerency. Thus, a Gallup poll released on March 13, 1938 found that 73 percent of respondents thought that a strong Navy would be more likely to keep the United States out of war than to get it into one.

13. That practice will be employed here too, along with the term Army Air Force. On June 20, 1941 the Army Air Corps officially became the Army Air Forces. This made no difference except to the service, people continuing to call it the Air Force.

14. According to a former chief historian of the Army there were over twenty such instances, plus another twelve in which the initiative for an important military step came from Roosevelt. Kent Roberts Greenfield, *American Strategy in World War II: A Reconsideration* (Malabar, FL; 1982), pp. 52-53. On the other hand, unlike Churchill, Hitler, and probably Stalin, he normally gave the services a free hand when it came to executing his policies.

15. Winston S. Churchill, *The Second World War: Volume 3, The Grand Alliance* (Boston; 1950), p. 353.

16. Winston S. Churchill, *The Second World War: Volume 1, The Gathering Storm* (Boston; 1948), p. 323.

17. A Gallup poll released on July 5, 1940 found that while 28 percent of respondents had no opinion, 71 percent of those who did approved of these appointments.

18. Geoffrey Perret, *There's a War to Be Won: The United States Army in World War II* (New York; 1991), pp. 14-15.

19. Winston S. Churchill to Franklin D. Roosevelt, July 31, 1940, quoted in Warren F. Kimball, ed., *Churchill & Roosevelt: The Complete Correspondence*, Vol. I (Princeton; 1984), p. 57.

20. Editorial, "If England Should Yield," *The Saturday Evening Post* (January 25, 1941), p. 26. As it happened, the Royal Navy took so long refitting these old destroyers that they were of little use during the crisis that led Churchill to acquire them.

21. Quoted in James MacGregor Burns, *Roosevelt: The Lion and the Fox* (New York; 1956), p. 441. *The Saturday Evening Post*, which had a circulation of 3.3 million at the time, echoed this view, accusing the President of seeking dictatorial powers. (February 15, 1941), p. 26.

22. Robert E. Sherwood, *Roosevelt and Hopkins, An Intimate History* (New York; 1948), p. 187.

23. Quoted in *ibid.*, p. 191.

24. Quoted in Robert Dallek, *Franklin D. Roosevelt and American Foreign Policy, 1932-1945* (New York; 1979), p. 252.

25. Burns, p. 26.

26. *The Public Papers and Addresses of Franklin D. Roosevelt, Vol. 9* (New York, 1941), p. 633.

27. The Almanac Singers, which included Pete Seeger and Woody Guthrie, released an album containing a song called "Plow Under," accusing the government of planning to have American boys slaughtered as surplus hogs had been under New Deal farm programs. See Carl Friedrich Joachim, "The Poison in Our System," *Atlantic Monthly* (June, 1941), p.

668. This was a result of the Stalin-Hitler Pact, which turned Communists into dedicated pacifists. After the Soviet Union was invaded in June 1941 the Almanac Singers became hawks.

28. Quoted in "Life on the Newsfronts of the World," *Life* (April 28, 1941), p. 32.
29. Waldo Heinrichs, *Threshold of War: Franklin D. Roosevelt and American Entry into World War II* (New York; 1988), p. 67.
30. Henry L Stimson and McGeorge Bundy, *On Active Service in Peace and War* (New York; 1948), p. 365.
31. Quoted in "Life on the Newsfronts of the World," *Life* (June 2, 1941), p. 26.
32. Editorial, "This Hitler Myth," (August 9, 1941), p. 26.
33. "LIFE on the Newsfronts of the World," *Life* (July 14, 1941), p. 20.
34. Here and throughout all references to the influence of Wilson's experience on Roosevelt's thinking are purely speculative. Warren Kimball, who has been studying FDR for thirty years and knows the Roosevelt papers from top to bottom, says there is not a scrap of evidence to support the theory that Roosevelt was determined to avoid Wilson's mistakes—compelling though it seems. In conversation with the author, September 4, 1991.
35. There was much confusion over this bill since many people thought it would extend selective service for a year and that its defeat would have ended the draft. Only the length of service for those drafted was at issue, not conscription itself. See Thomas H. Eliot, "Did We Almost Lose the Army?" *The New York Times* (August 12, 1991), p. A15. He was a member of Congress then and voted on the bill.

Chapter 3. The Lion and the Albatross

1. Edmund Morris, *The Rise of Theodore Roosevelt* (New York, 1979) tells this and other stories with great verve.
2. Roosevelt scholars are much in debt to James MacGregor Burns, *Roosevelt: The Lion and the Fox* (New York, 1956), for both the phrase and the concept behind it. Burns is still the only one of Roosevelt's biographers to have completed a full-length analytical study of him, and for a long time Burns was the only prominent scholar to look seriously at the less admirable side of Roosevelt's character, which some still refuse to do. What Burns did for the public man, Geoffrey C. Ward has done for the private, advancing our understanding considerably with two brilliant volumes—*Before the Trumpet* (New York, 1985) and *A First-Class Temperament* (New York, 1989)—that cover FDR's life up to 1928 and explain much about his character. Ward's books rely heavily on interviews, and since the number of people who knew FDR personally keeps shrinking, this is probably the most intimate study of Roosevelt that will ever be written. Together, Burns and Ward enable us to see FDR better in

ways than his contemporaries could, though some questions may never be answered.

3. Ward, *A First-Class Temperament*, p. 608.

4. Ward, *Before the Trumpet*, p. 296.

5. A good and affectionate account of the marriage told from Eleanor's point of view is Joseph P. Lash, *Eleanor and Franklin* (New York, 1971).

6. Quoted in Ward, *A First Class Temperament*, p. 772.

7. Though perhaps not quite so bad as Frederick W. Marks III makes them out to be in his acerbic *Wind Over Sand: The Diplomacy of Franklin Roosevelt* (Athens, GA, 1988).

8. Dean Acheson, *Present at the Creation: My Years in the State Department* (New York, 1969), p. 937.

9. James MacGregor Burns, *Roosevelt: The Soldier of Freedom, 1940–1945* (New York, 1970), p. 9.

10. Joseph Alsop, *FDR 1882–1945: A Centenary Remembrance* (New York, 1982), p. 9.

11. Quoted in Ward, *A First-Class Temperament*, p. 776.

12. The process is described in Robert Sherwood, *Roosevelt and Hopkins: An Intimate History* (New York, 1948). Sherwood was close to Hopkins and drew on his papers in writing this extremely useful, if partisan, book.

13. The two positions are ably summed up in Ernest K. Lindley, "The President's Tactics Provoke a Controversy," *Newsweek* (November 10, 1941), p. 21.

14. Quoted in Leonard Mosley, *Lindbergh: A Biography* (Garden City, NY, 1976), p. 353.

15. This is Leonard Mosley's position, *Ibid.*, p. 232.

16. In his *The Wartime Journals of Charles A. Lindbergh* (New York; 1970), pp. 81–82, Lindbergh described how, when asked in 1938 to help the French government procure more aircraft, he took the opportunity instead to rebuke French leaders for failing to recognize the hopelessness of their plight.

17. Quoted in Wayne S. Cole, *Charles A. Lindbergh and the Battle Against American Intervention in World War II* (New York, 1974), pp. 80–81.

18. Anne Morrow Lindbergh, *War Within and Without: Diaries and Letters of Anne Morrow Lindbergh, 1939–1944* (New York, 1980), p. 183. The entry is dated May 13, 1941.

19. Ed., "Mr. Mumford and the Liberals," *The New Republic* (April 29, 1940), p. 564.

20. Quoted in Cole, p. 130.

21. Anne Morrow Lindbergh, p. 176. The entry is dated May 9, 1941.

22. Quoted in Mosley, p. 516.

23. Anne Morrow Lindbergh, p. 179. The entry is dated May 9, 1941.

24. *Ibid.*, p. 138. The diary entry is for August 18, 1940.

25. Quoted in Cole, p. 162.
26. Anne Morrow Lindbergh, p. 223. The entry is dated September 14, 1941.
27. Quoted in Cole, p. 175.
28. Roosevelt kept Lindbergh out of the armed forces, but Henry Ford took him on as a consultant to the troubled bomber plant at Willow Run, Michigan. Later he wrangled a job as technical consultant to fighter groups in the Pacific, flying many combat missions as a civilian. Despite being ancient for a fighter pilot by contemporary standards (42), he shot down two Japanese aircraft—one in a dogfight. There is no denying Lindbergh's skill as a pilot, just as there is no getting around his political cretinism.

Chapter 4. The Force of Events

1. Samuel Eliot Morison, *The Rising Sun in the Pacific, 1931–April 1942*, Vol. III of *History of United States Naval Operations in World War II* (Boston, 1948), p. 10. This is the Navy's official history.
2. Quoted in Frederick W. Marks III, *Wind Over Sand: The Diplomacy of Franklin Roosevelt* (Athens, GA, 1988), p. 45.
3. The best biography is Godfrey Hodgson, *The Colonel: The Life and Wars of Henry Stimson, 1867–1950* (New York, 1990). For a history of the foreign policy establishment of which Root was a founder and Stimson a luminary, see Walter Isaacson & Evan Thomas, *The Wise Men: Six Friends and the World They Made* (New York, 1986).
4. Henry L. Stimson and McGeorge Bundy, *On Active Service in Peace and War* (New York, 1948).
5. Arnold C. Brackman, *The Other Nuremberg: The Untold Story of the Tokyo War Crimes Trials* (New York, 1987), p 17.
6. Quoted in Barbara W. Tuchman, *Stilwell and the American Experience in China, 1911–1945* (New York, 1971), p. 251.
7. Quoted in David Reynolds, *The Creation of the Anglo–American Alliance, 1937–1941* (Chapel Hill, NC, 1982), p. 11. At the same time, Reynolds points out, British diplomats had little understanding of the United States as a whole, tending to regard it as "almost an errant Dominion."
8. Quoted in Robert Dallek, *Franklin D. Roosevelt and American Foreign Policy, 1932–1945* (New York, 1979), p. 147.
9. *Ibid.*, p. 148.
10. The poll was released on January 16, 1938.
11. On this point see Jonathan G. Utley, *Going to War with Japan, 1937–1941* (Knoxville, TN, 1985), p. 80.
12. Robert Dallek, *Franklin D. Roosevelt and American Foreign Policy, 1932–1945* (New York, 1979), p. 242.
13. John Toland, *The Rising Sun: The Decline and Fall of the Japanese Empire* (New York, 1970), pp. 106–107. Iwakuro, who had been deeply involved

in negotiations with the United States, pleaded tirelessly in Tokyo for a policy of restraint.

14. *The Secret Diary of Harold L. Ickes: Vol. III, The Lowering Clouds, 1939–1941* (New York, 1954), p. 592. The entry is dated August 3, 1941.
15. *Ibid.*, p. 655.
16. Waldo Heinrichs, *Threshold of War: Franklin D. Roosevelt & American Entry into World War II* (New York, 1988), p. 144.
17. Quoted in Toland, p. 113.
18. Quoted in Heinrichs, p. 195.
19. Perhaps. There is no record of this conversation, and we have only Halifax's word for it. As Roosevelt could not guarantee intervention under these circumstances, whatever assurances he gave were probably hedged.
20. Utley, p. 182.
21. "U.S. Cheerfully Faces War with Japan," *Life* (December 8, 1941), p. 38.
22. "Chill of Crisis Comes to Capital," *Life* (October 27, 1941), p. 36.

Chapter 5. The Government Cannot Mobilize

1. See Jordan A. Schwarz, *The Speculator: Bernard M. Baruch in Washington, 1917–1965* (Chapel Hill, NC, 1981), an excellent biography.
2. Hugh Thomas, *Armed Truce: The Beginnings of the Cold War, 1945–1946* (New York, 1987), p. 153.
3. Eliot Janeway, *The Struggle for Survival: A Chronicle of Economic Mobilization in World War II* (New Haven, CT, 1951), p. 7.
4. Donald M. Nelson, *Arsenal of Democracy: The Story of American War Production* (New York, 1946), p. 87.
5. Quoted in James MacGregor Burns, *Roosevelt: The Soldier of Freedom, 1940–1945* (New York, 1970), p. 52.
6. See, for example, "The Kaiser Empire," *Life* (April 5, 1943), pp. 69–77.
7. For an account of how they were mass-produced, see Robert P. Kissel, "America's Wartime Liberty Ships Came Off the Assembly Line in Just Days," *World War II* (November, 1988), p. 12ff.
8. Quoted in J. Garry Clifford and Samuel R. Spencer, Jr., *The First Peacetime Draft* (Lawrence, KA, 1986), p. 194.
9. *Ibid.*, p. 224.
10. Edgar Snow, "They Don't Want to Play Soldier," *Saturday Evening Post* (October 25, 1941), p. 14.
11. Quoted in Ross Gregory, *America 1941: A Nation at the Crossroads* (New York, 1989), p. 47.
12. Quoted in "Ruml," *Life* (April 12, 1943), p. 36.
13. John Morton Blum, ed., *From the Morgenthau Diaries: Years of War 1941–1945* (Boston, 1967), p. 50.
14. See *ibid.*, pp. 49-64.
15. On their relationship, see Jeffrey M. Dorwart, *Eberstadt and Forrestal: A*

National Security Partnership (College Station, TX, 1992), a shrewd and far-ranging study.

16. Jordan A. Schwarz, *The Speculator: Bernard M. Baruch in Washington, 1917–1965* (Chapel Hill, NC, 1981), p. 432.
17. Quoted in Burns, p. 342.
18. Jackson J. Spielvogel, *Hitler and Nazi Germany: A History* (Englewood Cliffs, NJ, 1988), describes the Nazi state with briskness and efficiency.
19. Albert Speer, *Inside the Third Reich* (New York, 1970), p. 210.
20. Angus Calder, *The People's War: Britain, 1930–45* (London, 1969). This is a valuable history, although to an American it seems overly critical of the British war effort.
21. Paul A. C. Koistinen, "Warfare and Power Relations in America: Mobilizing the World War II Economy," in James Titus, ed., *The Home Front and War in the Twentieth Century: The American Experience in Comparative Perspective* (Washington, DC, 1984), pp. 91–110.
22. H. G. Nicholas, ed., *Washington Despatches, 1941–1945: Weekly Political Reports from the British Embassy* (Chicago, 1981), pp. xi–xii.

Chapter 6. Rout and Recovery

1. A recent contribution to this deplorable literature is John Toland, *Pearl Harbor and Its Aftermath* (Garden City, NY, 1982).
2. Thomas Fleming, "The Big Leak," *American Heritage* (December, 1987), pp. 64–71.
3. Edgar Snow, "Showdown in the Pacific," *The Saturday Evening Post* (May 31, 1941), p. 27ff; and "LIFE on the Newsfronts of the World," *Life* (July 28, 1941), p. 16. *Newsweek* also expected war, though it was much more optimistic. "Windup of Year's Maneuvers Finds Army Tough and Ready," *Newsweek* (December 8, 1941), p. 36.
4. "LIFE on the Newsfronts of the World," *Life* (March 3, 1941), p. 28.
5. John W. Dower, *War Without Mercy: Race & Power in the Pacific War* (New York, 1986).
6. See Edward S. Miller, "Kimmel's Hidden Agenda," *Military History Quarterly* (Autumn, 1991), pp. 36–43.
7. Samuel Eliot Morison, *History of United States Naval Operations in World War II*, Vol. III, *The Rising Sun in the Pacific, 1931–April 1942* (Boston, 1948), p. 132.
8. Carol Morris Petillo, *Douglas MacArthur: The Philippine Years* (Bloomington, IN, 1981).
9. Quoted in William Manchester, *American Caesar: Douglas MacArthur, 1880–1964* (New York, 1978), p. 269. The men's feeling of abandonment was understandable but mistaken. Americans were profoundly affected by the loss of the Philippines, as also by news of the men's suffering in Japanese prison camps. Isaiah Berlin, at the British Embassy in

Washington, was struck by the outpouring of sentiment when MacArthur returned to the Philippines in October 1944. "This event marks a great emotional climax; the scar left on America by the loss of the islands was deep [and the invasion of Leyte] has released a stream of pent-up feeling over the press and radio." H. G. Nicholas, ed., *Washington Despatches, 1941–1945* (Chicago, 1981), p. 435.

10. "Philippine Epic," Life (April 13, 1942), p. 25.

11. D. Clayton James, *The Years of MacArthur 1941–1945* (Boston, 1975), p. 90. This is the most thorough biography, yet even James cannot explain the pettiness and cruelty that characterized MacArthur at his worst.

12. Eric Larrabee, *Commander in Chief: Franklin Delano Roosevelt, His Lieutenants, and Their War* (New York, 1987), p. 12.

13. Samuel E. Morison, *History Of United States Naval Operations in World War II*, Vol. IV, *Coral Sea, Midway and Submarine Actions May 1942–August 1942* (Boston, 1949), p. 13.

14. No one at Station Hypo was rewarded for this great feat because codebreakers in Washington took the credit. Nimitz recommended Rochefort for a decoration, but he was sent to sea instead, and the Navy was deprived of his unique services for the balance of the war. See Ronald H. Spector, *Eagle Against the Sun* (New York, 1985), pp. 450–51.

15. Gordon W. Prange, Donald M. Goldstein, and Katherine V. Dillon, *Miracle at Midway* (New York, 1982), p. 387.

16. Prange, p. 281.

17. "American Victory Over Jap Fleet is Portrayed by Geddes Shipmodels," *Life* (June 22, 1942), p. 25.

18. "Made in America," Newsweek (June 29, 1942), pp. 18–19.

19. John Lardner, "Bombers and Fighters and Two and Two," *Newsweek* (June 29, 1942), p. 27.

20. William Manchester, *Goodbye, Darkness: A Memoir of the Pacific War* (Boston, 1979), p. 291.

Chapter 7. The People Are Willing

1. Quoted in C. Calvin Smith, *War and Wartime Changes: The Transformations of Arkansas, 1940–1945* (Fayetteville, AR), p. 12. Even before American entry into the war, local patriotism was such that after a Danville, Arkansas man beat a German immigrant to death for speaking up on behalf of the German people, a local grand jury refused to indict him for murder.

2. Milton Mayer, "Washington Goes to War," Life (January 5, 1942), p. 61.

3. "LIFE on the Newsfronts of the World," Life (July 6, 1942), p. 28.

4. "The Home Front," Newsweek (January 27, 1941), p. 32.

5. "Women Demand Greater Role in National Defense Program," *Newsweek* (August 11, 1942), pp. 33–34.

6. Quoted in James MacGregor Burns, *Roosevelt: The Soldier of Freedom 1940–1945* (New York, 1970), p. 433.

7. Quoted in Doris Weatherford, *American Women and World War II* (New York, 1990), p. 234. A valuable survey.

8. Ernest K. Lindley, "What's the Matter with Congress?" *Newsweek* (June 15, 1942), p. 32.

9. According to the Census Bureau, in 1990, 73.2 percent drove to work alone, 13.4 percent commuted in car pools, and 5.3 percent used public transportation.

10. Quoted in Weatherford, *op. cit.* Geoffrey Perrett, *Days of Sadness, Years of Triumph: The American People, 1939–1945* (Madison, WI, 1973) is a mine of information on scrap drives and victory gardens.

11. Anne Harmon, "World War II—Child's Eye View Years Later," *The Cape Codder Seniority* (Summer, 1992), pp 3–4.

12. Richard Polenberg, *War and Society: The United States, 1941–1945* (Philadelphia, 1972), p. 133,

13. Historian John Morton Blum echoes their belief that World War II was a lost opportunity. Roosevelt's Administration could have used it to promote a second and greater New Deal for the nation, and perhaps the world. Instead, Blum remarks: "The managers of the war did not use the war to convert the governed, or as a laboratory of democracy, or as a crusade for universal peace. The war used them. As a consequence, either the expectations of the governed, or the necessities of war as the governors construed them, dominated politics in the United States. At work at home or at arms abroad, Americans wanted it that way. The world would not turn brave or new that had such people in it." John Morton Blum, *V Was For Victory: Politics and American Culture in World War II* (New York, 1976), pp. 13–14.

14. Quoted in William L. O'Neill, *A Better World: the Great Schism: Stalinism and the American Intellectuals* (New York, 1982), pp. 64–65.

15. See Horace C. Peterson and Gilbert C. Fite, *Opponents of War, 1917–1918* (Madison, WI, 1957).

16. Clayton R. Koppes and Gregory D. Black, *Hollywood Goes to War: How Politics, Profits & Propaganda Shaped World War II Movies* (New York, 1987), p. 50.

17. Quoted in Blum, p. 27.

18. Lewis Gannett, "Books," in Jack Goodman, ed., *While You Were Gone: A Report on Wartime Life in the United States* (New York, 1940), p. 459.

19. Quoted in Lee Kennett, *For the Duration . . . : The United States Goes to War: Pearl Harbor–1942* (New York, 1985), p. 66.

20. "The Indian Ocean Becomes Newest Theater of War," *Life* (April 20, 1942), p. 28.

21. Today the Navy's uniformed head is called Chief of Naval Operations. The office existed then, too, but in a much weaker form. To resolve

ambiguities and possible conflicts, Roosevelt soon made King CNO as well as Cominch. See Thomas B. Buell, *Master of Sea Power: A Biography of Fleet Admiral Ernest J. King* (Boston, 1980), a first-rate analysis of this complex man.

22. Quoted in Samuel Eliot Morison, *The Battle of the Atlantic,* Vol. I *September 1939–May 1943* (Boston, 1984), p. 201. It was first published in 1947.
23. Wesley Frank Craven and James Lea Cate, Eds., *The Army Air Forces in World War II, Vol. II, Europe: Torch to Pointblank, August 1942 to December 1943* (Chicago, 1949), p. 384.
24. Morison, p. 203.
25. Richard Hough, *The Longest Battle: The War At Sea, 1939–45* (New York, 1986), p. 271.
26. Ronald Lewin, *Ultra Goes to War* (New York, 1978), p. 218.
27. Oddly enough, in his official history, Admiral Morison failed to mention any of these decisions, despite their extreme importance.
28. John Keegan, *The Second World War* (New York, 1990), p. 123.

Chapter 8. Operation Torch and the Great Debate over Strategy

1. Quoted in Arthur Bryant, *The Turn of the Tide, 1939–1943: A History of the War Years Based on the Diaries of Field-Marshal Lord Alanbrooke, Chief of the Imperial General Staff* (Garden City, NY, 1957), p. 234.
2. George McJimsey, *Harry Hopkins: Ally of the Poor and Defender of Democracy* (Cambridge, MA, 1987). This fine study takes advantage of documentation not available to Sherwood, whose own study remains invaluable because of his closeness to Hopkins. Thus, see also Robert Sherwood, *Roosevelt and Hopkins: An Intimate History* (New York, 1948).
3. Forrest C. Pogue, *George C. Marshall: Ordeal and Hope, 1939–1942* (New York, 1966), p. 305 the definitive biography.
4. Quoted in Martin Gilbert, *Winston S. Churchill: Vol. VII, Road to Victory, 1941–1945* (Boston, 1986), p. 88.
5. Quoted in Mark A. Stoler, *The Politics of the Second front: American Military Planning and Diplomacy in Coalition Warfare, 1941–1943* (Westport, CT, 1977), p. 37.
6. George F. Kennan, *American Diplomacy: 1900–1950* (Chicago, 1951), p. 73.
7. Quoted in Gilbert, p. 121.
8. Quoted in Thomas B. Buell, *Master of Sea Power: A Biography of Fleet Admiral Ernest J. King* (Boston, 1980), p. 209.
9. Quoted in Pogue, p. 330.
10. Quoted in Stephen E. Ambrose, *Eisenhower: Soldier, General of the Army, President-Elect, 1890–1952* (New York, 1983), p. 181. An outstanding and essential biography.

11. Eisenhower to John Russell Deane, August 27, 1942, published in *The Papers of Dwight David Eisenhower: The War Years* (Baltimore, MD, 1970), p. 503.
12. Eisenhower to Combined Chiefs of Staff, August 23, 1942, *Ibid.*, p. 488; and to George Van Horn Moseley, August 27, 1942, p. 504.
13. Eisenhower to Thomas Troy Handy, December 7, 1942, *Ibid.*, p. 811.
14. Quoted in Raoul Aglion, *Roosevelt and De Gaulle: Allies in Conflict, A Personal Memoir* (New York, 1988), p. 146.
15. Quoted in Warren Kimball, ed., *Churchill & Roosevelt: The Complete Correspondence: Vol. II: Alliance Forged, November 1942–February 1944* (Princeton, NJ, 1984), p. 5.
16. Winston S. Churchill, *The Second World War: Vol. 4, The Hinge of Fate* (Boston, 1950), p. 644.
17. Gaulle, Charles de, *The Complete War Memoirs of Charles de Gaulle* (New York, 1947), p. 385.
18. Quoted in Martin Gilbert, *Winston S. Churchill: Vol. VII, Road to Victory, 1941–1945* (Boston, 1986), p. 646.
19. De Gaulle, p. 470.

Chapter 9. The Sea of Dreams

1. Quoted in Forrest C. Pogue, *George C. Marshall: Organizer of Victory* (New York, 1973), p. 10.
2. Compare Pogue, pp 10–11, which draws on the actual reports Wedemeyer submitted to Marshall, with the opening pages of Albert C. Wedemeyer, *Wedemeyer Reports!* (New York, 1958).
3. Roundup is often dismissed on technical grounds, the argument being that 1944 was the earliest year in which an invasion of France could have been mounted. However, the following books offer compelling evidence that Roundup was indeed feasible: Walter Scott Dunn, Jr., *Second Front Now 1943* (Tuscaloosa, AL, 1980), and John Grigg, *1943: The Victory That Never Was* (New York, 1980).
4. Quoted in Arthur Bryant, *The Turn of the Tide: A History of the War Years Based on the Diaries of Field-Marshal Lord Alanbrooke, Chief of the Imperial General Staff* (Garden City, NY, 1957), p. 507.
5. Quoted in Martin Gilbert, *Winston S. Churchill, Volume VII, Road to Victory 1941–1945*, p. 436.
6. Quoted in Carlo D'Este, *Bitter Victory: The Battle for Sicily, 1943* (New York, 1988) p. 564.
7. See Stephen E. Ambrose, *Eisenhower: Soldier, General of the Army, President-Elect, 1890–1952* (New York, 1983), p. 260.

8. Quoted in Geoffrey Perrett, *There's a War to Be Won: The United States Army in World War II* (New York, 1991), p. 212.

9. Quoted in Lee Kennett, *G.I.: The American Soldier in World War II* (New York, 1987), p. 148.

10. Quoted in Mark A. Stoler, *The Politics of the Second Front: American Military Planning and Diplomacy in Coalition Warfare, 1941–1943* (Malabar, FL, 1977), p. 122.

11. Quoted in Hugh Thomas, *Armed Truce: The Beginnings of the Cold War, 1945–1946* (New York, 1987), p. 174.

12. Quoted in John Lewis Gaddis, *The United States and the Origins of the Cold War, 1941-1947* (New York, 1972), p. 163.

13. Quoted in Robert Sherwood, *Roosevelt and Hopkins: An Intimate History* (New York, 1948), p. 870.

14. An example of the first scholarly response is Foster Rhea Dulles, *America's Rise to World Power, 1898–1954* (New York, 1954). The most extreme revisionist statement is probably Gabriel Kolko, *The Politics of War: The World and United States Foreign Policy, 1943–1945* (New York, 1968). Revisionist charges that Washington was plotting to expand commercially into Eastern Europe have received more attention than they deserve, since they require one to believe that the United States was prepared to seriously antagonize Russia so as to wring profits out of some of the poorest countries in Europe. American leaders made mistakes, but they were not stupid.

15. Winston S. Churchill, *The Second World War: Vol. 6, Triumph and Tragedy* (Boston, 1953), p. 227.

16. Gaddis Smith, *American Diplomacy During the Second World War, 1941–1945* (New York, 1985), p. 149.

17. Quoted in Keith Eubank, *Summit at Teheran: The Untold Story* (New York, 1985), p. 462.

18. John Lewis Gaddis, *Strategies of Containment: A Critical Appraisal of Postwar American National Security Policy* (New York, 1982). A brilliant analysis.

19. Quoted in James MacGregor Burns, *Roosevelt: The Soldier of Freedom* (New York, 1970), p. 580.

20. Quoted in Warren F. Kimball, *The Juggler: Franklin Roosevelt as Wartime Statesman* (Princeton, NJ, 1991), p. 83.

21. Walter Lippmann, *U.S. Foreign Policy: Shield of the Republic* (Boston, 1943), p. 143.

22. Quoted in Ronald Steel, *Walter Lippmann and the American Century* (Boston, 1980), p. 407.

23. Warren F. Kimball, *The Juggler: Franklin Roosevelt as Wartime Statesman* (Princeton, NJ, 1991), p. 169.

24. Eubank is a severe critic of Roosevelt's performance. A more complex and sympathetic analysis can be found in Kimball, especially pp. 83–105.

Chapter 10. The Politics of Sacrifice

1. See Mark H. Leff, "The Politics of Sacrifice on the American Home Front in World War II," *The Journal of American History* (March, 1991), pp. 1296–1318.
2. The standard history is Irving Bernstein, *Turbulent Years: A History of the American Worker, 1933–41* (Boston, 1969).
3. John Morton Blum, *From the Morgenthau Diaries: Years of War, 1941–1945* (Boston, 1967), p. 30.
4. This figure is taken from Harold G. Vatter, *The U.S. Economy in World War II* (New York, 1985). Nelson Lichtenstein, *Labor's War at Home: The CIO in World War II* (New York, 1982) says the rise was from 9.5 million to 14.8 million.
5. Some historians have tried to argue that workers did not really gain financially from the war—but the aggregate figures fail to bear them out. Individual income exceeded consumer consumption which itself rose moderately, during the war by about $290 billion, of which $269 billion can be accounted for. It was absorbed in the following ways. Inflation took $84 billion, personal taxes $67 billion, individual holdings of government securities $49 billion, and savings $69 billion. Thus, although inflation and taxation eliminated 52 percent of surplus earnings, 41 percent remained for individuals to spend after the war, 7 percent having "disappeared." This information does not seem to support charges that the labor force was victimized by cruel wage restrictions.
6. Robert H. Zieger, *John L. Lewis: Labor Leader* (Boston, 1988). An excellent short study.
7. Quoted in *Ibid.*, p. 136.
8. "Where Do We Stand?" *Life* (May 17, 1943), p. 22.
9. Quoted in Donald R. McCoy, "Harry S. Truman: Personality, Politics, and Presidency," *Presidential Studies Quarterly* (Spring, 1982), p. 224.
10. Conversely, some labor historians maintain that Roosevelt actually coopted the CIO, which sold the workers out. The most interesting book with this point of view is George Lipsitz, *Class and Culture in Cold War America: "A Rainbow at Midnight"* (South Hadley, MA, 1982).
11. John Dos Passos, *State of the Nation* (Westport, CT, 1973), p 4. It was originally published in 1944.
12. John Keegan, *The Second World War* (New York, 1989), p. 218.
13. Alan Clive, *State of War: Michigan in World War II* (Ann Arbor, MI, 1979), p. 25.
14. Quoted in Lowell Juilliard Carr and James Edson Stermer, *Willow Run: A Study of Industrialization and Cultural Inadequacy* (New York, 1952), p. 9.
15. *Ibid*, p. 325. Stermer lived in the Bomber Trailer Park one winter, an experience that did much to fuel his indignation.

16. *Ibid.*, p. 311.
17. To German pilots the B-17 also seemed to have more firepower. Years later, one German fighter ace recalled that "[The] B-17 was the most respected airplane we had to fly against. There was always a wall of bullets. I never came home without holes in my aircraft." Quoted in William Neely, "Close Encounter," *American Heritage* (September 1991), p. 92. The article concerns a Fortress that made it back to base on only one engine and without brakes or rudder.
18. *The Wartime Journals of Charles A. Lindbergh* (New York, 1970), p. 645.
19. Robert J. Havighurst and H. Gerthon Morgan, *The Social History of a War-Boom Community* (New York, 1951), p. 296.
20. Quoted in Studs Terkel, *"The Good War": An Oral History of World War Two* (New York, 1984), p. 311.
21. See the unpublished manuscript by Jerry Strahan "Higgins: The Man, The Boat, The Industry."

Chapter 11. Minorities and Women

1. David S. Wyman, *Paper Walls: America and the Refugee Crisis, 1938–1941* (Amherst, MA, 1968), p. 212.
2. Haskel Lookstein argues that American Jews were to blame even so for not trying harder to save their European co-religionists. When war broke out, there were about 4.8 million Jews in America, and while they amounted to only 3.7 percent of the American people, they were concentrated in the 11 largest metropolitan areas, and especially in New York City, where 28 percent of the population was Jewish. This gave them a political clout that was never fully utilized. *Were We Our Brothers' Keepers?: The Public Response of American Jews to the Holocaust, 1938–1944* (New York, 1985).
3. This was true of anti-Semitic outrages committed before the war also. Richard Bernstein, "U.S. Articles on Prewar Jews of Germany Found Wanting," *New York Times* (May 20, 1988), p. 24. One explanation was that news of the Holocaust came mostly from Jewish sources and was therefore considered suspect, an attitude which lasted for most of the war. Also, because atrocity stories had been faked during World War I, Allied leaders in World War II were highly suspicious of such reports.
4. See Walter Isaacson & Evan Thomas, *The Wise Men: Six Friends and the World They Made* (New York, 1986).
5. Quoted in Jacob Heilbrunn, "The Real McCloy," *The New Republic* (May 11, 1992), p. 43.
6. Quoted in Peter Irons, *Justice at War* (New York, 1983), p. 29.
7. C. Calvin Smith, *War and Wartime Changes: The Transformation of Arkansas, 1940–1948* (Fayetteville, AR, 1986), p. 11.

8. Quoted in Audrie Girdner and Anne Loftin, *The Great Betrayal: The Evacuation of the Japanese–Americans during World War II* (Toronto, 1969), p. 211.
9. Quoted in Isaacson & Thomas, p. 199
10. Quoted in Richard M. Dalfiume's meticulous and thorough *Desegregation of the U.S. Armed Forces: Fighting on Two Fronts, 1939–1953* (Columbia, MO, 1969), p. 94.
11. John Modell, Marc Goulden, and Sigurdur Magnusson, "World War II in the Lives of Black Americans: Some Findings and an Interpretation," *Journal of American History* (December, 1989), pp. 838–48.
12. Roi Otterly, *New World A-Coming* (New York, 1968). A reprint of the 1943 edition.
13. Quoted in Karen Anderson, *Wartime Women: Sex Roles, Family Relations, and the Status of Women During World War II* (Westport, CT, 1981), p. 5. See also Susan M. Hartmann, *The Home Front and Beyond: American Women in the 1940s* (Boston, 1982).
14. Amy Kesselman, *Fleeting Opportunities: Women Shipyard Workers in Portland and Vancouver During World War II and Reconversion* (Albany, NY, 1990).
15. Nancy Gabin, "The Hand That Rocks the Cradle Can Build Tractors, Too," *Michigan History Magazine* (March/April 1992), p. 19.
16. Quoted in *Ibid.*, p. 14.
17. Quoted in Sherna Berger Gluck, *Rosie the Riveter Revisited: Women, The War, and Social Change* (Boston, 1987), p. 23.
18. Quoted in *Ibid.*, p. 246.
19. "Veronica Lake," *Life* (March 8, 1943), p. 39.

Chapter 12. *The Transformation of Everyday Life*

1. She was the mother of historian Stephen E. Ambrose, who writes about her in "The War on the Home Front," an unpublished paper.
2. Quoted in Judy Barret Litoff and David C. Smith, eds., *Since You Went Away: World War II Letters From American Women on the Home Front* (New York; 1991), p. 170.
3. Quoted in Studs Terkel, *"The Good War": An Oral History of World War II* (New York, 1984), p. 325.
4. Quoted in Litoff and Smith, p. 180.
5. "Boypower," *Life* (May 17, 1943), pp. 45–47.
6. Quoted in Lee Kennett, *For the Duration . . . The United States Goes to War: Pearl Harbor–1942* (New York, 1985), p. 141.
7. Allan Nevins, "How We Felt About the War," in Jack Goodman, ed., *While You Were Gone* (New York, 1946), p. 16.
8. Quoted in "Flip Corkin," *Life* (August 9, 1943), p. 42.
9. Raymond Rubicam, "Advertising," in *While You Were Gone*, p. 441.

10. Quoted in Clayton R. Koppes and Gregory D. Black, *Hollywood Goes to War: How Politics, Profits, and Propaganda Shaped World War II Movies* (New York, 1987), p. 123.
11. John W. Dower, *War Without Mercy: Race & Power in the Pacific War* (New York, 1986), p. 22.
12. Quoted in Koppes and Black, p. 79.
13. Bosley Crowther, "The Movies," in Goodman, p. 517.
14. David Culbert, ed., *Mission to Moscow* (Madison, WI, 1980), p. 41. The film showed, Culbert remarks, that even in wartime "There is a limit to what the traffic will bear."
15. Richard F. Shepard, "It Seems to Me I've Heard That Song Before," *New York Times* (March 19, 1989), p. H27.
16. Francis E. Merrill, *Social Problems on the Home Front: A Study of Wartime Influences* (New York, 1948).
17. Paul Fussell, *Wartime: Understanding and Behavior in the Second World War* (New York, 1989), pp. 96–114.
18. Quoted in Allan M. Brandt, *No Magic Bullet: A Social History of Venereal Disease in the United States Since 1880* (New York, 1985), p. 164.
19. Quoted in John Costello, *Virtue Under Fire: How World War II Changed Our Social and Sexual Attitudes* (Boston, 1985), p. 87.

Chapter 13. Two Wars in the Pacific

1. Douglas MacArthur, *Reminiscences* (New York; 1964), p. 173.
2. Quoted in Samuel Eliot Morison, *History of United States Naval Operations in World War II: Vol. IV: Coral Sea, Midway and Submarine Actions, May 1942–August 1942* (Boston, 1949), p. 246.
3. Quoted in Stephen E. Ambrose, *Eisenhower, 1890–1952*, p. 141. The entry is dated March 10, 1942.
4. Ronald G. Spector, *Eagle Against the Sun: The American War with Japan* (New York, 1985), p. 246. The best one-volume history of this struggle.
5. Some historians take the Navy's side in this dispute. See, for example, Stanley L. Falk, "Douglas MacArthur and the War Against Japan," in William M. Leary, ed., *We Shall Return: MacArthur's Commanders and the Defeat of Japan, 1942–1945* (Lexington, KY, 1988), pp. 1–22. In most cases a key justification of the Central Pacific strategy is that by taking the Marianas it enabled B-29s to bombard Japan. But, as we shall see, the bombing had little military value. Another justification is that attacking Saipan drew out the Japanese Fleet to its ruin in "the Great Marianas Turkey Shoot." This could have been accomplished just as well in SWPA. Thus, the main achievement of the Central Pacific drive ends up being the conquest of Okinawa, which is farther from Tinian and Guam than

from the Philippines, and could more easily have been assaulted from there.

6. James J. Fahey, *Pacific War Diary, 1942–1945* (Boston, 1963), p. 73.

7. William Manchester, *Goodbye Darkness: A Memoir of the Pacific War* (Boston, 1980), p. 298. Though written in the first person, this vivid history is mostly about battles the author did not participate in—a fact he reveals only at the end.

8. E. J. Kahn, Jr., "The Terrible Days of Company E," *Saturday Evening Post* (January 8, 1944) pp. 9ff.

9. Quoted in Jay Luvaas and John F. Shortal, "Robert L. Eichelberger: MacArthur's Fireman," in Leary, ed., p. 162.

10. Quoted in D. Clayton James, *The Years of MacArthur: Vol. II, 1941–1945,* (Boston, 1975), p. 279.

11. See Lida Mayo, *Bloody Buna* (Garden City, NY, 1974).

12. "Long War," *Life* (August 9, 1943), p. 28.

13. William J. Dunn, *Pacific Microphone* (College Station, TX, 1988), p. 205.

14. Quoted in Clayton D. James, *The Years of MacArthur, 1941–1945* (Boston, 1975), p. 448.

15. John Toland, for example, believes that 20,000 out of 30,000 civilians perished. See his *The Rising Sun: The Decline and Fall of the Japanese Empire* (New York, 1970), p. 590.

16. In his weekly report to the British government, Berlin wrote on August 12, 1944, of FDR's trip to Pearl Harbor: "Even rank-and-file Republicans express grudging admiration at this latest display of the President's skill as a political opportunist." H. G. Nicholas, ed., *Washington Dispatches: 1941, 1945* (Chicago, 1981), p. 401.

17. Quoted in Rafael Steinberg, et al., *Return to the Philippines* (Alexandria, VA, 1979), p. 63.

18. Quoted in James, p. 565.

19. Quoted in James MacGregor Burns, *Roosevelt: The Soldier of Freedom, 1940–1945* (New York, 1970), p. 545.

20. Quoted in Tuchman, p. 300.

21. Quoted in Michael Schaller, *The U.S. Crusade in China, 1938–1945* (New York, 1979), p. 165.

22. H. G. Nicholas, ed., *Washington Dispatches, 1941–1945: Weekly Political Reports from the British Embassy* (Chicago, 1981), p. 447.

23. Quoted in Schaller, p. 283.

Chapter 14. Air Power

1. *The Army Air Forces in World War II, Vol. One, Plans and Early Operations, January 1939 to August 1942.* Prepared under the Editorship of Wesley Frank Craven and James Lea Cate (Chicago, 1948), pp. 149–50.

2. Quoted in James Parton, *"Air Force Spoken Here:" General Ira Eaker and the Command of the Air* (Bethesda, MD, 1986), p. 109.

3. Michael Sherry speculates ingeniously on Roosevelt's motives in *The Rise of American Air Power* (New Haven, 1987), see especially his Chapter 4, "The Attractions of Intimidation," pp. 76–115.

4. For the war as a whole, out of every 100 RAF crewmen who attacked German targets, 60 would be killed and only twenty-four escape death, serious injury, or imprisonment. On their experiences see Max Hastings, *Bomber Command: The Myths and Reality of the Strategic Bombing Offensive, 1939–1945* (New York, 1979); Martin Middlebrook, *The Battle of Hamburg: Allied Bomber Forces Against a German City in 1943* (New York, 1981); and Anthony Verrier, *The Bomber Offensive* (New York, 1968).

5. Elmer Bendiner, *The Fall of Fortresses: A Personal Account of the Daring—and Deadly—American Air Battles of World War II* (New York; 1980), p. 174.

6. *Ibid.*, p. 234.

7. The AAF's policy of downplaying casualty rates greatly annoyed airmen, judging from a memoir published by two B-17 gunners during the bomber offensive. See Sgt. Bud Hutton and Sgt. Andy Rooney, *Air Gunner* (New York, 1944).

8. Quoted in Parton, p. 279.

9. Curtis E. LeMay, the war's leading bombardment tactician, devised the basic attack formation—the wedge shaped "Lead-High-Low combat box" consisting of either 18 or 21 bombers, in 1943, all that a heavy bomb group could put up on a given day. It was the minimum-sized unit for defensive purposes and the maximum that could be handled easily on a bomb run. Three such boxes made up a combat wing, as experience showed 63 was the largest number of bombers that could turn in formation. At that time LeMay commanded the 305th Bombardment Group, which he frequently led in battle. His adventures are described with annoying informality in *Mission with LeMay: My Story*, by General Curtis E. LeMay with MacKinlay Kantor (Garden City, NY, 1965).

10. Quoted in Martin Middlebrook, *The Nuremberg Raid, 30–31 March 1944* (New York, 1974), p. 25.

11. Verrier, p. 315.

12. The V-1 "Buzz-bomb" was a jet-powered, unmanned aircraft that carried 1,984 pounds of high explosive at 300 miles per hour, diving to the ground after flying a predetermined distance. It did little harm to Britain, but frightened the public, hence the pressure to attack its launching sites. It was followed by the V-2, the world's first ballistic missile. An amazing technical achievement, the V-2 had a small warhead and was highly inaccurate, so it too did little harm, except to British nervous systems. The Scud missile used by Iraq in the Gulf War is a direct descendant of the V-2, and, though more powerful, equally irrelevant as a weapon.

13. Just as there should have been American Lancasters, there ought to have been American Mosquitos, too. Its body was made entirely of wood,

enabling the Mosquito to fly over 400 MPH. Some models had pressurized cabins, and so could operate at 40,000 feet—higher than any German fighter. The Mosquito could carry over two tons of bombs, or a single two-ton blockbuster. Its speed enabled it to safely attack at low altitudes with a high degree of accuracy. It was the most cost-efficient weapon of the air war, being able to drop 4.5 times the weight of bombs as a similar investment in Lancasters. It also had the lowest loss rate of any bomber, amounting to one aircraft for every 2,000 sorties. As they were so rarely pursued, many flew unarmed, using the capacity gained thereby to extend their range or enlarge their bombload.

The B-17's outstanding merit was its ability to survive greater battle damage than any other heavy. In contrast, the vulnerable B-24 should never have been deployed in Europe. The opinion of pilots, it was confirmed by Pentagon "whiz kids," who through statistical analysis determined that the production of B-24s should be stopped, a finding arrived at, unfortunately for Liberator crews, too late to make much difference. See Deborah Shapley, *Promise and Power: The Life and Times of Robert McNamara* (Boston, 1993).

14. Allen Andrews, *The Air Marshals: Arnold, Dowding, Harris, Portal, Tedder and Goering in World War II* (New York, 1970). Andrews, an English historian, stops short of saying Harris should have been relieved after refusing to change his methods. However, he provides sufficient information to reach this conclusion.

15. Hamburg, the greatest success Bomber Command ever had, underlined the wastefulness of area bombing. In a series of attacks during July 1943, some 44,600 civilians and 800 enemy servicemen were killed, and 253,400 housing units destroyed, 56 percent of the city's total. After the war it was estimated that the resulting loss of war production was equal to the manufacturing output of the entire city for 1.8 months, the equivalent of 20 or so U-boats. To achieve this, Bomber Command lost 87 bombers and Eighth Air Force 17. This was a major victory. In its worst defeat the Nuremburg raid of March 30–31, 1944, Bomber Command lost 96 aircraft and accomplished nothing.

16. Sherry, p. 149.

17. Allan A. Michie, *The Air Offensive Against Germany* (New York, 1943), p. 57.

18. Quoted in Ronald Schaffer, *Wings of Judgment: American Bombing in World War II* (New York, 1985), p. 69.

19. When people outside of the Air Force required that heavy bombers be sent on specific missions, they nearly always chose wrongly. The attacks on U-boat pens and V-1 pads failed. Attacking Balkan capitals killed civilians without aiding the war effort. Heavy bomber raids in aid of the Transportation Plan were not very effective compared to the much more accurate fighter–bomber and medium bomber attacks. Several times in

Normandy, heavy bomber strikes were ordered up to support ground attacks, killing Allied soldiers by mistake while failing to stun the Germans enough to justify the effort. After the Allied breakout, heavies were never used in this way again.

20. Lord Zuckerman agreed with a recent study that Germany's rail system was more important to its economy than was the oil industry, and should have been given a higher priority. See his "The Doctrine of Destruction," *New York Review of Books* (March 29, 1990), pp. 33–35. The book in question is Alfred C. Mierzejewski, *The Collapse of the German Economy, 1944–1945: Allied Air Power and the German National Railway* (Chapel Hill, NC, 1989).

21. The vast expense and relative failure of strategic bombardment puts Goering's decision not to build heavy bombers in quite a different light. Believers in air power are fond of pointing out that the Blitz was sure to fail because the Germans attacked London with what was essentially a tactical air force. If Germany had possessed strategic bombers, it would only have duplicated the British experience of spending too much money for too little results. What supporters of air power prefer not to remember is that Germany's fighters and two engine bombers were on the brink of driving the RAF out of southern England when Hitler and Goering reassigned them to bombing London. Had the Luftwaffe been allowed to continue, Germany might have gained air superiority over the Channel. It was not that Germany had the wrong planes, but that its leaders employed them wrongly. John Killen, *A History of the Luftwaffe* (Garden City, NY, 1968), choosing to believe otherwise, faults Germany for not building a heavy bomber force.

Chapter 15. The GI

1. The preceding information is derived from Lee Kennett, *G.I. The American Soldier in World War II* (New York, 1987). An indispensable book.

2. Roger J. Spiller, "Shell Shock," *American Heritage* (May/June 1989), pp. 75–87.

3. Stephen E. Ambrose, *Band of Brothers: E Company, 506th Regiment, 101st Airborne from Normandy to Hitler's Eagle's Nest* (New York, 1992), p. 207.

4. Gerald N. Grob, "World War II and American Psychiatry," *The Psychohistory Review* (Fall 1990), pp. 41–46, deals thoughtfully with the implications of this success.

5. Samuel A. Stouffer, et al., *The American Soldier: Adjustment During Army Life. Vol. I* (Princeton, NJ, 1949), p. 433.

6. Hanson W. Baldwin, "Our Army in Western Europe," *Life* (December 4, 1944), p. 95.

7. *Ibid.*, p. 471.

8. Allan Bérubé, *Coming Out Under Fire: The History of Gay Men and Women in World War II* (New York, 1990). A pathbreaking work.
9. See Geoffrey Perret, *There's a War to Be Won: The United States Army in World War II* (New York, 1991), pp. 458–61, and John Costello, *Virtue Under Fire: How World War II Changed Our Social and Sexual Attitudes* (Boston, 1985).

Chapter 16. Overlord

1. Quoted in Forrest C. Pogue, *George C. Marshall: Organizer of Victory, 1943–1945* (New York, 1973) p. 321.
2. Quoted in Stephen E. Ambrose, *Eisenhower: Soldier, General of the Army, President-Elect, 1890–1952* (New York, 1983), p. 282.
3. Omar N. Bradley and Clay Blair, *A General's Life* (New York, 1983), p. 130.
4. Ladislas Farago, *Patton: Ordeal and Triumph* (New York, 1963) is a colorful biography. More accurate and scholarly is Martin Blumenson, ed., *The Patton Papers, 1940–1945* (Boston, 1974), which is based on Patton's own writings and includes a valuable commentary by the editor.
5. Patton gained these prize assignments despite his age, 56 at the time of his famous maneuvers in 1941. For almost all the other top American commanders, the luck of birthdate was an indispensable asset. Among Army officers, the best thing was to have been "West Point 1915"—known as "the class the stars fell on," owing to the large number of its men who became generals, Eisenhower and Bradley were both class of '45, exactly the right age for choice assignments. Most senior field commanders were in their fifties, while their superiors, like Marshall, MacArthur, and King were over 60, too old for combat leaders but not for supreme commanders. To be any older than King, 62 at the time of Pearl Harbor, no matter how brilliant or qualified, pretty much ruled out getting the kind of job that would make you famous.

   The chief exception to this rule was Lieutenant General Holland M. Smith, top Marine commander in the Pacific, saved as a result of FDR's personal intervention. The chief loss to the nation was General Fox Connor, whom Eisenhower called the ablest man he ever knew. Too young for high command in the First World War, he was too old in the Second.
6. Eisenhower to Walter Campbell Sweeney, December 28, 1943, in Alfred D. Chandler, Jr., ed., *The Papers of Dwight David Eisenhower: The War Years: III* (Baltimore, MD, 1970), p. 1630.
7. See Bill Mauldin, *Up Front* (New York, 1945), a classic of its kind which includes some of Mauldin's best cartoons. He describes his meeting with Patton, who felt Mauldin's cartoons inspired disrespect for the officer corps, in Bill Mauldin, *The Brass Ring* (New York, 1971), pp. 259–64.

8. Quoted in Martin Gilbert, *Winston S. Churchill: Road to Victory, 1941–1945* (Boston, 1986), p. 584.

9. Quoted in Ambrose, p. 301.

10. *Ibid.*, p. 309.

11. Bradley, p. 254.

12. Paul Kennedy, *The Rise and Fall of the Great Powers* (New York; 1987), p. 353.

13. Major General Levlin H. Campbell, quoted in "Answers to Prayers," *Newsweek* (December 14, 1942), p. 19.

14. Geoffrey Perret, *There's a War to Be Won: The United States Army in World War II* (New York, 1991), pp. 105–106.

15. Brendan Phibbs, *The Other Side of Time: A Combat Surgeon in World War II* (Boston, 1987), p. 75.

16. Russell F. Weigley, *Eisenhower's Lieutenants: The Campaign of France and Germany, 1944–1945* (Bloomington, IN, 1981), p. 10. A brilliant analytical narrative.

17. Weigley, p. 166.

18. Quoted in Russell F. Weigley, "To the Crossing of the Rhine," in David Curtis Skaggs and Robert S. Browning III, eds., *In Defense of the Republic: Readings in American Military History* (Belmont, CA, 1991), pp. 270–271,

19. Caleb Carr, "The American Rommel," *Military History Quarterly* (Summer 1992), pp. 77–85. In December Patton relieved Wood of his command and sent him back to the States, ostensibly because Wood's nerves were shot. Carr argues that, in reality, Wood had annoyed Patton with his frequent criticisms.

20. Perret, p. 340.

21. Martin Blumenson, "D-Day: Launching the 'Great Crusade'," in *In Defense of the Republic*, p. 309.

22. Omar Bradley and Clay Blair, *A General's Life* (New York, 1983), pp. 298–99. Martin Blumenson, a distinguished historian as well as Patton's biographer, goes so far as to suggest that closing the pocket in time would have won the war in the West. See "D-Day: Launching the 'Great Crusade'."

23. Quoted in Ambrose, *Eisenhower*, p. 333.

Chapter 17. Victory in Europe

1. Quoted in Martin Gilbert, *Winston S. Churchill: Road to Victory, 1941–1945* (Boston, 1986), p. 899.

2. Martin Van Creveld, "'Broad Front' or 'Knifelike Thrust'," in David Curtis Skaggs and Robert S. Browning III, eds., *In Defense of the Republic: Readings in American Military History* (Belmont, CA, 1991), p. 322.

3. James M. Gavin, *On to Berlin: Battles of an Airborne Commander, 1943–1946* (New York, 1978), p. 268.

4. Russell F. Weigley, *Eisenhower's Lieutenants: The Campaign of France and Germany* (Bloomington, IN, 1981), p. 371.
5. "How Big an Army," *Life* (March 8, 1943), p. 32, and "How Big an Army II" (March 15, 1943), p. 24.
6. Quoted in Will Lang, "Colonel Abe," *Life* (April 23, 1945), p. 47.
7. Brendan Phibbs, *The Other Side of Time: A Combat Soldier in World War II* (Boston, 1987), p. 76. Phibbs kept a diary, so the book is accurate in essence, but not in detail, since for dramatic and other purposes he changed names, unit designations, and apparently dates. For example, while he gives November 18 as his division's first day in combat, a standard reference work says it moved to the front on December 5 and relieved 4th Armored on December 7. Shelby L. Stanton, *Order of Battle U.S. Army, World War II* (Novato, CA, 1984), p. 65.
8. Phibbs, p. 77.
9. *Ibid.*, pp 80–81.
10. Quoted in Harold P. Leinbaugh and John D. Campbell, *The Men of Company K: The Autobiography of a World War II Rifle Company* (New York, 1985), pp. 72, 73.
11. Quoted in *Ibid.*, p. 73.
12. Theodore Draper, "Little Heinz and Big Henry," *The New York Times Book Review* (September 6, 1992), pp. 1ff. Draper served in the 84th.
13. Weigley, p. 464.
14. Quoted in Charles B. MacDonald, *A Time for Trumpets: The Untold Story of the Battle of the Bulge* (New York, 1985), p. 506.
15. Omar N. Bradley and Clay Blair, *A General's Life* (New York, 1983), p. 367.
16. Gavin, p. 246.
17. On Eisenhower's conduct of the battle see Stephen E. Ambrose, "The Bulge," *The Quarterly Journal of Military History* (Spring, 1986), pp. 22–33.
18. Quoted in Lee Kennett, *G.I. The American Soldier in World War II* (New York, 1987), p. 171.
19. Quoted in William K. Goolrick and Ogden Tanner, *The Battle of the Bulge* (Alexandria, VA, 1979), p. 189.
20. Bradley, p. 373.
21. Caleb Carr, "The American Rommel," *Military History Quarterly* (Summer 1992), p. 85.
22. Stephen E. Ambrose, *Eisenhower and Berlin, 1945: The Decision to Halt at the Elbe* (New York, 1967).
23. Bradley, p. 436.
24. Robert L. O'Connel, "The Visionaries of German Weaponry," *Military History Quarterly* (Spring, 1989), pp. 72–73.

Chapter 18. The War Winds Down at Home

1. "Congress," *Life* (February 21, 1944), p. 38.
2. "Miami Spectacle: Tourists jam resort in shameless display of wartime slackening," *Life* (February 21, 1944), p. 41.
3. "Last Call for War Aims," *Life* (March 6, 1944), p. 34.
4. *Ibid.*, p. 378.
5. Quoted in David McCullough, *Truman* (New York, 1992), p. 247. A superb biography.
6. Quoted in *Ibid.*, p. 614.
7. These figures, and much of the information here on Roosevelt and the press, come from Betty Houchin Winfield, *FDR and the News Media* (Urbana, IL, 1990).
8. Warren F. Kimball, *The Juggler: Franklin Roosevelt as Wartime Statesman* (Princeton, NJ, 1991), p. 15.
9. He was still doing this after the war, writing in his memoirs that the President's June 1944 checkup proved "There was nothing organically wrong," even though a serious cardiac condition had been identified in March. Ross T. McIntire, *White House Physician* (New York, 1946), p. 204.
10. H. G. Nicholas, ed., *Washington Dispatches 1941–45* (Chicago, 1981), p. 427.
11. "Election Battle," *Life* (October 9, 1944), p. 32.
12. *Ibid.*, p. 450. Remarkably, Berlin had never set foot on American soil before being assigned here in 1942.
13. Geoffrey Perret, *Days of Sadness, Years of Triumph: The American People, 1939–1945* (Madison, WI, 1973), p. 397.
14. General Frank T. Hines, chief of the Veterans Administration, had so informed a Congressional committee on February 27. See Paul D. Casdorph, *Let the Good Times Roll: Life at Home in America During WWII* (New York, 1989).
15. "Roosevelt," *Life* (April 23, 1945), p. 32.
16. Arthur M. Schlesinger, Jr., *The Politics of Upheaval* (Boston, 1960), pp. 656 and 657.

Chapter 19. The Destruction of Japan

1. The flag raising was a staged event, put on after the mountain had been secured. It duplicated an earlier raising of the flag under combat conditions, but for public relations purposes the second event was represented by the Navy as the first. His picture won a Pulitzer Prize for Rosenthal, and deservedly so, despite the minor deception. See Richard Severo, "Birth of a National Icon, but an Illegitimate One," *The New York Times* (October 1, 1991), p. C16.

2. Quoted in Bill D. Ross, *Iwo Jima: Legacy of Valor* (New York, 1985), p. 109.
3. Ronald H. Spector, *Eagle Against the Sun: The American War with Japan* (New York, 1985), p. 503.
4. Karal Ann Marling and John Wetenhall, *Iwo Jima: Monuments, Memories, and the American Hero* (Cambridge, MA, 1991), p. 123.
5. The official history, *The Army Air Forces in World War II. Vol. Five, The Pacific: Matterhorn to Nagasaki June 1944 to August 1945*, edited by Wesley Frank Craven & James Lea Cate (Chicago, 1945), though an excellent work in most respects, suggests that LeMay made the decision personally to go over to area bombing. However, Michael S. Sherry, *The Rise of American Air Power: The Creation of Armageddon* (New Haven, CT, 1987), has documented the pressure from Arnold and his staff to commence terror raids. Sherry, who interviewed LeMay, believes that he had some moral qualms about killing civilians. This is also suggested at points in Curtis E. LeMay with MacKinlay Kantor, *Mission with LeMay* (Garden City, NY, 1965), especially on pp. 425–26 in a discussion of the 1948 Berlin Airlift.
6. Quoted in LeMay, p. 353.
7. Clay Blair, Jr., *Silent Victory: The U.S. Submarine War Against Japan* (Philadelphia, 1975).
8. Geoffrey Perret, *There's a War to Be Won: The United States Army in World War II* (New York, 1991), p. 526.
9. George Feifer, *Tennozan: The Battle of Okinawa and the Atomic Bomb* (New York, 1992). This is an exceptionally gruesome account that justifies using the atomic bomb by making clear the price to be paid if Japan had been invaded.
10. Spector, p. 542.
11. The most extreme attack by an historian on the decision to drop the Bomb is Gar Alperovitz, *Atomic Diplomacy* (New York, rev. ed., 1985), which minimizes the number of expected casualties. Godfrey Hodgson, though highly critical of the decision, admits that invading Japan would have been costly. See his *The Colonel: The Life and Wars of Henry Stimson, 1867-1950* (New York, 1990), p. 326.
12. Quoted in Richard Rhodes, *The Making of the Atomic Bomb* (New York, 1986), p. 676.
13. Quoted in *Ibid.*, p. 638. The meeting took place on May 28, 1945.
14. Quoted in *Ibid.*, p. 742.
15. Quoted in *Ibid.*, p. 736.
16. See, for example, Alperovitz.
17. Quoted in David McCullough, *Truman* (New York, 1992), p. 442.
18. Lester Brooks, *Behind Japan's Surrender: The Secret Struggle That Ended an Empire* (New York; 1968).
19. Feifer, p. 583.

Chapter 20. The Reckoning

1. See William L. O'Neill, *American High: The Years of Confidence, 1945–1960* (New York, 1986).
2. A recent Hollywood fictional treatment, *Memphis Belle*, repeats most of the wartime falsehoods about the nature of strategic bombardment.
3. Harold P. Leinbaugh and John D. Campbell, *The Men of Company K: The Autobiography of a World War II Rifle Company* (New York, 1985).
4. Quoted in Judy Barrett Litoff and David C. Smith, eds., *Since You Went Away: World War II Letters from American Women on the Home Front* (New York, 1991) p. 277.
5. Quoted in *Ibid.*, p. 273
6. Quoted in Studs Terkel, *"The Good War": An Oral History of World War II* (New York, 1984), p. 560.
7. Quoted in Litoff, Smith, p. 52.
8. His superb essay, "Trans-National America," written during World War I, can be found in *The History of a Literary Radical & Other Papers by Randolph Bourne* (New York, 1956), pp. 260–284.

Index